Society

This book is offered to teachers of sociology in the hope that it will help today's students understand their place in our society and, more broadly, in tomorrow's world.

John J. Macionis

SECOND EDITION

Society
The Basics

JOHN J. MACIONIS

Kenyon College

Prentice Hall, Englewood Cliffs, New Jersey 07632

Library of Congress Cataloging-in-Publication Data

MACIONIS, JOHN J.
   Society : the basics / John J. Macionis. -- 2/E.
      p.   cm.
   Includes bibliographical references and index.
   1. Sociology.   I. Title.
HM51.M1657 1994
301--dc20   93–10848
                                         CIP
ISBN 0–13–042730–6

Acquisitions Editor: Nancy Roberts
Editor-in-Chief: Charlyce Jones Owen
Development Editors: Susanna Lesan and Diana Drew
Production Editor: Barbara Reilly
Marketing Manager: Maria DiVencenzo
Design Director: Anne T. Bonanno
Interior Design: Meryl Poweski
Cover Design: Jerry Votta
Page Layout: Karen Noferi
Prepress Buyer: Kelly Behr
Manufacturing Buyer: Mary Ann Gloriande
Photo Editor: Lorinda Morris-Nantz
Photo Research: Barbara Salz
Associate Editor: Sharon Chambliss
Editorial Assistant: Pat Naturale
Scheduler: Linda Spillane
Cover Art: *Crowd* by Diana Ong. Photo by Superstock, Inc.

 © 1994, 1992 by Prentice-Hall, Inc.
A Simon & Schuster Company
Englewood Cliffs, New Jersey 07632

Printed in the United States of America
10 9 8 7 6 5 4 3 2 1

ISBN   0-13-042730-6

Prentice-Hall International (UK) Limited, *London*
Prentice-Hall of Australia Pty. Limited, *Sydney*
Prentice-Hall Canada Inc., *Toronto*
Prentice-Hall Hispanoamericana, S.A., *Mexico*
Prentice-Hall of India Private Limited, *New Delhi*
Prentice-Hall of Japan, Inc., *Tokyo*
Simon & Schuster Asia Pte. Ltd., *Singapore*
Editora Prentice-Hall do Brasil, Ltda., *Rio de Janeiro*

Brief Contents

Contents

11

Economics and Politics 257

12

Family and Religion 289

Global Maps:
Windows on the World

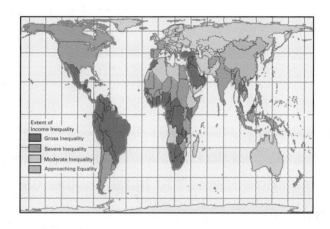

Boxes

A DECADE OF CHANGE

CRITICAL THINKING

SOCIOLOGY OF EVERYDAY LIFE

Preface

The world continues to change in surprising ways, making the revision of textbooks—especially in sociology—both necessary and challenging. The reality of the "new world order" seems to be steady transformation, as national economies become ever more linked, technology draws traditional cultures into a global conversation, and deeply rooted ethnic loyalties and blood feuds rise from the ashes of discarded political systems.

The United States, too, is changing. Even as our economy struggles out of recession, analysts warn that many jobs may be gone for good. A postindustrial (or postmodern) era is upon us in which our society will have to adapt to new kinds of work, face up to growing inequality, contend with new forms of communication, and make new demands of our schools (and of our textbooks).

It is in this context that we are proud to offer the second edition of *Society: The Basics*. The revision of a text—which in its first edition quickly became the most widely used book of its kind—raises high expectations. In this case, we are confident that this new edition offers a unique and unmatched introduction to sociology. This revision is the product of two years of evaluation, careful planning, and intensive work. Our goal in completing the revision has been to make *Society: The Basics* a book without equal: authoritative, comprehensive, and plain fun to read. We invite your consideration of what we

think you will agree is a textbook that ignites a sociological imagination in students, presents the many ways of life found in the United States, and explains our society's place in the changing world.

This text is derived from *Sociology*, fourth edition, which is far and away the most popular text in the discipline. Despite the enthusiastic reception given to *Sociology*—or perhaps because of it—many instructors expressed an interest in a brief version of the book. The result was *Society: The Basics*, a fifteen-chapter paperbound text that provides the essentials of sociological insight in a trim and inexpensive format.

Society: The Basics was not the first brief text in sociology, but it is distinctive. Authors (and sometimes freelance writers or editors) have produced most brief texts on the market simply by paring down a longer manuscript. Such cut-and-paste books may be attractively priced, but typically they do not earn the loyalty of instructors, who try them for a term only to return to more comprehensive books. By contrast, *Society: The Basics* resulted from thorough *rewriting* by the author. This is why it reads smoothly and seamlessly. Just as important, the author has retained in this brief format each and every major topic found in the longer, hardback version. There are no holes in the coverage; the presentations are simply more focused and direct, providing fundamentals without frills. We hope that short-text users will conclude that, in this case, less is truly more.

CONTENT

Two principles guided the crafting of *Society: The Basics*. First, this text acknowledges the diversity of today's students—African American, Hispanic, Asian American, and white; women and men; older learners as well as traditional younger students. This text is broadly inclusive in content, language, and tone, reflecting the author's own twenty-five years of teaching in various academic settings, including large universities, small colleges, community colleges, and even a police academy and a prison. From these experiences, I have learned that inclusiveness is good sociology because a text that is inviting to *all* categories of students provides more learning for *each* by portraying the rich variety of U.S. society.

Second, we asked instructors what they wish to include in their classes, and this research directed us to provide greatest coverage to those topics that are most widely taught in the introductory course. Chapter 1 ("Sociology: Perspective, Theory, and Method") explains how this discipline's distinctive point of view illuminates the world in a new and exciting way. In addition, the first chapter presents major theoretical approaches and explains the key methods sociologists use to test their ideas and insights.

The next five chapters examine core sociological concepts. Chapter 2 ("Culture") explains how and why our species has created variable and fascinating ways of life around the world. Chapter 3 ("Socialization: From Infancy to Old Age") investigates how humans the world over cultivate our humanity as we learn to participate in society. While highlighting the importance of the early years to the socialization process, this chapter describes significant transformations that occur over the entire life course, including old age. Chapter 4 ("Social Interaction in Everyday Life") presents a micro-level look at how people construct the daily realities that we so often take for granted. Chapter 5 ("Groups and Organizations") focuses on the setting of many of our most meaningful experiences—social groups. It also investigates the expansion of formal organization and suggests some of the problems of living in a bureaucratic age. Chapter 6 ("Deviance") analyzes how the routine operation of society simultaneously promotes both deviance and conformity.

The next four chapters provide coverage of social inequality—far more than available in any other brief text. Chapter 7 ("Social Stratification") introduces basic concepts that convey the variety of social hierarchy throughout history and around the world. The chapter then highlights dimensions of social difference in the United States today. Chapter 8 ("Global Inequality") demonstrates this text's commitment to global education by analyzing social stratification in the world as a whole. This chapter analyzes wealth and power inequalities between rich and poor societies and suggests how the regions of our world are becoming increasingly interdependent.

Society: The Basics also provides full-chapter coverage of two additional dimensions of social difference. Chapter 9 ("Race and Ethnicity") explores racial and ethnic diversity in the United States, as well as the social ranking of various categories of our population. Chapter 10 ("Sex and Gender") describes patterns of human sexuality and explains how societies transform the biological facts of sex into systems of gender stratification.

Next are three chapters that survey social institutions. Chapter 11 ("Economics and Politics") explains how the Industrial Revolution transformed the Western world, contrasts capitalist and socialist economic models, and investigates how economic systems are linked to a society's distribution of power. This chapter also contains coverage of the important issues of war and peace.

Chapter 12 ("Family and Religion") spotlights two institutions central to the organization and symbolism of social life. The chapter begins by focusing on the variety of families in the United States, making frequent comparisons to kinship systems in other parts of the world. Basic elements of religious life are discussed next, with an overview of recent religious trends.

Chapter 13 ("Education and Medicine") examines two institutions that have gained importance in the modern world. The historical emergence of schooling is addressed first, noting many ways in which educational systems are linked to other social institutions. Like education, medicine has become a central institution during the last century. The chapter concludes by explaining how various societies have devised distinctive strategies for promoting public health and exploring the health-care crisis here at home.

The final two chapters of the text focus on important dimensions of social change. Chapter 14 ("Population and Urbanization") spotlights the growth of population and the swelling of cities in the United States and, especially, in poor nations of the world. Chapter 15 ("Social Change and Modernity") explains why societies change, looks at how people forge social movements to encourage or to resist change, and assesses the benefits and liabilities of modern social patterns.

CONTINUITY: ESTABLISHED FEATURES OF *SOCIETY*: *THE BASICS*

Although brief texts have much in common, they are not all the same. The extraordinary success of *Society*: *The Basics* results from a combination of a dozen distinctive features.

Unsurpassed Writing Style

Most important, this text offers a writing style widely praised by students and faculty alike as elegant and engaging. *Society*: *The Basics* is an inviting text that encourages students to read—even beyond their assignments.

Intriguing Chapter Openings

A popular feature of the first edition was the engaging vignettes that began each chapter. These openings—which range from the "Buy American" campaign and the "family values" debate to the controversy surrounding the police beating of Rodney King—spark the interest of the reader as they introduce important themes. For this edition, almost half of the vignettes are new.

A Celebration of Social Diversity

Society: *The Basics* invites students from all social backgrounds to discover a fresh and exciting way to see their world and themselves. In addition to a full chapter on race and ethnicity, readers will hear throughout this text the diverse voices of our society—people of African, Asian, European, and Latino ancestry, as well as women and men of various class positions and at all points in the life course. Just as important, without flinching from the difficulties that marginalized people confront, this text does not treat these individuals as "social problems" but notes their achievements.

Inclusive Focus on Women and Men

Few brief texts devote a full chapter to the important concepts of sex and gender. *Society*: *The Basics* offers this and more, "mainstreaming" gender into *every* chapter, explaining that gender not only affects our answers

about how society works but also the way we frame questions in the first place.

Instructive and Engaging Examples

Reviewers consistently praise this text for offering high-quality examples and illustrations. On every page, class-tested examples and illustrations give life to concepts and theories and demonstrate to students the value of applying sociology to their everyday lives.

A Global Perspective

Along with its longer version *Sociology*, this text has taken a leading role in expanding the horizons of our discipline beyond the United States. Each chapter contains comparative material that focuses on the social diversity of our world. Just as important, *Society*: *The Basics* explains that many trends in the United States—whether they be musical tastes, the price of wheat, or growing disparity of income—are influenced by what happens elsewhere. More than ever before, understanding our society demands comprehending this nation's place in the larger global system.

Theoretically Clear and Balanced

This text makes theory easy. The discipline's major theoretical approaches are introduced in Chapter 1 and are systematically reapplied in later chapters. In addition to the social-conflict, structural-functional, and symbolic-interaction paradigms, chapters incorporate social exchange analysis, ethnomethodology, cultural ecology, and sociobiology.

Emphasis on Critical Thinking

Critical thinking skills include the ability to challenge common assumptions, formulate questions, identify and weigh appropriate evidence, and reach reasoned conclusions. This text empowers students to discover as well as to learn, to seek out contradictions as well as to formulate consistent arguments, and to forge connections among the various dimensions of social life.

Recent Sociological Research

Society: *The Basics* blends classical sociological statements with the latest research, as reported in leading publications in the field. Hundreds of new studies are included in this revision; on average, almost three-fourths of each chapter's citations are of articles and books published since 1980. As in the first edition, the statistical data are the most recent available: this revision's data are from the 1990 Census or newer sources.

Learning Aids

This text has specific features to help students learn. Each chapter begins with a **topic outline** that shows readers at a glance the content and organization of that chapter. **Key concepts,** identified within the text by bold-faced type, are each followed by *a precise, italicized definition.* An alphabetical listing of key concepts and their definitions appears at the end of each chapter, and a complete **glossary** is placed at the end of the book. Each chapter also contains a numbered **summary** to assist students in reviewing material and assessing their understanding.

Outstanding Images: Photography and Fine Art

The author has searched extensively for the finest images of the human condition and thoughtfully developed a unique program of photography and artwork. Not only are images of extraordinary quality, but they represent photographs and paintings by artists of various social backgrounds and historical periods. In addition to widely celebrated art by George Tooker and Vincent Van Gogh, for example, this edition has paintings by African-American artists Henry Tanner and Jacob Lawrence, Latino artists Frank Romero and Carmen Lomas Garza, and the Australian painter and feminist Sally Swain.

Thought-Provoking Theme Boxes

Although boxes are common to introductory texts, *Society: The Basics* provides a wealth of uncommonly good boxes. Each chapter typically contains two boxes, which fall into five types that strengthen the central themes of the text. *Social Diversity* boxes, new to this edition, focus on multicultural issues and enhance the voices of people of color and women. A *Decade of Change* boxes, also new to this revision, use recent census data to highlight important changes during the 1980s or to project trends for the 1990s. *Critical Thinking* boxes teach students to ask sociological questions about their surroundings, and help them to evaluate important, controversial issues. *Global Sociology* boxes provoke readers to think about their own way of life by examining the fascinating cultural diversity found in our world. *Sociology of Everyday Life* boxes show that, far from being detached from daily routines, many of sociology's most important insights involve familiar, everyday experiences.

INNOVATION: CHANGES IN *SOCIETY: THE BASICS,* SECOND EDITION

The following list outlines the new teaching features and other significant changes we have made in this new edition.

Placing Our Society in Global Perspective

Sociology has long revealed how individual lives are shaped by placement in their own society. As we approach the new century, sociology is extending its reach by showing how the United States is itself affected by our country's position in the world as a whole. An unfortunate fact is that, at present, our students know little about the rest of the world and the ways in which all nations are linked. Consider that, of some 12 million college students in this country, only about 50,000—less than 1 percent—have first-hand experience studying abroad. This pales in comparison to the 350,000 foreign students currently studying in the United States.

In three ways, this revision enhances the global sophistication of students. First, **this edition makes careful use of language.** We no longer use the term "Americans"—a word that literally designates two continents—to refer only to people in the United States. Thus, for example, the "American economy" is now more correctly termed the "U.S. economy." This may seem a small point, but it is appropriate recognition that we in this country are only one part of the Americas. The author has taken great care to avoid other examples of ethnocentric language.

Second, **this edition ties life in the United States to processes and trends in the larger world.** Various chapters explain, for example, how growing economic inequality in this country is linked to the globalization of the economy, and how the overall wealth of the United States is tied to our relations abroad. This global emphasis in no way lessens the text's focus on the United States; on the contrary, it provides a richer and more accurate understanding of our society.

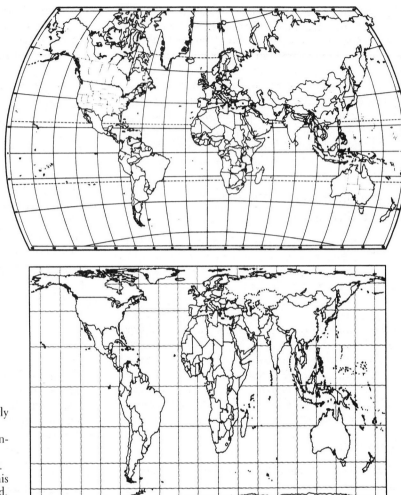

The Mercator projection (top), which correctly displays the *shape* of land masses, was vital to early sea-faring navigators. But it Eurocentrically inflates the dimensions of countries (like England) that are far from the equator. The Peters projection (bottom) is used in this text because it accurately presents the *size* (and, by implication, importance) of all nations.

Third, and most significantly, **this edition includes nineteen global maps.** This unique feature, which we call **Windows on the World,** provides truly sociological maps that reveal, in global perspective, patterns such as income disparity, favored languages, permitted marriage forms, the degree of political freedom, the incidence of HIV infection, the extent of child labor, prostitution, and illiteracy, and a host of other issues. A listing of all nineteen **Windows on the World** follows the table of contents.

We make a major commitment to world maps, first, because global learning begins by learning basic geography. Surveys tell us that many of our students cannot locate countries of the world. Students who do not know even in what *region* of the globe to find Somalia, Bosnia, or Bangladesh obviously cannot understand the human drama that is currently unfolding in these places. Second, students need to see ways in which rich and poor nations differ. Understanding the effects of industrialization requires investigating global birth rates, the extent of child labor, and what share of women are in the labor force. **Windows on the World** graphically display all these factors and more.

All maps distort reality, since they portray a three-dimensional world in two dimensions. However, for our purposes, some biases are better than others. **Windows on the World** are drawn in a new, non-Eurocentric projection devised by cartographer Arno Peters. Most of us are familiar with the Mercator projection (devised by the Flemish mapmaker Gerhardus Mercator, 1512–1594). Mercator sought to accurately present the *shape* of countries (a vital concern to early sea-faring navigators), but in doing so he distorted their *size*. His projection inflates the size of nations at greater distance from the equator so that Europe and North America have exaggerated dimensions (and, by implication, importance). By the same token, the Mercator map renders most Third-World countries smaller than they are. The Peters projection distorts the shape of some countries in service to the goal of displaying them all in their correct relative size.

Highlighting the Social Diversity of the United States

College students in this country have never been as socially diverse as they are today. Although this trend has brought change to sociology, many texts continue to provide aggregate data on "generic Americans," which is, at best, a short-hand fiction. By contrast, the new edition of *Society: The Basics* actively portrays this diversity by incorporating variables of gender, race, ethnicity, social class, and age into each chapter. This text continually shows how topics have different significance to various categories of people, encourages students to understand their own social identities, and helps them to reach intellectually beyond themselves toward others who are in some way different.

New Topics

Society: The Basics offers topic coverage that is unparalleled among short texts. The second edition is now even stronger, with dozens of new or expanded discussions. Here is a partial listing, by chapter, of new material:

1. The contributions of W. E. B. DuBois to sociology and how gender affects research
2. Afrocentrism and the multiculturalism debate
3. Where and why child labor continues in the world
4. How women and men use space differently
5. The importance of organizational environments
6. Date rape and sexual violence
7. How our society redistributed income and wealth during the 1980s
8. The Christopher Columbus controversy
9. Projections of a coming "minority-majority"
10. Why millions of Asian women are "missing"
11. The "Buy American" movement and a look at conservative African-American policy makers
12. An examination of Sweden, where families are weakest in all the industrial world
13. The school choice movement and the latest global data on HIV infection
14. Why birth rates are highest in the poorest countries
15. How anomie differs from alienation

The Latest Statistical Data

The 1990 Census data have been released and *Society: The Basics* has them. Each chapter has the most current statistics available—in many cases, for 1991 and even 1992—as well as hundreds of new research findings. On average, almost three-fourths of each chapter's citations refer to material published since 1980. This revision also includes recent current events, from the Rodney King incident, to the lingering recession, to the turmoil in the former Yugoslavia.

SUPPLEMENTS

This text is the heart of a comprehensive learning package that includes an unsurpassed range of proven instructional aids. John Macionis has supervised the development of all of the supplements, ensuring their quality and compatibility with the text. No other brief text offers so much high-quality material that will truly enhance teaching and learning.

The Annotated Instructor's Edition

Faculty can request *Society: The Basics* in an annotated instructor's edition (AIE). The AIE is a complete student text that has been enriched by the author with additional material on every page. Annotations include summaries of research findings, statistics that allow comparisons between the United States and other world nations, data concerning social diversity in this country, insightful quotations, and high-quality survey data from the National Opinion Research Center's (NORC) *General Social Survey*.

Data File

This is the "instructor's manual" that will interest even seasoned sociologists who have never used one before. Beyond chapter outlines and discussion questions, the

Data File contains the data and conclusions of recent research about the United States and other societies, summaries of current controversies and debates, and "briefs" on additional topics that expand the scope of every chapter of the text. The *Data File* has been prepared by Stephen W. Beach (Avila College) and John Macionis.

Prentice Hall Images in Sociology: Laser Videodisc

Using the latest technology, *Images in Sociology* presents illustrations both from within the text and from outside sources in an integrated framework appropriate for classroom use. These images include maps, graphs, diagrams, and other illustrations, as well as video segments taken from the *ABC News/Prentice Hall Video Library for Sociology*. See your local Prentice Hall representative for details on how to preview this videodisc.

Social Survey Software

This is the supplement that is changing the way instructors teach and students learn. *Social Survey Software* is an easy yet powerful program that allows users to investigate U.S. society and other nations; it employs the best source of survey data available, including the *General Social Survey*. John J. Macionis and Jere Bruner (Oberlin College) have prepared more than one hundred data sets that are keyed to the chapters of *Society: The Basics*. Karen Frederick and Jere Bruner have written an easy-to-understand student manual as well as a helpful instructor's manual to accompany the software. Both manuals have been updated for this revision. *Social Survey Software* supports multivariate analysis including controls, allowing investigators to analyze survey responses by gender, race, income level, education, and a host of other variables. *Social Survey Software* is executed on the CHIPendale student version microcomputer program developed by James A. Davis (Harvard University) and is available to operate in IBM and MacIntosh formats.

Test Item File

A completely new and improved test item file for this revision has been prepared by Edward Kick, University of Utah. This file is available in both printed and computerized forms. The file contains 1,500 items—100 per chapter—in multiple-choice, true-false, and essay formats. Questions are identified as more simple "recall" items or more complex "inferential" issues; the answers to all questions are page-referenced to the text. *Prentice Hall TestManager* is a test generator and classroom man-

agement system designed to provide maximum flexibility in producing and grading tests and quizzes. MicroTest III, MacIntosh Version, is available to MacIntosh users. Prentice Hall also provides a test preparation service to users of this text that is as easy as one call to our toll-free 800 number.

Core Test Item File

This general test item file consists of additional test questions appropriate for introductory sociology courses. All of the questions have been class tested, and an item analysis is available for every question.

Seeing Ourselves: Classic, Contemporary, and Cross-Cultural Readings in Sociology, Second Edition

Create a powerful and affordable teaching package by combining this brief text with *Seeing Ourselves*, the most popular collection of sociology readings available. John J. Macionis and Nijole V. Benokraitis (University of Baltimore) have selected and edited sixty-six selections organized in a format unique among all readers: a cluster of readings—classic statements, contemporary issues and research, and cross-cultural comparisons—for each major topic in this text. Classical statements include excerpts by Emile Durkheim, Karl Marx, George Herbert Mead, Max Weber, Georg Simmel, C. Wright Mills, W. E. B. DuBois, Mirra Komarovsky, Jessie Bernard, and others; contemporary readings highlight issues such as gender patterns in everyday speech, politics and research, how computers are changing the workplace, racial and ethnic bias in advertising, and the debate concerning pornography. Cross-cultural selections examine issues with an eye toward social diversity in the United States or in global perspective. This companion text is a low-cost resource that provides exceptional quality and unsurpassed flexibility for instructors who wish to supplement textbook reading with primary sources.

ABC News/Prentice Hall Video Library for Sociology Series I, II, III (Issues in Sociology) and IV (Global Culturalism)

Video is the most dynamic supplement you can use to enhance a class. But the quality of the video material and how well it relates to your course still makes all the difference. Prentice Hall and ABC News are now working together to bring you the best and most comprehensive video ancillaries available in the college market.

Through its wide variety of award-winning programs—*Nightline, Business World, On Business, This Week with David Brinkley, World News Tonight,* and *The Health Show*—ABC offers a resource for feature and documentary-style videos related to the chapters in *Society: The Basics.* The programs have extremely high production quality, present substantial content, and are hosted by well-versed, well-known anchors.

Prentice Hall and its authors and editors provide the benefit of having selected videos and topics that will work well with this course and text and include notes on how to use them in the classroom. An excellent video guide in the *Data File* carefully and completely integrates the videos into your lecture. The guide has a synopsis of each video showing its relation to the chapter and discussion questions to help students focus on how concepts and theories apply to real-life situations.

The New York Times Supplement

The New York Times and Prentice Hall are sponsoring *Themes of the Times,* a program designed to enhance student access to current information of relevance in the classroom.

Through this program, the core subject matter provided in the text is supplemented by a collection of time-sensitive articles from one of the world's most distinguished newspapers, *The New York Times.* These articles demonstrate the vital, ongoing connection between what is learned in the classroom and what is happening in the world around us.

To enjoy the wealth of information of *The New York Times* daily, a reduced subscription rate is available. For information, call toll-free: 1-800-631-1222.

Prentice Hall and *The New York Times* are proud to co-sponsor *Themes of the Times.* We hope it will make the reading of both textbooks and newspapers a more dynamic, involving process.

Other supplements available to aid in classroom teaching are

> *Prentice Hall Color Transparencies: Sociology Series III*
>
> Instructor's Guide to *Prentice Hall Color Transparencies: Sociology Series III*
>
> Film/Video Guide: *Prentice Hall Introductory Sociology,* Revised Edition

Study Guide
Prentice Hall StudyManager
Critical Thinking Audiocassette Tape

IN APPRECIATION

The conventional practice of designating a single author obscures the efforts of dozens of women and men that have resulted in *Society: The Basics.* Nancy Roberts, executive editor at Prentice Hall and valued friend, has contributed enthusiasm, support, and sound advice throughout the revision process. Susanna Lesan has played a vital role in the development of this text since its inception and has shouldered day-to-day responsibility for coordinating and supervising the editorial process. I also have a large debt to the members of the Prentice Hall sales staff, who gave the first edition of this text remarkable support. Thanks, especially, to Tracy Augustine, Roland Hernandez, and Maria Di Vencenzo, who have headed up our marketing campaigns. I also offer heartfelt thanks to Pat Naturale, Bill Webber, Charlyce Jones Owen, Will Ethridge, and Ed Stanford for all that they have done to make this text what it is today.

The production of *Society: The Basics* was supervised by Barbara Reilly, who has expended extraordinary time and energy, kept track of countless details, and tolerated no compromises along the way. The interior design of the book is the creative work of Meryl Poweski. Karen Noferi created each of the pages with exceptional skill. Copy editing of the manuscript was provided by Diana Drew and Amy Macionis. Barbara Salz did an excellent job of filling the author's requests for photos; she worked under the supervision of Lorinda Morris-Nantz, head of Prentice Hall's Photo Archives. Linda Spillane coordinated production schedules to ensure the on-time delivery of the text

It goes without saying that every colleague knows more about some topics covered in this book than I do. For that reason, I am grateful to the hundreds of people who have written to me to offer comments and suggestions; thanks, too, to the many students who have shared with me their reactions to the book. More formally, I wish to thank the following people who have reviewed some or all of this manuscript:

Leander Abbott, Cayuga Community College
Darrell D. Irwin, Loyola University

Ruben Martinez, University of Colorado at Colorado Springs

Christa Reiser, East Carolina University

Mary Kay Schleiter, University of Wisconsin at Parkside

Jennifer Crew Solomon, Winthrop University

I also wish to thank the following colleagues for sharing their wisdom in ways that have improved this book: Doug Adams (The Ohio State University), Kip Armstrong (Bloomsburg University), Rose Arnault (Fort Hays State University), Philip Berg (University of Wisconsin, La Crosse), Bill Brindle (Monroe Community College), John R. Brouillette (Colorado State University), Karen Campbell (Vanderbilt University), Gerry Cox (Fort Hays State University), Harrold Curl (Mount Vernon Nazarene College), James A. Davis (Harvard University), Helen Rose Fuchs Ebaugh (University of Houston), Heather Fitz Gibbon (The College of Wooster), Kevin Fitzpatrick (University of Alabama-Birmingham), Dona C. Fletcher (Sinclair Community College), Charles Frazier (University of Florida), Karen Lynch Frederick (Saint Anselm College), Jarvis Gamble (Owen's Technical College), Steven Goldberg (City College, City University of New York), Charlotte Gotwald (York College of Pennsylvania), Jeffrey Hahn (Mount Union College), Dean Haledjian (Northern Virginia Community College), Peter Hruschka (Ohio Northern University), Glenna Huls (Camden County College), Jeanne Humble (Lexington Community College), Harry Humphries (Pittsburg State University), Cynthia Imanaka (Seattle Central Community College), Patricia Johnson (Houston Community College), Ed Kain (Southwestern University), Irwin Kantor (Middlesex County College), Thomas Korllos (Kent State University), Rita Krasnow (Virginia Western Community College), Michael Levine (Kenyon College), George Lowe (Texas Tech University), Don Luidens (Hope College), Larry Lyon (Baylor University), Li-Chen Ma (Lamar University), Alan Mazur (Syracuse University), Meredith McGuire (Trinity College), Dan McMurry (Middle Tennessee State University), Jack Melhorn (Emporia State University), Joe Morolla (Virginia Commonwealth University), Craig Nauman (Madison Area Technical College), Toby Parcel (The Ohio State University), Anne Peterson (Columbus State Community College), Daniel Quinn (Adrian College), Nevel Razak (Fort Hays State College), Virginia Reynolds (Indiana University of Pennsylvania), Laurel Richardson (The Ohio State University), Ellen Rosengarten (Sinclair Community College), Howard Schneiderman (Lafayette College), Doug Schocke (Northern Virginia Community College), Ray Scupin (Lindenwood College), Harry Sherer (Irvine Valley College), Walt Shirley (Sinclair Community College), Glen Sims (Glendale Community College), Verta Taylor (The Ohio State University), Len Tompos (Lorain County Community College), Christopher Vanderpool (Michigan State University), Marilyn Wilmeth (Iowa University), Stuart Wright (Lamar University), Dan Yutze (Taylor University), Wayne Zapatek (Tarrant County Community College), and Frank Zulke (Harold Washington College).

Carol Singer, librarian at the National Agricultural Library in Washington, DC, skillfully secured statistical data for this revision. Amy Marsh Macionis, beyond providing thoughtful ideas on a daily basis, has made a substantial contribution to the editorial and production phases of this revision. Finally, I dedicate this edition of *Society: The Basics* to Whitney Linnea Macionis with the promise of a lifetime of love.

JJM

About the Author

John J. Macionis (pronounced ma-SHOW-nis) was born and raised in Philadelphia, Pennsylvania. He received his bachelor's degree from Cornell University and his doctorate in sociology from the University of Pennsylvania. His publications are wide-ranging, focusing on community life in the United States, interpersonal intimacy in families, effective teaching, the importance of global analysis to sociology, and the anatomy of humor. He is author of *Sociology*, the leading introductory textbook in the field, and he has coedited the companion volume to this text, *Seeing Ourselves: Classic, Contemporary, and Cross-Cultural Readings in Sociology* (both available from Prentice Hall). He is also coauthor of the popular urban text *The Sociology of Cities*.

John Macionis is currently professor of sociology at Kenyon College in Gambier, Ohio. He has served as chair of the Anthropology-Sociology Department, director of Kenyon's multidisciplinary program in humane studies, and chair of the college's faculty.

Professor Macionis teaches a wide range of upper-level courses but his favorite course is Introduction to Sociology, which he teaches every semester. He enjoys extensive contact with students, making an occasional appearance on campus with his guitar and inviting each of his students to enjoy a home-cooked meal. He also is a frequent visitor to other campuses and enjoys participating in teaching programs abroad. In the Fall of 1994, he will direct the Global Education course for the University of Pittsburgh's Semester at Sea, a program of world education based on a shipboard campus that circles the globe visiting ten countries.

John Macionis lives in rural Ohio with his wife Amy and children McLean and Whitney. Their home operates as a popular bed and breakfast where they enjoy visiting with old friends and making new ones.

The author welcomes comments and suggestions from faculty and students about this book. Write to Kenyon College, Gambier, Ohio 43022. His e-mail internet address is MACIONIS@KENYON.EDU

1

Sociology: Perspective, Theory, and Method

On a spring evening in New York's Central Park in 1989, a twenty-eight-year-old woman was jogging after a day of work in the city's financial district. As she passed a grove of sycamore trees, the quiet setting suddenly exploded into a chase as a gang of more than twenty teenage boys pursued her. Flushed with terror, the woman stumbled into a gully where she fought off her attackers while one youth battered her with a pipe and another stabbed her with a knife. Overpowered and seriously wounded, she was raped repeatedly. The attackers left their victim for dead, and she lay helpless and broken until found three hours later. Having lost much of her blood, she reached the hospital in a coma. After months of intensive care, she has made a courageous physical recovery.

Many people reacted to this incident with disbelief. Partly, this was because of the attack's brutality, and partly because the attackers were so young—fourteen to sixteen years of age. But most curiously, the boys could provide no reason for their crime beyond seeking excitement—what they called a night of "wilding." Thus this terrible event provoked people everywhere to confront the basic question: *What makes people do the things they do?*

There are, of course, many ways to look at human events. The *perspective*—or point of view—that we use

We can easily grasp the power of society over the individual simply by imagining how different our world would be had we been born in place of any of these children from around the globe.

determines which facts we see and suggests how we weave these facts together into coherent patterns of meaning. The police officers investigating the "wilding" case used one perspective to sort out who did what and to whom so they could make arrests. This point of view is concerned primarily with describing an event and responding to it in accordance with the law.

A psychiatrist offers another look at the boys' behavior. From a psychiatrist's point of view, the important issue is the state of mind that leads an individual to act so violently. In this case, the psychiatric perspective would isolate a different set of facts and prescribe a response based on appropriate medical principles.

A sociologist brings yet another perspective to understanding human behavior. A sociologist attempting to make sense of this incident might note that the offenders were males, that they were teenagers, and that they were members of an economically disadvantaged minority. Notice that the facts highlighted by the sociological perspective differ markedly from those noted by law enforcement officials or psychiatrists. The police are concerned with facts that pertain to this one, specific crime. Knowing that an offender is male is useful only if it leads to identifying *which* male was involved. Likewise, psychiatrists seek out the personal traumas that may have caused an explosive outburst by a particular person. Thus both police and psychiatrists share the assumption that, in important ways, each crime and every person are unique. By contrast, a sociologist looks at the behavior of any particular person and sees that *categories* of people act in distinctive ways.

This chapter introduces the sociological perspective and explains how sociologists tie this point of view to theory and scientific methods in order to study human behavior.

THE SOCIOLOGICAL PERSPECTIVE

The discipline of **sociology** is defined as *the scientific study of human social activity*. Sociologists use a distinctive point of view in their efforts to understand the social world.

Seeing the General in the Particular

Peter Berger (1963) describes the sociological perspective as *seeing the general in the particular*. This means that sociologists see general social patterns in the behavior of particular individuals. While acknowledging that each individual is unique, we also recognize that general social forces shape us into various *kinds* of people. In the Central Park jogger case, for example, the sociological perspective leads us to wonder if committing violent crime is more likely on the part of males than females, the young than the old, the disadvantaged as opposed to affluent people. Sociological research confirms that these conjectures are actually so.

Victimization rates, too, show society at work. Figure 1–1 provides a sociological insight into our chances of becoming a victim of homicide. First, the rate of victimization for African Americans (35.4 cases for every 100,000 people in this category in 1989) is more than *six times higher* than the rate for whites (5.4 per 100,000). Also notice that for both races, males are more likely than females to become homicide victims. Among whites, males (8.2) are almost three times more likely than females (2.8) to fall victim to homicide. For people of African descent, males (61.1) have a rate more than four times higher than that of females (12.9). As we shall see in Chapter 6 ("Deviance"), while whites commit

Figure 1–1 Rate of Death by Homicide, by Race and Sex, for the United States

Rates indicate the number of deaths by homicide for every 100,000 people in each category for 1989.
(*U.S. Bureau of the Census*)

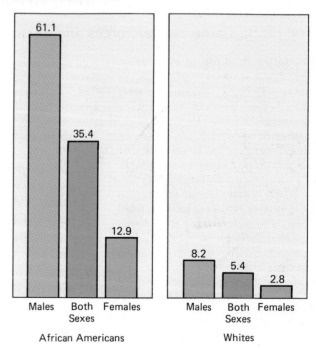

most crimes in the United States, disproportionate numbers of disadvantaged African-American men are involved in violent crime as offenders and as victims. Clearly, then, our particular life experiences are shaped by the general categories of society into which we fall.

Seeing the Strange in the Familiar

The sociological perspective shows us *the strange in the familiar.* This does not mean that sociologists focus on the bizarre elements of society but that we give up the familiar idea that human behavior is simply a matter of what people *decide* to do, in favor of the initially strange notion that society guides our thoughts and deeds.

For individualistic North Americans, learning to "see" how society affects us may take a bit of practice. Consider the seemingly personal matter of people's names. Historically, many U.S. celebrities changed their names as they began their careers. But are the names they use simply a matter of personal choice or are social forces at work? The box takes a critical look at what's in a name.

Individuality in Social Context

Sociological insights often challenge common sense by suggesting that human behavior is not as individualistic as we may think. For most of us, everyday awareness carries a heavy load of personal responsibility: we pat ourselves on the back when we succeed in our endeavors and kick ourselves when things go wrong. Proud of our individuality, even in painful times, we resist the idea that we or others act in socially patterned ways.

For this reason, it generally provokes controversy when someone suggests that "society" has a hand in a crime like the Central Park attack, described at the beginning of this chapter. In the weeks following the "wilding" incident, the U.S. press debated how much personal responsibility should be assigned to the attackers.

On one side of the controversy, social scientists pointed out that a wide range of social factors—including gender, youth, race, and social background—had to be considered in accurately assigning blame. But several nationally known commentators took an opposing view, claiming that *bad kids* alone were to blame for the repulsive act. They criticized sociologists for appearing to

SOCIAL DIVERSITY

The Name Game: Social Forces and Personal Choice

On the fourth of July in 1918, twins were born in Sioux City, Iowa, to Abe and Becky Friedman, who named their first-born twin Esther Pauline and her sister Pauline Esther. Today, these women are known to almost everyone, but by very different names: Ann Landers and Abigail ("Dear Abby") Van Buren.

These two women are among tens of thousands of people in the United States who have changed their names to further their careers. At first glance, a new name may seem to be simply a matter of personal preference. But using the sociological perspective, we see that most people tend to adopt *English-sounding* names. Why? Because our society has long accorded high social prestige to those of Anglo-Saxon background. How many of these well-known people can you identify from their original names?

1. Michael James Vijencio Gubitosi
2. Cherilyn Sarkisian
3. Jacob Cohen
4. Robert Allen Zimmerman
5. Patsy McClenny
6. Nathan Birnbaum
7. Frederick Austerlitz
8. George Kyriakou Panayiotou
9. Ana Mae Bullock
10. Issur Danielovitch Demsky
11. Mladen Sekulovich
12. Gerald Silberman
13. Bernadette Lazzarra
14. Karen Ziegler
15. Ramon Estevez
16. Henry John Deutschendorf, Jr.
17. Allan Stewart Konigsberg
18. Judy Cohen
19. Eugene Maurice Orowitz
20. William Claude Dukenfield

1. Robert Blake; 2. Cher; 3. Rodney Dangerfield; 4. Bob Dylan; 5. Morgan Fairchild; 6. George Burns; 7. Fred Astaire; 8. George Michael; 9. Tina Turner; 10. Kirk Douglas; 11. Karl Malden; 12. Gene Wilder; 13. Bernadette Peters; 14. Karen Black; 15. Martin Sheen; 16. John Denver; 17. Woody Allen; 18. Juice Newton; 19. Michael Landon; 20. W. C. Fields

side with the offenders by blaming everything but the individual perpetrators for the vicious attack (Will, 1989).

Such criticism tells us something about sociology and much about the United States. When a particular event causes pain and anguish, we want to know who is to blame and want to see guilty people punished. In this case, six teenage boys (of the twenty or so who participated) were charged with the crime. This action partially satisfied our passionate sense of anger. But are we seeing the whole picture?

Sociologists insist that the answer is no. Of course, sociological analysis does *not* defend committing violent crimes. But, in truth, no human behavior is solely the product of simple "free will" or mere "personal choice." While people make decisions, the available choices depend on a host of powerful social forces (as well as whatever biological and psychological factors may also be at work).

One example is gender. Would anyone imagine that teenage *girls* would be as likely as teenage boys to commit this kind of crime? As Chapter 6 ("Deviance") explains, males in the United States commit *nine times* as many violent crimes as females do. And what about age? Are middle-aged people as likely as teenagers to "choose" to attack innocent people? Hardly, as evidenced by the fact that people between the ages of fifteen and twenty-four represent only 14.5 percent of our nation's population but account for 40.4 percent of all violent crimes. Likewise, we know that categories of people who are poor—white and black alike—experience more violence, both as victims and offenders, than more affluent people do. Finally, crimes such as the Central Park attack are also remarkably *American*. More assaults and murders occur in New York and other U.S. cities in a week than occur in most European cities in a year. In fact, more people are killed by stray bullets in New York than die from deliberate attacks in the major cities of Europe.

Every society demands that people take some personal responsibility for their actions, and our society does this more than most. Thus we think that to blame "society" for a problem is to blame everyone—and no one. In this cultural climate of individualism, sociology injects a needed dose of realism. Embedded in society from the moment of our birth, we learn to think, feel, and act as products of a larger social world. To think sociologically, therefore, does not mean we become "bleeding hearts." Rather, thinking sociologically helps us understand ourselves and the world around us more fully and accurately.

Suicide: The most individual act. Nothing demonstrates the power of social forces to influence human behavior better than the study of suicide. What, after all, is more personal than taking one's own life? This is why Emile Durkheim (1858–1917), a pioneer of sociology, chose this as a topic of research. He was able to reveal social forces at work even in the apparent isolation of the ultimate self-destructive act.

Durkheim examined official records of suicide in and around his native France.[1] The statistics clearly showed that some categories of people are much more likely than others to take their own lives. Specifically, Durkheim found, men, Protestants, wealthy people, and the unmarried each had significantly higher suicide rates than did women, Catholics and Jews, the poor, and married people. Durkheim explained these differences by reasoning that suicide varied according to a person's degree of *social integration*. Low suicide rates, in other words, characterized the kinds of people who commonly have stronger ties to others. By contrast, high suicide rates were found among categories of people who are typically more individualistic.

In the patriarchal societies studied by Durkheim, men certainly had more autonomy than women. Whatever its advantages, explained Durkheim, this freedom lowers social integration, contributing to a higher suicide rate among men. Likewise, Catholic and Jewish practices foster stronger social ties and thus lower rates of suicide than do individualistic Protestant beliefs. The wealthy clearly have much more freedom than the poor, but with a predictably higher suicide rate. Finally, with weaker social bonds than married people, single people, too, are at greater risk of suicide.

A century later, statistical evidence still supports Durkheim's analysis. Figure 1–2 shows suicide rates for four categories in the U.S. population. Whites had 12.0 recorded suicides for every 100,000 people in 1989, almost twice the rate of African Americans (7.1). Also, for both races, suicide is more common among men than women. White men (19.6) are four times more likely than white women (4.8) to take their own lives. Among African Americans, the rate for men (12.5) is five times that for women (2.4). Following Durkheim's argument, we conclude that the higher suicide rate among whites and men (and especially white men) is due to their greater affluence and autonomy. By contrast, poorer people and those with limited choices are more

---

[1] This discussion is a much-abbreviated account of Durkheim's (1966; orig. 1897) considerably more complex analysis of suicide.

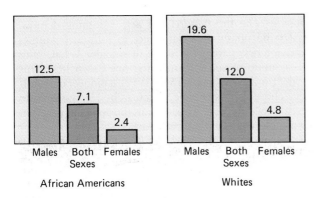

Figure 1–2 Rate of Death by Suicide, by Race and Sex, for the United States

Rates indicate the number of deaths by suicide for every 100,000 people in each category for 1989.
(*U.S. Bureau of the Census*)

socially rooted and have correspondingly lower suicide rates.

In this way, we see general social patterns in even the most personal actions of individuals. Social forces are complex, of course, as a comparison of Figures 1–1 and 1–2 shows. The social forces linked to race produce opposing patterns with regard to homicide and suicide. Disadvantaged African Americans suffer disproportionately from homicide; more privileged whites suffer more from suicide. Men of any race are more prone than women to both homicide and suicide.

The Importance of Global Perspective

Sociology's basic insight is that our placement in society profoundly affects our individual experiences. Extending this argument, the standing of the United States in the larger world affects everyone in this country.

In global perspective, the United States is among the world's richest nations, as Global Map 1–1 shows. The 1991 annual per-person income in the United States (including children as well as adults) stands at $19,133. This affluence opens a range of personal choices for us—in terms of housing, health care, education, and personal recreation—unknown to most of the world's people. As Chapter 8 ("Global Inequality") explains, billions of adults and children live with little choice in poor, strongly traditional communities. Thus the choices available to us follow from both our placement in one society and that society's standing in a world of nations.

Global sophistication is especially important today, as political changes sweep through Latin America, Eastern Europe, the former Soviet Union, the Middle East, and South Africa, and rapid economic development reshapes many countries in Eastern Asia. One reason the world is changing so quickly is that societies are increasingly interdependent: note, for example, that 80 percent of new jobs in this country now involve foreign trade (Council on International Educational Exchange, 1988).

The Sociological Perspective in Everyday Life

Although members of our society often overlook the power of social forces, some situations do prompt us to think sociologically even before we take a first sociology course.

Encountering social diversity. Recognizing cultural diversity stimulates the sociological perspective. We can hardly consider the life of a young woman in Saudi Arabia or a man living in the African nation of Botswana without thinking about what it means to live in the United States. Just as a foreign student on a U.S. college campus typically notices social patterns that natives take for granted, so a North American encountering the social diversity of the world gains a heightened awareness of social forces. Even facing the social diversity of our local community encourages us to look at ourselves with new eyes.

Marginality: Race and gender. Sociologists use the term *social marginality* to mean a condition of being excluded as an "outsider." We all feel we don't fit in from time to time; for some categories of people, however, standing apart from the mainstream is an everyday experience. The more acute people's social marginality, the more likely they are to embrace the sociological perspective.

No African American, for example, lives for long in the United States without learning how much race affects personal experiences. But because whites are the dominant majority, they think about race only from time to time and often imagine that race affects only African Americans rather than themselves as well.

Much the same is true of women, gay people, people with disabilities, and the very old. All those relegated to the outskirts of social life are likely to recognize social patterns others take for granted. They have stepped back from society (or perhaps, more correctly, society has stepped back from them) and therefore take a more sociological view of the world.

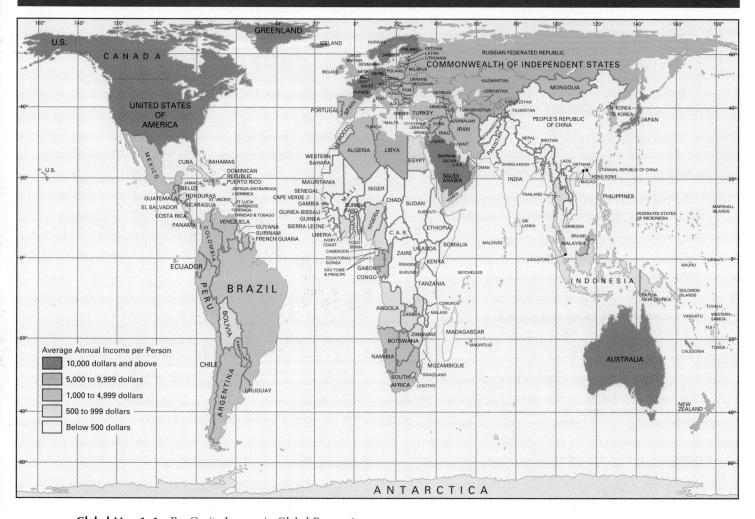

Global Map 1–1 Per Capita Income in Global Perspective

Comprehending the range of opportunities and obstacles that confronts us depends not only on understanding our place in a single society, but also on seeing our society's position in the world as a whole. Average people in the United States and Canada, where income is far higher than in most of the world, live longer and more comfortably than people who inhabit poor societies of Latin America, Africa, and Asia.

Social crisis. U.S. sociologist C. Wright Mills (1959) suggested that social disruption also sparks sociological thinking. For example, during the Great Depression of the 1930s, one-fourth of the labor force was out of work. In this catastrophic situation, unemployed workers could not help but see general social forces at work in their particular lives. Rather than claiming, "Something is wrong with me; I can't find a job," they were likely to say, "The economy has collapsed; there are no jobs to be found!"

The decade of the 1960s also enhanced sociological awareness in the United States. The civil rights, women's liberation, and antiwar movements each challenged accepted social patterns, highlighting ways in which people's lives are shaped by the political, economic, military, and technological elements of "the system." Although the merits of these movements may be debated, they certainly called attention to the ways in which the lives of women and men are shaped by social forces.

Worth noting, too, is that sociological thinking often fosters social change. The more we learn about the operation of "the system," the more we may wish to change it in some way. An introduction to sociology, then, helps us to understand—and perhaps to reshape—the world around us.

THE ORIGINS OF SOCIOLOGY

Like individual "choices," historical events rarely just happen; they are usually products of powerful social forces. So it was with sociology itself.

Although people have thought about society since the beginning of human history, sociology is one of the youngest academic disciplines—far younger than history, physics, or economics. Only in 1838 did the French social thinker Auguste Comte coin the term *sociology* for a new way of looking at the world.

Science and Sociology

The nature of society held the attention of virtually all the brilliant thinkers of the ancient world, including the Greek philosophers Plato (427–347 B.C.E.) and Aristotle (384–322 B.C.E.).[2] In the centuries that followed, the Roman emperor Marcus Aurelius (121–180), the medieval writer Christine de Pizan (c. 1363–1431), and the English playwright William Shakespeare (1564–1616) all reflected on the state of human society.

Yet these philosophers and theologians envisioned the "ideal" society; none tried to analyze society as it actually was. In creating their new discipline, pioneers Auguste Comte, Emile Durkheim, and others reversed these priorities. Although they remained concerned with how human society could be improved, the major goal of early sociologists was to understand how society actually operates.

---

[2] Throughout this text, the abbreviation B.C.E. designates "before the common era." This terminology is used in place of the traditional B.C. ("before Christ") in recognition of the religious plurality of our society. Similarly, in place of the traditional A.D. (anno Domini, or "in the year of our Lord"), the abbreviation C.E. ("common era") is employed.

Comte (1975; orig. 1851–1854) identified three stages in the historical emergence of scientific sociology. During the earliest *theological stage*, corresponding to the medieval era in Europe, people adopted a religious view that society expressed God's will. With the Renaissance, this theological approach gave way to what Comte called the *metaphysical stage*, in which people saw society as the product of natural forces. For instance, the English philosopher Thomas Hobbes (1588–1679) suggested that society was guided primarily by a rather selfish human nature. What Comte heralded as the final, *scientific stage* began as scientific thought—first seen in the work of Polish astronomer Copernicus (1473–1543), the Italian astronomer and physicist Galileo (1564–1642), and the English physicist and mathematician Isaac Newton (1642–1727). This approach was applied by Comte and others to the study of society. The term **positivism** means *a path to understanding based on science.* As a positivist, Comte believed that society had an inherent, underlying order that one could study and understand, just as physical scientists had learned that the natural world operates according to gravity and other identifiable principles.

Emerging as an academic discipline in the United States at the beginning of this century, sociology embraced Comte's ideas. Even today, most sociologists agree that science is a crucial element of sociology. But since Comte's time, we have learned that human behavior is often far more complex than natural events. That is, human beings are not just physical objects but creatures with considerable imagination and spontaneity whose behavior can never be fully explained by any rigid "laws of society."

Social Change and Sociology

Striking transformations in seventeenth- and eighteenth-century Europe drove the development of sociology. As the social ground trembled under their feet, people understandably focused their attention on society.

First came technological discoveries that produced a factory-based, industrial economy. In the Middle Ages, most people in Europe tilled fields near their homes or engaged in small-scale *manufacturing* (derived from Latin meaning "to make by hand"). But by the middle of the eighteenth century, factories appeared as inventors applied new sources of energy—including steam power—to the operation of large machines. Now, instead of laboring at home or in tightly knit groups, workers became part of a large and anonymous industrial labor force, toiling for strangers who owned the factories. This

The birth of sociology came at a time of rapid social change. The discipline developed in those regions of Europe where the Industrial Revolution most disrupted traditional ways of life, drawing people from isolated villages to rapidly growing industrial cities.

change in the system of production prompted a rapid breakdown of traditions that had guided small communities for centuries.

Second, as factories sprouted across England and the European continent, cities grew to unprecedented size. English industrialists were quick to turn farmland into grazing pastures for sheep—the source of wool for the textile mills. This so-called Enclosure Movement pushed countless people from the countryside toward cities in search of work in the new factories. Soon the small settlements of the medieval world were eclipsed by the great cities of the industrial era. These cities churned with strangers, in numbers that often overwhelmed available housing. Widespread social problems—including pollution, crime, and homelessness—further stimulated development of the sociological perspective.

A third change occurred in political thought. By the sixteenth century, every kind of tradition had come under spirited attack. In the writings of Thomas Hobbes (1588–1679), John Locke (1632–1704), and Adam Smith (1723–1790), we find less concern with moral obligations than with self-interest. Indeed, the key phrases in the new political climate—*liberty* and *rights*—highlighted not the group but the individual. Echoing the thoughts of Locke, our own Declaration of Independence clearly spells out that each citizen has "certain unalienable rights," including "life, liberty, and the pursuit of happiness."

The political revolution in France that began in 1789 sparked an even more dramatic break with political and social traditions. As he surveyed his own country after the French Revolution, the French social and political thinker Alexis de Tocqueville (1805–1859) exaggerated only slightly when he asserted that the changes amounted to "nothing short of the regeneration of the whole human race" (1955:13; orig. 1856). The new industrial economy, enormous cities, and fresh political ideas combined to draw attention to society; not surprisingly, the discipline of sociology flowered in precisely those countries—France, Germany, and England—where change was greatest.

Various sociologists reacted differently to these changes, just as they respond differently to society today. Although Auguste Comte celebrated the birth of scientific sociology, he feared that rapid change would overpower tradition and uproot long-established communities. His conservative sociology ended up seeking a rebirth of traditional family, rooted community, and conventional morality. Quite different were the ideas of German social critic Karl Marx (1818–1883), who despised traditional society. But Marx detested even more the concentration of industrial wealth in the hands of a small elite, while the masses faced only hunger and misery.

Although they differed in their assessments of changing social conditions, Comte and Marx were both part of the movement that established sociology as an academic discipline. The sociological perspective animates the work of each, showing that people's lives are framed by the social forces at work in a particular time and place.

SOCIOLOGICAL THEORY

The task of turning isolated observations into understanding brings us to another dimension of sociology: theory. A **theory** is *an explanation of how and why specific facts are related*. In his study of suicide, Emile Durkheim explained variations in suicide rates by observing that categories of people prone to suicide (including men, Protestants, wealthy people, and the unmarried) were those with low social integration.

In building theory, sociologists face a number of choices. What issues should we choose to study? How should we link facts together? In making sense of society, sociologists are guided by one or more general frameworks, or theoretical paradigms (Kuhn, 1970). A **theoretical paradigm** is *a set of fundamental assumptions that guides thinking and research*. Three major paradigms in sociology are the structural-functional paradigm, the social-conflict paradigm, and the symbolic-interaction paradigm.

The Structural-Functional Paradigm

The **structural-functional paradigm** is *a theoretical framework based on the assumption that society is a complex system whose parts work together to promote stability*. As its name suggests, the structural-functional paradigm makes two assertions. The first holds that society is composed of **social structures,** meaning *relatively stable patterns of social behavior*. Social structures range from broad patterns, including the family and religious systems, to face-to-face behavior like waving hello. The second is that each social structure has a **social function,** or *consequences for the operation of society as a whole*. Social structures—from economic production to a simple handshake—have a part in perpetuating society, at least in its present form.

The structural-functional paradigm owes much to the ideas of Auguste Comte, who sought to promote social integration during a time of dramatic change. A second architect of this theoretical orientation, the English sociologist Herbert Spencer (1820–1903), liked to compare society with the human body: as the skeleton, muscles, and various internal organs of the body each contribute to the survival of the human organism, so do social structures work together to keep society operating. This approach, then, leads sociologists to identify various social structures and to ask what part each plays in the operation of the whole system.

Several decades after Comte's death, Emile Durkheim further developed the structural-functional paradigm. As later chapters explain, Durkheim explored, as a guiding idea, how societies manage to tie countless individual lives together.

The work of Robert K. Merton, a contemporary U.S. sociologist, has refined the structural-functional approach, showing that any social structure usually has many functions, some more obvious than others. The **manifest functions** of a social structure refer to *consequences both recognized and intended by people in the society*. **Latent functions,** by contrast, are *consequences that are largely unrecognized and unintended*. Our growing reliance on automobiles during this century has had both kinds of consequences. The manifest functions of cars range from transporting people and goods to serving as status symbols that say something about a person's taste and bank account. One latent function of automobiles, which allow people to travel in relative isolation, is to reinforce our cultural emphasis on privacy and personal autonomy.

Merton makes a further point: it is unlikely that *all* the effects of a social structure will be positive. The term **social dysfunction** designates *undesirable effects on the operation of society*. One of the dysfunctions of our national reliance on private motor vehicles is that, with more than 180 million of them, air quality has suffered, especially in large cities. No doubt, too, the easy travel made possible by cars has eroded some of the strength of traditional families and local neighborhoods, changes many people lament.

Critical evaluation. The structural-functional paradigm has long been influential in sociology, although critics have revealed limitations of this approach. By focusing attention on societal unity, critics point out, structural-functionalism tends to overlook divisions based on social class, race, ethnicity, and gender, and to downplay how such divisions can generate tension and conflict. In addition, the structural-functional emphasis on stability tends to minimize important processes of social change. Overall, then, this paradigm takes a conservative stance toward society. As a critical response to this approach, another theoretical orientation in sociology has emerged: the social-conflict paradigm.

The Social-Conflict Paradigm

The **social-conflict paradigm** is *a theoretical framework based on the assumption that society is a complex system characterized by inequality and conflict that generate social change.* This orientation complements the structural-functional paradigm by highlighting not integration but social division. Using this paradigm, sociologists investigate how factors such as social class, race, ethnicity, gender, and age are linked to the unequal distribution of wealth, schooling, power, and prestige. Rather than identifying how social patterns work to promote the functioning of society as a whole, then, this approach concentrates on how these patterns benefit some people at the expense of others.

Social-conflict theorists view society as an arena in which conflict arises from the incompatible interests of various categories of people. Not surprisingly, dominant categories—the rich in relation to the poor, whites in relation to people of color, and men in relation to women—typically protect their privileges by supporting the status quo. Those with fewer advantages commonly try to bring about a more equitable distribution of social resources.

To illustrate, Chapter 13 ("Education and Medicine") details how secondary schools in the United States prepare some students for college and emphasize voca-

People whose gender or race put them at the margins of their society also contributed to the development of sociology. Harriet Martineau (1802–1876) (left), born to a rich English family, established her reputation as a sociologist with studies of slavery, factory laws, and women's rights. In the United States, Jane Addams (1860–1935) (middle) was a social worker active on behalf of poor immigrants. In 1889, Addams founded Hull House, a Chicago settlement house, where she engaged intellectuals and immigrants alike in discussions of the pressing problems of her day. Her contribution to the welfare of others earned Addams a Nobel Peace Prize in 1931. William Edward Burghardt DuBois (1868–1963) (right) was a bright child born to a poor Massachusetts family. He managed to enter Fisk University in Nashville and then Harvard, becoming the first person of color to earn a doctorate there. He is known for his study of the African-American community in Philadelphia at the turn of the century. Like Martineau and Addams, DuBois argued for linking research to human needs.

tional training for others. A structural-functional analysis might lead us to ask how society benefits from providing different types of schooling to students of differing academic abilities. The social-conflict paradigm offers a contrasting insight: "tracking" confers privileges on some students that it denies to others, thereby perpetuating social inequality.

Research guided by the social-conflict paradigm has shown that schools place students in college-preparatory tracks not just because of their intelligence but based on the privileged background of their families. Once ensured of becoming part of the educational elite with a college degree, most go on to occupations that confer both prestige and high income. By contrast, schools generally fill vocational tracks with students from modest backgrounds, sometimes with little regard for their academic potential. They receive no preparation for college, and thus, like their parents before them, they typically enter occupations that offer little prestige and low income. In both cases, the social standing of one generation is passed on to another, and this practice is justified in terms of alleged individual merit (Bowles & Gintis, 1976; Oakes, 1982, 1985).

Other examples of social conflict in the United States include labor strikes, the civil rights movement, and the drive for social equality by women. In each of these cases, the social-conflict paradigm points up how social structure fosters not stability but conflict between the forces of change and those seeking to maintain the status quo.

Finally, many sociologists who embrace the social-conflict paradigm attempt not only to understand society but to reduce social inequality. This was the central goal of Karl Marx, the social thinker who had a singularly important influence on the development of the social-conflict paradigm. Marx had little patience with those who sought to use science only to understand how society works. In a well-known declaration (inscribed on his monument in London's Highgate Cemetery), Marx asserted: "The philosophers have only interpreted the world, in various ways; the point, however, is to change it."

Critical evaluation. The social-conflict paradigm has developed rapidly in recent decades. Yet, like other approaches, it has come in for its share of criticism. Because this paradigm highlights power struggles, it gives little attention to social unity based on functional interdependence and shared values. In addition, say critics, the social-conflict approach advocates explicitly political goals in its drive for a more egalitarian society, thereby giving up the claim to scientific objectivity. Supporters of this paradigm counter that *all* social approaches have political consequences, albeit different ones.

Both the structural-functional and social-conflict paradigms envision society in broad, abstract terms, which sometimes seem quite distant from everyday experience. Thus, sociologists also employ a third theoretical paradigm, which views society more in terms of situational interaction. We now turn to this third approach.

The Symbolic-Interaction Paradigm

Both the structural-functional and social-conflict paradigms share a **macro-level orientation,** meaning *a concern with large-scale patterns that characterize society as a whole.* They take in the big picture, as you might investigate a city from the vantage point of a helicopter high above the ground, noting how highways facilitate traffic flow from one place to another or the striking contrasts between rich and poor neighborhoods. The symbolic-interaction paradigm differs by providing a **micro-level orientation,** meaning *a concern with small-scale patterns of social interaction in specific settings.* Exploring urban life in this way occurs at street level, observing face-to-face interaction in public parks or how individuals respond to homeless people. The **symbolic-interaction paradigm,** then, is *a theoretical framework based on the view that society is the product of the everyday interaction of individuals.*

How do millions of people weave their lives together into the drama of society? One answer, examined in detail in Chapter 2 ("Culture"), is that people are joined through common meanings we attach to everyday events and experiences. Sociologists guided by the symbolic-interaction approach view society as a complex mosaic of consensus and conflict emerging from our subjective perceptions and responses.

The symbolic-interaction paradigm rests, in part, on the work of Max Weber (1864–1920), a German sociologist who emphasized the need to understand a setting from the point of view of the people in it. On this foundation, others have constructed a number of specific approaches to learning about social life. Chapter 3 ("Socialization: From Infancy to Old Age") discusses the ideas of George Herbert Mead (1863–1931), who found the roots of human personality in social experience. Chapter 4 ("Social Interaction in Everyday Life") presents the work of Erving Goffman (1922–1982), whose *dramaturgical analysis* reveals how human beings resemble actors on a stage as they deliberately foster certain impressions in the minds of others. Other contemporary sociologists, including George Homans and Peter Blau, have developed *social-exchange analysis*. In their view, social interaction is guided by what each person stands to gain (and lose) from others. In the process of courtship, for example, individuals seek mates who offer them at least as much—in terms of physical attractiveness, intelligence, and social prestige—as they offer in return.

Critical evaluation. The symbolic-interaction paradigm helps to overcome a limitation typical of macrolevel approaches to understanding society. Without denying the reality of broad patterns such as "the family" and "social inequality," we must remember that society basically amounts to people interacting. Put another way, this micro-approach attempts to convey more of how individuals actually *experience* society.

Table 1–1 summarizes the distinctive features of the three theoretical paradigms. One paradigm may be more useful than another in a given situation, since each leads us to ask different kinds of questions. But the three taken together provide a more complete understanding about social life. The box on pages 14–15 illustrates how the structural-functional paradigm, the social-conflict paradigm, and the symbolic-interaction paradigm combine to produce a comprehensive analysis of sports.

SCIENTIFIC SOCIOLOGY

Refinements in sociological theory come from research. Spurred on by their curiosity, sociologists ask questions about how and why we behave as we do. To answer these questions, researchers rely on **science**, *a logical system that derives knowledge from direct, systematic observation*. Scientific knowledge, therefore, is based on **empirical evidence**, *facts we are able to verify with our senses*.

Sociological research often reveals that what we accept as "common sense" is not entirely true. Here are three examples of widely held attitudes that are contradicted by scientific evidence.

1. **Differences in the social behavior of women and men are "human nature."** Sociological investigation shows us that what we call "human nature"

Table 1–1   THE THREE MAJOR THEORETICAL PARADIGMS: A SUMMARY

Theoretical Paradigm	Orientation	Image of Society	Illustrative Questions
Structural-functional	Macro-level	A system of interrelated parts that is relatively stable based on widespread consensus as to what is morally desirable; each part has functional consequences for the operation of society as a whole	How is society integrated? What are the major parts of society? How are these parts interrelated? What are the consequences of each for the operation of society?
Social-conflict	Macro-level	A system characterized by social inequality; any part of society benefits some categories of people more than others; conflict-based social inequality promotes social change	How is society divided? What are major patterns of social inequality? How do some categories of people attempt to protect their privileges? How do other categories of people challenge the status quo?
Symbolic-interaction	Micro-level	An ongoing process of social interaction in specific settings based on symbolic communications; individual perceptions of reality are variable and changing	How is society experienced? How do human beings interact to create, sustain, and change social patterns? How do individuals attempt to shape the reality perceived by others? How does individual behavior change from one situation to another?

Sports: Playing the Theory Game

To people in the United States, sports seem indispensable to life. With almost everyone engaging in sports to at least some degree, the field has evolved into a multibillion-dollar industry. What insights can the three theoretical paradigms provide about this familiar element of life?

A structural-functional approach directs attention to the functions of sports for society as a whole. Manifest functions include providing recreation, offering a relatively harmless way to "let off steam," and contributing to the physical fitness of the population. Sports have important latent functions as well, from fostering social relationships, to generating tens of thousands of jobs, to celebrating competition, achievement, and success—ideas central to our way of life (Spates, 1976a; Coakley, 1990). When he said, "Winning is not everything, but making the effort to win is," Vince Lombardi was speaking not only as a football coach; he was also speaking for his entire society.

Sports has dysfunctional consequences as well. For example, colleges and universities intent on fielding winning teams sometimes recruit students for their athletic ability rather than their academic aptitude. This can pull down the academic standards of the school and may leave the athletes themselves little time to concentrate on anything but their sport.

A social-conflict analysis of sports begins by pointing out that sports are closely related to patterns of social inequality. Some sports, like tennis,

swimming, golf, and skiing, are expensive, so participation is largely limited to the well-to-do. By contrast, sports with mass appeal, including football, baseball, and basketball, are accessible to people of all income levels. In short, the games people play are not simply a matter of choice but also reflect their social standing.

In the United States, sports are oriented primarily toward males. Sexual discrimination has traditionally limited the athletic opportunities of females, even when they have the talent, interest, and economic means to participate. The first modern Olympic Games held in 1896, for example, excluded women from competition entirely (Mangan & Park, 1987). Until quite recently, Little League teams also barred girls in most parts of the country. Such discrimination has been defended by unfounded notions that women lack athletic ability or that women athletes risk losing their femininity. Thus our society encourages men to be athletes while expecting women to be attentive observers and cheerleaders. More women now play professional sports than ever before, yet they continue to take a back seat to men, particularly in sports that yield the greatest earnings and social prestige.

Our society long excluded people of color as well from professional sports, although the opportunity to earn a high income in athletics has expanded in recent decades. Major league baseball first admitted African-American players when Jackie Robin-

son broke the "color line" in 1947. By 1991, African Americans (12 percent of the total population) accounted for 18 percent of professional baseball players, 61 percent of all football players, and 72 percent of all basketball players (Center for the Study of Sport in Society, 1991).

The increasing proportion of people of African descent in professional sports reflects the fact that individual athletic performances cannot be diminished by white prejudice. It is also true that some people of color are drawn to athletics because of the relatively greater opportunity it affords (Steele, 1990).

Nonetheless, racial discrimination still shapes professional sports in the United States. For example, while people of color now fill the player ranks, almost all managers, head coaches, and owners of sports teams are still white. Furthermore, minority players hold few starring positions in professional sports: about 70 percent of African-American players in major league baseball patrol the outfield. In football and basketball, too, whites predominate in the central positions (Jones, 1987; Staples, 1987; Coakley, 1990).

From a social-conflict perspective, one might also wonder who benefits most from professional sports. Although millions of fans follow their teams, the vast earnings they generate are controlled by the small number of people (again, predominantly white men) for whom teams are income-producing property. Thus sports in the United States are bound up with inequalities based on gender, race, and economic power.

Turning to the symbolic-interaction paradigm, sports form a complex and changing pattern of interaction. Play is guided by a person's assigned position and by formal and informal rules of the game. But like all patterns of human behavior, sports are also partly spontaneous so that the precise outcome of a game cannot be predicted, and each player looks at the game from a unique perspective. Some people, for example, thrive in competitive situations while others perform badly under pressure. To some, sports offer a chance to win, while others turn to athletics as a means of building personal friendships (Coakley, 1986).

Furthermore, the behavior of team members changes over time. Rookies, for example, may feel quite self-conscious during the first few games in the big leagues. In time, however, most develop a more comfortable sense of team membership. This process of coming to feel at home in professional sports was slow and agonizing for Jackie Robinson, who recognized early on that many white players, and millions of white baseball fans, resented his presence in major league baseball (Tygiel, 1983). Eventually, however, his outstanding ability and his confident and cooperative manner won him the respect of the entire nation.

By noting how each of these paradigms differs in its approach to any

The painting *Pastime* by Gerald Garston suggests that baseball—the Great American Pastime—is more than mere diversion and entertainment. In addition, the sport provides valuable lessons about how we in the United States expect each other to think and behave.

issue, we do not mean to imply that one offers a more accurate analysis than another. Applied to various social issues, the different theoretical paradigms draw out fascinating debates and engaging controversies; the richest sociology, therefore, comes from using all three.

There are many kinds of truth. *The Emergence of Clowns* by U.S. artist Roxanne Swentzell presents the story of creation according to the Santa Clara Pueblo. Life began, they believe, when four clowns emerged onto the earth's surface, each facing in a different direction. All of the world's people have creation beliefs of some kind (including the Biblical accounts in *Genesis*). As members of a scientific society, we sometimes dismiss such stories as "myth." Whether or not they are entirely factual, they do convey basic truths about the way in which each society searches for human origins and struggles to find meaning in the universe. It is science, not "myth," that is powerless to address such questions.

is largely the product of the society in which we are raised. Further, researchers have discovered that definitions of "feminine" and "masculine" vary significantly from one society to another (see Chapter 10, "Sex and Gender").

2. **The United States and Canada are middle-class societies in which most people are more or less equal.** North America is rich by global standards. Research also reveals that the richest 5 percent of our population controls half of the country's property, while about half the population has little or no wealth at all. Chapters 7 ("Social Stratification") and 8 ("Global Inequality") provide details.

3. **People marry because they are in love.** It may come as a surprise to many people, but researchers have discovered that most marriages worldwide have little to do with love. In addition, as Chapter 12 ("Family and Religion") explains, we can safely predict that most people will fall in love with someone of a similar social background.

As these examples indicate, the sociological perspective—carried forward in scientific research—turns up unexpected facts and can help us to evaluate critically a wide range of information we encounter every day.

Concepts, Variables, and Measurement

A crucial element of science is the **concept,** *an abstract idea that represents some aspect of the world, inevitably in a somewhat simplified form.* Sociologists use concepts to identify key dimensions of social life, including "religion" and "the economy," and to categorize individuals in terms of their "gender," "race," or "social class."

A **variable** consists of *a concept whose value changes from case to case.* The familiar variable known as "price" varies from item to item in a supermarket. In a similar way, the concept of "social class" varies as we describe people as "upper class," "middle class," "working class," or "lower class."

Measurement means *determining the value of a variable in a specific case.* We can measure a variable as easily as stepping on a scale to discover our weight. Measuring sociological variables, however, is typically more difficult. A sociologist might assess social class, for example, by asking about someone's income, occupation, or education. But these three measures may yield inconsistent results.

An important rule of research holds that a researcher must *operationalize* all variables, that is, specify exactly what is to be measured in each case. In measuring social class, for example, researchers must decide precisely what aspect of social class is being measured and report this decision along with their findings.

A related issue arises when sociologists seek to describe a category of people using a variable like income. Clearly it is impractical to report the income of many people individually; more usefully, sociologists employ one or more numerical measures called *descriptive statistics*, described in the box.

Reliability and validity. Beyond carefully operationalizing variables, useful measurement also depends on reliability and validity. **Reliability** refers to *consistency in measurement*. If, for example, two measures of one community's religious attitudes produce different values, we suspect that one or both of them is not reliable.

Even consistent results, however, may not be valid. **Validity** refers to *measuring exactly what one intends to measure*. Say that you are interested in assessing how religious people are. You decide to do this by asking how often your respondents attend religious services. But are religiosity and attending services really the same? After all, people engage in religious rituals for any number of reasons, not all of them religious; some devout

believers, on the other hand, avoid organized religion entirely. Thus, even when a measure yields consistent results (having reliability), it can still miss the real, intended target (lacking validity). Because poor measurement undermines scientific precision, researchers must always pay close attention to reliability and validity.

Correlation and Cause

We gain insights about the social world as we begin to link variables together. **Correlation** means *a relationship between two (or more) variables*; in simple terms, we notice that when one variable changes so does the other. Ideally, sociological research seeks to understand not only *what* changes but also *why*. More useful than merely noting correlation, then, is mapping out relationships in terms of **cause and effect**, which means that *change in one variable is explained by change in another*. As we noted earlier, Emile Durkheim explained varying suicide rates for categories of people in terms of their corresponding degrees of social integration. In cause-

---

CRITICAL THINKING

What's Average? Three Statistical Measures

We often describe things or people in terms of averages—the average price of a gallon of gasoline, the average age of the U.S. population, and so on. Sociologists use three different statistical measures to describe what is average or typical.

Assume that we wish to describe the annual incomes of seven individuals in a night-school course:

$24,250	$27,000
$76,000	$15,500
$21,750	$18,500
$27,000	

The simplest of the three statistical

measures is the **mode**, defined as *the value that occurs most often in a series of numbers*. In this example, the mode is $27,000, since that value occurs twice, while the others occur only once. If each value were to occur only once, there would be no mode; if two values each occurred twice, there would be two modes.

A more common statistical measure, the **mean**, is calculated by taking *the arithmetic average of a series of numbers*. To find the mean, add all the values and divide by the number of cases. The sum of the seven incomes here is $210,000 which, divided by 7, results in a mean income of $30,000. Notice that the mean in-

come is actually higher than the income of six of the seven individuals; this shows how the mean is influenced by any extremely high or low value (in this case, the $76,000 income).

The **median** is *the value that occurs midway in a series of numbers or, simply, the middle case*. Here the median income for the seven people is $24,250, since three incomes are higher and three are lower. (With an even number of cases, the median would be halfway between the two middle cases.) Typically, the median gives the best picture of the income of the entire group because it is not affected by extreme scores.

and-effect relationships, we designate one factor as the **independent variable** (in this case, the degree of social integration), which means that it is *the variable that causes the change*. The **dependent variable** (here, the suicide rate) is *the variable that is changed*. Understanding cause and effect is valuable because it allows researchers to use what they know to *predict* what they don't know.

However, just because two variables change together does not necessarily mean that they have a cause-and-effect relationship. To take a simple case, more cars are stolen during months when the sale of ice cream rises, but there is no direct link between the two. Sociologists call a correlation *spurious*, or "false," if it is not based on cause and effect. Variables display spurious correlation because they are both affected by some third factor. In this case, rising temperatures increase auto thefts because people leave car windows open, just as warm weather encourages them to indulge in ice cream.

Researchers untangle cases of spurious correlation by utilizing *scientific control* to neutralize the effect of one variable so that the relationships among other variables can be determined. In our example, the effects of temperature might be controlled by studying auto thefts and ice cream consumption only on very hot days; doing so, no doubt, would reveal little of the original correlation.

In short, to conclude that variables are linked by cause and effect, we must demonstrate (1) that the two variables are correlated; (2) that the independent (or causal) variable precedes the dependent variable in time; and (3) that there is no evidence suggesting the correlation is spurious due to the effects of some third variable.

The Ideal of Objectivity

Another standard of sound scientific study is *objectivity*, or personal neutrality, in conducting research. The ideal of objective inquiry is allowing the facts to speak for themselves rather than being filtered through the personal values and biases of the researcher. In reality, of course, achieving complete neutrality is impossible for anyone. But carefully adhering to the logic of scientific research enhances objectivity. Researchers should also look inward to discern personal biases and state them explicitly along with their findings to help readers evaluate conclusions in the appropriate context.

The influential German sociologist Max Weber knew that personal values play a part in sociologists' selection of topics of study. But although investigations are, usually *value-relevant*, Weber argued, researchers must strive to be *value-free*. That is, they should be dispassionate and concerned with discovering truth *as it is* rather than as they think *it should be*. This, for Weber, exemplifies the essential difference between science and politics. Researchers must cultivate an open-minded readiness to accept the results of an investigation, whatever they might be.

Although widely supported, Weber's views are subject to two kinds of criticism. First, *researchers must always interpret their data*. No scientist's data speak for themselves; sociologists always face the task of constructing meaning from the facts they have gathered. Moreover, the best research springs from a lively sociological imagination as well as careful attention to the scientific method. Science, after all, is basically a series of procedures, like a recipe used in cooking. Just as it takes more than a good recipe to make a great chef, so scientific procedures never, by themselves, yield a great sociologist. In this sense, sociology is art as well as science (Nisbet, 1970).

A second criticism of Max Weber's goal of value-free research is the claim that *any and all research is political* (Gouldner, 1970a, 1970b). From this point of view, all knowledge has implications for the distribution of power in society. If sociologists cannot escape the political implications of their craft, they do have a choice about *which* values are worth supporting. Although this viewpoint is not limited to sociologists of any one political stripe, it predominates among social-conflict thinkers. It was, after all, Karl Marx who questioned the merit in understanding the world without the will to change it (1972:109; orig. 1845).

Research and Gender

In recent years, sociologists have become increasingly aware that research is affected by *gender*, the relative social standing of women and men. In the view of Margrit Eichler (1988), sound research can fall victim to four problems involving gender.

1. **Androcentricity.** Androcentricity (*andro* is the Greek word for "male"; *centricity* means "being centered on") refers to approaching an issue from a male perspective. This problem arises, for instance, when a researcher assumes that men are heads of households and directs questions to them, thereby ignoring the views of women. The parallel problem, *gynocentricity*—seeing the world from

A basic lesson of social research is that people react to being observed. Researchers can never be sure just how this will occur, however: some people become highly animated when they are the object of attention, while others become shy. In neither case does the researcher witness natural behavior.

a female perspective—limits sociological investigation as well, although this occurs less frequently in our male-dominated society.

2. **Overgeneralizing.** Historically, sociologists have used data obtained from men as the basis for claims about all people. This poses problems, for instance, when a researcher gathers information about a corporation from male officials and uses this to draw general conclusions about the corporate world. Overgeneralizing also occurs when a researcher investigating child-rearing practices collects data only from mothers and offers conclusions about "parenthood."

3. **Gender insensitivity.** Sometimes research completely overlooks the variable of gender, giving rise to another bias. For example, researchers looking into social isolation among elderly people in the United States would be remiss if they overlooked the fact that the majority of elderly men live with spouses while most elderly women live alone or with other relatives.

4. **Double standards.** Researchers should avoid evaluating people's attitudes or behaviors according to their sex. A double standard emerges when researchers describe a household as composed of a "man and wife," or systematically evaluate the work of one sex as more significant than that of the other.

5. **Interference.** Beyond Eichler's four ways that gender affects research, subjects can also interfere with research if they react to the sex of the researcher rather than to the research itself. For instance, while conducting research in Sicily, Maureen Giovannini (1992) reported that many men, guided by local traditions, responded to her as a *woman* rather than in the sex-neutral sense of a *researcher*. Their response prevented her from engaging in activities (such as private conversations with men) that were deemed inappropriate for single women.

Nothing stated here should discourage researchers from focusing on one sex or the other. Indeed, the pervasive attention to men at the expense of women in the past has led many of today's researchers to make special efforts to investigate the female world. But researchers—and others who read their work—must think critically about how gender can, and often does, shape the process of sociological investigation.

Research Ethics

Research provides knowledge but it also directly affects subjects—for better or ill. The American Sociological Association—the major professional association of sociologists in North America—has established guidelines that protect the rights, privacy, and safety of anyone involved in a research project. Sociologists are obligated to terminate any research, however valuable its possible results, if they suspect that they are violating these standards and placing subjects at risk.

One guideline is that sociologists should accurately present the purpose of their research to subjects, and disclose if they work for a particular political organization or business. Any such affiliation and sources of funding also must be disclosed in the publication of the research. In addition, all subjects in research are entitled to full anonymity, even if sociologists come under legal pressure to release confidential information. After completing their work, researchers should report their findings in full, with a complete description of how the study was conducted. Researchers should also provide all possible interpretations of their data, and point out the limitations of their conclusions (American Sociological Association, 1984).

RESEARCH METHODS

A **research method** is *a strategy for systematically carrying out research.* Here we introduce four commonly used methods of sociological investigation: experiments, surveys, participant observation, and use of existing sources. None is better or worse than any other. Just as a carpenter selects a particular tool for a particular task, distinctive strengths and weaknesses make each method suitable for specific kinds of research.

The Experiment

Research conducted by **experiment** *investigates cause-and-effect relationships under highly controlled conditions.* Experiments are typically devised to test a specific **hypothesis,** *an unverified statement of a relationship between two (or more) variables.* In everyday language, a hypothesis is an educated guess about how variables are linked. An experimenter gathers the empirical evidence needed to accept or reject the hypothesis in three steps: (1) measuring the dependent variable; (2) altering the independent variable; and (3) measuring the dependent variable again to see what, if any, change has occurred.

Successful experiments depend on careful control of all factors that might affect what is being measured. This is easiest in a laboratory, an artificial setting specially constructed for this purpose. But experiments in an everyday location—"in the field" as sociologists say—have the advantage of allowing researchers to observe subjects in their natural settings.

The Survey

A **survey** is *a research method in which subjects respond to a series of statements or questions in a questionnaire or an interview.* Perhaps the most widely used of all research methods, the survey is particularly well suited to studying what cannot be observed directly, such as political attitudes or religious beliefs.

A survey is directed at a **population,** *the people about whom a researcher seeks knowledge.* For example, if we wished to measure the average years of schooling among adults living in a particular city, all adult residents would then be the survey population. Sometimes every adult in the country can be the survey population, as in the familiar polls taken during political campaigns. Since contacting each of a vast number of people is all but impossible, researchers often study a **sample,** *a relatively small number of cases selected to represent an entire population.* National surveys commonly provide accurate estimates based on samples of only fifteen hundred people.

Selecting subjects, however, is only the first step in carrying out a survey. The next stage involves a specific plan for asking questions and recording answers. The most common way to do this is by using a **questionnaire,** *a series of written questions or items to which subjects respond.* Usually the researcher provides possible responses to each item and asks the subject to select only one (similar to a multiple-choice examination). Sometimes, though, a researcher may want subjects to respond in an entirely free way, perhaps seeking subtle shades of opinion. Of course, the researcher later has to make sense out of what can be a bewildering array of answers.

In an **interview,** *a series of questions or items a researcher administers personally to respondents,* subjects have considerable freedom to respond as they wish. Researchers often ask follow-up questions, both to probe a bit more deeply and to clarify the subject's answers. In doing this, however, a researcher must avoid influencing the subject even in subtle ways, such as raising an eyebrow when the subject begins to answer. Researchers often present their survey results in the form of tables. The box provides data from a recent survey along with some tips about how to read tables efficiently.

Table Reading: An Important Skill

A table provides a great deal of information in a small amount of space, so learning to read tables can increase your reading efficiency. Table 1–2 provides data from a survey of sexual activity among couples in the United States. Look first at the title to see what variables are included. This table describes sexual activity in terms of (1) the type of relationship involved (married couples, cohabiting heterosexual couples, and homosexual couples); (2) the duration of the relationship (under 2 years, 2 to 10 years, over 10 years); and (3) the sex of the respondent (female or male).

These three variables divide the table into three major parts, with six categories of people found in each part. For each category, the proportion that reported engaging (or not) in sexual activity outside of the rela-

tionship is presented; the two numbers add up to 100 percent.

The first part of the table shows that 13 percent of women married for less than two years reported having sexual activity outside of their relationship, while 87 percent reported not doing so. For women married between two and ten years, the corresponding figures are 22 percent and 78 percent. The percentages hold for women married for more than ten years. Comparable information is provided for all the other categories of people.

What do these data tell us? First, generally speaking, the longer the couple has been together, the more likely a partner is to engage in sexual activity with someone else (which the researchers describe using the morally neutral term, "nonmonogamy").

Second, men are more likely than women to be nonmonogamous. Third, cohabiting heterosexual partners are more likely to be nonmonogamous than married people are. Note, too, that the pattern among homosexual couples differs sharply by sex: gay men are far more likely to be nonmonogamous than are lesbian partners.

Finally, a critical reader should try to assess the overall quality of the research. Important clues include the identity and background of the researchers themselves (are they sociologists? newspaper reporters?), as well as bibliographical information (was the research published by an established journal? a group with some vested interest in the topic?). The research presented here is sound on both counts.

Table 1–2 SEXUAL ACTIVITY AMONG U.S. COUPLES, BY TYPE OF RELATIONSHIP, DURATION OF RELATIONSHIP, AND SEX OF RESPONDENT

Married Couples					Cohabiting Heterosexual Couples					Homosexual Couples				
	Reported Sexual Activity Outside Relationship					Reported Sexual Activity Outside Relationship					Reported Sexual Activity Outside Relationship			
Years Together	Females		Males		Years Together	Females		Males		Years Together	Females		Males	
	Yes	No	Yes	No		Yes	No	Yes	No		Yes	No	Yes	No
Under 2	13%	87%	15%	85%	Under 2	20%	80%	21%	79%	Under 2	15%	85%	66%	34%
2–10	22	78	23	77	2–10	42	58	47	53	2–10	38	62	89	11
Over 10	22	78	30	70	Over 10*	no data		no data		Over 10	43	57	94	6

* Too few cohabiting couples had been together for more than ten years.

SOURCE: Adapted from Philip Blumstein and Pepper Schwartz, *American Couples* (New York: William Morrow, 1983), p. 276. © 1983 by Philip Blumstein and Pepper W. Schwartz. Adapted by permission of William Morrow & Co.

Participant Observation

Participant observation is *a method in which researchers systematically observe people while joining in their routine activities.* This method works especially well in studying social life in some natural settings, from gambling casinos to religious seminaries. Cultural anthropologists, who make wide use of participant observation to study other societies, call this approach "fieldwork."

Researchers choose participant observation when they wish to explore some setting about which they have only a limited understanding. They often begin with few specific hypotheses to test, since researchers may not be sure what the important questions will turn out to be. Compared to experiments and surveys, then, par-

The exotic often excites the sociological imagination. Participant observation is well suited for exploring an unfamiliar setting such as this urban neighborhood in India. But research abroad demands extensive preparation. To begin, investigators must acquire necessary language skills, and they need to gain at least a basic understanding of the new culture. To minimize these difficulties, researchers often study communities with which they have at least some previous experience.

ticipant observation has few hard and fast rules. Flexibility can be an advantage, however, since researchers frequently must adapt to unexpected circumstances in an unfamiliar environment. Initially, the researcher concentrates on gaining entry into the setting without intruding on—and thereby changing—the routine behavior of others. In time, general impressions lead to specific questions that the researcher answers through systematically observing a way of life.

As its name suggests, participant observation has two facets. On the one hand, gaining an insider's viewpoint depends on becoming a participant in the setting—"hanging out" with others, attempting to act, think, and even feel the way they do. In contrast to other research methods, participant observation requires personal immersion in a social setting, not for a week or two, but for months or even years. On the other hand, the researcher must maintain the role of "observer," standing back from the action and applying the sociological perspective to social patterns that others take for granted.

Because the personal impressions of individual researchers play such a central role in participant observation, this method is sometimes criticized as lacking in scientific rigor. Yet its personal approach is also a strength; where a visible team of sociologists administering a formal survey might disrupt a setting, a sensitive participant-observer can often gain considerable insight into people's natural behavior.

Existing Sources

Each of the methods of conducting sociological investigation described so far involves researchers collecting their own data. In many cases, however, sociologists draw from existing sources, analyzing data originally collected by others.

The most widely used data are gathered by government agencies such as the Bureau of the Census. Data about other nations in the world are found in various publications of the United Nations and the World Bank. A wide range of such information is as near as the college library.

The advantage of using available data—whether government statistics or the work of other sociologists—is savings in time and money that otherwise would be needed to assemble information from scratch. Using existing sources is especially appealing to sociologists with low budgets, and the quality of data may turn out to be better than what many researchers could hope to obtain on their own.

Still, existing sources have their drawbacks. For one thing, data may not be available in the specific form a researcher may desire. Moreover, although government data are generally quite precise, the accuracy of existing data may be difficult to assess. Durkheim's nineteenth-century study of suicide, described earlier, is well-known research using existing records. But Durkheim was cautious, knowing that some "suicides" were actually accidents and some true suicides were never recorded as such.

Characteristics of the four major methods of sociological investigation we have introduced are summarized in Table 1–3.

Ten Steps in Sociological Research

The following ten steps can serve as guidelines for carrying out research projects in sociology.

1. **Define the topic you wish to investigate.** Ideas for social research can be found everywhere, if you remain curious and observe the world around you from the sociological perspective.
2. **Find out what has already been written about the topic.** You are probably not the first person to have an interest in a particular issue. Spend enough time in the library to learn what theories and methods others have applied to the topic. In looking over earlier research, be especially mindful of problems that may have come up before.
3. **Assess the requirements for carrying out the research.** What resources are necessary to support your research? How much time will you need? Are you working alone or with others? What sources of funding might be available to support your research? You must answer all these questions before you actually begin to design a research project.
4. **Specify the questions you are going to ask.** Is your plan to explore an unfamiliar social setting? To describe some category of people? To investigate cause-and-effect links among several variables? If your study is exploratory, identify general questions that will guide your work. If it is descriptive, specify the population and the characteristics of interest. If your study is explanatory, state the hypothesis to be tested and carefully operationalize each variable.
5. **Consider the ethical issues involved in the research.** Be alert for ethical concerns in the research. Can you promise anonymity to the subjects? If so, how can you ensure that anonymity will be maintained? Could the research injure anyone? How can you design the study to minimize the chances for such harm?
6. **Choose the research method.** Consider all major research strategies—as well as innovative combina-

Table 1–3   FOUR RESEARCH METHODS: A SUMMARY

Method	Application	Advantages	Limitations
Experiment	For explanatory research that specifies relationships among variables; generates quantitative data	Provides greatest ability to specify cause-and-effect relationships; replication of research is relatively easy	Laboratory settings have artificial quality; unless research environment is carefully controlled, results may be biased
Survey	For gathering information about issues that cannot be directly observed, such as attitudes and values; useful for descriptive and explanatory research; generates quantitative and/or qualitative data	Sampling allows surveys of large populations using questionnaires; interviews provide in-depth responses	Questionnaires must be carefully prepared and may produce low return rate; interviews are expensive and time-consuming
Participant observation	For exploratory and descriptive study of people in a "natural" setting; generates qualitative data	Allows study of "natural" behavior; usually inexpensive	Time-consuming; replication of re research is difficult; researcher must balance roles of participant and observer
Existing sources	For exploratory, descriptive, or explanatory research whenever suitable data are available	Saves times and expense of data collection; makes historical research possible	Researcher has no control over possible bias in data; data may not be suitable for current research needs

tions of approaches—before deciding how to proceed. Which method is best depends on the kinds of questions you are asking as well as the resources available to support your research.

7. **Put the method to work to gather data.** Assess the reliability and validity of all measurements. Be sure to record all information accurately and in a way that will make sense to you later (it may be some time before you actually write up the results of your work). Seek out sources of bias that might weaken the research.

8. **Interpret the findings.** What answers to the initial questions do the data suggest? Remember that there may be several ways to interpret the results of your study, consistent with different theoretical paradigms, and you should consider them all. Be alert to your own personal values or initial expectations, which affect how you make sense out of the data you collect.

9. **State the conclusions based on your findings.** Prepare a final report indicating what you have learned from the research. Consider how your work contributes both to sociological theory and to improving sociological methods of research. Finally, evaluate your work. What problems arose during the research process? What questions were left unanswered? How might your own biases have affected your conclusions?

10. **Publish your research!**

SUMMARY

1. The sociological perspective enables us to recognize that the lives of individuals are shaped by the forces of society. Because our way of life highlights individual choice, sociology can provide a "reality check" on what we view as common sense.

2. Auguste Comte gave sociology its name in 1838. Earlier social thought focused on what society *ought to be*; sociology was based on the use of scientific methods to understand society *as it is*.

3. Sociology emerged as a reaction to the rapid transformation of European societies during the eighteenth and nineteenth centuries. The rise of an industrial economy, the explosive growth of cities, and the emergence of new political ideas combined to weaken tradition and stimulate the development of the sociological perspective.

4. Theory helps us to construct meaning from sociological insights. Theory building is guided by one or more theoretical paradigms.

5. The structural-functional paradigm is a framework for exploring how social structures promote the stable operation of society. This approach tends to minimize conflict and change.

6. The social-conflict paradigm suggests that social inequality generates conflict and promotes change. This approach downplays the extent of social integration and social stability.

7. In contrast to these two macro-level approaches, the symbolic-interaction paradigm is a micro-level framework for studying social interaction in specific situations. At this level of analysis, society is subjective, highly variable, and somewhat unpredictable.

8. Sociological research employs the logic of science. Scientific facts are based on empirical evidence.

9. Measurement is the process of determining the value of a variable in any specific case. Sound measurement has both reliability and validity.

10. Science seeks to specify the relationships among variables. Ideally, researchers try to identify relationships of cause and effect in which change in an independent variable leads to a predicted change in a dependent variable.

11. The scientific ideal is objectivity. Although the issues researchers study typically reflect their interests, the goal of value-free research requires suspending personal values and biases as much as possible. However, some sociologists argue that all research involves political values, and that their work should promote desirable social change.

12. Because research can affect the well-being of subjects, investigators must observe ethical guidelines.

13. An experiment investigates the relationship between two (or more) variables under controlled, laboratory conditions.

14. A survey collects subjects' responses to items in questionnaires and interviews.

15. Participant observation involves direct study of a social setting for an extended period of time. The

researcher is both a participant in the setting and a careful observer of it.

16. The use of existing sources is often preferable to collecting one's own data; this method is of special interest to sociologists with limited research budgets.

KEY CONCEPTS

cause and effect a relationship between two variables in which change in one (the independent variable) causes change in another (the dependent variable)

concept an abstract idea that represents some aspect of the world, inevitably in a somewhat simplified form

correlation a relationship between two (or more) variables

dependent variable a variable that is changed by another (independent) variable

empirical evidence facts we are able to verify with our senses

experiment a research method that investigates cause-and-effect relationships under highly controlled conditions

hypothesis an unverified statement of a relationship between two (or more) variables

independent variable a variable that causes change in another (dependent) variable

interview a series of questions or items administered personally by a researcher to respondents

latent functions the unrecognized and unintended consequences of any social pattern

macro-level orientation a concern with large-scale patterns that characterize society as a whole

manifest functions the recognized and intended consequences of any social pattern

mean the arithmetic average of a series of numbers

measurement the process of determining the value of a variable in a specific case

median the value that occurs midway in a series of numbers or, simply, the middle case

micro-level orientation a concern with small-scale patterns of social interaction in specific settings

mode the value that occurs most often in a series of numbers

participant observation a research method in which investigators systematically observe people while joining in their routine activities

population the people about whom a researcher seeks knowledge

positivism a path to understanding based on science

questionnaire a series of written questions or items to which subjects respond

reliability the quality of consistency in measurement

research method a strategy for systematically carrying out research

sample a relatively small number of cases selected to be representative of an entire population

science a logical system that derives knowledge from direct, systematic observation

social-conflict paradigm a theoretical framework based on the assumption that society is a complex system characterized by inequality and conflict that generate social change

social dysfunction the undesirable consequences of any social pattern for the operation of society

social function the consequences of any social pattern for the operation of society as a whole

social structure any relatively stable pattern of social behavior

sociology the scientific study of human social activity

structural-functional paradigm a theoretical framework based on the assumption that society is a complex system whose parts work together to promote stability

survey a research method in which subjects respond to a series of statements or questions in a questionnaire or interview

symbolic-interaction paradigm a theoretical framework based on the view that society is the product of the everyday interaction of individuals

theoretical paradigm a set of fundamental assumptions that guides thinking and research

theory an explanation of how and why specific facts are related

validity the quality of measurement gained by measuring exactly what one intends to measure

variable a concept whose value changes from case to case

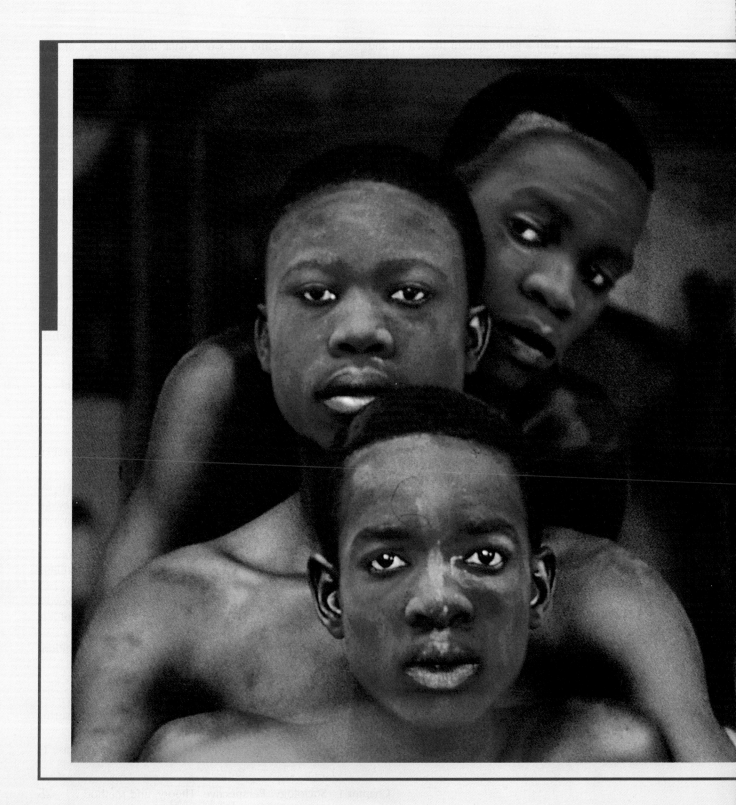

2

Culture

CHAPTER OUTLINE

A small aluminum motorboat chugged steadily along the muddy Orinoco River, deep in the vast tropical rain forest of southern Venezuela. Anthropologist Napoleon Chagnon was nearing the end of a three-day journey to the home territory of the Yąnomamö, one of the most technologically primitive societies on earth.

Some twelve thousand Yąnomamö live in scattered villages along the border between Venezuela and Brazil. Their way of life could hardly be more different from our own. The Yąnomamö are spirit worshipers who wear little clothing, live without automobiles or electricity, and have no form of writing. Until recent contact with outsiders, they used only handcrafted weapons like the bow and arrow to hunt for food. Thus Chagnon would be as strange to them as they to him.

By two o'clock in the afternoon, Chagnon had almost reached his destination. Under the hot sun, the anthropologist's clothes were soaked with perspiration; his face and hands were swollen from the bites of gnats that swarmed around him.

Chagnon's heart pounded as the boat slid onto the riverbank near a Yąnomamö village. Voices could be heard nearby. Chagnon and his guide climbed from the boat and walked toward the sounds, stooping as they pushed their way through the dense undergrowth. Chagnon describes what happened next:

> I looked up and gasped when I saw a dozen burly, naked, sweaty, hideous men staring at us down the shafts of their drawn arrows! Immense wads of green tobacco were stuck between their lower teeth and lips making them look even more hideous, and strands of dark green slime dripped or hung from their nostrils—strands so long that they clung to their [chests] or drizzled down their chins.
>
> My next discovery was that there were a dozen or so vicious, underfed dogs snapping at my legs, circling me as if I were to be their next meal. I just stood there holding my notebook, helpless and pathetic. Then the stench of the decaying vegetation and filth hit me and I almost got sick. I was horrified. What kind of welcome was this for the person who came here to live with you and learn your way of life, to become friends with you? (1983:10)

Fortunately for Chagnon, the Yąnomamö villagers recognized his guide and withdrew their weapons. Reassured that he would at least survive the afternoon, Chagnon was still shaken by his inability to make any sense of the people surrounding him. And this was to be his home for a year and a half! He wondered why he had forsaken physics to study human culture in the first place.

The 5 billion people living on earth are members of a single biological species: *Homo sapiens*. Even so, humans can be overwhelmed by how different we are from one another, differences not of biology but of culture. Entering the world of the Yąnomamö, Chagnon experienced a severe case of **culture shock,** *the personal disorientation accompanying exposure to an unfamiliar way of life.* Like most of us, Chagnon had been raised to keep his clothes on, even in hot weather, and to use a handkerchief when his nose was running, especially in front of others. The Yąnomamö clearly had other ideas about how to live. The nudity that embarrassed Chagnon was customary to them. The green slime hanging from their nostrils was caused by inhaling a hallucinogenic drug, a practice common among friends. The "stench" from which Chagnon recoiled in disgust no doubt smelled like "Home Sweet Home" to the inhabitants of that Yąnomamö village.

Human beings the world over have very different ideas about what is pleasant and repulsive, polite and rude, true and false, right and wrong. This capacity for startling difference is a wonder of our species: the expression of human culture.

CULTURE AND SOCIETY

Culture is defined as *the beliefs, values, behavior, and material objects shared by a particular people.* Sociologists distinguish between *nonmaterial culture,* which includes intangible human creations ranging from altruism to zen, and *material culture,* the tangible products of human society, everything from armaments to zippers. The terms *culture* and *society* are sometimes used interchangeably, but their precise meanings are different. Culture is a shared way of life or social heritage. **Society** refers to *people interacting within a limited territory guided by their culture.* Neither society nor culture can exist without the other.

In daily life, what we wear to work, when and what we eat, and how we enjoy spending our free time are all grounded in culture. Our culture infuses life with meaning, providing standards of success, beauty, and goodness, and fills us with reverence for a divine power, the forces of nature, or long-dead ancestors. Culture also shapes our personalities, creating many variations of what we commonly (yet inaccurately) describe as "human nature." The Yąnomamö are fierce and warlike, and they strive to develop these "natural" qualities in their children. The Semai of Malaysia, by contrast,

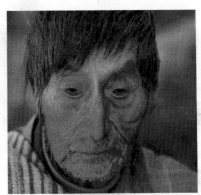

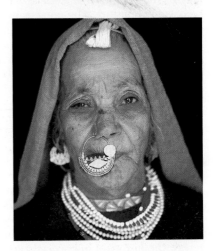

A global perspective reveals that human beings create varied ways of life. Such diversity begins with outward appearance: contrast the women shown here from Iran, Kenya, New Guinea, and Egypt, and the men from Taiwan (Republic of China), Peru, India, and New Guinea. Less obvious, but of even greater importance, are internal differences, since culture also shapes our goals in life, our sense of justice, and even our innermost personal feelings.

are so peace-loving that they rarely speak of violence. The cultures of the United States and Japan stress achievement and hard work; but most members of our society value competition and individualism, while the Japanese place great emphasis on cooperation and self-denying obedience to authority. In short, culture is a blueprint for virtually every dimension of our lives, from the might of enormous corporations to the meaning of a shy smile.

In everyday conversation, "culture" usually refers to art forms associated with elites, such as classical literature, music, dance, and painting. Sociologists, however, use the term to refer to *everything* that makes up a people's way of life—Motown as well as Mozart, fish sticks as well as fine cuisine, ping pong as well as polo.

Culture is distinctively human. Every other species of living creatures—from ants to zebras—behaves in uniform ways. To a world traveler, the enormous diversity of humanity contrasts sharply with the behavior of, say, cats, which is the same everywhere. Most living creatures respond to biological forces we call *instincts*, strategies for survival that change only over long periods of time. A few animals—notably chimpanzees and other related primates—have the capacity for basic elements of culture such as using simple tools and teaching these skills to their offspring. But our creative ability to shape the world far exceeds that of any other form of life, so that *only humans depend on culture rather than instinct to ensure the survival of their kind* (Harris, 1987).

To understand how this came to be, we must briefly review the history of our species on earth.

Culture and Human Intelligence

In a universe scientists estimate to be 15 billion years old, our planet is a relatively young 4.5 billion years of age, and the human species is a wide-eyed infant of only 40,000. We can trace our ancestry to the first forms of life that emerged a billion years after the earth was formed. One crucial turn in human history was the development of primates some 65 million years ago.

Primates evolved into highly intelligent life forms, with the largest brains relative to body weight of all living creatures. The human line diverged from that of our closest primate relatives, the great apes, some 12 million years ago. Our common lineage remains apparent, however, in traits that humans share today with chimpanzees, gorillas, and orangutans: great sociability; affectionate and long-lasting bonds; the ability to walk upright (normal in humans, but less common among other primates); and hands that manipulate objects with great precision.

Studying fossil records, scientists have concluded that the first creatures displaying human characteristics lived some 2 million years ago. These distant ancestors, with limited mental capacity, grasped cultural fundamentals like the use of fire, tools, and weapons. Although such "stone age" achievements seem modest, they signify the point at which our forebears embarked on a distinct evolutionary course, making culture the primary strategy for survival. As mental capacity expanded, we became the only species that names itself, and we are appropriately termed *Homo sapiens*, Latin for "thinking person."

Culture, therefore, is an evolutionary strategy for survival that emerged as our ancestors descended from the trees into the tall grasses of central Africa and began to walk upright and hunt in groups. Gradually the biological forces we call instincts were replaced by a more efficient survival scheme: *human beings gained the mental power to actively fashion the natural environment for themselves.* At this point, human nature no longer turned on instinct but on culture (Barash, 1981). Ever since, humans have made and remade their worlds in countless ways, which explains today's fascinating (and, as Napoleon Chagnon's experiences show, sometimes disturbing) cultural diversity.

THE COMPONENTS OF CULTURE

Although cultures vary greatly, they all have components in common, including symbols, language, values, and norms. We shall begin with the one that underlies the rest: symbols.

Symbols

The human world is grounded not in objects and action, but in *symbolic meaning*. A **symbol** is *anything that carries a particular meaning recognized by members of a society*. A whistle, a wall of graffiti, a flashing red light, a fist raised in the air are all symbolic. The human capacity to create and manipulate symbols comes through in the various ways a simple wink of the eye can convey interest, understanding, or insult.

As the basis of culture, symbols are the foundation of everyday reality. We become so familiar with the symbols of our own culture that we usually take them for granted. Often, however, we gain a heightened sense of the importance of our symbolic world when a symbol is used in an unconventional way, say, if a United States flag is burned at a political demonstration.

We also recognize the power of symbols when we enter an unfamiliar culture. Culture shock stems from our inability to attach meaning to our surroundings. Like Napoleon Chagnon confronting the Yąnomamö, we feel lost, unsure of how to act, and sometimes frightened—a consequence of being outside the symbolic web of culture.

The meanings of actions or objects vary from culture to culture. To people in North America, a baseball bat symbolizes sport and relaxation, but the Yąnomamö would probably see it as a well-carved club that arouses thoughts of war. A dog is a beloved household pet to millions of people in the United States, but a regular meal to millions in China. Likewise, the cows that are sacred to Hindus in India are routinely consumed in the form of "quarter-pounders" by hungry North Americans. Thus symbols not only bind people together but also separate people who live in the various societies of the world.

Sometimes everyday behavior that seems trivial to us gives offense to people elsewhere. Counting one's change is routine in New York, yet it would insult a shopkeeper in Tokyo. Similarly, sitting with one leg draped casually across the other is simply a relaxed pose in this country, but it gives offense to Iranians who, as Muslims, do not display the bottom of the foot because they define it as unclean.

Symbolic meanings also vary within a single society. The fur coat, a prized symbol of success to one person, may exemplify the inhumane treatment of animals to another. Opening a door for a woman may signify a common courtesy in the minds of some men yet symbolize male condescension and dominance to many women.

Language

The heart of a symbolic system is **language,** *a system of symbols with standard meanings that allows members of a society to communicate with one another.* All societies have a spoken language; some, including the Yąnomamö, lack a written language and communicate entirely through speech. Systems of writing are culturally variable: societies in the West write left to right, those in North

Africa and western Asia write right to left, and people in eastern Asia write from top to bottom.

Global Map 2–1 on page 32 shows regions using the world's three most widely spoken languages. Chinese is in use among 20 percent (roughly 1 billion) of the world's people. More precisely, although all Chinese people read and write with the same characters, they speak dozens of dialects. The "official" dialect is Mandarin (the dialect of Beijing, China's capital city), which is taught in schools throughout the People's Republic of China and the Republic of Taiwan. Cantonese (the language of Canton) is the second most common Chinese dialect. English is the mother tongue of about 10 percent (500 million) of the world's people, and Spanish is the official language of 6 percent (300 million) of people worldwide. Notice, too, that English is steadily becoming a global language, since it is given preference as a second tongue in most of the world's societies.

Language not only facilitates communication, but it also ensures the continuity of culture. Language is a cultural heritage in coded form, the key to **cultural transmission,** *the process by which culture is passed from one generation to the next.* Just as our bodies contain the genes of our ancestors, so our words and ideas are rooted in the lives of those who came before us. Language, then, gives us enormous power by providing access to the accumulated knowledge of centuries.

For most of human history, people transmitted culture through speech alone, which is often termed the *oral cultural tradition.* Not until five thousand years ago did humans devise writing and, in the United States a century ago, only a small elite was literate. Today, perhaps 25 million adults (about one in seven) in the United States cannot read and write very well. Among the poorest societies of the world, four out of five people cannot use written language.

Language skills not only put us in touch with the past, they unlock the human imagination. Connecting symbols in new ways, we can conceive of life other than as it is. Language—both spoken and written—distinguishes human beings as creatures aware of our limitations and ultimate mortality, yet able to dream and hope for a future better than the present.

The Sapir-Whorf hypothesis. If the Semai of Malaysia have few words of anger in their language, how do they imagine warfare? Certainly, they cannot do so as readily as the Yąnomamö, whose language is rich with terms for fighting. Since language provides the building blocks of reality, linguistic differences mean that mem-

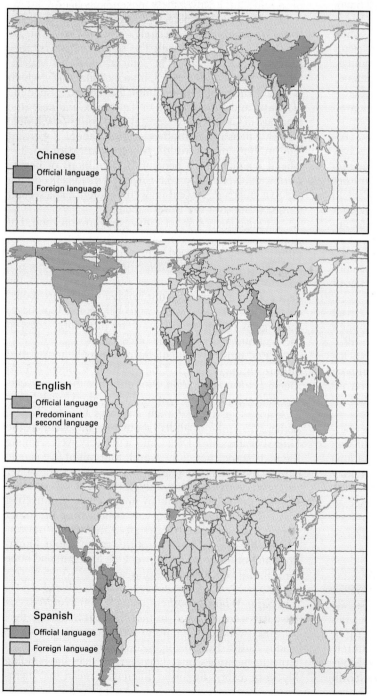

Global Map 2–1 Language in Global Perspective Chinese (including Mandarin, Cantonese, and dozens of other dialects) is spoken by one-fifth of the world's people, almost all of whom live in Asia.

English is the mother tongue or official language in several world regions, and has become the preferred second language in most of the world.

The largest concentration of Spanish speakers is in Latin America, and Spanish is the preferred second language of the United States.

bers of one culture experience the world differently from people in another symbolic world.

Two anthropologists who specialized in linguistic studies, Edward Sapir and Benjamin Whorf, claimed that language stands between us and the world, becoming our reality (Sapir, 1929, 1949; Whorf, 1956). Sapir and Whorf therefore suggested that thousands of human languages give rise to differing truths. This occurs because each language includes words or expressions that have no precise counterpart in another symbolic system. In addition, each language fuses symbols with particular emotions. Thus, as multilingual people can attest, a single idea may "feel" different if spoken in Spanish rather than in English or German (Falk, 1987). Formally, then, the **Sapir-Whorf hypothesis,** as this insight has come to be called, holds that *we know the world only in terms of our language.*

Of course, the Sapir-Whorf hypothesis recognizes the human capacity to generate new symbols as well as to employ familiar symbols in novel ways. Technological advances like the invention of computers have led to new words and phrases, including *byte, interface,* and *E-mail.* Political controversy, too, brings change to language. The desire for greater equality with whites has prompted African Americans to replace the tainted word *Negro* with the term *black* or *person of color.* After more than twenty years of increasing usage, this symbolic change has helped improve white people's perceptions of African Americans. If language shapes reality, humans retain the capacity to alter their language, and the corresponding reality it evokes.

Values

What accounts for the popularity of movie characters like James Bond, Dirty Harry, Rambo, or Thelma and Louise? Each is a rugged individual, suspicious of "the system," who relies primarily on personal skill and initiative. Together, they suggest that our culture celebrates an ideal of sturdy individualism, especially among men. Sociologists call such patterns **values,** *standards by which members of a culture define what is desirable or undesirable, good or bad, beautiful or ugly* (Williams, 1970:27). Values are evaluations and judgments, from the standpoint of the culture, of what ought to be. We see these broad guidelines at work in most aspects of everyday life.

Because the United States is a multicultural nation of immigrants, few values are shared by everyone. Even

Australian artist Sally Swain (1958–) altered a famous artist's painting to make fun of her culture's tendency to ignore the everyday lives of women. This spoof is entitled *Mrs. Renoir Cleans the Oven.*

so, a number of dominant values have emerged. Sociologist Robin Williams (1970) suggests that the following ten values stand at the core of our culture.

1. **Equal opportunity.** Our perception of fairness demands that everyone have the opportunity to get ahead, although, due to varying talents and efforts, people will not end up in the same situation. In other words, while not endorsing *equality of condition,* we do embrace *equality of opportunity.*

2. **Achievement and success.** Our way of life encourages competition. In this way, we reason, each person's share of success depends on merit. In the United States, to be successful makes one a worthy person, a "winner."

3. **Activity and work.** Our heroes, from Olympic skater Kristy Yamaguchi to film's famed archaeologist Indiana Jones, are "doers" who get the job done. Our culture values *action* over *reflection*, and favors working hard to control events over passively accepting one's "fate."

4. **Material comfort.** In global perspective, Western cultures stand out as materialistic. Members of our society quip that "money won't buy happiness" but most eagerly pursue wealth and its trappings all the same.

5. **Practicality and efficiency.** Just as our way of life values money, so we praise those who solve problems with the least effort. "Building a better mousetrap" is a cultural goal, especially when done in the most cost-effective way.

6. **Progress.** Members of our society traditionally have believed that the present is better than the past, and that the future is likely to be better still. Advertising sparks sales with claims that the "very latest" is the "very best."

7. **Science.** We frequently turn to scientists, convinced of the value of science to solve problems. We think of ourselves as rational people, which probably explains our cultural tendency (among men more than women) to devalue emotion and intuition as sources of knowledge.

8. **Democracy.** Citizens of the United States have rights that cannot be overridden by government. Our political system is based on the ideal of free elections in which all adults exercise their right to vote.

9. **Freedom.** Closely related to democracy, freedom as a cultural value favors individual initiative over collective conformity. While we acknowledge that everyone has responsibilities to others, we think that individuals should be free to pursue personal goals without unreasonable interference from anyone else.

10. **Racism and group superiority.** While claiming commitment to the values of equality and freedom, people in the United States also link personal worth to social class, race, ethnicity, and sex. Our culture values men above women, whites above people of color, and more privileged people above those who are disadvantaged. Although we may describe ourselves as a nation of equals, there is little doubt that some of us are "more equal than others."

Looking over this list, we see that some dominant cultural values contradict others (Lynd, 1967; Bellah et al., 1985). For example, we frequently find ourselves torn between the "me first" attitude of an individualistic, success-at-all-costs orientation and the contradictory need to be part of a community. In addition, the value we place on equality of opportunity for all has long conflicted with a tendency to promote or degrade others because of their race, sex, or social background. Such value conflict inevitably causes strain, leading to awkward balancing acts in our views of the world. Sometimes we decide that one value is more important than another; in other cases, we may simply learn to live with such inconsistencies.

Finally, values also change over time, bursting on the scene as short-lived trends or settling in as lasting orientations. For example, the traditional value we place on individual responsibility has recently been eroded by what some observers have tagged "a new culture of victimization." The box takes a closer look.

Norms

Through values, culture gives shape to ideas. Norms are *rules that guide behavior*. William Graham Sumner (1959; orig. 1906), an early U.S. sociologist, coined the term **mores** (pronounced MORE-ays; the rarely used singular form is *mos*) to refer to *norms that have great moral significance*. Mores, or *taboos*, are exemplified by our society's insistence that adults not engage in sexual relations with children.

But not all norms are so important. Sumner used the term **folkways** to designate *norms with little moral significance*. Examples include codes for dress, polite behavior, or other situations in which we allow each other considerable personal discretion. Because their significance is minor, violations of folkways typically result in mild penalties. A man who does not wear a tie to a formal dinner party may raise an eyebrow for violating folkways or "etiquette." By contrast, were he to arrive at the dinner party wearing *only* a tie, he would be violating cultural mores and inviting more serious sanctions.

Cultural norms, then, steer our behavior by defining what is proper and improper. Although we sometimes object to the conformity norms demand, these shared expectations make possible a sense of security and trust in our personal interactions. Norms thus form part of

A New "Culture of Victimization"?

A New York man recently jumped in front of a subway train and survived; soon after he collected $650,000 from the city, claiming the train failed to stop in time to prevent his serious injuries. In Washington, DC, after realizing that he had been videotaped smoking crack cocaine in a hotel room, the city's mayor blamed his woman companion for "setting him up" and suggested that he was being harassed by police because he is an African American. A New Jersey woman smoked more than one pack of cigarettes each day for forty years before developing lung cancer; she sued the cigarette manufacturer, claiming the company was responsible for her illness. In the most celebrated case of its kind, a San Francisco man gunned down that city's mayor and a city council member only to maintain that eating "junk food" (the so-called "Twinkie defense") had made him temporarily insane.

Surveying these and similar cases, sociologist Irving Horowitz proclaims the advent of a "new culture of victimization" saying, "Everyone is a victim these days; no one accepts responsibility for anything."

Consider the proliferation of "addictions." No longer limited to the compulsive use of drugs, we now hear about gambling addicts, compulsive overeaters and undereaters, sex addicts, and even people who excuse mounting credit-card debts as a symptom of shopping addiction. Bookstores now overflow with manuals to help people come to terms with alleged medical or psychological conditions ranging from "The Cinderella Complex" and "The Casanova Complex" to "Soap Opera Syndrome." And our courts are ever more clogged with lawsuits driven by the need to blame someone—and often to collect big money—for the kind of misfortune that we used to accept as part of life.

What's going on here? Is our culture changing? Historically, our cultural ideal was "rugged individualism," the notion that—for better or worse—people are responsible for whatever befalls them. But this value has weakened for a number of reasons. First, members of our society have become more aware (partly through the work of sociologists and other social scientists) of how society itself shapes the lives of everyone. Second, there has been a small revolution in the legal system by which many lawyers—especially since gaining the right to advertise their services in 1977—now encourage a sense of injustice among clients they hope to shepherd into court. And the number of million-dollar awards in the United States has risen twenty-five fold in the last twenty-five years. Third, there has been a proliferation of "rights groups" that have encouraged what sociologist Amitai Etzioni calls "rights inflation." Beyond the traditional constitutional liberties are many newly claimed rights, including those of hunters (as well as those of animals), the rights of smokers (and nonsmokers), the right of women to control their bodies (and the rights of the unborn), the right to own a gun (and the right to be safe from violence). Competing claims for unmet rights create victims on all sides.

Whether this change will take hold over the long term remains to be seen. But few cultural trends are entirely new. The current "culture of victimization" itself has roots in our society's long-standing optimism—the belief that everyone has the right to prosperity, success, and happiness. While our concern with individual rights has helped the United States confront clear cases of injustice, we also need to remember that individualism, taken to an extreme, has the potential to undermine society. As we have in the past, we will continue to delicately balance the rights of individuals and the responsibilities of members of a society.

SOURCES: Based on Etzioni (1991) and Taylor (1991).

the symbolic road map of culture, guiding us through countless social situations.

As we learn—or *internalize*—cultural norms, we build them into our personalities. This explains the experience of *guilt*—a negative judgment we make of ourselves for having violated a norm—as well as *shame*—the disturbing acknowledgment of others' disapproval. Learning norms is no doubt what writer Mark Twain had in mind when he remarked that human beings "are the only animals that blush . . . or need to."

"Ideal" and "Real" Culture

Values and norms do not describe actual behavior as much as prescribe how members of a society *should* act. We learn to recognize some difference between *ideal culture*, expectations embodied in values and norms, and *real culture*, the patterns that typically occur in everyday life. The vast majority of adults in the United States acknowledge the importance of sexual fidelity in marriage, for example, but at least one-third of married people are sexually unfaithful to their spouses at some point in their marriages. These discrepancies bring to mind the old saying, "Do as I say, not as I do."

TECHNOLOGY, CULTURE, AND SOCIETY

In addition to nonmaterial cultural elements such as values and norms, every culture encompasses a wide range of material creations (sometimes referred to as *artifacts*). The Yąnomamö gather material from the forest to build huts and make hammocks. They craft bows and arrows to hunt and defend themselves, fashion tools for raising crops, and use pigments to paint their bodies.

Examining a society's artifacts reveals that what people create expresses their cultural values; that is, material and nonmaterial elements of culture are closely related. Because warfare is central to their lives, the Yąnomamö value militaristic skills, carefully craft weapons, and prize the poison tips on their arrows. In the same way, we see our society's embrace of individuality and independence, for instance, in our long love affair with the automobile as well as the popular distaste for mass transportation. With 140 million cars registered in the United States, every person could climb in at once—with no one sitting in back!

A society is also shaped by **technology,** *the application of knowledge to the practical tasks of living.* In simple terms, humans use technology to fashion culture from the natural world. The more complex a society's technology, the more its members are able to shape the world for themselves. Gerhard and Jean Lenski (1991) have described **sociocultural evolution,** *the historical process of cultural change caused by technological innovation,* in terms of four levels of development.[1]

---

[1] This account examines only the major types of societies described by the Lenskis; see Lenski, Lenski, & Nolan, 1991.

Hunting and Gathering

The most basic productive technology is **hunting and gathering,** *the use of simple tools to hunt animals and gather vegetation.* From the time of our earliest human ancestors, most people lived this way until several centuries ago. Now hunting and gathering is found in only a few societies, including the Kaska Indians of northwest Canada, the Pygmies of central Africa, the Bushmen of southwestern Africa, the Aborigines of Australia, and the Semai of Malaysia.

Because their food production is inefficient, members of these societies focus on the search for game and edible plants. Societies remain small—generally only several dozen people in a family-like group. Hunting and gathering bands rove far from one another since food production requires a large amount of land. These nomads move on as they deplete the vegetation in one area, or in pursuit of migratory animals.

Everyone takes part in the search for food. The very young and the very old contribute what they can, leaving healthy adults to secure most of what is consumed. Women typically gather vegetation—the primary food source in these societies—while men do the hunting. Women and men thus have different roles, but they remain relatively equal in social importance (Leacock, 1978).

Hunting and gathering peoples have few formal leaders. They may recognize one person as a *shaman* who presides over spiritual concerns. But while this position provides prestige it affords no release from the daily responsibility to help procure food. Overall, hunting and gathering is a relatively simple and equitable way of life.

Limited technology leaves hunters and gatherers vulnerable to the forces of nature. Storms and droughts can easily destroy their food supply, and they have few effective ways to deal with accident and disease. Such high-risk living appears to encourage cooperation as a strategy for enhancing the odds of survival. Even so, many members of hunting and gathering societies die in childhood, and no more than half survive to the age of twenty.

Faced with depleted game and vegetation and the encroachment of people with complex technology, hunters and gatherers are fast vanishing from the planet. Fortunately, study of their way of life has already produced valuable information about humanity's sociocultural history and our fundamental ties to the natural world.

The members of hunting and gathering societies depend on nature for basic foods and building materials. Pastoral people have a somewhat higher standard of living based on the ability to domesticate animals. Members of agrarian societies use animal power to plow land and for a host of other tasks. People in industrial societies are the most productive of all, utilizing vastly more powerful energy sources; this allows people far greater choice in how they earn a living but also fosters materialism.

Horticulture and Pastoralism

Horticulture, *the use of hand tools to raise crops*, slowly began to transform the lives of hunters and gatherers between ten and twelve thousand years ago. The invention of the hoe and the digging stick (used to punch holes in the ground for seeds) first occurred in fertile regions of the Middle East and Southeast Asia; these tools were in use from Western Europe to China six thousand years ago. Central and South Americans, too,

learned to cultivate plants, but rocky soil and mountainous terrain prompted people like the Yanomamö to incorporate this new technology into traditional hunting and gathering (Fisher, 1979; Chagnon, 1983).

In especially arid regions, horticulture had little impact. There, however, societies turned to **pastoralism**, *the domestication of animals*. Numerous societies—in the Americas, Africa, the Middle East, and Asia—also combined horticulture and pastoralism.

Greater productivity from domesticating plants and

animals, first, allowed societies to expand to hundreds of members. While pastoral peoples remain nomadic, horticulturalists founded settlements linking thousands of people in trading networks.

A second effect of material surplus was to free some of the population from food production. This allowed societies to become internally complex, with people making crafts, engaging in trade, or serving as full-time priests. Compared to hunters and gatherers, pastoral and horticultural societies are also hierarchical. Wealth became concentrated in the hands of some families, who began to form a political system partly to protect their elite privileges.

Hunters and gatherers, who have little control over nature, generally believe that the world is inhabited by numerous spirits. Once humans gained control over plants and animals, however, they began to conceive of God as creator of the world. The pastoral roots of Judaism and Christianity are evident in the term "pastor" for some members of the clergy and the common view of God as "shepherd," overseeing the well-being of the world.

Agriculture

About five thousand years ago, further technological advances led to agriculture, *large-scale cultivation using plows drawn by animals.* Agrarian technology first appeared in the Middle East and gradually spread throughout the world. So important to human culture was the invention of the animal-drawn plow and the wheel, as well as writing, numbers, and the expanding use of metals, that historians regard this era as "the dawn of civilization" (Lenski, Lenski, & Nolan, 1991:160).

By turning the soil, plows allowed land to be farmed for decades, so people became rooted in permanent settlements. Large food surpluses, transported on animal-powered wagons, supported societies of unprecedented size, sometimes reaching 1 million people or more.

As they grew in size, societies gained in productive specialization, linking occupations through the exchange of money rather than simple barter. Expanding trade and the growth of cities generated a wide range of human opportunities, but also rendered social life more and more individualistic and impersonal.

Agriculture also fostered a dramatic increase in social inequality. The majority of people in most societies became slaves or serfs who labored for elites. Freed from the need to work, nobility cultivated a "refined" way

of life, based on the study of philosophy, art, and literature. Most commoners, by contrast, remained illiterate and centered their lives on their work. At all levels of society, the two sexes also became distinct as men gained pronounced power and privilege over women.

Technologically simple people live much the same the world over, with differences due mostly to variations in the natural environment. But agrarian technology, the Lenskis explain, provides sufficient control over the natural world to unleash human creativity, producing marked cultural diversity.

Industrialization

Industrialization, a focus of Chapter 11 ("Economics and Politics"), occurred as societies replaced the muscle power of animals and humans with advanced sources of energy. Formally, an **industrial society** is *a society that produces goods using sophisticated machinery powered by advanced fuels.* The introduction of steam-powered machines in England in 1765 expanded productivity once again and transformed cultural patterns in the process.

Agrarian people typically work in or near the home; industry, however, relocated work to factories under the supervision of strangers. Lost in the process of European industrialization were many traditional cultural values and customs that had guided agrarian life for centuries.

Industry made the world seem smaller. During the nineteenth century, railroads and steamships revolutionized transportation, moving people farther and faster than ever before. During the twentieth century, additional waves of change followed the invention of the automobile, radio, and television.

Industrial technology has raised living standards and extended lives for millions of the world's people. A larger share of people also benefit from schooling, because industrial production demands a literate and skilled labor force. Further, as Chapter 7 ("Social Stratification") explains, industrial societies steadily extended political rights to the population and achieved some lessening of economic inequality.

Despite the drawbacks of our way of life—including its individualism and focus on material goals—most members of industrial societies deem themselves more "advanced" than others who rely on simpler technology. Some facts support such a judgment. The average life expectancy in the United States, for example, now stands at more than seventy-eight years for women and seventy-one years for men. In contrast, Napoleon Chagnon reported, the life expectancy of the Yąnomamö was barely forty years.

We must take care, however, to avoid self-serving conclusions about cultures different from our own. Although the Yąnomamö are quite eager to obtain some of the trappings of industry—like steel tools and shotguns—they are generally well fed by world standards and most are quite satisfied with their world (Chagnon, 1983). We, on the other hand, endlessly manipulate the natural environment to suit ourselves. Advanced technology has produced work-reducing devices and seemingly miraculous forms of medical treatment, but it has also contributed to unhealthy levels of stress, threatened the planet's ecosystem, and created weapons capable of destroying in a flash everything that humankind has managed to achieve.

CULTURAL DIVERSITY

The combination of complex technology and a high rate of immigration has made the United States a remarkably multicultural society. Over the last 150 years, more than 60 million immigrants have come to this land. Early in this century, most came from Europe; in the 1990s, the majority are arriving from Asia and Latin America. More than ever before, the United States is truly a cultural kaleidoscope.

Subculture

A **subculture** consists of *cultural patterns that distinguish some segment of a society's population*. Jazz musicians, race-car drivers, Korean Americans, homeless people, and New Englanders all form subcultures. Cultural diversity of this kind also separates the "down home" residents of small towns from "cosmopolitan" city dwellers. Within large cities, subcultures abound; the gay communities of San Francisco and New York represent but one dimension of cultural difference.

In global perspective, subcultures most often correspond to ethnicity, and often generate conflict. Consider the recent fate of Yugoslavia, a small nation in southeastern Europe. Before its shattering civil war, this *one* small country made use of *two* alphabets, had *three* major religions, spoke *four* major languages, contained *five* major nationalities, was divided into *six* separate repub-

lics, and absorbed cultural influences from *seven* other nations with which it shared borders. Is it any wonder that the cultural conflict there has been so intense?

In the United States, children have long been taught that their country is a "melting pot" in which many nationalities blend into a single "American" culture. More correctly, subcultures involve not only *difference* but *hierarchy*. Often what we view as "dominant" cultural patterns are those of powerful segments of our society, while subcultures are traits of disadvantaged people. This dilemma has sparked a new approach to the study of culture in the country—multiculturalism.

Multiculturalism

In recent years, the United States has been facing up to the challenge of **multiculturalism**, *the recognition of our society's cultural diversity coupled with efforts to promote the equality of all cultural traditions*. We have long downplayed our cultural diversity, compressing many ways of life into unrealistically singular terms reflecting the culture of European (and especially English) immigrants. The legacy of this practice is a spirited debate over whether we should continue to stress what is common to our national experience, or highlight our internal diversity.

E Pluribus Unum, the familiar Latin words that appear on each piece of U.S. currency, roughly means "out of many, one." This motto not only symbolizes our national political confederation, but also describes the ideal of our nation's cultural history—creating a single way of life for immigrants from around the world.

But, from the beginning, instead of melting together into a single heritage, cultural diversity hardened into a hierarchy. At the top were the English social patterns and institutions of the dominant founders. Down the pecking order, people of other backgrounds were advised to model themselves after "their betters," so that the "melting" was more accurately a process of Anglicization. This hierarchy has led historians to highlight the descendants of the English and other Europeans, to describe events from their point of view, and to push to the margins the perspectives and accomplishments of Native Americans, people of African descent, and immigrants from Asia. In short, multiculturalists argue, the European way of life was long ago set up as the ideal against which all should be judged. This pattern is termed **Eurocentrism**, *the dominance of European (particularly English) cultural patterns*. Molefi Kete Asante, a leading

Conventional history has portrayed European expeditions to the so-called "New World" as sober efforts to bring religion and civilization to the childlike inhabitants of these societies. This message has long been a theme in European art, suggested here by a painting of the landfall of Columbus. More recently, historians have presented a more accurate view of events, explaining that the "explorers" were actually conquerors often intent on destroying existing civilizations in pursuit of wealth. The painting on the right suggests that the "discovery" of the Americas was more a pitched battle, illustrated by the assault on Tenochtitlán (today's Mexico City) by Hernando Cortés and his conquistadors.

advocate of multiculturalism, suggests that like "the fifteenth-century Europeans who could not cease believing that the earth was the center of the universe, many today find it difficult to cease viewing European culture as the center of the social universe" (1988:7).

Although no one can deny our culture's wide-ranging roots, multiculturalism is controversial because it demands that we rethink the norms and values at the core of our culture. One area of debate involves language. For a decade, Congress has debated a proposal to designate English as the official language of the United States. It has yet to decide the issue, although, by 1991, legislatures in sixteen states had done so. To some, "official English" may seem unnecessary, but the fact is that more than 30 million people—at least one in ten—speak a language other than English in their homes. And their ranks will swell to 40 million by the beginning of the next century. Spanish is our second national language, and other widely used tongues include Italian, German, French, Filipino, Japanese, Korean, and Vietnamese.

Just as important, how should our nation's schools teach about cultural diversity? It is among educators that the clash over multiculturalism has been most intense. Two basic positions have emerged from this discussion.

Proponents defend multiculturalism, first, as a way to capture a more accurate picture of our nation's *past*. Proposed educational reforms seek, for example, to correct simplistic praise directed at Christopher Columbus and other European explorers by recognizing the tragic impact of the European conquest on the native peoples of this hemisphere. As detailed in Chapter 9 ("Race and Ethnicity"), from the point of view of Native Americans, contact with Europeans unleashed five centuries of domination. Moreover, a multicultural approach would recognize the achievements of many women and men whose cultural backgrounds up to now have kept them on the sidelines of history.

Second, proponents claim, multiculturalism is a means to come to terms with our country's even more diverse *present*. During the 1980s, the Hispanic population of the United States increased by 50 percent, and the number of Asian Americans doubled. Children born in the 1990s may well live to see people of African, Asian, and Hispanic ancestry as a majority of this country's population.

Third, proponents assert that multiculturalism is a way to strengthen the academic achievement of black children and others who, from this point of view, find little personal relevance in traditional educational programs. To counter pervasive Eurocentrism, some educators are calling for **Afrocentrism**, *the dominance of African cultural patterns*, which they see as a corrective for centuries of ignoring the achievements of African societies.

Fourth and finally, proponents see multiculturalism as needed preparation for everyone to live in a world in which nations are increasingly linked. As various chapters of this book explain, social patterns at home are now closely linked to issues and events elsewhere. In short, multiculturalism teaches global connectedness.

Multiculturalism has provoked its share of criticism as well. The argument most commonly voiced by opponents is that any society remains cohesive only to the extent that cultural patterns are widely shared. Multiculturalism, in this view, fuels the "politics of difference," encouraging people to identify with only their own category rather than with the nation as a whole. In the curriculum, critics charge, multiculturalism erodes the claim to common truth by maintaining that ideas should be evaluated according to the race (and sex) of those who present them. There is no common humanity, in other words, only an "African experience," a "European experience," and so on.

Second, critics are skeptical that multiculturalism actually benefits minorities in the United States. On the one hand, multiculturalism seems to demand precisely the kind of racial segregation that our nation has struggled for decades to end. On the other hand, an Afrocentric curriculum may well deny children a wide range of important knowledge and skills by forcing them to study from a single point of view. Historian Arthur Schlesinger, Jr. (1991) puts the matter bluntly: "If a Kleagle of the Ku Klux Klan wanted to use the schools to handicap black Americans, he could hardly come up with anything more effective than the 'Afrocentric' curriculum."

Third, critics warn, multiculturalism has a political agenda. Rooted in left-wing politics, they explain, this approach threatens the political and economic freedoms that have attracted diverse people to the United States in the first place.

There is some common ground in this debate. Virtually everyone agrees that we all need to gain greater appreciation of our cultural diversity. Further, because minorities will be a majority of the population during the next century, multicultural education is needed now. But precisely where the balance is to be struck—between the *pluribus* and the *unum*—is likely to remain a divisive issue for some time to come.

Counterculture

Cultural diversity within a society sometimes takes the form of active opposition to at least some widely shared cultural elements. **Counterculture** refers to *cultural patterns that strongly oppose conventional culture*. People who embrace a counterculture may question the morality of the majority. Not surprisingly, the majority may swiftly condemn what is perceived as a threat.

Most of us are familiar with the youth-oriented countercultures of the 1960s. Hippies criticized mainstream culture as overly competitive and self-centered. Instead, they favored a collective and cooperative lifestyle in which "being" took precedence over "doing," and the capacity for personal growth—then called "expanded consciousness"—was prized over material possessions like homes and cars. Their disdain for the status quo prompted many hippies to "drop out" of the larger society, forming countercultural centers like the Haight-Ashbury district in San Francisco (Spates, 1976b, 1982, 1983).

Members of countercultures are often visibly different from others, in terms of language, greetings, dress, and music. To many members of the 1960s countercultures, for instance, blue jeans and "ethnic" clothing symbolized identification with the "common people" of our society. Rock and roll music flourished as a countercultural anthem, with far less of the respectability it enjoys today.

Countercultures still exist, although most maintain a lower profile than in the 1960s. In the United States, the Ku Klux Klan and other white supremacist groups promote violence and racial hatred in order to protect what they see as "real American values." In Europe, young "punks" express their contempt for established culture by displaying shaved heads or multicolored hairstyles, black leather clothing, and chains—all intended to offend more conventional members of society.

Cultural Change

The Greek philosopher Aristotle observed that "there is nothing permanent except change." Consider, for example, some recent changes in family life. More and more women are joining the labor force, and many are delaying marriage and childbearing, or remaining single and having children all the same. The current divorce rate is more than twice what it was fifty years ago. And over the last generation, the number of single-parent households has more than doubled so that a majority of our nation's children now live with only one parent for some period before they turn eighteen.

Table 2-1 presents another dimension of change, comparing the attitudes of first-year college students in 1968 with those of women and men matriculating in 1990. Some things have changed only slightly: about

Table 2–1 ATTITUDES AMONG STUDENTS ENTERING U.S. COLLEGES, 1968 AND 1990

		1968	1990	Change
Reasons to Go to College (Very Important)				
Gain a general education	male	60	56	−4
	female	67	69	+2
Learn more about things	male	69	68	−1
	female	74	77	+3
Get a better job	male	74	78	+4
	female	70	79	+9
Prepare for graduate or professional school	male	39	49	+10
	female	29	57	+28
Improve reading and writing skills	male	22	38	+16
	female	23	47	+24
Make more money	male	57	77	+20
	female	42	70	+28
Life Objectives (Essential or Very Important)				
Develop a philosophy of life	male	79	42	−37
	female	87	44	−43
Keep up with political affairs	male	52	47	−5
	female	52	39	−13
Help others in difficulty	male	50	51	+1
	female	71	71	0
Raise a family	male	64	68	+4
	female	72	71	−1
Be successful in my own business	male	55	50	−5
	female	32	38	+6
Be well off financially	male	51	78	+27
	female	27	70	+43

Note: To allow comparisons, data from early 1970s rather than 1968 are used for some items.

SOURCE: Richard G. Braungart and Margaret M. Braungart, "From Yippies to Yuppies: Twenty Years of Freshmen Attitudes," *Public Opinion*, Vol. 11, No. 3 (September-October 1988): 53–56; Alexander W. Astin, William S. Korn, and Ellyne R. Berz, *The American Freshman: National Norms for Fall 1990*, Los Angeles: U.C.L.A. Higher Education Research Institute, 1990.

the same share of students come to college in order to "gain a general education" and to "learn more about things." But the students of the 1990s seem relatively more interested than their parents' generation in gaining skills that will lead to high-paying jobs. Moreover, the political activism of the 1960s seems to have declined significantly in favor of the pursuit of personal success. Note that these changes have been greater among women than among men. This, no doubt, reflects the fact that the women's movement, concerned with social equality for the two sexes, intensified after 1968.

Change in one part of a cultural system typically sparks changes in others. Arlie Hochschild (1989:258) points out, "The gender revolution is primarily *caused* by changes in the economy, but people *feel* it in marriage." Such a linkage illustrates the principle of **cultural integration**, which holds that *the various parts of a cultural system are linked together.* Further, some parts of a cultural system change more quickly than others. William Ogburn (1964) observed that technological advances change material culture ("test-tube babies," for example) faster than nonmaterial elements (such as ideas about parenthood). Ogburn used the term **cultural lag** to refer to *inconsistencies in a cultural system resulting from the unequal rates at which various cultural elements change.* In a culture that now has the technical ability to allow one woman to give birth to a child by using another woman's egg, which has been fertilized in a laboratory with the sperm of a total stranger, what do the traditional terms *motherhood* and *fatherhood* mean?

Cultural changes are set in motion in three ways. The first is *invention,* the process of creating new cultural elements such as the telephone (1876), the airplane (1903), and the aerosol spray can (1941). The process of invention goes on constantly, as indicated by the thousands of applications received by the U.S. Patent Office each year.

Discovery, a second, closely related cause of change, involves recognizing and understanding something already in existence—from a distant star, to the foods of a foreign culture, to the athletic ability of women. Discovery often results from scientific research but sometimes by a stroke of luck, as when Marie Curie unintentionally left a "rock" on a piece of photographic paper in 1898 and discovered radium.

The third cause of cultural change is *diffusion,* the spread of both material and nonmaterial elements from one cultural system to another. Missionaries and anthropologists like Napoleon Chagnon have introduced many cultural elements to the Yąnomamö. Elements of our culture have spread throughout the world through diffusion: jazz, with its roots deep in the culture of African Americans; computers, first built in the mid-1940s in a Philadelphia laboratory; and even the U.S. Constitution, on which several other countries have modeled their own political systems. Conversely, much of what we assume is "American" is actually borrowed from other cultures. Ralph Linton (1937) has pointed out that most of our clothing and furniture, clocks, newspapers, money, and even the English language are derived from other cultures. As technology allows faster travel and communication, the rate of cultural diffusion will increase.

Ethnocentrism and Cultural Relativity

A question in the popular game Trivial Pursuit asks which beverage is the most popular drink in the United States. Milk? Soft drinks? Coffee? The answer is soft drinks, but all the beverages mentioned are favored by members of our culture. If the Masai of eastern Africa were to join the game, however, their answer might well be "blood." To us, of course, the idea of drinking blood is unnatural, if not downright revolting. On the other hand, a healthful glass of milk is actually detested by billions of people in the world, including the Chinese (Harris, 1985).

In a world of many cultures, how do we come to terms with other people's ways of living when they offend our own notions of what is proper? Anthropologists and sociologists caution us against **ethnocentrism,** *the practice of judging another culture by the standards of our own culture.* Some ethnocentrism is inevitable because our reality is rooted in our own culture. But evaluating an unfamiliar practice without understanding its cultural context can lead to misunderstanding and conflict. Ethnocentrism is a two-way street, of course. Just as we tend to dismiss those who differ from us, so others may judge us in the same way. Why, for example, have North Americans and Europeans traditionally called China the "Far East?" Such a term would have little meaning to the Chinese; "Far East" is an ethnocentric expression for what is far east *of Europe.* The Chinese, too, place themselves in the center of their world; the Chinese character that designates their nation is translated as "central state." Figure 2–1 on page 44 shows ethnocentrism at work in how people draw the world.

An alternative to ethnocentrism is **cultural relativism,** *the practice of evaluating any culture by its own standards.* Cultural relativism doesn't come easily, since it requires both understanding unfamiliar values and norms and breaking the grasp of a culture we have known all our lives. Still, the attempt is worth making for reasons of good will and self-interest. Success in the emerging global economy depends on cultural sensitivity and sophistication. When Coors first translated their slogan "Get loose with Coors" into Spanish, would-be customers were startled by words that meant "Get the runs with Coors." Similarly, Kentucky Fried Chicken was dismayed to learn that the Chinese viewed "finger-licking good" as hopelessly rude. And Coca-Cola's early attempts to entice the Japanese to buy their soft drink involved a translation of "Coke adds life" that startled Japanese readers as "Coke brings your ancestors back from the dead" (Westerman, 1989:32).

But cultural relativity can also pose problems. Virtually every kind of behavior is found somewhere in the world, yet does that mean that anything and everything is right just because *somebody* thinks so? What about the practice of Yąnomamö men who routinely offer their wives to others and beat women who displease them? Even in the unlikely event that Yąnomamö women accept this sort of treatment, should we say that, since truth is relative, these practices are right as long as the Yąnomamö themselves think so?

One might imagine, since we are all members of a single human species, that there must be some standards of fair conduct for people everywhere. But which ones? How can we resist imposing our own standards on everyone else? Sociologists have no simple answer to this dilemma, yet in a world where societies confront each other amid ever-present problems like hunger and war, this issue demands careful thought. On a smaller scale, this dilemma affects travelers abroad, as the box on page 45 explains.

THEORETICAL ANALYSIS OF CULTURE

Culture allows us to understand ourselves and the world around us. Sociologists, however, have the special task of understanding culture itself. To comprehend something as complex as culture requires several theoretical approaches.

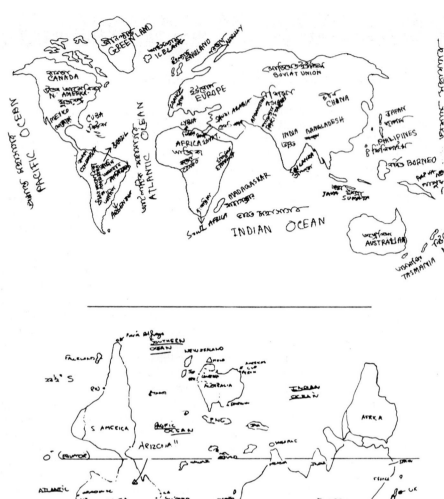

Figure 2–1 Ethnocentric Images of the World

One element of culture is how a person conceives of the world. The Eurocentric map, which places Europe in the center, is common in many parts of the world, reflecting Great Britain's historical dominance of the seas. Traditionally, European sea-farers measured their east-west location using as a standard the zero meridian of longitude, which runs north and south through Greenwich (near London). The top map, drawn by a student in India, is Eurocentric. The bottom map, typical of students in Australia, places what we in North America call "the Far East" in the center of the world; moreover, the world is drawn from the point of view of being "down under."

"The Traveler's Dilemma": How Should You Judge Another Culture?

Taiwan

Avoiding ethnocentrism requires resisting the temptation to judge another way of life by our own standards. But this is easier said than done, as travelers discover in many parts of the world.

Imagine, for instance, strolling the streets of Taipei, the capital city of Taiwan, the Republic of China. This island nation, about the size of the states of Maryland and Delaware combined, lies 150 miles off the shore of the Chinese mainland. It is a rapidly developing nation, but its culture is shaped by distinctive traditions and centuries of great poverty.

Taipei is frantic with activity. Pedestrians and motor scooters choke the streets. The city reaches a frenzied pace after dark, when tens of thousands of people flood the vast "night market." Countless outdoor stalls offer just about everything for sale. Vendors hawk familiar items such as clothing, fruits, and jewelry to the passing crowd; they also sell "snacks" such as chicken feet, and, even more shocking to the Western visitor, barbecued dogs. Children with withered limbs lie on the ground, begging from the people who swarm around them.

Nearby, the night market's infamous "Snake Alley" will push a visitor's sensibilities to the limit. For here, at least some would say, cruelty and violence are elevated to a sport. Visitors are drawn to a stall by a man beckoning over a loudspeaker. At the back of the stall, several televisions "warm up" the crowd displaying dog

fights in which the animals tear each other to pieces. The real show, however, begins as the master of ceremonies displays dozens of huge, live snakes. "Who will drink the venom?" he taunts in Chinese, again in Japanese, and then in English. One or two young men—eager to display courage to their comrades—push forward, money in hand. The man raises a snake overhead capturing everyone's attention, poking and taunting the animal to provoke its full viciousness. Suddenly, the snake's head is punctured by a hook suspended from the ceiling and—as it continues to flash back and forth—the man tears the skin from the snake's body, handing it to members of the audience. Then, using skills learned from hundreds of such displays, the master of ceremonies squeezes venom from the body of the snake into a small glass. Paying for the prize, a spectator

promptly chugs the fluid like so much whiskey. The crowd cheers. The process is repeated.

Snake Alley illustrates what might be called "the traveler's dilemma." On the one hand, ethnocentrism threatens to close off understanding, leading us to judge others simplistically and unfairly. On the other hand, cultural relativism suggests that right and wrong are simple matters of convention so that, in the end, morality seems arbitrary and meaningless.

Is there a resolution to "the traveler's dilemma?" First, resisting quick judgments, confront the unfamiliar with an open mind. We learn by being receptive to others' ways of living. Second, try to imagine events from *their* point of view. Witnessing the events of the night market, for instance, one might wonder if animals have a different significance in a society in which human poverty, hunger, and suffering are commonplace. Third, after a period of careful and critical thinking, try to reach some judgment of the cultural practice. After all, a world in which everyone passively accepted their surroundings would be frightening. But, in making your evaluation, bear in mind that, unless we are truly able to "stand in their shoes," we can never experience the world as others do. Fourth, and finally, try to evaluate more realistically our own way of life as well. Would an experience in the night market of Taipei change a visitor's view of fox hunts or boxing in the United States?

SOURCE: Based on the author's travels in Taipei.

Structural-Functional Analysis

The structural-functional paradigm depicts culture as a complex and relatively stable strategy for meeting human needs. This point of view borrows from the philosophical doctrine of *idealism* by asserting that values are the core of a culture (Parsons, 1966; Williams, 1970). A culture's values, as expressed in everyday routines, make life meaningful and bind people together. Beyond ideas, all other cultural traits have one or more functions that support a way of life.

Take the Amish, whose strongly religious communities across Pennsylvania, Ohio, and Indiana shun change and modern conveniences. The outsider is likely to be puzzled seeing Amish farmers tilling hundreds of acres with horse and plow rather than tractors. From the Amish point of view, however, rejecting modern technology makes sense because continuous labor—usually outside the home for men and inside for women—functions to maintain Amish discipline. Long days of shared work, along with meals and recreation at home, bind family members together and make local communities self-sufficient (Hostetler, 1980).

Of course, some Amish traits also have dysfunctional consequences. The practice of "shunning," by which people refuse to interact with anyone judged to have violated religious mores, enhances conformity but can also cause a serious rift in the community. In the extreme case, a cultural practice may even lead to a community's demise. The Shakers, another countercultural religious group that flourished in the nineteenth century, prohibited sexual relations among its members. Although they survived for decades by taking in new members from the outside world, the Shakers' failure to reproduce themselves ultimately led to their extinction.

Because people devise culture to meet their needs, we might expect to find humans around the world creating many of the same cultural patterns. The term **cultural universals** refers to *traits found in every culture of the world*. Comparing hundreds of cultures, George Murdock (1945) identified dozens of traits common to them all. One cultural universal is the family, which functions everywhere to control sexual reproduction and to oversee the care and upbringing of children. Another example is funeral rites, since all societies confront death. Jokes, too, exist in all cultures, at least partly because they provide a relatively safe means of relieving stress.

Critical evaluation. Structural-functional analysis has the strength of portraying culture as an organized system

We readily think of a funeral as a display of respect for a deceased person. The social function of funerals, however, has much more to do with the living. For survivors, funerals reaffirm a sense of unity and continuity in the face of separation and disruption.

to meet human needs. All cultures have much in common, but since there are many ways to meet almost any need, cultures around the world reveal striking diversity.

One limitation of structural-functional thinking is its tendency to stress a society's dominant cultural patterns, while directing less attention to cultural diversity. This is especially true with regard to cultural differences that arise from social inequality. By emphasizing cultural stability, in addition, this paradigm downplays the importance of change.

Social-Conflict Analysis

The social-conflict paradigm suggests that many cultural traits function to the advantage of some and the disadvantage of others. Thus, according to this view, a culture operates as a dynamic arena in which inequality among categories of people drives a continual power struggle.

Social-conflict analysis also asks why one set of values rather than another dominates a society. Many conflict theorists, especially those influenced by the work of Karl Marx, argue that culture is shaped by a society's system of economic production. "It is not the consciousness of men that determines their existence," Marx asserted, "it is their social existence that determines their consciousness" (1977:4; orig. 1859). In other words, the social-conflict paradigm draws on the philosophical doctrine of *materialism,* which holds that a society's system of material production (in the United States, an industrial-capitalist economy) has a powerful effect on all other dimensions of culture. Such a materialist approach contrasts with the idealist leanings of structural-functionalism.

Social-conflict analysis, then, would suggest that the competitive and individualistic values of this society reflect our capitalist economy and serve the interests of those who own factories and other productive enterprises. The culture of capitalism further teaches us to think that the rich and powerful have more talent and discipline than others, and therefore deserve their wealth and privileges. Viewing capitalism as somehow "natural" also discourages efforts to lessen economic disparity in the United States.

Social-conflict analysts claim that strains created by social inequality eventually transform cultural systems. The civil rights movement and the women's movement exemplify the drive for change supported by disadvantaged segments of the U.S. population. Both, too, have encountered opposition from defenders of the status quo.

Critical evaluation. The strength of the social-conflict paradigm lies in its suggestion that if cultural systems address human needs, they do so unequally. Put otherwise, this orientation holds that the main "function" of many cultural elements is to maintain the dominance of some people over others. This inequity, in turn, promotes change.

However, the social-conflict paradigm falls short by stressing the divisiveness of culture and understating the ways in which cultural patterns integrate members of a society. Thus we should consider both social-conflict and structural-functional insights to gain a fuller understanding of culture.

Cultural Ecology

Ecology is a branch of the natural sciences that explores the relationship between a living organism and its natural environment. **Cultural ecology,** then, is *a theoretical paradigm that explores the relationship between human culture and the physical environment.* This paradigm investigates how climate and the availability of natural resources shape cultural patterns.

Consider the case of India, a nation that contends with widespread hunger and malnutrition. The norms of India's predominantly Hindu culture prohibit the killing of cows, which are considered sacred animals. To North Americans who consume so much beef, this is puzzling. Why should Indians not eat beef to supplement their diet?

Marvin Harris (1975) claims that the cow's food value is greatly surpassed by its importance to India's ecology. Harris points out that cows cost little to raise since they consume grasses of no interest to humans. And cows produce two vital resources: oxen (the neutered offspring of cows) and manure. Unable to afford the high costs of machinery, Indian farmers depend on oxen to power their plows. From their point of view, killing cows would be as clever as farmers in the United States tearing down factories that build tractors. Furthermore, each year India processes millions of tons of cow manure into building material or burns it as fuel (this nation has little oil, coal, or wood). To kill cows, then, would deprive millions of Indians of homes and a source of heat. In India, then, protecting cows is ecologically sound.

Critical evaluation. Cultural ecology adds to our understanding of the interplay between culture and the natural environment. This approach can reveal how and why specific social patterns arise under particular physical conditions.

However, the physical environment rarely shapes cultural patterns in any simple or direct way. More correctly, the cultural and physical worlds interact, each shaping the other.

Sociobiology

Sociology has maintained a rather uneasy relationship with biology. In part, this stems from a rivalry between two disciplines that study human life. However, the friction runs much deeper because early biological assertions

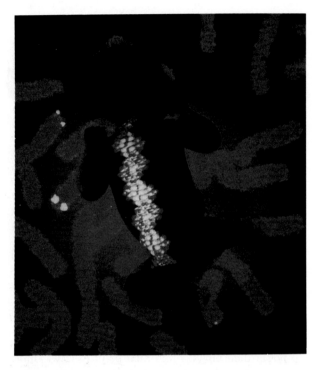

Debate continues about the role of biology in shaping human behavior. The truth is that scientists are only beginning to "map" genetic processes that guide physical development. Present evidence suggests biology can explain some variation in how individuals think and act. But the bigger picture is that our human nature demands that we create culture, and that we learn a way of life through social experience.

about human behavior—for example, that some categories of people are inherently "better" than others—were expressions of historical racism and ethnocentrism rather than legitimate science. Early sociologists provided evidence to refute such thinking.

By the middle of this century, sociologists had demonstrated that culture rather than biology is the major force shaping human behavior. In recent decades, however, new ideas linking culture to the principles of biological evolution have revived old debates. This research has created **sociobiology,** *a theoretical paradigm that explains cultural patterns in terms of biological forces*. While some sociologists are skeptical of this new paradigm, others think that it may provide useful insights into human culture.

The scientific view of how life developed on earth is based on the theory of evolution. In his book *On the Origin of Species*, Charles Darwin (1859) asserted that living organisms change over long periods of time as a result of *natural selection*, a matter of four simple principles. First, all living things live and reproduce within a natural environment. Second, genes—the basic units of life that carry traits of one generation into the next—vary randomly in each species. Genetic variation allows species to "try out" new life patterns in a particular environment. Third, this variation enables some organisms to survive better than others and to pass on their advantageous genes to their offspring. Fourth and finally, over thousands of generations, genetic patterns that promote survival and reproduction become dominant. In this way, as biologists say, a species *adapts* to its environment, and dominant traits represent the "nature" of the organism.

Sociobiologists suggest that the surprising number of cultural universals reflects our membership in a single biological species. How else can we explain, for example, the apparently universal pattern that we commonly call the "double standard" by which men engage in sexual activity more freely than women do? As sex researcher Alfred Kinsey put it, "Among all people everywhere in the world, the male is more likely than the female to desire sex with a variety of partners" (cited in Barash, 1981:49).

Speaking sociobiologically, nature has assigned different reproductive strategies to the two sexes. We all know that children result from joining a woman's egg with a man's sperm. But there are striking differences in the value of a single sperm to a man and a single egg to a woman. For healthy men, sperm represents a "renewable resource" produced by the testes throughout most of life. A man releases hundreds of millions of sperm in a single ejaculation—technically, enough to fertilize every woman in North America (Barash, 1981:47). A newborn female's ovaries, however, contain her entire lifetime allotment of follicles or immature eggs. Women commonly release just one mature egg cell from their ovaries each month. So, while men are biologically capable of fathering thousands of offspring, women are able to bear a relatively small number of children. Biologically, then, men reproduce their genes most efficiently through a strategy of sexual promiscuity. This strategy, however, opposes the reproductive interests of women. Each of a woman's relatively few pregnancies demands that she carry the child, give birth, and provide care for some time afterward. Thus, efficient reproduction on the part of the woman depends on selecting a man whose qualities will contribute to her child's survival and successful reproduction (Remoff, 1984).

No one doubts that the double standard plays a part in the historical domination of women by men (Barry, 1983). But sociobiology suggests that this cultural pattern, like many others, has an underlying bio-logic. Simply put, it has developed around the world because women and men everywhere benefit from distinctive reproductive strategies.

Critical evaluation. Because sociobiology is a new approach, its significance is still not clear. Potentially, this paradigm offers insights about the biological roots of some cultural patterns, especially those that are universal.

At present, however, sociobiology remains controversial for several reasons. First, because so-called biological facts historically have been used (or more precisely, *mis*used) to justify oppression of one race or sex, critics of sociobiology fear that this new paradigm may follow the same path. Defenders respond, however, that sociobiology has no connection to the past pseudoscience of racial superiority. On the contrary, sociobiology serves to unite rather than divide humanity by asserting that we all share a single evolutionary history.

Sexism—the assertion that males are inherently superior to females and are thus justified in having greater social power—also has no place in sociobiological thinking. Sociobiology does rest on the assumption that men and women differ biologically in some ways that no culture is likely to eliminate—if, in fact, any culture intended to. But, far from asserting that males are somehow more worthy than females, sociobiology emphasizes how both sexes are vital to human reproduction.

Second, say the critics, little evidence supports sociobiology's claims. Despite optimistic projections by Edward O. Wilson (1975, 1978), generally credited as the founder of this field, that research will demonstrate the biological roots of human culture, a generation of work has yet to reveal that biological forces *determine* human behavior in any strict sense. Rather, abundant evidence supports the conclusion that human behavior is *learned* within a cultural system. More likely, the value of sociobiology will lie in explaining why some cultural patterns are more prevalent than others.

CULTURE AND HUMAN FREEDOM

Finally, what are the consequences of culture for human freedom? Certainly humanity could not live without culture. But our symbolic capacity also makes possible the experience of alienation, which is unknown to other

Although organized social living is the key to realizing our human potential, we sometimes experience our culture as threatening and overwhelming. This alienation is evident in Tom Lea's (1907–   ) portrayal of a marine caught up in the agony of World War II.

forms of life. Cultural systems can also weigh heavily, creating a form of social inertia that carries forward from generation to generation, tying us to the past. Then, too, our culture supports marked social inequality, conferring great privilege on some and consigning others to poverty. Women of all social classes, too, have often felt powerless in the face of cultural patterns that reinforce the dominance of men.

Similarly, while our cultural insistence on competitive achievement encourages us to strive for excellence, it also isolates us from one another. Material comforts improve our lives in some ways, yet a preoccupation with things diverts us from the security and satisfaction of close relationships and the spiritual side of existence. And just as our emphasis on personal freedom ensures privacy and autonomy, our culture often denies us the support of a human community in which to share the problems of life (Slater, 1976; Bellah et al., 1985).

For better and worse, human beings are cultural creatures, just as ants and bees are prisoners of their biology (Berger, 1967). But there is a crucial difference. The burden of culture is *freedom*, the responsibility to shape the world for ourselves. Our creative capacity is evident in the cultural diversity of our own society, and the even greater human variety around the world. Furthermore, far from static, culture is ever-changing. And although it sometimes functions as a constraint, culture also presents a continual source of human opportunity. The more we discover about the workings of our culture, the greater our ability to use the freedom it offers us.

SUMMARY

1. Culture refers to patterned ways in which humans live together. Some animals display limited culture; only humans rely on culture to survive. Society refers to people's interaction, which is guided by culture.

2. Culture developed over the long course of human evolution as the brain gradually grew larger. Although basic elements of culture appeared 2 million years ago, complex civilization emerged only during the last ten thousand years.

3. Culture relies on symbols. Language is the symbolic system by which we pass culture from generation to generation.

4. Values are standards that shape our orientation to the world. Norms guide specific behavior; mores have greater moral significance than folkways.

5. Culture is shaped by technology. Technological development follows four stages of sociocultural evolution: hunting and gathering, horticulturalism and pastoralism, agriculture, and industry.

6. Culture involves not only common patterns but also diversity. A subculture is a distinctive pattern that characterizes a segment of society; counterculture is strongly at odds with widely accepted cultural patterns.

7. Multiculturalism refers to efforts to enhance appreciation of cultural diversity.

8. Invention, discovery, and diffusion all generate cultural change. Cultural lag results as parts of a cultural system change at varying rates.

9. Ethnocentrism involves judging others using standards of our own culture. By contrast, cultural relativism means understanding other cultures using their own standards.

10. Structural-functional analysis views culture as a relatively stable system built on core values. Any cultural trait is understood in terms of its function in maintaining the entire social system.

11. The social-conflict paradigm envisions culture as a dynamic arena of inequality and conflict. Cultural traits typically benefit some categories of people more than others.

12. Cultural ecology studies how culture is shaped by the natural environment. Sociobiology investigates links between culture and our species' evolutionary past.

13. Culture can constrain human needs and ambitions, yet it provides us with the capacity and freedom to shape and reshape our world.

KEY CONCEPTS

Afrocentrism the dominance of African cultural patterns

agriculture a way of life based on large-scale cultivation using animal-drawn plows

counterculture cultural patterns that strongly oppose conventional culture

cultural ecology a theoretical paradigm that explores the relationship between human culture and the physical environment

cultural integration the close relationship among various parts of a cultural system

cultural lag inconsistencies in a cultural system resulting from the unequal rates at which various cultural elements change

cultural relativism the practice of evaluating any culture by its own standards

cultural transmission the process by which culture is passed from one generation to the next

cultural universals traits found in every culture

culture the beliefs, values, behavior, and material objects shared by a particular people

culture shock the personal disorientation accompanying exposure to an unfamiliar way of life

ethnocentrism the practice of judging another culture by the standards of our own culture

Eurocentrism the dominance of European (especially English) cultural patterns

folkways norms that have little moral significance

horticulture a way of life based on the use of hand tools to raise crops

hunting and gathering a way of life based on the use of simple tools to hunt animals and gather vegetation

industrial society a society that produces goods using sophisticated machinery powered by advanced fuels

language a system of symbols with standard meanings that allows members of a society to communicate with one another

mores norms that have great moral significance

multiculturalism the recognition of our society's cultural diversity coupled with efforts to promote the equality of all cultural traditions

norms rules by which a society guides the behavior of its members

pastoralism a way of life based on the domestication of animals

Sapir-Whorf hypothesis the assertion that people perceive the world only in terms of the symbols provided by their language

society people interacting within a limited territory guided by their culture

sociobiology a theoretical paradigm that explains cultural patterns in terms of biological forces

sociocultural evolution the historical process of cultural change caused by technological innovation

subculture cultural patterns that distinguish some segment of a society's population

symbol anything that carries a particular meaning recognized by members of a society

technology the application of knowledge to the practical tasks of living

values culturally defined standards of desirability, goodness, and beauty that serve as broad guidelines for social life

Henry Ossawa Tanner, 1893. The Banjo Lesson. Oil on Canvas. Hampton University Museum, Hampton, Virginia.

3

Socialization: From Infancy to Old Age

CHAPTER OUTLINE

On a cold winter day in 1938, a concerned social worker drove to a farmhouse in rural Pennsylvania and found a five-year-old girl hidden in a second-floor storage room. Anna sat rigidly in a chair with her arms tied above her head. Her limbs were like matchsticks—so thin and frail that she could not use them (Davis, 1940:554).

Anna had been born to an unmarried woman of twenty-six who lived with her father. Enraged by his daughter's "illegitimate" motherhood, at first he refused to even have the child in his house. Anna therefore spent the early months of her life in the custody of various welfare agencies. Finally, because her mother was unable to pay for this care, and her grandfather was unwilling, Anna was returned to the home where she was not wanted.

The grandfather's hostility and the mother's indifference resulted in Anna living alone in a room where she received little attention and just enough milk to keep her alive. There she stayed, with virtually no human contact, for five years.

Upon learning of the discovery of Anna, sociologist Kingsley Davis traveled immediately to see the child, who had been taken to a county home. He was appalled at her condition; the emaciated child could not laugh, speak, or even smile. Anna was completely apathetic, as if alone in an empty world (Davis, 1940).

THE IMPORTANCE OF SOCIAL EXPERIENCE

Here is a deplorable but instructive case of a human being deprived of social contact. Although physically alive, Anna had none of the capabilities associated with full humanity. Anna's story illustrates that, without social experience, an individual develops no capacity for thought, emotion, or meaningful behavior.

Sociologists use the term **socialization** to refer to *lifelong social experience by which individuals develop their human potential and learn patterns of their culture.* As Chapter 2 ("Culture") explained, the behavior of other species of life is biologically determined; only humans depend on culture for survival. Social experience is also the foundation of **personality**, *a person's fairly consistent patterns of thinking, feeling, and acting.* Personality is constructed from our surroundings and how we learn to respond to them. As personality develops, we simultaneously become distinctive individuals and

share a culture. Without social experience, as the case of Anna shows, personality simply does not emerge.

Social experience is as vital for society as it is for individuals. Through the lifelong process of socialization, society transmits culture from one generation to the next.

Nature and Nurture

Virtually helpless at birth, the human infant needs others to provide care and nourishment and to teach patterns of culture. Although Anna's short life makes these facts clear, a century ago most people mistakenly believed that human behavior was the product of biology.

Charles Darwin's groundbreaking studies of evolution, conducted in the mid-nineteenth century and described in the last chapter, led most people to think that human behavior was instinctive, simply the "nature" of our species. Such notions are still with us. People sometimes claim, for example, that our economic system reflects "instinctive human competitiveness," that some people are "born criminals," or that women are emotional while men are rational (Witkin-Lanoil, 1984).

Darwin's work was also misconstrued by people trying to understand distinctive social arrangements around the globe. Centuries of world exploration and empire building brought Western Europeans into contact with people whose customs differed markedly from their own. They readily attributed these unfamiliar practices and beliefs to biological differences rather than to cultural diversity. Thus Europeans and North Americans considered the members of technologically simple societies as biologically less evolved and, thus, less human. This self-serving and ethnocentric view justified brutal colonial subjugation. It is easy to enter another society, exploit its resources, and even enslave its people if you think they are not human in the same sense that you are.

In this century, naturalistic explanations of human behavior came under fire. Psychologist John B. Watson (1878–1958) devised an approach called *behaviorism*, which held that human behavior is not instinctive but learned. Arguing that all the world's cultures have the same biological foundation, Watson rejected the notion that cultural diversity reflects any evolutionary distinctions. Rather, Watson argued, human behavior is malleable, and will respond to virtually any environment imaginable.

Watson, therefore, rooted human behavior in *nurture* rather than nature. Endorsing this view, anthropologist Margaret Mead concluded that global differences

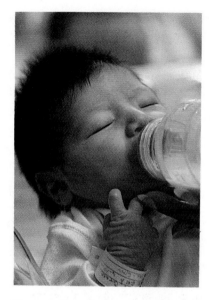
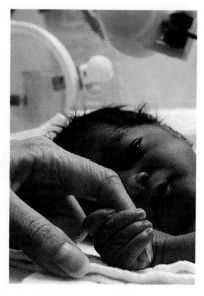
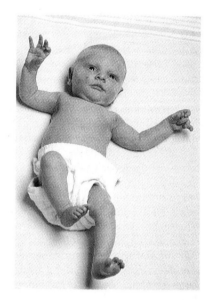

Human infants display various reflexes, biologically based patterns of behavior that enhance survival. The sucking reflex actually begins before birth and enables the infant to obtain nourishment. The grasping reflex, triggered by placing a finger on the infant's palm, causes the hand to close. This response helps the infant to maintain contact with a parent and, later on, to grasp objects. The Moro reflex, a response to being startled, causes the infant to swing both arms outward and then bring them together on the chest. This action, which disappears during the first months of life, probably developed among our evolutionary ancestors so that a falling baby could grasp the body hair of a parent.

in human behavior—like individual differences in a single community—are "almost entirely to be laid to differences in conditioning, especially during early childhood, and this conditioning is culturally determined" (1963:280; orig. 1935).

Today, social scientists are cautious about describing *any* human behavioral trait as instinctive. This does not mean that biology plays no part in human behavior. Human life, after all, depends on the functioning of the human body. We know that children share biological traits with their parents, especially physical attributes such as height, weight, hair and eye color, and facial features. Heredity also plays a role in the transmission of intelligence and personality characteristics (such as how one reacts to stimulation). The potential to excel in activities such as art and music has a genetic component as well. However, what we do with our inherited potential depends on social experiences (Plomin & Foch, 1980; Goldsmith, 1983). On balance, then, nurture matters much more than nature in shaping human behavior. Or perhaps we should say that, as human beings, it is

our nature to create, learn, and modify culture. Thus, nature and nurture stand not so much in opposition as they are intertwined.

Social Isolation

For obvious ethical reasons, researchers cannot subject human beings to experimental isolation. But research on the effects of social isolation has involved nonhuman primates.

Psychologists Harry and Margaret Harlow (1962) placed rhesus monkeys—whose behavior is in some ways surprisingly similar to that of human beings—in various conditions of social isolation to observe the consequences. They found that complete social isolation (with adequate nutrition) for a period of even six months was sufficient to cause developmental disturbances. When reintroduced to others of their kind, these monkeys were fearful and defenseless against aggression.

The Harlows also placed infant rhesus monkeys

in cages with an artificial "mother" constructed of wire mesh and a wooden head and the nipple of a feeding tube where the breast would be. These monkeys, too, were subsequently unable to interact with other monkeys. But when the artificial "mother" was covered with soft terry cloth, the infant monkeys clung to it, deriving some emotional benefit from the closeness; this reduced the developmental harm. The experiment revealed the profound developmental importance of the simple act of affectionately cradling an infant.

The Harlows made two further discoveries. First, as long as they were surrounded by other infants, monkeys were not adversely affected by the absence of a mother. This shows that deprivation of social experience, not the specific absence of a mother, has devastating effects. Second, the Harlows found that, when socially isolated for shorter periods of time (about three months), infant monkeys eventually regained normal emotional patterns after rejoining others. The damage of short-term isolation, then, can be overcome; longer-term isolation, however, appears to cause irreversible emotional and behavioral damage.

The later development of Anna is roughly consistent with the research of the Harlows. After being discovered, Anna experienced extensive social contact, and

soon began to show some improvement. When Kingsley Davis (1940) revisited her after ten days, he noted that she was more alert and displayed some human expression, even smiling with obvious pleasure. Over the next year, Anna made slow but steady progress, as she experienced the humanizing effects of socialization, showing more interest in other people and gradually gaining the ability to walk. After a year and a half, she was able to feed herself, walk alone for short distances, and play with toys.

Yet it was becoming apparent that Anna's five years of social isolation had left her permanently damaged. At age eight her mental and social development had only reached that of a child a year and a half old. Only as she approached the age of ten did she begin to use language. Complicating the situation, Anna's mother was mentally disabled, so that Anna may have been similarly disadvantaged. The puzzle was never solved, however, because Anna died at age ten of a blood disorder, possibly related to her long years of abuse (Davis, 1940).

A second, similar case reveals more about the long-range effects of social isolation. At the same time that Anna was discovered, another girl of about the same age was found under strikingly similar circumstances.

The personalities we develop depend largely on the environment in which we live. When a child's world is shredded by violence, the damage can be profound and lasting. This drawing was made by a four-year-old living in a low-income neighborhood of Washington, DC. What are the likely effects of such an environment on a child's self-confidence and capacity to trust others?

After more than six years of virtual isolation, this girl—known as Isabelle—revealed the same lack of human responsiveness as Anna (Davis, 1947). Isabelle made more rapid progress than Anna, however. One week after an intensive program was begun, Isabelle was attempting to speak, and a year and a half later, her vocabulary consisted of almost two thousand words. Psychologists observed Isabelle's progress through what is normally six years of development during two years of intensive effort. By the time she was fourteen, Isabelle was attending sixth-grade classes in school, apparently on her way to an approximately normal life.

The fate of Anna and Isabelle demonstrates that social experience is crucial for the development of human personality. Human beings are resilient creatures, sometimes able to recover from even the crushing experience of prolonged isolation. But there seems to be a point—precisely when is unclear from the small number of cases studied—at which isolation in infancy results in developmental damage, including a reduced capacity for language, that cannot be fully repaired.

UNDERSTANDING SOCIALIZATION

Several pioneers have explored the complex process of socialization. Three of the most important models of human development are presented here.

Sigmund Freud: The Elements of Personality

Sigmund Freud (1856–1939) lived in Vienna at a time when most Europeans thought human behavior was a matter of biological forces. Freud began his career as a physician but soon dedicated himself to analyzing human personality. Increasingly drawn to the treatment of psychological problems, Freud's towering achievement was the development of psychoanalysis.

Freud contended that biology plays an important part in the human personality, although he never reduced human behavior to simple biological instincts. For Freud, instinct meant general human needs or drives. One such need is for bonding, which Freud termed the life instinct, or *eros* (ancient Greece's god of love). Another is an aggressive drive he called the death instinct, or *thanatos* (derived from Greek meaning "death"). Freud asserted that these opposing forces ignite tension—mostly at the unconscious level—in our personality.

Freud incorporated both basic human needs and the influence of society into a model of personality with three parts: id, ego, and superego. The **id** represents *the human being's basic drives,* which are unconscious and demand immediate satisfaction. (The word *id* is Latin for "it," suggesting the tentative way Freud explored the human mind; it also derives from the Greek word *es,* meaning "primal urge.") Rooted in our biology, the id is present at birth, so that a newborn is basically a bundle of needs—for attention, touching, and food. Since society opposes such a self-centered orientation, the id's desires inevitably meet with resistance, which is why children soon grasp the meaning of "no."

To lessen frustration, a child learns to approach the world more realistically. This is accomplished through the ego, which gradually becomes differentiated from the id. The **ego** (Latin for "I") represents *a person's conscious efforts to balance the innate pleasure-seeking drives and the demands of society.* The ego arises as we gain awareness of our distinct existence and face up to the fact that we cannot have everything we want.

Finally, the human personality develops the **superego** (Latin meaning "above" or "beyond" the ego), which is *internalized cultural values and norms.* Superego is, simply put, the presence of culture in the individual, which is experienced as conscience. Through the superego, we understand *why* we cannot have everything we want. First expressed as the awareness of parental control, the superego matures as the child comes to recognize the cultural system, realizing that parents, too, must respond to society's moral mandates.

From a child's point of view, the world first appears as a bewildering array of physical sensations and need satisfactions. As the superego develops, the child's comprehension reaches beyond pleasure and pain to the moral concepts of right and wrong. In other words, an infant initially can feel good only as physical sensation. Later the child can feel good for behaving in culturally appropriate ways and, conversely, feel bad (the experience of guilt) for breaking the rules.

If the ego successfully manages the opposing forces of the id and the superego, the personality is considered to be well adjusted. If this conflict is not successfully resolved, personality disorders can result. Freud viewed childhood as the critical period for the formation of an individual's basic personality, and he believed that conflicts experienced during this stage of life often linger as an unconscious source of personality problems later on.

Freud termed society's efforts to control human

drives *repression*. Some repression is inevitable, he claimed, since society must coerce people into looking beyond themselves. A compromise Freud called *sublimation* transforms selfish drives into more socially acceptable behavior. For example, the sexual urges may lead to marriage, and aggression can be expressed in a sports stadium.

Critical evaluation. Freud's work sparked controversy in his own lifetime, and some of that debate still smolders today. His own society vigorously repressed sexuality, and few of Freud's contemporaries were prepared to confront this dimension of life, much less to acknowledge it as a basic drive. More recent critics of Freud's work argue that his thinking depicts humanity strictly in male terms with a distorted view of women (Donovan & Littenberg, 1982). Despite these critiques, it is widely acknowledged that Freud's ideas have influenced virtually everyone who subsequently examined the human personality. Of special importance to sociology is his notion that we internalize social norms, and that childhood experiences have lasting importance in the socialization process.

Jean Piaget: Cognitive Development

Swiss psychologist Jean Piaget (1896–1980) also stands among the foremost social psychologists of this century. His theory and research centered on human *cognition*—how people think and understand. Early in his career, Piaget became fascinated with the behavior of his own three children, wondering not only what they knew, but *how* they understood the world. He identified four age-linked stages of cognitive development.

The first is the **sensorimotor stage,** *the level of development at which individuals have only sensory-based experience.* For roughly the first two years of life, the infant knows the world only by touching, looking, sucking, and listening. At this stage, then, infants fail to appreciate what Piaget termed *object permanence*, the fact that objects continue to exist even if they are beyond sensory range. Infants may react with despair, for example, when an adult leaves the room, as if that person had ceased to exist. Until this stage is complete, children have a very fragile level of confidence about the world.

Second, lasting from about age two to seven, is the **preoperational stage,** *the level of development at which individuals first use language and other symbols.* Symbols are the child's doorway into a vast world of meanings extending beyond the immediate senses. At

In a well-known experiment, Jean Piaget demonstrated that children over the age of seven entered the concrete operational stage of development as they came to recognize that the quantity of liquid remained the same when poured from a wide beaker into a tall one.

this point, children can appreciate fantasy and fairy tales (Kohlberg & Gilligan, 1971; Skolnick, 1986). But young children attach only specific names and meanings to objects, identifying a particular toy, for example, but not describing toys in general. That is, they cannot yet grasp abstract concepts such as beauty, size, or weight.

In one of his best-known experiments, Piaget placed two identical glasses filled with the same amount of water on a table and asked several five- and six-year-olds if the amount in each was the same. They acknowledged that it was. The children then watched Piaget take one of the glasses and pour its contents into a taller, narrower glass, raising the level of the water. He asked again if each glass held the same amount. The typical five- or six-year-old now insisted that the taller glass held more water. But children over the age of seven, who are able to think more abstractly, realized that the amount of water in the two different-shaped glasses remained the same.

Next, in Piaget's model, is the **concrete operational stage,** *the level of development at which individuals begin logical reasoning.* During this stage, typically corresponding to the years between about seven and eleven, children start to connect facts in terms of cause and effect. They also learn that more than one symbol can be attached to a single event; "Wednesday," for instance, can also be "My birthday!" However, the thinking of children remains centered on concrete events and objects. They may understand that hitting brothers without provocation will bring punishment, but they generally cannot imagine a situation in which hitting a brother would be fair or understand why parents punish.

The fourth level in Piaget's model is the **formal operational stage**, *the level of development at which individuals think abstractly and with imagination*. By about the age of twelve, children can report not only wanting to be, say, a teacher someday, but they can describe such work as "challenging" and "satisfying." This capacity for abstract thought also allows the child to comprehend metaphors. Hearing the phrase "A penny for your thoughts" might prompt a younger child to think of money, but an older child will recognize a gentle invitation to intimacy.

Critical evaluation. If Freud envisioned human beings as torn by the opposing forces of biology and society, Piaget saw the mind as active and creative so that children steadily gain the ability to shape their own social world (cf. Corsaro & Rizzo, 1988). His contribution to understanding socialization lies in showing that this capacity unfolds gradually as the result of both biological maturation and increasing social experience.

In global perspective, there is some question about whether Piaget's stages and time frame apply to people everywhere. For instance, living in a society that changes very slowly is likely to inhibit the ability to imagine the world being very different. In addition, Carol Gilligan (1982) has suggested that boys and girls do not develop in precisely the same way. She claims that boys generally grasp abstract standards of right and wrong while girls tend to evaluate events morally according to how they affect others. Finally, among both women and men, a substantial proportion of adults never reach the formal operational stage (Kohlberg & Gilligan, 1971). Regardless of biological maturity, people who encounter little creative and imaginative thinking in others are unlikely to develop this capacity in themselves.

George Herbert Mead: The Social Self

What exactly is social experience? George Herbert Mead (1863–1931) spent much of his life answering this vital question. Mead's approach (1962; orig. 1934), termed *social behaviorism*, starts with the notion that environment shapes behavior, and highlights the centrality of symbols to human behavior.

Mead's central concept is the **self**, *a dimension of personality composed of an individual's active self-aware-ness*. Mead's genius lay in seeing the self as inseparable from society, a connection explained in a series of steps. First, Mead asserted, the self develops from social experience. The self has no biological component and does not exist at birth. Mead rejected the view that humans have biological drives (as Freud asserted) or develop only with biological maturation (as Piaget claimed). For Mead, the self gradually arises as the individual comes into contact with others. In the absence of social experience—as isolated children show us—the body grows but no self emerges.

Second, Mead claimed, social experience is *symbolic interaction*, or the exchange of symbols. A wave of the hand, a spoken word, or a broad smile are all symbolic. Thus, while Mead agreed with psychologist John B. Watson that human behavior is shaped by the environment, he maintained that humans are unique in our symbolic capacity. A dog, for example, can be trained to respond to a specific stimulus, but the dog attaches no meaning to this behavior. Human beings, by contrast, are as sensitive to intention as we are to action. In short, a dog responds to *what you do*, but a human imagines *what you have in mind* as you do it. Thus one can train a dog to go to the corner and carry back an umbrella. But, grasping no intention behind the command, a dog unable to find an umbrella would never look for a raincoat instead, as a human being would.

Third, humans comprehend intention by learning to *take the role of the other*. Seeing ourselves from another person's point of view, we can anticipate the other's response to us. This mental process precedes even a simple act such as throwing a ball. Imagining the other's response—in this case, catching the ball—is how one directs a throw.

Furthermore, how we think of ourselves has much to do with how others think of us. Charles Horton Cooley, one of Mead's colleagues, pointed out that other people serve as a social mirror or looking glass in which we imagine ourselves as they see us. Cooley (1964; orig. 1902) used the phrase **looking-glass self** to mean *a conception of self based on the responses of others*. We come to know ourselves, in other words, from how others think and act toward us. We are unlikely to think of ourselves as, say, trustworthy unless we find support for this perception from others.

Mead's fourth argument is that, by taking the role of another, we become *self-reflective*. This means the self has a dual nature. As subject, a self initiates social action, making humans innately active and spontaneous.

"Peek-a-boo" reveals the inability of very young children to accomplish what Mead calls taking the role of the other. Children assume that, "since I cannot see you, you cannot see me." After gaining this capacity, however, youngsters commonly play "dress-up," exploring the role of one other person, usually a parent. Complex team sports require the child to simultaneously take the role of many others. Thus only when they have had considerable social experience can children play games such as soccer.

For simplicity, he dubbed this subjective side of the self the *I* (the subjective form of the personal pronoun). The self is also object, as we imagine ourselves from the viewpoint of others. Mead called the objective side of the self the *me* (the objective form of the personal pronoun). Combining the two we distill the essence of social experience: the self initiates interaction (as the I) and simultaneously imagines this action (the me) through taking the role of the other. That is, we initiate behavior that we subsequently guide by "seeing" ourselves through the response of others.

The key to developing the self, then, is gaining sophistication in taking the role of the other. Like Freud and Piaget, Mead thought that early childhood was crucial in this process. He did not, however, link the development of the self closely to age. Mead consistently minimized the importance of biological forces, claiming that the complexity of the self simply derived from amassing social experience.

Mead explained that infants with limited social experience respond to others only in terms of *imitation*. That is, they mimic behavior without understanding underlying intentions and so, as yet, they have no self. As children learn to use language and other symbols, the self appears in the form of *play*. Play involves assuming roles modeled on significant people—such as parents—who are sometimes termed *significant others*. Playing "Mommy" or "Daddy," for instance, helps children imagine the world and themselves from a parent's point of view.

Further social experience teaches children to take the roles of several others simultaneously. Able to initiate different actions in response to different others, children move from simple play involving one role to more complex *games* involving many roles at one time.

A final developmental step depends on children learning to see themselves as society in general does. Figure 3–1 shows how this works as an extension of the ability to engage in play and games. Children recognize that all members of their society share many of the same norms and values. Once these cultural patterns are incorporated into the self, they are able to respond to themselves as they imagine *any* other person in *any* situation would. Mead used the term **generalized other** to refer to *widespread cultural norms and values used as a reference in evaluating ourselves.*

The emergence of self does not conclude the socialization process. Quite the contrary: we change throughout our lives as a result of changing social experiences. Just as important, Mead stressed, social life is *interac-*

tional: as society shapes us, so we can "act back" on others. As active and creative beings, Mead concluded, we play a large part in our own socialization.

Critical evaluation. George Herbert Mead's contribution to the understanding of socialization lies in showing that symbolic interaction is the foundation of both self and society.

Mead's view can be criticized for being radically social—meaning that it recognizes no biological element in the self. In this, he stands apart from Freud (who identified general drives in the organism) and Piaget (whose stages of development are tied to biological maturation).

Although Mead's concepts of the I and the me resemble Freud's terms id and superego, the approaches differ in two respects. First, Freud rooted the id in the biological organism, while Mead rejected any link between the self and biology (although he never clearly spelled out the origin of the "I"). Second, Freud's concept

of the superego and Mead's concept of the me both reflect the power society wields over our lives, but Freud's superego is locked in continual combat with the id. Mead's concept of the me, by contrast, operates in concert with the I (Meltzer, 1978).

AGENTS OF SOCIALIZATION

We are affected in at least a small way by every social experience we have. However, several agents of socialization have pronounced importance, as we shall now explain.

The Family

For most people, the family has the greatest impact on socialization. Infants are almost entirely dependent on others, and this responsibility typically falls on family members. Through physical contact, verbal stimulation, and responsiveness, parents foster the development of children (Belsky, Lerner, & Spanier, 1984). The family remains the center of a child's world, at least until the onset of schooling, and continues to shape personality later in life (Riley, Foner, & Waring, 1988).

Not all socialization in the family is intentional. Children learn constantly from the environment adults unconsciously create. Whether children believe they are strong or weak, smart or stupid, loved or simply tolerated—and whether they believe the world to be trustworthy or dangerous—largely depends on the signals they get from parents.

Socialization also involves parents conferring their social position on their children. That is, parents place children socially in terms of class position, religion, race, and ethnicity. In time, all these elements of social identity are incorporated into the self.

Why is class position important? Beyond the resources parents make available to children, Melvin Kohn (1977) found that working-class parents stress behavioral conformity in rearing their children. Middle-class parents, by contrast, tolerate a wider range of behavior and show greater concern for the intentions and motivations that underlie their children's actions. Kohn explained that working-class parents have less education and are more likely to hold jobs in which they are closely supervised. In turn, they demand obedience and conformity in their children. With more schooling, middle-class

Figure 3–1 Building on Social Experience
George Herbert Mead described the development of self as the process of gaining social experience. This is largely a matter of taking the role of the other with increasing sophistication.

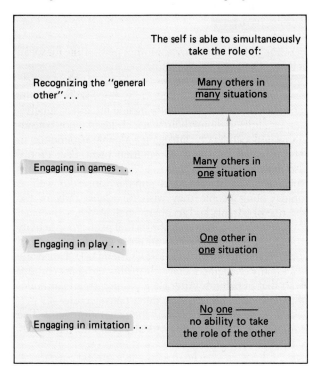

The self is able to simultaneously take the role of:

Recognizing the "general other"... — Many others in <u>many</u> situations

Engaging in games... — Many others in <u>one</u> situation

Engaging in play... — <u>One</u> other in <u>one</u> situation

Engaging in imitation... — <u>No one</u> — no ability to take the role of the other

people usually have jobs that provide more autonomy and encourage the use of imagination. These parents are likely to inspire this same creativity in their children. In many ways, parents teach children to follow in their footsteps, adapting to the constraints or privileges of their inherited social positions.

Schooling

Schooling presents children with unfamiliar people and new experiences. Encountering greater social diversity heightens children's awareness of their own social identities and, as researchers have observed, school children soon begin to form play groups made up of one sex and one race (Lever, 1978; Finkelstein & Haskins, 1983).

Schools initially teach basic skills such as reading, writing, and arithmetic and later offer advanced knowledge that students will need to assume a specialized role in their complex society. Beyond formal lessons, however, the school's so-called *hidden curriculum* imparts important cultural values. School activities such

A young person of color in a predominantly white society often finds difficult the task of forging a positive self-image. Amid negative racial messages from their environment, some young people struggle to feel that they *are important*. The art *I Am Somebody* expresses this struggle in the life of the artist, Glenn Ligon.

as spelling bees and sports encourage competition and showcase success. Children also receive countless messages that their society's culture is both practically and morally good. Raphaela Best (1983) cites the importance of gender in school, noting that boys engage in more physical activities and spend more time outdoors, while girls tend to be more sedentary, often helping the teacher with various housekeeping chores. Gender differences continue through college as women tend toward the arts or humanities, while men are encouraged to study the physical sciences. Further, informal campus culture provides more support for the academic achievement of men, while making romantic life more central to women (Holland & Eisenhart, 1990).

For most youngsters, school introduces the new experience of being evaluated in reading or sports according to universal standards rather than on the basis of personal relationships, as is often the case in families. Finally, school is generally a child's first experience with rigid formality. The school day is based on a strict time schedule, subjecting students to impersonal regimentation and fostering traits, such as punctuality, required for success in many large organizations where students will work later in life.

Peer Groups

In school, children discover another new setting for social activity, the **peer group,** defined as *a group whose members have interests, social position, and age in common.*

The peer group differs from the family and the school by allowing children to escape the direct supervision of adults. Among their peers, children enjoy considerable independence, and gain valuable experience in forging social relationships on their own. Peer groups also draw out interests that may not be shared by adults (such as styles of dress and popular music) as well as topics young people may wish to discuss only in the absence of parents and teachers (such as drugs and sex).

The ever-present possibility that peer-group activity would not be condoned by adults accounts for parents' concern about who their children's friends are. Especially in a rapidly changing society, the influence of peer groups rivals that of parents. After all, the interests and attitudes of parents and children may differ considerably—as suggested by the familiar phrase "the generation gap." The importance of peer groups typically peaks during adolescence when young people begin to break away from their families and to think of themselves as responsible adults.

Even during adolescence, however, parental influence on children remains strong. While peers may guide short-term choices in dress and music, parents retain more sway over long-term aspirations. For example, one study found that parents had more influence than even best friends on young people's educational aspirations (Davies & Kandel, 1981).

Finally, a neighborhood or school is typically a social mosaic of many peer groups. As Chapter 5 ("Groups and Organizations") explains, members often perceive their own peer group in positive terms while viewing others negatively. Many peer groups, then, contribute to socialization as individuals conform to one group while opposing others. Then, too, people are strongly influenced by peer groups they would like to join. For example, upon entering a new school, a young man who excels at basketball may wish to join the basketball players' social crowd. He is likely to adopt what he sees as the social patterns of this group in the hope of eventual acceptance. Sociologists call this strategy **anticipatory socialization,** *social learning directed toward gaining a desired position.* Later in life, careers also involve anticipatory socialization. For instance, a young lawyer who hopes to become a partner in her firm may display attitudes and behavior characteristic of partners to encourage her acceptance into this exclusive group.

The Mass Media

The **mass media** are *impersonal communications directed to a vast audience.* The term "media" is derived from Latin meaning "middle," so media serve to connect people. In industrial societies, television, radio, newspapers, and magazines all reach tens of millions of people. These media have an enormous effect on our attitudes and behavior; television, especially, has become a powerful arbiter of taste and attitudes.

Back in 1950, only about 9 percent of U.S. households had a television set; by 1990, this proportion had soared to 98 percent (only 93 percent had telephones), and surveys indicate that the average household has a television turned on for seven hours a day (U.S. Bureau of the Census, 1990). Children watch television before they learn to read, and they end up spending more hours

in front of a TV screen than they do in school or interacting with parents (Anderson & Lorch, 1983; Singer, 1983; Singer & Singer, 1983).

Television does more than entertain us; it also programs many of our attitudes and beliefs. Television has traditionally portrayed men and women according to cultural stereotypes, showing, for instance, men in positions of power and women only as mothers or subordinates (Cantor & Pingree, 1983; Ang, 1985). Similarly, television shows have long presented affluent people in favorable terms, while depicting less affluent people (Homer Simpson is a recent example) as ignorant and wrongheaded (Gans, 1980). Television also affects us by what it ignores, such as the lives of the poor and of homosexual people. In this way, television sends a message that such people do not matter or, worse still, that they do not exist at all.

People of color tend to watch more television than whites, but until recently minorities have been all but absent from programming. The successful 1950s comedy *I Love Lucy,* for example, was shunned by all the major television producers because it featured Desi Arnaz—a Cuban—in a starring role. Even now, shows depict minorities in ways attractive to white middle-class viewers (like the affluent black family on *The Cosby Show*). This situation is improving as advertisers recognize the marketing potential of appealing to a multicultural audience (Wilson & Gutiérrez, 1985). The box on page 64 offers a critical look at how mass media advertising has historically portrayed minorities in terms of negative images and stereotypes.

Television has unquestionably enriched our culture in many respects, bringing into our homes a wide range of entertaining and educational programming. Furthermore, this "window on the world" has strengthened our awareness of diverse cultures and our understanding of current public issues. At the same time, the power of television generates controversy, especially when it supports traditional stereotypes.

Public Opinion

Public opinion refers to *the attitudes of people throughout a society about one or more controversial issues.* Although family members and peers have particular importance to socialization, our attitudes and behavior also reflect what we think are the views widely held in our society.

When Advertising Offends: Another Look at Aunt Jemima

Companies advertise in order to sell products. However, some ad campaigns offend rather than persuade their audience by portraying certain categories of people in inaccurate and unfair ways.

A century ago, the vast majority of consumers in the United States were white, and many were uneasy with the growing racial and cultural diversity of their country. Businesses commonly exploited this discomfort by depicting racial and cultural minorities in ways that were clearly condescending. In 1889, for example, a pancake mix appeared featuring a servant mammy named "Aunt Jemima." Although recently modified, this logo remains because the product still holds a commanding share of the market. Likewise, the hot cereal "Cream of Wheat" is still symbolized by the black chef Rastus, and "Uncle Ben" is familiar to millions of people as a brand name for rice. To many, such caricatures—which, after all, originally depicted the black slaves of white people—are insensitive at best.

Changes for the better have occurred in advertising. The stereotypical Frito Bandito, familiar to older television viewers, was abandoned in 1971 by Frito-Lay amid complaints that it cast Hispanics as bumbling bandits. A host of other such images has also disappeared as U.S. businesses confront the growing voice and financial power of minorities. Taken together, Americans of African, Hispanic, and Asian descent now comprise 20 percent of the population, and will constitute a majority before the end of the next century.

Many of today's minorities are immigrants, people who rely heavily on television to learn about their new society. This makes them especially susceptible to advertising. For reasons of fairness, as well as good business sense, companies are backing away from marketing strategies that compromise human dignity.

SOURCE: Based on Westerman (1989).

The mass media track the latest trends, and there is little doubt that both adults and children mimic these patterns. For example, the clothing industry's success in marketing new fashions several times a year illustrates people's tendency to adopt, within their budgets, what the trend makers define as desirable.

Public opinion often minimizes and demeans cultural diversity in the United States. We have all heard "people say" that homosexuals are "weird," that noncompetitive men "lack character," and that assertive women are "pushy." It is worth remembering that no one conforms completely to so-called dominant values or popular viewpoints. Nonetheless, what others think—or what we *think* they think—affects how we see ourselves.

Industrial societies encompass agents of socialization beyond those described here. Religious organizations, the workplace, the military, and social clubs all affect our thoughts and actions. As a result, socialization is inevitably inconsistent: this process is not a simple matter of learning, but a complex balancing act in which we encounter a wide range of ideas as we try to forge our own distinctive attitudes and personalities.

SOCIALIZATION AND THE LIFE COURSE

Socialization continues throughout different stages of the life course, in childhood, through adolescence and early adulthood, and, finally, into old age. Each stage has distinctive characteristics.

Childhood

In industrial societies, *childhood*—roughly the first twelve years of life—is ideally a time of freedom from the responsibilities of the adult world. Centuries ago, however, children's lives were much like those of adults. Historian Philippe Ariès (1965) explains that, in medieval Europe, as soon as children could survive without constant care, they were expected to fend for themselves. This meant that poor children worked long and hard, just as adults did. Global Map 3–1 on page 66 shows that this pattern persists today in poor societies throughout Latin America, Africa, and Asia.

The notion of children working long hours may be startling because our common sense suggests that youngsters are very different from adults—inexperienced in the ways of the world and biologically immature. But much of this difference is rooted in society, not biology. Because technologically complex societies are more affluent, everyone does not need to work. In addition, such societies extend childhood to allow time for learning many complex skills required of adults. These facts prompt us to define children and adults in contrasting ways, with "irresponsible" children looked after by "responsible" adults (Benedict, 1938). In global perspective, however, this pattern does not always hold. The traits assigned to childhood—and even whether this stage of life exists at all—are one variable dimension of culture.

More recently, researchers have documented that childhood is changing once again, this time becoming shorter. Especially among affluent families, children are subjected to mounting pressures to dress, speak, and act like adults (Elkind, 1981; Winn, 1983). Evidence of this "hurried child" pattern includes ten-year-old boys in designer jeans, and girls of the same age adorned with jewelry and makeup. The mass media now carry into a child's world not only sexuality, but violence and a host of issues that were considered a generation ago to be strictly adult topics. Pressure to grow up quickly is also found in the home as greater numbers of mothers work, requiring their children to fend more for themselves. Furthermore, today's parents are often delighted if their children can read or discuss world events before their peers can. Schools also promote rapid maturation by emphasizing achievement, which reflects positively on both parents and teachers. In the view of child psychologist David Elkind (1981), the "hurried child" pattern can be detrimental if children must confront issues that they lack the experience to understand, let alone successfully resolve.

Adolescence

As childhood emerged as a distinct stage of life in industrial societies, adolescence became a buffer stage between childhood and adulthood, corresponding roughly to the teenage years. This time of life offers the opportunity to gain independence and to learn specialized, adult activities.

We generally associate adolescence with emotional and social turmoil; young people spar with their parents and struggle to develop their own identities. Since adolescence generally begins at the same time as the onset of puberty, we often attribute the emotional turmoil of this stage of life to physiological change. However, the instability of adolescence also reflects inconsistencies in socialization. For example, adults expect teens to be increasingly self-reliant, yet adults view adolescents as unequipped for the occupations that would give them financial independence. The adult world also gives adolescents mixed signals about sexuality—the mass media glorify sex, while parents urge restraint. Consider, also, that an eighteen-year-old male may face the adult responsibility of going to war, but he lacks the adult right to drink alcohol. Without denying the role of biological forces in adolescence, then, we must recognize that this is a time of social contradictions when people are no longer children but not yet adults.

Finally, like all periods of the life course, adolescence varies according to social background. Young people from working-class families often move directly into the adult world of work and parenthood after completing high school. Those from wealthier families, however, have the resources to attend college and perhaps graduate school, which may push adolescence into the later twenties and even the thirties (Skolnick, 1992). Poverty, too, can extend adolescence. Especially in the inner cities, many young minorities cannot attain adult standing because jobs are not available.

Adulthood

Adulthood, which begins at some point between the late teens and early thirties depending on social background, is typically the period during which most of life's accomplishments occur. Having completed schooling, people embark on careers and raise families of their own. Personalities are largely formed by the onset of adulthood, although marked transformations in an individual's social environment—such as unemployment,

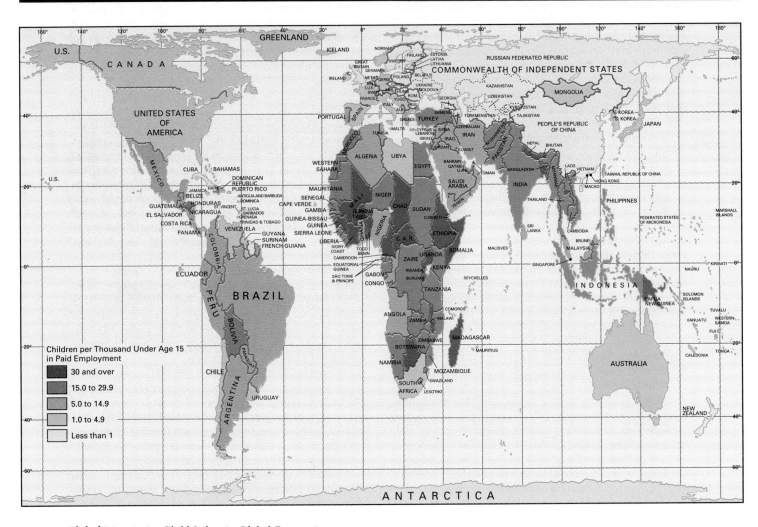

Global Map 3–1   Child Labor in Global Perspective

Industrialization has the effect of prolonging childhood and discouraging children from engaging in work and other activities deemed suitable only for adults. Thus child labor is relatively uncommon in the United States and other industrial societies. In less industrialized nations of the world, however, children form a vital economic asset and they typically begin working as soon as they are able.

divorce, or serious illness—may result in significant personality changes (Dannefer, 1984).

Early adulthood—until about age forty—is generally a time of working toward many goals set earlier in life. Young adults learn to manage for themselves a host of day-to-day responsibilities that had been taken care of by parents or others. In addition, early adulthood typically involves establishing intimacy with another person who may have just as much to learn. This is also a period of juggling conflicting priorities and demands on time: parents, spouse, children, and work (Levinson et al., 1978). Women, especially, face the realization that "doing it all" can be extremely difficult, since our culture expects women to assume primary responsibility for child rearing and household chores, even while performing demanding occupations outside the home.

By middle adulthood—roughly between the ages of forty and sixty—people may begin to feel that marked improvements in life circumstances are less likely. Greater reflection thus characterizes middle adulthood, as people assess their achievements in light of earlier expectations. They also become more aware of the fragility of health at this age, which is taken for granted among the young. Women who have already spent many years raising a family can find middle adulthood especially trying. Children have grown up and require less attention, husbands become absorbed in their careers, leaving some women with spaces in their lives that are difficult to fill. Women who divorce during middle adulthood may confront serious economic problems (Weitzman, 1985). For all these reasons, many women in middle adulthood return to school and begin careers. Since 1970, women between thirty-five and forty-four have been the fastest-growing segment of the U.S. labor force (U.S. Bureau of the Census, 1991).

The traditional conception of femininity also stresses the importance of physical attractiveness. Both older men and older women face the reality of physical decline, but our society's traditional socialization of women to pursue beauty makes wrinkles, weight gain, and loss of hair generally more traumatic for them (Wolf, 1990). Men, of course, have their own particular difficulties in middle adulthood. Some are disappointed by their limited achievements, others realize that the price of career success has been neglect of family or personal health (Farrell & Rosenberg, 1981).

Socialization in our youth-oriented culture has convinced many people that life ends at forty. But as average life expectancy in the United States increases, such limiting notions about growing older are changing. Major life transformations may become less likely, but the potential for learning and new beginnings still infuses life with meaning.

Old Age

Old age comprises the later years of adulthood and the final stage of life, beginning about the mid-sixties. As Figure 3–2 on page 68 shows, about one in eight members of our society is over the age of sixty-five, so that the elderly now outnumber teenagers. By 2020, our population beyond the age of fifty will soar by 75 percent, while the number of people under fifty will rise a scant 2 percent (Wolfe, 1991). The "oldest old"—people eighty-five and over—are the fastest-growing segment of our population; their numbers will increase six-fold over the next century.

The "graying of the United States" will have profound consequences for everyone. More and more people will depend on Social Security and other pension programs, medical facilities will be increasingly burdened, and elderly people will be more evident in everyday life. Many middle-aged people (especially women) already think of themselves as a "sandwich generation," because they will spend as much time caring for aging parents as they did for their young children. Finally, the graying of the United States has sparked the growth of the relatively new field of **gerontology** (from the Greek word *geron*, meaning "old person"), which is *the study of aging and the elderly*.

For most of our population, gray hair, wrinkles, loss of height and weight, and an overall decline in strength and vitality begin in middle age (Colloway & Dollevoet, 1977). After about age fifty, bones become brittle, and falls that had been of little consequence earlier in life can result in disabling injuries that take longer to heal. In addition, a substantial proportion of the elderly suffer from chronic illnesses such as arthritis that limit activity, and life-threatening conditions such as heart disease and cancer. Moreover, while only 5 percent of middle-aged people have visual impairments, 10 percent of the elderly do. The frequency of hearing problems jumps from 15 percent among middle-aged people to 30 percent of the elderly. Both impairments are more common among men than women (National Center for Health Statistics, 1990). Declining ability to taste and smell also affects eating habits, sometimes causing poor nutrition (Eckholm, 1985).

Although health problems unquestionably increase with advancing age, the bigger picture shows that most elderly people are not physically disabled. Only one in ten reports trouble walking, and one in twenty requires the intensive care provided by a hospital or nursing home. No more than 1 percent of the elderly are bedridden. Overall, 70 percent of people over the age of sixty-five assess their health as "good" to "excellent," while 30 percent characterize their condition as "fair" or "poor" (National Center for Health Statistics, 1990).

As with all stages of life, growing old involves not

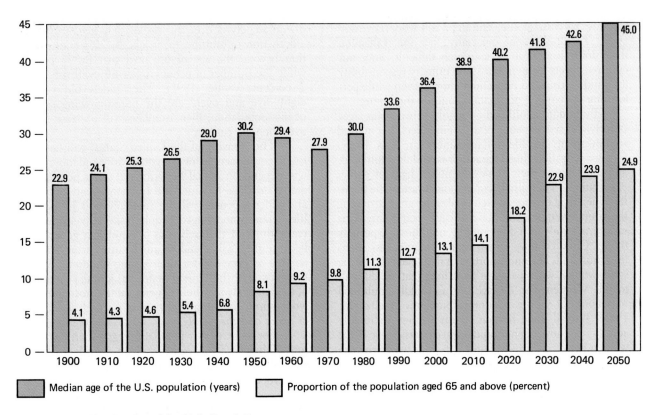

Figure 3–2 The Graying of the U.S. Population
(Spencer, 1989; U.S. Bureau of the Census, 1991)

just biological change but shifting cultural expectations. In preindustrial societies, old age typically confers great influence and respect because the elderly control most land and other wealth, and they bask in their society's respect for wisdom gained over a lifetime (Sheehan, 1976; Hareven, 1982). A preindustrial society, therefore, tends to be a **gerontocracy,** *a form of social organization in which the elderly have the most wealth, power, and privileges.*

Industrialization, however, diminishes the social standing of the elderly. They typically live apart from their grown children, and rapid social change renders much of what they have learned obsolete, at least from the point of view of the young. A problem of industrial societies, then, is **ageism,** *prejudice and discrimination against the elderly.*

For all these reasons, growing old in the United States is a challenging experience. For children, adolescents, and younger adults, growing older means entering new roles and taking on fresh responsibilities. Old age,

however, follows the opposite path: leaving roles that have provided social identity and prestige. Although retirement sometimes fits the common image of restful recreation after years of work, it can also pull men and women out of familiar routines, so that they lose the self-worth derived from work and sometimes suffer from outright boredom. Like any life transition, retirement demands learning new ways of living and simultaneously *un*learning earlier routines. A similar transition is required of a nonworking wife or husband who must accommodate a spouse now spending more time in the home.

Poverty among the elderly has dropped sharply, from 33 percent in 1960 to 12 percent in 1990 (U.S. Bureau of the Census, 1991). Since 1985, in fact, poverty has been lower among the elderly than among the nonelderly (Stone, 1986). The Decade of Change box on the following page takes a closer look at how government programs improved the fortunes of the elderly during the 1980s.

The Elderly: A Financial Windfall

A generation ago, society's poor were most likely to be the elderly; today, children are at greatest risk of poverty. There are many reasons for this change, including better health, which helps older people earn more, and better pension programs for those who have retired. But government policies play a big part since, during the 1980s, federal programs favored the old over the young as never before.

Given the increasing number of elderly people—and their growing political clout—federal spending (including Social Security) that directly benefited the elderly soared during the 1980s by half, to account for 47 percent of all government spending. By 1990, as spending for defense eased, assisting the elderly became our single greatest national expense. On the other hand, spending for children actually fell by 4 percent during the 1980s to roughly 11 percent of total government expenditures.

As the figure shows, median household income fell during the 1980s among young people. But advancing age brought income gains during the 1980s, with elderly house-

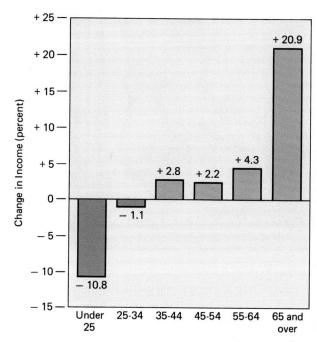

Change in Median Household Income 1980–1990, by Age
(U.S. Bureau of the Census)

holds gaining most of all. As the proportion of our population over the age of sixty-five rises, this trend is likely to continue.

A reasonable question, in light of

this windfall, is whether we should continue to favor the oldest members of our society and risk slighting the youngest—those who now suffer most from poverty.

Death and Dying

Throughout most of human history, death was a familiar fact of human life because of a low standard of living and simple medical technology. Although death can still occur at any time in industrial societies (especially among the poor), about 70 percent of people die after the age of sixty-five. Therefore, even though more and more senior citizens look forward to decades of life,

patterns of socialization in old age involve the recognition of impending death.

After observing many dying people, Elisabeth Kübler-Ross (1969) described death as an orderly process involving five stages. Because our culture tends to ignore the reality of death, people's first reaction to the prospect of their demise is usually *denial*. The second stage is *anger* as the person begins to accept the impending death but sees it as a gross injustice. In the third stage, anger

The infancy of photography in the 1840s was also a time of deadly epidemics in the United States, with between one-third and one-half of children dying before the age of ten. Many grieving parents rushed to capture their dead children on film. The post-mortem photograph, in most cases the only picture ever taken of someone, suggests a far greater acceptance of death during the nineteenth century. In this century, death has become rare among the young, so that dying is separated from life as a grim reality that people do their best to deny.

gives way to *negotiation*, the attitude that one might yet escape death through a bargain struck with God. The fourth stage is *resignation*, often accompanied by psychological depression. Finally, a complete adjustment to death requires *acceptance*. At this point, no longer paralyzed by fear or gloom, the person sets out constructively to make use of whatever time remains.

As the share of our population in old age increases, we can expect attitudes toward death to change. Today, death is physically removed from public life so that most people have never seen a person die. While our ancestors typically died at home, most people now die in unfamiliar and impersonal hospitals or rest homes (Ariès, 1974). Even hospitals segregate dying patients in a special part of the building, and hospital morgues are located well out of sight of patients and visitors (Sudnow, 1967).

Thus the historical acceptance of death has largely been replaced by a sense of fear and anxiety about dying. No doubt, this has prompted an increase in medical research aimed at prolonging the life of the elderly. But we may be reaching a turnaround. Many elderly people are less fearful of death than they are at the prospect of being kept alive to no good purpose by doctors wielding high technology. In short, people want control over their deaths no less than they want control over their lives.

Consequently, patients and families are now taking the initiative, choosing to forego available medical technology to prolong life or "heroic measures" to resuscitate a dying person. Living Wills—statements of what medical procedures an individual wants or refuses under specific conditions—are becoming widespread. Certainly, there are dangers in this practice. Family members may exert subtle pressure on a failing parent to refuse medical care, for example, because others wish to escape emotional stress or be spared a financial burden. Patients, family members, and doctors now face moral and medical decisions about dying; to assist them, many hospitals offer the services of biomedical ethics committees composed of medical specialists, social service professionals, and members of the clergy. The trend seems clear: if decline and death remain inevitable, people at least can make choices about when, where, and how they will die.

Critical evaluation. This brief examination of the life course leads to two general conclusions. First and most important, although linked to the biological process of aging, essential characteristics of each stage of the life course are socially constructed. For this reason, any period of life may be experienced differently by members of various cultures. Second, each stage presents characteristic problems and transitions that involve learning something new and, in many cases, unlearning what has become familiar.

Finally, the fact that societies organize social experience according to age does not negate the effects of other social forces, such as class, race, ethnicity, and gender. Thus, the general patterns described are all subject to modification as they apply to various categories of people.

RESOCIALIZATION: TOTAL INSTITUTIONS

This chapter has focused on socialization as it applies to the vast majority of individuals living in countless familiar settings. Almost 1 million people, however, experience a special type of socialization that takes place because they are confined—often against their will—in prisons or mental hospitals. This is the special world of a **total institution,** *a setting in which individuals are isolated from the rest of society and manipulated by an administrative staff.*

According to Erving Goffman (1961), total institutions control the full round of daily life for their residents (often called "inmates"), including eating, sleeping, working, and playing. Rigid routines subject inmates to standardized food, sleeping quarters, and activities, and the staff applies formal rules to inmate behavior in every setting.

Total institutions impose regimented routines with the goal of **resocialization,** *deliberate socialization intended to radically alter the individual's personality.* The power of a total institution lies in depriving inmates of any other source of social experience. Isolation is achieved through walls and fences, barred windows, locked doors, and control of the telephone, mail, and visitors. Cut off in this way, the inmates inhabit a staff-controlled world, where officials seek to produce change—or at least compliance.

Resocialization is a two-part process. First, the staff attempts to erode the new inmate's established identity. This involves a series of experiences Goffman (1961:14) describes as "abasements, degradations, humiliations, and profanations of self." For example, staff require inmates to surrender personal possessions, including the clothing and grooming articles normally used to maintain a distinctive appearance. In their place, inmates receive standard-issue items and standardized haircuts that make everyone more alike. The staff also processes new inmates by searching, weighing, fingerprinting, and photographing them, and by issuing them a serial number. Once inside the walls, individuals also surrender their privacy: guards are often on hand as inmates undress as part of the admission procedure, and the staff conducts routine surveillance and searches of inmates' living quarters. These "mortifications of self" undermine the identity and autonomy that the inmate brings to the total institution from the outside world.

The second part of the resocialization process involves efforts at rebuilding a new self. The staff does this by manipulating inmates with rewards and punishments. The privilege of keeping a book or receiving a visitor may seem trivial from the vantage point of outsiders, but in the rigid environment of the total institution, they can be powerful motivations toward conformity. Furthermore, the duration of incarceration in a prison

or mental hospital typically depends on the extent to which the inmate cooperates with the staff. Goffman emphasizes that conformity in a total institution must reflect not only outward behavior but inward motivation, lest an inmate be punished for having "an attitude problem."

Resocialization in a total institution can bring about considerable change in an inmate. The rebuilding of a person's self is extremely difficult, however, and no two people are likely to respond to any environment in precisely the same way (Irwin, 1980). Therefore, some inmates may experience "rehabilitation" or "recovery" (meaning change that is officially approved), while others gradually sink into an embittered state because of the perceived injustice of their incarceration. Sometimes, over a long period of time, the rigidly controlled environment of a total institution may render people completely *institutionalized,* incapable of the independence required for living in the outside world.

SOCIALIZATION AND HUMAN FREEDOM

Through socialization, society shapes how we think, feel, and act. If society has such power over us, in what sense are we free? This chapter ends with a closer look at this important question.

Children and adults throughout North America delight in watching the Muppets, stars of television and film. Observing the expressive antics of Kermit the Frog, Miss Piggy, and the rest of the troupe, one almost believes that these puppets are real rather than objects animated from backstage. The sociological perspective suggests that human beings are like puppets in that we, too, respond to the backstage guidance of society. Indeed, more so, in that society affects not just our outward behavior but our innermost feelings.

But our analysis of socialization also reveals where the puppet analogy breaks down. Viewing human beings as the puppets of society leads to the trap that Dennis Wrong (1961) has called an "oversocialized" conception of the human being. In part, Wrong reminds us, we are biological as well as social creatures, and to the extent that any biological force affects our being (as Freud suggested), we can never be entirely shaped by society.

The fact that human beings may be subject to *both* biological and social influences, however, hardly advances the banner of human freedom. Here is where the ideas of George Herbert Mead are of crucial importance. Mead recognized the power of society to act on human beings, but he argued that human spontaneity and creativity empower us to continually *act back* on society. Thus the process of socialization affirms the human capacity for choice as we reflect, evaluate, and act. Therefore, although the process of socialization may initially suggest that we respond like puppets to forces beyond our control, Peter Berger points out that "unlike the puppets, we have the possibility of stopping in our movements, looking up and perceiving the machinery by which we have been moved" (1963:176). Doing this, we can act to change society by, so to speak, pulling back on the strings. And, Berger adds, the more we utilize the sociological perspective to study how the machinery of our society works, the freer we are.

SUMMARY

1. Socialization is a process through which social experience makes us fully human. Socialization is also the means by which society transmits culture to each new generation.

2. A century ago, people thought most human behavior was grounded in biological instinct. Today, however, we understand human behavior to be mostly a result of nurture rather than nature.

3. The damaging effects of social isolation in humans and other primates reveal the importance of social experience to human development.

4. Sigmund Freud envisioned the human personality in three parts. The id expresses general human drives, which Freud claimed were innate. The superego represents cultural values and norms as internalized by the individual. The ego mediates competition between the needs of the id and the cultural restraints of the superego.

5. Jean Piaget believed that human development reflects both biological maturation and increasing social experience. He asserted that child development involves four major stages: sensorimotor, preoperational, concrete operational, and formal operational.

6. To George Herbert Mead, social experience nurtures the self, which Mead characterized as partly autonomous (the I) and partly guided by society (the me).

7. Charles Horton Cooley used the term looking-glass self to recognize that our self-image is influenced by how we perceive others responding to us.

8. Commonly the first setting of socialization, the family has primary importance for shaping a child's attitudes and behavior.

9. School exposes children to greater social diversity and introduces them to the experience of being evaluated according to impersonal standards of performance. In addition to formal learning, the hidden curriculum teaches cultural lessons about race and gender.

10. Peer groups free children from adult supervision. Peer groups take on increasing significance in adolescence.

11. The mass media, especially television, are important in the socialization process. The average child in the United States now spends more time watching television than attending school.

12. Public opinion plays a role in the socialization process because popular attitudes influence our individual views and values.

13. Evidence supports the conclusion that the characteristics of all stages of life—from childhood to old age—are, to a significant degree, socially constructed and variable from society to society.

14. Old age involves marked transitions, including retirement from work. While the elderly have high prestige in preindustrial societies, industrial societies are more youth-oriented.

15. Members of industrial societies typically die in old age. Adjustment to the death of a spouse (an experience more common to women) and acceptance of the inevitability of one's own death are part of socialization for the elderly.

16. Total institutions such as prisons and mental hospitals have the goal of resocialization—radically changing the inmate's personality.

17. Socialization demonstrates the power of society to shape our thoughts, feelings, and actions. Yet, the relationship between self and society is a two-way process: each shapes the other through social interaction.

KEY CONCEPTS

ageism prejudice and discrimination against the elderly

anticipatory socialization social learning directed toward gaining a desired position

concrete operational stage Piaget's term for the level of human development at which individuals begin logical reasoning

ego Freud's designation of a person's conscious attempts to balance the pleasure-seeking drives of the human organism and the demands of society

formal operational stage Piaget's term for the level of human development at which individuals think abstractly and with imagination

generalized other George Herbert Mead's term for widespread cultural norms and values used as a reference in evaluating ourselves

gerontocracy a form of social organization in which the elderly have the most wealth, power, and privileges

gerontology the study of aging and the elderly

id Freud's designation of the human being's basic drives

looking-glass self Cooley's term referring to a conception of self derived from the responses of others

mass media impersonal communications directed to a vast audience

peer group a group whose members have interests, social position, and age in common

personality a person's fairly consistent patterns of thinking, feeling, and acting

preoperational stage Piaget's term for the level of human development at which individuals first use language and other symbols

public opinion the attitudes of people throughout a society about one or more controversial issues

resocialization deliberate socialization intended to radically alter the individual's personality

self George Herbert Mead's term for the dimension of personality composed of an individual's active self-awareness

sensorimotor stage Piaget's term for the level of human development at which individuals have only sensory-based experience

socialization the lifelong process of social experience by which individuals develop their human potential and learn patterns of their culture

superego Freud's designation of the presence of culture within the individual in the form of internalized values and norms

total institution a setting in which individuals are isolated from the rest of society and manipulated by an administrative staff

4

Social Interaction in Everyday Life

If you stop to think about it, a cemetery has a hard time selling its product. Brochures—like the one that just arrived in the mail—announce "limited-time offers"; in this case, $395 will buy two burial spaces in the "Garden of the Praying Hands." But there is something wrong with trying to sell burial plots as if they were cars, even though many people (sooner or later) need them. For one thing, someone opening the morning mail still might be grieving over the death of a family member, and hardly needs to be reminded of the loss. More generally, there are social rules that demand that we treat death with a special respect. People selling cemetery plots must be as dignified and low-key as possible, acting quite differently from the way dealers typically hawk automobiles. Consider, as examples, some of the following lines common to the car business that you will *never* read in cemetery advertising:[1]

1. We're dealing.
2. How do we keep prices low? Volume.
3. Doing business at the same location for years.
4. Our customers never go anywhere else.
5. We're having a midnight madness sale.
6. The boss says everything must go.
7. Push it, pull it, tow it in.

Such contrasts are among the fascinating patterns that compose everyday life, the topic of this chapter. The chapter begins by presenting many of the building blocks of our common experiences, continues by exploring the almost magical way in which face-to-face interaction generates reality, and concludes with a look at humor and what our jokes tell us about ourselves.

The key concept throughout is **social interaction,** *the process by which people act and react in relation to others.* Social interaction is the key to creating the reality we perceive. We interact, moreover, according to particular social guidelines.

SOCIAL STRUCTURE: GUIDING EVERYDAY LIFE

Earlier chapters have provided ample evidence of the power of society to shape our lives. Even so, we resist the idea that human behavior is socially patterned. Living

---

[1] This opening is adapted from a news feature by Mike Harden (1989).

in a culture that prizes self-reliance, few of us readily admit to being part of any kind of system. Instead, we emphasize individual responsibility for behavior and highlight the unique elements of our personalities. But behaving in patterned ways does not threaten our individuality. Quite the contrary: social structure actually promotes our individuality.

First, as Chapter 3 ("Socialization: From Infancy to Old Age") explained, our humanity only flowers in social interaction, producing distinct personalities as people blend their unique qualities with the values and norms of the larger culture. Second, in the absence of social structure, the world would be disorienting and frightening. After all, entering an unfamiliar setting inhibits us from freely expressing ourselves. Stepping onto a college campus for the first time, for example, we feel understandable anxiety at not knowing quite what to expect. We look to others, therefore, for clues about what sort of behavior is appropriate. Only after we understand the behavioral standards that apply to the situation can we comfortably "act like ourselves."

Social structure also places some constraints on everyday life, since established patterns inevitably discourage what is unconventional. North American society, for example, still retains the expectation that men will be dominant and assertive, and that women will adopt a deferential and supportive stance. By pressuring each of us to fit neatly into "feminine" or "masculine" categories, social structure gives us identity, but at the cost of limiting individual freedom.

Yet social structure *guides* rather than *determines* human behavior. A cello and a saxophone are each designed to make only certain kinds of sounds. Similarly, "fatherhood" or any other social structure encourages a certain kind of behavior. Like musical instruments, however, any social arrangement can be "played" in a wide range of creative ways.

STATUS

Among the most important components of social interaction is **status,** *a recognized social position that an individual occupies.* Every status involves various rights, duties, and expectations. Sociologists use the term "status" somewhat differently from its everyday meaning of "prestige." In common usage, a bank president has "more status" than a bank teller; sociologically speaking, however, both "president" and "teller" are statuses or social positions within the organization of the bank.

In many traditional societies, people cannot interact until they assess one another's social standing. In villages throughout India, caste position is a master status; therefore, individuals alert others to their social identity by wearing caste marks on their foreheads.

Statuses establish relationships in any setting. In the college classroom, for example, professors and students have distinct, well-defined rights and duties in relation to one another. Similarly, family life is based on a host of "relations," including mother, father, son, daughter, and so on.

We each simultaneously occupy many statuses. The term **status set** refers to *all the statuses a person holds at a particular time*. A teenage girl is a *daughter* to her parents, a *sister* to her brother, a *friend* to others in her social circle, and a *goalie* to members of her hockey team. Just as status sets branch out in different directions, so they change over the life course. A child turns into a parent, a student becomes a lawyer, and people marry to become husbands and wives, sometimes becoming single again as a result of divorce or death. Joining an organization or finding a job enlarges our status set; retirement or withdrawing from activities diminishes it. Individuals gain and lose dozens of statuses over a lifetime.

Statuses are a key part of how we define ourselves. Occupational status, for example, is a major element of most people's self-concept. Even after retirement, for instance, a woman may still think of herself as a professor, continue to engage in many academic routines on the campus, and be similarly defined by others.

Ascribed and Achieved Status

Sociologists make a useful distinction between two kinds of statuses. An **ascribed status** is *a social position a person receives at birth or assumes involuntarily later in the life course*. Examples of statuses ascribed at birth are being a daughter, a Hispanic, a Canadian, or the Prince of Wales. Statuses ascribed as part of the aging process include becoming a teenager, a senior citizen, or a widow or widower. All ascribed statuses are matters about which people have little or no choice.

By contrast, an **achieved status** refers to *a social position that a person assumes voluntarily and that reflects a significant measure of personal ability and choice*. Examples of achieved statuses are being an honors student, an Olympic athlete, a wife or husband, a computer programmer, or a gambler.

Most statuses involve a combination of ascription and achievement. That is, people's ascribed statuses influence the statuses they achieve. Children cannot be lawyers, since this status is open only to adults. And adults who complete law school are likely to have been born into relatively privileged families. More generally, a person of a privileged gender, age, race, or ethnicity has more opportunity to achieve desirable statuses than does someone without such advantages. By the same token, many less desirable statuses, such as criminal, homeless person, or drug addict are more easily "achieved" by people disadvantaged by ascription.

Master Status

Among the many statuses a person holds at any time, one often overshadows all the others. A **master status** is *a social position with exceptional importance for iden-*

tity, often shaping a person's entire life. A master status may result from any combination of ascription and achievement. In our society, a person's occupation—largely due to achievement—is often a master status closely linked to education, income, and family background. No doubt, this is why adults typically introduce themselves by stating their occupations along with their names. Other master statuses, however, are based on ascription. For a Rockefeller or a Kennedy, family name is what stands out in the minds of others.

Serious disease can also be a master status resulting in social isolation, as people with cancer or acquired immune deficiency syndrome (AIDS) often learn. Most societies of the world also limit the opportunities of women and people of color, whatever their abilities, so that gender and race can also serve as master statuses. Additionally, people with physical disabilities may feel dehumanized because others perceive them as little more than the sum of their handicaps. In the box, several people describe this problem.

ROLE

Besides status, a second major component of social interaction is **role,** *normative patterns of behavior for those holding a particular status.* Ralph Linton (1937) described a role as the dynamic expression of a status. Every status confers various obligations and privileges that shape the role. The student role, for example, involves responsibilities to professors and other students, as well as entitling the student to devote much time to personal enrichment through academic study. In short, then, people *occupy* a status and *perform* a role.

Cultural norms suggest how a person with a particu-

SOCIAL DIVERSITY

Physical Disability as Master Status

Interviewed in his late thirties, David Clark has spent most of his life in a wheelchair. Stricken with polio when he was ten months old, he lives and works in Corning, New York. Being defined as different or incomplete has clearly affected how he sees himself.

All the stares you get from the public used to really bother me when I was younger. But either it doesn't happen as much nowadays, or parents have taught their children better about disabilities, or else I'm older and more immune to it, I don't know. It doesn't bother me now like it used to; it used to really bother me. But I really think people are better educated now about disabilities and they don't look as much and make you feel like you're a freak, which is the way I felt when I was younger and they were looking at you like you didn't belong there, what's your problem?

Donna Finch is twenty-nine years old, holds a master's degree in social work, and lives with her husband and son in Muskogee, Oklahoma. She is also blind.

Most people don't expect handicapped people to grow up, they are always supposed to be children. . . . [Y]ou aren't supposed to date, you aren't supposed to have a job, somehow you're just supposed to disappear. I'm not saying this is true of anyone else, but in my own case I think I was more intellectually mature than most children, and more emotionally immature. I'd say that not until the last four or five years have I felt really whole.

Rose Helman is an elderly woman living near New York City. She suffers from spinal meningitis and is also blind.

You ask me if people are really different today than in the '20s and '30s. Not too much. They are still fearful of the handicapped. I don't know if fearful is the right word, but uncomfortable at least. But I can understand it somewhat; it happened to me. I once asked a man to tell me which staircase to use to get from the subway out to the street. He started giving me directions that were confusing, and I said, "Do you mind taking me?" He said, "Not at all." He grabbed me on the side with my dog on it, so I asked him to take my other arm. And he said, "I'm sorry, I have no other arm." And I said, "That's all right, I'll hold onto the jacket." It felt funny hanging onto the sleeve without the arm in it.

SOURCE: Orlansky & Heward (1981).

lar status should act. As noted in Chapter 2 ("Culture"), however, real culture only approximates ideal culture, so that *role performance* varies from *role expectation* due to an individual's social background and unique personality.

Like a status, a role is *relational*, organizing our behavior toward some other person. The parent's role, for example, is centered on caring for a child. Correspondingly, the role of daughter or son consists largely of obligations toward a parent. Other examples of such role pairs include wives and husbands, baseball pitchers and catchers, physicians and patients, and performers and members of an audience.

Because we hold many statuses simultaneously—a status set—we perform multiple roles. The total number of roles usually exceeds the number of statuses because each status can involve several roles in relation to various other people. Robert Merton (1968) introduced the term **role set** to identify *a number of roles attached to a single status*. Figure 4–1 depicts four statuses of one individual, each linked to a different role set. First, the woman occupies the status of "wife," with a "conjugal role" (such as confidant and sexual partner) toward her husband, with whom she would share a "domestic role" in the household. Second, she also holds the status of "mother," with a "maternal role" toward her children and a "civic role" in organizations such as the PTA. Third, as a professor, the "teaching role" is directed toward students, and through the "colleague role" she engages other academics. Fourth, her "researcher role" in the laboratory provides the data for her publications as an author. Figure 4–1, of course, lists only some status and role sets; people generally occupy dozens of statuses at one time, each linked to a role set.

A global perspective reveals that the key roles people use to define their lives differ significantly from society to society. In agrarian countries, for example, most people work in agriculture, and have few of the occupational choices found in industrial societies. Another dimension of difference is housework. As Global Map 4–1 on page 80 shows, in many nations of the world, the lives of women are centered on housework, more so in poor societies and less so in industrial societies.

Conflict and Strain

The personal performances required by an array of role sets often make heavy demands on a person's time and energy. This holds especially true for members of indus-

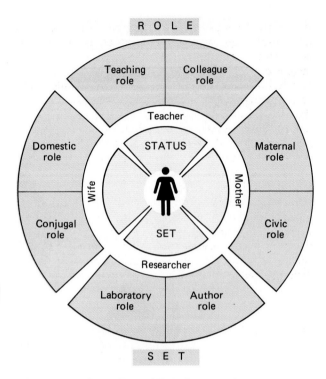

Figure 4–1 Status Set and Role Set

trial societies in which people routinely assume many specialized statuses and an even greater number of roles. Sociologists use the concept of **role conflict** to refer to *incompatibility among roles corresponding to two or more statuses*. We experience role conflict when we find ourselves pulled in various directions by all our obligations at a single point in time. As mothers and fathers who work outside the home can testify, carrying out the demanding roles of parent and breadwinner can sometimes seem all but impossible.

Even the many roles linked to a single status make competing demands on us. The concept of **role strain** refers to *incompatibility among the roles corresponding to a single status*. A plant supervisor may wish to be an approachable friend to other workers. At the same time, however, to ensure worker performance the supervisor may have to resort to occasional discipline, dictating a measure of personal distance. In short, performing the roles of even a single status often requires something of a "balancing act."

Individuals handle problems of conflicting roles in a number of ways. One strategy is to define some roles as more important than others. A new mother,

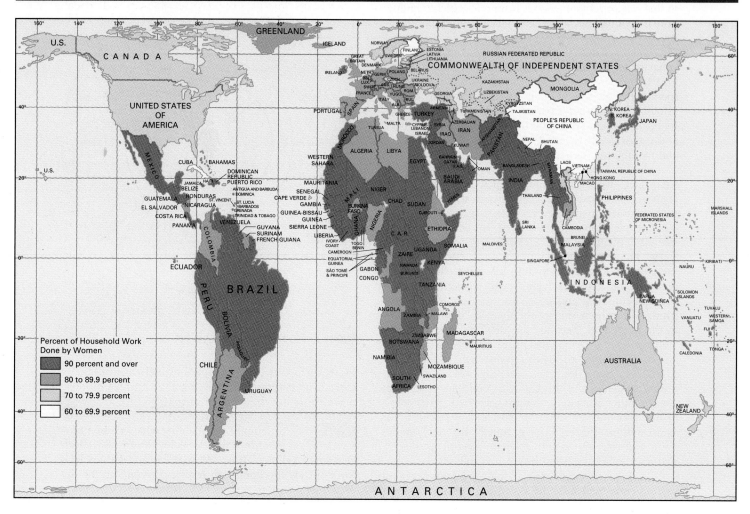

Global Map 4–1   Housework in Global Perspective

Throughout the world, a major component of women's routines and identities involves housework. This is especially true in poor societies of Latin America, Africa, and Asia, where women are not typically in the paid labor force. But our society also defines housework and child care as "feminine" activities, in spite of the fact that a majority of U.S. women are in the paid labor force.

for instance, might devote most of her efforts to parenting and put her career on hold, at least for the present. Of course, resolving role conflict in this way depends on being able to afford not to work—an option unavailable to many mothers.

Setting priorities also reduces strain among roles linked to a single status. Adopting this approach, for example, a father may decide that maintaining a close and trusting relationship with his child is more important than enforcing cultural norms as a disciplinarian.

Another strategy for minimizing role conflict is to "insulate" roles from one another (Merton, 1968). No role is ignored, but people "compartmentalize" their lives by performing roles linked to one status at one time and those corresponding to another status later on. The familiar notion of "leaving the job at the office" when people go home to the family illustrates this pattern.

Role Exit

Recent research has focused on *role exit*, the process by which people disengage from important social roles. Helen Rose Fuchs Ebaugh (1988) began to study role exit as she herself left the life of a Catholic nun to become a university sociologist. Interviewing ex-nuns, ex-doctors, ex-husbands, and ex-alcoholics, Ebaugh identified elements common to the process of "becoming an ex."

According to Ebaugh, the process begins as people experience mounting doubts about their ability or willingness to perform a role. As they consider alternatives, they ultimately reach a turning point that marks a new direction. In the subsequent "ex-role," they disengage from the previous situation, building a new sense of self, evident in changing appearance and behavior (an ex-nun, for example, begins to wear stylish clothing and pursue a social life). "Exes" must also assist others accustomed to dealing with the "ex" in an earlier role—often not easy since new roles may be unfamiliar and awkward for everyone concerned. Often, there is much for the "ex" to learn. Ebaugh reports, for example, that nuns who begin dating after decades in the church are startled to discover that today's sexual norms are quite different from those they knew as teenagers.

In modern society, fewer and fewer people expect to spend their entire lives in one job or one marriage. The study of role exit, therefore, promises to attract greater attention.

THE SOCIAL CONSTRUCTION OF REALITY

More than fifty years ago, Italian playwright Luigi Pirandello created the character of Angelo Baldovino—a brilliant man with a rather checkered past. In the play *The Pleasure of Honesty*, Baldovino enters the fashionable home of the Renni family and offers this peculiar introduction:

Inevitably we construct ourselves. Let me explain. I enter this house and immediately I become what I have to become, what I can become: I construct myself. That is, I present myself to you in a form suitable to the relationship I wish to achieve with you. And, of course, you do the same with me. . . . (1962:157–58)

Pirandello is suggesting that, while situations are guided by status and role, each of us has considerable ability to shape how they unfold. Put another way, "reality" is not as fixed as we might think (Berger & Luckmann, 1967).

The phrase **social construction of reality** refers to *the process by which individuals creatively build reality through social interaction*. This idea is familiar as the foundation of the symbolic-interaction paradigm in sociology, detailed in Chapter 1 ("Sociology: Perspective, Theory, and Method"). In this context, Angelo Baldovino's remark suggests that, as an encounter begins, quite a bit of "reality" is not yet clear in anyone's mind. Pirandello's character thus uses his ability to "present himself" in terms he thinks will suit his purposes. As others do the same, the process of negotiating reality proceeds.

Given the presence of culture, social interaction typically yields considerable agreement about how to define a situation. But participants rarely have exactly the same perceptions of events. Impressions vary because social interaction draws together people with different purposes and interests, each of whom will seek a particular outcome.

Steering reality in this way is what we mean by "street smarts." In his biography *Down These Mean Streets*, Piri Thomas recalls moving to a new apartment in Spanish Harlem, which soon brought him into contact with the local street gang. Returning home one evening, young Piri found himself cut off by Waneko, the gang's leader, and a dozen others.

"Whatta ya say, Mr. Johnny Gringo," drawled Waneko.

Think man, I told myself, *think your way out of a stomping. Make it good.* "I hear you 104th street coolies are supposed to have heart," I said. "I don't know this for sure. You know there's a lot of streets where a whole 'click' is made out of punks who can't fight one guy unless they all jump him for the stomp." I hoped this would push Waneko into giving me a fair one. His expression didn't change.

"Maybe we don't look at it that way."

Crazy, man. I cheer inwardly, the cabron *is falling into my setup. . . .* "I wasn't talking to you," I said. "Where

I come from, the pres is president 'cause he got heart when it comes to dealing."

Waneko was starting to look uneasy. He had bit on my worm and felt like a sucker fish. His boys were now light on me. They were no longer so much interested in stomping me as seeing the outcome between Waneko and me. "Yeah," was his reply. . . .

I knew I'd won. Sure, I'd have to fight; but one guy, not ten or fifteen. If I lost, I might still get stomped, and if I won I might get stomped. I took care of this with my next sentence. "I don't know you or your boys," I said, "but they look cool to me. They don't feature as punks."

I had left him out purposely when I said "they." Now his boys were in a separate class. I had cut him off. He would have to fight me on his own, to prove his heart to himself, to his boys, and most important, to his turf. He got away from the stoop and asked, "Fair one, Gringo?" (1967:56–57)

This situation reveals the drama—sometimes subtle, sometimes savage—by which human beings creatively build reality. We all know that there are limits to what even the most skillful personality can achieve. Should a police officer have come upon the fight that ensued between Piri and Waneko, both young men might well have ended up in jail. Clearly, not everyone enters a negotiation with equal standing; the police officer would probably have the last word simply because of a status that holds greater power than theirs (Molotch & Boden, 1985).

The Thomas Theorem

Piri Thomas won acceptance that evening. Having been defined as worthy, he was now one of the group, and from that moment his social identity was changed. W. I. Thomas (1966:301; orig. 1931) captured the essence of such events in what is known as the **Thomas theorem**: *situations that are defined as real are real in their consequences.* Applied to social interaction, his insight means that although reality is initially "soft" as it is fashioned, it can become "hard" in its effects. The Thomas theorem calls into question the bit of childhood wisdom "Sticks and stones can break my bones, but names can never hurt me." More correctly, how we define other people often has real effects on what they become.

Reality-Building in Global Perspective

People do not construct everyday experience "out of thin air." Rather, we creatively manipulate elements in the surrounding culture. For this reason, residents of Spanish Harlem build somewhat different realities from those living on the affluent East Side of Manhattan. In global perspective, reality varies even more, so that social experiences common to, say, women in Saudi Arabia would seem bizarre to many women in the United States. Similarly, social reality changes over time. People living in ancient Japan forged social worlds very different from those typical of the Japanese today.

Because social reality is grounded in the surrounding culture, any object or action is subject to different interpretations from place to place. The meanings attached to the two sexes, stages of the life course, or even to the days of the week vary around the world. Researcher Wendy Griswold (1987) asked respondents from the West Indies, Great Britain, and the United States to interpret several novels. She found that the messages her readers drew differed and, furthermore, were consistent with their basic "blueprint" of culture. What people see in a book—or anything else—is guided by their social world.

This variability of human experience leads to an interesting question: since people everywhere are members of a single species, don't we share the same basic feelings? According to a number of researchers who have conducted cross-cultural investigations of human emotions, the answer is yes—and no—as the box on pages 84–85 explains.

Ethnomethodology

It is hardly surprising that we take for granted most of the reality we create. After all, what would everyday life be like if we questioned every situation we experienced? For some sociologists, however, challenging conventional patterns of behavior yields rich insights about the organization of everyday life.

Ethnomethodology is a specialized approach within the symbolic-interaction paradigm. The term itself has two parts: the Greek *ethno* refers to shared culture, and "methodology" denotes a system of methods or principles. Combining them makes **ethnomethodology,** *the*

Cultures frame reality differently. This man lay on the street in Bombay, India, for several hours and then quietly died. In the United States, such an event would probably have provoked someone to call the rescue squad. In a poor society in which death on the streets is a fact of everyday life, however, many Indians responded not with alarm but with simple decency by stopping to place incense on his body before continuing on their way.

study of the everyday, common-sense understandings people have of the world.

Ethnomethodology was devised in the 1950s by Harold Garfinkel, a sociologist dissatisfied with the then-widespread view of society as a broad "system." Instead, Garfinkel wanted to explore how we create rules and expectations in familiar, everyday situations (Heritage, 1984). For example, people readily expect certain behavior when sitting down to dinner in a restaurant, beginning a final examination, or driving onto a freeway. As important as such conventional understandings may be, Garfinkel (1967) maintained that few of us ever think much about them.

In the rebellious social climate of the 1960s, Garfinkel developed a distinctive technique for exposing the typically unacknowledged patterns of everyday life: *break the rules.* In other words, a good way to tease out conventional realities is to deliberately ignore them.

Garfinkel (1967) and his students mapped everyday life by refusing to "play the game." Some entered stores and insisted on bargaining for standard-priced items; others recruited people into simple games (like tic-tac-toe) only to intentionally flout the rules; still others initiated conversations and slowly moved closer and closer until they were almost nose to nose with their quarry. At the very least, this rule violation caused bewilderment;

often it provoked "victims" to anger. The fact that rule violation causes anxiety or irritation, Garfinkel reasoned, only shows the importance of everyday norms.

Because of its provocative character and focus on commonplace experiences, ethnomethodology has gained a reputation as being less-than-serious research. Even so, this unorthodox approach has succeeded in heightening awareness of many patterns of everyday life.

DRAMATURGICAL ANALYSIS: "THE PRESENTATION OF SELF"

Erving Goffman (1922–1982) shared with Garfinkel an interest in the patterned character of everyday life. Goffman argued that people socially constructing reality have much in common with actors performing on a stage. Thinking much like a director scrutinizing the action in a theater, Goffman pioneered **dramaturgical analysis,** *the investigation of social interaction in terms of theatrical performance.*

Dramaturgical analysis offers a fresh look at two now-familiar concepts. In this theoretical scheme, a status mirrors a part in a play, and a role serves as a script,

GLOBAL SOCIOLOGY

Emotions: Are Feelings the Same Everywhere?

On a New York sidewalk, a woman reacts angrily to the skateboarder who hurtles past her. Her facial expression, accompanied by a few choice words, broadcasts a strong emotion that any New Yorker easily can recognize. But would an observer from New Guinea be able to interpret her emotion? In other words, do people everywhere have similar emotions and do they express them in the same way?

Paul Ekman (1980) and his colleagues studied emotions in a number of countries around the world—even among members of a small society in New Guinea. From this research, they concluded that people the world over feel the same basic emotions—including anger, fear, happiness, disgust, surprise, and sadness. Moreover, these researchers learned that people around the globe express these feelings using the same distinctive facial gestures. To Ekman, this commonality points to the fact that much emotional life is universal—rather than culturally specific—with the display of emotion biologically rooted in our facial features, muscles, and central nervous system.

But the reality of emotions is only partly rooted in our biology. Ekman notes three ways in which emotional life differs in global perspective. First, what *triggers* an emotional response varies from one culture to another. Whether a particular situation is defined as an insult (causing anger), a loss (calling out sadness), or a mystical event (provoking surprise) depends on culture. In other words, people in various societies may react quite differently to the same event.

Second, people *display* emotions according to the norms of their culture. Every society has its own rules about when, where, and to whom people may exhibit certain emotions. Members of our society, for example, typically approve of emotional expression in the home among family members, but consider such behavior out of place at work. Similarly, we expect children to show emotions to parents, although parents are taught to guard their emotions in front of children.

Third, cultures differ in terms of how people *cope* with emotions. Some societies encourage people to express their feelings, while others belittle emotions and demand that

their members suppress them. Societies also display significant gender differences in this regard. Our culture tends to label emotional expression as feminine, expected of women but a sign of weakness among men. In other societies, however, this sex typing of emotions is less pronounced or even reversed.

In sum, emotional life in cross-cultural perspective has both common and variable dimensions. People the world over experience the same basic emotions. But what sparks a particular emotion, how and where a person expresses it, and how people define emotions in general all vary as matters of culture. In global perspective, therefore, everyday life differs not only in terms of how people think and act, but how they infuse their lives with feeling.

SOURCES: Ekman (1980a; 1980b), Lutz & White (1986), and Lutz (1988).

---

supplying dialogue and action for each character. In any setting, then, each of us is partly the actor, partly the audience. Goffman called the intricate drama of everyday life the **presentation of self,** meaning *ways in which individuals, in various settings, try to create specific impressions in the minds of others.* This process, sometimes termed *impression management,* contains several distinctive elements (Goffman, 1959, 1967).

Performances

As we present ourselves to others, we convey information—consciously and unconsciously—about how we wish to be understood. Goffman called these efforts, taken together, a *performance.* Dress (costume), objects people carry (props), tone of voice, and gestures are all part of a performance. Setting, too, affects a performance.

To most people in the United States, these facial expressions convey anger, fear, joy, disgust, surprise, and sadness. But do people elsewhere in the world define them in the same way? Research suggests that all human beings experience similar basic emotions and display them to others in the same ways. But culture plays a part by specifying the situations that trigger one or another emotion.

People may joke loudly on the sidewalk, for example, but assume a more reverent manner when they enter a church. Equally important, individuals often design settings, such as homes or offices, to invoke desired reactions in others. A setting is a stage that enhances a person's performance by providing numerous specific pieces of information.

Consider, for example, how a physician's office conveys appropriate information to an audience of patients. Physicians enjoy considerable prestige and power in the United States, a fact evident to patients immediately upon entering the office. First, the physician is nowhere to be seen. Instead, in what Goffman describes as the "front region" of the setting, the patient encounters a receptionist who functions as a gatekeeper, deciding if and when the patient can meet the physician. A quick look around the doctor's waiting room, with patients (often impatiently) waiting to gain entry to the inner sanctum, leaves little doubt that the medical team controls events.

The physician's private office and examination room are the "back region" of the setting. Here the patient confronts a wide range of props, such as medical books and framed degrees, that reinforce the impression that the physician is in charge. In the office, the physician usually remains seated behind a desk—the larger it is, the greater the statement of power—while the patient is provided with only a chair.

The physician's appearance and manner convey still more information. The usual costume of white lab coat may have the practical function of keeping clothes from becoming soiled, but its primary function is to let others know at a glance the physician's status. A stethoscope around the neck or a black medical bag in hand has the same purpose. A doctor's highly technical terminology—occasionally necessary, but frequently mystifying—also emphasizes the hierarchy in the situation. The use of the title "Doctor" by patients who, in turn, are frequently addressed only by their first names also underscores the physician's dominant position. The overall message of a doctor's performance is clear: "I can help you, but you must allow me to take charge."

Nonverbal Communication

Novelist William Sansom describes the performance of a fictional Mr. Preedy, an English vacationer on a beach in Spain:

> He took care to avoid catching anyone's eye. First, he had to make it clear to those potential companions of his holiday that they were of no concern to him whatsoever. He stared through them, round them, over them—eyes lost in space. The beach might have been empty. If by chance a ball was thrown his way, he looked surprised; then let a smile of amusement light his face (Kindly Preedy), looked around dazed to see that there were people on the beach, tossed it back with a smile to himself and not a smile *at* the people. . . .
>
> . . . [He] then gathered together his beach-wrap and bag into a neat sand-resistant pile (Methodical and Sensible Preedy), rose slowly to stretch his huge frame (Big-Cat Preedy), and tossed aside his sandals (Carefree Preedy, after all). (1956; cited in Goffman, 1959:4–5)

In this performance, Mr. Preedy offers a great deal of information about himself to anyone caring to observe him. Notice that he does so without uttering a single word. This illustrates the process of **nonverbal communication**, *communication using body movements, gestures, and facial expressions rather than spoken words.*

Our movements and gestures convey much information to others, as suggested by the more common term *body language.* Facial expressions have special importance to nonverbal communication. Smiling, for example, symbolizes pleasure, although we distinguish between the casual, lighthearted smile of Kindly Preedy on the beach, a smile of embarrassment, and the full, unrestrained smile of self-satisfaction we often associate with the "cat who ate the canary."

Eye contact is another important element of nonverbal communication. Generally, eye contact is a prelude to social interaction. Someone across the room "catches our eye," sparking a conversation. Avoiding the eyes of another, by contrast, discourages communication. Hands, too, speak for us. Common hand gestures in our culture convey, among other things, an insult, a request for a ride, an invitation for someone to join us, or a demand that others stop in their tracks. Gestures also supplement spoken words. Pointing in a menacing way at someone, for example, gives greater emphasis to a word of warning, as shrugging the shoulders adds an air of indifference to the phrase "I don't know," and rapidly waving the arms lends urgency to the single word "Hurry!"

Most nonverbal communication is culture-specific. Bodily gestures have different meanings from place to place, so that many gestures significant to North Americans mean nothing—or something very different—to members of other societies, as explained in Chapter 2 ("Culture"). For instance, what we call the "A-Okay" gesture, with thumb touching forefinger, means "You're a zero" to the French and symbolizes a crude word for "rectum" to many Italians (Ekman, Friesen, & Bear, 1984).

Individuals express many elements of nonverbal communication deliberately. Sometimes, however, the information we unintentionally give off contradicts our intended performance. Listening to her teenage son's explanation for returning home at a late hour, for example, a mother begins to doubt his words because he avoids her eyes. The guest on a television talk show claims that his recent divorce is "the best thing that ever happened to me," but the nervous swing of his leg suggests otherwise. No body gesture directly conveys deceit, but such inconsistent messages—especially likely when strong emotions are involved—are clues to decep-

Professionals typically carry out their performances in carefully crafted settings. By prominently displaying several degrees and certificates behind her desk, this physician informs her patients that she expects to take charge of the interaction.

tion. A trained observer can discern discrepancies in a performance in much the same way that a lie detector measures the subtle physical changes in breathing, pulse rate, perspiration, and blood pressure that signal the stress of telling lies (Ekman, 1985).

Gender and Personal Performances

Because they are socialized to be less assertive than men, women tend to be especially sensitive to nonverbal communication. In fact, gender is a central element in personal performances. Based on the work of Nancy Henley, Mykol Hamilton, and Barrie Thorne (1992), we can extend the conventional discussion of personal performances to spotlight the importance of gender.

Demeanor. Goffman (1967) explains that *demeanor*—general conduct or deportment—is affected by a person's power. Simply put, the more power people have, the greater their personal discretion in how to act. Office behavior such as swearing, removing shoes, or putting feet up on the desk may well be appropriate for the boss, but rarely for subordinates (Henley, Hamilton, & Thorne, 1992). Similarly, people in positions of dominance interrupt the performances of others with impunity, while those subject to their power must display deference by becoming silent (Smith-Lovin & Brody, 1989).

For women, who generally occupy positions of low power, demeanor is a matter of particular concern. As Chapter 10 ("Sex and Gender") explains, about half the working women in the United States have clerical or service jobs that place them under the control of supervisors, who are usually men. Women, then, must craft their personal performances more formally than men, and display a greater degree of deference in everyday interaction.

Use of space. How much space does a personal performance require? Here again, power plays a key role, and using more space conveys a nonverbal message of personal importance. According to Henley, Hamilton, and Thorne (1992), our society has long measured femininity by how little space women occupy (the standard of "daintiness"), while men enhance their masculinity by controlling as much territory as possible.

The concept of **personal space** refers to *the surrounding area over which a person makes some claim to privacy*. In the United States, we maintain somewhat larger personal space than people in more densely populated societies such as Japan; we typically remain at least several feet from others. But in daily life, men readily intrude on the personal space of women. A woman's intrusion into a man's personal space, however, may be construed as a sexual overture. Here again, women have less power to define a specific reality than men do.

Women and men use space in different ways, a fact that is reflected in our clothing and demeanor. Because controlling space is a measure of power, men typically take up as much space as they can—even while relaxing—while women try to use as little as possible.

Staring, smiling, and touching. Eye contact encourages interaction. Women more than men work to maintain interaction, generally sustaining more eye contact. One exception is *staring*. Men often make women the objects of stares, which reflects both the dominance of men and their tendency to define women as sexual objects.

Although frequently conveying pleasure, *smiling* can also project a wide range of meaning. In a male-dominated world, women often smile to indicate appeasement or submission. For this reason, Henley, Hamilton, and Thorne maintain, women smile more than men; in extreme cases, smiling may reach the level of nervous habit.

Finally, *touching* constitutes an intriguing social pattern. Mutual touching generally conveys intimacy and caring. Apart from close relationships, however, touching is generally something men do to women. A male physician touches the shoulder of his female nurse as they examine a report, a young man who has just begun dating touches the back of his woman friend as he guides her across the street, or a male skiing instructor unnecessarily touches his female students. In such examples the touching may evoke little response, but it

amounts to a subtle ritual by which men express their dominant position in an assumed hierarchy that subordinates women.

Idealization

Complex motives underlie human behavior. Even so, Goffman suggests, performances tend to *idealize* our intentions. That is, we try to convince others that our actions reflect culturally ideal standards rather than more self-serving motives.

Idealization is easily illustrated by returning to the world of physicians and patients. In a hospital, physicians engage in a performance commonly described as "making rounds." Entering the room of a patient, the physician often stops at the foot of the bed and silently examines the patient's chart. Afterwards, physician and patient briefly converse. In ideal terms, this routine involves a physician making a personal visit to inquire about a patient's condition.

In reality, something less exemplary is usually going on. A physician who sees perhaps thirty-five patients a day may remember little about most of them. Reading the chart gives the physician the opportunity to rediscover the patient's identity and medical problems. Openly acknowledging the impersonality of much medical care would undermine the culturally ideal perception of the physician as deeply concerned about the welfare of others. Idealizing the behavior of physicians also encourages patients to "follow doctor's orders," which, they assume, are in their own best interest. No doubt this is often the case. But, as Chapter 13 ("Education and Medicine") explains, physicians often prescribe drugs, order tests, admit patients to hospitals, and perform surgery with a keen awareness of what's in it for themselves (Kaplan et al., 1985).

Idealization is woven into the fabric of everyday life in countless ways. Physicians and other professionals typically idealize their motives for entering their chosen careers. They describe their work as "making a contribution to science," perhaps "answering a calling from God," or "serving the community." Rarely do such people concede the less honorable, although common, motives of seeking the high income, power, and prestige these occupations confer. More generally, we all smile and make polite remarks to people we do not like. Such small hypocrisies ease our way through social interactions. Even when we suspect that others are putting on an act, we are unlikely to openly challenge their performance, for reasons that we shall explain next.

Embarrassment and Tact

The presidential candidate enters the room and stumbles over the rug; the eminent professor consistently mispronounces a simple word; the visiting dignitary rises from the table to speak, unaware of the napkin that still clings to her dress. As carefully as individuals craft their performances, slipups of this kind frequently occur. The result is *embarrassment*, or discomfort following a spoiled performance. Goffman describes embarrassment simply as "losing face."

Embarrassment looms as an ever-present danger because, first, idealized performances typically contain some deception. Second, most performances involve a complex array of elements, any one of which if badly done can shatter the intended impression.

Curiously, an audience typically overlooks flaws in a performance, thereby allowing the individual to avoid embarrassment. We discreetly inform a man that his zipper is open (creating limited embarrassment) only to help him avoid an even greater loss of face. In Hans Christian Andersen's classic fable "The Emperor's New Clothes," the child who blurts out that the emperor is naked tells the truth, but is scolded for being rude.

Members of an audience not only ignore flaws in a performance, Goffman explains, they often help the performer recover from them. *Tact* is an effort to help another person "save face." After hearing a supposed expert make an embarrassingly stupid remark, for example, people may be tactful in a variety of ways. They may ignore the statement, acting as if it was never made. They may laugh, indicating that they dismiss what was said as a joke. Or a listener might gently respond, "I'm sure you didn't mean that," suggesting that the statement will be discounted so as not to destroy the expert's overall performance.

Why is tact so common? Simply because embarrassment provokes discomfort not simply for the actor but for *everyone*. Just as members of a theater audience feel uneasy when an actor forgets a line, people who observe a social blunder are reminded of how fragile their own performances often are. Socially constructed reality thus functions like a dam holding back a sea of chaotic possibility. Should one person's performance spring a leak, others tactfully assist in making repairs. Everyone, after all, is engaged in jointly building reality, and no one wants it to be suddenly swept away.

Goffman's research shows that although individuals interact with a considerable degree of individuality and spontaneity, everyone's social interactions are constructed out of similar patterned elements. Almost four hundred years ago, William Shakespeare wrote:

> All the world's a stage,
> And all the men and women merely players.
> They have their exits and their entrances,
> And one man in his time plays many parts.
> (*As You Like It*, V)

Hand gestures vary widely from one culture to another. Yet a chuckle, grin, or smirk in response to someone's performance is universally defined as not taking the person seriously. Therefore, the world over, people who cannot restrain their mirth tactfully cover their faces.

Although human behavior may not be as rigidly scripted as a stage performance, each individual does play many parts in a lifetime that reflect both social structure and a unique personality. While human behavior certainly involves more than stage and script, Shakespeare's observation still contains a good measure of truth.

INTERACTION IN EVERYDAY LIFE: TWO ILLUSTRATIONS

We have now examined a number of dimensions of social interaction. The final sections of this chapter illustrate these lessons by focusing on two important, yet quite different, elements of everyday life.

Language: The Gender Issue

As explained in Chapter 2 ("Culture"), members of a society use language to weave the symbolic web we call culture. Language conveys not just *manifest* meaning—that is, what is explicitly stated—but also *latent* messages about social reality. One latent dimension of language involves gender. Language defines men and women differently in at least three ways (Henley, Hamilton, & Thorne, 1992).[2]

Language and power. A young man drives into the gas station, eager to display his new motorcycle, and proudly asks, "Isn't she a beauty?" On the surface, the question has little to do with gender. Yet, why does the fellow use the pronoun "she" rather than "he" to refer to his prized possession?

The answer has to do with power. Men often use language to establish control over their surroundings. That is, a man attaches a female pronoun to a motorcycle, car, yacht, or other object because it reflects *ownership*. Male ownership of female things is part of our culture: try reversing the pronoun to see how awkward it sounds.

The interplay of power and language comes through clearly in how people are named. Traditionally in the United States, as in many other parts of the world, a woman takes the family name of the man she marries.

While few today consider this an explicit statement of a man's ownership of a woman, many think it does reflect male dominance. For this reason, an increasing proportion of women have retained their own name (more precisely, the family name obtained from their father) or merged two family names.

Language and value. Language tends to attach greater value to what is defined as masculine. This pattern is deeply rooted in the English language, in ways that few women or men realize. For instance, the positive adjective "virtuous," meaning "morally worthy" or "excellent," is derived from the Latin word *vir* meaning "man." Contrarily, the disparaging adjective "hysterical" comes from the Greek word *hyster*, meaning "uterus."

In many more familiar ways, language also confers different value on the two sexes. Traditional masculine terms such as "king" or "lord" have retained their positive meaning, while some traditionally comparable terms, such as "queen," "madam," or "dame" have now assumed negative connotations. Language both mirrors social attitudes and helps perpetuate them.

Similarly, use of the suffixes "ette" and "ess" to denote femininity generally devalues a word. For example, a *major* has higher standing than a *majorette*, as does a *host* in relation to a *hostess*. And, certainly, men's groups with names such as the Los Angeles Rams carry more weight than women's groups with names like the Radio City Music Hall Rockettes.

Language and attention. Language also shapes reality by directing attention to what is masculine. Consider the use of personal pronouns. In the English language, the plural pronoun "they" neutrally refers to both sexes. But the corresponding singular pronouns "he" and "she" are sex linked. According to traditional grammatical practice, "he" (also, the possessive "his" and the objective "him") is widely used to refer to *all people*. Thus, we assume that the masculine pronoun in the bit of wisdom "He who hesitates is lost" refers to women as well as men. But are masculine pronouns truly inclusive, or do they serve to direct attention to what is masculine? A growing body of research suggests that people tend to respond to generic male pronouns as if only males were involved. To many women—especially those with feminist leanings—encountering male pronouns carries the message that females are of peripheral importance (MacKay, 1983).

Over the years, advocates of gender equality have urged creation of a gender-neutral, third-person singular personal pronoun. A century ago, one language critic

---

[2]The following sections draw primarily on Henley, Hamilton, & Thorne, 1992. Additional material is taken from Thorne, Kramarae, and Henley, 1983, and MacKay, 1983, and others as noted.

offered the new word "thon" (from "that" + "one") to solve the pronoun problem, as in "the confident person is thon who is well prepared" (Converse, 1884; cited in Kramarae, Thorne, & Henley, 1983:175). More recently, the plural pronoun "they" has gained currency as a singular pronoun ("*Everyone* should do as *they* please"). This usage is controversial because it violates grammatical rules. Yet, in an age of growing concern over gender-linked bias, some evolution of the English language seems likely.

Humor: Playing With Reality

Humor plays a vital part in everyday life. Comedians are among our favorite entertainers, most newspapers contain cartoon pages, and even professors and the clergy include humor in their performances. Like many aspects of daily living, however, humor is largely taken for granted. While everyone enjoys a good joke, few people think about what makes something funny or why humor is found among humans everywhere in the world. Many of the ideas developed in this chapter provide insights into the character of humor, as we shall now see.[3]

The foundation of humor. People create humor by deliberately and playfully contrasting incongruous realities. We will call one version of reality *conventional*, because it is consistent with what people usually expect in some situation. Let's call the other version of reality *unconventional*, since it contains some significant violation of cultural norms or values. In simple terms, humor arises when contradiction, ambiguity, and "double meanings" characterize our definitions of some situation. Note how this principle works in these simple pieces of humor:

> Steve Martin muses: "I like a woman with a head on her shoulders. *I hate necks!*"

> A car pulls alongside a steaming wreck and the driver calls out: "Have an accident?"
> "No thanks," comes the reply. "*Just had one!*"

In each example, the first sentence sets up the conventional reality. A man seeks a woman who is sensible and intelligent. One driver expresses concern for another.

---

[3]The ideas advanced in this discussion are those of the author (1987), except as otherwise noted. The general approach draws on work presented earlier in this chapter, especially the ideas of Erving Goffman.

There is nothing startling here. The second sentence in each example, however, injects the unconventional meaning that collides with what we take for granted. In the first joke, Steve Martin's assertion "I hate necks!" suddenly transforms the entire statement into an unexpectedly grotesque image. Similarly, the motorist who replies "Just had one" transforms an offer of help into an absurd invitation to further injury. The foundation of all humor lies in intentionally contrasting reality in this way.

This simple pattern comes through in the off-hand joking of comedian Groucho Marx:

> "This morning, I shot a lion in my pajamas. What the lion was doing in my pajamas I'll *never* know . . ."

Or how about one of the many "lawyer jokes" of recent years:

> #1: "How do you know lawyers are lying?"
> #2: "I don't know, how?"
> #1: "Their lips move . . ."

Here, again, we find these jokes containing two major elements, a conventional assertion followed by an unconventional one. The more powerful the incongruity between the two definitions of reality, the greater the humor. The humor that opened this chapter flows from contrasting the hucksterism of car dealers with the formality and dignity expected of those who provide funeral services.

When telling jokes, then, people try to strengthen this opposition in various ways. Groucho Marx, George Burns, Gracie Allen, and other comedians of the screen frequently do this by presenting the first, conventional remark in conversation with another actor, then turning toward the audience (or the camera) while delivering the second, unconventional line. This "shift of channel" underscores the incongruity of the two parts. Fashioning the strongest incongruity also leads comedians to pay careful attention to their performances: the precise words they use, as well as the timing of each part of the delivery. A joke is "well told" if the comic creates the sharpest possible opposition between the realities, just as humor falls flat in a careless performance. Since the key to humor lies in the opposition of realities, it is not surprising that the climax of a joke is called the *punch line*.

The dynamics of humor: "Getting it." Someone who does not understand both the conventional and unconventional realities embedded in a joke may complain,

Because humor is based on incongruous definitions of reality, the most common format for comedy is "funny person–straight person." Here, one comic disrupts social conventions to the consternation of the other. The Smothers Brothers are among the many comedians to generate laughter in this way, with Tommy playing the fool to Dicky's dismay.

"I don't get it." To "get" humor, a member of an audience must understand the two realities involved well enough to perceive their incongruity.

But there is something more to getting a joke, because some of the information listeners must grasp is usually left unstated. The audience, therefore, must pay attention to the *stated* elements of the joke, figure out the *unstated* elements, and then complete the joke in their own minds. Consider the following exchange, from the well-known television show "Cheers":

SAM: "Diane, you're drunk."
DIANE: "Yes, Sam, and you're stupid, but I'll be sober in the morning."

In this case, "getting" the joke depends on following the logic to recognize that Diane's line really ends with the unstated words, ". . . and you'll *still* be stupid."

A more complex joke is the following, written on the wall of a college rest room:

Dyslexics of the World, Untie!

This joke demands much more of the audience. One must know, first, that dyslexia is a condition in which people routinely reverse letters; second, one must identify the line as an adaptation of Karl Marx's call to the world's workers to unite; third and finally, one must recognize "untie" as an anagram of "unite," as one might imagine a dyslexic person would write it.

More complicated still is the following joke, which requires knowledge of three specialized words:

#1: "What do you get when you cross an insomniac, an agnostic, and a dyslexic?"
#2: "I don't know, what?"
#1: "A person who stays up all night wondering if there is a dog."

Why would an audience be required to make this sort of effort in order to understand a joke? Simply because our reaction to a joke is heightened by the pleasure of having been clever enough to "get it." Additionally, "getting" the joke confers on the audience favored "insider" status. These insights also explain the frustration that accompanies not getting a joke: anxiety about mental inadequacy coupled with a sense of being shut out of the pleasure shared by others. Not surprisingly, "outsiders" in such a situation sometimes fake "getting" the joke, only to ask for an explanation later, which others may tactfully provide.

But, as the old saying goes, if a joke has to be explained, it won't be very funny. Besides taking the edge off the language and timing on which the *punch* depends, an explanation relieves the audience of mental involvement, substantially reducing their pleasure.

The topics of humor. People everywhere smile and laugh, providing ample evidence that humor is a universal human trait. But since people live in diverse cultures, they differ in what they find funny. Musicians frequently perform for receptive audiences around the world, suggesting that music may be the "common language" of humanity. Comedians rarely do this, confirming that humor does not travel well.

What is humorous to the Chinese, then, may be lost on most people in the United States. To some degree, too, the social diversity of our society means that people

Because humor involves challenging social realities, "outsiders"—particularly ethnic and racial minorities—have always been disproportionately represented among America's comedians. The Marx Brothers, sons of Jewish immigrants, delighted in revealing the pretensions of the Protestant upper class.

find humor in different situations. New Englanders, southerners, and westerners have their own brands of humor, as do Hispanics and Anglos, fifteen- and forty-year-olds, bankers and construction workers.

In all these cases, however, humor deals with topics that lend themselves to double meanings or controversy. For example, the first jokes many of us learned as children concerned what our culture defines as a childhood taboo: sex. The mere mention of "unmentionable acts" or even certain parts of the body can dissolve young faces in laughter.

The controversy inherent in humor often walks a fine line between what is funny and what is considered "sick." During the Middle Ages, the word *humors* (derived from the Latin *humidus*, meaning "moist") referred to a balance of bodily fluids that determined a person's health. Most cultures value the ability to take conventional definitions of reality lightly (in other words, having a "sense of humor"). In fact, empirical evidence supports the old saying "Laughter is the best medicine": maintaining a sense of humor does contribute to a person's physical health by decreasing stress (Robinson, 1983; Haig, 1988). At the extreme, however, people who always take conventional reality lightly risk being defined as deviant or even mentally ill (mental hospitals have long been dubbed "funny farms").

Every social group considers some topics too sensitive for humorous treatment. A violation may result in the comedian being admonished for telling a "sick" joke,

one that pokes fun at a situation that is expected to be handled with reverence. Some topics, in other words, are "off limits" because people expect them to be understood in only one way. People's religious beliefs, tragic accidents, or appalling crimes are the stuff of "sick" jokes.

The functions of humor. From a structural-functional point of view, humor acts as a social "safety valve" in every society, allowing people to release potentially disruptive sentiments with little consequence. Put another way, jokes express ideas that might be dangerous if taken seriously, as in the case of racial and ethnic jokes. Called to account for a remark that could be defined as offensive, a person may defuse the situation by simply stating, "I didn't mean anything by that—it was just a joke!" Likewise, rather than taking offense at another's behavior, a person might use humor as a form of tact, smiling as if to say, "I could be angry at this, but I'll assume you were only kidding."

Like drama and art, humor also allows a society to challenge established ideas and to explore alternatives to the status quo. Sometimes, in fact, humor promotes social change by loosening the hold of convention.

Humor and conflict. While humor holds the potential to liberate, it can also be used for subjugation. Men who tell jokes about feminists, for example, may well be voicing some measure of hostility toward the interests of women (Benokraitis & Feagin, 1986; Powell & Paton, 1988). Similarly, jokes at the expense of gay people reveal tensions surrounding sexual orientation in the United States.

"Put down" jokes, which make one category of people feel good at the expense of another, are common around the globe. After collecting and analyzing jokes from many societies, Christie Davies (1990) concluded that conflict among ethnic groups is a driving force behind humor virtually everywhere. Typically, jokes label some disadvantaged category of people as stupid or ridiculous, thereby imputing greater wisdom and skills to those who share the humor. In the United States, Poles have long been the "butt" of jokes, as have Newfoundlanders ("Newfies") in eastern Canada, the Irish in Scotland, the Scots in England, the Sikhs in India, the Hausas in Nigeria, the Tasmanians in Australia, and the Kurds in Iraq.

Disadvantaged people, of course, also make fun of the powerful. Women in the United States have long joked about men, just as African Americans portray whites in humorous ways, and poor people poke fun at the rich. Throughout the world, people target their lead-

ers with humor, and officials in some countries take such jokes seriously enough to vigorously repress them.

Probing beneath the surface, then, we discover that humor is serious business. Michael Flaherty (1984, 1990) points out that socially constructing reality is constant and demanding work. Furthermore, the reality that emerges may suffer by comparison to what we imagine the world should be. As long as we maintain a sense of humor, however, we are never prisoners of our present lives. Rather, in laughter we assert our freedom to recast the world, if only in our minds. And, in doing so, we actually do change the world—and ourselves—just a little.

These very different issues—the impact of gender in our language and humor—are both important dimensions of everyday life. Each demonstrates our power to socially construct a world of meaning and then react to what we have made. Each also demonstrates the value of sociological thinking for understanding—and more actively participating in—this process.

SUMMARY

1. Social life is patterned in various ways. By guiding behavior within culturally approved bounds, social structure helps to make situations more understandable and predictable.

2. A major component of social structure is status. In an entire status set, a master status has particular significance.

3. In principle, ascribed statuses are involuntary, while achieved statuses are earned. In practice, however, many statuses are both ascribed and achieved.

4. Role is the dynamic expression of a status. Like statuses, roles are relational, guiding people as they interact.

5. When roles corresponding to two or more statuses are incompatible, role conflict results. Likewise, incompatibility among various roles linked to a single status (a role set) causes role strain.

6. The phrase "social construction of reality" conveys the important idea that people build the social world as they interact.

7. The Thomas theorem holds that a situation defined as real is real in its consequences.

8. People build social reality using elements of their culture and available social resources.

9. Ethnomethodology is a means of discovering the structure of everyday social situations by violating rules of expected behavior.

10. Dramaturgical analysis explores everyday life in terms of theatrical performances.

11. People speak, use body language, and fashion physical settings to assist their performances. Often performances idealize underlying intentions.

12. Women and men craft their situational behavior differently based on their relative social power.

13. Social behavior carries the ever-present danger of embarrassment. Tact is a common response to a "loss of face" by others.

14. Language is a major tool of reality-building. In various ways, language defines women and men in different terms, generally to the advantage of men.

15. Humor is based on the contrast between conventional and unconventional social realities. Because comedy is framed by a specific culture, people throughout the world find humor in different situations.

KEY CONCEPTS

achieved status a social position that a person assumes voluntarily and that reflects a significant measure of personal ability and choice

ascribed status a social position that a person receives at birth or assumes involuntarily later in the life course

dramaturgical analysis the investigation of social interaction in terms of theatrical performance

ethnomethodology the study of the everyday, common-sense understandings that people have of the world

master status a social position with exceptional importance for identity, often shaping a person's entire life

nonverbal communication communication using body movements, gestures, and facial expressions rather than spoken words

personal space the surrounding area over which a person makes some claim to privacy

presentation of self Goffman's term for the ways in which individuals, in various settings, try to create specific impressions in the minds of others

role normative patterns of behavior for those holding a particular status

role conflict incompatibility among the roles corresponding to two or more statuses

role set a number of roles attached to a single status

role strain incompatibility among roles corresponding to a single status

social construction of reality the process by which individuals creatively build reality through social interaction

social interaction the process by which people act and react in relation to others

status a recognized social position that an individual occupies

status set all the statuses a person holds at a particular time

Thomas theorem the assertion that situations that are defined as real are real in their consequences

5

Groups and Organizations

CHAPTER OUTLINE

While playing in front of her New Hampshire home, nine-year-old Alicia Martin rolled her ball into the next yard. Annoyed at the child's carelessness, her eighty-eight-year-old neighbor refused to return the ball. Alicia's parents then did the properly American thing: they *sued* their neighbor, winning a court judgment for $30.20.

This story is becoming more typical as neighbors in the United States make increasing use of lawyers and the courts to settle issues that once were resolved with some hasty apologies and a handshake. The number of lawyers in the United States has soared to 1 million: one for every three hundred people in the country. Each year, people file some 18 million lawsuits in state and federal courts, one for every ten adults.

What does it tell us about ourselves that the United States has 70 percent of the world's lawyers, while most other societies have few such professionals, and some have none at all? Even among industrial nations, the United States produces attorneys twice as fast as Great Britain, three times the pace of Germany, and twenty-five times the rate of Japan (Cohn, 1991; Johnson, 1991).

Our country's reliance on formal litigation, of course, has many causes beyond the large number of attorneys. As a nation, we embrace the notion of individual rights, which makes us quick to think our rights or interests are infringed. More broadly, the United States has become a vast system of countless, complex organizations. At the same time, we are an impersonal society, in which individuals recognize few obligations to their neighbors and, in many cases, do not even want to know them. Our desire for privacy has grown so much that more than one-fourth of all households in the United States have unlisted telephone numbers. In large cities like Los Angeles, the proportion is as high as two-thirds.

This chapter examines the importance of *social groups*, the clusters of people around whom we carry out much of our daily lives. As we shall explain, the scope of group life has expanded during this century, from the families and neighborhoods of the past to the vast bureaucracies and businesses that sociologists call *formal organizations*. We now turn to how groups and organizations operate, and the impact of these social units on our lives.

SOCIAL GROUPS

Virtually everyone moves through life with a sense of belonging; that is the experience of group life. A **social group** is defined as *two or more people who identify and interact with one another*. As human beings, we continually join together in couples, families, circles of friends, neighborhoods, teams, churches, businesses, clubs, and numerous large organizations. Whatever the form, groups encompass people who share experiences, loyalties, and interests. In short, while maintaining their individuality, the members of social groups also think of themselves as a special "we."

Not every collection of individuals forms a group. People who happen to be at the same place at the same time but interact little and lack a sense of belonging are correctly termed an *aggregate*. Riders on a subway train are an example of an aggregate, not a group. People who have some status in common, such as "mother," "sergeant," "homeowner," or "Roman Catholic" are also not a group but a *category*. They do not make up a group because, while they may be aware of others like themselves, most are strangers who never interact.

People in an aggregate or category *could* become a social group, if the right circumstances gave them a common identity and caused them to interact. When a subway train recently crashed beneath the streets of New York City, for example, passengers were prompted by their common plight toward group awareness, helping each other survive the ordeal.

Primary and Secondary Groups

Acquaintances commonly greet one another with a smile and the simple phrase "Hi! How are you?" The response is usually a well-scripted, "Just fine, thanks. How about you?" This answer, of course, is often far from truthful. In fact, providing a detailed account of how you *really* are doing might well prompt the other person to make a hasty and awkward exit.

Social groups fall into one of two types according to their members' degree of personal concern for each other. According to Charles Horton Cooley, a **primary group** is *a small social group in which relationships are personal and enduring*. Bound together by strong and lasting loyalties, which Cooley termed *primary relationships*, people in primary groups share many activities, spend a great deal of time together, and feel that they know one another well. As a result, they typically display genuine concern for each other's welfare. The family is the most important primary group in any society.

Cooley called personal and tightly integrated groups *primary* because they are among the first groups we experience in life. In addition, the family and peer groups

Around the world, families are the most significant primary group. Weddings are among the various rituals that reaffirm the primary bonds of family life, linking the generations with ties of identification and duty. Here members of a wedding party in Monrovia, Liberia commemorate their celebration through a family portrait.

also hold primary importance in the socialization process, shaping attitudes and behavior and providing comfort and security. We look to members of our primary groups for clues to our social identity as well, which is why members of such groups almost always think of themselves as "we."

Although members of primary groups provide a wide range of benefits to one another, they generally think of their group as an end in itself rather than as a means to other ends. For example, we readily call on family members or close friends to help us move into a new apartment, without expecting to pay for their services. And we would do the same for them. A friend who never returns a favor, however, is likely to leave us feeling "used" and questioning the depth of the friendship.

Finally, members of a primary group engage each other as unique individuals. We usually do not care who cashes our check at the bank or drives the cross-town bus. Yet members of primary groups are not interchangeable and are bound to one another by emotion

and loyalty. Although brothers and sisters experience periodic conflict, they always remain siblings.

In contrast to the primary group, the **secondary group** is *a large and impersonal social group based on a specific interest or activity.* Examples of secondary groups include people who work together in an office, enroll in the same college course, live in a given neighborhood, or belong to a particular political organization.

In most respects, secondary groups have precisely the opposite characteristics of primary groups. *Secondary relationships* usually involve little personal knowledge of one another and weak emotional ties. Secondary groups vary in duration, but are frequently of short term, beginning and ending without particular significance. Students in a college course, for example, may or may not see each other again after the semester ends. Because secondary groups focus on a special interest or activity, members have little chance to develop a broad concern for one another's overall welfare. In some cases, such as co-workers who share an office, relationships may edge from secondary to primary with the passing of time. People in a secondary group sometimes think of themselves as "we," but the boundary that distinguishes members from nonmembers is usually far less clear than in primary groups.

While primary relationships have a *personal orientation*, secondary relationships have a *goal orientation*. This does not mean that secondary ties need be formal and unemotional. On the contrary, social interactions among students, co-workers, and business associates can be enjoyable even if they are rather impersonal.

Put otherwise, primary-group members define each other according to *who* they are; members of secondary groups look to one another for *what* they are, that is, what they can do. In secondary groups, we are always mindful of what we offer others and what we receive in return. This "keeping score" comes through most clearly in business relationships. Likewise, neighbors typically expect that a neighborly favor will be reciprocated. On the other hand, if people feel themselves injured or short changed in a secondary relationship, they might even turn to the courts for satisfaction—a less likely response in a primary relationship.

The goal orientation of secondary groups encourages members to carefully craft their behavior. In these roles, then, we remain characteristically impersonal and polite. The secondary relationship, therefore, is one in which the question "How are you?" may be asked without really wanting a truthful answer.

The characteristics of primary and secondary

groups are summarized in Table 5–1. Using these two ideals as ends of a continuum, we can describe any real group as primary or secondary to some degree. Some family relationships, after all, are more primary than others, and not all business relationships are equally secondary.

By spotlighting primary and secondary ties, we can track changes in society itself. In general, primary relationships dominate life in preindustrial societies. Strangers stand out in the social landscape. By contrast, secondary ties take precedence in modern, industrial societies, where people assume highly specialized social roles. In today's world, we routinely engage in impersonal, secondary relationships with strangers—people about whom we know very little and may never meet again (Wirth, 1938).

Group Leadership

Social groups vary in the extent to which members recognize leaders, people charged with responsibility to direct the group's activities. Some friendship groups grant one person the clear status of leader; others do not. In families, parents have leadership roles, although husband and wife may disagree about who is really in charge. In many secondary groups, such as corporations, leadership is likely to involve a formal chain of command.

Table 5–1   PRIMARY GROUPS AND SECONDARY GROUPS: A SUMMARY

	Primary Group	Secondary Group
Quality of relationships	Personal orientation	Goal orientation
Duration of relationships	Usually long term	Variable; often short term
Breadth of relationships	Broad; usually involving many activities	Narrow; usually involving few activities
Subjective perception of relationships	As an end in itself	As a means to an end
Typical examples	Families; close friendships	Co-workers; political organizations

We may think that leaders possess extraordinary personal abilities, but research over several decades has failed to produce convincing evidence of so-called "natural leaders." Instead of reflecting individual traits, leadership has more to do with the needs of the group itself (Ridgeway, 1983; Ridgeway & Diekema, 1989).

Two different leadership roles commonly emerge in groups (Bales, 1953; Bales & Slater, 1955). **Instrumental leadership** refers to *group leadership that emphasizes the completion of tasks*. Group members look to instrumental leaders to "get things done." **Expressive leadership**, by contrast, *emphasizes collective well-being*. Expressive leaders are concerned less with the performance goals of a group than with providing emotional support to members and minimizing conflict among them.

Because they concentrate on performance, instrumental leaders usually forge secondary relationships with group members. Instrumental leaders give orders and reward or punish people according to their performance. Expressive leaders, however, cultivate more primary relationships. They offer sympathy for a member having a tough time, work to keep the group united, and lighten serious moments with humor. While successful instrumental leaders gain a distant *respect*, expressive leaders generally enjoy more personal *affection*.

In the past, this differentiation of leadership has been linked to gender. In traditional families, for example, cultural norms have bestowed instrumental leadership on men. As fathers and husbands, they have assumed primary responsibility for family income, making major decisions, and disciplining children. As mothers and wives, women have taken the expressive leadership role, with the expectation that they will lend emotional support and maintain peaceful family relationships (Parsons & Bales, 1955). This division of labor partly explains why many children have greater respect for their fathers, but closer personal ties with their mothers (Macionis, 1978). But changes in family life have blurred the gender-linked distinction between leadership roles and, in other settings as well, women and men are assuming both types of leadership roles.

Decision-making styles also characterize leaders. *Authoritarian leaders* focus on instrumental concerns, make decisions on their own, and demand strict compliance from subordinates. Although this leadership style wins little affection from the group, members may praise an authoritarian leader in a crisis situation requiring immediate decisions and strong group discipline. *Democratic leaders* are more expressive, and try to include everyone in the decision-making process. While less successful when a crisis leaves little time for discussion, democratic leaders can otherwise draw on the ideas of all members to forge reflective and imaginative responses to the tasks at hand. *Laissez-faire leaders* (from the French phrase meaning roughly "to leave alone") tend to downplay their position and power, allowing the group to function more or less on its own. Laissez-faire leaders are generally the least effective in promoting group goals. Leadership style in any particular case depends, in large part, on the needs of the group itself (White & Lippitt, 1953; Ridgeway, 1983).

Group Conformity

Groups influence the behavior of their members, often promoting conformity. Some amount of group conformity provides a secure feeling of belonging; group pressure, however, can be considerable and sometimes unpleasant. Even groups of strangers can foster conformity, as a classic experiment by Solomon Asch (1952) showed.

Asch's research. Asch (1952) formed groups of six to eight people, allegedly to study visual perception. He arranged with all but one member of the group to create a situation in which the remaining subject would be pressured to accept conclusions that were quite unreasonable. Asch asked group members, one at a time, to match a "standard" line, as shown in Figure 5–1 on "Card 1," to one of three lines on "Card 2." Anyone with normal vision could see that the line marked "A" on "Card 2" was the correct choice. Initially, everyone gave correct answers. Then, Asch's secret accomplices began responding incorrectly, making the naive subject bewildered and uncomfortable. Asch found that more than one-third of subjects placed in this awkward situation chose to conform to the others by answering incorrectly. Many of us are apparently willing to compromise our own judgment to avoid the discomfort of being different from others, even from people we do not know.

Milgram's research. In the early 1960s, Stanley Milgram—a one-time student of Solomon Asch—conducted a controversial conformity experiment of his own. In his initial study (Milgram, 1963, 1965; Miller, 1986), a researcher explained to pairs of subjects that they were engaging in a study of memory. One subject was assigned the role of "teacher" and the other—who was an insider to the study—became the "learner."

The learner sat in a forbidding contraption resembling an electric chair with electrodes attached to one

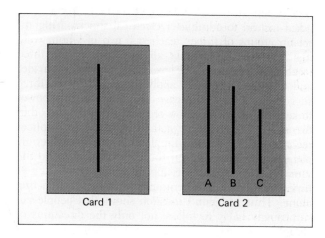

Figure 5–1 The Cards Used in Asch's Experiment in Group Conformity
(*Asch, 1952:452–53*)

arm. The researcher instructed the teacher to read pairs of words, later repeating each first word and asking the learner to recall the corresponding second word. As mistakes occurred, the researcher instructed the teacher to shock the learner using a "shock generator," a realistic-looking device marked to regulate electric current from 15 volts (labeled "mild shock") to 450 volts (marked "Danger: Severe Shock" and "XXX"). Beginning at the lowest level, the teachers were told to increase the shock by 15 volts every time the learner made a mistake. The experimenter explained to the teacher that the shocks were painful but caused no permanent damage.

The results are striking evidence of the ability of leaders to obtain compliance. None of the forty subjects assigned in the role of teacher during the initial research even questioned the procedure before applying 300 volts, and twenty-six of the subjects—almost two-thirds—went all the way to 450 volts. In subsequent trials, Milgram's subjects administered shocks to people who verbally objected, to those who protested that they had heart conditions, and to individuals who screamed and then feigned unconsciousness. Not surprisingly, many subjects found the experiment extremely stressful, the source of the controversy ever since. No less disturbing is the implication of Milgram's research that people who commit atrocities against fellow human beings—as some Nazi and Soviet soldiers did during World War II—are more or less typical people who are "just following orders."

Milgram (1964) then modified his research to see if the group conformity documented by Asch's matching lines experiment would be exhibited when subjects were asked instead to administer electrical shocks. Milgram set up groups of three "teachers," two of whom were his accomplices. Milgram allowed each of the three teachers to suggest a shock level when an error was made, and told the teachers to apply the *lowest* of the three suggestions. This strategy gave the naive subject the power to keep the shock level low regardless of what the other two subjects suggested. For their part, the accomplices recommended increasing the shock level with each error, placing group pressure on the naive subject to do the same. As a result, subjects applied voltages three to four times higher than in experiments when they were acting alone. Thus Milgram's research shows that people are surprisingly likely to follow not only the directions of "authority figures," but also groups of ordinary people.

Janis's research. Even the experts succumb to pressure for group conformity, according to Irving L. Janis (1972, 1989). Janis contends that a number of foreign-policy errors, including the failure to foresee the Japanese attack on Pearl Harbor in World War II, the disastrous U.S. plan to invade Cuba in 1961, and our ill-fated involvement in the Vietnam War, were the results of group conformity among our highest-ranking political leaders.

We often think that group "brainstorming" improves decision making. However, Janis explained that group thinking sometimes backfires. Rather than examining a problem from many points of view, group members often seek consensus, thereby narrowing the range of options. Moreover, once settled on a position, group members may come to see anyone with another view as the "opposition." Janis called this process **"groupthink,"** *a limited understanding of an issue due to group conformity.*

Janis claims that "groupthink" led the Kennedy administration to invade Cuba—a plan that failed, provoking international criticism of the United States. Arthur Schlesinger, Jr., former adviser to President John Kennedy, confessed guilt "for having kept so quiet during those crucial discussions in the Cabinet Room," but added that the group discouraged anyone from challenging even what seemed "nonsense" (Janis, 1972:30, 40).

Of course, U.S. officials are not the only leaders who can be blinded by group consensus. In 1991, a group of eight top government officials carried out a short-lived seizure of power in the former Soviet Union. Despite access to vast amounts of information through government agencies, these leaders failed to anticipate the reaction of their opponents, or the depth of popular opposition to their attempted coup.

Reference Groups

Frequently we evaluate ourselves using a **reference group,** *a social group that serves as a point of reference for making evaluations and decisions.* A young man who imagines his family's response to a woman he is dating is using his family as a reference group. Similarly, a banker who assesses her colleagues' reactions to a new loan policy is using her co-workers as a point of reference.

As these examples suggest, reference groups can be both primary and secondary. And because we are often strongly motivated to conform to a group, the attitudes of group members can greatly affect personal evaluations. This is true both of groups we belong to and those we would like to join, as the discussion of *anticipatory socialization* in Chapter 3 ("Socialization: From Infancy to Old Age") suggests.

Stouffer's research. Samuel A. Stouffer (1949) conducted a classic study of reference group dynamics during World War II. In a survey, Stouffer asked soldiers to evaluate the chances of promotion for a competent person in their branch of the service. Common sense suggests that soldiers serving in outfits with a high promotion rate would be optimistic about future advancement. Yet survey responses revealed just the opposite: soldiers in branches of the service with low promotion rates were actually more encouraged about chances for advancement.

The key to this paradox is that the soldiers measured their progress against specific groups. Those in branches with lower promotion rates compared their advancement with people like themselves; that is, although they had not been promoted, neither had many others, so they did not feel deprived. Soldiers in a service branch with a higher promotion rate, however, could easily think of people who had been promoted sooner or more often than they had. Using these people for reference, even soldiers who had been promoted were likely to feel they had come up short. These were the soldiers who voiced more negative attitudes in their evaluations.

Stouffer's research demonstrates that, regardless of our situation in *absolute* terms, our subjective sense of well-being is *relative* to some specific reference group (Merton, 1968; Mirowsky, 1987).

Ingroups and Outgroups

Differences among groups, in political outlook, social status, even manner of dress, may lead us to embrace one while avoiding others. Across the United States,

Many ingroups and outgroups are based on dimensions of inequality. In Joseph Decker's (1853–1924) painting *Our Gang* (1886), the artist shows how readily race can lead some people to experience social marginality. The African-American boy has his back against a wall covered with weathered posters that seem to point to him like a finger of accusation (Decker originally named this painting *The Accused*). The reality of race in the United States is that people of color often find themselves cast in the role of an outgroup.

Our Gang, 1886. Oil on canvas, 10¾ x 20 (27.3 x 50.8). Signed in lower right corner: J. Decker (illegible). Private Collection.

for example, students wear high-school jackets to indicate that, to them, school is an important social group. Students attending another school may become the targets of derision simply because they belong to a rival group.

This illustrates an important process of group dynamics: the opposition of ingroups and outgroups. An 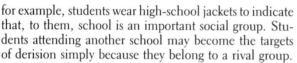 **ingroup** is *an esteemed social group commanding a member's loyalty.* An **outgroup,** by contrast, is *a scorned social group toward which one feels competition or opposition.* A town's Democrats generally think of themselves as an ingroup in relation to local Republicans. Ingroups and outgroups work on the principle that "we" have valued traits that "they" lack. Tensions among groups sharpen their boundaries and give people a clearer social identity. However, research has shown that the members of ingroups hold overly positive views of themselves and unfairly negative views of various outgroups (Tajfel, 1982).

Power plays a part in group dynamics. For example, whites have historically viewed people of color as an outgroup and subjected them to social, political, and economic disadvantages. Internalizing these negative attitudes, people of African, Hispanic, Asian, and Native-American descent often struggle to overcome negative self-images based on stereotypes widespread among the white majority.

Group Size

If you are the first person to come to a party, you can observe some fascinating group dynamics. Until about six people enter the room, everyone generally shares a single conversation. But as more people arrive, the group soon divides into two or more smaller clusters. It is apparent that size plays a crucial role in how group members interact.

To understand why, consider the mathematical connection between the number of people in a social group and the number of relationships among them, as shown in Figure 5–2 on page 104. Two people form a single relationship; adding a third person results in three relationships; a fourth person yields six. Adding people one at a time—a process mathematicians describe as an *arithmetic progression*—rapidly increases the number of relationships in a *geometric progression*. By the time six people join one conversation, fifteen different relationships connect them, so the group usually divides at this point.

German sociologist Georg Simmel (1858–1918) focused his research on social dynamics in the smallest social groups. Simmel (1950; orig. 1902) used the term **dyad** (from the Greek word for *pair*) to designate *a social group with two members.* In the United States, love affairs, marriages, and the closest friendships are dyadic. Simmel identified two special qualities of the dyad. First, they are typically less stable than larger groups. Both members of a dyad must actively participate in the relationship; if either withdraws from the dyad, the group collapses. Because the stability of marriage is important to society, we support this dyad with legal and often religious ties. By contrast, a large group is inherently more stable. A volunteer fire company, for example, does not collapse even if several members drop out.

Second, social interaction in a dyad is typically

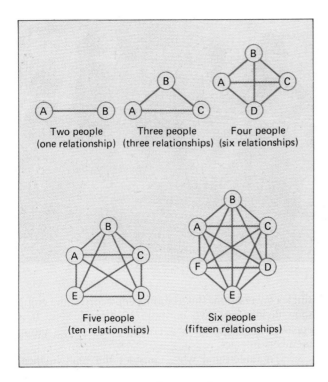

Figure 5–2 Group Size and Relationships

more intense than in other groups. In a one-to-one relationship, neither member shares the other's attention with anyone else. For this reason, dyads have the potential to be the most meaningful social bonds we ever experience. Because marriage in our culture is dyadic, strong emotional ties generally unite husbands and wives. As Chapter 12 ("Family and Religion") explains, however, in other societies marriage can involve more than two people. In that case, the marriage is more stable although the many marital relationships, viewed individually, are probably less strong.

Simmel also analyzed the **triad**, *a social group with three members.* A triad contains three relationships, each uniting two of the three people. Any two members, then, can form a majority coalition, transforming the triad into a dyad with a "third wheel." Two members who develop a romantic interest, for example, quickly understand the old saying "Two's company, three's a crowd."

Despite characteristic problems, however, a triad is more stable than a dyad. If the relationship between any two of the group's members becomes strained, the third can act as a mediator to restore the group's vitality.

Similarly, members of a dyad (such as a married couple) often seek out a third person (a trusted friend or counselor) to air tensions between them.

Social groups with more than three members tend to be even more stable because even if several members lose interest, the group's existence is not directly threatened. Larger social groups usually develop formal roles guided by rules and regulations that stabilize their operation. Yet, larger groups inevitably lack intense personal interaction, for this is possible only in the smallest groups.

Thus there is no ideal size for a social group. A dyad offers unsurpassed emotional intensity, while a group of several dozen people will be more stable and capable of accomplishing larger, more complex tasks (Slater, 1958; Ridgeway, 1983).

Social Diversity and Group Dynamics

Race, ethnicity, and gender also affect group dynamics, especially the likelihood that members will interact with outsiders. Peter Blau (1977, 1982; South & Messner, 1986) points to three ways in which social diversity influences intergroup contact.

First, Blau claims that, the larger a group, the more likely members will maintain relationships only with one another. To illustrate, increasing the number of international students on campus may promote social diversity, but it also enables these students to maintain their own distinctive social group. For the same reason, members of smaller ethnic communities are more likely to marry out of their group than members of larger communities (Gurak & Fitzpatrick, 1982).

Second, Blau argues that the more internally heterogeneous a group is, the more likely it is to interact with outsiders. Members of campus groups that recruit people of various social backgrounds, then, typically have more intergroup contact than those who choose members of a particular type.

Third, Blau contends that physical considerations also affect social contacts. To the extent that a social group is physically segregated from others (by having its own dorm or dining area, for example), its members are less likely to engage others.

Networks

A **network** is *a web of weak social ties.* Unlike members of a social group, people in networks usually feel little sense of membership and have only occasional contact.

The boundaries of networks are also less clear than those of groups.

Some networks approximate groups, as among college chums who maintain their friendship by mail and telephone. More commonly, however, networks involve weak ties, often including people we know of—or who know of us—but with whom we interact rarely (Granovetter, 1973). As one woman with a widespread reputation as a community organizer explains, "I get calls at home, someone says, 'Are you Roseann Navarro? Somebody told me to call you. I have this problem . . .' " (Kaminer, 1984:94).

Network ties may be weak, but they are sometimes a valuable resource. Nan Lin (1981) discovered that subjects he surveyed used networks to find a job more than any other single resource. He also found that men whose fathers held important occupational positions gained the greatest advantages from networks. This finding underscores the fact that networks link people of similar social background, thereby perpetuating their level of social privilege.

Peter Marsden (1987) determined that the most extensive social networks are maintained by young, well-educated urbanites. Women's and men's networks tend to be the same size, he added, but women have more ties to relatives so that their networks carry less clout than the "old-boy" networks do. Because many women work in settings where men outnumber them, they are now paying more attention to building career networks for themselves (Speizer, 1983; Coppock, 1987).

FORMAL ORGANIZATIONS

A century ago, social life was centered in small groups—the family, friends, and neighbors. Today, central to our lives are **formal organizations,** *large, secondary groups organized to achieve specific goals.* Formal organizations such as corporations or government agencies differ from small primary groups not just in being impersonal but also in having a decidedly planned or formal atmosphere, and they operate to accomplish specific tasks.

With its population exceeding 250 million, our society performs countless jobs ranging from educating expectant parents to delivering the mail. Most of these responsibilities are carried out by formal organizations, which develop a life and culture of their own beyond the individual members who may come and go.

Today's college campuses value social diversity. One of the challenges of multiculturalism is ensuring that all categories of students are integrated into campus life. This is not always easy. Following Blau's theory of group dynamics, as the number of minority students increases, these individuals are able to form a group unto themselves, perhaps interacting less with others.

Types of Formal Organizations

According to how members are linked to an organization, Amitai Etzioni (1975) has identified three organizational types. *Normative organizations* pursue goals that their members consider morally worthwhile, offering members personal satisfaction, perhaps social prestige, but no monetary reward. Sometimes called *voluntary associations,* these include community service groups (such as the PTA, the Lions Club, the League of Women Voters, and the Red Cross), political parties, and religious organizations. Because our society has historically excluded women from much of the paid labor force, they have traditionally played a greater part than men in civic and charitable organizations.

Coercive organizations have involuntary members subject to punishment (a prison) or treatment (a mental hospital). Coercive organizations have extraordinary physical features, such as locked doors, barred windows, and security personnel (Goffman, 1961). Designed to segregate people as inmates or patients for a period of time, they sometimes seek to radically alter the attitudes and behavior of people confined within their walls.

According to Etzioni, people join *utilitarian organizations* in pursuit of material rewards. Large business enterprises, for example, generate profits for their owners and income in the form of salaries and wages for their employees. While utilitarian organizations offer greater individual freedom than coercive organizations, they provide less autonomy than normative organizations. Most people have little choice but to spend half of their waking hours at work, where they have only limited control over their jobs.

From differing vantage points, a particular formal organization can fall into *all* of these categories. A mental hospital, for example, is a coercive organization to a patient, a utilitarian organization to a psychiatrist, and a normative organization to a hospital volunteer.

Origins of Bureaucracy

Formal organizations date back thousands of years to the use of religious and political administrations by elites to control their people. Formal organizations also collected taxes, administered military campaigns, and constructed monumental structures like the Great Wall of China and the pyramids of Egypt.

The effectiveness of these early organizations was limited, however, by the traditional character of preindustrial societies. The influential German sociologist Max Weber defined **tradition** as *sentiments and beliefs about the world that are passed from generation to generation.* Members of traditional societies use the past to guide their thought and behavior. Such conservatism, Weber found, restrained organizational efficiency.

Modern society, by contrast, encourages formal organization. Weber characterized the contemporary world view as one of **rationality,** *deliberate, matter-of-fact calculation of the most efficient means to accomplish a particular task.* A rational world view is indifferent to the past, so that tradition is simply another bit of information without any special claim on individuals. Patterns of thought and behavior are based on calculation of their consequences for the present.

The key to the rise of the "organizational society" is the process Weber termed **rationalization,** *the change from tradition to rationality as the dominant mode of human thought.* Modern society, he claimed, became "disenchanted" as sentimental ties to the past gave way to greater reliance on scientific thinking, advancing technology, and the organizational structure called *bureaucracy.*

Characteristics of Bureaucracy

Bureaucracy is *an organizational model designed to efficiently perform tasks.* Bureaucratic officials formulate and modify policy to make an organization as efficient as possible. To appreciate the efficiency of bureaucratic organization, consider our country's telephone system. Each of more than 160 million telephones can be used to reach any other telephone in homes, businesses, and automobiles within seconds. Of course, the telephone system depends on technological developments such as electricity and computers. But equally important is the organizational capacity to keep track of every telephone call—noting which phone called which other phone, when, and for how long—and presenting all this information to millions of telephone users in the form of a monthly bill.

In global context, the availability of facsimile (fax) machines and other forms of electronic communication is a good indicator of the extent of bureaucratic organization. As shown in Global Map 5–1 on page 108, these devices are most common in the United States and Canada, Western Europe, Japan, and Australia and New Zealand. In most nations of the world, however, this equipment is limited to government officials, large businesses, and urban elites. Thus the proliferation of bureaucracy is closely tied to economic development.

What traits promote organizational efficiency? Max Weber (1978; orig. 1921) identified six elements of the ideal bureaucratic organization.

1. **Specialization.** Most of our ancestors were preoccupied with securing food and shelter. Bureaucratic societies, by contrast, assign people highly specialized roles that correspond to organizational offices.

2. **Hierarchy of offices.** Bureaucratic offices form a hierarchy, according to their responsibilities. Each person is supervised by "higher-ups" in the organization while, in turn, supervising those in lower positions.

3. **Rules and regulations.** Bureaucratic operations are guided by rationally enacted rules and regulations. Ideally, a bureaucracy seeks to operate in a completely predictable fashion.

4. **Technical competence.** Bureaucratic officials must have the technical competence to carry out their duties. Bureaucracies typically recruit new members according to set criteria and, later, monitor

Although formal organization is vital to modern, industrial societies, it is far from new. Twenty-five centuries ago, the Chinese philosopher and teacher K'ung Fu-Tzu (known to Westerners as Confucius) endorsed the idea that government offices should be filled by the most talented young men. This led to what was probably the world's first system of civil service examinations. Here, would-be bureaucrats compose essays to demonstrate their knowledge of Confucian texts.

their performance. Such impersonal evaluation contrasts sharply with the custom, through most of human history, of favoring relatives—whatever their talents—over strangers.

5. **Impersonality.** Bureaucracy places rules ahead of personal feelings. Ideally, offices provide uniform treatment for each client and worker. From this detached approach stems the notion of the "faceless bureaucrat."

6. **Formal, written communications.** An old adage suggests that the heart of bureaucracy is not people but paperwork. Rather than face-to-face talk, bu-

reaucracy relies on formal, written memos and reports, which accumulate into vast *files*. Such documents guide an organization in roughly the same way that personality guides an individual.

Bureaucracy Versus Small Groups

Members of small groups, especially primary groups like the family, value one another in a personal sense. By contrast, bureaucrats value their organization and each other as a way to get a job done.

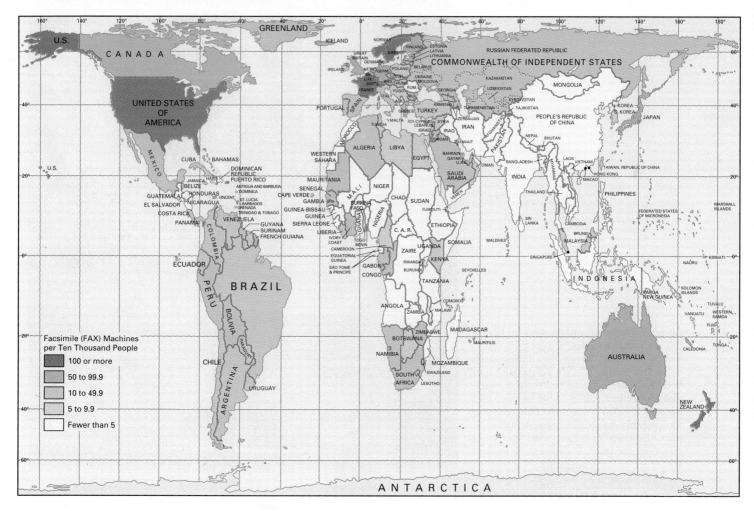

Global Map 5–1 Data Transmission in Global Perspective

The expansion of formal organization depends partly on available technology. Facsimile (fax) machines and other devices for transmitting data are most widespread in economically developed regions of the world, including the United States, Canada, Western Europe, Japan, and Australia. In poor societies, such devices are all but unknown. Note, too, that the wealthy elite in small nations like Kuwait make use of advanced technology to support their global business operations.

Facsimile (FAX) Machines per Ten Thousand People
- 100 or more
- 50 to 99.9
- 10 to 49.9
- 5 to 9.9
- Fewer than 5

Bureaucratic organization promotes efficiency by carefully recruiting personnel and demanding conformity to set rules and regulations. In small, informal groups, by contrast, members have considerable discretion to respond to each other personally, without regard for rules or rank. Table 5–2 summarizes differences between small social groups and large formal organizations.

The Informal Side of Bureaucracy

In Weber's ideal bureaucracy, officials deliberately regulate every activity. Realistically, however, organizational behavior often diverges from the rules. In some cases, innovation and informality help meet legitimate needs overlooked by regulations. In other situations, such as cutting corners in one's job, informal behavior undermines efficiency (Scott, 1981). Actual operations, then, do not always reflect bureaucratic blueprints.

Although power formally resides in offices, studies of U.S. corporations reveal that the interpersonal skills of individuals have a tremendous impact on organizational outcomes (Halberstam, 1986). Authoritarian, democratic, and laissez-faire types of leadership—described earlier in this chapter—also reflect individual personality as much as any organizational plan. Then, too, decision making does not always conform to a defined hierarchy and official regulations. As the recent savings and loan scandal reveals, officials and their friends may personally benefit from abuse of organizational power. In many organizations, furthermore, people in leadership positions rely on subordinates to handle much of their own work. Many secretaries, for example, have more day-to-day responsibility than their job title and salary suggest.

Communication offers another example of organizational informality. Formally, memos and other written documents disseminate information through the chain of command. Typically, however, individuals cultivate informal networks or "grapevines" that spread information much faster, if not always as accurately. Grapevines are particularly important to subordinates because elites often attempt to conceal important information from them.

Sometimes employees of formal organizations simply ignore bureaucratic structures to advance their own interests. A classic study of the Western Electric factory in Chicago revealed that few workers reported employees who violated rules, as the rules demanded (Roethlisberger & Dickson, 1939). On the contrary, those who *did* were

Table 5–2 SMALL GROUPS AND FORMAL ORGANIZATIONS: A COMPARISON

	Small Groups	Formal Organizations
Activities	Members typically engage in many of the same activities	Members typically engage in various highly specialized activities
Hierarchy	Often informal or nonexistent	Clearly defined, corresponding to offices
Norms	Informal application of general norms	Clearly defined rules and regulations
Criteria for membership	Variable, often based on personal affection or kinship	Technical competence to carry out assigned tasks
Relationships	Variable; typically primary	Typically secondary, with selective primary ties
Communications	Typically casual and face to face	Typically formal and in writing
Focus	Person oriented	Task oriented

socially isolated, labeled by other workers as untrustworthy "squealers." Although the company formally set productivity standards, workers informally created their own definition of a fair day's work, criticizing those who exceeded it as "rate-busters" and others who fell short as "chiselers."

Such informal social structures suggest that many people reject bureaucratic rigidity. They also show that we have the creative capacity to humanize even the most formally defined social situations.

Limitations of Bureaucracy

Weber touted the ideal bureaucracy as a model of efficiency. Still, real-life formal organizations certainly have their limitations, even when it comes to performance of specific tasks. Anyone who has ever tried to replace a lost driver's license, return defective merchandise to

George Tooker's (1920–) painting *Government Bureau* is a powerful statement about the human costs of bureaucracy. The artist depicts members of the public in monotonous similitude—reduced from human beings to mere "cases" to be disposed of as quickly as possible. Set apart from others by their positions, officials are "faceless bureaucrats" concerned more with numbers (notice their hands on calculators) than with providing genuine assistance.

George Tooker, Government Bureau, *1956. Egg tempera on gesso panel. 19⅝ x 29⅝ inches. The Metropolitan Museum of Art. George A. Hearn Fund, 1956.(56.78).*

a discount chain store, or change an address on a magazine subscription knows that large organizations can be maddeningly unresponsive to individual needs.

Of course, no organizational system will ever completely eradicate human failings. Moreover, some problems occur because organizations are *not* truly bureaucratic. But, as Weber himself recognized, even the pure form of bureaucracy has limitations. Perhaps the most serious limitation of bureaucracy is its potential to *dehumanize* those it purports to serve. To operate efficiently, each client must be treated impersonally as a standard "case." In other words, in striving for efficiency, the organization loses the ability to provide individual attention to clients or customers.

Weber also feared that bureaucratic impersonality would *alienate* those who worked in large organizations. He described the bureaucrat as "a small cog in a ceaselessly moving mechanism" (1978:988; orig. 1921). Although formal organizations are intended to serve humanity, Weber worried that humanity would end up serving formal organizations.

The ambivalence of many people toward bureaucracy, then, comes as no surprise. On the one hand, formal organizations advance many of our widespread cultural values (see Chapter 2, "Culture"), including efficiency, practicality, and achievement. On the other hand, bureaucracies threaten cherished ideals of democracy and individual freedom. In addition, the growth

of bureaucratic organization has prompted a decline in individual privacy (Long, 1967; Smith, 1979). The box provides details.

Bureaucratic waste and incompetence. *"Work expands to fill the time available for its completion."* Enough truth underlies C. Northcote Parkinson's (1957) tongue-in-cheek assertion that it is known today as Parkinson's Law.

To illustrate, assume that a bureaucrat processes fifty passport applications in an average day. If one day this worker had only twenty-five applications to examine, how long would the task take? The logical answer is half a day; but Parkinson's Law suggests that if a full day is available to complete the work, a full day is how long it will take. After all, few members of formal organizations are going to seek out extra work to fill their spare time. What they do is try to appear busy, which only prompts organizations to take on more employees. The time and expense required to hire, train, supervise, and evaluate a larger staff makes everyone busier still, setting in motion the vicious cycle we call "bureaucratic bloat." Ironically, the larger organization may accomplish no more real work than it did before.

Laurence J. Peter (Peter & Hull, 1969) devised the Peter Principle, which states that *bureaucrats are promoted to their level of incompetence.* The logic here is simple: employees competent at any level of the organi-

Bureaucracy: A Threat to Personal Privacy?

A century ago, people who wanted personal privacy built a fence around their houses and hung "Beware of Dog" signs on the gates. Today, however, fences and dogs do little to protect people in the United States from a distinctly modern kind of intrusion. And more people now have access to more information about each one of us than nosey neighbors of the past could imagine.

Why? Because of the growth of formal organizations. Bureaucracy is essential to a vast and complex society, but the cost is ever-larger banks of personal information. Automobile drivers must be licensed, but doing so requires gathering information about everyone who legally operates a vehicle. The Internal Revenue Service, the Social Security Administration, and programs that benefit veterans, students, the poor, and un-

employed people each must collect extensive information.

The explosive growth of credit in the economy has further fueled the drive for information. In the past, local merchants offered credit to customers with no more paperwork than an I.O.U. Today, people in the United States carry 1 billion credit cards, enabling them to obtain credit from total strangers.

The Information Revolution has spawned a new business: maintaining files about people's place of residence, marital status, employment, income, debts, and history of paying their bills on time. Further eroding personal privacy, computers now share information more widely and more rapidly than ever before. Because addresses can easily be added to mailing lists, so-called junk mail now makes up half of all correspondence. Of greater

concern, information circulates from organization to organization, generally without the knowledge or consent of the people in question.

In response, many states have adopted laws giving citizens the right to examine records kept about them by employers, banks, and credit bureaus. The U.S. Privacy Act of 1974 also limits the exchange of information among government agencies. Additionally, citizens can examine information contained in most government files and offer corrections that become part of the record.

Existing laws have slowed the erosion of personal privacy, but even expanded legislation is unlikely to reverse this trend. The price of relying on formal organizations may be the sacrifice of much personal privacy.

SOURCES: Smith (1979) and Miller (1991).

---

zational hierarchy are likely to be promoted to higher positions. Eventually, however, they reach a position where they are in over their heads, and they are no longer eligible for advancement. This dooms them to a future of inefficiency. Compounding the problem, by the time they rise to a place in the hierarchy that is beyond their abilities, they probably have acquired enough skill to avoid demotion or dismissal by hiding behind rules and regulations, by taking credit for work actually performed by their more competent subordinates, or by building up a network of well-connected allies.

Bureaucratic ritualism. For many of us, the term *bureaucracy* conjures up images of *red tape* (derived from the red tape used by eighteenth-century English officials to wrap official parcels and records; Shipley, 1985). Red tape refers to a tedious preoccupation with organizational procedures. Robert Merton (1968) considers red tape to be one kind of group conformity. His term **bureau-**

cratic ritualism signifies a *preoccupation with rules and regulations to the point of obstructing organizational goals.*

Ritualism impedes performance by stifling people's creativity and imagination, robbing the organization of talent and thinking needed to meet changing circumstances (Whyte, 1957; Merton, 1968). In bureaucratic ritualism, we see one form of the alienation that Max Weber feared would arise from modern organizations.

Bureaucratic inertia. Weber noted that "once fully established, bureaucracy is among the social structures which are hardest to destroy" (1978:987; orig. 1921). **Bureaucratic inertia,** *the tendency of bureaucratic organizations to endure over time,* means that they take on a life of their own and persist whether they are useful or not. After completing its original task, an organization often redefines its goals to provide a livelihood for its members. The National Association for Infantile Paralysis, sponsor of the well-known March of Dimes, funded research that led to a cure for polio in the early 1950s. But after the appearance of the Salk vaccine, rather than disbanding, the organization redirected its efforts toward other medical problems, including birth defects, and still exists today. In short, bureaucratic inertia often leads formal organizations to justify themselves, sometimes even after they have outlived their usefulness.

Oligarchy

Robert Michels (1876–1936) is credited with observing that bureaucracy fosters **oligarchy,** *the rule of the many by the few* (1949; orig. 1911). Early societies lacked the organizational means for even the most power-hungry ruler to control everyone. The development of more complex formal organizations, however, enhanced the opportunities of a small elite to control society. According to what Michels called "the iron law of oligarchy," the pyramid-like structure of bureaucracy places a few leaders in charge of entire government organizations.

Weber linked bureaucracy's strict hierarchy of responsibility to efficiency. Michels added that it discourages democracy. While organizational officials should subordinate personal interests to organizational goals, people who occupy powerful positions can—and often do—use their access to information and the media to promote their personal interests. Oligarchy, then, thrives in the hierarchical structure of bureaucracy, and undermines people's confidence in their elected leaders.

Political competition and governmental checks and balances in this nation's system of government prevent the flagrant oligarchy found in some societies. Among national office holders, incumbents certainly enjoy enormous advantages of power and funding over challengers. In 1990, all but one incumbent senator was returned to office by the voters. Two years later, even with widespread political discontent, all but nineteen of 349 incumbents in Congress won reelection.

Social Diversity and Organizations

Rosabeth Moss Kanter (1977; Kanter & Stein, 1979) has shown that gender and race play an important part in organizational structure. In most organizations, there is a dominant category of people (usually white men) who operate as an ingroup enjoying greater acceptance, credibility, and access to social networks. By contrast, women, people of color, and those from economically disadvantaged backgrounds often feel like members of

The notion that organizations can muster vast resources to perpetuate themselves was called into question by the rapid and sweeping changes in Eastern Europe and the former Soviet Union. Oligarchies, it turns out, are more vulnerable to popular opposition than the thinking of Robert Michels suggests they are.

a socially isolated outgroup who are taken less seriously and given slimmer chances for promotion. These people may feel uncomfortably visible and think that they must work twice as hard as those in dominant categories simply to maintain their present standing, let alone advance to a higher position.

The opportunity to advance is a key dimension of organizational life. According to Kanter, organizations that offer everyone a chance for promotion turn their employees into "fast-trackers" with greater commitment to the organization. By contrast, "dead-end" jobs produce only "zombies" with little aspiration or loyalty.

Kanter adds that power and opportunity encourage flexible leadership that builds the morale of subordinates. People who have little power, by contrast, often jealously guard what privileges they do have and rigidly supervise subordinates. Table 5–3 summarizes Kanter's conclusion that organizations must "humanize" their structure to bring out the best in their workers and improve the "bottom line."

Humanizing Bureaucracy

Humanizing bureaucracy refers to *organizational efforts to develop human resources.* Research by Kanter (1977, 1983, 1989; Kanter & Stein, 1980) and others (cf. Peters & Waterman, Jr., 1982) shows that humanizing bureaucracy produces both happier employees and healthier profits. Based on the discussion so far, we can identify three paths to more humane organizations:

1. **Social inclusiveness.** The social composition of the organization should make no one feel out of place because of gender, race, or ethnicity. The performance of all employees will improve to the extent that no one is subject to social exclusion.

2. **Sharing of responsibilities.** Humanizing bureaucracy means relaxing rigid, oligarchical structures by spreading power and responsibility more widely. Knowing that superiors are open to suggestions encourages all employees to think creatively, increasing organizational effectiveness.

3. **Expanding opportunities for advancement.** Reducing the number of employees stuck in dead-end jobs encourages workers to perform better, to share ideas, and to try new approaches. No position should be ruled out as the start of an upward career path.

Critical evaluation. Kanter's work takes a fresh look at the concept of bureaucracy as it applies to business organizations. Perhaps rigid formality made more sense in the past, when uneducated workers were simply a source of physical labor. But today, workers can contribute a wealth of ideas to bolster organizational efficiency if the organization encourages and rewards innovation.

Although Kanter's suggested changes are controversial, such efforts offer significant returns. Comparing rigidly bureaucratic companies to competitors with more flexible organizational structures, Kanter (1983) found that flexibility increases profits. She argues, therefore, that bureaucratic structure limits an organization's success by treating employees as a group to be controlled rather than as a resource to be developed.

Organizational Environment

How organizations operate depends not just on their internal structure but on the **organizational environment,** *any external factors that affect its operation.* Environmental factors include technology, politics, the economy, available work force, and other organizations.

For example, modern organizations could not exist without the technology of telephone systems, facsimile (fax) machines, copiers, and computers. Today's organizations are also changing as the proliferation of personal computers gives employees access to more information than ever before and also allows executives to monitor the activities of workers (Markoff, 1991).

Similarly, political and economic changes often

Table 5–3 KANTER'S RESEARCH: A SUMMARY

	Advantaged Employees	Disadvantaged Employees
Social composition	Being represented in high proportions helps employees to fit in more easily and to enjoy greater credibility; they experience less stress, and are usually candidates for promotion	Being represented in low proportions puts employees visibly "on display" and results in their not being taken seriously; they tend to fear making mistakes and losing ground rather than optimistically looking toward advancement
Power	In powerful positions, employees contribute to high morale and support subordinates; such employees tend to be more democratic leaders	In positions of low power, employees tend to foster low morale and restrict opportunities for subordinates to advance; they tend to be more authoritarian leaders
Opportunity	High opportunity encourages optimism and high aspirations, loyalty to organization, use of higher-ups as reference groups, and constructive responses to problems	Low opportunity encourages pessimism and low aspirations, weak attachment to the job, use of peers as reference groups, and ineffective griping in response to problems

SOURCE: Based on Rosabeth Moss Kanter, *Men and Women of the Corporation* (New York: Basic Books, 1977), pp. 246–49.

Japan is a fascinating blend of the old and the new. Traditional loyalties and patterns of deference—of the young toward the old and of women toward men—are still evident in modern, corporate life.

have dramatic consequences for the operation of an organization. Many industries now face a host of new environmental standards; likewise, all organizations are buoyed or burdened by periodic economic growth and recession (Pennings, 1982). The size and composition of the surrounding populace also affect organizations. The average age, typical education, and social diversity of a local community shape both the available work force and the market for an organization's products or services. Finally, other organizations also contribute to the organizational environment. People who operate a hospital, for example, must contend with the insurance industry as well as organizations representing doctors, nurses, and other hospital workers. And to remain competitive a hospital must keep abreast of the equipment, procedures, and prices at other nearby facilities (Fennell, 1980).

In short, organizations everywhere are linked in many ways to their surrounding societies. This is especially evident when making global comparisons.

Japanese Organizations

The remarkable success of Japanese corporations has sparked debates about organizational structure. Since the end of World War II, Japan's economic growth has surged five times faster than our own. Although only the size of the state of Montana, Japan produces 60 percent as much[1] as the entire United States.

Businesses in Japan reflect that nation's strong collective identity and solidarity. While people here prize rugged individualism, the Japanese value cooperation. This cohesiveness results in relatively low levels of social problems—such as alcoholism, violence, and drug abuse—compared to more rootless and competitive societies like the United States (Ouchi, 1981). This solidarity also explains Japan's remarkably small number of lawyers, as noted at the beginning of this chapter. The Japanese try to settle disputes according to traditional norms rather than by resorting to formal legal procedures.

This social solidarity makes formal organizations in Japan remarkably personal, rather like extremely large primary groups. In the United States, by comparison, although a few companies have tried to model themselves on Japanese organizational principles, even humanized bureaucracy has many more secondary relationships. Indeed, as the box suggests, U.S. workers often oppose highly personal Japanese policies.

William Ouchi (1981) highlights five distinctions between formal organizations in Japan and their counterparts in industrial societies of the West. In each case, the Japanese organization has a more collective orientation.

1. **Hiring and advancement.** Organizations in the United States hold out promotions and higher salaries as prizes won through individual competition. In Japan, however, organizations hire new school graduates together as a group and assign them comparable salaries and responsibilities. Only after several years is anyone likely to be singled out for special advancement. This corporate approach generates a common identity, or team spirit, among employees of the same age.

2. **Lifetime security.** Employees in the United States rarely remain with one company for their entire careers; rather, we expect to move from one company to another in pursuit of personal goals. U.S. companies are also quick to lay off employees in the face of economic setbacks. By contrast, Japanese corporations typically hire workers for life, so companies and their employees have strong, mutual loyalties. Japanese companies also avoid layoffs by retraining workers for other jobs in the organization.

---

[1]Comparison based on Gross Domestic Product (GDP).

The Japanese Model: Will It Work in the United States?

What the company wants is for us to work like the Japanese. Everybody go out and do jumping jacks in the morning and kiss each other when they go home at night. You work as a team, rat on each other, and lose control of your destiny. That's not going to work in this country.

John Brodie
President, United Paperworkers Local 448
Chester, Pennsylvania

Who can argue with the economic success of the Japanese? Competition from Asia (and, increasingly, from Europe) is forcing companies in the United States to reconsider long-held notions about corporate operations, from the assembly line right up to the board room. Among the most interesting examples of new "transplant organizations" are Japanese manufacturing plants built here in this country. Manufacturing plants operated in the U.S. by Honda, Nissan, and Toyota employ more than 250,000 people and achieve the same degree of efficiency and quality that have won these companies praise in Japan. Yet some voices in industry—workers, union leaders, and managers— are speaking as bitterly about transplanting Japanese organizational techniques as they are about importing Japanese cars.

To a large extent, organizational life reflects the surrounding culture, and experts are generally skeptical that organizational patterns can be transplanted easily from one society to another. However, stirred by the economic power of Japanese corporations, the United States work force has increasingly experimented with Japan's organizational techniques, such as quality control groups.

Many U.S. workers dislike the notion of worker participation, which they see as increasing their workload. While still responsible for building cars, for instance, workers are now asked to worry about quality control, unit costs, and overall company efficiency—tasks traditionally shouldered by management. Moreover, some employees do not want to move from job to job, since learning new skills is demanding and sometimes threatening. Many union leaders are

also suspicious of any plans formulated by management, even those purporting to share power. Some managers, too, have been slow to adopt worker participation programs. Sharing power to procure supplies, direct production, and even schedule vacations does not come easily to executives used to more top-down decision-making practices. Finally, in an age of corporate takeovers and short-term profits, company owners may not wish to invest time and money in restructuring organizations.

Nonetheless, worker-participation programs are changing the U.S. workplace. A recent government survey found that, despite some outright resistance, 70 percent of large businesses had initiated at least some programs of this kind. The advantages go right to the bottom line, since profits are usually higher when workers have a say in decision making. And most employees in worker-participation programs—even those who may not want to sign up for morning jumping jacks—seem significantly happier about their jobs. Workers who have long used only their bodies are now enjoying the opportunity to use their brains as well.

SOURCES: Hoerr (1989) and Florida & Kenney (1991).

---

3. **Holistic involvement.** While we tend to keep business and personal life distinct, Japanese organizations play a broad role in their employees' lives. Companies may provide dormitory housing or offer mortgages for the purchase of homes, and sponsor a wide range of social events in which workers participate. Employee interaction beyond the workplace strengthens collective identity and offers respectful Japanese workers an opportunity to voice suggestions and criticisms in more casual settings.

4. **Nonspecialized training.** Bureaucratic organization in the United States is based on specialization. But a Japanese organization trains employees in all phases of its operation, with the expectation that employees will remain with the organization for life. Ideally, this general training helps workers

understand how each job relates to the organization's overall operation (Sengoku, 1985).

5. **Collective decision making.** Typically, a handful of executives make key decisions in the U.S. corporation. Although Japanese business leaders take responsibility for their company's performance, they involve workers in decisions that affect them. This cooperation is encouraged by relatively greater economic equality between management and workers: the salary differential between Japanese executives and workers is far less than that found in the United States. Additionally, Japanese companies create semi-autonomous working groups, or "quality circles." These, too, afford all employees in Japan managerial responsibilities.

Taken together, these traits generate a strong sense of organizational loyalty. The cultural emphasis on *individual* achievement in the United States thus finds its parallel in Japanese *groupism*. Workers tie their personal interests to those of the organization, and the company, in turn, places a high value on meeting employee needs.

GROUPS AND ORGANIZATIONS IN GLOBAL PERSPECTIVE

In recent years, the emphasis in the study of formal organizations has shifted from the organizations themselves to the environment in which they operate. In part, this change stems from a growing global focus in research, which shows that the structure and performance of organizations reflect a host of broad societal factors.

Despite Max Weber's depiction of bureaucracy as a singular form, organizations actually developed quite differently in various world regions. In Europe and the United States, most businesses began as small family enterprises. But as Western societies were rocked by the Industrial Revolution, the way of thinking Weber termed "rationalization" defined nepotism (favoritism shown to a family member) or other primary relationships as barriers to organizational efficiency.

But the development of formal organizations in Japan followed a different route. Historically, that society was even more socially cohesive, organized by family-based loyalties. As Japan industrialized, people there found no threat to efficiency in primary relationships, as Westerners did. On the contrary, the Japanese modeled their large businesses on the family and, as that nation modernized, traditional family loyalties were transferred to corporations. Perhaps Japanese workers are now becoming more individualistic; yet the Japanese model still demonstrates that organizational life need not be impersonal.

Beyond Japan, organizations throughout the world are taking on particular forms based on distinctive environments. Businesses in Poland are gaining vitality as that country opens to global trade. European nations as a whole are engaged in forming a new multinational economic system. Organizations in the People's Republic of China have come under renewed control by that nation's communist party. In the former Soviet Union, associations of all kinds are coming out from under rigid political control for the first time in three-quarters of a century. In some respects, each of these developments is likely to have an effect on organizational patterns in the United States.

As some analysts point out, organizations in our society are still the envy of the world for their efficiency; after all, where on earth does the mail arrive as quickly and dependably as in the United States (Wilson, 1991)? But global diversity and change demand that we be wary of any "absolute truths" about formal organizations and, just as important, that we be curious about the possibilities for reorganizing our future.

SUMMARY

1. Social groups are important building blocks of society, fostering common identity among members.

2. Primary groups are small and person-oriented; secondary groups are typically large and goal-oriented.

3. Instrumental leadership is concerned with a group's goals; expressive leadership focuses on the collective well-being of members.

4. The process of group conformity is well documented by researchers. Because members often seek consensus, groups do not necessarily generate a wider range of ideas than do individuals working alone.

5. Individuals use reference groups—both ingroups and outgroups—to make decisions and evaluations.

6. Georg Simmel argued that dyads have a distinctive intensity, but lack stability because of the effort necessary to maintain them. A triad can easily dissolve into a dyad by excluding one member.

7. Peter Blau explains that group size, homogeneity, and physical segregation each affect group behavior.

8. Social networks are grouplike relational webs whose members usually have little common identity and uncertain interaction.

9. Formal organizations are large, secondary groups that seek to perform complex tasks efficiently. Depending on their members' reasons for joining, formal organizations can be termed normative, coercive, or utilitarian.

10. Bureaucratic organization expands in modern societies and allows the efficient performance of many complex tasks. Bureaucracy is based on specialization, hierarchy, rules and regulations, technical competence, impersonal interaction, and formal, written communications.

11. Limitations of bureaucracy include the inability to deal efficiently with special cases, depersonalizing the workplace, and fostering ritualism among some employees. Max Weber also recognized that bureaucracy tends to resist change.

12. Formal organizations tend toward oligarchy. Rosabeth Moss Kanter's research has shown that the concentration of power and opportunity in U.S. corporations can compromise organizational effectiveness.

13. Humanizing bureaucracy means recognizing that people are any organization's greatest resource. To develop human resources, organizations must not allow people of one gender or race to dominate decision making; rather, responsibility and opportunity should be available at all levels.

14. Organizations operate not only according to their internal structures but also based on their external environments, responding to technological, political, and economic factors.

15. Formal organizations in Japan differ from the Western, bureaucratic model because of the collective spirit of Japanese culture. Formal organizations in Japan are based on more personal ties than are their counterparts in the United States.

KEY CONCEPTS

bureaucracy an organizational model designed to efficiently perform tasks

bureaucratic inertia the tendency of bureaucratic organizations to persist over time

bureaucratic ritualism a preoccupation with organizational rules and regulations to the point of obstructing organizational goals

dyad a social group with two members

expressive leadership group leadership that emphasizes collective well-being

formal organization a large secondary group that is organized to achieve specific goals

"groupthink" limited understanding of some issue due to group conformity

humanizing bureaucracy organizational efforts to develop human resources

ingroup an esteemed social group commanding a member's loyalty

instrumental leadership group leadership that emphasizes the completion of tasks

network a web of weak social ties

oligarchy the rule of the many by the few

organizational environment any external factors that affect the operation of an organization

outgroup a scorned social group toward which one feels competition or opposition

primary group a small social group in which relationships are personal and enduring

rationality deliberate, matter-of-fact calculation of the most efficient means to accomplish any particular task

rationalization Max Weber's term for the change from tradition to rationality as the dominant mode of human thought

reference group a social group that serves as a point of reference for making evaluations and decisions

secondary group a large and impersonal social group based on some special interest or activity

social group two or more people who identify and interact with one another

tradition sentiments and beliefs about the world that are passed from generation to generation

triad a social group with three members

6

Deviance

CHAPTER OUTLINE

Sirens sliced through the night as police cruisers joined in angry pursuit of the 1988 Hyundai as it sped through a suburban neighborhood in Los Angeles. As the black-and-white cars closed in on their quarry, a helicopter chattered overhead, its powerful floodlight bathing the surreal scene in a shimmering brilliance.

Twenty-five-year-old Rodney Glen King, the lone occupant of the Hyundai, brought his car to a halt, opened his door, and stumbled into the street. In an instant, police swarmed around him, and a sergeant lunged forward, staggering King with the discharge of a 50,000-volt Taser stun gun. Unarmed and now help-less, King fell to the pavement. As eleven police officers looked on, three others took turns kicking King and striking him with their clubs as he tried to protect himself. By the time the beating ended, King had sustained a crushed cheekbone, a broken ankle, damage to his skull, a burn on his chest, and internal injuries.

The capture and beating of an unemployed Afri-can-American construction worker by the police might have attracted little notice except for one extraordinary coincidence: the resident of a nearby apartment building had observed the event—through the eyepiece of his video camera. In a matter of hours, the violent confronta-tion was being replayed on television screens across the United States.

The King incident touched off a firestorm of public debate over the operation of police departments in Los Angeles and elsewhere. To some critics, the scene was all too familiar: a black man being brutalized by white police for little or no reason. Other critics declared that the King episode was notable only because the police had been caught in the act; during the previous year, the Los Angeles police department had paid out $10 million to compensate citizens who claimed they had been victims of abuse.

The officers involved in the King incident soon stood charged with assault with a deadly weapon and use of excessive force. But, a year later, a jury acquitted the four of wrongdoing—a verdict that touched off the worst rioting this country has seen in two decades. Inner-city neighborhoods in Los Angeles went up in flames, leaving more than fifty people dead, thousands injured, and hundreds of millions of dollars in damages.

Every society struggles to establish some notion of justice, to reward people who play by the rules, and to punish those who step out of line. But, as the Rodney King incident and its aftermath so vividly demonstrate, the line that separates good and evil is no simple matter of black and white. This chapter investigates many of

Despite evidence provided by an amateur videotape of the incident, a California court of law acquitted four police officers in the beating of Rodney King in Los Angeles in 1992. The aftermath of the verdict was widespread rioting that suggests definitions of right and wrong are rarely simple matters of black and white.

the questions that underlie this case: Why do societies create moral standards in the first place? Do such codes actually control deviance? Why are some people more likely than others to be charged with offenses? And what are the purposes and problems of our criminal justice system? We begin by defining several basic concepts.

WHAT IS DEVIANCE?

Deviance is *the recognized violation of cultural norms.* Norms guide virtually all human activities, so the concept of deviance is also quite broad. One distinctive category of deviance is **crime,** *the violation of norms formally enacted into criminal law.* Even criminal deviance spans a wide range, from minor traffic violations to serious offenses such as rape and murder.

Deviance encompasses many other types of non-conformity as well, some of which most people view as mild (left-handedness or boastfulness, for example) while we consider others more serious (mental illness or flunking out of school). To some who are in the majority, being a member of a racial or ethnic minority may seem deviant. In addition, the poor—who may find it difficult to conform to many conventional middle-class patterns—are also widely defined as deviant. Even

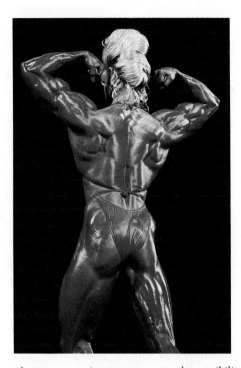

Each and every normative pattern creates the possibility for deviance. Many societies retain traditional norms that women should be soft and submissive; in this context, women who develop their physical strength—or those who are assertive—may be viewed as deviant.

physical traits may be considered abnormal. Men with many highly visible tattoos may court criticism, as do women with any tattoo at all. Being unusually tall or short, or grossly fat or exceedingly thin, may brand a person as deviant. Physical disabilities also set a person apart as nonconforming.

Most examples of nonconformity that come readily to mind involve *negative* definitions. However, since we all have shortcomings, we often define especially righteous people as deviant even if we accord them a measure of respect (Huls, 1987). Overall, then, deviance involves some difference in others, whether negative or positive, which causes us to react to them as "outsiders" (Becker, 1966).

All of us are subject to **social control,** *attempts by society to regulate the thought and behavior of individuals*. Like deviance itself, social control takes many forms. Socialization, the focus of Chapter 3, involves a lifelong process of social control in which family, peer groups, and the mass media influence people's attitudes and actions. A more complex and formal type of social control is the **criminal justice system,** which *responds to alleged violations of the law using police, courts, and state-sanctioned punishment.* A society exerts social control by responding positively to conformity—including praise from parents, high grades in school, and positive recognition from people in the community—and reacting negatively to deviance—ranging from personal criticism to legal prosecution. Both positive reinforcement for socially accepted actions and fear of incurring society's wrath promote conformity to conventional patterns of thought and behavior.

The Biological Context

How do people come to be conformists or deviants in the first place? As noted in Chapter 3 ("Socialization: From Infancy to Old Age"), people during the nineteenth century understood their behavior as an expression of biological instincts. Not surprisingly, then, early investigations of criminality focused on biological causes.

In 1876 Caesare Lombroso (1835–1909), an Italian physician who worked in prisons, suggested that criminals were physically distinctive—with low foreheads, prominent jaws and cheekbones, protruding ears, lots of body hair, and unusually long arms that made them resemble our apelike ancestors. In essence, Lombroso viewed criminals as evolutionary throwbacks to lower forms of life. Toward the end of his career he acknowledged the social roots of criminality, but his early assertion that some people were literally born criminals was extremely popular, especially among powerful people who were not inclined to face up to flaws in society that might be responsible for criminal deviance (Jones, 1986).

But Lombroso failed to recognize that his "criminal" physical traits also existed in the population as a whole. Several decades later the British psychiatrist Charles Buckman Goring (1870–1919) probed the matter more carefully, comparing thousands of convicts and noncriminals. He found great physical variation within both groups, but no overall physical differences, distinguishing criminals from noncriminals, of the kind suggested by Lombroso (1972; orig. 1913).

Although Lombroso's work had been discredited, others continued to search for biological explanations of criminality. William Sheldon (1949) suggested that a person's build plays a role in criminality. He described three general types of body structure: *ectomorphs*, who are tall, thin, and fragile; *endomorphs*, who are short and fat; and *mesomorphs*, people both muscular and athletic. After analyzing the body structure and criminal history of hundreds of young men, Sheldon reported a correlation between criminality and the mesomorphic body type. Criminality, according to Sheldon, was linked to a muscular, athletic build.

Sheldon and Eleanor Glueck (1950) agreed. The Gluecks cautioned, however, that mesomorphic body structure is not necessarily a *cause* of criminality. Mesomorphic males, they suggested, are somewhat more likely to be raised with little affection and understanding from family members and consequently show less sensitivity toward others and tend to react aggressively to frustration. Young men with muscular builds also have the physical capacity to become the "bullies on the block" (Gibbons, 1981). If we expect muscular and athletic boys to be more physically aggressive than others, people may treat them accordingly, thereby provoking aggressive behavior in a self-fulfilling prophecy.

More recently, increasing knowledge of genetics has fueled interest in biological causes of criminality. To date, research suggests that no simple genetic flaw causes criminality (Hook, 1973; Vold & Bernard, 1986; Suzuki & Knudtson, 1989). More likely, the researchers conclude, overall genetic composition in combination with social influences explains some variation in criminality (Rowe, 1983; Rowe & Osgood, 1984; Wilson & Herrnstein, 1985; Jencks, 1987). Sociobiologists (see Chapter 2, "Culture") claim that biological factors partly account for why males engage in more violence than females do and why family violence targets disabled or foster children more than healthy or natural children (Daly & Wilson, 1988). Clearly, however, whatever biological forces may be at work are enhanced or inhibited by the social environment.

Critical evaluation.   Biological theories try to explain crime in terms of people's physical traits. Early biological research focused on rare and abnormal cases, which under any circumstances could explain only a small share of crimes. More recent sociobiological research suggests that biology plays some part in criminality but, as yet, we know too little about genetics and human behavior to support causal connections.

In any case, an individualistic biological approach cannot explain how some kinds of behavior come to be defined as deviant in the first place. Therefore, although there is much to be learned about how human biology may affect behavior, research currently places far greater emphasis on social influences on human behavior (Gibbons & Krohn, 1986; Liska, 1991).

Personality Factors

Like biological theories, psychological explanations of deviance spotlight the individual, focusing on abnormalities in the personality. Though some anomalies are hereditary, psychologists think that most result from socialization. Since personality is shaped by social experience, psychologists argue that deviance stems from "unsuccessful" socialization.

Walter Reckless and Simon Dinitz (1967) linked juvenile delinquency to the personality traits of young boys. These researchers claimed that delinquent urges can be contained by boys who have developed strong moral standards and a positive self-image. Reckless and Dinitz called their idea *containment theory.*

The researchers began by interviewing boys about twelve years of age, some of whom teachers thought were likely to engage in delinquent acts and some who were tapped as less prone to delinquency. The "good boys" seemed to share a strong conscience (or superego, in Sigmund Freud's terminology), generally coped well with frustration, and identified positively with cultural norms and values. The "bad boys" had a weaker conscience, tolerated less frustration, and identified less strongly with conventional culture. Over a four-year period, the researchers found, the "good boys" experienced fewer contacts with the police than the "bad boys." All the boys studied were from areas where delinquency was widespread, so the researchers concluded that boys who managed to stay out of trouble had personalities that worked like an "internal buffer" to resist norm violation (Reckless, 1970:401).

Critical evaluation.   Psychological research has linked deviance to distinctive personality patterns. However, because the vast majority of serious crimes are committed by people who are psychologically normal, we must question the value of this approach. Also, in global perspective, the personality traits people deem "normal" or "abnormal" vary from society to society. Finally, psychological research sheds little light on why, among people who behave in the same manner, some are defined as deviant while others are not.

Both biological and psychological approaches fall short in thinking of deviance as an individual attribute. Researchers with these orientations fail to explore how people construct conceptions of right and wrong or to investigate the deviant person's standing in society. We now address these issues as we turn to the social foundations of deviant behavior.

The Social Foundations of Deviance

Although we tend to view deviance in terms of the free choice or personal failings of individuals, all behavior—deviance as well as conformity—is guided by society. There are three *social* foundations of deviance.

1. **Deviance exists only in relation to cultural norms.** No thought or action is inherently deviant; it becomes so only when judged against particular norms. In the traditional village communities of Sicily, for example, norms demand the use of violence to avenge an insult to family honor (Wolfgang & Ferracuti, 1982). In that culture, peacefully ignoring an insult is defined as deviant. In the United States, legal norms forbid the use of violence in this way. What is viewed as honorable in one place, then, may result in arrest and prosecution in another.

As norms change, so does deviance. A century ago, when the lives of most women in the United States were linked to the home, the "career woman" was widely considered unfeminine and odd. Today, however, most women work outside the home and receive widespread support for that choice.

2. **People become deviant as others define them that way.** Each of us violates cultural norms, perhaps even to the extent of breaking the law. For example, most of us have at some time walked around talking to ourselves or "borrowed" supplies, such as pens or paper, from the workplace. Whether such actions are sufficient to define us as mentally ill or criminal depends on how others perceive, define, and respond to any given situation.

3. **Both norms and the way people define situations involve social power.** As explained later in this chapter, Karl Marx viewed norms, and especially law, to be a strategy used by powerful people to protect their interests. For example, the owners of an unprofitable factory have a legal right to close their business, even if doing so puts thousands of people out of work. If workers commit an act of vandalism that closes the same factory for even

On May 4, 1970, Ohio National Guard troops trained their weapons on students who had gathered for an antiwar demonstration at Kent State University. A minute of gunfire left four students dead and nine wounded. Widespread opinion held that the shootings were justified, although regrettable, as a firm response to the disruptive campus protests that were taking place at the time. No criminal prosecution of any soldier occurred in the wake of this tragic event.

a single day, however, they are subject to criminal prosecution. Similarly, a homeless person who stands on a street corner denouncing the government risks arrest for disturbing the peace; a presidential candidate during an election campaign does the same thing while receiving extensive police protection. In short, norms and their application are linked to social inequality.

THE FUNCTIONS OF DEVIANCE: STRUCTURAL-FUNCTIONAL ANALYSIS

The key insight of the structural-functional paradigm is that deviance is a necessary element of every social system. In a pioneering study of deviance, Emile Durkheim (1964a, orig. 1895; 1964b, orig. 1893) asserted that there is nothing abnormal about deviance, since it performs four essential functions.

1. **Deviance affirms cultural values and norms.** Culture turns on moral choices as people define some attitudes and behavior as preferable to others. Conceptions of "right" can exist only in relation to corresponding conceptions of "wrong." For example, what is honorable stands alongside what is evil just as every law defines a crime. In short, deviance is inevitably linked to the process of sustaining cultural values.
2. **Responding to deviance clarifies moral boundaries.** In defining people as deviant, members of a society set the boundary between right and wrong. For example, a college marks the line between academic honesty and cheating by invoking disciplinary procedures to condemn plagiarism.
3. **Responding to deviance promotes social unity.** People typically react to serious deviance with collective outrage. In doing so, Durkheim explained, we reaffirm the moral ties that bind us. For example, many people in the United States joined in a surge of patriotism as we condemned the 1990 invasion of Kuwait by Iraq.
4. **Deviance encourages social change.** Deviant people, claimed Durkheim, patrol a society's moral boundaries, suggesting alternatives to the status quo and encouraging change. Today's deviance, he

noted, may well become tomorrow's morality (1964a:71).

For all these reasons, Durkheim concluded, deviance is a vital dimension of social organization. From the structural-functional perspective, in sum, there is nothing abnormal about deviance.

Merton's Strain Theory

While some deviance is inevitable in all societies, Robert Merton (1938, 1968) argues that excessive deviance results from particular social arrangements. Merton's theory is concerned with our society's *goals* (such as financial success) and the *means* (including education and hard work) available to achieve them. The essence of conformity, from this point of view, is pursuing conventional goals by approved means.

But not everyone who desires conventional success has the opportunity to achieve it. Young people raised in poor inner-city neighborhoods, for example, may see little hope of becoming successful if they "play by the rules." As a result, they may seek wealth through one or another kind of crime—say, by dealing cocaine. Merton called this type of deviance *innovation*—the attempt to achieve a culturally approved goal (wealth) using unconventional means (drug sales). Table 6–1 shows that innovation involves accepting the goal of success while rejecting the conventional means of becoming rich.

Table 6–1 MERTON'S STRAIN THEORY OF DEVIANCE

Individual Responses to Dominant Cultural Patterns	Cultural Goals	Cultural Means
Nondeviant Response		
Conformity	Accept	Accept
Deviant Responses		
Innovation	Accept	Reject
Ritualism	Reject	Accept
Retreatism	Reject	Reject
Rebellion	Reject current goals but promote new ones	Reject current means but promote new ones

SOURCE: Based on Robert K. Merton, *Social Theory and Social Structure* (New York: Free Press, 1968), pp. 230–46.

This kind of deviance, explains Merton, results from "strain" between our society's pronounced emphasis on material success and the limited opportunity it provides to become successful. The poor, especially, may respond to this dilemma by engaging in what is conventionally defined as theft, selling illegal drugs, or some other kind of crime.

The inability to become successful by normative means may also prompt another type of deviance that Merton calls *ritualism* (see Table 6–1). Ritualists resolve the strain of being unable to realize cultural goals by abandoning them in favor of almost compulsive efforts to be "respectable." In essence, they embrace the rules to the point that they lose sight of meaningful goals in life. Lower-level bureaucrats, Merton suggests, often succumb to ritualism as a way of gaining respectability despite their limited achievements. In Merton's view, such deviance stems from giving up the pursuit of success; however, ritualists may gain the reputation of being "good citizens" because they rigidly adhere to the rules.

A third type of deviance in our society is *retreatism*—a failure to succeed that results from rejecting both the goals and the means of success. Retreatists are society's dropouts. They include some alcoholics and drug addicts, and some of the street people found in most U.S. cities. The deviance of retreatists lies in unconventional living and, perhaps more seriously, accepting this situation.

The fourth response to failure is *rebellion*. Like retreatists, rebels reject both the cultural definition of success and the normative means of achieving it. Rebels, however, go further by advocating radical alternatives to the existing social order. Whether they express their unconventional vision in political or religious language, rebels withdraw from society forming a counterculture that is widely viewed as deviant.

Deviant Subcultures

Richard Cloward and Lloyd Ohlin (1966) extended Merton's theory in their investigation of delinquent youth. They maintain that criminal deviance results not simply from limits to legitimate opportunity for success but also from readily accessible illegitimate alternatives. In other words, they explain deviance and conformity in terms of the *relative opportunity structure* young people face in their lives.

The life of Al Capone, a notorious gangster of the Prohibition era (which ran from 1920 to 1933), illus-

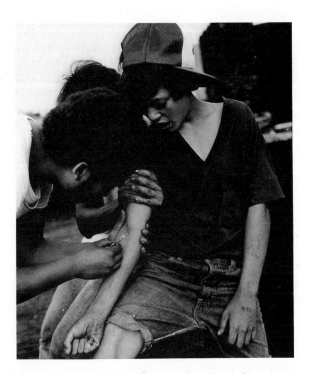

No social class stands apart from others as being by nature either criminal or free from criminality. According to various sociologists, however, people with less stake in society and less optimism about their own future typically exhibit less resistance to some kinds of deviance. Photographer Stephen Shames captured this scene in the Bronx, New York, in 1983.

trates this concept. As a poor immigrant, Capone was denied legitimate paths to success, such as a college education. Yet his world did provide illegitimate opportunity for success as a bootlegger. Where relative opportunity favors what Merton might call "organized innovation," Cloward and Ohlin predict the development of *criminal subcultures*. These subcultures confer knowledge, skills, and other resources people need to succeed in unconventional ways.

But in poor and transient neighborhoods, where chances for success by any means are slim, delinquency is likely to surface in the form of *conflict subcultures* where violence explodes as an expression of frustration and a claim to prestige. Alternatively, among those who fail to achieve success, even using criminal means, *retreatist subcultures* may arise. Consistent with Merton's analysis, such subcultures comprise dropouts who may use alcohol or other drugs.

Albert Cohen (1971) suggests that criminality is most pronounced among lower-class youths because society offers them little opportunity to achieve success in conventional ways. Without legitimate avenues to wealth and all its trappings, these young people struggle for self-respect by forging a deviant subculture that defines them in more positive ways. These subcultures, Cohen says, "define as meritorious the characteristics [these youths] *do* possess, the kinds of conduct of which they *are* capable" (1971:66). In contrast to the dominant cultural value of being rich and well educated, a deviant subculture may extol being reckless and tough. In short, members of a deviant subculture publicly flout conventional norms while carefully conforming to their own standards.

Walter Miller (1970) adds that deviant subcultures are likely to have six focal concerns: (1) *toughness*, the value placed on physical size, strength, and athletic skills, especially among males; (2) *trouble*, arising from frequent conflict with teachers and police; (3) *smartness*, the ability to succeed on the streets, to out-think or "con" others, and to avoid being similarly taken advantage of; (4) *excitement*, the search for thrills, risk, or danger as a release from a daily routine that is predictable and unsatisfying; (5) *fate*, a sense that people lack control over their own lives; and (6) *autonomy*, a desire for freedom expressed as resentment toward figures of authority.

Hirschi's Control Theory

A final argument that builds on Durkheim's analysis of deviance is Travis Hirschi's (1969) *control theory*. Hirschi assumes that everyone finds deviance tempting. What requires explanation, then, is not deviance, but *conformity*. He suggests that conformity arises from four types of social controls.

1. **Attachment.** Strong attachments to family, peer group, and school encourage conformity; weak relationships to others put people more at risk of deviance.
2. **Commitment.** The higher one's commitment to legitimate opportunity, the greater the advantages of conformity. A young person who seems bound for college, with good career prospects, has a high stake in conformity. By contrast, someone with little confidence in future success has a low investment in conformity and is more likely to follow a deviant path.
3. **Involvement.** Extensive involvement in legitimate activities such as holding a job, going to school, or playing sports inhibits deviance. People with little legitimate involvement—who simply "hang out" waiting for something to happen—have time and energy for deviant activity.
4. **Belief.** Strong beliefs in conventional morality and respect for authority figures also restrain tendencies toward deviance; people with weak beliefs are more vulnerable to whatever temptation deviance presents.

Hirschi's analysis explains many kinds of deviant behavior, and it has gained support from subsequent research (Wiatrowski, Griswold, & Roberts, 1981; Sampson & Laub, 1990). Here, again, a person's social standing is crucial in generating a stake in conformity or allowing everyday temptations to cross the line into deviance.

Critical evaluation. Durkheim's pioneering work in the functions of deviance remains central to sociological thinking. Even so, recent critics point out that a community does not always come together in reaction to crime; sometimes people living in high-crime neighborhoods have a chilling fear of engaging their neighbors (Liska & Warner, 1991).

Various theories derived from Durkheim's analysis—especially Merton's strain theory—have enjoyed widespread support. But Merton's theory has also been criticized for explaining some kinds of deviance (theft, for example) better than others (such as crimes of passion or mental illness). In addition, Merton provides only a few clues as to why an individual would choose one response to strain over another. Finally, not everyone seeks success in conventional terms of wealth. As explained in Chapter 2 ("Culture"), members of our society embrace many different cultural values and are motivated by various notions of personal success.

The general argument of Cloward and Ohlin, Cohen, Miller, and Hirschi—that deviance reflects the opportunity structure of society—has been confirmed by subsequent research (cf. Allan & Steffensmeier, 1989). However, these theories, too, fall short in assuming that everyone shares the same cultural standards for judging right and wrong. Moreover, we must be careful not to define deviance in terms that unfairly focus attention on poor people. If crime is defined to include stock fraud as well as street theft, criminals are more likely to include affluent individuals. Finally, all structural-functional theories imply that everyone who breaks the rules will be defined as deviant. Becoming deviant, however, is actually a highly complex process, as the next section explains.

THE LABEL OF DEVIANCE: THE SYMBOLIC-INTERACTION APPROACH

The symbolic-interaction paradigm directs attention to how people construct reality in countless situations. Applied to deviance, this theoretical paradigm reveals that definitions of deviance and conformity are surprisingly flexible.

The central contribution of symbolic-interaction analysis is **labeling theory**, *the assertion that deviance and conformity arise in the response of others*. While common sense suggests that deviance lies in what someone does, in other words, this approach grounds deviance in how others react. Because reactions vary according to a host of factors, labeling theory stresses the relativity of deviance, pointing out that people may define the same behavior in any number of ways. Howard S. Becker therefore claims that deviance is nothing more than "behavior that people so label" (1966:9).

Consider these situations: a woman takes an article of clothing from a roommate; a married man at a convention in a distant city sleeps with a female prostitute; a member of Congress drives home intoxicated after a party. The first situation could be defined as carelessness, borrowing, or theft. The consequences of the second situation depend largely on whether the news of his behavior follows the man back home. In the third situation, is the official an active socialite or a dangerous drunk? The social construction of reality, then, is a highly variable process of detection, definition, and response.

People sometimes contend with deviant labels because of events beyond their control. For example, victims of violent rape may be labeled deviant because of the misguided assumption that they encouraged the offender. Similarly, people with serious diseases may be branded as deviant by those who cannot cope with their illness. Individuals with acquired immune deficiency syndrome (AIDS), for instance, are sometimes shunned by employers, friends, and even family members.

Edwin Lemert (1951, 1972) explains that many episodes of norm violation are insignificant and transitory, provoking little reaction from others and with little effect on a person's self-concept. Lemert calls such passing episodes *primary deviance*. If other people do take notice of someone's deviance, however, that person may engage in further deviance as a coping strategy. Such *secondary deviance* may take the form of defending deviant actions, lying about them, or getting used to them. Thus, secondary deviance, which can have far greater consequences for social identity and self-definition, is set in motion by people's reaction to some norm violation. Initial labeling, then, can encourage individuals to develop deviant identities, thereby fulfilling the expectations of others. The box on page 128 shows how a young woman, initially labeled as deviant for being overweight, gradually became engulfed in a complex deviant identity.

Stigma

Emerging secondary deviance marks the start of what Erving Goffman (1963) called a *deviant career*. Typically, this involves acquiring a **stigma**, *a powerfully negative label that radically changes a person's social identity and self-concept*. Stigma operates as a master status (see Chapter 4, "Social Interaction in Everyday Life"), overpowering other dimensions of social identity so that a whole, complex person is reduced in the minds of an audience to a discredited deviant.

Stigma sometimes affects entire categories of people. These include not only lawbreakers but people of certain races and social classes, as well as people with physical disabilities or those who lead unconventional lives in some other respect.

Attaching stigma may involve a formal process Harold Garfinkel (1956) terms a *degradation ceremony*. A criminal prosecution, for example, has many of the characteristics of a high-school graduation, except that people stand before others to be formally labeled in a negative rather than positive way.

Stigma can also be deepened as a person is subject to **retrospective labeling**, *the interpretation of someone's past consistent with present deviance* (Scheff, 1984). For example, after discovering that a man who has taught at a boys' school for years has sexually molested a child, others rethink his past, perhaps musing, "He always did want to be around young boys." Retrospective labeling involves a highly selective view of a person's past, guided more by the present stigma than by any attempt to be fair. But this process may nonetheless deepen a deviant identity.

Being Overweight: A Study in Deviant Labeling

Joan, a sociologist, begins her story by explaining that she was born to two overweight parents. Probably through no fault of her own, she became heavy as a child. Yet she was unaware of being overweight—or of what it meant to others—until she began school.

> In the first grade, it was painfully pointed out to me—for the first time in my life—that I was different from other children. Other children's taunts of "fatty" and "pig" first brought shock, pain, tears, and later, guilt. I remember being afraid of the other children to the point of not wanting to walk home alone, and my mother frequently walked the one block from my home to the school to get me.
>
> The teasing, however, did not cause me to stop eating, for I still did not realize the connection between eating and being overweight. Instead, I started to develop . . . coping and protective devices which became quite elaborate later.

Ironically, Joan's "coping devices" deepened her deviant identity. She learned, for example, to avoid the embarrassment of engaging in sports (no one wanted her as a teammate) by pretending to be sick. Gradually, her deviant identity expanded:

> I also learned that by being "sick" I could avoid facing other people. . . . While in the third grade, I was in the school nurse's office almost every day with a wide range of ailments.

Another coping mechanism was lying. When her mother asked how much she weighed, Joan answered according to what she thought her mother would believe rather than revealing her actual weight. She knew her parents disliked lying, but she preferred to think of herself as a liar than as fat. Yet, this self-protection backfired:

> Like all good things, my deception came to an end when it was discovered during a visit to the doctor for a physical. Right up to the point of stepping on the scale . . . I had my mother convinced I weighed almost fifteen pounds less. The anxiety caused by the lying was terrible, but it was nothing compared with the way I felt when they found out. I cried hysterically. . . . The doctor suggested that my parents send me to a psychiatrist if I couldn't diet, which they did not do. This recommendation shocked me, and I entered high school with a much different picture of myself. At last I knew I was deviant; I accepted the fact, and I began to act accordingly.

In high school Joan deepened her deviant role, shunned and dateless. Unable to lose weight, she came to accept a negative self-image. Being heavy was no longer the problem; she saw *herself* as an outcast undeserving of friends. Entering college, Joan sought out others similarly labeled as deviant—her roommate was a woman who was partly blind and who was known to have undergone extensive psychiatric treatment; another friend was physically disabled. These were unhappy years.

> I think my college depression can best be summarized by the way I felt when both my roommate and my paraplegic friend had dates on Friday night and I didn't. The only outlet I found that night for the anger I felt was the candy vending machine in the basement of the dormitory. How ironic that I should perpetuate the very thing that was helping to keep me home by eating candy.

There is no happy ending to Joan's story. She has now lost a great deal of weight and gained considerable understanding of her past. Yet she finds that her deviance has become so incorporated into her self-concept that her life simply hasn't changed:

> I now weigh 129 pounds and plan to lose at least another 10 pounds. The loss in weight, however, has not been accompanied by any increase in dates or change of mental attitude, and I fear that it is really my internal makeup that is deviant. I still feel fat, and no matter how many times my friends or parents tell me how nice I look, I don't believe them. . . . I do not know how to get dates, let alone what type of behavior is expected on a date.
>
> If I sound bitter, it's because I am tired of having to do all the changing. I don't like the fact that I have allowed my life to be regulated by the opinions and expectations of other people. . . . If nothing else, I hope I have shown to what extent being obese, and others' reactions to obesity, as well as the various rationalizations one entertains under these circumstances, can influence and even create a lifestyle.

SOURCE: Adapted from Anonymous, in Jacobs (1974:69–72).

The long-term effects of being stigmatized can be considerable. Even after losing weight, for instance, Joan still thought of herself as unattractive. Yet Joan also expresses determination to resist the negative judgments of others. Many people with physical disabilities, gay people, and members of racial minorities have countered stigma by recognizing and emphasizing their positive personal qualities.

Labeling and Mental Illness

Labeling theory is especially applicable to mental illness since a person's mental condition is difficult to define. Psychiatrists often assume that mental disorders have a concrete reality similar to diseases of the body. There is truth to this, insofar as heredity, diet, stress, and chemical imbalances in the body do account, in part, for mental disturbances. However, what we call "mental illness" is also a matter of social definitions sometimes made with the intention of enforcing conformity to conventional standards (Thoits, 1985).

Is a woman who believes that Jesus rides the bus to work with her every day seriously deluded or merely expressing her religious faith in a highly graphic way? If a man refuses to bathe, much to the dismay of his family, is he insane or simply choosing an unconventional way to live? Is a homeless woman who refuses to allow police to take her to a city shelter on a cold night mentally ill or simply trying to live independently?

Psychiatrist Thomas Szasz charges that the label of insanity is widely applied to what is actually only "difference"; therefore, he claims, the notion of mental illness should be abandoned (1961, 1970; Vatz & Weinberg, 1983). Illness, Szasz argues, afflicts only the body, making mental illness a myth. Being "different" in thought or action may irritate others, but it is no grounds on which to define someone as sick. To do so, Szasz claims, simply enforces conformity to the standards of people powerful enough to get their way.

Szasz's views have provoked controversy; many of his colleagues reject the notion that all mental illness is a fiction. Others have hailed his work, however, for pointing out the danger of abusing medical practice in the interest of promoting conformity. Most of us, after all, have experienced periods of extreme stress or other mental disability at some time in our lives. Such episodes, although upsetting, are usually of passing importance. If, however, they form the basis of a social stigma, they

The world is full of people who are unusual in one way or another. This man spends his days driving the streets of New York with a religious message. Should we define his opinions, and his unconventional way of expressing them, as simple eccentricity or are they evidence of mental illness?

may lead to further deviance as a self-fulfilling prophecy (Scheff, 1984).

The Medicalization of Deviance

Labeling theory has prompted a historical shift in the way we understand deviance. Over the last fifty years, the growing influence of medicine—especially psychiatry—in the United States has encouraged the **medicalization of deviance,** *the transformation of moral and legal issues into medical matters.* In essence, this amounts to changing labels. In moral terms, we define people and their actions as "bad" or "good." However, the scientific objectivity of medicine replaces moral judgments with a clinical diagnosis of being "sick" or "well."

Changing views on alcoholism illustrate this process. Until the middle of this century, an alcoholic was viewed widely as morally deficient, a "drunk" too weak to act responsibly. Gradually, however, specialists redefined alcoholism as a medical problem. Now it is generally viewed as a disease, affecting people who are "sick" rather than "bad." Similarly, obesity, drug addiction, child abuse, adultery, and even stealing—each of which used to be a moral issue—are today defined by some people as illnesses for which "victims" need help rather than punishment.

Whether deviance is defined as a moral or medical issue has a number of profound consequences. First, consider *who responds* to deviance. An offense against common morality typically provokes a reaction from members of the community or the police. Applying medical labels, however, transfers the situation to the control of clinical specialists, including counselors, psychiatrists, and physicians. Second, we must address *how people respond* to deviance. A moral approach defines the deviant as an "offender" subject to punishment; medically, however, "patients" cry out for treatment. Therefore, while punishment is designed to fit the crime, treatment is tailored to the patient and may involve virtually any therapy that might prevent future deviance (von Hirsh, 1986.) Third, and most important, we must look at *the personal competence of the person labeled as deviant.* Morally, people may do wrong but they understand their actions and must face the consequences. Medically, sick people are defined as personally incompetent and unaware of what is in their own best interest. Thus, they become vulnerable to involuntary treatment. For this reason alone, attempts to define deviance in medical terms should be made with extreme caution.

Differential Association Theory

Related to the issue of how we define others' behavior is the question of how we learn to understand our own. Edwin Sutherland (1940) suggested that all behavior, including deviance, is learned through association with others, especially in primary groups. At some point, people are exposed to forces promoting criminality as well as those supporting conformity. The likelihood that a person will engage in criminal activity, then, depends on the frequency of association with those who support norm violation compared with those who endorse conformity. This is Sutherland's theory of *differential association.*

Critical evaluation. Labeling theory links deviance not to *action* but to the *reaction* of others. Thus an audience labels some people as deviant while choosing to ignore the same behavior in others. The concepts of stigma, secondary deviance, and deviant career imply that the label of deviance can be incorporated into a lasting self-concept.

Yet labeling theory has several limitations. First, because this theory takes a highly relative view of deviance, it glosses over the fact that some kinds of behavior,

like murder, are condemned virtually everywhere (Wellford, 1980). Labeling theory is thus most usefully applied to less serious deviance, such as certain kinds of sexual behavior and mental illness. Second, the consequences of deviant labeling are unclear: research is inconclusive as to whether deviant labeling encourages subsequent deviance or discourages further violations (Smith & Gartin, 1989). Third, not everyone resists the label of deviance; some people actually may want to be defined as deviant (Vold & Bernard, 1986). For example, individuals may engage in civil disobedience leading to arrest to call attention to social injustice. Fourth, we have much to learn about how people respond to those labeled as deviant. One study found that the stigma of being a former mental patient typically resulted in social rejection only in cases in which an individual was considered dangerous (Link et al., 1987).

Sutherland's differential association theory has had considerable influence in sociology, but provides little insight into why society's norms and laws define certain kinds of activities as deviant in the first place. This important question is addressed by social-conflict analysis, described in the next section.

DEVIANCE AND INEQUALITY: SOCIAL-CONFLICT ANALYSIS

The social-conflict paradigm links deviance to social inequality. This approach suggests that *who* and *what* is labeled as deviant are based largely on relative power.

Alexander Liazos (1972) points out that deviance brings to mind "nuts, sluts, and 'preverts' " who share the trait of powerlessness. Bag ladies (not tax evaders) and unemployed men on street corners (not those who profit from wars) carry the negative stigma of difference. Similarly, the peer groups of poor youths are dangerous "street gangs," while those of affluent young people are fashionable "cliques."

Social-conflict theory explains this pattern in three ways. First, the norms—including laws—of any society generally reflect the interests of the rich and powerful. People who threaten the wealthy, either by taking their property or by advocating a more egalitarian society, may find themselves defined as "thieves" or "political radicals." Karl Marx, one major architect of this approach, argued that all social institutions by and large support the capitalist economic system and protect the

Artist Frank Romero (1941–   ) painted *The Closing of Whittier Boulevard* based on a recollection of his youth in East Los Angeles. To many young Hispanics, identified here by their distinctive "low-rider" cars, police represent a hostile Anglo culture likely to use heavy-handed tactics to discourage them from venturing out of their neighborhood.

Frank Romero. The Closing of Whittier Boulevard, 1984. Oil on canvas. 72 x 120 inches. Collection of Peter Schindler.

interests of the rich, capitalist class. Richard Quinney makes the point succinctly: "Capitalist justice is by the capitalist class, for the capitalist class, and against the working class" (1977:3).

Second, even if their behavior is called into question, the powerful have the resources to resist deviant labels. Corporate executives who might order or condone the dumping of hazardous wastes are rarely held personally accountable for these acts. While such mischief poses dangers for all of society, it is rarely defined as an individual's criminal act.

Third, the widespread belief that the law is right and good obscures the political character of our legal system. For this reason, we may condemn the *unequal application* of the law but give little thought to whether the *laws themselves* are inherently unfair (Quinney, 1977).

Deviance and Capitalism

Steven Spitzer (1980) argues that deviant labels are applied to people who impede the operation of capitalism. First, because capitalism is based on private control of property, people who threaten the property of others—especially the poor who steal from the rich—are prime candidates for labeling as deviants. Conversely, the rich who exploit the poor are unlikely to be defined as deviant. Landlords, for example, who charge poor tenants high

rents and legally evict those who cannot pay are not considered a threat to society; they are simply "doing business."

Second, because capitalism depends on productive labor, those who cannot or will not work risk deviant labeling. Many members of our society think of people who are out of work—even if through no fault of their own—as deviant.

Third, capitalism depends on respect for figures of authority, so people who resist authority are generally labeled as deviant. Examples are children who skip school or talk back to parents and teachers, adults who do not cooperate with employers or police, and anyone who opposes "the system."

Fourth, capitalism rests on the widespread acceptance of the status quo; those who undermine or challenge the capitalist system are subject to deviant labeling. In this category fall antiwar activists, environmentalists, labor organizers, and anyone who endorses an alternative economic system.

To turn the argument around, people label positively whatever enhances the operation of capitalism. Winning athletes, for example, have celebrity status because they express the values of individual achievement and competition vital to capitalism. Additionally, Spitzer notes, we define using drugs of escape (marijuana, psychedelics, heroin, and crack) as deviant, while embracing drugs that promote adjustment to the status quo (such as alcohol and caffeine).

People who are a "costly yet relatively harmless burden" on society, says Spitzer, include Robert Merton's retreatists (for example, those addicted to alcohol or other drugs) and the elderly, and people with physical disabilities, mental retardation, and mental illness. These people are subject to control by social welfare agencies. But those who directly threaten the capitalist system, including the inner-city "underclass" and revolutionaries—Merton's innovators and rebels—come under the purview of the criminal justice system and, in times of crisis, military forces such as the National Guard.

Note that both systems apply labels that place responsibility for social problems on the people themselves. Welfare recipients are deemed unworthy freeloaders; poor people who vent their rage at their plight are labeled as rioters; anyone who actively challenges the government is branded a radical or a communist; and those who attempt to gain illegally what they cannot otherwise acquire are called common thieves.

White-Collar Crime

Until 1989, few people other than Wall Street stockbrokers had ever heard of Michael Milken. Yet Milken had accomplished a stunning feat, becoming the highest paid U.S. worker in half a century. In a single year, his salary and bonuses totaled $550 million—*about $1.5 million a day*—placing Milken behind only Al Capone, whose 1927 earnings topped $600 million in current dollars (Swartz, 1989). Milken had something else in common with Capone: the government seized much of his fortune and sent him to jail for violations of securities and exchange laws.

Milken's activities exemplify **white-collar crime**, defined by Edwin Sutherland in 1940 as *crimes committed by people of high social position in the course of their occupations* (Sutherland & Cressey, 1978:44). White-collar crime rarely involves uniformed police converging on a scene with drawn guns and does not include crimes such as murder, assault, or rape that are committed by people of high social position. Instead, this concept refers to crimes committed by powerful people making illegal use of their occupational positions to enrich themselves or others, often causing significant public harm in the process (Hagan & Parker, 1985; Vold & Bernard, 1986). For this reason, sociologists sometimes call white-collar offenses that occur in government offices and corporate board rooms *crime in the suites* compared to *crime in the streets*.

The public harm wreaked by false advertising, marketing of unsafe products, embezzlement, and bribery

Marijuana use is not illegal simply because it is harmful. In fact, smoking tobacco is far more dangerous since it contributes to more than 300,000 premature deaths each year. The legal standing of a drug depends on many factors, including whether it promotes social adjustment or encourages escape and what potential profit it represents for businesses.

of public officials extends far beyond what most people realize. Some researchers contend that white-collar crime causes greater public harm than all street crimes combined (Reiman, 1990). Estimates of the economic costs of business-related crimes range up to several hundred billion dollars a year—an amount far exceeding the economic loss from common theft (Reid, 1982; Reiman, 1984; U.S. Department of Justice, 1987). Similarly, more people in the United States die from work-related injuries and diseases than are murdered by street criminals (Simon & Eitzen, 1990).

Sutherland argued that harmful actions by corporate executives or public officials usually end up in a civil hearing rather than in a criminal courtroom. *Civil law* regulates economic affairs between private parties, while *criminal law* defines every individual's moral responsibility to society. In civil settlements, then, a "loser" pays for damage or injury but no one is labeled a criminal. Further, since corporations have the legal standing of persons, white-collar offenses commonly involve the organization as a whole rather than specific individuals. Today, as at the time of Sutherland's research, elite deviance rarely results in criminal labeling of powerful people.

Although the recent savings and loan scandal ended up costing the U.S. public some $180 billion dollars— $1,000 for every adult in the country—authorities prosecuted only a handful of individuals. In recent years, more rich and powerful lawbreakers have gone to jail for their crimes. But when white-collar criminals face the music, the odds favor lenient sentences. Only about 6 percent of embezzlers convicted in the U.S. District Court system spend a single day in prison; most are placed on probation (U.S. Bureau of Justice Statistics, 1990). White-collar polluters also have reason to scoff at the law: the federal government jailed only ninety people for all federal environmental crimes between 1986 and 1991 (Gold, 1991).

The main reason for such leniency is that, as Sutherland noted years ago, the public displays far less concern about white-collar crime than about street crime. Corporate crime, in effect, victimizes everyone and no one. White-collar criminals do not stick a gun in anyone's ribs, and the economic costs are usually spread throughout the population.

Critical evaluation. According to social-conflict theory, the inequality of wealth and power that pervades capitalist societies guides the creation and application of laws and other norms. This theory also suggests that the criminal justice system and social welfare organizations act as political agents controlling categories of people who threaten the capitalist system.

Like other approaches to deviance, however, social-conflict theory has its critics. First, this approach assumes that laws and other cultural norms benefit only the rich and powerful. But laws also protect workers, consumers, and the environment, sometimes in opposition to the interests of capitalists. A second criticism holds that social-conflict theory's attention to the social injury caused by the powerful does not square with public concern with street crime. Third, this approach implies that criminality arises only to the extent that a society treats its members unequally. According to Durkheim, however, all societies generate deviance and, in societies far more economically equal than our own, criminality exists all the same.

We have presented various sociological explanations for crime and other types of deviance. Table 6–2 summarizes the contributions of each approach.

Table 6–2 SOCIOLOGICAL EXPLANATIONS OF DEVIANCE: A SUMMARY

Theoretical Paradigm	Major Contribution
Structural-functional analysis	While what is deviant may vary, deviance itself is found in all societies; deviance and the social response it provokes serve to maintain the moral foundation of society; deviance can also direct social change
Symbolic-interaction analysis	Nothing is inherently deviant but may become defined as such through the response of others; the reactions of others are highly variable; the label of deviance can lead to the emergence of secondary deviance and deviant careers
Social-conflict analysis	Laws and other norms reflect the interests of powerful members of society; those who threaten the status quo are likely to be defined as deviant; social injury caused by powerful people is less likely to be defined as criminal than social injury caused by people who have little social power

Date Rape: Exposing Dangerous Myths

Completing a day of work during a business trip to the courthouse in Tampa, Florida, thirty-two-year-old Sandra Abbott[1] pondered how she would return to her hotel. An attorney with whom she had been working—a pleasant enough man—made a kind offer of a lift. As his car threaded its way through the late afternoon traffic, their conversation was animated. "He was saying all the right things," Abbott recalled, "so I started to trust him." He wondered if she would join him for dinner; she happily accepted. After lingering over an enjoyable meal, they walked together to the door of her hotel room. The new acquaintance angled for an invitation to come in, but Abbott hesitated. Sensing that he might have more than conversation on his mind, she explained being old-fashioned about relationships. He could come in, she finally agreed, but only for a little while, and with the understanding that talk was *all* they would do.

Sitting on the couch in the room, soon Abbott was overcome with drowsiness. Feeling comfortable in the presence of her new friend, she let her head fall gently onto his shoulder and, before she knew it, she fell

[1]A pseudonym; the facts of this case are from Gibbs (1991a).

asleep. That's when the attack began. Abbott was startled back to consciousness as the man thrust himself upon her sexually. She shouted "No!" but he paid no heed. Abbott describes what happened next:

> I didn't scream or run. All I could think of was my business contacts and what if they saw me run out of my room screaming rape. I thought it was my fault. I felt so filthy, I washed myself over and over in hot water. Did he rape me?, I kept asking myself. I didn't consent. But who's gonna believe me? I had a man in my hotel room after midnight. (Gibbs, 1991a: 50)

Abbott knew that she had said "No!" and thus had been raped. She notified the police, who conducted an investigation and turned their findings over to the state attorney's office. But the authorities backed away from Abbott. In the absence of evidence like bruises, a medical examination, and torn clothes, they responded, there was little point in prosecuting.

The case of Sandra Abbott is all too typical. Even today, in most incidences of sexual attack, a victim makes no report to police, and no offender is arrested. The woman faces the bitter reality of simply trying as

best she can to put a traumatic experience behind her.

The reason for this inaction is that many people have a misguided understanding of rape. Three inaccurate notions about rape are so common in the United States that they might be called "rape myths." A first myth is that rape involves strangers. A sexual attack brings to mind young men who lurk in the shadows and suddenly spring on their unsuspecting victims, much like the gang of young New Yorkers who attacked the Central Park jogger as described at the beginning of Chapter 1 ("Sociology: Perspective, Theory, and Method"). But this pattern is the exception rather than the rule: experts report that only one in five rapes involves strangers. For this reason, people have begun to speak more realistically about *acquaintance rape* or, more simply, *date rape*. A rape is typically committed by a man who is known to, and even trusted by, his victim. But common sense dictates that being a "friend" (or even a husband) does not prevent a man from committing murder, assault, or rape.

A second myth about rape is that women provoke their attackers. Surely, many people think, a woman claiming to have been raped must have done *something* to encourage

Deviance and Gender

Anne Campbell points out that no variable is related to deviance more than gender: her own research, for example, shows that the vast majority of gang members are men. Curiously, however, analysis of crime and

other deviance rarely takes gender into account. Let us now highlight how gender figures in to some of the theories that we have already discussed.

Robert Merton's strain theory, for example, defines cultural goals in terms of financial success. Traditionally, however, this preoccupation with material things has

The 1992 rape conviction of heavyweight boxing champion Mike Tyson—now inmate number 922335 in the Indiana penal system—suggests that our society is taking the problem of sexual violence against women more seriously.

the man, to lead him on, to make him think that she really wanted to have sex. In the case described above, didn't Sandra Abbott agree to have dinner with the man? Didn't she willingly admit him to her room? Such thinking often paralyzes victims, so that women themselves experience self-doubt about their actions after having been raped. But by having dinner with a man—or even inviting

him into her hotel room—she had hardly given consent to have sex with him any more than these actions constitute an invitation to have him beat her with a club.

A third myth is the notion that rape is simply sex. If there is no knife held to a woman's throat, or if she is not bound and gagged, then how can sex be a crime? The answer is simply that *forcing a woman to have sex without her consent is rape*. To accept the idea that rape is sex one would also have to see no difference between brutal combat and playful wrestling. In the absence of consent, as Susan Brownmiller (1975) explains, rape is not sex but violence. Beyond the brutality of being physically violated, date rape also undermines a victim's sense of trust.

The more people believe rape myths, the more women will become victims of sexual violence. The ancient Babylonians stoned married women who fell victim to rape, claiming that the women had committed adultery. To a startling extent, ideas about rape have not changed over thousands of years, which helps to explain why, even today, most rapes go unreported to police and, even when authorities are notified, prosecutions and convictions are rare. At present, perhaps one in twenty

rapes results in an offender being sent to jail.

Nowhere has the issue of date rape been more widely discussed than at colleges and universities. The campus is distinctive in several respects: students have easy access to one another, the collegiate setting encourages trust (and, often, sexuality), and many young people have much to learn about relationships and about themselves. While this open environment promotes communication, it also allows for an alarming level of sexual violence. Studies estimate that one in six college women will be raped before she graduates.

To eliminate sexual violence we must begin by exposing the myths about rape. In addition, the campus must be transformed so that women and men interact with dignity and equality. Serious questions involve the role of alcohol in campus social life, and the effect of traditional cultural patterns that define sex as sport. A crucial step in the right direction is for everyone to understand two simple truths: forcing sex without a woman's consent is rape, and when a woman says "no," she means just that.

SOURCES: Gibbs (1991a, 1991b).

been more a cultural trait of men while women have been socialized to define success in terms of relationships—as good daughters, wives, and mothers (Leonard, 1982).

Labeling theory offers various insights into how gender influences our definitions of deviance. Since the behavior of women and men is judged by different standards, the very process of labeling stems from sex-linked biases. Further, Edwin Schur (1983) explains that because society generally places men in positions of power over women, men often escape direct responsibility for their actions that victimize women. Frequently, men who engage in sexual harassment or more serious assaults against women are tagged with only mildly deviant labels; sometimes, they suffer no adverse consequences and, in some quarters, they may even gain social approval for their actions. By contrast, women who are victimized may have to convince an unsympathetic audience that they are not to blame for what happened. Research confirms that whether people define a situation as deviance—and, if so, whose deviance it is—depends on the sex of both the audience and the actors (King & Clayson, 1988). The box on pages 134–35 takes a closer look at the issue of date rape, in which many women and men are standing up for an end to a double standard that has long threatened the well-being of women.

Ironically, in light of its concern with social inequality, social-conflict analysis has also neglected the importance of gender. If oppression fostered by capitalism is a primary cause of crime, why do women (who generally occupy a lower economic position than their male counterparts) commit far *fewer* crimes than men do? The next section, which examines crime rates in the United States, answers this question.

CRIME

Speak of crime and people immediately conjure up images of unsavory characters ducking into alleyways, waiting to prey on unsuspecting victims. But crime covers a surprisingly wide range of behaviors. In centuries past, a commoner who simply looked at the Chinese emperor in public faced serious charges. Today a citizen of the People's Republic of China who expressed support for the nation's historic royalty would likely face criminal prosecution. The judicial system in the United States has also undergone considerable change, supporting slavery for two centuries, for example, then condemning racial discrimination.

Generally, then, crime is the violation of the criminal law enacted by local, state, or federal government. Technically, all crimes are composed of two distinct elements: the *act* itself (or, in some cases, the failure to do what the law requires) and *criminal intent* (in legal terminology, *mens rea*, or "guilty mind"). Intent is a matter of degree, ranging from a deliberate action to negligence in which an individual behaves (or fails to act) in a manner that the person may reasonably expect to produce harm. The legal system weighs the degree of intent in determining whether, for example,

someone who kills another is guilty of first-degree murder, second-degree murder, or negligent manslaughter (Reid, 1982).

Types of Crime

In the United States, the Federal Bureau of Investigation gathers information on criminal offenses. Two major types of crimes make up the "crime index."

Crimes against the person are *crimes that involve personal violence or the threat of violence.* Such "violent crimes" include murder and nonnegligent manslaughter (legally defined as "the willful killing of one human being by another"), aggravated assault ("an unlawful attack by one person on another for the purpose of inflicting severe or aggravated bodily injury"), forcible rape ("the carnal knowledge of a female forcibly and against her will"), and robbery ("taking or attempting to take anything of value from the care, custody, or control of a person or persons by force or threat of force or violence and/or putting the victim in fear").

Crimes against property are *crimes that involve theft of property belonging to others.* "Property crimes" include burglary ("the unlawful entry of a structure to commit a [serious crime] or a theft"), larceny-theft (the unlawful taking, carrying, leading, or riding away of property from the possession of another"), auto theft ("the theft or attempted theft of a motor vehicle"), and arson ("any willful or malicious burning or attempt to burn the personal property of another").

A third category of offenses, not used in calculating the crime index, is **victimless crime**, *violation of law in which there is no readily apparent victim.* Examples of "crimes without complaint" are illegal drug use, prostitution, and gambling. However, "victimless crime" is often a misnomer. How victimless is a crime when young people purchasing drugs may be embarking on a life of crime to support a drug habit? How victimless is a crime if a young pregnant woman smoking crack causes the death or permanent injury of her baby? How victimless is a crime when a young runaway is lured into prostitution and then brainwashed into thinking that's her only way to live? And how victimless is a crime when a gambler falls so deeply into debt that he cannot make the mortgage payments or afford food for his family? In truth, the people who commit such crimes can themselves be both offenders and victims.

Because public opinion about such activities varies so much, the laws regulating victimless crimes differ

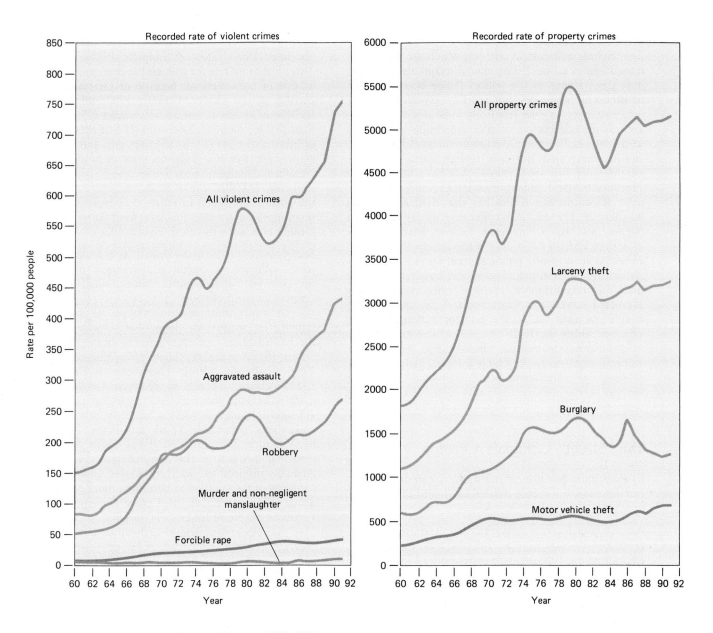

Figure 6–1 Crime Rates in the United States, 1960–1991
(*U.S. Federal Bureau of Investigation, 1992*)

from place to place. In the United States, gambling is legal in Nevada, Atlantic City, New Jersey, and a few other places; prostitution is legal only in part of Nevada; homosexual (and some heterosexual) behavior is legally restricted in about half of the states. Where such laws do exist, enforcement is generally uneven.

Criminal Statistics

Statistics gathered by the Federal Bureau of Investigation show that crime rates increased dramatically during the 1970s, declined during the early 1980s, and rose again after 1984. Figure 6–1 shows this trend.

Crime statistics should be read with caution since they include only certain offenses, which are sometimes tagged "index crimes." The official record also includes only cases known to the police. Police become aware of almost all homicides, but assaults—especially among acquaintances—are far less likely to be reported. Police records include even a smaller proportion of property crime, especially when thefts involve items of little value. Some victims may not even realize that a crime has occurred, or they may assume they have little chance of recovering their property even if they notify the police.

Rape statistics reflect less than half of all such assaults (cf. Harlow, 1991). Because of the traditional stigma attached to innocent victims, many women choose to remain silent after being attacked. However, in recent years greater public support for rape victims—including better training of police and hospital personnel and the establishment of rape crisis centers—has prompted more victims to come forward, contributing to a 25 percent rise in the number of forcible rapes reported during the 1980s.

One way to evaluate official crime statistics is a *victimization survey*, in which a representative sample of people is asked about being victimized. According to these surveys, actual criminality occurs at a rate about three times higher than what official reports indicate.

The "Street" Criminal: A Profile

By examining government statistics, we can draw a general description of people arrested for violent and property crimes.

Age. Official crime rates rise sharply during adolescence and the early twenties, declining thereafter (Hirschi & Gottfredson, 1983; Krisberg & Schwartz, 1983). People between the ages of fifteen and twenty-four represent only 15 percent of our population, but they accounted for 45 percent of all arrests for serious crimes in 1991: 43.1 percent for violent crimes and 45.4 percent for property crimes.

Gender. Official statistics suggest that crime is an activity pursued by males much more than females. Although each sex constitutes roughly half the population, males were 3.5 times more likely than females to be arrested for serious crimes in 1991: 74.6 percent of property crime arrests were of males; 25.4 percent, females. For violent crimes, the disparity was even greater: 88.6 percent males and 11.4 percent females. Research suggests that this

disparity is less pronounced among people of lower social standing (Hagan, Gillis, & Simpson, 1985).

The arrest rate for women has been moving closer to that of men, perhaps because of increasing sexual equality in our society. Between 1982 and 1991, the *increase* in arrests of women was greater (35.9 percent) than that for men (15.2 percent) (U.S. Federal Bureau of Investigation, 1992). In addition, girls and boys show comparable patterns of delinquency in families where females and males are accorded relative equality (Hagan, Simpson, & Gillis, 1987). Research also confirms that the greatest difference in crime rates between the two sexes appears in societies that most limit the social opportunities of women (Blum & Fisher, 1980).

Social class. People in the United States associate criminality with poverty. Sociological research suggests that rich and poor alike commit crimes, albeit somewhat different *kinds* of offenses.

A disproportionate number of people of low social standing are arrested for violent and property crimes in the United States and elsewhere (Wolfgang, Figlio, & Sellin, 1972; Clinard & Abbott, 1973; Elliot & Ageton, 1980; Braithwaite, 1981; Thornberry & Farnsworth, 1982; Wolfgang, Thornberry, & Figlio, 1987). This fact partly reflects the historical tendency to view poor people as unworthy compared to those whose wealth and power make them "respectable" (Tittle & Villemez, 1977; Tittle, Villemez, & Smith, 1978; Elias, 1986). Some contend that this bias in the criminal justice system has gradually diminished, with criminality among various segments of the population becoming more equal. Evidence also suggests that street crime disproportionately *victimizes* people of lower social position.

Although crime plagues many inner-city neighborhoods, only a small proportion of less-advantaged people are ever convicted of crimes because most crimes are committed by relatively few hard-core offenders (Wolfgang, Figlio, & Sellin, 1972; Elliot & Ageton, 1980; Wolfgang, Thornberry, & Figlio, 1987). Additionally, as John Braithwaite (1981) notes, the correlation between social standing and criminality depends on what kind of crime one is talking about. If the focus shifts from street crime to white-collar crime, the "common criminal" is of much higher social position.

Race. Official statistics indicate that 69.0 percent of arrests for index crimes in 1991 involved whites. However, African Americans were arrested more often than whites in proportion to their numbers, representing about 12 percent of the population and 29.0 percent of index

In Saudi Arabia, women may not vote, drive a car, or appear in public without being veiled. Given this rigid regulation, crimes by women are rare. In the United States, women have relatively more freedom about what they do and how they dress. This greater choice is reflected in crime rates that are steadily moving closer to those of men.

crime arrests. Whites comprised 66.4 percent of arrests for property crimes, versus 31.3 percent for blacks; among those arrested for violent crime 53.6 percent were white and 44.8 percent African American (U.S. Federal Bureau of Investigation, 1992).

Just as most people have long considered criminality the province of the poor, they have also associated crime with people of color (and, particularly, young, black males). This despite overwhelming evidence that most crimes are committed by whites.

Clear conclusions about crime and race are difficult to reach for three reasons. First, African Americans are overly criminalized to the extent that prejudice related to class or color prompts police to arrest blacks more readily than whites, and leads citizens more readily to report people of color to police as suspected offenders. The same prejudices may operate in the courtroom. In the long run, even small biases by law enforcement officials and the public distort the official link between race and crime (Liska & Tausig, 1979; Unnever, Frazier, & Henretta, 1980; Smith & Visher, 1981).

Second, race in the United States closely relates to social standing, which, as we have already shown, affects the likelihood of engaging in street crimes. After studying criminal patterns in twelve large U.S. cities, Judith and Peter Blau (1982) concluded that criminality—especially violence—is fueled by income disparity or the sting of poverty in the midst of affluence. Being poor in a rich society, they reasoned, leads people to perceive society as unjust and to disregard its laws. Because unemployment among African-American adults is two to three times higher than among whites, and because *almost half* of black children grow up in poverty (in contrast to about one in six white children), we should expect proportionately higher crime rates for African Americans (Sampson, 1987).

Third, as noted earlier, white-collar crimes are excluded from the official crime index. If our definition of crime were broadened to include insider stock trading, toxic waste dumping, embezzlement, bribery, and cheating on income tax returns, the proportion of white criminals would rise dramatically.

Crime in Global Perspective

By world standards, the United States has a lot of crime. Marshall Clinard (1978) observed that in Switzerland murders are relatively rare even in the largest cities. By contrast, New York City led all U.S. cities with 2,154 murders in 1991. Rarely does a day pass with no murder in New York; typically more New Yorkers are hit by stray bullets than are gunned down deliberately in cities elsewhere in the world.

Although crime rates rose in Europe more than in the United States during the 1980s, crime pervades our society to a much greater extent than it does in European countries. Global comparisons suffer because nations define crimes differently and not every country collects data with care. But comparisons suggest the rate of property crime in the United States is twice that in Europe, the homicide rate is five times higher, and the rape rate is seven times higher. Figure 6–2 graphically illustrates global rates of rape and robbery. Although the patterns differ for each crime, the general conclusion is that the United States contends with more crime than virtually any other country in the world (Kalish, 1988).

Elliott Currie (1985) suggests that crime is one product of our culture's emphasis on individual economic success, frequently at the expense of family and community cohesion. Currie also notes that, unlike some European nations, the United States neither guarantees families a minimum income nor publicly funds child-care programs. Such public policy decisions, in his view, erode the fabric of our society, fuel frustration among society's have-nots, and thus encourage criminal behavior. Furthermore, Currie asserts that the high level of unemployment and underemployment tolerated in the United States (and increasingly in Europe) helps create a category of perpetually poor people whose opportunities to make money are often limited to criminal pursuits. The key to reducing crime, he concludes, lies in *social change*, not in hiring more police and building more prisons.

Another contributing factor to violence in the United States is widespread private ownership of guns. About 60 percent of the 20,000 murder victims annually in the United States are killed by guns. In recent years, high-power, military-type weaponry has prompted police organizations and citizen groups to press for gun control. Public support propelled the passage in 1991 of the so-called Brady Bill, named after James Brady, the presidential press secretary shot along with Ronald Reagan in 1981. No one thinks reining in the gun trade will end crime in the United States. There are already about as many guns in the hands of private individuals as there are people in the United States. Further, Elliott Currie reminds us that the causes of violence go far beyond the availability of guns. He points out that the number of Californians killed each year by knives exceeds the number of Canadians killed annually by weapons of all kinds. Most experts do think, however, that gun control will be a step in the right direction.

We know that rampant poverty and rapid population growth are pushing up crime rates in the largest cities of the world, including São Paulo, Brazil, and that drug wars continue to inflict violence on the people of Colombia. By and large, however, crime rates in less-developed societies are lower than in the United States. These lower rates reflect the traditional character of less-developed societies; there, strong families and cohesive residential areas informally control crime (Clinard & Abbott, 1973; *Der Spiegel*, 1989). By the same token, however, traditional social patterns promote crimes like prostitution by curbing the opportunities available to women. Global Map 6–1 on page 142 shows the extent of prostitution in various world regions.

THE CRIMINAL JUSTICE SYSTEM

Through the criminal justice system, society formally responds to crime. We shall briefly introduce the key elements of this system: police, the courts, and the punishment of convicted offenders.

The Police

The police are usually the point of contact between the public and the criminal justice system. In principle, the police maintain public order by uniformly enforcing the law. In reality, 736,000 full-time police officers

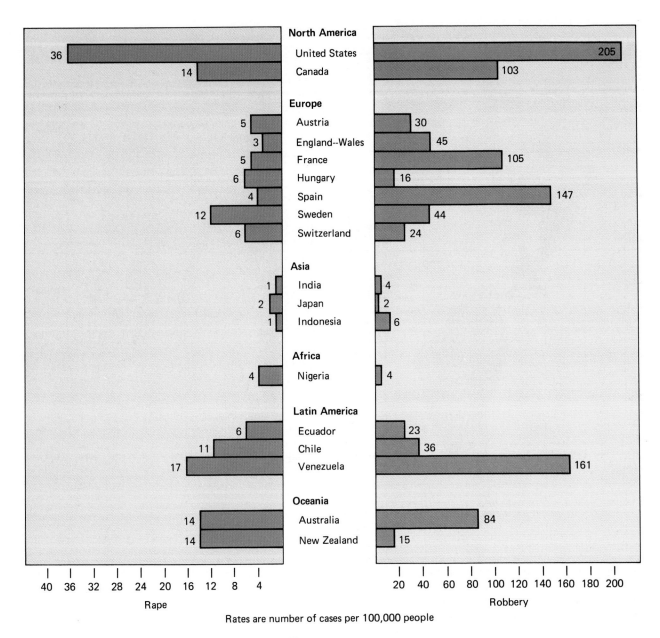

Figure 6–2 Global Comparisons: Rates for Rape and Robbery
(Interpol data, as reported by Kalish, 1988)

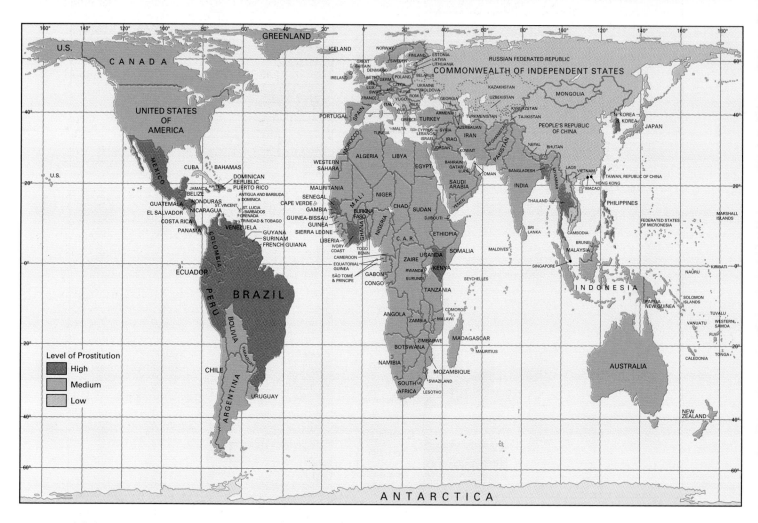

Global Map 6–1   Prostitution in Global Perspective

Roughly speaking, prostitution is widespread in societies of the world where women have low social standing in relation to men. Officially, at least, the now defunct socialist regimes in Eastern Europe and the Soviet Union, as well as the People's Republic of China, boasted of gender equality, including the elimination of "vice" such as prostitution. By contrast, in much of Latin America, a region of pronounced patriarchy, prostitution is commonplace. In many Islamic societies, where patriarchy is also strong, religious forces temper this practice. Western, industrial societies also display a moderate amount of prostitution.

in the United States (in 1991) cannot effectively monitor the activities of 250 million people. As a result, the police exercise considerable discretion about which situations warrant their attention and how to handle them.

Police discretion means, on the one hand, that officers have a good deal of latitude in decision making because of the magnitude of their responsibilities. On the other hand, however, the ability of police to pursue a situation as they see fit also fosters unequal treatment of some categories of people, as suggested by the Rodney King incident in Los Angeles, described at the beginning of this chapter. The challenge of professional police work is using official power to enhance rather than undermine public well-being.

How, then, do police carry out their duties? In a study of police behavior in five cities, Douglas Smith and Christy Visher (1981; Smith, 1987) identified six factors that influence police when confronted with apparent crime. Because they must often act quickly, police rely on external cues to guide their actions. First, the more serious they perceive the situation to be, the more likely they are to make an arrest. Second, police assess the victim's preference as to how the matter should be handled. In general, if a victim demands that police make an arrest, they are likely to do so. Third, police more often arrest suspects who appear uncooperative. Fourth, they are more likely to arrest suspects with whom they have had prior contact, presumably because this suggests guilt. Fifth, the presence of bystanders increases the likelihood of arrest. According to Smith and Visher, this is because police want to appear in control of the situation, and also because an arrest moves the interaction from the street (the suspect's turf) to the police department (where law enforcement officers have the edge). Sixth, all else being equal, police are more likely to arrest people of color than whites. Smith and Visher concluded that police generally consider people of African or Hispanic descent as either more dangerous or more likely to be guilty. In the researchers' view, this perception contributes to the disproportionately high arrest rates among these categories of people.

Finally, the concentration of police relative to population is greatest in cities with high minority populations and those with large income disparities between rich and poor (Jacobs, 1979). This finding squares with Judith and Peter Blau's (1982) conclusion that striking inequality promotes criminal violence. Thus police are concentrated where a volatile mix of social forces encourages disruption.

The Courts

After arrest, a suspect's guilt or innocence is determined by a court. In principle, our courts rely on an adversarial process involving attorneys—one representing the defendant and another the state (or "the people")—and a judge who monitors adherence to legal procedures. In practice, however, about 90 percent of criminal cases are resolved prior to court appearance through **plea bargaining,** *a legal negotiation in which the prosecution reduces a charge in exchange for a defendant's plea of guilty.* For example, a defendant charged with burglary may agree to plead guilty to the lesser charge of possession of burglary tools; another charged with selling cocaine may go along with pleading guilty to mere possession.

Plea bargaining is so widely used because it spares the system the time and expense of a court trial. A trial is usually unnecessary if there is little disagreement as to the facts of the case. By selectively trying only a small proportion of the cases, the courts can also channel their resources into those deemed most important (Reid, 1991).

But in the process, defendants (who are legally presumed innocent) are pressured to plead guilty. A person can demand a trial, of course, but only at the risk of receiving a more severe sentence if found guilty. In essence, then, plea bargaining undercuts the right of defendants as it circumvents the adversarial process. According to Abraham Blumberg (1970), defendants who lack understanding of the criminal justice system, as well as those unable to afford a good lawyer, are likely to suffer from this system of "bargain-counter justice."

Punishment

In 1831 the officials in an English town hanged a nine-year-old boy for the crime of setting fire to a house (Kittrie, 1971:103). The history of the United States records 281 youths executed for crimes committed as juveniles, most recently a young man in Texas for a murder committed when he was seventeen. Some two dozen other juveniles are currently on death row pursuing their legal rights to appeal.

Such cases spark controversy because young people are widely regarded as having diminished capacity for crime. These situations also press us to explain why societies punish in the first place. Four justifications are commonly offered.

Dutch painter Vincent Van Gogh (1853–1890) strongly identified with suffering people that he found around him. Perhaps this is why he placed his own likeness in this portrait of the dungeon-like prisons of the nineteenth century. Since then, the stark isolation and numbing depersonalization of prison life have changed little. Prisons are still custodial institutions in which officials make few efforts at rehabilitation.

Retribution. The most important justification for punishing is **retribution,** *inflicting on an offender suffering comparable to that caused by the offense.* An act of social vengeance, retribution is grounded in a view of society as a system of moral balance. When criminality upsets this balance, punishment restores the moral order, as suggested by the ancient dictum "An eye for an eye."

Retribution is the oldest justification for punishment. During the Middle Ages, crime was widely viewed as sin—an offense against God as well as society—and therefore it warranted harsh punishment. While contemporary critics of retribution sometimes charge that this

policy lacks the force to reform the offender, it still remains a strong justification for punishment.

Deterrence. A second justification for punishment is **deterrence,** *the attempt to discourage criminality through punishment.* Deterrence is based on the Enlightenment notion that humans are calculating and rational creatures. From this point of view, people engage in deviance for personal gain, but they will forego such acts if the pains of punishment outweigh the pleasures of deviance.

Initially, deterrence arose as the banner of reformers seeking to end what they saw as excessive punishments based on retribution. Why put someone to death for stealing, critics reasoned, if the crime can be discouraged by a lesser penalty? As the concept of deterrence gained widespread acceptance, execution and physical mutilation of criminals were gradually replaced by milder forms of punishment such as imprisonment.

Punishment may deter in two ways. *Specific deterrence* demonstrates to the individual offender that crime does not pay. Through *general deterrence,* the punishment of one person serves as an example to others.

Rehabilitation. The third justification for punishment, **rehabilitation,** involves *reforming the offender to preclude subsequent offenses.* Rehabilitation as a justification for punishment paralleled the development of the social sciences in the nineteenth century. Crime, the thinking goes, springs from an unfavorable social environment, perhaps pervaded by poverty or a lack of parental supervision. Thus, just as offenders learn to be deviant, they learn to obey the rules if placed in the right setting. *Reformatories* or *houses of correction* serve as a controlled environment to help offenders learn proper behavior (recall the description of total institutions in Chapter 3, "Socialization: From Infancy to Old Age").

Rehabilitation resembles deterrence by motivating the offender to conform. But rehabilitation emphasizes constructive improvement while deterrence and retribution make the offender suffer. In addition, while retribution demands that the punishment fit the crime, rehabilitation focuses on the distinctive problems of each offender. Thus identical offenses would call for similar acts of retribution but different programs of rehabilitation.

Social protection. A final justification for punishment is **social protection,** or *rendering an offender incapable of further offenses either temporarily through incarceration or permanently by execution.* Like deterrence, social protection is a rational approach to punishment and seeks to protect society from crime.

Table 6–3 summarizes these four justifications for punishment.

Critical evaluation. No society operates without some system to punish deviance. Assessing the actual consequences of punishment, however, is no simple task.

The value of retribution relates to Durkheim's ideas about the functions of deviance, presented earlier in this chapter. Recall that Durkheim believed that responding to deviance is the way people sustain their shared morality. Punishing a person for a moral offense, moreover, unites a society through a common sense of justice. For this reason punishment was traditionally carried out in public. Public executions occurred in England until 1868; the last public execution in the United States took place in Kentucky in 1936. Today the mass media ensure public awareness of executions carried out inside prison walls (Kittrie, 1971). Nonetheless, it is difficult to prove scientifically that punishment upholds social morality. Often it advances one conception of social morality at the expense of another, as when people who object to military service are imprisoned.

Perhaps the most serious question about the effectiveness of our system of criminal justice is raised by this country's high rate of **criminal recidivism,** *subsequent offenses by people previously convicted of crimes.* A recent study of people released from prison found that within three years 63 percent had been rearrested and 41 percent had been returned to prison (U.S. Bureau of Justice Statistics, 1989). Such high recidivism suggests that punishment may not deter crime. Another problem is that only about one-third of all crimes are reported to the police and, of these, only about one in five results in an arrest. The old adage that "crime doesn't pay" rings rather hollow, since only a small proportion of offenses ever result in punishment.

General deterrence is even more difficult to investigate scientifically, since we have no way of knowing how people might act if they were unaware of punishments meted out to others. In the debate over capital punishment, now permitted in thirty-six states, critics point to research suggesting that the death penalty has limited value as a general deterrent. They add that the United States is the only Western industrial society that still executes serious offenders (Sellin, 1980; van den Haag & Conrad, 1983; Archer & Gartner, 1987; Lester, 1987; Bailey & Peterson, 1989).

Efforts at rehabilitation have sparked controversy as well. Prisons accomplish short-term social protection simply by keeping offenders off the streets, but they do very little to reshape attitudes and behavior in the long

Table 6–3	FOUR JUSTIFICATIONS OF PUNISHMENT: A SUMMARY
Retribution	The oldest justification of punishment that still holds sway today. Punishment is atonement for a moral wrong by an individual; in principle, punishment should be comparable in severity to the deviance itself.
Deterrence	An early modern approach, deviance is viewed as social disruption, which society acts to control. People are viewed as rational and self-interested, so that deterrence requires that the pains of punishment outweigh the pleasures of deviance.
Rehabilitation	A modern approach linked to development of the social sciences, deviance is viewed as the product of social problems (such as poverty) or personal problems (such as mental illness). Social conditions are improved and offenders subjected to intervention appropriate to their condition.
Social protection	A modern approach easier to implement than rehabilitation. If society is unable or unwilling to improve offenders or reform social conditions, protection from further deviance is afforded by incarceration or execution.

term. For this reason, penologists now concede that prisons rarely rehabilitate inmates (Carlson, 1976). Perhaps this is to be expected, since according to Sutherland's theory of differential association, placing a person among criminals for a long period of time should simply strengthen criminal attitudes and skills. The prison environment is also destructive because of widespread physical and sexual violence. Finally, inmates returning to the outside world also contend with the stigma of being ex-convicts, an obstacle to successful integration in the larger society. One study of young offenders in Philadelphia found that boys who were punished severely, and were therefore more likely to acquire a criminal stigma, later committed both more crimes and more serious ones (Wolfgang, Figlio, & Sellin, 1972).

In sum, we should never assume that the criminal justice system—the police, courts, and punishment—can effectively stop crime. The reason, echoed throughout this chapter, is simple: crime—in fact, all kinds of deviance—is more than the acts of "bad people." It is bound up with the operation of society itself.

SUMMARY

1. Deviance refers to norm violations that span a wide range, from mild breaches of etiquette to serious violence.

2. Biological analysis, from Lombroso's research in the nineteenth century to ongoing research in human genetics, has yet to produce much insight into the causes of deviance.

3. Psychological explanations of deviance focus on abnormalities in the individual personality, which arise from either biological causes or the social environment. Psychological theories help to explain some kinds of deviance.

4. Social forces produce nonconformity because deviance (a) exists in relation to cultural norms, (b) involves a process of social definition, and (c) is shaped by the distribution of social power.

5. Sociology links deviance to the operation of society rather than the deficiencies of individuals. Using the structural-functional paradigm, Durkheim identified several functions of deviance for society as a whole.

6. The symbolic-interaction paradigm is the basis of labeling theory, which holds that deviance arises in the reaction of some audience to a person's behavior. Labeling theory explains that acquiring the stigma of deviance can generate secondary deviance and a deviant career.

7. Social-conflict theory directs attention to the relationship between deviance and inequality. Following the approach of Karl Marx, this paradigm holds that laws and other norms reflect the interests of the most powerful members of a society. Social-conflict theory also focuses on white-collar crimes that cause extensive social harm; offenders, however, are rarely defined as criminals because of their privileged social positions.

8. Official statistics indicate that arrest rates peak in adolescence, then drop steadily with advancing age. Overall, males are arrested about 3.5 times as often as females are for serious street crimes: three-fourths of property crime arrests are of males, as are almost nine of ten arrests for violent crimes.

9. People of lower social position tend to commit more street crime than those with greater social privilege. When white-collar crimes are included among criminal offenses, however, this disparity in overall criminality diminishes.

10. More whites than African Americans are arrested for street crimes. However, African Americans are arrested more often than whites in proportion to their respective numbers. Eliminating racial bias from the criminal justice system would lessen this disparity.

11. The police exercise considerable discretion in their work. Research suggests that factors such as the seriousness of the offense, the presence of bystanders, and the accused being male or a person of color make arrest more likely.

12. Although ideally an adversarial system, U.S. courts predominantly resolve cases through plea bargaining. An efficient method of handling cases when the facts are not in dispute, plea bargaining nevertheless places less powerful people at a disadvantage.

13. Punishment has been justified in terms of retribution, deterrence, rehabilitation, and social protection. Because its consequences are difficult to evaluate scientifically, punishment—like deviance itself—sparks considerable controversy among sociologists and the public as a whole.

KEY CONCEPTS

crime the violation of norms formally enacted into criminal law

crimes against the person (violent crimes) crimes against people that involve violence or the threat of violence

crimes against property (property crimes) crimes that involve theft of property belonging to others

criminal justice system a reaction to alleged violations of the law through the use of police, courts, and state-sanctioned punishment

criminal recidivism subsequent offenses committed by people previously convicted of crimes

deterrence the attempt to discourage criminality through punishment

deviance the recognized violation of cultural norms

labeling theory the assertion that deviance and conformity arise in the response of others to some act

medicalization of deviance the transformation of moral and legal issues into medical matters

plea bargaining a legal negotiation in which the prosecution reduces a charge in exchange for a defendant's guilty plea

rehabilitation reforming the offender to preclude further offenses

retribution inflicting on an offender suffering comparable to that caused by the offense

retrospective labeling the interpretation of someone's past consistent with present deviance

social control attempts by society to regulate the thought and behavior of individuals

social protection rendering an offender incapable of further offenses either temporarily through incarceration or permanently by execution

stigma a powerfully negative label that radically changes a person's social identity and self-concept

victimless crime violation of law in which there is no readily apparent victim

white-collar crime crimes committed by people of high social position in the course of their occupations

7

Social Stratification

CHAPTER OUTLINE

On April 10, 1912, the ocean liner *Titanic* left the docks of Southampton, England, on its maiden voyage across the North Atlantic to New York. A proud symbol of the new industrial age, the towering ship carried twenty-three hundred passengers, some enjoying luxury that most travelers today could barely imagine. Crowded into the lower decks, however, were poor immigrants, journeying to what they hoped would be a better life in the United States.

On April 14, reports of icebergs in the area reached the ship, but the crew paid little notice. Then, near midnight, as the ship steamed swiftly and silently westward, a lookout was stunned to see a massive shape rising out of the dark ocean directly ahead. Moments later, the ship collided with a huge iceberg, almost as tall as the *Titanic* itself, which ripped open the starboard side of the ship as if it were a giant tin can. Sea water exploded into the ship's lower levels, and within twenty-five minutes people were packing the lifeboats. At that point, the fate of the great ship was sealed. By 2 A.M. the bow of the *Titanic* was submerged with the stern high above the water. There, silently observed by the lucky ones in lifeboats, hundreds of helpless passengers solemnly passed their final minutes before the ship disappeared into the frigid water (Lord, 1976).

The tragic loss of more than sixteen hundred lives shocked the world. Looking back dispassionately at this terrible event from a sociological perspective, however, we see that some categories of passengers had much better odds of survival than others. Of those holding first-class tickets, more than 60 percent survived, primarily because they were on the upper decks, where warnings were sounded first and lifeboats were readily accessible. Only 36 percent of the second-class passengers were saved, and of the third-class passengers on the lower decks, only 24 percent escaped drowning. On board the *Titanic*, class turned out to mean more than the degree of luxury of accommodations: it was truly a matter of life or death.

The fate of those aboard the *Titanic* dramatically illustrates the enormous differences that social inequality can make in the way people live, or sometimes whether they live at all. This chapter introduces a number of concepts and sociological ideas concerning social stratification and provides an overview of social inequality in the United States. Chapter 8 ("Global Inequality") enlarges our perspective by exploring how our society fits into a worldwide system of wealth and comfort, on the one hand, and poverty and suffering, on the other.

WHAT IS SOCIAL STRATIFICATION?

Every society is marked by inequality, with some people having more money, housing, education, health, and power than others. **Social stratification** refers to *a system by which a society ranks categories of people in a hierarchy.* Social stratification involves four fundamental principles.

1. **Social stratification is a characteristic of society, not simply a function of individual differences.** Social stratification involves how a society distributes what it produces. Technologically simple hunting and gathering societies produced so little that people were more or less equal in social standing. In industrial societies, complex technology allows bountiful production, but resources may be distributed quite unequally to people regardless of their individual abilities.

    Did a higher percentage of the first-class passengers on the *Titanic* survive because they were better swimmers than second- and third-class passengers? Hardly. They fared better because of their privileged position on the ship. Similarly, children born into wealthy families are more likely than those born into poverty to enjoy health, to become academic achievers, to succeed in their life's work, and to live well into old age. Neither rich nor poor children are responsible for creating social stratification, yet this system shapes the lives of them all.

2. **Although variable in form, social stratification is universal.** Social stratification is found everywhere. Yet its character and intensity are highly variable. As we shall explain, social stratification in the world's agrarian societies tends to be more rigid than that common to industrial nations. Some differences also distinguish systems of social inequality among today's industrial societies.

3. **Social stratification persists over generations.** Because social stratification is linked to the family, children assume the social position of their parents. The concept of **social mobility** refers to *a change of position in a stratification system.* But in industrial societies like the United States, and especially in agrarian societies, most people spend their lives at about the same social position, passing their standing on to their children.

4. **Social stratification is supported by patterns of belief.** Any system of social stratification defines some kinds of inequality as fair. Just as stratification itself varies around the world, so do its legitimizing beliefs. Within a society, people with the most social privileges express the strongest support for their society's system of social inequality, while those with fewer resources are more likely to seek change.

CASTE AND CLASS SYSTEMS

Sociologists often compare the world's systems of social inequality using two opposing standards: those that are relatively "closed" and allow for little social mobility, and those that are relatively "open," offering considerable opportunity for change in social standing (Tumin, 1985).

The Caste System

A **caste system** amounts to *social stratification based on ascription*. A pure caste system would grant individuals no social mobility at all; birth alone would determine their destiny. Not surprisingly, then, people living in caste-like systems recognize that their social category affects every dimension of everyday life.

An illustration: India.   The nation of India—especially the traditional Hindu villages in which 80 percent of its population still lives—exemplifies a caste-like system. In India, people are born into one of several thousand caste groups, which define one's standing in the local community.

Birth determines the fundamental shape of people's lives. First, traditional castes are linked to occupation, so that families in each caste perform one type of work from generation to generation. Although some vocations (such as farming) are open to all, castes are identified with the work their members do (priests, barbers, leather workers, and so on).

Second, maintaining caste boundaries demands that each person marries someone with the same standing. Sociologists call this pattern *endogamous* marriage ("endo" stems from the Greek, meaning "within"). The Indian tradition directs parents to select their children's marriage partners, often when the children are quite young. Only occasionally does a child of one caste (usu-

We experience the effects of social hierarchy directly and personally as triumph or failure. This idea is captured in this haunting photograph, a universal portrait of suffering, by Sebastiao Salgado. The essential sociological insight is that, however strongly we feel its effects, social standing is largely a consequence of the way in which a society (or a world of nations) structures opportunity and reward. In short, we are all products of social stratification.

ally a female) marry a person of higher position (Srinivas, 1971).

Third, cultural beliefs shore up this caste system. In India, Hindu traditions define acceptance of fate as a moral duty so that people must carry out their life's work, whatever it may be. Caste systems are typical of agrarian societies because such beliefs foster the habits of diligence and discipline that agriculture demands. Cultural norms also guide social relationships by defining higher caste groups as relatively "pure" compared to "unclean" lower caste groups. Hindu beliefs that a member of a higher caste is symbolically polluted by contact with a member of a lower caste keeps members of various categories apart and virtually precludes intermarriage.

Since the Industrial Revolution, beliefs that rank entire categories of people in this way have gradually weakened. As later chapters explain, such views represent various "isms"—racism, sexism, ageism—that are increasingly denounced as unjust. More than fifty years ago, India officially outlawed caste; nonetheless, it remains embedded in rural social life.

Another society dominated by caste is South Africa, whose racially-based system of *apartheid* is still legally in force. The box on pages 152–53 explains that, despite recent reforms, the white minority continues to dominate the black majority.

South Africa: Race as Caste

At the southern tip of the African continent lies South Africa, a territory about the size of Alaska, with a population of almost 40 million. Long inhabited by people of African descent, the region was colonized by Dutch traders in the mid-seventeenth century. Early in the nineteenth century, a new wave of British colonization pushed the descendants of these Dutch settlers inland. By the beginning of this century, the British had gained control of the country, calling it the Union of South Africa. In 1961 the Republic of South Africa formally severed ties with the United Kingdom and became politically independent.

But freedom was a reality only for the white minority. To ensure their political control, the whites continued the policy of *apartheid*, or separation of the races. A common practice for many decades, apartheid had been enshrined in law in 1948 so that whites could deny the black majority

South African performer John Clegg has blended familiar rock and roll with traditional African music and dancing. For his efforts, the apartheid government banned him on the grounds that his work brought the races together. In the currently more liberal climate, however, Clegg has enjoyed unprecedented popularity.

South African citizenship, ownership of land, and any voice in the government. Under this policy, blacks became a subordinate caste, receiving only the schooling needed to perform

the low-paying jobs shunned by whites. Under such conditions, blacks were able to earn, on average, only one-fourth what whites received. A final plank in the platform of apartheid was the forcible resettlement of millions of blacks to so-called homelands, dirt-poor districts set aside by whites to confine and control blacks. The overall effect was devastating on the black majority. In a land rich with natural resources, most blacks lived close to abject poverty.

The prosperous white minority has defended its privileges by viewing blacks as social inferiors. Increasingly, however, whites have been forced to rely on a system of brutal military repression to maintain their power. Without formal rights, blacks suspected of opposing white rule have been subject to arbitrary arrest and indefinite detention.

Despite its severity, this repression has not kept blacks—and a growing number of sympathetic whites—from challenging apartheid. Violent confrontations have been frequent, espe-

The Class System

A caste system bolsters stable, agrarian life; industrial societies, by contrast, depend on individual initiative and the development of specialized talents. Industrialization does not abolish inequality, but it does change its character, from a caste system to a **class system,** *social stratification based on individual achievement.*

Social "classes" are not as rigidly defined as castes. As people gain skills and schooling, they are likely to experience at least some social mobility, which blurs class distinctions. Social categories also break down as people migrate from rural areas to industrial cities, lured by better jobs and the chance for advanced education.

Class systems stand on a different conception of fairness: talent and effort, rather than birth, should determine social position. People tend to think of their careers as a matter of individual choice rather than a duty passed from generation to generation, as members of caste systems do. Greater individuality also translates into more freedom in marriage, with parents playing a lesser role in children's selections of their mates.

Greater freedom and mobility confer on members of class systems lower **status consistency,** *consistent standing across various dimensions of social inequality.* Where ranking follows from birth (caste systems), people have the same relative standing with regard to wealth, power, and prestige. Class systems, with their greater

cially among younger blacks impatient for political and economic opportunity. Also, by 1990, some 200 U.S. corporations had severed direct economic ties with South Africa. This foreign divestment has staggered the South African economy, hurting both blacks and whites in the process. But it has accomplished its primary objective: to pressure that government to begin the dismantling of apartheid.

Recent reforms permit South Africans of mixed race and Asians a limited voice in government. Blacks can now form labor unions, and enter a number of occupations once restricted to whites. All people now have the right to own property. Additionally, officials have abolished a host of "petty apartheid" regulations that segregated blacks and whites in public places, including beaches and hospitals. In 1990, the release from prison of Nelson Mandela and the legalization of the anti-apartheid African National Congress opened the political system and raised the hope for more basic change. And, in 1992,

a majority of white voters endorsed, in principle, the gradual ending of apartheid.

The reforms enacted thus far have prompted traditionalists to charge that the government is selling out white interests. But, to date, the basic structure of apartheid remains intact. The legal right to own property means little to millions of blacks who barely have enough to eat; opening hospitals to all South Africans is an empty gesture for those who cannot afford medical care; reducing workplace discrimination offers little real opportunity to men and women without much schooling. The harsh reality is that more than one-third of all black adults cannot find any work at all and, by the government's own estimate, half of all blacks live in desperate conditions.

The worst off are the 7 million *ukuhleleleka*, which means "marginal people" in the Xhosa language. In Soweto-by-the-Sea, an idyllic-sounding community, thousands live crammed into shacks built of dis-

carded material like packing cases, corrugated metal, cardboard, boards, and pieces of pipe. There is no electricity for lights or refrigeration; without plumbing, people haul sewage in buckets; women line up awaiting their turn at a single tap that provides water for more than one thousand people. Jobs are hard to come by, partly because Ford and General Motors have closed their factories in nearby Port Elizabeth, and partly because people keep migrating to the town from regions where life is even worse. The lucky ones find work that pays $200 a month.

To those who struggle to survive, the pace of change is agonizingly slow. Defenders of government reforms urge patience, and point to real progress toward breaking down apartheid. For the present, however, South Africa remains a society divided.

SOURCES: Based on Fredrickson (1981), Wren (1991), and Contreras (1992).

social mobility, have less status consistency. In the United States, some people with prestigious occupations (such as priests or professors) accumulate little wealth and only moderate social power. Such inconsistencies make the boundaries between classes less clear than those separating castes.

An illustration: Great Britain. There are no pure caste or class systems; every society combines elements of these two forms. Great Britain has a class system that began to take form with the coming of the Industrial Revolution. But it also shows the effects of centuries as an agrarian society.

During the Middle Ages, Great Britain had a caste-

like system of three *estates*. A hereditary nobility, or *first estate*, accounting for only 5 percent of the population, controlled most of the land—the chief form of wealth (Laslett, 1984). Typically, nobles had no occupation at all; to be "engaged in trade" or any other work for income was deemed "beneath" them. Well tended by servants, nobles used their extensive leisure time to cultivate refined tastes in art, music, and literature.

Vast landholdings were preserved from generation to generation by the law of *primogeniture* (from Latin meaning "first born"). This law mandated that property be passed only to the eldest son rather than divided among all children. Under this system, however, younger noble sons were forced to support themselves. Some entered the clergy—the *second estate*—where spiritual power was supplemented by the church's extensive landholdings. Others became military officers or lawyers, or took up other occupations that have come down to us today as "honorable" callings for "gentlemen." In an age when few women could expect to earn a living on their own, a daughter of nobility depended for her security on marrying well.

Below the nobility and the clergy, the vast majority of men and women formed the *third estate*, or commoners. With little property, commoners or serfs worked parcels of land owned by nobles. Unlike the nobility and the clergy, commoners had little access to schooling, so most remained illiterate.

As the Industrial Revolution gradually transformed England's economy, some commoners, especially those in cities, gained wealth and power rivaling—and sometimes surpassing—that of the nobility. Rapid economic growth, along with broader political rights and more schooling, soon blurred traditional social rankings as a class system emerged.

Yet the legacy of Britain's feudal past remains in today's social hierarchy. Although many members of Great Britain's small upper class enjoy wealth largely achieved through their own efforts, other descendants of traditional nobility maintain inherited wealth, savor the highest prestige, attend expensive, elite universities, and wield considerable power in British society. Moreover, a traditional monarch stands as Britain's head of state, and Parliament's House of Lords is composed of "peers" of noble birth. This, despite the fact that actual control of government now resides in the House of Commons, made up of commoners who are more likely to have achieved their position through individual effort than through ascription.

Below today's upper class, perhaps one-fourth of the British people fall into the "middle class." A few enjoy enough income from professions and business to be included in the roughly 10 percent of Britons who own stocks and bonds (Sherrid, 1986). Below the middle class, across a boundary that cannot be precisely defined, lie the half of all Britons known as "working class." As in the United States, these people earn modest incomes, commonly from manual labor. Although the British economy expanded during the 1980s, traditional industries such as coal mining and steel production declined, subjecting many working-class families to unemployment and plunging some into poverty. The remaining one-fourth of the British people are poor, without steady work and adequate income. They are concentrated in the nation's northern and western regions, which are plagued by economic decay.

Today's Great Britain displays typical class-system traits: unequally distributed wealth, power, and prestige, with some people moving upward while others slip downward. In one legacy of a long-established estate system, however, social mobility occurs less frequently in the United Kingdom than in the United States (Kerckhoff, Campbell, & Winfield-Laird, 1985). The relative rigidity of British stratification is exemplified in the importance attached to accent as a mark of social position. Distinctive patterns of speech develop in any society as categories of people are socially segregated from one another over long periods. In Great Britain, families of longstanding affluence and those living in chronic poverty speak so differently that they seem to be, as the old saying goes, a single people divided by a common language.

Classless Societies?

Industrialization transforms traditional caste systems into class systems. But have some industrial societies with socialist economies moved beyond class to become classless? The former Soviet Union, for example, long made this claim.

The Union of Soviet Socialist Republics (U.S.S.R.) emerged from a 1917 revolution that ended a feudal estate system ruled by a hereditary nobility. The Russian Revolution transferred control of most farms, factories, and other productive property from private owners to the state. Following the ideas of Karl Marx, Soviet leaders contended that private ownership of productive property gives rise to social classes. If private ownership is abolished, they maintained, then so are social classes.

But the former Soviet Union did have a social hierarchy, topped by high government officials who presided over intellectuals and professionals, manual workers, and, at the lowest ranking, the rural peasantry. Sweeping transformations of the socialist societies of Eastern Europe and the Soviet Union itself in the late 1980s and early 1990s seriously undermined the notion that these nations were classless. More correctly, a powerful ruling class of party officials—served by military leaders and scientists—had for decades managed these societies. In the Soviet Union, where the Communist Party retained a monopoly of power between 1917 and 1991, roughly 6 percent of the people were party members, enjoying privileges unavailable to others such as vacation homes, chauffeured automobiles, and access to many consumer goods (Zaslavsky, 1982; Theen, 1984). The children of this elite also had special educational advantages and occupational opportunities.

And what about social mobility in so-called classless societies? During this century there has been more upward social mobility in the Soviet Union than in Great Britain, Japan, or even the United States. This reflects both the lesser amount of concentrated wealth passed from generation to generation and also the expansion of both factories and government agencies that pulled upward many members of the Soviet working class and rural peasantry. This movement exemplifies what sociologists call **structural social mobility,** *a shift in the social position of large numbers of people due more to changes in society itself than to individual efforts.*

Although the former Soviet society was not truly classless, it is fair to say that this country lacked the extremes of wealth and poverty found in Great Britain and the United States. This is because Soviet elites had extensive *power* more than *wealth.* With the dramatic changes in this country—which can truly be called the Second Russian Revolution—state power has been greatly reduced in favor of more private control of the economy. The long-term effects of this change, the new leadership hopes, will be economic prosperity and more political democracy. It may also mean, if Western societies are a guide, greater disparities in income.

Institutions, Ideology, and Inequality

The caste system of Great Britain lasted for centuries; even more striking, for two thousand years most people in India accepted the idea that they should be privileged or poor due to the accident of birth. We might wonder how stratified societies can persist so long without distributing their resources more equally.

The ancient Greek philosopher Plato (427–347 B.C.E.) explained that justice was mostly a matter of agreement about who should have what. Members of a society learn to view their system of social stratification as basically "fair." On the other side of this argument stood Karl Marx, who argued that inequality is fundamentally unjust. Social institutions, he contended, perpetuate and try to justify unequal shares of wealth and power. Linked by marriage, for example, well-to-do families funnel wealth from generation to generation. Society then protects inherited wealth through legal rights to private property backed up by the state. With both re-

The economic confusion of the former Soviet Union is portrayed here as the bust of Lenin scowls high above the floor of Moscow's commodities trading center. The introduction of a market system has reshaped social stratification in Russia, replacing traditional Communist Party officials with a new economic elite.

sources and ideas under the institutional control of a society's elite, Marx concluded, efforts to create a more equitable social order face formidable barriers.

Though Plato looked more favorably on social hierarchy than Marx did, both thinkers recognized that stratification depends on **ideology,** *cultural beliefs that reflect and support the interests of certain categories of people.* Any idea is ideological to the extent that its consequences favor some people over others. Ideology may include self-serving ideas deliberately generated by some privileged group. But, most often, it takes the form of established cultural patterns that justify social hierarchy, thereby entitling certain people to privileges denied to others. Through socialization, most of us learn to accept our society's ideas about fairness; those who do challenge them commonly question their own position in the system rather than the system itself.

As a society's economy and technology change, so do the ideas that justify social stratification. Caste systems, dependent on the routine labor of most people, define each person's work as a moral responsibility, all but ruling out the chance to change one's ranking. With the Industrial Revolution, however, a new economic elite promoted the idea that individual merit, rather than birth, was the proper criterion for reward. The poor, who had been the objects of charity under feudalism,

In medieval Europe, people typically accepted striking social differences, which divided them from birth until death, as part of a divine order for the world. This fifteenth-century painting by the Limbourg brothers—part of a book offered to the brother of the king—portrays life as orderly and cyclical. In this example, showing indoor life during January, the Duke of Berry is seated near the fireplace surrounded by a host of attendants who cater to his every whim. The firescreen behind him appears to give him a halo, surely intended by the artists to suggest a common notion of the time that nobles enjoyed their privileges by grace of God.

were degraded by industrial capitalism as personally undeserving.

Human history reveals how difficult it is to change systems of social stratification. Our own society, for example, still subjects women to caste-like expectations that they perform tasks out of altruism and duty, while men are financially rewarded for their efforts (in a more class-like fashion). To illustrate, just consider the differences in power, prestige, and financial rewards between a family cook, usually a woman, and a chef, typically a man. However, challenges to the status quo continue to arise as traditions weaken and people recognize their political consequences. For example, historic notions of a woman's place today are losing their power to deprive women of opportunities. Thus, while sexual equality is still not a reality in the United States, there is little doubt that the sexes are steadily becoming more equal. The continuing struggle for racial equality in South Africa also exemplifies widespread rejection of apartheid, which was never widely accepted by blacks, and it is losing support as a "natural" system among whites who reject ideological racism (Friedrich, 1987).

THE FUNCTION OF SOCIAL STRATIFICATION

Why are societies stratified at all? One answer to this question, consistent with the structural-functional paradigm, is that social stratification has vital consequences for the operation of society. This assertion was developed half a century ago by Kingsley Davis and Wilbert Moore (1945).

The Davis–Moore Thesis

In 1945 Davis and Moore proposed a theory of social stratification that remains influential to this day. The *Davis–Moore thesis* holds that all societies are stratified to some degree because inequality has beneficial effects.

In their effort to discover these consequences, Davis and Moore begin by pointing out that societies encompass many occupational positions of varying importance. Some jobs are performed easily by virtually anyone, while the most important positions can be performed only by people with rare talents who have received long and expensive education and training. Such functionally important positions also subject individuals to considerable pressure and day-to-day responsibility.

By rewarding the performance of important tasks with income, prestige, power, and leisure time, a society encourages the discovery and development of human resources. Further, such differential rewards motivate people to engage in the most significant activities possible. To illustrate, if a society values the work of a Supreme Court justice more than that of a government clerk, it will accord greater benefits to the member of the High Court. In short, effective performance of key social roles depends on a system of unequal rewards, which creates social stratification. According to the Davis–Moore thesis, a society could be egalitarian, but only to the extent that its members are prepared to have *any* person perform *any* job. Equality would also demand that someone who carries out a job well be rewarded no more than another who performs poorly. Logic dictates that a system of equal rewards would not motivate people toward their best efforts and would thereby reduce a society's productive efficiency.

The Davis–Moore thesis tries to explain why *some* kind of stratification exists everywhere; it does not endorse any particular system of inequality or suggest precisely what reward should be attached to any occupational position. Davis and Moore merely state that rewards must function to draw talent to the most important positions.

The thesis implies that societies become more productive as they approach **meritocracy**, *stratification linking rewards to personal merit.* Societies define "merit" (from Latin, meaning "worthy of praise") differently, however. Since most members of agrarian caste systems work in low-skill agriculture, the "merit" they reward is dutifully working and remaining "in one's place," whatever the rank. By contrast, members of highly specialized industrial societies strive much more to cultivate individual potential. Ideally, this requires class systems to provide *equality of opportunity* to everyone, even though *equality of condition* will not result, given individual differences. Meritocracy makes societies more productive and also enhances social mobility, blurring class boundaries.

Notice, however, that no class system tries to be a pure meritocracy. Why? Because rewarding only the ambition and achievement of individuals tends to undermine the social fabric of family and community, threatening a society's cohesion. We favor members of our families, in other words, whether or not they are especially capable individuals. In short, the need for social integration encourages some caste elements even within industrial class systems.

Critical evaluation. Although the Davis–Moore thesis has made a lasting contribution to sociological analysis,

Melvin Tumin (1953) argues that it is flawed in several respects. First, Tumin points to the difficulty of specifying the functional importance of any occupation. For example, our belief that physicians are valuable to society partly results from a policy of limiting the number of people entering the medical profession (through medical school admission policies) to ensure that physicians remain in great demand.

Further, do we really reward functional importance? Basketball player Michael Jordan, for example, earned about $24 million in 1992, twenty times as much as the combined salaries of the nine-member Supreme Court. Is his work as a star athlete and product-pitchman that useful to our society? To take another example, U.S. corporate executives pay themselves salaries and bonuses much higher than those of Japanese executives, even though many of Japan's corporations outperform their U.S. counterparts. Clearly some people manipulate market forces to their own advantage. On the other end of the spectrum, Rachel Stuart offers prenatal counseling to poor women in rural Louisiana, helping them to deliver healthy babies. Preventing a single premature baby can save the government as much as $200,000 in medical bills, yet Stuart receives only about $4,000 a year for her work (Werman, 1989).

A second charge made by Tumin is that Davis and Moore fail to mention how social stratification can *prevent* the development of individual talents. Society does reward individual talent to some degree, but families also transfer wealth and power from generation to generation regardless of personal abilities. Additionally, for women, people of color, or others with limited opportunities, stratification ensures that much talent and ability will never be discovered.

Third, by suggesting that social stratification benefits all of society, the Davis–Moore thesis sidesteps ways in which social inequality promotes conflict and even outright revolution. This assertion leads us to the social-conflict paradigm, which provides a very different explanation for the persistence of social stratification.

STRATIFICATION AND CONFLICT

Social-conflict analysis argues that, rather than benefiting society as a whole, social stratification ensures that some people gain advantages at the expense of others. This analysis draws heavily on the ideas of Karl Marx; additional contributions were made by Max Weber.

This cartoon, entitled "Capital and Labour," appeared in the English press in 1843, when the ideas of Karl Marx were first gaining attention. It links the plight of that country's coal miners to the privileges enjoyed by those who owned coal-fired factories.

Karl Marx: Class Conflict

The striking inequality of the early Industrial Revolution both saddened and angered Karl Marx. Through the technological miracle of industrialization, humanity could finally envision a society free from want. Yet, industrial capitalism had done little to improve the lives of most people. Marx devoted his life to explaining a glaring contradiction: how a society that was so rich could have so many people who were so poor.

In Marx's view, social stratification is rooted in people's relationships to the means of production. Either they are *owners* of productive property or they *provide labor* for enterprises controlled by others. In feudal Europe, the nobility and clergy owned the productive land, and the peasantry supplied continual labor. The rise of industrial capitalism changed only the identity of the contending classes. Class systems are dominated by **capitalists,** *people who own factories and other productive businesses.* Capitalists (sometimes termed the *bourgeoisie,* a French word meaning "of the town") use their property to gain profits. To do this, they employ the **proletariat,** *people who sell their productive labor.* Members of the industrial proletariat work for the wages needed to live.

Faced with irreconcilable interests and separated by great disparities in wealth and power, Marx maintained that the two classes would inevitably clash in a thunderous confrontation.

Marx's analysis drew heavily on his observations of capitalism in the nineteenth century, when powerful new productive forces had elevated some to great wealth while subjecting many more to monotonous toil for low wages. During this period, wealthy U.S. capitalists like Andrew Carnegie, J. P. Morgan, and John Jacob Astor (one of the few rich passengers to perish on the *Titanic*) lived in fabulous mansions filled with priceless art and staffed by dozens of servants. Even by today's standards, their incomes were staggering. Carnegie, for example, made more than $20 million in 1900—at a time when the average worker earned perhaps $500 a year in wages—and his fortune would be worth $7.5 billion today (Baltzell, 1964; Gordon, 1992).

In time, Marx believed, the working majority would organize to overthrow such capitalists once and for all. Capitalism was sowing the seeds of its own demise, Marx reasoned, by steadily reducing the living standards of the working majority. Just as important, under capitalism, workers have little control over the process or product of their labor. Thus, Marx asserted, work produced **alienation,** *the experience of powerlessness in social life,* rather than serving as an expression of personal creativity. In place of capitalism, Marx envisioned a *socialist* system he thought would respond to the needs of all—rather than merely boosting the profits of the few. Thus Marx, a relentless critic of the present, looked to the future with hope, claiming (1972:362; orig. 1848): "The proletarians have nothing to lose but their chains. They have a world to win."

Critical evaluation. By explaining how social inequality, and especially the capitalist economic system, generates conflict between classes, Marx's analysis has had enormous influence on sociological thinking in recent decades. Its revolutionary implications also render it highly controversial.

Marx's approach has come under strong criticism for denying the crucial element of the Davis–Moore thesis: that motivating people to perform various social roles well requires a system of unequal rewards. Marx separated reward from performance, endorsing an egalitarian system based on the principle "to each according to need, from each according to ability" (1972:388). Critics suggest that this approach accounts for the low productivity of socialist economies around the world.

Further, the revolutionary change Marx considered inevitable failed to materialize. Here lies perhaps the most important critique of his ideas. The next section explores why the socialist revolution Marx predicted and promoted has not occurred, at least in advanced capitalist societies.

Why No Marxist Revolution?

Capitalism is still thriving, in spite of Marx's prediction to the contrary. But Western capitalism has evolved in at least some of the ways Marx anticipated.

Workers in the United States have not overthrown capitalism for several reasons (Dahrendorf, 1959). First, in the century since Marx lived, the capitalist class has grown fragmented. Nineteenth-century companies were typically owned by *families*; today they are owned by more numerous *stockholders*. Further, a large managerial class, whose members may or may not own a significant. share of the companies they manage, has also emerged. As a result, an increasing number of people have a direct stake in preserving the capitalist system.

Second, Marx's industrial proletariat has also been transformed by the so-called white-collar revolution. As Chapter 11 ("Economics and Politics") explains, a century ago most people in the U.S. labor force filled the ranks of **blue-collar occupations,** *work that involves mostly manual labor,* in factories or on farms. Today, most of the labor force holds **white-collar occupations,** *work that involves mostly mental activity.* These jobs include positions in sales, management, and other service work, frequently in large, bureaucratic organizations. While these white-collar workers have much in common with the industrial working class described by Marx, most do not think of themselves in those terms. For much of this century, then, the white-collar revolution has prompted many men and women to perceive their social positions as higher than those of their parents and grandparents. As a result of this structural social mobility, our society seems less sharply divided between the rich and poor than it did during Marx's lifetime (Edwards, 1979; Gagliani, 1981; Wright & Martin, 1987).

Third, the plight of workers is not as desperate today as it was a century ago. Despite setbacks for many workers during the 1980s, living standards have improved significantly since Marx's time. Moreover, workers have won the right to organize into labor unions that negotiate regularly with management, sometimes using threats of work slowdowns and strikes. If not always peaceful, then,

worker-management disputes are now institutionalized.

Fourth, during the last century, the government extended legal protection to workers. Government programs such as unemployment insurance, disability protection, and Social Security also provide workers with substantially greater financial security than the capitalists of the last century were willing to grant them.

Taken together, these developments suggest that despite marked stratification, capitalism has smoothed many of its own rough edges. Consequently, social conflict today is less intense than it was a century ago.

Advocates of social-conflict analysis respond with four key points (Miliband, 1969; Edwards, 1979; Giddens, 1982; Domhoff, 1983; Stephens, 1986). First, wealth remains highly concentrated as Marx contended, with about half of all privately controlled corporate stock owned by 1 percent of our population. Second, the jobs produced by the white-collar revolution often offer no more income, security, or satisfaction than factory jobs did a century ago. This is especially true of clerical jobs commonly held by women. Third, although labor organizations certainly have advanced the interests of workers over the last half century, regular negotiation between workers and management does not signal the end of class conflict. Many of the concessions workers have won came about precisely through the turmoil Marx described, and workers still struggle to hold on to what they already have. Today, for instance, half of U.S. workers still have no employer pension program. Fourth, workers may have gained some legal protection, but the law has neither changed the overall distribution of wealth in this country, nor helped "average" people to use the legal system to the same advantage as the rich do.

Therefore, social-conflict theorists conclude, the fact that no socialist revolution has taken place in the United States hardly invalidates Marx's analysis of capitalism. Our cultural values, emphasizing individualism and competition, may have curbed revolutionary aspirations, but, as we shall see shortly, pronounced social inequality persists in the United States, as does social conflict—albeit less overtly and violently than a century ago.

Table 7–1 summarizes the two contrasting explanations of social stratification.

Max Weber: Class, Status, and Power

Max Weber agreed with Karl Marx that social stratification sparks social conflict, but he disagreed with Marx in several important respects.

Table 7–1   TWO EXPLANATIONS OF SOCIAL STRATIFICATION: A SUMMARY

Structural-Functional Paradigm	Social-Conflict Paradigm
1. Social stratification keeps society operating. The linkage of greater rewards to more important social positions benefits society as a whole.	Social stratification is the result of social conflict. Differences in social resources serve the interests of some and harm the interests of others.
2. Social stratification encourages a matching of talents and abilities to appropriate positions.	Social stratification ensures that much talent and ability within society will not be utilized at all.
3. Social stratification is both useful and inevitable.	Social stratification is useful to only some people; it is not inevitable.
4. The values and beliefs that legitimize social inequality are widely shared throughout society.	Values and beliefs tend to be ideological; they reflect the interests of the more powerful members of society.
5. Because systems of social stratification are useful to society and are supported by cultural values and beliefs, they are usually stable over time.	Because systems of social stratification reflect the interests of only part of the society, they are unlikely to remain stable over time.

SOURCE: Adapted in part from Arthur L. Stinchcombe, "Some Empirical Consequences of the Davis–Moore Theory of Stratification," *American Sociological Review*, Vol. 28, No. 5 (October 1963): 808.

Weber considered Marx's two-class model simplistic. Instead, he viewed social stratification as the interplay of three distinct dimensions. First is economic inequality—the issue so vital to Marx—which Weber termed *class* position. Weber's use of "class" refers not to crude categories, but to a continuum on which anyone could be ranked from high to low. Second is *status*, meaning amount of social prestige. Third, Weber noted the importance of *power* in the social hierarchy.

Marx treated social prestige and power as elements derived from economic position, so he saw no reason to treat them as distinct dimensions of inequality. But Weber asserted that status consistency in modern societies is sometimes quite low: a local official, say, might wield considerable power yet have little wealth or social prestige. Weber's central contribution, then, is showing that stratification in industrial societies is a multidimensional ranking rather than merely the clash of two classes. Following Weber's thinking, sociologists often use the term **socioeconomic status** to refer to *a composite social ranking based on various dimensions of social inequality*.

A population that varies widely on each of these three dimensions of social inequality displays a virtually infinite array of social groupings, all of which pursue their own interests. Thus, unlike Marx, who saw conflict between classes, Weber considered social conflict as a more complex, subtle, and variable process.

Weber also suggested that each of his three dimensions of social inequality stands out at different points in history. Agrarian societies, he maintained, emphasize *prestige* in the form of honor or symbolic purity. Members of these societies gain prestige by conforming to norms corresponding to their rank. Industrial capitalism generates striking *economic* differences, tying the importance of money to social standing. Mature industrial societies (especially socialist societies) witness a surging growth of the bureaucratic state and accord tremendous *power* to high-ranking officials.

Weber's concern with the growth of bureaucracy (detailed in Chapter 5, "Groups and Organizations") led him to disagree with Marx about the future of industrial-capitalist societies. Marx, who focused on economics, thought that societies could eradicate stratification by abolishing private ownership of productive property. Weber doubted that overthrowing capitalism would significantly diminish stratification in modern societies, because of the growing importance of power in formal organizations. In fact, Weber thought that a socialist revolution might well increase inequality by expanding government and concentrating power in the hands of a political elite. Recent popular uprisings against entrenched socialist bureaucracies in Eastern Europe lend support to Weber's analysis.

Critical evaluation.   Sociologists in the United States have embraced Weber's multidimensional approach to inequality. Some analysts (particularly those influenced by Marx) concede that social class boundaries have become less pronounced, but maintain that striking patterns of inequality persist in this country, as they do in other industrial societies. Moreover, as we shall explain presently, the extent of economic inequality in the United States has increased in recent years; this economic polarization may foster a renewed emphasis on "classes" rather than the subtle shadings of a "multidimensional hierarchy."

STRATIFICATION AND TECHNOLOGY: A GLOBAL SURVEY

We can weave together a number of observations made in this chapter by considering the relationship between a society's technology and its form of social stratification. This analysis draws on Gerhard and Jean Lenski's model of sociocultural evolution, detailed in Chapter 2 ("Culture"), as well as both the structural-functional and social-conflict approaches (Lenski, 1966; Lenski, Lenski, & Nolan, 1991).

Simple technology limited the production of hunters and gatherers to what was necessary for day-to-day living. While some individuals were more productive than others, group survival depended on sharing by everyone. With little or no surplus, therefore, no categories of people emerged as better off than others.

Technological advances historically generate a productive surplus, while intensifying social inequality. In horticultural and pastoral societies, a small elite controls most of the resources. Agrarian technology based on large-scale farming generates greater abundance, but because this surplus is shared unequally, various categories of people lead strikingly different lives. The favored strata—the hereditary nobility—frequently wield godlike power over the masses.

In industrial societies, however, social inequality declines to some extent. Prompted by the need to develop individual talents, democratic thinking takes hold in these societies, eroding the power of elites. Also, the greater productivity of industrial technology gradually raises the living standards of the historically poor majority. Specialized work encourages the expansion of schooling, sharply reducing illiteracy. And, as already noted, technological advances transform much blue-collar labor into white-collar work with greater prestige. All these transformations help to explain why Marxist revolutions occurred in agrarian societies—such as Russia (1917), Cuba (1959), and Nicaragua (1979)—where social inequality is historically most pronounced, rather than in industrial societies, as Marx predicted more than a century ago.

Initially, industrialization increases the concentration of wealth—the pattern so troublesome to Marx. In time, however, the share of property in the hands

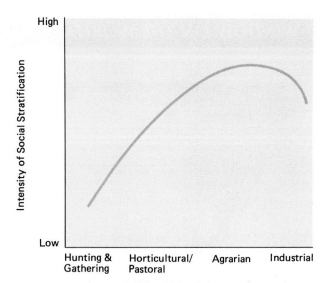

Figure 7–1 Social Stratification and Technological Development: The Kuznets Curve

The Kuznets Curve suggests that greater technological sophistication is generally accompanied by more pronounced social stratification. The trend reverses itself, however, as industrial societies gradually become more egalitarian. Rigid caste-like distinctions are relaxed in favor of greater opportunity and equality under the law. Political rights are more widely extended, and there is even some leveling of economic differences. The Kuznets Curve may also be usefully applied to the relative social standing of the two sexes.

of the very rich declines slightly. Estimates suggest that the proportion of all wealth controlled by the richest 1 percent of U.S. families peaked at about 36 percent in 1929, falling to about 25 percent by the 1980s (Williamson & Lindert, 1980; Beeghley, 1989).

Additionally, the domination of women by men, generally strongest in agrarian societies, gradually diminishes with industrialization. The drive for gender equality derives from the demand for individual talent in the industrial economy coupled with more widespread education. Thus a belief in basic human equality steadily pushes aside traditional patriarchy.

In short, reducing the intensity of social stratification is actually functional for industrial societies. This historical pattern, recognized by Nobel Prize–winning economist Simon Kuznets (1955, 1966), is illustrated by the "Kuznets Curve" (Figure 7–1).[1]

[1] The ideas of Simon Kuznets are discussed by Peter Berger (1986:43–46), whose interpretations are reflected in what appears here.

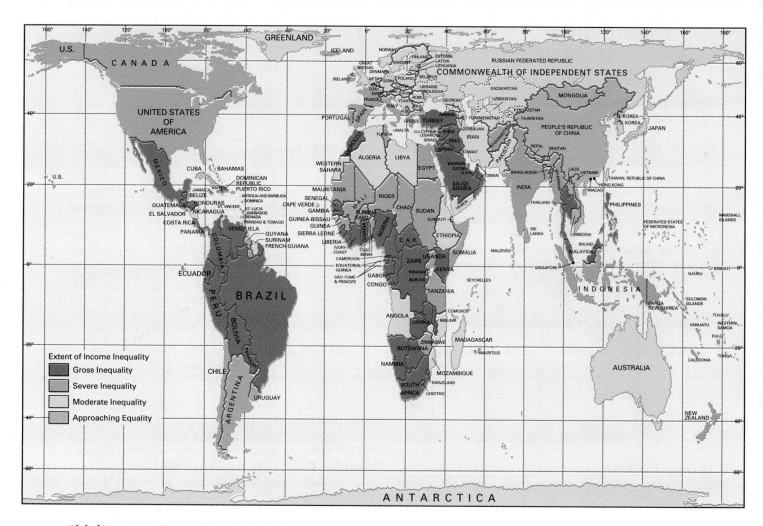

Global Map 7–1 Income Disparity in Global Perspective

Societies of the world differ in the rigidity and intensity of social stratification as well as in their overall standard of living. This map highlights income inequality. Generally speaking, countries that have had centralized, socialist economies (including the People's Republic of China, the former Soviet Union, and Cuba) display the least income inequality, although their standard of living has been relatively low. Industrial societies with predominantly capitalist economies, including the United States and most of Western Europe, have higher overall living standards, accompanied by severe income disparity. The less industrialized societies in Latin America and Africa (including Mexico, Brazil, and Zaire) exhibit the most pronounced inequality of income.

Confirming the validity of the "Kuznets Curve" is Global Map 7–1, which shows the extent of income disparity in today's world. The map reveals that agrarian societies generally have greater income disparity than industrial societies like Japan and the United States.

Of course, the trend identified by Kuznets does not necessarily mean that industrial societies will become less and less stratified. In fact, we have seen some resurgence of economic concentration in recent years. The remainder of this chapter will explore in detail social inequality in the United States.

INEQUALITY IN THE UNITED STATES

We have long considered members of our society to be basically equal. Unlike Japan or most European nations, the United States never had a feudal aristocracy. With the significant exception of our racial history, we have never known a rigid caste system.

Even so, U.S. society is highly stratified. The rich not only control most of the money, but they also benefit from more schooling, better health, and they consume a greater share of almost all goods and services than others do. Such privilege contrasts sharply with the poverty of millions of women and men who struggle from day to day simply to survive. The notion of "middle-class America" simply doesn't square with the facts.

Income, Wealth, and Power

One important dimension of economic inequality involves **income**, *wages or salary from work and earnings from investments*. The government reports that the median U.S. family income[2] in 1991 was $35,939. Figure 7–2 on page 164 shows the distribution of family income in the United States. Note that the 20 percent of families with the highest earnings receive 44.2 percent of all income, while the bottom 20 percent make only about 4.5 percent. At the very top, the highest-paid 5 percent of families (who earn at least $100,000 annually) secured 17.1 percent of all income, more income than the lowest-paid 40 percent (15.2 percent).

[2] Reported for households rather than families, median income is somewhat lower: $30,126 in 1991. Most of the difference is due to size, with households averaging 2.63 people compared to 3.17 for families.

This income disparity increased during the 1980s to the greatest level since World War II. As the box on page 165 explains, this growing economic concentration was a result of changes in the economy, new tax policies, and cuts in social programs that assist low-income people (Levy, 1987; Jaeger & Greenstein, 1989; Reich, 1989; DeParle, 1991b).

Income is but one component of the broader economic factor of **wealth**, *an individual's or family's total financial assets*. Wealth—in the form of stocks, bonds, real estate, and other privately owned property—is distributed even less equally than income is. Figure 7–3 shows the approximate distribution of wealth in the United States in 1990. The richest 20 percent of U.S. families own roughly four-fifths of the country's entire wealth. High up in this privileged category are the wealthiest 5 percent of families—the "super-rich," who control over half of all wealth. Richer still—with wealth into the tens of millions—1 percent of our families possess about one-third of this country's wealth. And at the very top of the wealth pyramid, the *three* richest families have a combined wealth totaling $35 billion, which equals the total property of more than a million "average" people (Joint Economic Committee, 1986; *Forbes*, 1992).

The wealth of the average U.S. family is about the same as the median annual income for families, or $35,000 (U.S. House of Representatives, 1991). Lesser wealth is also different in kind. The richest people hold their property in the form of stocks and other income-producing investments. The wealth of average people resides primarily in property that produces no income, such as a home. When financial assets are balanced against debts for the lowest ranking 40 percent of families, wealth simply does not exist. As the negative number in Figure 7–3 shows, the bottom 20 percent actually live in debt.

In the United States, wealth stands as an important source of power. Therefore, the small proportion of families that controls most of the wealth also has the ability to shape the agenda of the entire society. As explained in Chapter 11 ("Economics and Politics"), some sociologists argue that such concentrated wealth undermines democracy because the political system serves the interests of the small proportion of "super-rich" families.

Occupational Prestige

Beyond generating income, occupation also serves as an important source of social prestige. We commonly evaluate each other according to the kind of work we

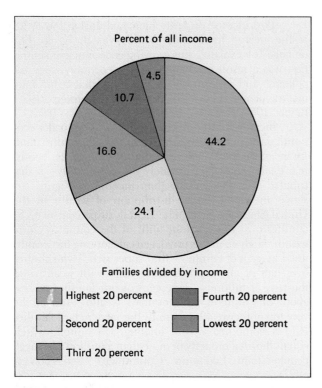

Figure 7–2 Distribution of Income in the United States, 1991
(U.S. Bureau of the Census, 1992)

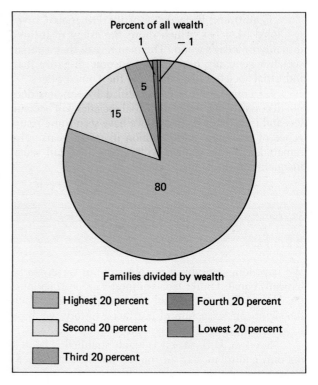

Figure 7–3 Distribution of Wealth in the United States, 1990
(Based on sources cited in footnote 4)

do, envying and respecting some, shunning and looking down on others. Work, in our society, is an important measure of human worth.

Sociologists have long monitored the relative social prestige of various occupations (Counts, 1925; Hodge, Treiman, & Rossi, 1966; N.O.R.C., 1991). Based on a survey of U.S. adults, Table 7–2 on page 166 shows that high-prestige occupations—such as physicians, lawyers, and engineers—generally confer high income. These occupations also require considerable ability, education, and training. By contrast, less prestigious work— as a salesperson or bus driver, for example—not only pays less, but usually requires less ability and schooling. Occupational prestige rankings follow similar patterns in all industrial societies.[3]

In any society, the most privileged categories of people tend to have occupations that yield the greatest prestige. Starting from the beginning in Table 7–2 (that is, from the most prestigious jobs), one passes more than a dozen occupations before finding one ("registered nurse") in which most workers are women. As Jessie Bernard (1981) explains, women are highly concentrated in *pink-collar* jobs. These service jobs—such as secretary, waitress, and hairdresser—tend to fall near the bottom of the prestige hierarchy.

---

[3] I am grateful to Dr. Li-Chen Ma of Lamar University for providing cross-cultural comparisons.

---

[4] This distribution is based on data from the Office of Management and the Budget (*Social Indicators, 1973*) and the Joint Economic Committee (1986), modified by the author on the basis of the Survey of Consumer Finances carried out in 1983 and 1989–90 by the Federal Reserve Board (cf. Kennickell & Shack-Marquez, 1992). Worth noting is the relative ease with which social scientists may obtain income data from the government and the frustrating difficulty of securing data about wealth.

Economic Transformation: Trends in Income Disparity

Were the 1980s a decade of prosperity or a time when the rich got richer while the poor fell further behind? As with many controversies, there is some truth on each side.

First, the standard of living in the United States stalled early in the 1970s, when skyrocketing oil prices threw the economy into a tailspin. Average family income bottomed out in 1982 and rebounded for the rest of the decade. In 1990, median family income topped $33,000, an all-time high when adjusted for inflation. From this point of view, the 1980s was a decade of economic expansion.

But averages mask the different experiences of various categories of people. At the upper extreme, the 1980s brought a bonanza to the rich. The earnings share of the highest-income one-fifth of families stretched from about 41.5 percent (1980) to more than 44 percent (1990). The proportion of total income received by the lowest three-fifths of families, however, shrunk slightly. The figure illustrates this change by showing income dollars through the decade. The highest-income fifth of U.S. families saw a rapid rise in median annual earnings from about $64,600 in 1980 to $82,300 in 1990, up 27 percent. Families in the second 20 percent, on average, showed a modest 6 percent upturn, gaining $2,000 in income over the decade. For the remaining 60 percent, income declined by about $600 in the 1980s; this amounted to a 9 percent loss for people in the lowest-income fifth of the population. During the 1980s, then, the rich moved further away from

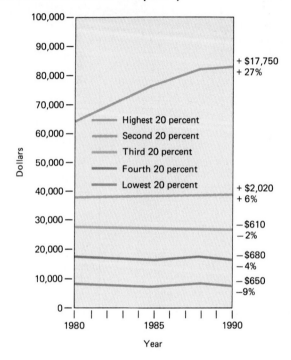

Median After-Tax Income, U.S. Families, 1980–1990 (in estimated 1992 dollars, adjusted for inflation)
(*Congressional Budget Office*)

the poor—and also the middle class.

How could overall family income increase during the 1980s when a majority of U.S. families saw their income fall? Because the rise in income among the richest people was great enough to pull up the average for everyone. The highest-paid 1 percent of families—the uppermost tip of the top 20 percent shown in the figure—had median earnings of $325,000 in 1980; by 1990, however, the inflation-controlled income of this economic elite had doubled to $650,000 (although only half of 1980's richest families were still among this elite group in 1990). As explained presently, much of this rise was due to the global expansion of the U.S.

economy, benefiting corporate executives and large stockholders, while hurting rank-and-file factory workers, many of whom lost their jobs as companies transferred production abroad.

Changes in the tax structure during the 1980s amplified the effect of changes in the economy. Total taxes on income dropped 5 percent for the highest-income fifth of families, yet rose 15 percent for the fifth with the lowest income. All things considered, the 1980s were boom times for our economic elite. The next tier of families with above-average incomes also made gains, but far smaller than those of the very rich. For most families, however, the 1980s saw income slipping as living costs and taxes rose.

Table 7–2 THE RELATIVE SOCIAL PRESTIGE OF SELECTED OCCUPATIONS IN THE UNITED STATES

White-collar Occupations	Prestige Score	Blue-collar Occupations	White-collar Occupations	Prestige Score	Blue-collar Occupations
Physician	86			47	Mail carrier
Lawyer	75		Musician/composer	47	
College/university professor	74			46	Secretary
Architect	73		Insurance agent	45	
Chemist	73		Photographer	45	
Physicist/astronomer	73		Bank teller	43	
Aerospace engineer	72		Buyer, farm products	42	
Dentist	72			42	Tailor
Geologist	70			42	Welder
Clergy	69			41	Apprentice electrician
Psychologist	69			41	Locomotive engineer
Pharmacist	68			40	Farmer
Optometrist	67			40	Telephone operator
Registered nurse	66		Auctioneer	39	
Secondary-school teacher	66			39	Carpenter
Accountant	65			39	Furniture finisher
Air traffic controller	65			38	Mining explosives worker
Athlete	65			38	TV repairperson
Electrical engineer	64			37	Security guard
Elementary-school teacher	64			36	Brick/stone mason
Mechanical engineer	64			36	Child care worker
Economist	63		File clerk	36	
Industrial engineer	62			36	Hairdresser
Veterinarian	62			35	Baker
Airplane pilot	61			35	Upholsterer
Computer programmer	61			34	Bulldozer operator
Sociologist	61			34	Meter reader
Editor/reporter	60			32	Bus driver
	60	Police officer		32	Hotel clerk
Actor	58			31	Auto body repairperson
Radiologic technician	58		Apparel retail salesperson	30	
Dietician	56			30	Truck driver
Statistician	56		Cashier	29	
Forester and conservationist	55			28	Elevator operator
Radio/TV announcer	55			28	Garbage collector
Librarian	54			28	Taxi driver
	53	Aircraft mechanic		28	Waiter/waitress
	53	Firefighter		27	Bellhop
Postmaster	53			27	Freight handler
Dental hygienist	52			25	Bartender
Painter/sculptor	52			23	Farm laborer
Social worker	52			23	Household servant
Draftsman	51			23	Midwife
	51	Electrician		22	Door-to-door salesperson
Computer operator	50			22	Janitor
Funeral director	49			19	Car washer
Realtor	49			19	News vendor
Bookkeeper	47			09	Shoe shiner
	47	Machinist			

SOURCE: Adapted from *General Social Surveys, 1972–1991: Cumulative Codebook* (Chicago: National Opinion Research Center, 1991), pp. 827–35.

Schooling

Industrial societies generally define schooling as a right, but all young people in the United States do not have an equal opportunity for formal education. Table 7–3 indicates the schooling of our population aged twenty-five and over in 1991. While more than three-fourths had completed high school, only 21.4 percent were college graduates.

Formal education promotes not just personal development, it also affects a person's occupation and income. Most (but not all) of the white-collar occupations shown in Table 7–2 that offer high income and prestige require a college degree or other advanced education. Similarly, most blue-collar jobs are held by people with less schooling.

Ancestry, Race, and Gender

Although our class system does reward individual talent and initiative, who we are at birth greatly influences what we become later in life.

Ancestry determines our point of entry into the social hierarchy. The family into which we are born has a strong bearing on our future schooling, occupation, and income. Studies of our country's richest individuals—those with hundreds of millions of dollars in wealth—suggest that about half derived their fortunes primarily from inheritance (Thurow, 1987; Queenan, 1989). The "inheritance" of poverty and the lack of opportunity that goes with it just as surely shape the future of those in need.

Race is strongly related to social position in the United States. Whites have a higher overall occupational standing than blacks, and also receive more schooling. These differences are reflected in median income: African-American families earned on average $21,548 in 1991, which is about 57 percent of the $37,783 earned by the average white family (U.S. Bureau of the Census, 1992). Differences in family patterns account for much of this income disparity. Comparing only families that include a married couple, African-American families earn 84 percent as much as white families do.

Over time, this income differential creates a considerable "wealth gap," with average wealth among African Americans (about $4,100) about 10 percent of the $43,300 found among whites (O'Hare, 1989). Finally, even among affluent families, race makes a difference, as the box on page 168 explains.

Table 7–3 SCHOOLING OF U.S. ADULTS, 1991 (AGED 25 AND OVER)

	Women	Men
Not a high-school graduate	21.7%	21.4%
8 years or less	10.3	11.0
9–11 years	11.4	10.4
High-school graduate	78.4%	78.5%
High school only	41.0	36.0
1–3 years college	18.6	18.2
College graduate or more	18.8	24.3

SOURCE: U.S. Bureau of the Census, 1992.

Ethnicity also relates to social stratification. Traditionally, people of English ancestry have had the most wealth and greatest power. The rapidly growing Hispanic population in the United States, by contrast, has long been disadvantaged. In 1991, median income among Hispanic families was $23,895, 63 percent of the comparable figure for all whites. A detailed examination of how race and ethnicity affect social standing is presented in Chapter 9 ("Race and Ethnicity").

Societies also place men and women in different social positions. Of course, both sexes are born to families at every social level. Yet women claim less income, wealth, and occupational prestige, and place slightly lower in educational achievement than men (Bernard, 1981; Lengermann & Wallace, 1985). Even more important, as we shall explain later, households headed by women are ten times more likely to be poor than those headed by men. Chapter 10 ("Sex and Gender") fully examines the link between gender and social stratification.

SOCIAL CLASSES IN THE UNITED STATES

As we have seen, rankings in a rigid caste system are obvious to all. Defining the social categories in a more fluid class system, however, poses a number of challenges. Taking Karl Marx's lead, we might identify only two major social classes; other sociologists, however, have identified as many as six (Warner & Lunt, 1941) or even seven (Coleman & Rainwater, 1978). Another approach, following Max Weber, would be to conclude that our society has no clear classes but rather is stratified along a multidimensional continuum.

Two Colors of Affluence: Do Blacks and Whites Differ?

The typical African-American family earns only about 57 percent of the income of the average white family. This creates a strong link between race and poverty. But there is another side to the black community—an affluent side—that expanded during the 1980s.

The number of affluent African-American families—with annual incomes over $50,000—is increasing rapidly. In 1991, more than 1 million black families were financially privileged. Adjusted for inflation, this represents a five-fold increase over two decades before. Today, 15 percent of African-American families (more than 2 million adults and their children) are affluent. About 16 percent of Hispanic families are affluent, too, although twice as many non-Hispanic white families have this much income.

But black and white affluence is not the same. First, rich people of color are not *as rich* as affluent whites.

Just over 40 percent of rich white families (14 percent of all white families) earn more than $75,000 a year; only 30 percent of affluent African-American families (5 percent of all black families) reach this level of income. Second, blacks more than whites achieve affluence through *multiple incomes*—from two em-

ployed spouses, or employed parents and children. Third, affluent blacks generally *earn* their income rather than deriving it from investments. Three-fourths of affluent white families had unearned investment income, compared to only one-half of affluent black families.

Beyond differences in income, affluent blacks still contend with social barriers based on color. Even African Americans with the money to purchase a home, for example, may find they are unwelcome as neighbors. For this reason, affluent blacks are more likely to live in central-city areas (56 percent) than in the suburbs (40 percent). Affluent whites are much more concentrated in suburbs (61 percent).

Affluent people come in all colors. Yet, the social significance of race affects the lives of the rich just as it shapes the lives of the rest of us.

SOURCES: O'Hare (1989) and U.S. Bureau of the Census (1991).

The difficulty in defining classes in the United States arises from the relatively low status consistency in our society. Especially toward the middle of the hierarchy, a person's social position on one dimension may contradict standing on another (Gilbert & Kahl, 1987). Into what class would we place a member of the clergy who enjoys high prestige, but has moderate power and little wealth? And what of a lucky gambler who accumulates lots of money yet has little power and never completed high school? To make matters more complex, the social mobility characteristic of class systems—again, most pronounced near the middle—can change social standing during anyone's lifetime, further blurring class boundaries. Keeping these problems in mind, we can describe four general rankings: the upper class, the middle class, the working class, and the lower class.

The Upper Class

The upper class includes 3 or 4 percent of the population. The yearly income of upper-class families is at least $100,000 and can exceed ten times that much. In many cases, this high income is derived from inherited wealth. In 1992, *Forbes* magazine profiled the richest four hundred people in the United States, estimating their combined wealth at $300 billion. These richest people had a minimum net worth of $265 million and included seventy-three billionaires. The upper class thus comprises what Karl Marx termed "capitalists" who own most of the nation's productive property.

Adding to their wealth and power, many members of the upper class work as top executives in large corporations and as high government officials. The upper class also gains the most education, typically in expensive and highly regarded schools and colleges. Historically, the upper class has been composed largely of white Anglo-Saxon Protestants (WASPs), although today this is less often the case (Baltzell, 1964, 1976, 1988).

People in the *upper-upper class*, sometimes termed "society" or "bluebloods," include about 1 percent of the nation's population (Warner & Lunt, 1941; Coleman & Neugarten, 1971; Rossides, 1990). Membership is almost always the result of birth, as suggested by the old quip that the easiest way to become an "upper-upper" is to be born one. These families possess enormous wealth, primarily inherited rather than earned. For this reason, members of the upper-upper class are said to have *old money*.

Set apart by their wealth, members of the upper-upper class live in exclusive neighborhoods, such as Beacon Hill in Boston, the Rittenhouse Square section of Philadelphia, the Gold Coast of Chicago, and Nob Hill in San Francisco. Their children typically attend private secondary schools with others of similar background, completing their formal education at high-prestige colleges and universities. In the historical pattern of European aristocrats, they study liberal arts rather than vocationally directed subjects. Women of the upper-upper class often engage in volunteer work for charitable organizations. While helping the larger community, these activities also forge networks that broaden this elite's power (Ostrander, 1980, 1984).

The remaining 2 or 3 percent of the upper class fall into the *lower-upper class*. For these families, earnings rather than inheritance is the primary source of wealth. While so-called "new rich" families generally live in expensive houses or condominiums, they are still excluded from the highest-prestige clubs and associations of "old-money" families.

The Middle Class

The middle class includes 40 to 45 percent of the U.S. population. Because it is so large and embodies the aspirations of many more people, the middle class exerts tremendous influence on our culture. Television and other mass media usually show middle-class men and women, and most commercial advertising is directed at these "average" consumers. The middle class encompasses far more ethnic and racial diversity than the upper class.

Families in the top third of this category are some-times designated as the *upper*-middle class, based on their above-average income in the range of $50,000 to $100,000 a year. This allows upper-middle-class families to gradually accumulate considerable property—a comfortable house in a fairly expensive area, several automobiles, and some investments. Virtually all upper-middle-class people receive college educations, and postgraduate degrees are common. Many work in white-collar fields such as medicine, engineering, and law, or as business executives. Lacking the power of the richest people to influence national or international events, members of the upper-middle class often play an important role in local political affairs.

The rest of the middle class typically work in less prestigious white-collar occupations (as bank tellers, lower-level managers, and sales clerks) or in highly skilled blue-collar jobs (including electrical work and carpentry). Family income falls between $30,000 and $50,000 a year—depending on how many family members are working—which roughly equals the median income for U.S. families ($35,939 in 1991). Middle-class people generally accumulate a small amount of wealth over the course of their working lives, and most eventually own a house. Middle-class men and women are likely to be high-school graduates, but only some will be able to send their children to college. Limited income means that children of middle-class parents who do go to college generally attend state-supported schools.

The Working Class

Comprising about one-third of the population, working-class people have lower incomes than those in the middle class and virtually no accumulated wealth. In Marxist terms, the working class forms the core of the industrial proletariat. The blue-collar occupations of the working class generally yield a family income of between $15,000 and $30,000 a year, somewhat below the national average. Working-class families thus find themselves vulnerable to financial problems brought on by unemployment or illness.

Working-class jobs typically provide less personal satisfaction, and workers are usually subject to continual supervision by superiors (Edwards, 1979). Such jobs also provide fewer benefits such as medical insurance and pension plans. About half of working-class families own their homes, usually in lower-cost neighborhoods. College is an expense only a few can afford.

Television programming in the United States has typically portrayed people in a relatively narrow range of the class structure, from lower-upper class to middle class. In the last decade or so, however, an increasing number of shows have featured working-class families—belated recognition of the fact that at least one-third of all families in this country think of themselves in these terms. Roseanne Arnold, herself from a working-class family, is the star of one of the most popular shows on television.

The Lower Class

The remaining 20 percent of our population make up the lower class. Little income renders their lives unstable and insecure. In 1991, 35.7 million people (14.2 percent of the population) were officially classified as poor. Millions more—the so-called "working poor"—are only marginally better off. The poor typically work in low-prestige jobs that provide little intrinsic satisfaction. Only some manage to complete high school; a college degree is usually out of reach.

The lower class experiences considerable social segregation, especially when the poor belong to racial or ethnic minorities. Such segregation appears most starkly in urban areas where large numbers of poor people live in deteriorating neighborhoods or rental housing shunned by the other social classes. Lower-class children learn early on the harsh reality that most people place little value on their accomplishments and consider them only marginal members of society. Observing the struggles of their parents and other lower-class adults, they may lose hope of breaking the cycle of poverty. Lower-class life, then, often generates self-defeating resignation to being cut off from the resources of an affluent society (Jacob, 1986).

Some simply give up. Most poor people, however, work desperately—often at two or three jobs—to make ends meet. In a study conducted in a northern city, Carol Stack (1975) discovered that, far from lacking initiative and responsibility, many poor people devise ingenious means to survive. They do so, she concluded, because they simply have no choice.

THE DIFFERENCE CLASS MAKES

Social stratification affects nearly every dimension of social life. Health is one of the most important correlates of social standing. Children born into poor families are several times more likely to die—from disease, accidents, or violence—during their first year of life than children born into privileged families (Gortmaker, 1979; Children's Defense Fund, 1991). Among adults, people with above-average incomes are twice as likely to describe their health as excellent as are low-income people. Affluence supports longer life expectancy by providing more nutritious foods, a safer and less stressful environment, and more comprehensive medical care.

Cultural values, too, vary somewhat from class to class. Women and men with the highest social standing have an unusually strong sense of family history since their wealth and social prestige have been passed down from generation to generation (Baltzell, 1979). Because their social standing is guaranteed as a birthright, the "old rich" also tend to be understated in their manners and tastes, while "new rich" people make extensive use of homes, cars, and clothes as *status symbols* that "make a statement" about their owners.

People with greater personal and financial security also display more tolerance than their less privileged counterparts toward controversial behavior on "family values" issues like premarital sexual activity and homosexuality. Similarly, working-class people grow up with greater supervision and more rigid discipline, which they continue to experience on the job as adults. This encourages greater conformity to conventional beliefs and practices (Kohn, 1977; Humphries, 1984).

Political attitudes also are class-linked. Generally, more privileged people support the Republican Party while less advantaged people favor the Democrats (Wolfinger, Shapiro, & Greenstein, 1980). A desire to protect their wealth prompts people who are well off to take a more conservative approach to economic issues. Thus, members of the higher social classes tend to favor a free-market economy unregulated by government. On social issues, such as support for the Equal Rights Amendment, abortion, and other feminist concerns, however, affluent people tend to be more liberal. People of lower social standing show the opposing pattern, favoring liberal economic policies and conservative social goals (Nunn, Crockett, & Williams, 1978; Erikson, Luttbeg, & Tedin, 1980; Syzmanski, 1983; Humphries, 1984).

Finally, family life is also shaped by social class. Generally, lower-class families are somewhat larger than middle-class families, due to earlier marriage and less use of birth control. Upper-class families, too, have more children, partly because they can afford added child-rearing expenses. Divorce is more common among disadvantaged couples because of stresses resulting from low income and unemployment (Kitson & Raschke, 1981; Fergusson, Horwood, & Shannon, 1984). Working-class marriages reveal a rigid division of tasks between husband and wife, while middle-class marriages are more egalitarian (Bott, 1971). Finally, the number of households containing women and their children increased rapidly during the last decade. This is significant because women raising children without husbands are at high risk of poverty. This vulnerability is greatest among poor African Americans, although more women at all social levels are grappling with the economic problems of single parenthood.

SOCIAL MOBILITY

Ours is a dynamic society marked by a significant measure of mobility. Earning a college degree, securing a higher-paying job, or succeeding in a business endeavor contribute to *upward social mobility*, while dropping out of school, losing a job, or failing to sustain a business may signal *downward social mobility*. *Horizontal social mobility*—as people change their occupation, for example,

without changing their overall social standing—also appears frequently in class systems.

Changes in society as a whole also affect social mobility. During the first half of this century, for example, industrialization expanded the economy, raising the standard of living for millions of people. Even without being very good swimmers, so to speak, people were able to "ride a rising tide of prosperity." As explained presently, *structural social mobility* in a downward direction has more recently dealt many people economic setbacks.

Sociologists distinguish between one-generation and multigenerational transitions. **Intragenerational social mobility** refers to *a change in social position occurring during a person's lifetime*. **Intergenerational social mobility**, *the social standing of children in relation to their parents*, has special significance because it often reflects changes in society that affect virtually everyone.

Social Mobility: Myth and Reality

In few societies do people dwell on social mobility as much as in the United States: historically, moving ahead has been central to "the American Dream." Our social hierarchy rests largely on the notion that people have the opportunity to realize their individual potential (Kleugel & Smith, 1986).

Using the broad categories of blue-collar and white-collar jobs, studies of intergenerational mobility (that, unfortunately, have focused almost exclusively on men), show that almost 40 percent of the sons of blue-collar workers attain white-collar jobs and almost 30 percent of sons born into white-collar families end up doing blue-collar work. Looking more closely at specific occupations, we find that 80 percent of sons show some social mobility in relation to their fathers (Blau & Duncan, 1967; Featherman & Hauser, 1978). In global perspective, we find roughly the same degree of social mobility in other industrial societies (Lipset & Bendix, 1967; McRoberts & Selbee, 1981; Kaelble, 1986).

Until recently, at least, the trend in social mobility has more commonly been upward than downward. Structural social mobility accounted for most of this upward movement as better-paying white-collar jobs steadily replaced the blue-collar and farming work more common several generations ago. When an individual does experience social mobility, however, the change is usually incremental rather than dramatic. This means that members of our society rarely move "from rags to riches," or the other way around.

But no patterns apply equally to everyone. African Americans traditionally have experienced less upward social mobility than whites (Featherman & Hauser, 1978; Pomer, 1986). Both people of African and Hispanic descent ended the 1980s with little or no gains in real income, due to declining wage levels and rising unemployment. In comparison to whites, blacks fell further behind: African-American families earned 65 percent of what white families did in 1980, sliding to 57 percent by 1990 (Jacob, 1986; DeParle, 1991b). For Hispanics, the comparable figures were 73 percent and 63 percent.

Women also have less opportunity for upward mobility than men do since most women hold clerical positions (such as secretaries) and low-paying service jobs (such as waitresses). The 1980s saw a narrowing of the "gender gap" in earnings, with women receiving 60 percent as much as men in 1980, and 74 percent as much in 1991 (an all-time high). Much of this convergence, however, was due to a drop in men's earnings during the decade with the income of women remaining about the same (U.S. Bureau of the Census, 1992).

The Global Economy and the U.S. Class Structure

The assumption that everyone has a shot at upward social mobility is deeply rooted in our culture. For much of our history, economic expansion has fulfilled the promise of prosperity by raising the overall standard of living. Beginning about 1970, however, this upward trend ended, with the average worker gaining little in real income since then. Take the case of a typical fifty-year-old man working full time. Between 1958 and 1973, his income rose from $21,000 to $32,000 (in 1990 dollars). Between 1973 and 1990, however, this worker's income stagnated, even as the cost of necessities like housing and medical care rose sharply (Levy, 1987; DeParle, 1991a). In short, more and more people now seem to be trying simply to hold on to what they have.

The brisk pace of economic expansion, long taken for granted, has now slowed for a generation, creating what some analysts call *the middle-class slide*. Figure 7–4 shows median U.S. family income from 1950 to 1991 in constant 1991 dollars. Between 1950 and 1973,

Figure 7–4 Median Income, U.S. Families, 1950–1991
(*U.S. Bureau of the Census*)

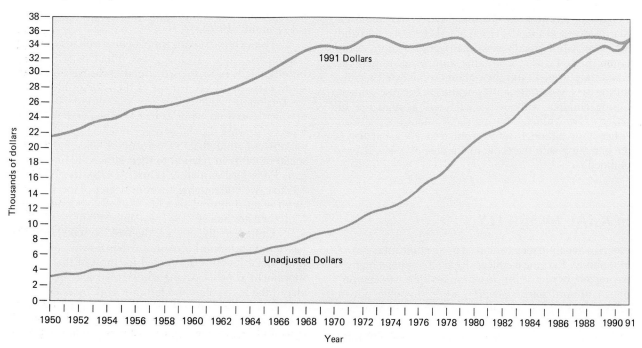

median family income grew by almost 65 percent; however, it has remained roughly stable since then (U.S. Bureau of the Census, 1992).

Underlying the "middle-class slide" is a global economic transformation. Much of the industrial production that offered U.S. workers high-paying jobs a generation ago has been transferred overseas, while a growing proportion of new jobs at home fall into the category of "service work" requiring little skill and providing minimal income (Blumberg, 1981; Rosen, 1987; Thurow, 1987). The United States now serves as a vast market for industrial goods—such as cars, and popular items like stereos and cameras—produced in Japan, Korea, and other countries. At home, traditionally high-paying corporations like USX (formerly U.S. Steel) have fallen on such hard times that they now employ fewer people than McDonald's. Echoing this shift toward lower-paying work, one study predicts that the fastest-growing job categories in the 1990s will be cashiers, nurses, maintenance workers, and truck drivers (Howe & Strauss, 1991). The expansion of global corporations has sparked upward mobility for the small number of rich men and women who manage and invest in multinational companies; note, for example, that leading stock market indexes tripled during the 1980s. But this process has hurt moderate-income workers whose factory jobs have been "exported" overseas (Reich, 1989).

"The deindustrialization of America" has shaken the confidence of many people. Compared to a generation ago, far fewer now expect to improve their social position, and a growing number worry about being able to match their parents' standard of living. Even home ownership—long a key component of the American Dream—slipped slightly during the 1980s from 66 percent to 64 percent. And this has happened while women and men are working harder than ever: half of today's families have two or more people in the labor force, double the proportion in 1950. Against this backdrop of mixed economic performance, we turn now to the growing problem of poverty in the United States.

POVERTY IN THE UNITED STATES

Social stratification simultaneously creates "haves" and "have-nots." Poverty, therefore, inevitably exists in all systems of social inequality. The concept of poverty, however, takes two different forms. **Relative poverty,** which is universal, refers to *deprivation in relation to*

A widespread stereotype links poverty to people of color in the inner cities of the United States. Although minorities are more likely to be disadvantaged, most poor people in the United States are white. Furthermore, although inner cities have the greatest concentration of poverty, rural people are actually at higher risk of poverty than their urban counterparts.

the greater resources of others. **Absolute poverty,** on the other hand, is *deprivation of resources that is life-threatening.* Absolute poverty is the more serious, if solvable, human problem.

As the next chapter ("Global Inequality") explains, the global dimensions of absolute poverty place the lives of some 1 billion human beings—one in five of the earth's people—at risk. Even in the affluent United States, the wrenching reality of poverty results in hunger, inadequate housing, and poor health.

The Extent of U.S. Poverty

Historically, poverty in this country has been going down, although the ranks of the poor have swelled in recent years. In 1991, the government listed 36 million people—

14.2 percent of the population—as poor. To be poor, the annual income for a family of four living in a city must not exceed $13,924. This standard approximates three times the estimated minimum expense for food. But not all families are even this "well off": one recent study noted that 40 percent of the poor live on less than half the official poverty level (Littman, 1989; Children's Defense Fund, 1991). Another 12 million people are *marginally poor*, falling within 25 percent of this poverty line.

Poverty means hunger, which is a daily reality for some 20 million people in the United States (Schwartz-Nobel, 1981; Physicians' Task Force on Hunger, 1987). The Children's Defense Fund, a poverty advocacy organization, estimates that ten thousand children die each year for various reasons stemming from poverty, making low income the leading cause of death among the youngest members of our society. The advocacy group calculates the cost of wiping out child poverty in this country at $28 billion a year—an enormous sum, to be sure, but no more than what we have been spending each year to bail out the savings and loan industry. It also does not exceed the *added* income received by the richest 1 percent of U.S. families as a result of recent changes in our tax laws.

Who Are the Poor?

Although no single description covers all poor people, poverty is pronounced among certain segments of our population.

Age. The burden of poverty falls most heavily on children. In 1991, 21.8 percent of people under age eighteen (some 14 million children) were poor. From another perspective, 40 percent of the poor are under the age of eighteen.

A generation ago, the elderly were at greatest risk for poverty. In 1991, however, the poverty rate for women and men over the age of sixty-five was 12.4 percent (yielding 3.8 million elderly poor). This rate is below the overall poverty rate of 14.2 percent. About 11 percent of the poor are elderly people.

Race and ethnicity. Two-thirds of all poor people are white; about 30 percent are black. But in relation to their overall numbers, people of color are about three times as likely as whites to be poor. In 1991, 33 percent of African Americans (about 10 million people) lived in poverty, compared to about 29 percent of Hispanics

(more than 6 million), 14 percent of Asians and Pacific Islanders (1 million), and 9 percent of non-Hispanic whites (about 17 million). During the 1980s, the "poverty gap" between the races increased (U.S. Bureau of the Census, 1992).

Since both young people and people of color are disproportionately poor, minority children are at high risk of poverty. About 22 percent of all boys and girls under the age of 18 were poor in 1991; this includes 17 percent of white children, 40 percent of young Hispanics, and 46 percent of black youths.

Gender and family patterns. Of all poor people over eighteen, 63 percent are women, and 37 percent are men. This disparity reflects the fact that women who head households bear the brunt of poverty. On their shoulders falls the financial burden of raising children, and for those willing and able to work, low-paying jobs are the norm. Of all poor families, 54 percent are headed by women with no husband present. In marked contrast, only 5 percent of poor families are households headed by single men. **The feminization of poverty** refers to *the trend by which women represent an increasing proportion of the poor.*

Area of residence. The highest concentration of poverty is found in our central cities where 20 percent of people are poor. For the entire urban area, however, the poverty rate was 14 percent in 1991, lower than the 16 percent found in rural places. Generally speaking, living in cities raises living standards because job opportunities and social services are concentrated there. Suburban areas, too, have their share of poverty (10 percent), although this figure is far less than the comparable proportion in inner cities.

Explaining Poverty

The presence of tens of millions of poor people in one of the world's most affluent societies raises serious social and moral concerns. Two general approaches to the problem of poverty are described below.

The poor are primarily responsible for their own poverty. Throughout our history, people in the United States have embraced the notion that individuals are largely responsible for their social standing. This view assumes that our society offers considerable opportunity for anyone able and willing to take advantage of it. The poor, then, are those with fewer skills, less schooling, lower motivation, or, perhaps, a debilitating drug addiction—in sum, people who are somehow undeserving.

Every society embraces notions of how we *like* to see ourselves, while only occasionally taking a more objective look at what we really are. John George Brown (1831–1913) made a fortune a century ago as a painter who portrayed the world as most people wanted to see it. Others, including photographer Jacob Riis (1849–1914), found far less financial reward for capturing something closer to the truth. This is his now-famous image of "street arabs" who survived as best they could on the mean streets of the growing industrial cities.

Anthropologist Oscar Lewis (1961) employs a variant of this approach in his analysis of Latin American poverty. Lewis claims that the poor become entrapped in a *culture of poverty* that fosters resignation to one's plight as a matter of fate. Socialized within this environment, children come to see little point in aspiring to a better life. The result is a self-perpetuating cycle of poverty. Looking at U.S. inner cities with the same point of view, Edward Banfield (1974) adds that concentrations of poor people generate a distinctive lower-class subculture that inhibits personal achievement. One element of this subculture, he claims, is a present-time orientation, which encourages living for the moment rather than engaging in hard work, saving, and other behavior likely to promote upward social mobility. Banfield therefore portrays the poor as irresponsible, reaping what they deserve.

Society is primarily responsible for poverty. An alternative position, argued by William Ryan (1976), holds that society—not the poor—is primarily responsible for poverty because of how it distributes resources. In global perspective, societies that distribute resources more equally than our country does (including Sweden and Japan) have far less poverty. From Ryan's point of view, then, any lack of ambition on the part of poor people is less a cause of poverty than a *consequence* of being poor. He argues that Banfield's analysis amounts to "blaming the victims" for their own suffering. Ryan maintains that providing more economic opportunity to the poor and engineering more social equality should be high priorities.

Critical evaluation. Each of these explanations of poverty has won public support and has advocates among government policy makers. Asking the public at large about this debate, we find that 33 percent of U.S. adults think government should take the lead in attacking poverty; another 20 percent counter that poor people should take care of themselves; the remaining 40 percent express sympathy for both views (N.O.R.C., 1991).

Supporters of the personal responsibility position advocate working harder to encourage equality of opportunity in the United States, but they otherwise adopt a laissez-faire approach toward the poor. Advocates of ac-

African-American artist Henry O. Tanner (1859–1937) captured the humility and humanity of impoverished people in his painting *Thankful Poor.* This insight is important in a society that tends to dismiss poor people as morally unworthy and deserving of their bitter plight.

Henry O. Tanner, Thankful Poor, 1894. Oil on canvas. 35 x 44". William H. and Camille O. Cosby Collection. Philadelphia Museum of Art.

tive government intervention claim that we should reduce poverty by redistributing income more equally. This might be accomplished through programs ranging from comprehensive child care to help poor mothers gain job training to a guaranteed minimum income level for every U.S. family.

Little hard evidence conclusively validates either of these approaches. Looking at data reflecting patterns of work among the poor, we see that half of the heads of poor families did not work at all during 1991. In fact, only one in six heads of families in poverty worked steadily (at least fifty weeks) during that year (U.S. Bureau of the Census, 1992). This would seem to support the view that the poor are simply unable or unwilling to work.

But *why* do many of the poor not work? Most women who are poor claim they cannot work because they need to care for their children. In the United States, few employers provide child-care programs for workers, and few low-paid workers can afford to obtain child care on their own. Most poor men contend that there are no jobs to be found; illness or disability has sidelined them, or, if elderly, they have retired. Overall, poor adults feel they have few options (Popkin, 1990).

But not all poor people are jobless. The 16 percent (1.2 million) heads of households who work full time are included in the *working poor;* these men and women labor for at least fifty weeks of the year yet cannot escape poverty. Another 25 percent of these heads of households (1.8 million people) work 27 to 49 weeks, and an additional 4 percent (300,000 people) are on the job fewer than 26 weeks. Such "working poverty" places the poor in a double bind: their jobs pay only low wages needed to live but consume time and energy they would need to gain training or schooling that might open new doors (Levitan & Shapiro, 1987). Keep in mind that, at the current minimum wage level of $4.25, even two adults working full time can barely support a family above the official poverty line.

No one doubts that individual ability and initiative play a part in shaping everyone's social position. On balance, though, evidence points to society—not individual character traits—as the primary source of poverty. Some poor people lack ambition. Overall, however, the poor are *categories* of people—women heads of families, minorities, people isolated from the larger society in inner-city areas—without the same opportunities as others.

Homelessness

Homelessness is caused by poverty and our society's failure to ensure an adequate supply of affordable housing. There is no precise count of homeless people. The Census Bureau carried out a tally of the homeless during the night of March 20, 1991, and found 178,828 people at shelters and 49,793 people on streets where the poor are known to congregate. But Census Bureau officials cautioned that this represented only a portion of the total homeless population. A completed tally—in rural areas as well as cities—would probably reach 500,000 *on any given night* with three times this number—1.5 million people—homeless *at some time during the course of a year* (Kozol, 1988; Wright, 1989).

The familiar stereotypes of homeless people—men sleeping in doorways and women carrying everything they own in shopping bags—have recently been undermined by the reality of the "new homeless," those thrown out of work because of plant closings, people forced out of apartments by rising rents, and others whose wages cannot meet mortgage or rent payments. Today, no stereotype of the homeless paints a complete picture because such people are now a highly varied category of our population.

But virtually all homeless people have one thing in common: *poverty*. For that reason, the approaches already used in explaining poverty also apply to homelessness. One side of the debate places responsibility on *personal traits* of the homeless themselves. Perhaps one-third of homeless people are mentally ill; others are addicted to alcohol or other drugs. Some, for whatever reason, are unable to cope in a complex and highly competitive society (Bassuk, 1984; Whitman, 1989). Those on the other side of the debate suggest that homelessness results from *societal factors*, including a lack of low-income housing and our economy's growing number of low-income jobs (Kozol, 1988; Schutt, 1989). Advocates of this position are quick to point out that one-third of all homeless people are now entire families, and children are the fastest-growing category of the homeless.

No one disputes that a large proportion of homeless people are personally impaired to some degree, although how much is cause and how much effect is difficult to untangle. But structural changes in the U.S. economy, coupled with limited government support for lower-income people, contribute substantially to homelessness.

Class and Welfare, Politics and Values

This chapter has focused on social stratification and presented many facts about social inequality in the United States. In the end, however, conclusions about wealth and poverty also turn on politics and values. Understandably, the notion that social standing reflects personal merit is most popular among well-off people. The opposing idea that society should distribute wealth and other resources more equally finds greatest favor among those with fewest advantages (Rytina, Form, & Pease, 1970; N.O.R.C., 1991).

Most members of our society find some truth in the assertion that people are responsible for their own life circumstances. When a random sample of adults was asked, "How important is hard work for getting ahead in life?" almost 90 percent responded that it was "essential" or "very important" (N.O.R.C., 1991:541). Such cultural values encourage us to see successful people as personally meritorious and the poor as personally deficient. Richard Sennett and Jonathan Cobb (1973) term this judgment, applied to the poor, the *hidden injury of class*. In other words, poverty erodes people's self-image while, for others, privilege is a personal "badge of ability." With this attitude in mind, it is easy to understand why our society has historically viewed social welfare programs as "handouts" for the "undeserving" that undermine individual initiative (Waxman, 1983; Handler & Hasenfeld, 1991). Accepting public assistance thus becomes personally demeaning, which helps explain why half the people eligible for various forms of needed benefits do not even apply for them (U.S. Bureau of the Census, 1991).

Curiously, our value system paints a more positive picture of government benefits provided to "deserving" wealthy people. Current law, for example, allows homeowners to deduct from their income all the interest paid on home mortgages and real estate tax payments in calculating their income tax. The savings realized from this policy—which, of course, goes into the pockets of people affluent enough to own their own homes—amounts to some $50 billion annually, at least *five times* the amount of government funds used to help house the poor. Our cultural tendency to equate privilege with personal merit leads us to wink at "wealthfare" while denouncing welfare to the poor. Such attitudes are important because they guide government efforts to deal with the problem of poverty.

Finally, the drama of social stratification extends far beyond the borders of the United States. The most striking social disparities are found not by looking at one country but by comparing living standards in various parts of the world. As we shall see, poverty worldwide is both more widespread and more severe than it is in this country. In Chapter 8, we broaden our investigation of social stratification by focusing on global inequality.

SUMMARY

1. Social stratification involves ranking categories of people in a hierarchy. Caste systems, common in agrarian societies, are based on ascription and permit little or no social mobility. Class systems, characteristic of industrial societies, allow more social mobility based on individual achievement.

2. The Davis–Moore thesis states that social stratification is universal because it is useful to a society. In class systems, unequal rewards encourage the most able people to assume the most important occupational positions. Critics of the Davis–Moore thesis note (a) the difficulty in objectively determining the functional importance of occupational positions; (b) that stratification prevents many people from developing their abilities; and (c) that stratification often generates social conflict.

3. For Karl Marx, conflict in industrial societies involves the bourgeoisie, who own the means of production and seek profits, and the proletariat, who provide labor in exchange for wages. While the socialist revolution that Marx predicted has not occurred in industrial societies such as the United States, some sociologists point out that our society is still marked by pronounced social inequality and substantial class conflict.

4. Max Weber envisioned social stratification in terms of three dimensions of inequality: economic class, social status or prestige, and power. Together, these three dimensions form a complex hierarchy of socioeconomic standing.

5. Gerhard and Jean Lenski observe that, historically, technological advances have been associated with more pronounced social stratification. A limited reversal of this trend occurs in advanced industrial societies, as represented by the "Kuznets Curve."

6. Social inequality in the United States involves disparity in income, wealth, occupational prestige, and schooling.

7. The upper class, which is small (3 to 4 percent of the population), includes this nation's richest and most powerful individuals. Comprising this group are the upper-upper class, the "old rich," who inherit wealth, and the lower-upper class, or "new rich," who derive most of their wealth from earned income.

8. The middle class (40 to 45 percent) enjoys reasonable financial security, but only the upper-middle class has significant wealth. Members of the working class (33 percent) have below-average incomes, typically from blue-collar work, and are less likely than middle-class people to obtain a college education.

9. The lower class (20 percent) includes individuals near or below the official poverty line. People of color, Hispanics, and women are disproportionately represented in the lower class.

10. Some social mobility is common in the United States as it is in other industrial societies; typically, however, only small changes occur from one generation to the next.

11. The growing global economy has helped increase the wealth of rich families in the United States, but has stalled or even reduced the standard of living of other people.

12. Some 36 million people in this country are officially classified as poor. About 40 percent of the poor are children under the age of eighteen. Most poor people are white, but African Americans and Hispanics are disproportionately represented among the poor. The share of poor families headed by women is growing.

13. The "culture of poverty" thesis suggests that poverty is perpetuated by the personal flaws of the poor themselves. Critics of this view argue that poverty is caused by the unequal distribution of wealth in society.

KEY CONCEPTS

absolute poverty a deprivation of resources that is life-threatening

alienation the experience of powerlessness in social life

blue-collar occupation lower-prestige work that involves mostly manual labor

capitalist one who owns a factory or other productive enterprise

caste system social stratification based on ascription

class system social stratification based on individual achievement

feminization of poverty the trend by which women represent an increasing proportion of the poor

ideology cultural beliefs that reflect and support the interests of certain categories of people

income wages or salary from work and earnings from investments

intergenerational social mobility the social standing of children in relation to their parents

intragenerational social mobility a change in social position occurring during a person's lifetime

meritocracy stratification linking rewards to personal merit

proletariat people who sell their productive labor

relative poverty deprivation in relation to the greater resources of others

social mobility a change of position in a stratification system

social stratification a system by which a society ranks categories of people in a hierarchy

socioeconomic status a composite social ranking based on various dimensions of social inequality

status consistency consistent standing across various dimensions of social inequality

structural social mobility social mobility of large numbers of people due more to changes in society itself than to individual efforts

wealth the total amount of money and valuable goods that any person or family controls

white-collar occupation higher-prestige work that involves mostly mental activity

David Alfaro Siquieros, Echo of a Scream, 1937. Duco on wood. 48 x 36". Collection, The Museum of Modern Art, New York. Gift of Edward M. M. Warburg.

8

Global Inequality

Half an hour from the center of Cairo, Egypt's capital city, the bus turned onto a dirt road and jerked to a stop. It was not quite dawn, and the Mo'edhdhins would soon climb the minarets of Cairo's many mosques to call the Islamic faithful to morning prayer. Genuinely bewildered, the driver turned to the busload of students from the United States and their instructor. "Why," he asked, mixing English with some Arabic, "do you want to be here? And in the middle of the night?"

Why, indeed? No sooner had we stepped down from the bus than smoke and stench, the likes of which we had never before encountered, overcame us. Eyes squinting, handkerchiefs pressed against noses and mouths, we climbed the path ascending mountains of trash and garbage that extended for miles. We were entering the Cairo Dump, where one of the world's largest cities of 15 million people deposits its trash and garbage.[1] We walked stiffly and with great care, since the only light came from small fires smoldering around us. Suddenly, spectral shapes appeared out of the shadows. After a moment, we identified them as dogs peering curiously through the curtain of haze. As startled as we were, they quickly turned and vanished into the thick air. Ahead of us, we could see blazing piles of trash circled by people seeking warmth and companionship.

Human beings actually inhabit this inhuman place, creating a surreal scene, like the aftermath of the next war. As we approached, the fires cast an eerie light on their faces. We stopped some distance from them, separated by a vast chasm of culture and circumstances. But smiles eased the tension, and soon we were sharing the warmth of their flames. At that moment, the melodious call to prayer sounded across the city.

The people of the Cairo Dump, called the Zebaleen, belong to a religious minority—Coptic Christians—in a predominantly Muslim society. Barred by religious discrimination from many jobs, the Zebaleen use donkey carts and small trucks to pick up refuse throughout the city and bring it here. The night-long routine reaches a climax at dawn when hundreds of Zebaleen gather at the dump, swarming over the new piles seeking out anything of value. That morning, we watched men, women, and children fill their baskets with pieces of screen, bits of ribbon, scraps of discarded food—enough to get them through another day. Watching in silence,

we became keenly aware of our sturdy shoes and warm clothing, and self-conscious that our watches and cameras represented more money than most of the Zebaleen earn in a year.

Although unfamiliar to most North Americans, the Zebaleen of the Cairo Dump are hardly unique. Their counterparts live in the Philippines, India, Mexico—in fact, in most nations on earth. In poor societies around the globe, as we shall see, poverty is not only more widespread than in the United States, but also far more severe.

THE THREE WORLDS

To gain a broader understanding of social inequality, then, we must look beyond the United States. While we recognize that pronounced social differences divide members of our society (see Chapter 7, "Social Stratification"), the average U.S. family is quite well off by world standards. Even most people below the official poverty line enjoy a much higher standard of living than the majority of those in the poorest nations on earth. We begin our study of global inequality by separating the world's societies into three broad categories or "worlds."

First, however, a word of caution. To place the roughly 187 nations on earth into three sweeping categories ignores striking differences in their ways of life. The societies in each category have rich and varied histories, speak dozens of languages, and encompass diverse peoples whose cultural distinctiveness serves as a source of pride. However, the three broad categories employed in this chapter are widely used to organize world nations based on (1) their level of technological development and (2) their political and economic system.

The First World

The term **First World** refers to *industrial societies that have predominantly capitalist economies.* They are not called "first" because they are "better" or "more important" than other nations, but rather because the Industrial Revolution came first to these nations, beginning two centuries ago, vastly increasing their productive capacity. For example, the economic activity surrounding the care of household pets in the United States today exceeds the entire economic output of medieval Europe. This is reflected in a relatively high standard of living for the average person in a First-World society.

---

[1] This portrayal of the Cairo Dump is based on the author's experiences in Cairo. It also draws on the discussion found in Spates & Macionis (1987) and conversations with James L. Spates, who has also visited the Cairo Dump.

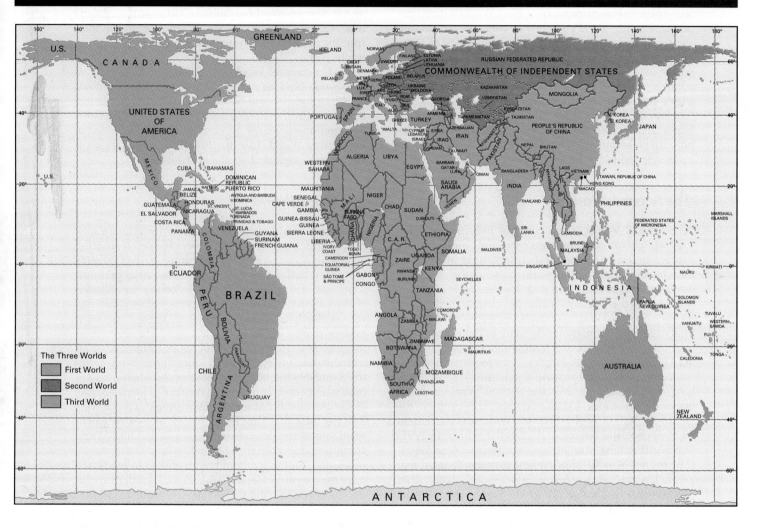

Global Map 8–1 The Three Worlds

Global Map 8–1 identifies countries of the First World. Shown in blue, this region encompasses the nations of Western Europe, including the United Kingdom (made up of England, Scotland, Wales, and Northern Ireland). It was in southeastern England that early industrialization appeared by 1775. Also part of the First World are the United States and Canada in North America, where the Industrial Revolution was under way around 1850. On the African continent, the advanced economic development of South Africa places this country (at least its *white minority*) in the First World. Also ranking in the First World is Japan, the most economically powerful nation in Asia. And, in the geographic region known as Oceania, Australia and New Zealand also belong to the First World.

Collectively, the First World covers roughly 25 percent of the earth's land area, includes parts of five continents, and mostly lies in the Northern Hemisphere. In 1993, the population of the First World was about 800 million, just over 15 percent of the earth's people.

By global standards, the First World is not densely populated.

The industrial capacity of First-World nations explains why the world's income is concentrated among the small share of humanity. The economies of these nations are predominantly capitalist, so that a market system (or "private enterprise"), rather than government, controls most production. Since World War I, the United States has been the dominant nation (often called a "superpower") of the First World. Because the United States and its Western European allies are linked by political and economic alliances, the First World is sometimes referred to by the shorthand term "the West."

The Second World

The **Second World** is composed of *industrial societies that are currently transforming socialist economies into market systems*. Industrialization took hold in much of this broad region of the world only in the twentieth century. This accounts, in part, for the lesser economic strength of the Second World in relation to the First World. Second-World nations have less powerful industrial capacities; proportionately more of their people live in rural areas and work in agricultural production. (Chapter 11, "Economics and Politics," compares the performance of capitalist and socialist economies.)

In Global Map 8–1, the Second World is designated by red stripes. During the twentieth century, the dominant nation in the Second World was the Union of Soviet Socialist Republics (U.S.S.R.), which, in 1992, was recast as the Commonwealth of Independent States. The former Soviet Union's military strength rivaled that of the United States, giving it "superpower" status. After World War II, the Soviet Union took control of the nations of Eastern Europe including Poland, the German Democratic Republic (East Germany), Czechoslovakia, Hungary, Romania, and Bulgaria. During 1989, most of Eastern Europe was transformed by the popular overthrow of established socialist governments, the opening of borders to the West, and the call for Western-style market systems. Within a year, the "two Germanies" were rejoined, and the united Germany is now shown as part of the First World. In 1991, change accelerated in the Soviet Union as well, ending the historic monopoly on power enjoyed by that nation's Communist Party. After the Baltic republics of Estonia, Latvia, and Lithuania won their independence, ten of the twelve remaining republics of the former Soviet Union formed a new feder-

ation. Reform toward a market economy is currently under way throughout these republics. The future course of the Second World is unclear; perhaps the concept of a "second world" may soon be obsolete. In the short run, the political systems of these countries are continuing to evolve.

The Second World spans roughly 15 percent of the world's land area. Most of it lies in the Commonwealth of Independent States, geographically the largest nation on earth, stretching from Europe to Asia. Roughly 500 million people or 10 percent of humanity live in the Second World. Like the First World, this region is not densely populated by global standards.

The Third World

The **Third World** encompasses *primarily agrarian societies in which most people are poor*. In these countries, economic activity centers on farming; in fact, slightly more than half of the world's people are rural peasants. Many are staunchly traditional, following the folkways of their ancestors. Industrial technology plays a minimal role in the lives of such people; its limited impact is evident mostly in Third-World cities. Therefore these societies are less productive by world standards. This pattern holds true even though some Third-World countries—notably the oil-rich nations of the Middle East—have an extremely high average standard of living because of the great wealth of *some* of their people. Global Map 8–1 indicates that the Third World, shown in green, spans most of the globe. In our hemisphere, Third-World countries range from the poor but industrializing nation of Mexico, on the southern border of the United States, to all the nations of Central America and South America. Moving across the Atlantic Ocean, the continent of Africa (except for white South Africa) falls into the Third World. Included, too, is the Middle East, except Israel, and all of Asia, with the exception of Japan.

The Third World represents about 60 percent of the earth's area including most of the countries near and below the equator. More significantly, 75 percent of the world's 5.6 billion people live in the Third World. Population density is high: ten times higher in India, for example, than in the United States. Because of its large and rapidly increasing population, as well as low economic productivity, the Third World faces poverty on a massive scale. Hunger, unsafe housing, and high rates of disease all plague Third-World nations.

Less-developed societies have no single economic

When natural disasters strike rich societies, property loss is great but loss of life is low; in poor societies, the converse is true. A cyclone recently devastated coastal Bangladesh, killing tens of thousands of people who had little choice but to live in regions prone to flooding. Tragically, most of those who survived the storm remained there, hoping against the odds to escape further catastrophe.

system in common. Some poor countries, such as the People's Republic of China (with 1.3 billion people, the world's most populous nation), maintain predominantly socialist economies. Other nations, like India and Egypt, blend elements of socialism and capitalism. Still others, including Brazil and much of Latin America, are primarily capitalist. In all cases, however, these countries struggle against a tide of devastating poverty.

GLOBAL POVERTY

Poverty always means suffering. In global perspective, however, poverty is by far most acute in the Third World. This does not mean that deprivation in the United States is a minor issue. Especially in a rich society, the lack of food, housing, and health care for tens of millions of people—many of them children—amounts to a national tragedy. Yet, in global perspective, poverty in the Third World is *more severe* and *more extensive* than in the United States.

The Severity of Poverty

Poverty in the Third World is more severe than it is in rich societies such as the United States. The data in Table 8–1 on page 186 suggest why. The first column

of figures shows the gross domestic product (GDP)[2] for selected countries. Industrial societies typically have a high economic output mainly due to their productive industrial technology. A large, First-World nation like the United States had a 1990 GDP of more than $5 trillion; the GDP of the former Soviet Union, a large Second-World country, stood at about $2 trillion. The rest of the table shows that Third-World countries, with little industrial technology, had far lower GDPs.

The second column of figures in Table 8–1 indicates "per-person income" for these countries, calculated by dividing the country's total annual income by the total population. The resulting figures for First-World nations are relatively high—topping $20,000 for the United States, for example. Income levels in Second-World societies are significantly lower than those in the First World. But the most dramatic difference occurs

---

[2] Gross domestic product refers to all the goods and services produced by a society's economy in a given year. Income earned abroad by individuals or corporations is excluded from this measure, differentiating GDP from gross national product (GNP) that includes foreign earnings. For countries that invest heavily abroad (Kuwait, for example) GDP is considerably less than GNP; for countries in which other nations invest heavily (Hong Kong), GDP is considerably higher than GNP. For societies that both invest heavily abroad and have considerable foreign investment (including the United States) the two measures are comparable. For the present purpose, simply notice the striking differences in the power of the various world economies.

Table 8–1   WEALTH AND WELL-BEING
IN GLOBAL PERSPECTIVE, 1990

Country	Gross Domestic Product ($ billion)	Per-Person Income ($)	Quality of Life Index
First World			
Japan	2,818	23,810	.993
Canada	488	19,030	.983
Sweden	167	21,570	.982
United States	5,156	20,910	.976
United Kingdom	717	14,610	.967
Germany	1,189	20,440	.959
Second World			
Czechoslovakia	50	9,709	.920
Hungary	29	8,260	.911
Soviet Union	2,000	8,662	.908
Bulgaria	16	2,320	.899
Poland	68	6,879	.863
Third World			
Latin America			
Argentina	200	2,160	.854
Mexico	400	2,010	.838
Brazil	319	2,540	.759
Colombia	39	1,200	.757
Nicaragua	3	850	.612
El Salvador	6	1,070	.524
Bolivia	5	620	.416
Africa/Middle East			
Saudi Arabia	80	6,020	.697
Lebanon	3	1,150	.592
Iran	150	3,200	.577
Egypt	32	640	.394
Cameroon	11	1,000	.328
Zaire	10	260	.299
Nigeria	29	250	.242
Burkina Faso	2	350	.081
Sierra Leone	220	890	.048
Asia			
Hong Kong	53	10,300	.934
South Korea	211	4,400	.884
Thailand	69	1,220	.713
P. R. of China	417	350	.614
Pakistan	36	370	.311
India	235	340	.308
Bangladesh	20	180	.186

SOURCES: United Nations Development Programme, *Human Development Report 1991*, New York: Oxford University Press, 1991; The World Bank, *World Development Report 1991: The Challenge of Development*, New York: Oxford University Press, 1991.

in the Third World. Here, per-person income levels are commonly below $2,000 a year. At approximately $180, the per-capita income in Bangladesh amounts to less than 1 percent of that found in the United States. In simple terms, this means that the typical person in this poor Asian nation labors all year to make what the average worker in the United States earns in several days.[3]

The third column of Table 8–1 provides a measure of the quality of life in various nations. The index used here, calculated by the United Nations, factors in income, education (adult literacy and average years of schooling), and longevity (how long people typically live). Index values are decimals that fall between hypothetical extremes of 1 (highest) and zero (lowest). Japan has the highest rating of world societies (.993), and the African nation of Sierra Leone has the lowest (.048). The United States has a quality of life index of .976, placing us ninth in the world (The World Bank, 1991).

One key reason that quality of life differs so dramatically among the societies of the world is that economic productivity is lowest in precisely the regions of the globe where population is greatest. Figure 8–1 shows the division of global income and population for each of the three "worlds." The First World is by far the most advantaged with two-thirds of the world's income consumed by just 15 percent of the planet's people. The people of the Second World are less well off, but they, too, claim a disproportionately large share of global income. In the Third World, 20 percent of global income supports a full 75 percent of humanity. Factoring together income and population, for every dollar earned by a Third-World worker, a person in the Second World takes home five dollars and a worker in the First World receives sixteen dollars.

Bear in mind that, beyond sweeping global patterns, each society is *internally* stratified. The net result is that the most affluent North Americans live worlds apart from the most disadvantaged people on our planet, such as Cairo's Zebaleen, described in the chapter opening.

Relative versus absolute poverty. A distinction made in the last chapter has an important application to global inequality. Members of rich societies generally focus

---

[3] The per-person income figures for the poorest of the world's societies are understated to the extent that they exclude products grown for home consumption or bartered with others. But even if the figures are doubled to neutralize this bias, per capita income of Third-World societies remains well below that of rich nations.

on the *relative poverty* of some of their members, highlighting how some people lack resources that are taken for granted by others. Relative poverty, by definition, exists in every society, even in the First World. But especially important in global perspective is the concept of *absolute poverty*, a lack of resources that is life-threatening. Most commonly, absolute poverty means lacking the minimum level of nutrition necessary for health and long-term survival.

In a rich society like the United States, most people described as poor are deprived in the relative sense. But absolute poverty, too, exists in the United States. Inadequate nutrition that leaves children vulnerable to illness or even outright starvation is a stark and tragic reality. By global standards, however, immediate life-threatening poverty strikes a very small proportion of the U.S. population. By contrast, Third-World societies face a severe problem of absolute poverty, involving one-fifth of the population—almost 1 billion people—who lack nutrition adequate for a safe and productive life.

The Extent of Poverty

Poverty in the Third World is more extensive than it is in the United States. Chapter 7 ("Social Stratification") indicated that about 14 percent of the U.S. population is officially classified as poor. In the societies of the Third World, however, *most* people live no better than our nation's poor and, at any given time, about 20 percent of the people are near absolute poverty. In some parts of the world (such as East Asia), the extent of absolute poverty is not so great; in other regions (rural areas in Central America and in much of eastern Africa, for example), half the population may be ill-nourished. In the world as a whole, 100 million people have no shelter and approximately 1 billion people do not eat enough to allow them to work regularly. Of these, at least 800 million are at risk for their lives (Sivard, 1988; Helmuth, 1989; United Nations Development Programme, 1991).

Global Map 8–2 on page 188 illustrates the level of nutrition common to various world regions. If anything, the problem in the First World is too much nutrition; on average a person in the West consumes more than 3,500 calories daily, which contributes to obesity and related health problems. People in much of the Third World, by contrast, suffer from inadequate nutrition. Especially in parts of central Africa, the problem of hunger is critical.

Put more bluntly, people die—every minute of every day—from lack of basic nutrition. In the ten min-

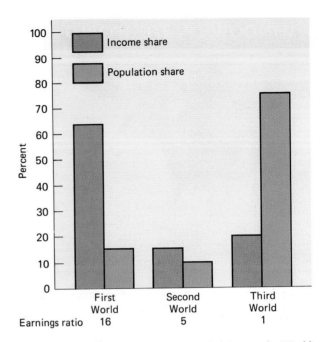

Figure 8–1 The Relative Share of Global Income by World Region

utes it takes to read through this section of the chapter, about three hundred people in the world will die of starvation. This amounts to more than 40,000 people a day, or 15 million people each year. Even more than in the United States, the burden of poverty in the Third World falls on children. In the entire Third World, about one child in four dies before reaching age five.

Two further comparisons suggest the human toll of global poverty. First, at the end of World War II, the United States obliterated the Japanese city of Hiroshima with an atomic bomb. The global loss of life from starvation equals the Hiroshima death toll *every three days*. Second, the death toll from hunger in just the last five years equals the number of deaths from war, revolution, and murder during the last 150 years (Burch, 1983). Given the magnitude of this problem, easing world hunger is one of the most serious responsibilities facing humanity today.

Third-World Women: Work and Poverty

Even more than in rich societies, Third-World women are disproportionately the poorest of the poor. In societies poor to begin with, the opportunities for women are

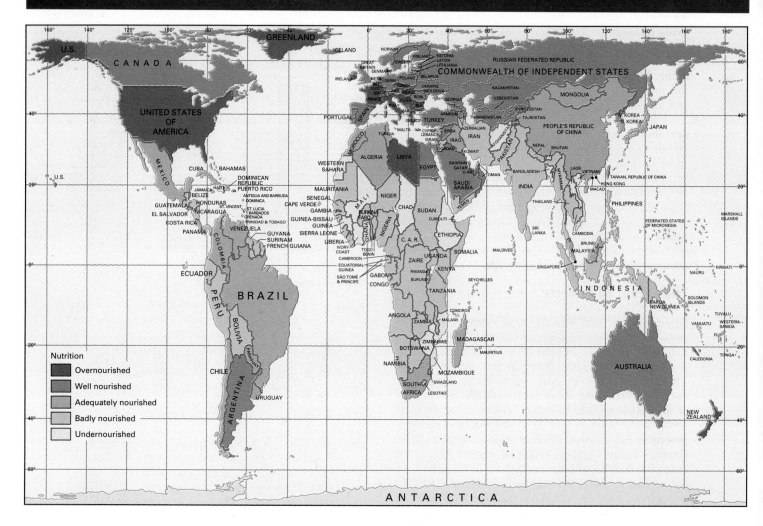

Global Map 8–2 Nutrition in Global Perspective

To remain healthy, an average, active adult requires 2,500 to 3,000 calories a day in food energy. Women and men in many poor societies are not well nourished: hundreds of millions of people survive on fewer than 2,000 calories daily despite engaging in extensive physical labor. By contrast, members of rich societies are typically overnourished—consuming in excess of 3,500 calories each day—just as they are less active physically. Although not as immediately life threatening as undernourishment, overconsumption contributes to obesity and a host of longer-term health problems.

Life for both women and men throughout the Third World is more often than not a matter of continual labor to meet basic needs. But inequality based on gender is greater in agrarian societies than it is in industrial nations. Therefore, a scene like this one, in which women work long and hard in agricultural work under the supervision of men, is common in poor countries.

sharply limited by traditions that accord them primary responsibility for child rearing and maintaining the household.

Especially in rural regions of the Third World, women work long hours—typically twelve hours a day compared to about eight hours for men (House of Representatives, 1988). Much of women's work—cleaning and repairing the home, gathering firewood, traveling to and from the market, tending to the needs of children, and preparing meals for the family—remains "invisible" to those who monitor the labor force. In comparison to rich societies, in the Third World more of women's work is not paid, making the economic position of women correspondingly weaker.

Even Third-World women who work for pay are at a greater disadvantage than their counterparts in rich societies. As Chapter 10 ("Sex and Gender") details, in the United States and the rest of the industrialized world, women receive less income for their labor than men do. In the largely agrarian societies of the Third World, where traditional subordination of women to men is more pronounced, the differential in salary between the two sexes is even greater. In the Third World, women have less access to education than men have, a pattern that is disappearing in many industrial societies (United Nations, 1988). Lacking education, women have far fewer options to change their lives.

Finally, the United Nations estimates that 90 percent of land in the Third World is formally owned by men (in rich societies, men control a lesser proportion

of wealth). In reality, wives and mothers exert considerable control over property that formally belongs to husbands and sons. Nevertheless, strong traditions reinforced by law give men ultimate control of the land, the chief source of wealth in agrarian societies.

Overall, then, Third-World poverty is both severe and extensive. The burden of poverty is not only heavy, it is shared unequally: women and children are among the most disadvantaged.

Correlates of Global Poverty

What accounts for the intense poverty of the Third World? The rest of this chapter weaves together explanations from various facts about poor societies.

1. **Technology.** The Third World is largely agrarian, lacking the productive power of industrial technology. Energy from human muscles or beasts of burden falls far short of that generated by steam, oil, or nuclear fuels. This simple technology limits the use of heavy machinery. Moreover, a focus on farming, rather than on specialized production, stunts the development of human skills and abilities.

2. **Population growth.** As Chapter 14 ("Population and Urbanization") explains in detail, Third-World societies have the highest birth rates in the world.

Despite high death rates from poverty, the populations of many poor societies of Africa, for example, double every twenty-five years. In these countries, half the people are teenagers or younger, so that they are just entering their childbearing years. Population growth, therefore, is inevitable. Even a fast-developing economy will not be able to support future surges in population. Typically, then, economic growth is overwhelmed by population increase, curbing the rise in living standards.

3. **Cultural patterns.** Societies yet to industrialize usually embrace tradition. Families and neighborhood groups pass down folkways and mores from generation to generation. Adhering to long-established ways of life, such people resist innovations—even those that promise a richer material life.

   The members of poor societies often accept their fate, bleak though it may be, in order to maintain a sense of family vitality and cultural heritage. While such attitudes discourage development, they bolster strong social bonds. The box explains why traditional people in India respond to their poverty differently than poor people in the United States generally do.

4. **Social stratification.** The modest wealth of Third-World societies is distributed very unequally among their populations. Chapter 7 ("Social Stratification") explained that social inequality is generally more pronounced in agrarian societies, where land is a vital resource, than in industrial societies. In many Asian and Latin American countries, for example, 10 percent of landowners control half the land, while half of all farming families have little or no land of their own (Hartmann & Boyce, 1982; Barry, 1983). Such concentration of wealth has prompted widespread demands for land reform.

5. **Global power relationships.** A final cause of global poverty lies in the relationships among the nations of the world. Much Third-World wealth has ended up in the hands of the First World. Historically, this can be traced to **colonialism,** *the process by which some nations enrich themselves through political and economic control of other nations.* The nations of Western Europe colonized and maintained control over much of Latin America for more than 300 years; much of Africa endured a century of colonial rule; parts of Asia were also colonized for long periods. Some analysts claim that this global exploitation allowed some nations to *develop* economically while others were deliberately *underdeveloped.*

Even though most former colonies now are politically independent, a continuing pattern of **neocolonialism** (*neo* comes from Greek, meaning "new") amounts to *a new form of economic exploitation that involves not formal political control but the operation of multinational corporations.* **Multinational corporations,** detailed in Chapter 11 ("Economics and Politics"), are *huge businesses that operate in many countries.* These corporations now wield such tremendous economic power that corporate decision makers can—and often do—influence the political systems in countries where they do business.

GLOBAL INEQUALITY: THEORETICAL ANALYSIS

There are two major explanations for the unequal distribution of the world's wealth and power—modernization theory and dependency theory. Each suggests not only why so many of the world's people are poor, but why we as North Americans enjoy such comparative advantages.

The two explanations overlap to some extent. Both acknowledge enormous inequality on our planet, and suggest that changes are needed to guarantee the future security of humanity, rich and poor alike. Yet, by emphasizing different factors, each reaches a different conclusion about the causes and remedies of global poverty.

Modernization Theory

Modernization theory is *a model of economic and social development that explains global inequality in terms of differing levels of technological development among societies.* Modernization theory developed in the 1950s, a decade of fascination with technology in the United States and a time of hostility to U.S. interests in much of the Third World. Socialist nations of the Second World were warning Third-World countries that they could not make economic progress under the influence of the capitalist First World. In response, U.S. policy makers framed a broad defense of the First World's free-market

India: A Different Kind of Poverty

Most North Americans know that India is one of the poorest societies of the world: typical personal income in this Asian nation stands at only $340 a year (see Table 8–1). Although there are rich people in India, one-third of the world's hungry people live in this vast society. But few members of our society can comprehend the reality of poverty in this Asian nation. Most of the country's 750 million people live in conditions far worse than those of us who are labeled "poor." A traveler's first experience of Indian life is sobering and sometimes shocking; in time, the outsider also learns that, in India, people experience poverty differently as well.

Arriving in Madras, one of India's largest cities, a visitor immediately recoils from the smell of human sewage, which hangs over the city like a malodorous cloud and makes much of the region's water unsafe to drink. The sights and sounds, too, are strange and intense—the streets are choked by motorbikes, trucks, carts pulled by oxen, and waves of people. Along the roads, vendors sit on burlap cloth hawking fruits, vegetables, and prepared foods. Seemingly oblivious to the surrounding urban chaos, people work, talk, bathe, and sleep in the streets. The cities of India literally teem with millions of homeless people.

Third-World societies may be poor, but they are characterized by strong traditions and vital families that place everyone in a network of social support. Thus many people endure poverty with the help of their kin, which contrasts to the often isolating poverty in the United States.

Madras is dotted by more than a thousand shanty settlements, where perhaps half a million people live in huts constructed of branches, leaves, and discarded materials. These shanties offer little privacy and no refrigeration, running water, or bathrooms. The visitor from the United States understandably feels uneasy entering such a community, since the poorest sections of inner cities in the United States abound with frustration and, oftentimes, outright violence. But here, too, India offers a sharp contrast. No angry young people hang out at the corner, no drugs pervade the area, and there is a surprising absence of danger. Instead, the social units of shantytowns—strong families of children, parents, and sometimes grandparents—extend a smile and a welcome. In traditional societies like India, ways of life change little, even over many generations. Moreover, the lives of traditional Indians are shaped by *dharma*—the Hindu concept of duty and destiny—that presses people to accept their fate, whatever it may be. Mother Teresa, who has won praise for her work among the poorest of India's people, goes to the heart of the cultural differences: "Americans have angry poverty; in India, there is worse poverty, but it is a happy poverty."

No one who lives on the edge of survival can be called truly "happy." The deadly horror of poverty in India, however, is eased by the strength of families and traditional communities, a sense of purpose to life, and a world view that encourages each person to accept whatever society offers. As a result, the U.S. visitor comes away from the first encounter with Indian poverty in confusion: "How can people be so poor, and yet apparently content, vibrant, and so *alive*?"

SOURCE: Based on the author's research in Madras, India, November, 1988.

economy that has shaped official foreign policy toward poor nations ever since.[4]

Historical perspective. According to modernization theory, the *entire world* was poor as recently as several centuries ago. Because poverty is the norm throughout human history, then, *affluence*—not deprivation—demands an explanation.

Affluence came within reach of a small segment of humanity during the twilight of the Middle Ages as economic activity expanded in Western Europe. Burgeoning urban trade, exploration of other parts of the world, and finally the Industrial Revolution transformed Western Europe and, soon after, North America. Industrial technology and the innovations of countless entrepreneurs created new wealth on a grand scale. At the outset, modernization theorists concede, this wealth benefited only a few. Yet industrial technology was so productive that gradually the standard of living of even the poorest people began to rise. The specter of absolute poverty, which had cast a menacing shadow over humanity for its entire history, was finally routed.

Since then, the standard of living in the region where the Industrial Revolution first began has continued to improve. Today, the fruits of industrialization are widely enjoyed in the First World and, to a lesser extent, in the Second World. But without industrial technology, the Third World maintains the same low productivity it has had throughout history.

The importance of culture. Why didn't people the world over share in the Industrial Revolution so that they, too, could enjoy material plenty? Modernization theory holds that people are likely to exploit new technology only in a *cultural environment* that emphasizes the benefits of materialism and innovation.

The greatest barrier to economic development, therefore, is *traditionalism*. In societies that celebrate strong family systems and revere the past, ancient ways provide powerful guides to understanding the present and shaping the future. Predictably, this creates a form of "cultural inertia" that keeps societies from adopting new technologies that would improve their material standard of living. For example, Western innovations and technological advances have encountered fierce resistance in Iran because they threaten traditional Islamic family relationships, customs, and religious beliefs.

---

[4] The following discussion of modernization theory draws primarily on Rostow (1978), Bauer (1981), and Berger (1986).

Max Weber (1958; orig. 1904–1905) argued that, toward the end of the Middle Ages, Western Europe developed a distinctive cultural environment that favored change. As explained in Chapter 12 ("Family and Religion"), this progress-oriented culture characterized societies where the Protestant Reformation had transformed traditional Catholicism. Material affluence, which the Catholic Church had regarded with suspicion, became a sign of personal virtue, and the growing importance of individualism steadily eroded the traditional emphasis on kinship and community. Taken together, these changing cultural patterns nurtured the Industrial Revolution, which allowed one segment of humanity to prosper.

Rostow's stages of modernization. Modernization theory does not condemn poverty-stricken regions of the globe to a future as poor as their past. As technological advances diffuse around the world, all societies are gradually converging on one general form: the industrial model. According to W. W. Rostow (1978), the process of modernization follows four general stages.

1. **Traditional stage.** Initially, cultural traditions are strong, so poor societies resist technological innovation. Socialized to venerate the past, people in traditional societies cannot easily imagine how life could be different. They build their lives around their families and local communities, granting little individual freedom to one another, which, of course, inhibits change. Life is often spiritually rich, but lacking in material abundance.

    A century ago, much of the world was in this initial stage of economic development. The Asian nation of Bangladesh and the African country of Burkina Faso, still at the traditional stage, remain impoverished to this day.

2. **Take-off stage.** Reaching this point, societies experience a weakening of traditions, and the economy begins to grow. A limited market emerges as people produce not just for their own consumption but to profitably trade with others. Paralleling these developments is a greater achievement orientation, which often comes at the expense of family ties and time-honored norms and values.

    Great Britain reached this stage by about 1800; the United States entered "take-off" by 1820. Developing nations of the Third World, like Thailand in eastern Asia, are now at this stage. Rostow argues that economic "take-off" depends on progressive influences—including foreign aid, the in-

Early in the nineteenth century, exhausting and dangerous work was a fact of childhood in England. An unknown artist portrayed the perilous coal mines of Britain in this 1844 painting. Initially, the Industrial Revolution did little to improve the lives of children, who had historically labored just as adults did. Gradually, however, as machinery reduced the need for labor, the role of children was transformed so that they left the mines and factories for schools.

troduction of advanced technology and investment capital, and schooling abroad—that only rich nations can provide.

3. **Drive to technological maturity.** By this time, a society is in full pursuit of a higher standard of living. An active, diversified economy is driven by a population eager to enjoy the benefits of industrial technology. At the same time, however, people begin to realize (and sometimes lament) that industrialization is eroding traditional life in families and local communities. Great Britain reached this point by about 1840, the United States by about 1860. Today, Mexico and the People's Republic of China are among the nations driving to technological maturity.

By this stage, absolute poverty is greatly reduced. Cities swell to great size, occupational specialization renders relationships less personal, and heightened individualism often sparks movements for expanded political rights. Societies approaching technological maturity also recognize the need to provide basic schooling for all their people, and advanced training for some. Increasingly, tradition is discredited, further accelerating social change.

Moreover, the position of women steadily becomes more equal to that of men. In the short run, however, this development confronts women with new problems. Economic growth draws some men to cities, sometimes leaving women and children to fend for themselves. Further, under the influence of the Western media, women are now defined more as objects of sexual attention, a fact that contributes to a rising rate of divorce and desertion as men turn to younger, more physically attractive women. In the long run, however, modernization provides women with more opportunities for schooling and work outside the home (Alam, 1985; Mink, 1989).

4. **High mass consumption.** Economic development through industrial technology steadily raises living standards. This occurs, Rostow argues, as mass production stimulates mass consumption. The United States reached this stage of development by the beginning of the twentieth century. Other First-World societies were not far behind. For example, Japan became a military power early in this century. After recovering from the destruction of World War II, the Japanese enjoyed high mass

All over the world, poverty falls hardest on children because they are the most vulnerable. But the ordeal of child poverty is especially severe in the Third World for two additional reasons. First, these countries have far fewer resources to distribute among their people. Second, children represent a larger share of the population; in many poor nations, 60 percent of the people are no older than their teens.

consumption, and Japan now rivals the United States as the world's leading economic power. The former Soviet Union claimed to be approaching this stage by about 1950, but that nation's sluggish economy since then still limits the availability of even basic goods and services. Fast nearing this level of economic development are some of the most prosperous East Asian societies of the Third World: South Korea, Taiwan, Hong Kong, and Singapore.

The role of rich nations. Modernization theory claims that the First World plays an important role in global economic development. Far from being the *cause* of the abject poverty that afflicts much of humanity, rich

societies hold the key to *solving* global inequality in the following ways.

1. **Assisting in population control.** As we have already noted, population growth is greatest in the poorest societies of the world. First-World nations can help curb global population by exporting birth control technology and promoting its use. Once economic development is under way, birth rates should decline as they have in industrial societies.

2. **Increasing food production.** Modernization theory suggests that "high-tech" farming methods, exported from rich societies to poor nations, will raise agricultural yields. Such techniques—collectively referred to as the *Green Revolution*—involve the use of new hybrid seeds, modern irrigation methods, chemical fertilizers, and pesticides for insect control.

3. **Introducing industrial technology.** Technology transfers should involve industry as well as agriculture. Rich nations can accelerate economic growth in poor societies by introducing machinery and computer technology, which improves productivity and also helps to transform the labor force of poor countries from agricultural work to skilled industrial and service work.

4. **Providing foreign aid.** Investment capital from rich nations can boost the prospects of poor societies striving to reach the "take-off" stage. Developing countries can use foreign aid to purchase high technology—fertilizers and irrigation projects to raise agricultural productivity, and power plants and factories to improve industrial output.

Critical evaluation. Modernization theory has influential supporters among social scientists (Parsons, 1966; W. Moore, 1977, 1979; Bauer, 1981; Berger, 1986). By identifying how industrialization affects other dimensions of social life, this approach has helped to explain how and why industrialization changes a society. Modernization theory has also been important to government officials; for decades, it has shaped the foreign policy of the United States and other First-World nations. Proponents maintain that a number of poor societies have made impressive strides with the assistance of rich countries. This is especially true of Asia, where South Korea, Taiwan, the former British colony of Singapore, and the current British colony of Hong Kong each has an impressive record of economic development. Similarly, concerted efforts to modernize by nations like Turkey,

Mexico, and Argentina have improved their living standards.

From the outset, however, modernization theory came under fire from socialist nations of the Second World as a thinly veiled defense of capitalism. By the 1960s, a growing number of critics in First-World societies also detected major flaws in this approach. Perhaps the most serious failing, critics claim, is that modernization theory has fallen short of its own standards of success, since global inequality is still pervasive.

A second criticism is that modernization theory tends to ignore global forces that thwart Third-World development today. Modernization theory holds that the opportunities for growth are greater today than in the past because rich nations can offer assistance to the Third World. However, critics claim that political and economic barriers to development have emerged in the two centuries since Europe's Industrial Revolution that ensure the perpetuation of global poverty. In essence, they argue, the First World industrialized from a position of global *strength*; the Third World cannot be expected to modernize from a position of global *weakness*.

Third, critics maintain, by treating rich and poor societies as worlds unto themselves, modernization theory offers little insight into ways that the global economy links all nations. For example, as suggested in Chapter 7 ("Social Stratification"), the expansion of multinational corporations around the globe has brought a windfall to wealthy people in the United States; at the same time, the production of industrial goods abroad has brought decline to many traditional U.S. industries such as steel and automobiles, eroding the economic security of rank-and-file workers.

Fourth, critics contend that modernization theory holds up the First World as the standard by which the rest of humanity should be judged, thus betraying an ethnocentric bias. As Chapter 15 ("Social Change and Modernity") explains, "progress" thus amounts to reducing the cultural diversity of our world by promoting a materialistic, Western way of life around the globe.

Fifth, and finally, modernization theory draws criticism for suggesting that the causes of global poverty lie almost entirely in the poor societies themselves. This amounts to "blaming the victims" for their own plight. Instead, critics argue, an analysis of global inequality should focus as much attention on the behavior of *rich* nations as that of poor nations (Wiarda, 1987).

From these concerns has emerged a second approach to understanding global inequality: dependency theory.

Dependency Theory

Dependency theory is *a model of economic and social development that explains global inequality in terms of the historical exploitation of poor societies by rich societies.* This analysis places primary responsibility for global poverty on rich nations. Dependency theory holds that rich societies have impoverished the Third World so that today poor nations are *dependent* on richer ones. The roots of this destructive process, which continues today, extend back several centuries.

Historical perspective. Before the Industrial Revolution, there was little of the affluence present in some of the world today. Dependency theory asserts, however, that most of the people living in what we now call the Third World were actually better off economically in the past than they are now. André Gunder Frank (1975), a noted proponent of this approach, argues that the development of rich societies paralleled the *underdevelopment* of poor societies.

Dependency theory is built on the crucial insight that the economic positions of the rich and poor nations of the world are linked and cannot be understood in isolation from one another. This, the dependency theorists argue, is the key error of modernization theory: suggesting that poor societies are lagging behind rich ones on a single "path of progress." According to dependency theory, the increasing prosperity of the First World has come largely at the expense of the Third World. In short, some nations have become rich *only because others have become poor*. This complex process, which began centuries ago with the onset of global commerce, continues in much of the world today.

The importance of colonialism. Half a millennium has passed since Europeans set out to explore the "New World" of North America to the west, the massive continent of Africa to the south, and Asia to the east. The United States, itself originally a British colony, later colonized the Virgin Islands, Haiti, Puerto Rico, and part of Cuba in the Western Hemisphere, and Guam and the Philippines in Asia.

Across the United States, 1992 marked the quincentennial of the voyage of Christopher Columbus, who set out from Portugal believing that he could reach the Orient by sailing west. The unintended outcome of Columbus's voyage—what Europeans called "the discovery of the New World"—has long been celebrated as a stunning achievement. In recent decades, however, historians

When Worlds Collide: The Christopher Columbus Controversy

For generations, teachers across the United States instructed young people that the Italian explorer Christopher Columbus (1446–1505) was the man who "discovered" what Europeans dubbed "the New World." Conventional accounts explain that as Columbus forged a link between Europe and the Americas [two continents whose names honor Amerigo Vespucci (1452–1512), who accompanied Columbus on his fateful voyage], he introduced "civilization" to a land that had never known Christianity and instituted "advanced" political and scientific ideas in place of backwardness. In short, according to conventional history, Columbus tamed a savage wilderness with a civilizing culture, and set the New World on the path to economic development.

As Americans throughout the hemisphere recently observed the five-hundred-year anniversary of Columbus's voyage, spirited controversy surrounded the legacy of this historical figure. Against the backdrop of conventional history, the story of Columbus and his expedition is literally

One side of the "Christopher Columbus controversy" is illustrated by artist Diego Rivera (1886–1957) in his mural *Colonial Domination.* As this painting expresses in graphic detail, the arrival of Europeans to this hemisphere initiated considerable conflict and violence, placing the Americas under the political control of European nations for more than three hundred years.

being rewritten by scholars informed by multiculturalist perspectives. These critics challenge the heroic stature of Columbus on a number of counts.

First, although Columbus's dis-

---

have sketched a more complete understanding of this fateful collision of two worlds, as the box explains.

Overt colonialism has largely disappeared from the world. Most Latin American nations achieved political independence during the first half of the nineteenth century, and most African and Asian colonies gained their freedom during this century. However, according to dependency theory, political liberation has not meant economic autonomy. Far from it: poor societies maintain economic relationships with rich nations that carry on the colonial pattern. This neocolonialism is fueled by a capitalist world economy.

Wallerstein's capitalist world economy. Immanuel Wallerstein (1974, 1979, 1983, 1984) developed a model of the "capitalist world economy" to explain the origins of contemporary global inequality.[5] Wallerstein's term *world economy* suggests that interacting national economies comprise a global economic system. He argues that this global economy results from economic expansion rooted in the First World that has steadily spilled

[5] While based largely on Wallerstein's ideas, this section also is informed by the work of Frank (1980, 1981), Delacroix & Ragin (1981), and Bergesen (1983).

covery certainly changed the course of history, it was nonetheless quite accidental. Columbus sailed from Spain thinking that Japan and Asia were only three thousand miles to the west. Contrary to popular opinion, most educated people in the late fifteenth century knew that the world was round, but no one was sure of our planet's size. The westward route from Europe to Asia is actually three times what Columbus imagined, with the American continents in between. Thus when Columbus and the crews of his three wooden ships stumbled onto the Bahamian Islands at the eastern edge of the Americas, they weren't sure what they had found.

Second, critics point out, this world was "new" only to the Europeans; the Americas had been inhabited for tens of thousands of years by a host of distinctive societies that originated in Asia. The notion that Europeans "discovered" the "new world" illustrates how, from the outset, our history has been Eurocentric, that is, viewed from a European perspective (see Chapter 2, "Culture").

Third, the consequences of contact between Europeans and the indigenous cultures of the Americas were stunning and one-sided. Columbus represented a way of life that was both aggressive and materialistic. From the outset, he expected his voyage to bring him riches and power. By comparison to the Europeans, the people who received Columbus were gentle. Their society, too, was hierarchical, but they lived more peacefully and displayed a reverence for nature. Columbus enforced his rule with determination and frequently acted with brutality. He set a pattern for later colonizers as he systematically looted gold and silver from the lands he controlled, subjugating native peoples for slave labor. Even more tragically, Europeans unintentionally introduced to the Americas diseases against which native peoples had no natural defenses. Taken together, violence and disease took a frightening toll, decimating indigenous populations within several generations. The labor shortage caused by this loss of life set the stage for another disastrous

collision of different worlds: the slave trade by which Europeans and Africans transported human beings from Africa to the Americas to be sold into bondage.

The European conquest forever changed the course of life in the Americas. In at least some respects, the collision of two worlds in 1492 had long-term consequences that were positive. Useful instances of cultural diffusion resulted, including the introduction of horses from Europe to the Americas and the presentation by Native Americans of corn and potatoes (but also tobacco) that soon became popular in Europe. Further, with time, entire new societies—including the United States—emerged as a product of European settlement. But, from the point of view of the original inhabitants of the Americas, contact with Europeans initiated a five-hundred-year nightmare: a loss of traditional culture, centuries of oppressive colonization, and the virtual obliteration of many societies.

SOURCES: Sale (1990) and Gray (1991).

---

beyond national boundaries over the last five hundred years. The dominant character of this global system is capitalist.

Wallerstein terms the nations of the First World the *core* of the world economy. Based on their global colonialism, these core societies prospered as raw materials were funneled to Western Europe where they fueled the Industrial Revolution. Today, multinational corporations operate profitably around the globe by drawing wealth to North America, Western Europe, Australia, and Japan.

By contrast, the Third World encompasses countries at the *periphery* of the world economy. Drawn into the world economy by colonial exploitation, these poor countries continue to support industrial societies by providing inexpensive labor and a vast market for First-World products.

According to Wallerstein, the world economy benefits the First World (by generating profits) and harms the Third World (by perpetuating poverty). The world economy thus imposes a state of dependency on poor nations, which remain under the control of rich ones. This dependency is caused primarily by the following three factors.

1. **Narrow, export-oriented economies.** Unlike core nations, Third-World countries have economies that are not diversified. Historically, colonial powers forced local farmers to stop growing a variety of crops for local consumption in favor of producing a few raw materials for export. Coffee and fruits from Latin American countries, oil from Nigeria, hardwoods from the Philippines, and palm oil from Malaysia are some of the products central to the economies of poor nations. Multinational corporations maintain this pattern today as they purchase raw materials cheaply in poor societies and process them profitably in core societies.

2. **Lack of industrial capacity.** Without an industrial base, poor societies face a double bind: they count on selling inexpensive raw materials to rich nations, from whom they buy whatever expensive manufactured goods they can afford. In a classic example of this dependency, British colonialists encouraged the people of India to raise cotton, but prohibited them from manufacturing their own cloth. Instead, Indian cotton was shipped to textile mills in Birmingham and Manchester in England, woven into cloth, and sent back for profitable sale in India.

    Underdevelopment theorists also blast the Green Revolution, widely praised by modernization theory, for fostering dependency. To promote agricultural productivity, poor countries must purchase expensive fertilizers, pesticides, and mechanical equipment from core nations. Typically, rich countries profit most from this exchange.

3. **Foreign debt.** These unequal trade patterns push the Third World deeper and deeper in debt to industrialized nations. Collectively, the Third World owes First-World countries roughly $1 trillion, including hundreds of billions of dollars owed to the United States. This staggering debt can destabilize a country's economy; many poor nations are already reeling from high unemployment and rampant inflation.

    Caught in the "debt trap," some Third-World countries have tried to renegotiate loans, and a few have stopped making payments entirely. Cuba, for example, refused to make further payments on its $7 billion foreign debt in 1986. Because this threatens the economic growth of rich nations, countries such as the United States strongly oppose such actions.

The role of rich nations. Nowhere is the difference between modernization theory and dependency theory sharper than in the role they assign to rich nations. Modernization theory maintains that rich societies create new wealth through technological innovation. The economic success of the First World generates prosperity, not poverty. Therefore, according to this view, as Third-World nations modernize, absolute poverty will decrease. By contrast, dependency theory argues that rich societies have unjustly seized the wealth of the world for their own purposes. That is, the *over*development of some of the globe is directly tied to the *under*development of the rest of it.

Dependency theorists dismiss the idea that First-World programs of population control, agricultural and industrial technology, and foreign aid help poor societies. Instead, they contend, rich nations act simply in pursuit of profit. Selling technology makes money, and foreign aid typically goes to ruling elites (rather than the poor majority) in exchange for maintaining a favorable "business climate" for multinational corporations (Lappé, Collins, & Kinley, 1981).

Additionally, dependency theory maintains, the capitalist culture of the United States encourages people to think of poverty as natural or inevitable. Following this line of reasoning, poverty results from "natural" processes including having (too many) children, and disasters such as droughts. World hunger activists Frances Moore Lappé and Joseph Collins (1986) argue that global poverty is far from inevitable; rather, it results from deliberate policies. They point out that the world already produces enough food to allow every person on the planet to grow quite fat. Moreover, India and most of Africa *export* food in spite of the fact that most of their people go hungry.

According to Lappé and Collins, the contradiction of poverty amid plenty stems from a First-World policy of producing food for profits, not people. That is, rich nations cooperate with elites in the Third World to grow and export profitable crops such as coffee while simultaneously curbing the production of staples consumed by local families. Governments of poor societies support this "growing for export" because they need food profits to repay massive foreign debt. At the core of this vicious cycle, according to Lappé and Collins, is the capitalist corporate structure of the First World.

Critical evaluation. Dependency theory makes the important observation that no society develops (or fails to

In 1992 and 1993, the United States deployed armed forces to Somalia on the east coast of Africa. The crisis in Somalia is an illustration of how intense poverty and political turmoil often go hand in hand. While the foreign soldiers were able to secure a period of relative peace during which food shipments were distributed, they could do little about this nation's underlying economic calamity.

develop) in isolation, and this approach highlights how the global economy shapes the destiny of all nations. Dependency theorists point to Latin America and elsewhere, claiming that development simply cannot proceed under present international conditions. Addressing global poverty, they conclude, demands more than internal change within poor societies. Rather, these theorists call for reform of the entire global economy so it operates in the interests of the majority of people.

Critics of the dependency approach, however, take issue with several assertions. First, critics charge, dependency theory treats wealth as a zero-sum commodity, as if no one gets richer without someone else getting poorer. Not so, critics contend, since farmers, small-business owners, and industrialists can and do create new wealth through their drive and imaginative use of new technology. After all, they point out, the world's wealth has grown many times over during this century.

Second, critics reason, if dependency theory were correct in condemning the First World for creating global poverty, then nations with the strongest ties to rich societies should be the poorest. However, the most impoverished nations of the world (Ethiopia, for example) have had little contact with rich societies. Similarly, they con-

tinue, a long history of trade with rich countries has dramatically improved the economies of Singapore, South Korea, Japan, and Hong Kong (which became a British colony in 1841 and will remain so until 1997).

Third, critics contend that dependency theory is simplistic for pointing the finger at a single factor—world capitalism—as the sole cause of global poverty. Directing attention to forces *outside* of poor societies, dependency theory casts poor societies as passive victims, ignoring factors *inside* these countries that contribute to their economic plight. Sociologists have long recognized the vital role of culture in shaping human behavior. World cultural patterns vary greatly; some societies embrace change readily and others staunchly resist economic development. If, for example, Iran's fundamentalist form of Islam deliberately discourages economic ties with other countries, capitalist societies can hardly be blamed for that nation's economic stagnation. Nor can rich societies be saddled with responsibility for the reckless behavior of foreign leaders who engage in far-reaching corruption or militaristic campaigns to enhance their own power (examples include the regimes of Marcos in the Philippines, Duvalier in Haiti, Noriega in Panama, and Saddam Hussein in Iraq). Some governments also restrict

Hong Kong, which will remain a British colony until 1997, is an economic marketplace that operates as freely as any on earth. Modernization theorists tout Hong Kong as a monument to the power of capitalism to generate wealth. Dependency theorists, however, point out that while many people live well in Hong Kong, the city has a daunting problem of poverty. In the Aberdeen district, shown here, hundreds of children are growing up on ramshackle boats in a floating neighborhood that lacks even basic sanitation.

food supplies as a weapon in internal political struggles (this occurred in Somalia, Ethiopia, and the Sudan in Africa). Other regimes (including many in Latin America and Africa) have done little to improve the status of women or control population growth.

Fourth, critics chide dependency theorists for downplaying economic dependency fostered by the former Soviet Union. The Soviet army seized control of most of Eastern Europe during World War II and subsequently dominated these nations politically and economically. Critics of dependency theory see the popular uprisings against Soviet-installed governments, beginning in 1989, as rebellions against Soviet domination and the ensuing economic dependency.

A fifth criticism holds that dependency theory lacks clear policy implications. Most dependency theorists urge poor societies to end all contact with the First World, and to nationalize foreign-owned industries. On a broader scale, dependency theory implies that global

poverty could be eliminated by a world overthrow of international capitalism. What form emerging economies would take, and whether they would be capable of meeting the economic needs of a growing world population (in light of the historic shortcomings of socialist economies) remains unclear.

THE FUTURE OF GLOBAL INEQUALITY

People in the United States, sociologists included, are discovering many ways in which our lives are caught up in global trends. We read, for instance, that U.S. corporations are investing abroad while business interests from abroad are buying up more and more of this country. As Chapter 7 ("Social Stratification") explained, the increasingly global economy is polarizing our society as

Table 8–2 MODERNIZATION THEORY AND DEPENDENCY THEORY: A SUMMARY

	Modernization Theory	Dependency Theory
Historical pattern	The entire world was poor just two centuries ago; the Industrial Revolution brought affluence to the First World; as industrialization gradually transforms the Third World, all societies are likely to become more equal and alike.	Global parity was disrupted by colonialism, which developed the First World and simultaneously underdeveloped the Third World; barring change in the world capitalist system, rich nations will grow richer and poor nations will become poorer.
Primary causes of global poverty	Characteristics of Third-World societies cause poverty, including lack of industrial technology, traditional cultural patterns that discourage innovation, and rapid population growth.	Global economic relations—historical colonialism and the operation of multinational corporations—have enriched the First World while placing the Third World in a state of economic dependency.
Role of rich nations	First-World countries can and do assist Third-World nations through programs of population control, technology transfers that increase food production and stimulate industrial development, and by providing investment capital in the form of foreign aid.	First-World countries have concentrated global resources to their own advantage while producing massive foreign debt in the Third World; rich nations represent a barrier to economic development in the Third World.

it boosts the fortunes of the rich while cutting factory jobs and putting downward pressure on wages.

As this chapter has noted, however, social inequality is far more striking in global context. The concentration of wealth among First-World countries, in contrast to the grinding poverty in the Third World, may well end up being the most pressing dilemma facing humanity in the twenty-first century. But the role of the global economy in this problem remains a hotly contested issue. To some analysts, rich nations can draw poor countries toward prosperity; to others, rich nations have locked the Third World into an endless cycle of misery.

Faced with these two divergent approaches to understanding global equality, we might well wonder which is correct. But the truth is that each view has some merit as well as inherent limitations. Table 8–2 summarizes key arguments made by each approach.

In sorting out the truth, we must also consider empirical evidence. In some regions of the world, especially the "Pacific Rim" of eastern Asia, the market forces endorsed by modernization theory are raising living standards rapidly and substantially. At the same time, other societies of the Third World, especially central Africa and parts of Latin America, are experiencing economic turmoil that frustrates hopes for market-based development.

The Third-World societies that have surged ahead economically have two factors in common. First, they are relatively small.[6] Combined, the Asian societies of South Korea, Taiwan, Hong Kong, Singapore, and Japan equal only about one-fifth of the land area and population of India. The economic problems smaller countries face are more manageable; consequently, small societies more effectively administer programs of development. Second, these "best case" societies have cultural traits in common, especially an emphasis on individual achievement and economic success. In other areas of the world, where traditions inhibit individual achievement, even smaller nations have failed to turn development opportunities to their advantage.

The major "paths to development" advanced by modernization and dependency theories are both currently undergoing significant transformation. On the one hand, few societies seeking economic growth now favor a market economy completely free of government regulation. This view challenges modernization theory, which has favored a free-market approach over government-directed initiatives. Also, as recent upheavals in the for-

---

[6] This argument was suggested by Professor Alan Frishman of Hobart College.

mer Soviet Union and Eastern Europe demonstrate, a global reevaluation of socialism is currently under way. These events, following decades of poor economic performance and political repression, make many Third-World societies wary of this path to development. Because dependency theory has historically supported socialist economic systems, changes in world socialism will surely generate new thinking here as well.

In the short term, no plan for development is likely to effectively reduce the pressing problems of world hunger and rapid population growth. Looking to the next century, however, there are reasons for hope. The approaches described in this chapter identify the two keys to lessening global inequality. One insight, revealed by modernization theory, is that world hunger is at least partly a *problem of production and technology*. There

can be little doubt that a higher standard of living for a swelling world population will require greater agricultural and industrial productivity. The second insight, derived from dependency theory, is that global inequality is also a *problem of distribution and politics*. Even with higher productivity, in other words, the plight of the world's poor will be unchanged unless decisions are made to distribute this bounty more equitably.

As debate over global inequality continues, people are coming to recognize that the security of everyone in the world depends on reducing the destabilizing extremes of global poverty. We can only hope that, as the Cold War between the superpowers winds down, energy and resources will be redirected to the needs of the vast majority of humanity trapped in a desperate struggle for survival.

SUMMARY

1. Adopting a global perspective, we see the full extent of social stratification. A shorthand way to comprehend this inequality is to divide the globe into "three worlds," broad categories based on patterns of economic development. The First World encompasses industrialized, capitalist societies, including the United States; the Second World is composed largely of socialist societies in transition to market-based systems, including the Commonwealth of Independent States; the Third World represents the poor societies that have yet to industrialize.

2. In addition to relative poverty, the Third World grapples with widespread, absolute poverty. The typical member of a Third-World society struggles to survive on an income far below that of the average person in the United States.

3. Poverty places about 20 percent of the Third-World population—at least 800 million people—at risk. Some 15 million people, many of them children, die annually due to lack of nutrition.

4. Nearly everywhere in the world, women are more likely than men to be poor. In agrarian societies, women's relative and absolute disadvantages are greater than in industrial societies such as the United States.

5. The poverty of Third-World societies is a complex problem rooted in a lack of industrial technology,

rapid population growth, traditional cultural patterns, internal social stratification, and global power relationships that inhibit development.

6. Modernization theory maintains that poor societies seeking economic development must overcome the inertia of traditional cultural patterns and acquire advanced productive technology.

7. Modernization theorist W. W. Rostow identifies four stages of development: traditional, take-off, drive to technological maturity, and high mass consumption.

8. Arguing that rich societies hold the keys to creating wealth, modernization theory cites four ways rich nations can assist poor nations: through population control, food-producing technologies, industrial development, and investment and other foreign aid.

9. Critics of modernization theory argue that this approach has produced only limited economic development in the world, while ethnocentrically assuming that poor societies can follow the path to development taken by rich nations centuries ago.

10. Dependency theory claims global wealth and poverty are directly linked to the historical operation of the capitalist world economy.

11. The dependency of Third-World countries is rooted in colonialism. In this century, neocolonialism represents the continued exploitation of politi-

cally independent societies of the Third World through the operation of multinational corporations.

12. Immanuel Wallerstein views the First World as the advantaged "core" of the capitalist world economy and the poor societies of the Third World as the global "periphery."

13. Three key factors—export-oriented economies, a lack of industrial capacity, and foreign debt—perpetuate Third-World dependency on rich nations.

14. Critics of dependency theory argue that this approach overlooks the success of many nations in creating new wealth. Contrary to the implications of this approach, these critics maintain, the poorest societies are not those with the strongest ties to the First World.

15. Both modernization and dependency approaches offer useful insights into the origins of global inequality. Some evidence supports each view. Less controversial is the urgent need to address the various problems brought on by worldwide poverty.

KEY CONCEPTS

colonialism the process by which some nations enrich themselves through political and economic control of other nations

dependency theory a model of economic and social development that explains global inequality in terms of the exploitation of poor societies by rich societies

First World industrial societies with predominantly capitalist economies

modernization theory a model of economic and social development that explains global inequality in terms of differing levels of technological development among world societies

multinational corporation a large business that operates in many countries

neocolonialism a new form of economic exploitation involving not formal political control but the operation of multinational corporations

Second World industrial societies that are transforming socialist economies into market systems

Third World primarily agrarian societies in which most people are poor

9

Race and Ethnicity

Sitting at his kitchen table, the Croatian farmer recounts the tale of horror he has heard in the village.[1] His wife and neighbors look on silently, nodding from time to time to signal agreement. The farmer tells his rapt audience that a band of Serbs attacked a bus full of Croats in a village near Zagreb; they blocked the road, forced the vehicle to stop, and then pulled the Croats from the bus one by one, beating and kicking them. One man clubbed an old woman to death—the farmer pauses, shuddering with anger—and his Serb accomplices just stood there watching. Such brutality, he storms, shows that the Serbs are not people but animals. Others in the small kitchen murmur that the fighting in Croatia will continue as long as the Serbs commit such acts of aggression.

As civil war has engulfed part of the former Yugoslavia, stories like this one have been proliferating. Serbian efforts at "ethnic cleansing"—forcibly expelling Muslims and non-Serbs from the region—are a grim reminder that ethnicity has long fueled violence throughout the world. In recent years, as the heavy hand of government control was lifted from Eastern Europe, blood feuds have once again pitted people against one another. Beyond the Balkans, where Croats and Serbs are at war, Ukrainians, Moldavians, Azerbaijanis, and a host of other ethnic peoples in the former Soviet Union struggle to recover their cultural identity after decades of subjugation by the Russian majority. In the Middle East, negotiations continue to end decades of conflict between Arabs and Jews. In South Africa, democratic government struggles to take hold after centuries of racial separation. Throughout the Americas, the five-hundredth anniversary of the initial contact between native people and Europeans served as an occasion to confront and try to resolve old wounds.

All over the world, human beings are divided—and sometimes propelled to violence—by culture, color, and social heritage. Surely one of the greatest ironies is that those characteristics that most define us as individual human beings are the very traits that sometimes prompt people to degrade themselves with hatred and violence toward others.

In the United States, as elsewhere, race and ethnicity both trumpet personal identity and provoke conflict. This chapter examines the meaning of race and ethnicity, explains how these social constructs have shaped our

history, and suggests why they continue to play such a central role—for better or worse—in the world today.

THE SOCIAL SIGNIFICANCE OF RACE AND ETHNICITY

People in the United States and elsewhere frequently confuse the terms "race" and "ethnicity." For this reason, we begin with important definitions.

Race

A *race* is *a category composed of men and women who share biologically transmitted traits that are defined as socially significant.* Races are commonly distinguished by physical characteristics such as skin color, hair texture, shape of facial features, and body type. All humans are members of a single biological species, but biological variations that we describe as "racial characteristics" emerge over thousands of generations from living in different geographical areas of the world (Molnar, 1983). In hot regions, for example, humans developed darker skin that offers protection from the sun; in temperate regions, humans have lighter skin.

Over the course of history, migration carried genetic characteristics once common to a single region through much of the world. In places that have been "crossroads" of human migration, like the Middle East, people display remarkable racial variation. More isolated locales, such as Japan, exhibit far more racial uniformity. No society, however, is genetically pure; in fact, racial mixture occurs all the time as a result of contact among the world's people.

Trying to make sense of what can be bewildering human variety, nineteenth-century biologists developed a three-part scheme of racial classification. They labeled people with relatively light skin and fine hair *Caucasian*; they applied the term *Negroid* to those with darker skin and coarser, curlier hair; and they described people with yellow or brown skin and distinctive folds on the eyelids as *Mongoloid*. Such terms are misleading, however, because we now know that there are no biologically pure races. In fact, the world traveler notices gradual and subtle variations from region to region all around the globe. The people commonly called "Caucasians" or "whites" actually display skin color that ranges from light (in the Nordic countries) to dark (in India), and the same variation occurs among so-called "Negroids" and

---

[1] This chapter opening is adapted from an account by Celestine Bohlen (1991).

The range of biological variation in human beings is far greater than any system of racial classification allows. To see this fact, simply try to place all of the people pictured here into simple racial categories.

"Mongoloids." Many Caucasians in southern India actually have darker skin than many blond Negroid aborigines of Australia.

Although we readily distinguish between "black" and "white" people, research confirms that the population of the United States, too, is genetically mixed. Over many generations, the genetic traits of Negroid Africans, Caucasian Europeans, and Mongoloid Native Americans have spread widely through our population. Many "black" people, therefore, have a large proportion of Caucasian genes, and many "whites" have at least some Negroid genes. In short, then, race is not a black-and-white issue.

The prime importance of race lies in the widespread tendency to rank people by genetic traits in systems of social inequality. People have long defended this practice by asserting that physical traits are linked to innate intelligence and other mental abilities, although no sound scientific evidence supports such beliefs. With so much at stake, however, no wonder societies strive to make social rankings clear and enforceable. Earlier in this century, for example, many states in the South labeled as "colored" anyone who had at least one thirty-second

African ancestry (that is, one African-American great-great grandparent or any closer ancestor). Today, laws permit parents to declare the race of their child.

Ethnicity

Ethnicity is *a shared cultural heritage*. Members of an *ethnic category* usually have a common place of ancestral origin, a traditional language, and a historic religion which, together, confer a distinctive social identity. The United States is a multi-ethnic society in which English is the favored language, but millions of people speak Spanish, Italian, German, French, or other languages in their homes. The United States and Canada are predominantly Protestant societies, but most people of Spanish, Italian, and Polish ancestry are Roman Catholic, while many others of Greek, Ukrainian, and Russian ancestry are affiliated with the Eastern Orthodox Church. More than 6 million Jewish Americans (with ancestral ties to various nations) share a religious history. Similarly, several million women and men in the United States have a Muslim religious heritage.

The Coming Minority-Majority

During the 1980s, Manhattan, the central borough of New York City, gained a "minority-majority." This means that people of African, Asian, and Hispanic descent, together with other minorities, became a majority of the population. The same thing has occurred in St. Louis, in Fresno, California, and in 186 counties across the United States (about 6 percent of the total). In less than a century from now, if current patterns hold, minorities will be a majority in the United States as a whole.

Why? The table shows that the entire U.S. population increased by almost 10 percent during the 1980s. The rate of increase for non-Hispanic whites, however, was lower at 6 percent. The number of Asians or Pacific Islanders grew fastest, more than doubling primarily because of high levels of immigration. The Hispanic population increased by more than half, a result of both immigration and a high birth rate. Up, too, was the number of Native Americans (37.9 percent) and the number of African Americans (13 percent).

Overall population growth of the United States during the 1980s was highly concentrated. More than half

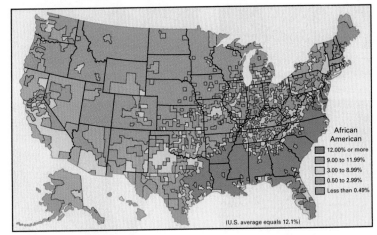

Percent African American, Hispanic American, and Asian American, by County, 1990

(*American Demographics Desk Reference Series, No. 1, June 1991, pp. 8, 14, 16*)

the increase took place in just three states: California, Florida, and Texas. As the maps illustrate, it is these states and others around them that have large minority populations: 1990 census data show that counties with the highest proportions of African Americans fall in the Southeast, while Hispanics are concentrated in the Southwest, and Asian Americans on the West Coast.

When the twentieth century began, most people in the United States thought of "minorities" as people of German, Irish, or Italian background. Ironically, during the twenty-first century, such people of European ancestry (other than Hispanics) may again become minorities as a host of others—those often termed *people of color*—become a majority in the United States.

Race and ethnicity, then, are quite different: one is biological, the other cultural. But the two may go hand in hand. Japanese Americans, for example, have distinctive physical traits and—for those who maintain a traditional way of life—cultural attributes as well. Finally, people can change their ethnicity. For instance, Polish immigrants who discard their cultural background over time may cease to have a particular ethnicity. Assuming people mate with others like themselves, however, the physical traits of race persist for generations.

Minorities

A racial or ethnic **minority**[2] is *a category of people, distinguished by physical or cultural traits, who are socially disadvantaged.* Minorities are of many kinds, including people with physical disabilities and (as Chapter

---

[2] We use the term "minority" rather than "minority group" because, as explained in Chapter 5 ("Groups and Organizations"), a minority is a category, not a group.

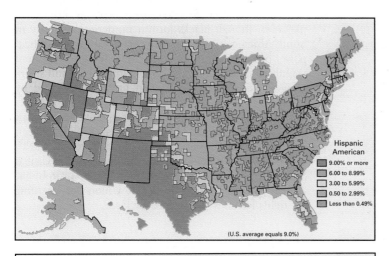

Hispanic
American

■ 9.00% or more
■ 6.00 to 8.99%
□ 3.00 to 5.99%
□ 0.50 to 2.99%
■ Less than 0.49%

(U.S. average equals 9.0%)

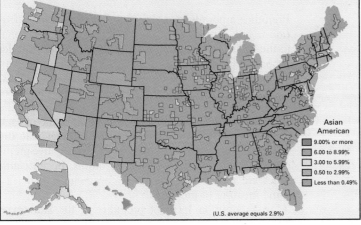

Asian
American

■ 9.00% or more
■ 6.00 to 8.99%
□ 3.00 to 5.99%
□ 0.50 to 2.99%
■ Less than 0.49%

(U.S. average equals 2.9%)

Percent Change in Population by Racial and Ethnic Category, 1980–1990	
Category	1980–1990 Increase
Asian or Pacific Islander	107.8%
Hispanic	53.0%
American Indian, Eskimo, or Aleut	37.9%
African American	13.2%
All other minorities	45.1%
White (non-Hispanic)	6.0%
Entire U.S. population	9.8%
SOURCE: U.S. Bureau of the Census, 1991.	

10, "Sex and Gender," suggests) women. Table 9–1 on page 210 tallies racial and ethnic minorities in the United States as recorded by the 1990 census. About 80 percent of the U.S. population is non-Hispanic whites. But the absolute numbers and share of population for virtually every minority grew rapidly during the 1980s. As the box explains, within a century various minorities, taken together, may well form a *majority* of the U.S. population.

Minorities have two major characteristics. The first

has to do with culture: they share a *distinct identity*. Because race is highly visible (and virtually impossible for a person to change), people of African descent in the United States or Chinese in South Africa generally have a keen awareness of their race. The significance of ethnicity (which can be changed) is more variable. Throughout U.S. history, some people (such as Reform Jews) have downplayed their ethnicity, while others (Orthodox Jews, for example) have maintained distinctive cultural traditions and neighborhoods.

Table 9–1 RACIAL AND ETHNIC CATEGORIES IN THE UNITED STATES, 1990

Racial or Ethnic Classification	Approximate U.S. Population	Percent of Total Population
African descent	29,986,060	12.1
Hispanic descent*	22,354,059	9.0
Mexican	13,495,938	5.4
Puerto Rican	2,727,754	1.1
Cuban	1,043,932	0.4
Other Hispanic	5,086,435	2.1
Native-American descent	1,959,234	0.8
American Indian	1,878,285	0.8
Eskimo	57,152	<
Aleut	23,797	<
Asian or Pacific Islander descent	7,273,662	2.9
Chinese	1,645,472	0.7
Filipino	1,406,770	0.6
Japanese	847,562	0.3
Asian Indian	815,447	0.3
Korean	798,849	0.3
Vietnamese	614,547	0.2
Hawaiian	211,014	<
Samoan	62,964	<
Guamanian	49,345	<
Other Asian or Pacific Islander	821,692	0.3
White	199,686,070	80.3
German	57,986,000	23.3
Irish	38,740,000	15.6
English	32,656,000	13.1
Italian	14,715,000	5.9
French	10,321,000	4.1
Polish	9,366,000	3.8
Other white	35,902,070	14.5

* People of Hispanic descent can be of any race.
< Indicates less than 1/10 of one percent.

SOURCE: U.S. Bureau of the Census, 1991.

or ethnicity often serves as a master status (as described in Chapter 4, "Social Interaction in Everyday Life") that overshadows personal accomplishments and sparks unfair treatment from others.

Minorities usually constitute a small share of a society's population, but there are exceptions. For example, even though blacks form a numerical majority in South Africa, they are deprived of economic and political power by whites. In the United States, women represent slightly more than half the population but are still struggling to gain opportunities and privileges enjoyed by men.

As suggested by this chapter's opening story about turmoil in the former Yugoslavia, social conflict between minorities and the majority springs up all over the world. Categories of people—African Americans in the United States, Kurds in Iraq, Christians in Egypt, Sikhs in India, Azerbaijanis in the former Soviet Union—are fighting for rights formally guaranteed by law.

Prejudice and Stereotypes

Prejudice amounts to *a rigid and irrational generalization about a category of people.* Prejudice is irrational to the extent that people hold strong, inflexible attitudes supported by little or no direct evidence. Prejudice can be directed toward people of a particular social class, sex, sexual orientation, age, political affiliation, race, or ethnicity. Prejudices are *prejudgments* that can be positive or negative, and most people hold some of each type. Our positive prejudices lead us to exaggerate the virtues of people like ourselves, while our negative prejudices condemn people who differ from us. Because attitudes are rooted in our culture, everyone has at least some measure of prejudice.

A common form of prejudice is the **stereotype** (*stereo* is derived from Greek meaning "hard" or "solid"), *a prejudiced description of some category of people.* Because stereotypes often involve emotions of love (generally toward members of ingroups) and hate or fear (toward outgroups), they are hard to change even in the face of contradictory evidence. For example, some people have a stereotypical understanding of the poor as lazy and irresponsible freeloaders who would rather sit back and accept welfare than work to support themselves (N.O.R.C., 1991). But, as explained in Chapter 7 ("Social Stratification"), this stereotype flies in the face of the fact that more than half of poor people in our nation are children, working adults, and elderly people.

The second has to do with power: minorities experience *subordination.* Chapter 7 ("Social Stratification") explained that minorities typically have lower incomes and less occupational prestige and education. But not all members of a minority are equally disadvantaged. Some Hispanics, for example, are quite wealthy, certain Chinese Americans are celebrated business leaders, and a number of African Americans are included among our nation's leading scholars. But even the most successful individuals suffer from their minority standing. Race

Societies devise stereotypes for virtually every racial and ethnic minority, and such attitudes become rooted in culture. As the opening to this chapter illustrates, conflict between Serbs and Croats has long been fueled by stereotypes. In the United States, many white people stereotype people of color in much the same way that wealthy people stereotype the poor, as lacking motivation to improve their own lives (N.O.R.C., 1991). Such attitudes assume that poverty is mostly a matter of personal deficiency and, more to the point, they ignore the fact that most poor people in the United States are white and that most minorities work as hard as anyone else and are *not* poor. In this case the bit of truth in the stereotype is that minorities are more likely than whites to be poor. But by building a rigid attitude out of a few selected facts, stereotypes distort reality.

Racism

A powerful and destructive form of prejudice, **racism** refers to *the belief that one racial category is innately superior or inferior to another*. Racism has pervaded world history: the ancient Greeks, various peoples of India, and many societies of East Asia viewed people unlike themselves as inferior. Racism has also been widespread in the United States where, for centuries, the enslavement of people of African descent was supported by notions of their innate inferiority. Today, overt racism has been weakened by a more egalitarian culture, yet it still persists, albeit in more subtle forms, and research continues to document the injury and humiliation that racism causes to people of color (Feagin, 1991).

In the past, Great Britain, France, Spain, and

The efforts of these four women advanced the United States toward the goal of equal opportunity regardless of a person's color. Sojourner Truth (1797–1883) (right), born a slave, became an influential preacher and later directed her charisma to the abolitionist cause. Near the end of the Civil War, President Abraham Lincoln honored her at the White House. Harriet Tubman (1820–1913) (bottom left), after escaping from slavery, masterminded the flight from bondage of hundreds of African-American men and women. She was one of the most successful participants in what came to be known as the "Underground Railroad." Ida Wells-Barnett (1862–1931) (bottom middle), born to slave parents, was outspoken in pursuit of social equality in the ante-bellum era. After becoming a partner in a Memphis newspaper, she was a tireless crusader against the practice of lynching that terrorized people of color throughout the United States. Marian Anderson (bottom right) (1897–1993) had an exceptional voice, which became part of her church choir when she was six years old. For years, Anderson's career was restrained by racial prejudice. Thus, when she sang in the White House (1936), and on the steps of the Lincoln Memorial to a crowd of almost 100,000 people (1939), she symbolically broke an important "color line."

the United States defended their colonial empires abroad with the argument that subjugated people were inferior beings. European explorers similarly demeaned Native Americans, whose land they seized. In this century, racism animated the Nazi regime in Germany. Nazi racial doctrine proclaimed a so-called "Aryan race" of blond-haired, blue-eyed Caucasians that was allegedly superior to all others and destined to rule the world. Such racism supported the murder of anyone deemed inferior, including some 6 million European Jews and millions of Poles, gypsies, and homosexuals.

More recently, racial conflict has intensified in Europe as whites confront millions of immigrants, many from former colonies (Glenn & Kennedy-Keel, 1986). Similarly, in the United States the 1980s was marked by increasing racial tensions in cities and on college campuses across the country. Racism—in thought and deed—remains a serious social problem here and elsewhere.

Individual versus institutional racism. Stokely Carmichael and Charles Hamilton (1967) point out that we typically think of racism in terms of the acts of specific individuals who hatefully and violently lash out at others. This, argue Carmichael and Hamilton, constitutes *individual racism*. But even greater harm is done by *institutional racism*, which refers to policies that guide the operation of schools, hospitals, the police force, and the workplace. For example, some saw in the beating of Rodney King by police in Los Angeles (see the opening vignette in Chapter 6, "Deviance") a case of wrongdoing by specific officers; to others, however, the incident epitomized a wide-ranging program of police violence directed at the city's black community. According to Carmichael and King, institutional racism is more insidious than the individual brand because racism embedded in social structure goes largely unrecognized, masking as the accepted acts of "established and respected" authority figures.

Theories of Prejudice

If prejudice has little basis in a rational assessment of facts, what are its origins? Social scientists have provided various answers to this vexing question.

Scapegoat theory of prejudice. One explanation, commonly termed *scapegoat theory*, holds that prejudice is the product of frustration among people who are them-

selves disadvantaged (Dollard, 1939). A white woman unhappy with the low wages she earns in a textile factory, for example, may direct hostility not at the powerful people who employ her but at powerless minority co-workers. Prejudice of this kind will not go far toward improving the woman's situation in the factory, but it serves as a relatively safe way to vent anger and it may give her the comforting sense that at least she is superior to someone.

A **scapegoat** is thus *a person or category of people, typically with little power, unfairly blamed for the troubles of others.* Because they are in no position to fight back, minorities are easy targets as scapegoats. For example, the Nazis used Jews as scapegoats, blaming them for all of Germany's ills.

Authoritarian personality theory. T. W. Adorno (1950) and others claim that extreme prejudice forms a personality trait in some individuals. This conclusion is supported by research showing that people who display strong prejudice toward one minority are usually prejudiced against all minorities. Such people exhibit *authoritarian personalities*, rigidly conforming to conventional cultural values, envisioning issues as clear-cut matters of right and wrong, and displaying strong ethnocentrism. People with authoritarian personalities also look on society as naturally competitive and hierarchical, with "better" people (such as themselves) inevitably dominating those who are weaker.

By contrast, Adorno found, people who are tolerant toward one minority are likely to be accepting of all. They tend to be more flexible in their moral judgments and feel uncomfortable in any situation in which some people exercise arbitrary power over others.

The researchers note that authoritarian personalities tend to develop in people with little education and those raised by cold and demanding parents. Socialized in this way, they theorize, children may become angry and anxious, and ultimately, as adults, hostile and aggressive toward scapegoats—others they define as their social inferiors.

Cultural theory of prejudice. A third approach contends that while extreme prejudice may characterize certain people, some prejudice is embedded in popular cultural values. As Chapter 2 ("Culture") notes, the social superiority of particular categories of people stands as a core value in the United States (Williams, 1970). Multiculturalists challenge this hierarchy, suggesting the need to broaden our traditionally Eurocentric attitudes to appreciate the culture of those of non-European backgrounds (Asante, 1987, 1988).

Emory Bogardus (1968) studied the effects of culturally rooted prejudice for more than forty years. He devised the concept of *social distance* to assess how closely people are willing to interact with members of various racial and ethnic categories. He found that most people view various racial and ethnic categories in much the same way, presumably because such attitudes are normative in our culture. We hold the most positive views of people of English, Canadian, and Scottish background, Bogardus explains, and welcome close relationships including marriage with them. Attitudes are somewhat less favorable toward the French, Germans, Swedes, and Dutch. According to Bogardus, the most negative prejudices target people of African and Asian descent; our culture discourages close social ties with them.

The fact that such evaluations are widespread suggests that prejudice is not simply a trait of abnormal people, the implication of Adorno's research. Rather, it is routinely expressed by people well adjusted to a "culture of prejudice."

Conflict theory of prejudice. A fourth approach views prejudice as the product of social conflict. According to this theory, prejudice is ideology used to justify the oppression of minorities. To the extent that people denigrate illegal Hispanic immigrants in the Southwest, for example, they will feel justified in paying these immigrants low wages for hard work.

Conflict theories of prejudice take various forms. According to one argument, based on Marxist theory, elites foster prejudice as a strategy for dividing workers. There is ample evidence in U.S. history that white workers have used minority co-workers as scapegoats; this process serves the interests of capitalists insofar as racial division decreases the chances that *all* workers will join together to advance their common interests (Geschwender, 1978; Olzak, 1989).

A more conservative argument made by Shelby Steele (1990) holds that minorities themselves spark conflict to the extent that they encourage a climate of *race consciousness* as a political strategy to gain power and privileges. Race consciousness, Steele explains, amounts to the claim that historically victimized people are now entitled to special considerations based on race. While this may yield short-term gains for minorities, he cautions, such policies frequently touch off a backlash from whites who see "special treatment" on the basis of race or ethnicity as unfair.

Discrimination

Closely related to prejudice is **discrimination,** *treating various categories of people unequally.* While prejudice refers to attitudes, discrimination is a matter of action. Like prejudice, discrimination can be either positive (providing special advantages) or negative (placing obstacles in the way of categories of people). Discrimination also varies along a continuum, ranging from subtle to blatant.

Prejudice and discrimination often occur together, but not always. A prejudiced personnel manager, for example, may refuse to hire minorities. Robert Merton (1976) describes such a person as an *active bigot* (see Figure 9–1). Fearing legal action, however, the prejudiced personnel manager may not discriminate, thereby remaining a *timid bigot.* What Merton calls *fair-weather liberals* discriminate without being prejudiced, as in the case of our manager discriminating only because it's profitable. Finally, Merton's *all-weather liberal* is free of both prejudice and discrimination.

Institutional discrimination. Like prejudice, discrimination involves not just individuals but social structure. **Institutional discrimination** refers to *discrimination that is a normative and routine part of the operation of a society.* As minorities in the United States have learned through painful experience, traditional ideas of people's "place" are sometimes deeply established in the operation of various social institutions, including the workplace, schools, and the courts.

Until 1954, for example, the principle of "separate

Figure 9–1 Patterns of Prejudice and Discrimination
(Discrimination and National Welfare, *Robert M. MacIver, ed. © 1949 Institute for Religious and Social Studies. Permission of HarperCollins Publisher, Inc.*)

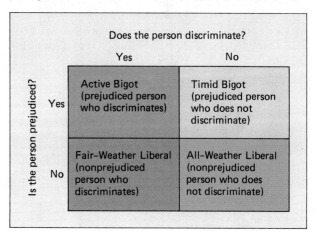

but equal" justified the practice of educating black and white children in different schools. Although the education received by African-American children was, in fact, far inferior to that enjoyed by whites, the law upheld this educational caste system. Such institutional discrimination was formally banned by the Supreme Court in the 1954 landmark decision *Brown* v. *The Board of Education of Topeka*. Racial discrimination has proven difficult to end in the United States, however; almost forty years after the *Brown* ruling, most young people still attend racially imbalanced schools.

Prejudice and Discrimination: The Vicious Cycle

Prejudice and discrimination reinforce each other. W. I. Thomas offered a simple explanation of this fact, noted in Chapter 4 ("Social Interaction in Everyday Life") as the Thomas theorem: *if situations are defined as real, they are real in their consequences* (1966:301; orig. 1931).

Thomas recognized that stereotypes become real to people who believe them, sometimes even to those victimized by them. Prejudice on the part of whites toward people of color, for example, does not produce *innate* inferiority but it can produce *social* inferiority, consigning the minority to poverty, low-prestige occupa-

tions, and racially segregated housing. If this disadvantage is interpreted by whites as evidence that people of color do not measure up to their standards, a new round of prejudice and discrimination is unleashed. Prejudice and discrimination thereby form a *vicious cycle*—each perpetuating the other over time, even from generation to generation.

MAJORITY AND MINORITY: PATTERNS OF INTERACTION

Patterns of interaction between minorities and more privileged members of a society can be described in terms of four models: pluralism, assimilation, segregation, and genocide.

Pluralism

Pluralism is *a state in which people of all races and ethnicities are distinct but have social parity*. This means that, while people may differ in appearance or social heritage, they all enjoy the same overall social standing.

The United States is pluralistic in the sense that ours is a multiracial and multicultural society. Indeed,

The ritual of Kwanza, devised in 1968, has gained popularity in recent decades as a celebration of African-American heritage. Observed soon after Chanukah and Christmas, Kwanza combines Jewish and Christian elements in a distinctly African ritual that builds the strength of families and communities.

many of us take pride in our countless "ethnic villages" where people celebrate the cultural traditions of their immigrant ancestors (Greeley, 1971; Gans, 1982). In New York these include Spanish Harlem, Little Italy, and Chinatown; in Philadelphia, Polish Kensington and Italian "South Philly"; in Chicago, Vietnamese "Little Saigon"; and in Los Angeles, Hispanic East Los Angeles.

Nevertheless, the United States is far from pluralistic for three reasons. First, while many people appreciate their cultural heritage, only a small proportion want to live apart from others exclusively with their "own kind" (N.O.R.C., 1991). Second, our tolerance for social diversity is limited. One reaction to the growing proportion of minorities in the United States, for example, has been a social movement seeking to make English this country's official language. Third, as we shall see later in this chapter, various racial and ethnic categories have strikingly unequal social standing.

Assimilation

Assimilation is *the process by which minorities gradually adopt patterns of the dominant culture.* Assimilation involves changing modes of dress, values, religion, language, or friends.

Many people have traditionally viewed the United States as a "melting pot" in which various nationalities were fused into an entirely new way of life. This melting-pot characterization is misleading, however. Rather than everyone "melting" into some new cultural pattern, minorities have typically adopted the traits of the dominant culture established by the earliest settlers. They did so to improve their social position and to escape some of the prejudice and discrimination directed against foreigners (Newman, 1973). This is not to deny the rich contributions to our culture made by various minorities; cultural contact, however, generally involves more change on the part of those with less power.

Because assimilation is a cultural process, it involves changes in ethnicity but not in race. For example, many descendants of Japanese immigrants have discarded their traditional way of life but still have their racial identity. However, distinctive racial traits diminish over generations as the result of **miscegenation,** *the biological process of interbreeding among racial categories.* While resistance to such biological mixing remains strong—for example, only one in 250 marriages in the United States involves black and white partners—miscegenation (often outside of marriage) has occurred throughout U.S. history.

Segregation

Segregation refers to *the physical and social separation of categories of people.* Sometimes minorities, especially religious orders like the Amish, voluntarily segregate themselves. Usually, however, minorities are involuntarily segregated by others who exclude them. Various degrees of segregation characterize neighborhoods, schools, occupations, hospitals, and even cemeteries. While pluralism fosters distinctiveness without disadvantage, segregation enforces separation to the detriment of a minority.

Racial segregation has a long history in the United States, involving centuries of slavery, and racially linked lodging, schooling, and transportation. Decisions such as the 1954 *Brown* case have reduced overt and *de jure* (Latin meaning "by law") discrimination in the United States. However, *de facto* ("in fact") segregation continues (Saltman, 1991; Wilson, 1991).

Recent urban research by Douglas Massey and Nancy Denton (1989) documented a pattern of racial segregation in which black neighborhoods cluster together into a larger ghetto in the inner city that allows

Only a full century after the abolition of slavery in the United States did the federal government take action to dismantle the "Jim Crow" laws that continued to enforce the separation of people of European and African ancestry in all aspects of public life. During the 1950s and 1960s, these laws, which formally segregated hotels, restaurants, parks, buses, and even drinking fountains, were finally abolished. Even so, de-facto racial segregation in housing and schooling remains a reality for millions of people of color in the United States.

residents little social contact with the outside world. Such *hypersegregation*, they concluded, is more common among African Americans than among any other minority in the United States.

Segregation and the second-class citizenship that accompanies it are understandably opposed by minorities. Sometimes the action of even a single individual can have lasting consequences. On December 1, 1955, Rosa Parks was riding a bus in Montgomery, Alabama, sitting in a section designated by law for African Americans. When a crowd of white passengers boarded the bus, the driver asked four blacks to give up their seats to whites. Three did so, but Rosa Parks refused. The driver left the bus and returned with police, who arrested her for violating the racial segregation laws. She was later convicted in court and fined $14. However, her action touched off a boycott of city buses by the black community, which ultimately brought an end to this form of segregation (King, 1969).

Genocide

Genocide is *the systematic killing of one category of people by another*. This brutal form of racism and ethnocentrism violates nearly every recognized moral standard; nonetheless, it has recurred time and again in human history.

Genocide figured prominently in centuries of contact between Europeans and the original inhabitants of the Americas. From the sixteenth century on, the Spanish, Portuguese, English, French, and Dutch forcefully established vast colonial empires. The native populations of North and South America were decimated after colonization began and Europeans moved to gain control of their wealth. Some were victims of calculated killing; most succumbed to diseases brought here by Europeans and against which native peoples had no natural defenses (Butterworth & Chance, 1981; Matthiessen, 1984; Sale, 1990).

Genocide has also occurred in the twentieth century. Unimaginable horror befell European Jews in the 1930s and 1940s during Adolf Hitler's reign of terror, known as the Holocaust. The Nazis exterminated more than 6 million Jewish men, women, and children. Between 1975 and 1980 the Communist regime of Pol Pot in Cambodia slaughtered anyone thought to represent capitalist cultural influences. Condemned to death were people who knew any Western language and even those who wore eyeglasses, viewed as a symbol of capitalist culture. In the "killing fields" of Cambodia, 2 million

people (one-fourth of the population) perished (Shawcross, 1979).

These four patterns of minority-majority contact exist together in a society. For example, we proudly point to patterns of pluralism and assimilation but only reluctantly acknowledge the degree to which our society has been built on segregation (of African Americans, for example) and genocide (of Native Americans).

The remainder of this chapter suggests how these four types of minority-majority contact have shaped the history and present social standing of major racial and ethnic categories in the United States.

RACE AND ETHNICITY IN THE UNITED STATES

Give me your tired, your poor,
Your huddled masses yearning to breathe free,
The wretched refuse of your teeming shore,
Send these, the homeless, tempest-tossed to me:
I lift my lamp beside the golden door.

These words by Emma Lazarus, inscribed on the Statue of Liberty, express the ideals of human dignity, personal freedom, and opportunity. But, as the history of this country's racial and ethnic minorities reveals, our nation's golden door has opened more widely for some than for others.

Native Americans

The term *Native Americans* refers to the hundreds of distinct societies—including Aleuts, Cherokee, Zuni, Sioux, Mohawk, Aztec, and Inca—who were the original inhabitants of the Americas. Thousands of years ago, migrating peoples crossed a land bridge from Asia to North America where the Bering Strait (off the coast of Alaska) lies today, and they gradually spread throughout the Western Hemisphere. When the first Europeans arrived late in the fifteenth century, Native Americans numbered in the millions and had a thirty-thousand-year history in this hemisphere. By the beginning of the twentieth century, after years of subjugation and outright genocide, the "vanishing Americans" numbered a mere 250,000 (Dobyns, 1966; Tyler, 1973).

Native Americans were first referred to as *Indians*

by Christopher Columbus (1446–1506), who landed in the Bahama Islands while searching for India. Columbus found the indigenous people to be passive and peaceful, a stark contrast to the more materialistic and competitive Europeans (Matthiessen, 1984; Sale, 1990). Even as Europeans seized the land of Native Americans, they justified such actions by painting their victims as thieves and murderers (Unruh, 1979; Josephy, 1982).

After the Revolutionary War, the new United States government adopted a pluralist approach to Native-American societies and sought to gain more land through treaties. Payment for land was far from fair, however, and when Native Americans resisted surrender of their homelands, superior military power was used to evict them. Thousands of Cherokees, for example, died on a forced march—the Trail of Tears—from their homes in the southeastern United States to segregated reservations in the Midwest. By the early 1800s, few Native Americans remained east of the Mississippi River.

After 1871, the United States made Native Americans wards of the government and tried to resolve "the Indian problem" through forced assimilation. Native Americans continued to lose their land, and they were well on their way to losing their culture as well. Reservation life fostered dependency, replacing ancestral languages with English and eroding traditional religion in favor of Christianity. Officials transferred many children from their parents to boarding schools, operated by the Bureau of Indian Affairs, where they were resocialized as "Americans." The U.S. government also gave local control of reservations to the few Native Americans who supported such policies, and officials distributed reservation land—traditionally held collectively—as the private property of individual families (Tyler, 1973). In the proc-

A century to the day after the December 29, 1890 killing of almost three hundred Native-American men, women, and children at Wounded Knee, South Dakota by soldiers of the 7th Cavalry, members of the Sioux braved a sub-zero wind chill to retrace the path taken by their ancestors. The Wounded Knee massacre marked the end of Native-American resistance to white settlement in the United States, and it has come to symbolize the tragic and shameful victimization of Native Americans at the hands of European settlers.

ess, some whites managed to grab still more land for themselves.

Not until 1924 were Native Americans entitled to citizenship. Since then, the government has encouraged their migration from reservations. Some have adopted mainstream cultural patterns and married non–Native Americans. Many large cities now have sizable Native-American populations. As shown in Table 9–2, however, median family income for Native Americans was far below the U.S. average in 1990, and relatively few Native Americans earn a college degree.

From in-depth interviews with Native Americans in a Western city, Joan Albon (1971) concluded that many are disadvantaged by little schooling, few marketable skills, and dark skin that provokes prejudice and discrimination. Additionally, she noted, some Native Americans lack the individualism and competitiveness that contribute to success in the United States. This passivity stems from both traditional values and long dependence on government assistance.

Like other racial and ethnic minorities in the United States, Native Americans have recently reasserted pride in their culture and have banded together seeking

Table 9–2 THE SOCIAL STANDING OF NATIVE AMERICANS, 1990

	Native Americans	Entire United States
Median family income	$20,025	$33,500
Proportion in poverty	30.9%	10.7%
Median education (years; age 25 and over)	N/A	12.7
Completion of four or more years of college (age 25 and over)	9.3%	21.4%

SOURCE: U.S. Bureau of the Census.

greater opportunity. Since 1990, Native-American organizations have reported a surge in new membership applications from people who had long downplayed their heritage but now draw pride from their roots (Johnson, 1991). In lawsuits against the federal government, Native Americans have pressed for return of lands seized in the past, and they have sought self-rule over reservation lands. In some instances, violent confrontations with federal officials have erupted. Few Native Americans support this means of addressing grievances, but the vast majority share a profound sense of injustice endured at the hands of whites (Josephy, 1982; Matthiessen, 1983).

White Anglo-Saxon Protestants

White Anglo-Saxon Protestants (WASPs) were not the first people to inhabit the United States, but they came to dominate this nation once European settlement began. Most WASPs are of English ancestry, but Scots and Welsh are also included. Roughly one in five of our people—more than 50 million in all—can claim some WASP background.

Historically, WASP immigrants were highly skilled and motivated toward achievement by what we now call the Protestant work ethic. Because of their numbers and power, WASPs were not subject to the prejudice and discrimination experienced by other categories of immigrants. The historical dominance of WASPs has been so great that, as noted earlier, assimilation into U.S. society has meant becoming more like the WASPs (Gordon, 1964).

Many WASPs responded to growing social diversity in the nineteenth century with hostility toward new arrivals they deemed "undesirable foreigners." Nativist political movements sought to legally limit the flow of immigrants. WASPs who could afford to pursued a personal solution to the "problem" by isolating themselves in exclusive suburbs and social clubs, far from those they deemed their social inferiors. Thus the 1880s—the decade in which the Statue of Liberty first welcomed immigrants to the United States—also saw the founding of the first country club (with all WASP members). Soon afterward, WASPs began publishing the *Social Register* (1887), a listing of members of "society," and established various genealogical societies such as the Daughters of the American Revolution (1890) and the Society of Mayflower Descendants (1894). These efforts served to socially distance wealthy WASPs from other immigrants (Baltzell, 1964).

By mid-century, WASP wealth and power showed signs of decline (Baltzell, 1964, 1976, 1988). This changing trend was symbolized in 1960 by the election of John Fitzgerald Kennedy as the first non-WASP (Irish-Catholic) president of the United States. But WASPs remain influential because of their extensive schooling, high-prestige occupations, and above-average incomes, and the majority of people in the upper-upper class are still WASPs (Greeley, 1974; Baltzell, 1979; Roof, 1981; Neidert & Farley, 1985). The WASP cultural legacy also persists: English remains the dominant language of the United States, and Protestantism is the majority religion. Our legal system, too, reflects its English origins. Perhaps the historical dominance of WASPs is most evident in the widespread use of the terms "race" and "ethnicity" to describe everyone but them.

African Americans

Although African Americans accompanied Spanish explorers to the New World in the fifteenth century, accounts of black history in the United States usually begin in 1619, when a Dutch trading ship brought twenty Africans to Jamestown, Virginia (Holt, 1980). Whether these people arrived as slaves or as indentured servants, people obligated to perform labor for a specified period in return for passage across the Atlantic Ocean, being of African descent on these shores soon became virtually synonymous with being a slave. In 1661 the first law recognizing slavery was passed in Virginia (Sowell, 1981).

In the colonies' agrarian economy, slavery was the foundation of the plantation system. Whites prospered not only as plantation owners, but also as slave traders—a business legal until 1808. Some 10 million Africans were forcibly brought to various countries in the Americas; about 400,000 entered the United States (Sowell, 1981). Hundreds of slaves were chained on board small sailing ships as human cargo during a voyage of several weeks across the Atlantic Ocean. Filth and disease killed many; others were driven to suicide. Overall, perhaps half died en route (Tannenbaum, 1946; Franklin, 1967).

Surviving the journey was a mixed blessing, bringing a life of servitude as the property of white owners. Most slaves engaged in farming, although some worked in cities at a variety of trades (Franklin, 1967). Work usually lasted from daybreak until sunset—longer during the harvest. The law gave slave owners the right to impose whatever discipline they deemed necessary to ensure that slaves labored continuously. Even the killing of a slave

The message of the Civil Rights movement was never stated more simply or clearly than it is here. The claim "I Am a Man"—regardless of color or class—is a bold challenge to the racism that continues to compromise the basic humanity of millions of women and men in the United States.

by an owner rarely prompted legal action. Owners also divided slave families at public auctions where human beings were bought and sold as pieces of property. By eliminating any opportunity for slaves to be schooled, owners further tightened control over slaves, who remained dependent on their masters for all their basic needs (Sowell, 1981).

There were free persons of color in both the North and the South, small-scale farmers, skilled workers, and small-business owners (Murray, 1978). But the lives of most African Americans stood in glaring contradiction to the principles of equality and freedom on which the United States was founded. The Declaration of Independence states:

> We hold these Truths to be self-evident, that all Men are created equal, that they are endowed by their Creator with certain unalienable Rights, that among these are Life, Liberty, and the Pursuit of Happiness. . . .

Most white Americans did not apply these ideals to blacks. In the Dred Scott case in 1857, the U.S. Supreme Court answered the question, "Are blacks citizens?" by writing, "We think they are not, and that they are not included, and were not intended to be included, under the word 'citizens' in the Constitution, and can therefore claim none of the rights and privileges which that instrument provides for and secures for citizens of the United States" (Blaustein & Zangrando, 1968:160). Thus arose what Swedish sociologist Gunnar Myrdal (1944) termed the *American dilemma*: the denial of basic rights and freedoms to an entire category of people. To resolve this dilemma, many whites simply defined African Americans as innately inferior.

In 1865 the Thirteenth Amendment to the Constitution outlawed slavery. Three years later the Fourteenth Amendment reversed the Dred Scott ruling, granting citizenship to all people born in the United States. The Fifteenth Amendment, ratified in 1870, stated that neither race nor previous condition of servitude should deprive anyone of the right to vote. However, so-called Jim Crow laws still segregated U.S. society into two racial castes (Woodward, 1974). Especially in the South, whites beat and lynched blacks (and some whites) who challenged the racial hierarchy.

The twentieth century has brought dramatic changes to African Americans. In the decades after World War I, tens of thousands of women and men left the rural South for jobs in northern factories. While they did find more economic opportunity, they did not escape racial prejudice and discrimination, which placed them lower in the social hierarchy than white immigrants arriving from Europe at the same time (Lieberson, 1980). In the 1950s and 1960s, a national civil rights movement

Table 9–3 THE SOCIAL STANDING OF AFRICAN
AMERICANS, 1991

	African Americans	Entire United States
Median family income	$21,548	$35,939
Proportion in poverty	32.7%	14.2%
Median education (years; age 25 and over)	12.4	12.7
Completion of four or more years of college (age 25 and over)	11.5%	21.4%

SOURCE: U.S. Bureau of the Census.

of blacks and sympathetic whites attacked racism, and encouraged landmark judicial decisions that outlawed segregated schools and overt discrimination in employment and public accommodations. In addition, the "black power movement" gave African Americans a renewed sense of pride, as more people were no longer willing to be defined in terms of the white culture.

Gains notwithstanding, people of African descent continue to occupy a subordinate position in the United States, as shown in Table 9–3. The median income of African-American families in 1991 ($21,548) was 57 percent of that earned by white families ($37,783).[3] Black families are also three times as likely as white families to be poor. In general, African Americans made significant economic gains from the 1940s through the 1960s; the 1970s brought economic stagnation, and much of the 1980s saw a decline in economic position (Jacob, 1986; Jaynes & Williams, 1989; Littman, 1989; Welniak & Littman, 1989).

In part, this recent downturn reflects the loss of millions of factory jobs—a vital resource for workers in this nation's inner cities. Thus black unemployment stands at more than twice the level among whites; among African-American teenagers in many cities, the figure exceeds 40 percent (Jacob, 1986; Lichter, 1989; U.S. Bureau of the Census, 1991).

In 1960, the median schooling for women and men over the age of 25 was 8.2 years for blacks compared to 10.9 years for whites. By 1991 this gap had almost closed: the respective figures were 12.4 years and 12.8 years. Even so, African Americans remain only half as

likely as whites to complete four years of college. During the 1980s, the number of African Americans enrolled in college and graduate schools rose slightly, with about one-third of high-school graduates entering college, compared with one-fourth a decade earlier (U.S. Bureau of the Census, 1992).

Further concern springs from evidence that schooling sparks less upward mobility among blacks than it does among whites (Blau & Duncan, 1967; Tienda & Lii, 1987). Almost one in three black families in the United States is now securely anchored in the middle class with an annual income of at least $35,000, and one in seven is affluent, earning $50,000 or more. But these gains stand out against the persistent poverty of millions of African Americans—especially single women and children—who are part of an economically desperate underclass (Wilson, 1984; O'Hare, 1989; Patterson, 1991).

The political clout of African Americans has increased, paralleling the number of registered voters and elected officials. Black migration to cities, along with white movement to the suburbs, has provided the political muscle to elect black mayors in half of this nation's ten largest cities. At the national level, however, people of color hold scarcely 1 percent of elected positions. After the 1992 elections, thirty-nine blacks (of 435) sat in the House of Representatives and one black person (of 100) was in the Senate.

In sum, for more than 350 years, people of African ancestry in the United States have struggled for social equality. As a nation, we can certainly take pride in how far we have come in this pursuit. A century ago slavery was outlawed and, during this century, much overt discrimination was legally banned. In his 1913 assessment of African Americans in the United States, W.E.B. DuBois expressed pride in the extent of black achievement, but cautioned that racial bigotry remained strong. Clearly this is still the case. One response to this problem is the government policy of affirmative action, or preferential treatment for categories of people historically subjected to prejudice and discrimination. The box examines this controversial policy.

Asian Americans

Although Asian Americans share some racial traits, enormous cultural diversity marks this category of people. The 1990 census placed their number at more than 7 million—approaching 3 percent of the population. The

---

[3] The figure would be 84 percent if only two-parent families were included.

220   Chapter 9   Race and Ethnicity

CRITICAL THINKING

Affirmative Action: Problem or Solution?

After World War II, the U.S. government funded higher education for veterans of all races. The G.I. Bill held special promise for African Americans and, by 1960, some 350,000 had gone to college with government funding. But these men and women were not finding the kinds of jobs for which they were qualified.

The government responded with a program that came to be known as "affirmative action." Under the Kennedy Administration in the early 1960s, affirmative action meant throwing a broader "net of opportunity" to find qualified minorities that the government knew were out there. This program won support for helping thousands of African Americans gain jobs in line with their skills. But, by the 1970s, critics complained, affirmative action was coming to mean "group preferences" for minorities.

Few people object to affirmative action's mandate that employers encourage applications from people of all races and ethnicities in their search for talent, and that they carefully monitor hiring and promotion to eliminate discrimination. But this practice slowly moved toward the controversial idea of quotas that ensure that minorities hold jobs in proportion to their numbers in the overall population. Under a quota system, some minority members are guaranteed favorable treatment regardless of how they stack up against other appli-

cants. In effect, say critics, an employer is required to find the best *minority*, rather than the best *person*, for a job. Rigid quota systems have been rejected by U.S. courts, but the law supports preferences based on race and ethnicity as a means of increasing the proportion of minorities in settings that have historically excluded them.

A related policy is *race-norming* test scores of applicants for jobs or promotions. This practice involves ranking test scores in racial categories, so that, say, African-American applicants compete only against members of their own race. Rankings are then combined so that someone who ranks at the top of any racial category will appear at or near the top of the overall listing, above others of a different race who had a higher score but were further down on their own racial list.

Advocates of all forms of affirmative action applaud these practices as fair and necessary correctives for historical discrimination. Everybody alive today, they argue, has been affected by privileges accorded or denied to their parents and grandparents. "Special treatment," then, is nothing new and is necessary for those denied opportunity through no fault of their own. Only in this way, advocates claim, can we break the vicious cycle of prejudice and discrimination.

Opponents of affirmative action concede that minorities have histori-

cally been treated unfairly, but they see affirmative action as *reverse discrimination*. Why should today's whites—most of whom are far from privileged—be penalized for past discrimination for which they were in no way responsible? Opponents also point out many minorities have overcome historical barriers to opportunity through hard work, not requests for special treatment. Giving entire categories of people preferences, opponents conclude, inevitably compromises standards, fosters race consciousness, provokes a hostile backlash from whites, and undermines the real accomplishments of minorities. Moreover, the critics add, affirmative action generally benefits minorities with more schooling while doing little for the persistently poor who really need assistance.

As applied to African Americans, the U.S. population tends to oppose affirmative action policies, as the following survey item suggests:

> Some people think that blacks have been discriminated against for so long that the government has a special obligation to help improve their living standards. Others believe that the government should not be giving special treatment to blacks. (N.O.R.C., 1991:327)

The numbers 1 through 5 show the range of opinion in relation to the three responses.

1 (10.2%)	2 (11.1%)	3 (30.6%)	4 (18.6%)	5 (26.0%)
I strongly agree that the government is obligated to help blacks.		I agree with both answers.		I strongly agree that the government shouldn't give blacks special treatment.

No Response = 3.5%   *Total* = 1,017 *respondents*

SOURCE: Survey data from N.O.R.C., *General Social Surveys* (Chicago: National Opinion Research Center, 1991), p. 327.

According to some analysts, communities gather strength and people gain social confidence through emphasizing racial and ethnic identity. From another point of view, however, these processes heighten divisions within our society and fuel social conflict. Resolving the tension between appreciating our distinctive heritage and respecting our common humanity will continue to challenge us into the next century.

largest category of Asian Americans are people of Chinese ancestry (1.6 million), followed by those of Filipino (1.4 million), Japanese (850,000), and Asian-Indian (815,000) background. Most Asian Americans live in the West, with four in ten residing in California.

Migration from China and Japan to the United States began over a century ago. More recent immigrants from Asia include Filipinos, Koreans, and Vietnamese. Overall, Asian Americans are this country's fastest-growing minority, accounting for almost half of all immigration to the United States.

Asian immigrants—especially young people—have commanded both attention and respect as high achievers. Many of their elders, too, have made significant economic and social strides. Yet some people express hostility to Asian Americans despite—or sometimes because of—their outstanding achievement. Moreover, as we shall

see, the "model minority" label obscures the poverty of some Asian Americans.

Chinese Americans. Chinese immigration to the United States began with the economic boom of the California Gold Rush in 1849. With new towns and businesses springing up overnight, entrepreneurs met their pressing need for cheap labor by employing some 100,000 Chinese immigrants in the decades that followed. Most were young, hard-working men willing to take lower-status jobs shunned by whites (Ling, 1971). But the economy soured in the 1870s, and desperate whites found themselves competing with the Chinese for jobs. Suddenly the industriousness of the Chinese posed a threat. Repeating a well-known pattern, economic hard times fueled prejudice and discrimination (Boswell, 1986).

Soon, laws barred the Chinese from many occupations. Courts also withdrew legal protections, unleashing vicious campaigns by some whites against the so-called "Yellow Peril" (Sowell, 1981). The entire country seemed to line up against the Chinese, as captured in a popular phrase of the time that a person "didn't have a Chinaman's chance" (Sung, 1967:56).

In 1882, the U.S. government passed the first of several laws curtailing Chinese immigration. This action created domestic hardship because, of the Chinese already in the United States, men outnumbered women by twenty to one (Hsu, 1971; Lai, 1980). This sex imbalance sent the Chinese population plummeting to only 60,000 by 1920. Chinese women already in the United States, however, were in high demand and they soon became far less submissive to men (Sowell, 1981).

Responding to their plight, some Chinese moved eastward; many more sought the relative safety of urban Chinatowns (Wong, 1971). There Chinese traditions flourished, and kinship networks, called *clans*, offered financial assistance and greater political strength. At the same time, those living in a Chinatown had less incentive to learn English or pursue cultural assimilation.

With the onset of World War II, a renewed need for labor increased the opportunities of the Chinese (Lai, 1980). In 1943 President Roosevelt ended the ban on Chinese immigration and extended the rights of citizenship to Chinese Americans born abroad. Many responded by moving out of Chinatowns and seeking assimilation. In turn-of-the-century Honolulu, for example, 70 percent of the Chinese people lived in Chinatown; today, the figure is closer to one in five.

By 1950, many Chinese Americans had achieved

considerable upward social mobility. No longer restricted to self-employment in laundries and restaurants, more people now work in high-prestige occupations. Their achievement has been outstanding in science and technology, fields in which many Chinese Americans—including several Nobel Prize winners—have excelled (Sowell, 1981). As shown in Table 9–4, the median family income of all Asian Americans in 1990 ($42,240) was above the national average ($33,500). Chinese Americans have above-average incomes, although not to the extent that Japanese Americans do. Note, however, that the higher income of Chinese Americans, as well as that of other categories of Asian Americans, reflects a larger number of family members in the labor force. Chinese Americans also have a remarkable level of educational achievement, with twice the national average of college graduates (U.S. Bureau of the Census, 1992).

Despite this record of success, many Chinese Americans still grapple with serious problems. Overt prejudice and discrimination have subsided, but some racial hostility persists. Poverty among Chinese Americans, which stands above the national average, is especially serious among those who remain in Chinatowns and still work in restaurants or other low-paying jobs. This fact has sparked a debate over whether racial and ethnic enclaves exploit or economically assist their residents (Sowell, 1981; Portes & Jensen, 1989; Zhou & Logan, 1989).

Japanese Americans. Japanese immigration to the United States began slowly in the 1860s, reaching only 3,000 by 1890. Most of these immigrants made their way to the Hawaiian Islands (a state since 1959) where they were welcomed as laborers on sugar plantations.

The U.S. government defended the internment of Japanese Americans in the western United States during World War II as necessary to ensure national security. But this policy also expressed the racial hostility that whites commonly directed toward people of Asian ancestry at this time.

Early in this century, however, as Japanese immigration rose and workers demanded better pay, whites sought to curb their immigration (Daniels, 1971). In 1908 the United States signed an agreement with Japan limiting immigration of men—the chief economic threat—while allowing women to immigrate to ease the sex-ratio imbalance. In the 1920s, laws mandating segregation and prohibiting interracial marriage virtually ended further Japanese immigration. No foreign-born person of Japanese ancestry could become a U.S. citizen until 1952.

Japanese and Chinese immigrants differed in three ways. First, far fewer Japanese came to this country. Second, the Japanese knew much more about the United States before migrating than the Chinese did, which encouraged assimilation (Sowell, 1981). Third, few Japanese immigrants clustered in cities; instead, most became farmers.

Japanese ownership of farms threw California into crisis. By 1913, racial hostility had driven lawmakers to ban any "noncitizen" from owning farmland. Foreign-born Japanese (called the *Issei*) responded by placing farmland in the names of their U.S.-born children (*Ni-*

Table 9–4	THE SOCIAL STANDING OF ASIAN AMERICANS, 1990	
	Asian Americans	Entire United States
Median family income	$42,240	$33,500
Percent in poverty	12.2%	10.7%
Median education (years; age 25 and over)	13.7	12.7
Completion of four or more years of college (age 25 and over)	39.0%	21.4%

SOURCE: U.S. Bureau of the Census.

sei), who were automatically U.S. citizens under the Constitution. Others leased farmland with great success.

The Japanese faced their greatest crisis after December 7, 1941, when the nation of Japan destroyed much of the U.S. naval fleet at Hawaii's Pearl Harbor. Rage toward Japan was directed at the Japanese living in the United States. New fears that Japanese people would commit acts of espionage and sabotage mixed with old racial hatreds. The result: Executive Order 9066, an unprecedented program of detention for people of Japanese descent. This act, intended to protect the national security of the United States, designated areas of the West Coast as military zones from which 110,000 people of Japanese ancestry (90 percent of the total) were relocated to remote, inland reservations.

While concern about national security always rises in times of war, this policy was criticized, first, because it targeted an entire category of people, not one of whom was ever convicted of any disloyal act. Second, roughly two-thirds of those imprisoned were *Nisei*—U.S. citizens by birth—whose rights were undermined by fear and racism (Kitano, 1985). Third, the United States was also at war with Germany and Italy, yet no comparable action was taken against whites of German or Italian ancestry.

Relocation meant selling homes, furnishings, and businesses on short notice for pennies on the dollar. As a result, almost the entire Japanese-American population was devastated economically. In the detention camps—surrounded by barbed wire and armed soldiers—families were crowded into single rooms, often in buildings that had previously been used for livestock (Fujimoto, 1971; Bloom, 1980). The internment ended in 1944, when the Supreme Court declared the program unconstitutional. In 1988 Congress awarded $20,000 to each victim of this policy as token compensation and recognition of the economic loss and personal suffering endured by Japanese Americans.

After World War II, Japanese Americans staged a dramatic recovery. Having lost their traditional businesses, they pursued schooling and entered a wide range of new occupations with remarkable success. The median income of Japanese-American households is very high—even by Asian-American standards—being more than 30 percent above the national average. And the rate of poverty among Japanese Americans is only half that for the United States as a whole.

Upward social mobility has encouraged cultural assimilation. The third and fourth generations of Japanese Americans (the *Sansei* and *Yonsei*) rarely live in residential enclaves, as many Chinese Americans still do, and a significant number have married non–Japanese Americans. In the process, many have abandoned their traditions, including the ability to speak Japanese. But a high proportion of Japanese Americans participate in ethnic associations as a way of maintaining their ethnic identity (Fugita & O'Brien, 1985). Assimilation by Japanese Americans, while beneficial in some respects, leaves many caught between two worlds, yet belonging to neither. As one Japanese-American man put it, "I never considered myself 100 percent American because of obvious physical differences. Nor did I think of myself as Japanese" (Okimoto, 1971:14).

Hispanic Americans

In 1990, Hispanics numbered at least 22 million, representing one in twelve people in the United States. While some Hispanics trace their roots to Spain, most have some combination of Spanish, African, and Native-American ancestry, and their cultures vary accordingly. About 60 percent (at least 13 million) are Mexican Americans, commonly called *Chicanos*. Puerto Ricans are next in population size (3 million), followed by Cuban Americans (1 million). Many other societies of Latin America are represented in smaller numbers. Because of a high birth rate and continuing immigration, the Hispanic population is currently increasing by almost a million a year. If this trend continues, Hispanics may outnumber African Americans in the United States early in the next century (Moore & Pachon, 1985).

The social standing of Hispanics improved in some respects during the 1980s. There has been a substantial increase in managerial and professional positions among Hispanic men and an even sharper rise in such jobs among Hispanic women (Schwartz, 1989). But, overall, Hispanic family income remained steady during the decade. As the following sections reveal, however, some categories of Hispanics have fared better than others.

Mexican Americans. Some Chicanos are descendants of people who were living in a part of Mexico that was annexed by the United States after the Mexican-American War (1846–1848). Most Mexican Americans, however, are recent immigrants. Between 1970 and 1990, more immigrants came to the United States from Mexico than from any other nation. The official total stands at almost 15 million, but the actual figure is probably far higher because large numbers of Mexican Americans enter the United States illegally and are not counted by the Census Bureau.

Mexican Americans play an important role in the economy of the United States, even though meager benefits accrue to them. Many have provided inexpensive labor, especially as farm workers; many more hold other low-paying jobs. Table 9–5 shows that in 1990 the median family income for Mexican Americans was $23,240, about 69 percent of the comparable national figure of $33,500 (a drop from 74 percent in 1980). In 1990, one-fourth of Chicano families were classified as poor— more than twice the national average but less than the proportion of African Americans living in poverty. Finally, despite gains since 1980, Mexican Americans still acquire significantly less education than U.S. adults as a whole.

Puerto Ricans. Puerto Rico has been a possession of the United States since the Spanish-American War ended in 1898. In 1917, islanders became U.S. citizens, and Puerto Ricans now move freely to and from the mainland (Fitzpatrick, 1980).

New York City is the center of Puerto Rican life in the continental United States. From about 500 in 1910, the Puerto Rican population of New York rose to 70,000 by 1940. After World War II, regular airline service between New York City and San Juan, Puerto Rico's capital, kindled even greater migration so that today there are more than 2 million Puerto Ricans in the continental United States, half of whom reside in New York's Spanish Harlem.

However, life in New York has not met the expectations of many Puerto Ricans, and about half of that city's Puerto Rican community live in poverty (Moore & Pachon, 1985). Adjusting to cultural patterns on the mainland—including, for many, learning English—is one major challenge; Puerto Ricans with darker skin also encounter prejudice and discrimination. As a result, about as many families return to Puerto Rico annually as arrive from the island.

This "revolving door" pattern hampers assimilation. About three-fourths of Puerto Rican families in the United States speak Spanish at home, compared with about half of Mexican-American families (Sowell, 1981; Stevens & Swicegood, 1987). Speaking only Spanish maintains a strong ethnic identity but it also limits economic opportunity. Puerto Ricans also have the highest incidence of women-headed households among Hispanics, which contributes to low income (Reimers, 1984). Table 9–5 shows that in 1990 the median household income for Puerto Ricans was $18,008, just 54 percent of the national average. Throughout the 1980s, therefore, Puerto Ricans were the most socially disadvantaged Hispanic minority.

Cuban Americans. Large numbers of Cubans came to the United States after the 1959 Marxist revolution led by Fidel Castro. By 1972, aided by special legislation, 400,000 Cubans had emigrated (Perez, 1980). Most settled in Miami, some in New York. Those who fled Castro's Cuba were generally not the "huddled masses" described on the Statue of Liberty, but highly educated business and professional people. They wasted little time building much the same success in the United States that they had enjoyed in their homeland (Fallows, 1983). Table 9–5 shows that the median household income for Cuban Americans in 1990 was $31,439—well above that of other Hispanics yet still below the national standard. Poverty among Cuban Americans is also substantially higher than average.

Many people of Cuban descent manage a delicate balancing act—achieving success in the larger society

Table 9–5 THE SOCIAL STANDING OF HISPANIC AMERICANS, 1990

	All Hispanics	Mexican Americans	Puerto Ricans	Cuban Americans	Entire United States
Median family income	$23,431	$23,240	$18,008	$31,439	$33,500
Proportion in poverty	25.0%	25.0%	37.5%	13.8%	10.7%
Median education (years; age 25 and over)	12.0	10.8	12.0	12.4	12.7
Completion of four or more years of college (age 25 and over)	9.2%	6.2%	10.1%	18.5%	21.4%

SOURCE: U.S. Bureau of the Census.

....QUE PASA LITTLE HAVANA?

Hispanic Americans represent a majority of the residents of Miami, Florida. In the Little Havana district of the city, Cuban immigrants have blended their traditional way of life with the surrounding cultures.

while retaining much of their traditional culture. Of all Hispanics, Cubans are the most likely to speak Spanish in their homes; eight out of ten families do (Sowell, 1981). Culturally assertive and living in visible communities like Miami's Little Havana, Cubans endure hostility from some whites who denounce them as outsiders taking over the locals' domain. As a bumper sticker states bluntly, "Will the last American to leave Miami remember to bring the flag?"

The 1990 census placed the total number of Cuban Americans at more than a million. Substantial population growth during the 1980s followed the so-called Mariel boat lift, the influx of 125,000 refugees from Mariel Harbor in Cuba. Several thousand of these "boat people" had been released from Cuban prisons and mental hospitals, and they became the focus of mass-media accounts fueling prejudice against Cuban Americans (Clark, Lasaga, & Regue, 1981; Portes, 1984).

Typically poorer and less well educated than those who arrived a generation earlier, these recent immigrants clashed with the better established Cuban community in Miami (Fallows, 1983). But they too are quickly putting down roots. Soon after their arrival, most applied for resident status so that their relatives abroad could also be admitted to the United States.

White Ethnic Americans

The 1960s gave us the term *white ethnics*, recognition of the evident ethnic heritage of many white people. White ethnics—a term linked to the working class—

are non-WASP people whose ancestors lived in Germany, Ireland, Italy, or other European nations. More than half of the U.S. population falls into one or another white ethnic category.

Unprecedented immigration from Europe during the nineteenth century greatly increased the social diversity of the United States. Initially, the Germans and Irish predominated. Italians, and Jews from many European countries, followed. Despite cultural differences, all shared the hope that the United States would offer greater political freedom and economic opportunity than they had known in their homelands. The belief that "the streets of America are paved with gold" turned out to be a far cry from the reality experienced by the vast majority of immigrants. Jobs were not always easy to find, and most demanded hard labor for low wages.

Economic problems were aggravated by prejudice and discrimination, which rose with the increasing tide of immigration. Nativist organizations opposed the entry of non-WASP Europeans and they denounced those already here. Newspaper ads seeking workers in the mid-nineteenth century often carried a warning to new arrivals: "None need apply but Americans" (Handlin, 1941:67).

Some of this prejudice and discrimination actually involved class, since immigrants were typically poor and many had only a poor command of English. But even distinguished achievers faced hostility. Fiorello La Guardia, the son of Italian and Jewish immigrants who served as mayor of New York between 1933 and 1945, was once rebuked by President Herbert Hoover in words that reveal unambiguous ethnic hatred:

You should go back where you belong and advise Mussolini how to make good honest citizens in Italy. The Italians are preponderantly our murderers and bootleggers. . . . Like a lot of other foreign spawn, you do not appreciate the country that supports and tolerates you. (Mann, 1959, cited in Baltzell, 1964:30)

Nativists were finally victorious. Between 1921 and 1968, the government applied immigration quotas to each foreign country. The greatest restrictions were placed on southern and eastern Europeans—people likely to have darker skin and greater cultural differences with the dominant WASPs (Fallows, 1983).

In response to widespread bigotry, white ethnics followed the pattern of forming supportive residential enclaves. Some also gained footholds in specialized trades: Italian Americans entered the construction industry; Irish Americans worked in various building trades and took civil service jobs; Jews predominated in the garment industry; many Greeks (like the Chinese) worked in the retail food business (Newman, 1973).

White ethnics who prospered assimilated more easily into the larger society, while many working-class people still live in traditional neighborhoods. Despite continuing problems, white ethnics have achieved considerable success. Many descendants of immigrants who labored in sweatshops and lived in overcrowded tenements now hold respectable positions—both socially and economically. As a result, many take great pride in their ethnic heritage.

U.S. MINORITIES: A HUNDRED-YEAR PERSPECTIVE

The United States has been, and is likely to remain, a land of immigrants. Its striking cultural diversity stems from immigration, which peaked at the beginning of this century and subsided with World War I (1914–1918) and restrictive legislation enacted during the 1920s (Easterlin, 1980).

For most of those who came to this country, the first half of this century brought gradual economic gains and at least some cultural assimilation. The government also granted basic freedoms that earlier had been denied, extending citizenship to Native Americans (1924), to foreign-born Chinese Americans (1943), and to Japanese Americans (1952). In the 1950s, African Americans or-

ganized the civil rights movement in response to centuries of oppression.

Immigration to this country has risen again to about 400,000 people annually, the same as during the "Great Immigration" a century ago (although newcomers now enter a country with five times as many people). But now most immigrants come not from Europe but from Latin America and Asia. During the 1980s, Mexicans, Filipinos, and Koreans arrived in the largest numbers.

New arrivals confront problems of prejudice and

This country's immigration policies have changed over time; today, as in the past, we have also seen fit to apply different standards to different categories of people. A recent case in point is Haitians who have fled their Caribbean nation because of poverty and political turbulence. The U.S. government has refused to allow most Haitians to enter this country, claiming that they are not true political refugees. Critics ask whether this policy would stand if the people in question were not both poor and dark skinned.

discrimination as did those who came before them. Also, like European immigrants of the past, many now struggle to enter the "golden door" of the United States without giving up their traditional culture. Some have also built racial and ethnic enclaves: the Little Havana and Korea-town of today stand alongside the Little Italy and German-town of the past. New arrivals also share the hope of their predecessors that racial and ethnic diversity will be considered a matter of difference but not a badge of inferiority.

SUMMARY

1. Race involves a cluster of biological traits that form three broad categories: Caucasians, Negroids, and Mongoloids. There are, however, no pure races. Ethnicity is based on shared cultural heritage. Minorities are those—including people of certain races and ethnicities—who are both socially distinct and socially disadvantaged.

2. Prejudice is an inflexible and distorted generalization about a category of people. Racism, a powerful form of prejudice, asserts that one race is innately superior or inferior to another.

3. Discrimination involves action—treating various categories of people differently.

4. Pluralism exists to the extent that distinct racial and ethnic categories have equal social standing. Assimilation is a process by which minorities gradually adopt the patterns of the dominant culture. Segregation is the physical and social separation of categories of people. The segregation of minorities is typically involuntary. Genocide refers to the extermination of one category of people by another.

5. Native Americans—the original inhabitants of the Americas—have endured genocide, segregation, and forced assimilation. Today their social standing is well below the national average.

6. WASPs predominated among the original European settlers of the United States, and they continue to enjoy high social standing today.

7. African Americans experienced two centuries of slavery. Emancipation in 1865 led to rigid segregation by law. Despite equality under the law, African Americans are still relatively disadvantaged today.

8. People of Chinese and Japanese ancestry have suffered as a result of both racial and ethnic differences. Today, however, both categories have above-average income and schooling.

9. Hispanics represent many ethnicities sharing a Spanish heritage. Mexican Americans are the largest Hispanic minority, heavily concentrated in the Southwest. Puerto Ricans, most of whom live in New York, are poorer. Cubans, concentrated in Miami, constitute the most affluent category of Hispanics.

10. White ethnic Americans include non-WASPs of European ancestry. While making gains during the last century, many white ethnics are still struggling for economic security.

11. Immigration has increased in recent years. No longer primarily from Europe, immigrants now come mostly from Latin America and Asia.

KEY CONCEPTS

assimilation the process by which minorities gradually adopt patterns of the dominant culture

discrimination treating various categories of people unequally

ethnicity a shared cultural heritage

genocide the systematic killing of one category of people by another

institutional discrimination patterns of discrimination that are a normative and routine part of the operation of a society

minority a category of people, distinguished by physical or cultural traits, who are socially disadvantaged

miscegenation the biological process of interbreeding among racial categories

pluralism a state in which people of all races and ethnicities are distinct but have social parity

prejudice a rigid and irrational generalization about a category of people

race a category composed of men and women who share biologically transmitted traits that are defined as socially significant

racism the belief that one racial category is innately superior or inferior to another

scapegoat a person or category of people, typically with little power, unfairly blamed for the troubles of others

segregation the physical and social separation of categories of people

stereotype a prejudiced description of some category of people

10

Sex and Gender

CHAPTER OUTLINE

Unity Dow smiled at her friends and supporters as the court decision was announced; there were hugs and handshakes all around. Dow, a thirty-two-year-old lawyer and citizen of the African nation of Botswana, had won the first round in her efforts to overturn the laws by which, she maintains, her country defines women as second-class citizens.

The law that sparked Unity Dow's suit against her government regulates how citizenship is extended to children. Traditionally in Botswana, family membership is traced through men—that is, children are part of their father's family line, but not their mother's. This *patrilineal* system is the model of the nation's citizenship law as well, and has special significance for anyone who marries a citizen of another country as Unity Dow did. Under the law, a child of a Botswanan man and a woman of another country would be a citizen of Botswana, since legal standing passes through the father. But the child of a Botswanan woman and a foreign man is denied citizenship. Because she is married to a man from the United States, Unity Dow's children had no citizen's rights in the country where they were born.

The significance of the Dow case goes far beyond citizenship, challenging all laws that treat men and women unequally. In rendering the decision in Dow's favor, High Court Judge Martin Horwitz declared, "The time that women were treated as chattels or were there to obey the whims and wishes of males is long past." In support of his decision, Horwitz pointed to the constitution of Botswana, which guarantees fundamental rights and freedoms to women as well as men. Arguing the government's case against Dow, Ian Kirby, a deputy attorney general, claimed that the Botswanan constitution does allow a legal distinction between women and men. He readily conceded that the citizenship laws—and a host of other statutes—favor men, but, he added, this pattern is consistent with Botswanan culture, which has long given men power over women. To challenge such traditions in the name of Western feminism, he continues, is nothing more than cultural imperialism by which some people seek to subvert their country's way of life by advancing ideas popular elsewhere.

Women from numerous African nations attended the Dow court case, many traveling great distances to observe what they considered to be historic change. The case is complex, and will be debated for years to come. Few doubt that it is the first of many similar lawsuits to come—in various African societies—that will have the goal of social equality between the sexes (Dow, 1990; Shapiro, 1991).

To many people in the United States, the Dow case may seem strange, since the notion that men and women are entitled to equal rights and privileges is widely endorsed here. But, as this chapter will explain, in our own society, the two sexes are far from equal in many respects. In fact, it is the United States, and not Botswana, that has no constitutional guarantee of equal standing under the law for women and men.

SEX AND GENDER

Many people think that differences in the social standing of men and women reflect innate differences between the sexes. As this chapter will explain, however, the different social experiences of women and men are more a creation of society than biology. To begin, we shall explore the key concepts of sex and gender.

Sex: A Biological Distinction

Sex refers to *the division of humanity into biological categories of female and male.* Sex is determined at the moment a child is conceived through sexual intercourse. The female ovum and the male sperm, which join to form a fertilized embryo, each contain twenty-three pairs of chromosomes—biological codes that guide physical development. One of these pairs determines the child's sex. The mother always contributes an X chromosome; if the father contributes an X chromosome, a female embryo (XX) develops, whereas a Y results in a male embryo (XY).

Within six weeks of conception, sex differentiation in the embryo begins. If the embryo is male, testicular tissue produces testosterone, a hormone that stimulates the development of the male genitals. Without testosterone, the embryo develops female genitals. At birth, males and females are distinguished by **primary sex characteristics**, *the genitals*, used to reproduce the human species. When they reach puberty, in the early teens, people become capable of reproduction. At this point, humans experience further biological differentiation, developing **secondary sex characteristics**, *physical traits, other than the genitals, that distinguish physiologically mature females and males*. To accommodate pregnancy, giving birth, and nurturing infants, adolescent females develop wider hips, breasts, and soft fatty tissue, thereby providing a reserve supply of nutrition for pregnancy and breast

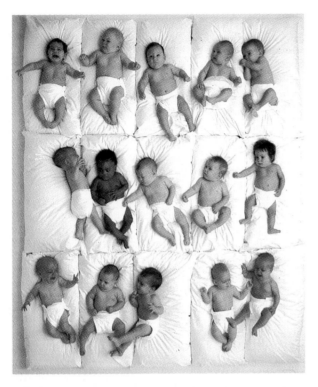

Sex is a biological distinction that develops prior to birth. Gender is the meaning that a society attaches to being female or male. That is, the range of human feelings, thoughts, and behavior is divided into what is defined as feminine or masculine. Moreover, gender differences are also a matter of power, as what is masculine typically has social priority over what is feminine. Gender differences are not evident among infants, of course, but the ways in which we think of boys and girls set in motion patterns that will continue for a lifetime.

feeding (Brownmiller, 1984). Usually slightly taller and heavier than females from birth, adolescent males typically develop more muscles in the upper body, more extensive body hair, and voices deeper in tone. These are only general differences, however. Many males are smaller and lighter than many females; some males have less body hair than some females; and some males speak in a higher tone than some females.

In rare cases, a hormone imbalance before birth produces a **hermaphrodite** (a word derived from Hermaphroditus, the offspring of the mythological Greek gods Hermes and Aphrodite, who embodied both sexes), *a human being with some combination of female and male internal and external genitalia.* Members of our culture often regard hermaphrodites with confusion and

even disgust. In contrast, the Pokot of eastern Africa are indifferent to what they define as a simple biological error, and the Navajo look on hermaphrodites with awe, viewing them as the embodiment of the full potential of both the female and the male (Geertz, 1975).

Finally, some people choose to change their sex. Hermaphrodites may have genital surgery to gain the appearance (and occasionally the function) of a sexually normal man or woman. Surgery may also be considered by **transsexuals,** *people who feel they are one sex though biologically they are the other.* Tens of thousands of transsexuals in the United States have surgically altered their genitals to escape the sense of being "trapped in the wrong body" (Restak, 1979, cited in Offir, 1982:146).

Sexual Orientation

Sexual orientation is *the manner in which people experience sexual arousal and achieve sexual pleasure.* For most living things, sexuality is biologically programmed. In humans, however, sexual orientation is bound up in the complex web of culture. The norm in all industrial societies is *heterosexuality* (*hetero* is a Greek word meaning "the other of two"), by which a person is attracted to the opposite sex. However, *homosexuality* (*homo* is the Greek word for "the same"), by which a person is sexually attracted to others of the same sex, is not uncommon.

More broadly, all cultures endorse heterosexuality, although many tolerate—and some even encourage—homosexuality. Among the ancient Greeks, for instance, elite male intellectuals celebrated homosexuality as the highest form of relationship, while devaluing relations with women, whom they considered to be incapable of philosophical discussion. Heterosexuality was thus seen as little more than a reproductive necessity and men who did not engage in homosexuality were defined as deviant. But because homosexual relations do not permit reproduction, no record exists of a society that favored homosexuality over heterosexuality (Kluckhohn, 1948; Ford & Beach, 1951; Greenberg, 1988).

Tolerance of *gay* people (a label homosexuals adopted in the 1960s) has increased during this century. In 1974 the American Psychiatric Association removed homosexuality from its listing of mental disorders. Gays were subject to increasing prejudice and discrimination during the 1980s, however, when the deadly disease AIDS became publicly identified with homosexual men. Today, 70 percent of adults in the United States continue to view homosexuality as morally wrong, but the same proportion think our society should allow gays and straights equal opportunities in the workplace (Salholz, 1990; N.O.R.C., 1991:257). For their part, many organizations of gay people are struggling to overcome the stereotypes of gay men and gay women (commonly called *lesbians*). Supporters of gay rights now use the term *homophobia* (with Greek roots meaning "fear of sameness") to designate an irrational fear of gay people (Weinberg, 1973). This label implies that people intolerant of gays, rather than those who engage in homosexuality, are misguided.

The pioneering research by Alfred Kinsey (1948, 1953) suggested that about 4 percent of men and roughly 2 percent of women have an exclusively same-sex orientation. Some researchers estimate that 10 percent of people in the United States—15 to 20 million adults—have a homosexual orientation strong enough to designate themselves as "gay" (Kirk & Madsen, 1989). At least twice this number have had at least one erotic experience with someone of the same sex. Sexual orientations, then, are not mutually exclusive; some people have a *bisexual* (combining homosexual and heterosexual) orientation.

How does a person develop a particular sexual orientation? There is growing evidence that sexual orientation is rooted in biological factors present at birth and is further reinforced by the hormone balance in the body as we grow (Gladue, Green, & Hellman, 1984; Weinrich, 1987; Isay, 1989). Still other research points to the importance of the social environment in encouraging sexual attitudes and behaviors (Troiden, 1988). According to these researchers, humans are born with the capacity and desire to be sexual, but *how* we express our sexuality is learned as our personality develops in society. Most likely, both nature and nurture play a part. To complicate matters further, sexual orientation is not established in precisely the same way for everyone. One influential study concluded that a complete explanation for sexual orientation simply does not exist at present (Bell, Weinberg, & Kiefer-Hammersmith, 1981).

Gender: A Cultural Distinction

Gender refers to *human traits linked by culture to each sex.* Gender guides how females and males think about themselves, how they interact with others, and what positions they occupy in society as a whole.

Gender deals not only with difference but also with *power.* Gender affects who makes decisions in families as well as in the Senate, it shapes patterns of income, and it influences who gains opportunities in the workplace. Like class, race, and ethnicity, therefore, gender is a major dimension of social inequality.

People may assume that gender simply reflects biological differences between females and males. But there is no "superior sex." Beyond the primary and secondary sex characteristics already noted, men have more muscle in the arms and shoulders, and the average man can lift more weight than the average woman can. Furthermore, the typical man has greater strength over short periods of time. Yet, women do better than men in some tests of long-term endurance because they can draw on the energy derived from greater body fat. Women also outperform men in life itself. The Census Bureau reports that the average life expectancy for males born in 1990 is 72.1 years, while females can expect to live 79.0 years.

Researchers have found that adolescent males exhibit greater mathematical ability, while adolescent females outperform males in verbal skills. But there is no difference in overall intelligence between females and males (Maccoby & Jacklin, 1974; Baker et al., 1980; Lengermann & Wallace, 1985).

Biologically, then, females and males have limited differences, with neither sex naturally superior. Nevertheless, the deep-rooted *cultural* notion of male superiority may seem so natural that we assume it proceeds inevitably from sex itself. But society, much more than biology, is at work here, as the global variability of gender attests.

Cultural variability in gender. Researchers investigating the roots of gender were drawn to collective settlements in Israel called *kibbutzim.* There, people have deliberately organized themselves to give females and males comparable social standing.

In the kibbutz (the singular form), both sexes perform a range of work including child care, building repair, cooking, and cleaning. Boys and girls are raised in the same way and, from the first weeks of life, live in dormitories under the care of specially trained personnel. To members of kibbutzim, then, sex is defined as irrelevant to much of everyday life.

Some observers suggest that the two sexes in the kibbutzim have been returning to more traditional social roles. Sociobiologists (see Chapter 2, "Culture") wonder if subtle but persistent biological dispositions may undermine efforts at gender equality (Tiger & Shepher, 1975). Even if this were so, the kibbutzim clearly show that cultures have wide latitude in defining what is feminine and masculine. They also exemplify how, through conscious efforts, a society can promote sexual equality.

Comparative research on gender was also carried out earlier in this century by anthropologist Margaret Mead. To the extent that gender reflects the biological facts of sex, she reasoned, the human traits defined as feminine and masculine should be the same everywhere; if gender is cultural, these conceptions should vary.

Mead's best-known research of this kind involved three societies in New Guinea (1963; orig. 1935). In the mountainous home of the Arapesh, Mead observed men and women with remarkably similar attitudes and behavior. Both sexes, she reported, were cooperative and sensitive to others—in short, what our culture would term "feminine." Among the Mundugumor, who lived to the south, Mead also found females and males to be alike; however, the Mundugumor culture of head hunting and cannibalism stood in striking contrast to the gentle ways of the Arapesh. Both sexes were typically selfish and aggressive, traits we define as more "masculine." Finally, traveling west to observe the Tchambuli, Mead discovered a culture that, like our own, defined females and males differently. Yet the Tchambuli *reversed* many of our notions of gender, raising females to be dominant and rational, while males were taught to be submissive, emotional, and nurturing toward children.

From this comparison, Mead concluded, first, that culture determines the extent to which the sexes differ and, second, what one culture defines as maculine may be considered feminine by another. Mead's research thus supports the conclusion that gender is a variable creation of society.

A broader study of more than two hundred preindustrial societies by George Murdock (1937) revealed some global agreement about which tasks are feminine or masculine. Hunting and warfare, Murdock found, generally fall to men, while home-centered tasks such as cooking and child care tend to be defined as women's work. With their simple technology, preindustrial societies must take advantage of men's typically greater size and short-term strength; because women bear children, their activities focus more on domestic duties.

But beyond these general patterns, Murdock also found variation. Some preindustrial societies consider agriculture—their main source of production—to be men's work; just as many encourage women to farm, and most divide this responsibility among both men and women. Which sex engaged in other tasks—from building shelters to applying tattoos—Murdock found varied from culture to culture.

In every society, people assume some tasks are "naturally" feminine while others are just as obviously masculine. But, in global perspective, we see remarkable variety in such social definitions. These men of Africa's Ivory Coast are engaged in what they think of as the masculine routine of "washing day."

Evidence suggests that societies have defined only a few specific activities as masculine or feminine. And as societies industrialize, and depend less on muscle power, gender distinctions become less pronounced (Lenski, Lenski, & Nolan, 1991). In sum, gender simply varies too much across cultures to be considered a simple expression of the biological categories of sex.

Patriarchy and Sexism

Although conceptions of gender vary, one pattern characterizes all societies to some degree: **patriarchy** (literally, "the rule of fathers"), *a form of social organization in which males dominate females.* Despite mythical tales of societies dominated by female "Amazons," the pattern of **matriarchy,** *a form of social organization in which females dominate males*, is not at present part of the human record (Gough, 1971; Harris, 1977; Kipp, 1980; Lengermann & Wallace, 1985). While some degree of patriarchy may be universal, however, world societies reveal significant variation in the relative power and privilege of females and males.

An important ideological underpinning of patriarchy is **sexism,** *the belief that one sex is innately superior to the other*. Patriarchy historically has been supported by a belief in the innate superiority of men who, therefore, legitimately dominate women. As Table 10–1 shows, sexism has much in common with racism, a key concept in Chapter 9 ("Race and Ethnicity"). Just

as racism constitutes an ideology that justifies whites dominating people of color, so sexism supports the domination of (allegedly inferior) women by (allegedly superior) men.

Sexism burdens all of society by stunting the talents and abilities of women—half the population. Men, too, suffer from sexism because, as Marilyn French (1985) argues, patriarchy compels men to relentlessly seek control—not only of women, but of themselves and the entire world. Such impossible goals extract a high price among males in terms of accidents, stress, and heart attacks. The so-called Type A personality—characterized by impatience, driving ambition, and competitiveness, and known to be linked to heart disease—is behavior that our culture defines as masculine (Ehrenreich, 1983).

Table 10–1 SEXISM: ECHOES OF RACIAL STEREOTYPES

	Women	African Americans
Link to highly visible personal traits	Secondary sex characteristics.	Skin color.
Assertion of innate inferiority	Women are mentally inferior. Women are irresponsible, unreliable, and emotional.	Blacks are mentally inferior. Blacks are irresponsible, unreliable, and pleasure-seeking.
Assertion that those who are disadvantaged are content with their "proper place" in society	"A woman's place is in the home." All women really enjoy being treated "like a woman."	"Blacks should remain in their place." Blacks are content living just as they do.
Assertion that victims are under the protection of their oppressors	"Men put women on a pedestal."	Whites "take care of" blacks.
Coping strategies on the part of victims	Behavior flattering to men; letting men think they are better even when they are not. Hiding one's real feelings. Attempting to outwit men.	Deferential behavior toward whites; letting whites think they are better even when they are not. Hiding one's real feelings. Attempting to outwit whites.
Barriers to opportunity	Women don't need an education. Confined to "women's work." Women should stay out of politics.	Blacks don't need an education. Confined to "black occupations." Blacks should stay out of politics.
Criticism of those who do not "stay in their place"	Assertive women are "pushy." Ambitious women are trying to be like men. Women as traditional targets of violence by men.	Assertive blacks are "uppity." Ambitious blacks are trying to be like whites. Blacks as traditional targets of violence by whites.

SOURCES: Adapted from Helen Mayer Hacker, "Women as a Minority Group," *Social Forces*, Vol. 30 (October 1951): 60–69; and "Women as a Minority Group: Twenty Years Later," in Florence Denmark, ed., *Who Discriminates Against Women?* (Beverly Hills, CA: Sage, 1974), pp. 124–34.

Furthermore, insofar as men try to control others, they lose the ability to experience intimacy and trust (French, 1985). As one researcher put it, although becoming masculine is supposed to separate "the men from the boys," in practice it separates men from men (Raphael, 1988:184).

Overall, when human feelings, thoughts, and actions are rigidly scripted according to a culture's conceptions of gender, people cannot develop and freely express the full range of their humanity. In Western culture, males are strongly pressured to be assertive, competitive, and in control, a weighty burden for many to bear. Females are constrained to be submissive, dependent, and self-effacing, regardless of their individual talents and personalities.

Is patriarchy inevitable? The answer is no because, generally speaking, technological advance has lessened gender inequality. In technologically simple societies, women have little control over pregnancy and childbirth, limiting the scope of their lives; similarly, men's greater height and short-term strength are vital resources. Technological advances—including birth control and reliance on industrial machinery—give members of industrial societies greater choice in defining the relation between the sexes. Today, in many societies, biological differences offer little justification for patriarchy.

Categorical social inequality—whether based on race, ethnicity, or sex—also comes under attack in the more egalitarian culture of industrial societies. In most industrial nations, laws mandate that women and men have equal opportunity in most occupations and that they receive equal pay for equal work. Nonetheless, as we shall see presently, the two sexes continue to hold different jobs; further, women still have primary responsibility for maintaining the household, while men wield the lion's share of economic and political power.

A good indicator of the extent of patriarchy is how much housework is done by women: the greater the relative social standing of men, the larger the proportion of housework women do. A glance back at Global Map 4–1 (page 80) confirms that industrial societies are somewhat less patriarchal than less-developed nations. Nowhere, however, is housework shared equally.

Some researchers claim that biological factors encourage different behaviors and motivations in the two sexes, making the complete eradication of patriarchy difficult, if not impossible (Goldberg, 1974, 1987). Many sociologists acknowledge that biological differences between the sexes have *some* effect on human behavior (Rossi, 1985). But the consensus is that gender is primar-

ily a social construction and, as such, is subject to change. Simply because patriarchy has been part of the human past, then, does not mean that it must inevitably shape our future.

To understand the persistence of patriarchy, we now examine how deeply gender is rooted in society, from the way children learn to think of themselves, to differences in income and power between men and women as adults.

GENDER AND SOCIALIZATION

From birth until death, human feelings, thoughts, and actions reflect social definitions of the sexes. As children interact with others, they quickly learn that their society defines females and males as different kinds of human beings; by about the age of three or four, they apply gender standards to themselves (Kohlberg, 1966; Bem, 1981). Table 10–2 lists traits that traditionally have defined females and males not only as different but in *opposing* terms. Polarizing humanity is still widespread in the United States, although research suggests that most young people resist defining themselves in consistently "feminine" or "masculine" terms (L. Bernard, 1980).

Just as gender affects how we think of ourselves, so it teaches us to *act* according to cultural conceptions of what is masculine and feminine. **Gender roles** (or

Table 10–2 TRADITIONAL NOTIONS OF GENDER IDENTITY

Feminine Traits	Masculine Traits
Submissive	Dominant
Dependent	Independent
Unintelligent and incapable	Intelligent and competent
Emotional	Rational
Receptive	Assertive
Intuitive	Analytical
Weak	Strong
Timid	Brave
Content	Ambitious
Passive	Active
Cooperative	Competitive
Sensitive	Insensitive
Sex object	Sexually aggressive
Attractive because of physical appearance	Attractive because of achievement

sex roles) are *attitudes and activities that a culture links to each sex.* Gender roles, then, express gender identity. In other words, insofar as our culture defines masculinity in terms of ambition and competition, we expect males to engage in team sports and seek out positions of leadership. To the extent that femininity involves deference and nurturing, we expect females to be good listeners and supportive of others.

Gender and the Family

The first question people usually ask about a newborn child is, "Is it a boy or a girl?" The question is important because the answer involves not just sex but the likely direction of the infant's entire life.

In fact, gender is at work even before the birth of a child, since parents generally hope to have a boy rather than a girl (Lengermann & Wallace, 1985). In China and other strongly patriarchal societies, female embryos are at risk because parents may abort them hoping to produce a boy, whose social value is greater.

Sociologist Jessie Bernard (1981) suggests that, soon after birth, family members introduce infants to the "pink world" of girls or the "blue world" of boys. In practice, both fathers and mothers encourage sons to be strong, aggressive achievers while raising daughters to be weaker and less assertive (Witkin-Lanoil, 1984). Parents may convey these expectations unconsciously in the way they handle their children. A researcher at an English university presented an infant dressed as either a boy or a girl to a number of women. Videotapes revealed that the women handled the "female" child tenderly, with frequent hugs and caresses, while treating the "male" child more aggressively, often lifting him up high in the air or bouncing him on the knee (Bonner, 1984). Other research shows that mothers have more overall physical contact with infant boys than with infant girls (Major, 1981). The message is clear: the female world revolves around passivity and emotion, while the male world places a premium on independence and action.

Gender and the Peer Group

As children reach school age, their lives spill outside the family and they forge ties with others their own age. Peer groups further distinguish the pink and blue worlds of girls and boys. The box explains how play groups shaped one young boy's sense of himself as masculine.

Janet Lever (1978), who spent a year observing fifth graders at play, concluded that female and male peer groups provide girls and boys with distinctive socialization. Boys, Lever reported, engage more in team sports—such as baseball and football—that involve many roles, complex rules, and clear objectives such as scoring a run or a touchdown. These games are nearly always competitive, producing winners and losers. Male peer activities reinforce masculine traits of aggression and control.

SOCIOLOGY OF EVERYDAY LIFE

Masculinity as Contest

By the time I was ten, the central fact in my life was the demand that I become a man. By then, the most important relationships by which I was taught to define myself were those I had with other boys. I already knew that I must see every encounter with another boy as a contest in which I must win or at least hold my own. . . . The same lesson continued (in school), after school, even in Sunday School. My parents, relatives, teachers, the books I read, movies I saw, all taught me that my self-worth depended on my manliness, my willingness to stand up to the other boys. This usually didn't mean a physical fight, though the willingness to stand up and "fight like a man" always remained a final test. But the relationships between us usually had the character of an armed truce. Girls weren't part of this social world at all yet, just because they weren't part of this contest. They didn't have to be bluffed, no credit was gained by cowing them, so they were more or less ignored. Sometimes when there were no grownups around we would let each other know that we liked each other, but most of the time we did as we were taught.

SOURCE: Silverstein (1977).

By contrast, girls play hopscotch or jump rope, or simply talk, sing, or dance together. Spontaneous activities with fewer formal rules, such games rarely have "victory" as their ultimate goal, and girls rarely oppose one another. Instead of teaching girls to be competitive, female peer groups promote interpersonal skills of communication and cooperation—presumably the basis for family life.

Carol Gilligan (1982) reports similar results in research concerning how children engage in moral reasoning. Boys reason according to rules and principles. For them, "rightness" means "playing by the rules." In the female world, morality is more a matter of maintaining close relationships with others. Such distinctive patterns of moral reasoning clearly are reinforced by the different peer-group activities of boys and girls.

Gender in School

Even before children enter school, what they read promotes distinctions of gender. A generation ago, one group of researchers found children's books typically made males the focus of attention (Weitzman et al., 1972). They found the ratio of males to females in illustrations was ten to one. Three times as many book titles mentioned males as females. Males engaged in diverse, interesting activities, while females usually stayed home and were concerned with pleasing males. More like dolls than living beings, the girls in these books were mostly attractive and compliant objects, sources of support and pleasure to males.

In the last decade, growing awareness that childhood learning shapes adult lives has led to changes. Today's books for children portray females and males in a more balanced way.

In addition to what children read, a school's curriculum encourages children to embrace appropriate gender patterns. In high school, topics of study reflect the different roles females and males expect to assume as adults. Instruction in typing and home-centered skills such as nutrition and sewing has long been provided to classes composed almost entirely of girls. Classes in woodworking and auto mechanics, conversely, are still mostly for boys.

In college, females and males follow this same pattern, tending toward different majors. Traditionally, the natural sciences—including physics, chemistry, biology, and mathematics—have been defined as part of the male province. Women have been expected to major

in the humanities (such as English), the fine arts (painting, music, dance, and drama), or the social sciences (including anthropology and sociology). New areas of study are also likely to be sex linked. Computer science, for example, with its grounding in engineering, logic, and abstract mathematics, has predominantly attracted male students (Klein, 1984); courses in gender studies, by contrast, tend to enroll females.

Gender and the Mass Media

Since it first captured the public imagination in the 1950s, television has placed the dominant segment of our population—white men—at center stage. Racial and ethnic minorities were all but absent from television

Some recent advertising reverses traditional gender definitions by portraying men as the submissive sex objects of successful women. Although the reversal is new, the use of gender stereotypes to sell consumer products is very old indeed.

until the early 1970s, and only in the last decade have programs featured people of color and women in prominent roles.

The brilliant detectives, fearless explorers, and skilled surgeons still are most frequently men. Women, by contrast, continue to be portrayed as relying on men. Researchers have also documented the fact that women are more often the targets of comedy (Busby, 1975). Finally, the mass media have long depicted women as objects that men value primarily for their sexual attractiveness.

Change has come most slowly to advertising, which sells products by conforming to widely established cultural patterns. Advertising thus presents the two sexes, more often than not, in stereotypical ways. Historically, ads have presented women in the home, happily using cleaning products, serving foods, modeling clothing, or trying out appliances. Men, on the other hand, predominate in ads for cars, travel, banking services, industrial companies, and alcoholic beverages. The authoritative "voiceover" in television and radio advertising is almost always male (Busby, 1975; Courtney & Whipple, 1983).

GENDER AND SOCIAL STRATIFICATION

Beyond socialization, gender is closely linked to privilege and power. **Gender stratification** refers to *the unequal distribution of wealth, power, and privilege between the two sexes.* The lower social standing of women can be seen, first, in the world of work.

Working Women and Men

In 1991, 66.4 percent of people in the United States over the age of fifteen were working for income: 76.2 percent of men and 57.4 percent of women (U.S. Bureau of Labor Statistics, 1991). In 1900, only about one-fifth of women were in the labor force; as shown in Figure 10–1, that proportion rose rapidly in recent decades. Furthermore, three-fourths of the women in the labor force in 1991 worked full time. The traditional view that earning an income is a "man's role" thus no longer holds true.

Figure 10–1   Men and Women in the U.S. Labor Force
(*U.S. Bureau of Labor Statistics*)

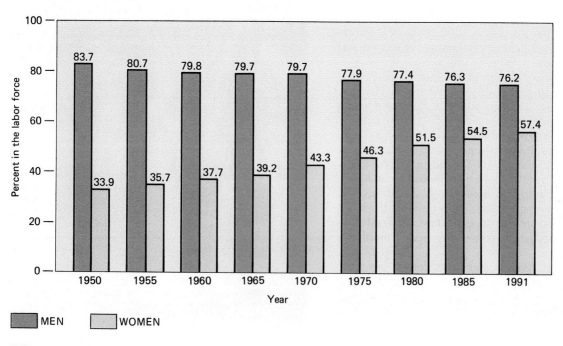

Among the factors at work in the changing U.S. labor force are the computer revolution, declining family size, and more flexible norms regarding appropriate roles for women. In addition, a slump in the standard of living for many families during the last fifteen years has prompted women to enter the labor force in order to boost family income. In 1991, about 60 percent of married couples had two incomes. In global perspective, the United States and other industrial societies consider women working for income to be the rule rather than the exception; as Global Map 10–1 on page 242 shows, however, this is not the case in many of the poorer societies of the world.

Even in the United States, many people still think that women in the labor force are single or, if married, without children. Of all married women 58 percent work outside the home, and the proportion stays the same for married women with children under six. Among married women with children between six and seventeen years of age, 73 percent were employed. For divorced women with children, the comparable figures were higher still: 70 percent of women with younger children and 85 percent of women with older children (U.S. Bureau of the Census, 1991). A gradual increase in employer-sponsored child-care programs is giving more women and men the opportunity to combine working and parenting, a trend that is especially important for divorced mothers.

Gender and occupations. While the proportions of women and men in the labor force are converging, the work done by the two sexes remains quite different. The U.S. Bureau of Labor Statistics (1991) reports that women enter a small range of occupations, with almost half falling into one of two general categories. First, clerical work occupies 28 percent of working women, including secretaries, typists, and stenographers. From another perspective, 80 percent of these "pink-collar" jobs are held by women. Second, service jobs employ 18 percent of women; these positions include waitressing and other food-service employment as well as nursing and related health-care work. Both types of employment provide low income and offer limited opportunities for advancement.

Table 10–3 shows the ten occupations with the highest concentrations of women in 1991. While more women are employed, then, they remain segregated in the labor force because our society links work to gender (Roos, 1983; Kemp & Coverman, 1989; U.S. Bureau of Labor Statistics, 1992).

Men predominate in most job categories beyond the ten occupations listed in the table. Jobs with the highest proportion of men are in the trades: 99.5 percent of brick masons, stone masons, structural metal workers, and heavy-equipment mechanics are male. Men also predominate in jobs that provide high income, prestige, and power. For example, more than 90 percent of engineers, 80 percent of physicians and lawyers, 65 percent of computer specialists, and 60 percent of corporate managers are men. Only a few women appear as the top executives of the largest U.S. corporations.

Interestingly, however, 30 percent of small businesses are now owned and operated by women and the share is rising rapidly. Ninety percent of these businesses are sole proprietorships with a single employee (Ando, 1990; O'Hare & Larson, 1991; U.S. Bureau of the Census, 1992). Even so, many of these talented entrepreneurs are showing that women can write their own success stories, sometimes creating greater opportunities than those offered by larger, male-dominated companies.

Overall, then, gender stratification shapes the workplace. This hierarchy is easy to spot in the job setting: male physicians are assisted by female nurses, male exec-

Table 10–3 JOBS WITH THE HIGHEST CONCENTRATIONS OF WOMEN, 1991

	Occupation	Number of Women Employed	Percent in Occupation Who Are Women
1.	Dental hygienist	83,832	99.8%
2.	Secretary	3,753,090	99.0%
3.	Prekindergarten and kindergarten teachers	439,215	98.7%
4.	Dental assistant	173,814	98.2%
5.	Receptionist	849,625	97.1%
6.	Child-care worker/ private household	328,780	96.7%
7.	Child-care worker	933,120	96.0%
8.	Housekeeper and servant/ private household	386,074	95.8%
9.	Typist	562,041	95.1%
10.	Licensed practical nurse	422,750	95.0%

SOURCE: U.S. Bureau of Labor Statistics, *Employment and Earnings*, Vol. 39, No. 1, January 1992, pp. 185–90.

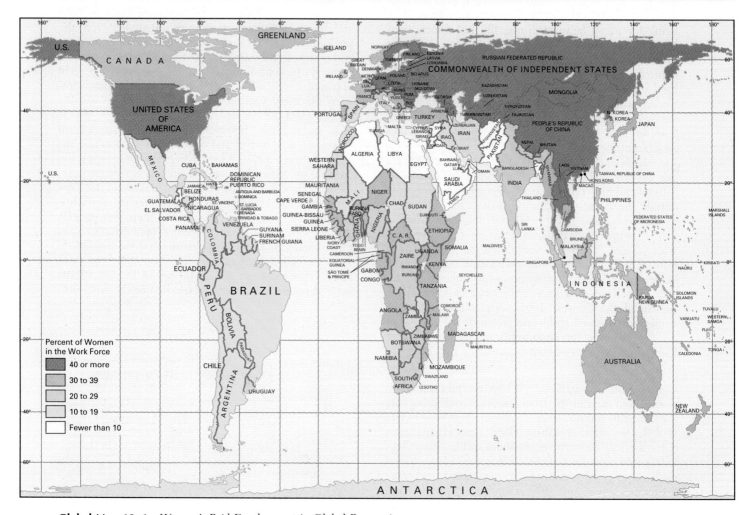

Global Map 10–1 Women's Paid Employment in Global Perspective

In 1991, women comprised 45.4 percent of the labor force of the United States—up almost 10 percent over the last generation. Throughout the industrialized world, at least one-third of the labor force are women. In poor societies, however, women work even harder than they do in this country, but they are less likely to have paid employment. In Latin America, for example, women represent only about 15 percent of the paid labor force; in Islamic societies of northern Africa and the Middle East, the figure is even lower.

utives have female secretaries, and male airline pilots work with female flight attendants. And, in any field, the greater a job's income and prestige, the more likely it is that the position will be held by a man. For example,

women make up 99 percent of kindergarten teachers; 86 percent in the elementary grades; 55 percent at the secondary-school level; and 41 percent of professors in colleges and universities (U.S. Bureau of Labor Statistics,

1992). At the top of the pyramid, about 12 percent of college and university presidents are women, who usually preside over smaller institutions, many enrolling only women (American Council on Education, 1984).

Housework: Women's "Second Shift"

As we have already noted, housework—maintaining the home and caring for children—is the province of women throughout the world. In the United States, housework has always embodied a cultural contradiction: touted as essential to family life on the one hand, carrying little reward or social prestige on the other (J. Bernard, 1981).

Surprisingly, women's rapid entry into the labor force has prompted little change in the pattern of responsibility for housework. One estimate indicates that the hours of housework performed by women have declined only slightly in recent decades and the proportion of housework shared by men has remained the same (Fuchs, 1986). Typically, couples share the disciplining of children and managing finances, but little else. Men routinely perform home repairs and mow the lawn; women see to the daily shopping, cooking, and cleaning. Thus women commonly return from the workplace to face a "second shift" of unpaid work on the home front

(Schooler et al., 1984; Benokraitis & Feagin, 1986; Hochschild, 1989).

A contradiction underlies this pattern: while most men support the idea of women entering the labor force, they resist modifying their own behavior in support of their partners (Komarovsky, 1973). Only in rare cases, such as the Israeli kibbutzim, is housework shared to any great extent. Even in Sweden, a society that stands out as progressive in this respect, only one in five couples shares housework equitably (Haas, 1981).

Gender, Income, and Wealth

Because women predominate in clerical and service jobs while men hold most business and professional positions, women earn less than men do. In 1991, the median earnings for women working full time were $21,245, while men working full time earned $30,331. This means that, for every dollar earned by men, women earned about 70 cents. Among full-time workers, 62 percent of women earned less than $25,000, whereas the same share of men earned more. At the other extreme, men were five times more likely than women (6.8 percent versus 1.4 percent) to earn more than $75,000 (U.S. Bureau of the Census, 1992).

This earning disparity stems primarily from the

African-American artist Jacob Lawrence (1917–   ) painted *Ironers* (1943) to depict the daily lives of women in his working-class neighborhood in New York's Harlem. The painting suggests that the work women perform in the labor force often parallels the tasks they perform in the home.

Jacob Lawrence, Ironers, 1943. Gouache on paper, 21½ x 29½ (54.6 x 74.9). Signed in the bottom right: J. Lawrence 43. Private Collection. Photo courtesy Terry Dintenfass Gallery, NYC.

different jobs held by men and women. In effect, jobs and gender interact so that jobs with less clout are considered "women's work" and, turning the argument around, jobs have less value to the extent that they are performed by women (Parcel, Mueller, & Cuvelier, 1986). During the 1980s, this disparity was challenged by people advocating a policy of "comparable pay for comparable worth," which means that people should be paid not according to the historical double standard but based on the worth of what they do. Such a policy, claim advocates, would go a long way toward closing the income gap between women and men.

A second cause of this gender-based income disparity has to do with the family. Both sexes have children, of course, but parenthood is more a barrier to the careers of women than it is to the advancement of men. Pregnancy, childbirth, and raising small children keep some younger women out of the labor force altogether at a time when men of the same age stand to make significant occupational gains. As a result, women workers have less job seniority than their male counterparts (Fuchs, 1986). Moreover, women who choose to have children may be reluctant or unable to maintain fast-paced jobs that require evening and weekend work. Career mothers therefore may seek less demanding jobs that offer a shorter commuting distance, flexible hours, and child-care services (Schwartz, 1989). The box examines a recent—and controversial—proposal to benefit corporate women.

The two factors noted so far—type of work and family responsibilities—account for roughly two-thirds of the earnings disparity between women and men. A third factor, then, accounting for much of the remainder of the income gap is discrimination against women (Pear, 1987). Because it is illegal, discrimination is often subtle; nonetheless, it places an economic burden on working women (Benokraitis & Feagin, 1986). Corporate women, for example, often encounter a "glass ceiling," a barrier not formally acknowledged by the company, but one that prevents women from rising above middle management.

For several reasons, then, women earn less than men even within a single occupational category. As shown in Table 10–4, the gender gap varies from job to job, but in only three of these job classifications do women earn more than 70 percent of what men take home.

Finally, perhaps because women typically outlive men, many people think that women own most of this country's wealth. Government statistics tell a different story: 57 percent of individuals with $1 million or more

Table 10–4 EARNINGS OF FULL-TIME U.S. WORKERS, BY SEX, 1991*

Selected Occupational Categories	Median Income (dollars)		Women's Income as a Percentage of Men's
	Men	Women	
Executives, administrators, and managers	$41,635	$26,928	65%
Professional specialties	$42,358	$30,487	72%
Technical workers	$32,029	$22,497	70%
Sales	$30,597	$17,254	56%
Precision production, craft, and repair workers	$27,508	$18,554	67%
Clerical and other administrative support workers	$27,037	$19,444	72%
Transportation workers	$25,194	$19,448	77%
Machine operators and tenders	$23,604	$14,965	63%
Service workers	$19,933	$12,148	61%
Farming, forestry, and fishing workers	$14,978	$10,205	68%
All occupations listed above	$29,421	$20,553	70%

* Workers aged 15 and over.

SOURCE: U.S. Bureau of the Census, *Current Population Reports*, Series P-60, No. 180, Washington, DC: U.S. Government Printing Office, 1992.

in assets are men, although widows are highly represented. The distribution (57 percent men, 43 percent women) is the same among people with more modest wealth ($250,000 to $1 million) (U.S. Bureau of the Census, 1991). Recently, *Forbes* magazine listed only fifty-two women (13 percent) among our country's four hundred richest individuals in 1992.

Gender and Education

In the past, higher education was deemed irrelevant for women, whose lives revolved around the home. In 1990, however, 54 percent of associate's and bachelor's degrees were earned by women, with the remaining 46 percent

Corporate Women: The "Mommy-Track" Controversy

The facts of corporate life are changing. Once the preserve of male executives and female support workers, more management positions are now being occupied by women. This is good news for corporations, because women are among the top college and business school graduates in the United States. The end of the post–World War II baby boom has reduced the supply of corporate workers, while the rapid growth in administrative positions in the new "information economy" has increased the demand for talented people. Overall, there are no longer enough men (and far fewer *good* men) to fill all the positions. Speaking purely in terms of the bottom line, U.S. corporations need women.

At the same time, the corporate world is decidedly unfriendly to women. Felice N. Schwartz—founder and president of Catalyst, an organization that seeks to develop the careers of women—explains that by trying to make women equal to men in the workplace, we have chosen to all but ignore *maternity*, the most crucial difference between the two sexes. Many young adults want to divide their time and energy between a career and young children. Currently, Schwartz claims, doing this is easy for men, but almost impossible for women. As evidence, she points out that, by age forty, 90 percent of male executives have children, but only 35 percent of female executives do. Men face no conflict between family and career as long as their wives take responsibility for child care.

Businesses have long been uneasy about women employees having children because, under current policies, motherhood takes women away from their jobs. Professional women usually consider having children in their early thirties, after corporations have invested almost a decade in training them. Paradoxically, when a corporate woman becomes a mother, her company typically pressures her to decide between the company and her family. But the choice is unfair because women usually want *both* career and family. Currently, many mothers end up leaving their careers; when that occurs, both corporations and women lose out.

The solution to the problem, Schwartz suggests, is for corporations to develop two tracks for women executives, a "career track" and a "career and family track." Women who wish to put their careers first (even if they have children) should be identified early and given as much opportunity and encouragement as the best and most ambitious men.

"Career and family women"—the majority of women, in Schwartz's view—value their careers, but are willing to forego some professional advancement to care for their children. These women are vital to a company, especially in the middle-management positions currently staffed by less successful men. Positions of moderate responsibility, with part-time, flex-time, or job-sharing options, allow women to combine career and child rearing. A "career and family" option also allows mothers to return to the "career track" at a later time. In any case, such a program allows corporations to recover their investment from past training and gain future benefits from loyal workers whose personal needs are being met.

Schwartz's proposal generated a heated controversy. Some critics fear that creating "mommy tracks" simply strengthens the stereotype that women are less attached to careers than men are. Such a plan, they continue, is unlikely to be applied to men and will end up hurting rather than helping corporate women.

Schwartz disagrees. Women, she claims, have demonstrated that they are the equal of men in any kind of work. About 40 percent of management positions are now held by women, who make further gains every year. Thus corporations must give women more choices about their jobs. If careers and children are no longer in conflict, corporations will enjoy more productive and satisfied employees.

SOURCE: Schwartz (1989).

earned by men (National Center for Education Statistics, 1991).

As noted earlier, men and women still tend toward different courses of study in college, although less so than in the past. In 1970, for example, only 17 percent of the bachelor's degrees in natural sciences, computer science, and engineering were awarded to women; by 1990 the proportion had almost doubled, nearing one-third.

Women now enjoy more opportunities for post-graduate education, often a springboard to high-prestige jobs. Today, counting all areas of study, women earn slightly more master's degrees (51.1 percent) than men. Furthermore, a growing number of women are pursuing programs that until recently were virtually all male. For example, in 1970 only a few hundred women received Master of Business Administration (M.B.A.) degrees; in 1990, the number exceeded 23,000 (34 percent of degrees) (Kaufman, 1982; National Center for Education Statistics, 1991).

However, men still outnumber women in many professional fields. In 1990, men received two-thirds of doctorates (although women earned 52 percent of all Ph.D.s in sociology). Men also earned 60 percent of law degrees (LL.B. and J.D.), 66 percent of medical degrees (M.D.), and 74 percent of dental degrees (D.D.S. and D.M.D.) (Center for Education Statistics, 1991). In a culture that still defines high-paying professions (and the drive and competitiveness needed to succeed in them) as masculine, some women are discouraged from undertaking professional education (Fiorentine, 1987). Nonetheless, the proportion of women in professional schools and the professions is rising steadily.

Gender and Politics

A century ago, virtually no women held elected office in the United States. Women were barred by law from voting in national elections in Canada until 1917, and in the United States until 1920. A few women were candidates for political office, however, even before they could vote. The Equal Rights Party supported Victoria Woodhull for the U.S. presidency in 1872; perhaps it was a sign of the times that she spent election day in a New York City jail. Table 10–5 cites milestones in women's gradual movement into political life.

Today, several thousand women serve as mayors of cities and towns across the United States, and tens of thousands more hold responsible administrative posts

---

Table 10–5 SIGNIFICANT "FIRSTS" FOR WOMEN IN U.S. POLITICS

1872	First woman to run for the presidency (Victoria Woodhull) represents the Equal Rights Party.
1917	First woman elected to the House of Representatives (Jeannette Rankin of Montana).
1924	First women elected state governors (Nellie Tyloe Ross of Wyoming and Miriam Ferguson of Texas); both followed their husbands into office.
	First woman to have her name placed in nomination for the vice presidency at the convention of a major political party (Lena Jones Spring).
1931	First woman to serve in the Senate (Hattie Caraway of Arkansas); completed the term of her husband upon his death and was reelected in 1932.
1932	First woman appointed to a presidential cabinet (Frances Perkins, Secretary of Labor).
1964	First woman to have her name placed in nomination for the presidency at the convention of a major political party (Margaret Chase Smith).
1972	First black woman to have her name placed in nomination for the presidency at the convention of a major political party (Shirley Chisholm).
1981	First woman appointed to the U.S. Supreme Court (Sandra Day O'Connor).
1984	First woman to be successfully nominated for the vice presidency (Geraldine Ferraro).
1988	First woman chief executive to be elected to consecutive third term (Madeleine Kunin, governor of Vermont).
1992	Political "Year of the Woman" yields record number of women in the Senate (six) and the House (forty-eight), as well as (1) first African-American woman to win election to U.S. Senate (Carole Mosely Braun of Illinois); (2) first state (California) to be served by two women Senators (Barbara Boxer and Dianne Feinstein); (3) first Puerto Rican woman elected to the House (Nydia Valasquez of New York).

SOURCE: Adapted from Sandra Salmans, "Women Ran for Office Before They Could Vote," *New York Times*, July 13, 1984, p. A 11, and news reports.

---

in the federal government (Mashek & Avery, 1983; Schreiner, 1984). Only recently has change become evident at the highest levels of politics, although a majority of citizens claim that they would support a woman for any office, including the presidency. After the 1992 elections, three of the fifty state governors were women (6 percent); in Congress, forty-eight of 435 members of the House of Representatives (11 percent) and six of 100 senators (6 percent) were women.

What became known as "The Year of the Woman" in U.S. politics did produce some significant change as fifty-four women took their place in Congress after the 1992 elections, up from thirty-one the year before.

Minority Women

If minorities (see Chapter 9, "Race and Ethnicity") are socially disadvantaged, are minority women doubly so? Generally speaking, yes. First, there is the disadvantage associated with race and ethnicity. For example, in 1991, median annual income for African-American women working full time was $19,134—89 percent as much as the $21,555 earned by white women. Hispanic women earned $16,548—77 percent as much. Second, there is the obstacle associated with sex. Thus, African-American women earned 85 percent as much as African-American men, while Hispanic women earned about 83 percent as much as Hispanic men. Combining these disadvantages, African-American women earned 62 percent as much as white men and Hispanic women earned 54 percent as much (U.S. Bureau of the Census, 1992).

The reduced income of minority women reflects their lower position on the occupational ladder in comparison to white women. Women of color are most likely to hold lower-paying jobs (Bonilla-Santiago, 1990). Further, whenever the economy sags, as it has in recent years, minority women are especially likely to experience declining income and unemployment.

Chapter 7 ("Social Stratification") explained that women are becoming a larger proportion of the American poor. Poverty is especially dramatic among minority women, partly because of a higher incidence of single parenthood. In 1990, 28.4 percent of households headed by white women (with no husband present) were poor, compared to 51.2 percent of comparable African-American households and 49.7 percent of Hispanic households.

Are Women a Minority?

Chapter 9 ("Race and Ethnicity") defined a minority as a category of people both socially disadvantaged and physically or culturally distinct. In a patriarchal society, women fit this definition, since they contend with a number of social barriers because of their sex.

Even so, most white women do *not* think of themselves as members of a minority (Hacker, 1951; Lengermann & Wallace, 1985). This is partly because, more than racial and ethnic minorities, white women belong to families at higher social levels. Yet, within every social class, women typically have less income, wealth, education, and power than men do. In fact, patriarchy makes women dependent for much of their social standing on men—first their fathers and later their husbands (Bernard, 1981).

Violence Against Women

Perhaps the most wrenching kind of suffering endured by women is violence. As Chapter 6 ("Deviance") explained, official statistics paint criminal violence as overwhelmingly the actions of men—hardly surprising, since aggressiveness is a trait our culture defines as masculine. Furthermore, much male violence is directed at women, an offshoot of devaluing what is culturally defined as feminine.

The most common location for gender-linked violence is the home. Richard Gelles (cited in Roesch, 1984) argues that, with the exception of the police and the military, the family is the most violent group in the United States. Although both sexes suffer from family violence, by and large women sustain more serious injuries than men (Straus & Gelles, 1986; Schwartz, 1987; Gelles & Cornell, 1990).

Violence toward women also occurs in casual relationships. As Chapter 6 ("Deviance") pointed out, most sexual violence does not involve strangers; most rapes,

Ireland is one of the few industrial societies in the world in which abortion is constitutionally banned. Irish law forbids physicians even from giving out information about how to obtain an abortion abroad. When fourteen-year-old Ann Lovett became pregnant—as the result of rape—the government initially denied her request to travel to England to terminate the pregnancy. International protest eventually drove officials to relent and Lovett did receive the abortion she sought.

for instance, are perpetrated by men known (and sometimes trusted) by women. Sexual violence, in short, is built into our way of life. Dianne F. Herman (1992) argues that the wolf whistles that intimidate women on the streets, the pinch in a crowded subway, and the physical assault that occurs in the home all express our "rape culture." Violence of all kinds, Herman maintains, is a male strategy to dominate women. Sexual violence, then, is fundamentally about *power* rather than sex, and that is why it is properly studied as a dimension of gender stratification.

Sexual harassment. The 1991 Senate confirmation hearings of Supreme Court Justice Clarence Thomas drew national attention to the concept of **sexual harassment,** widely defined as *comments, gestures, or physical contact of a sexual nature that are deliberate, repeated, and unwelcome.* Anita Hill, a law professor and former colleague, alleged that Thomas had harassed her during the time they worked together for the federal government. The Senate never clearly resolved the specific allegations made by Hill and vigorously denied by Thomas, but people across the United States lined up on one side or the other as the episode touched off a national debate that promises to significantly redefine workplace behavior.

Both men and women can be victims of sexual harassment. For two reasons, however, victims of harassment are typically women. First, our culture encourages men to be sexually assertive and to perceive women in sexual terms; social interaction in the workplace, on the campus, and elsewhere, then, can readily take on sexual overtones. Second, most individuals in positions of power—including business executives, physicians, bureau chiefs, assembly line supervisors, professors, and military officers—are men who typically oversee the work of women. Surveys carried out in widely different work settings reveal that half of women respondents report recently experiencing unwanted sexual attention (Loy & Stewart, 1984; Paul, 1991).

Sexual harassment is sometimes blatant and direct: a supervisor may solicit sexual favors from an employee coupled with threat of reprisals if the advances are refused. Courts have declared such *quid pro quo* sexual harassment (the Latin phrase means "one thing in return for another") to be illegal because it is a form of discrimination that violates civil rights and interferes with people's efforts to earn a living.

However, the problem is often a matter of subtle behavior—sexual teasing, off-color jokes, pin-ups displayed in the workplace—none of which any individual may intend to be harassing to a specific subordinate or co-worker. But, in effect, such actions may add up to creating a *hostile environment* (Cohen, 1991; Paul, 1991). Sexual harassment of this kind is far more complex because it is inherently ambiguous, with the behavior in question seen in a different light by each party. For example, a man may view his romantic interest in a co-worker as a compliment to her; she, on the other hand, may find his behavior offensive and a hindrance to her job performance.

Certainly many women have long chafed at subtle forms of harassment. Untangling precisely what behavior can and cannot be punished as the source of a hostile working environment, however, demands clearer standards of proper conduct than exist at present. Creating such guidelines—and educating the public to embrace them—is likely to take some time, since it involves defining new forms of deviance (Cohen, 1991; Majka, 1991). In the end, courts (and, ultimately, the court of public opinion) will have to draw the line between what is "reasonable friendliness" and behavior that is "unwarranted harassment."

Pornography. An additional source of sexual violence is *pornography.* Defining pornography has long challenged scholars and law makers alike. The Supreme Court empowers local cities and counties to decide for themselves what violates "community standards" of decency and lacks any redeeming social value. There is little doubt, however, that pornography (loosely defined) is popular in the United States: x-rated videos, 900 telephone numbers providing sexual conversation, and a host of sexually explicit magazines together constitute a 7-billion-dollar-a-year industry.

Traditionally, we have viewed pornography as a *moral* issue, involving how people express their sexuality. National survey data show that 60 percent of the U.S. population still think that "sexual materials lead to a breakdown of morals" (N.O.R.C., 1991:258).

A more recent view holds that pornography demeans women. That is, pornography constitutes a *political* issue because it fosters the notion that men should control both sexuality and women. Catharine MacKinnon (1987) has branded pornography as a fundamental underpinning of male dominance in the United States because it portrays women in dehumanizing and subservient fashion as the playthings of men. Worth noting, in this context, is that the term pornography is derived from the Greek word *porne,* meaning a harlot who acts as a man's sexual slave.

A related charge is that pornography promotes acts of violence against women. Anyone who has viewed "hard-core" videos can find this assertion plausible. Yet, demonstrating a scientific cause-and-effect relationship between what people look at and how they act is difficult. However, research does support the contention that pornography tends to make men think of women as objects rather than people (Mallamuth & Donnerstein, 1984; Attorney General's Commission on Pornography, 1986). The public at large shares this concern about the effects of pornography, with 55 percent of adults reporting the opinion that pornography encourages people to commit rape (N.O.R.C., 1991:258).

The pornography issue also raises concerns about safeguarding the rights of free speech and artistic expression. But the coalition of conservatives (who oppose pornography on moral grounds) and progressives (who condemn it for political reasons) is likely to maintain pressure to restrict this kind of material.

THEORETICAL ANALYSIS OF GENDER

Each of sociology's major theoretical paradigms addresses the significance of gender in social organization.

Structural-Functional Analysis

The structural-functional paradigm views society as a complex system of many separate but integrated parts. From this point of view, notions about gender are strategies for the operation of society.

As explained in Chapter 2 ("Culture"), the earliest hunting and gathering societies had little power over the forces of biology. Lacking effective birth control, women contended with frequent pregnancies and ongoing responsibilities of child care (Lengermann & Wallace, 1985). As a result, social norms encouraged women to center their lives around home and children. Likewise, to take advantage of men's greater short-term strength, norms guided them toward the pursuit of game and other tasks away from the home. Over many generations, this sex-based division of labor became institutionalized, built into the structure of society and taken for granted.

Industrial technology opens up a vastly greater range of cultural possibilities. Human muscle power no longer serves as a vital source of energy, so the physical strength of men loses much of its earlier significance. At the same time, the ability to control reproduction gives women greater choice in shaping their lives. Modern societies come to see that traditional ideas about gender waste an enormous amount of human talent; yet change comes slowly because gender-based behavior is deeply embedded in social mores.

In addition, as Talcott Parsons (1951, 1954) has explained, gender differences help to integrate society—at least in its traditional form. Gender, Parsons claimed, defines a *complementary* set of roles that links women and men into family units that, in turn, build the larger society. Women take charge of family life, managing the household and raising children; men connect the family to the larger world through their work in the labor force.

For generations, our society's evaluation of women in terms of physical appearance instead of job performance contributed to unequal occupational opportunities. By turning the tables, this educational poster helps people to see how grossly unfair this practice really is.

"Hire him. He's got great legs."

SEX DISCRIMINATION ISN'T FUNNY
SUPPORT THE NATIONAL ORGANIZATION FOR WOMEN
28 EAST 56 STREET N.Y.C. 10022

Parsons further argued that distinctive socialization teaches females and males their appropriate gender identity and skills needed for adult life. Destined for the labor force, boys are taught to be rational, self-assured, and competitive—a complex of traits Parsons described as *instrumental*. To prepare girls for child rearing, their socialization stresses *expressive* qualities, such as emotional responsiveness and sensitivity to others.

Finally, according to Parsons, society promotes gender-linked behavior through various means of social control. People incorporate cultural definitions about gender into their own identities, so that violations of gender norms produce guilt. Society further encourages gender conformity by conveying subtle and not-so-subtle messages that straying too far from accepted standards courts rejection by members of the opposite sex. In simple terms, women are likely to view nonmasculine men as sexually unattractive, while unfeminine women risk rejection by men.

Critical evaluation. Structural-functionalism advances a theory of complementarity by which gender integrates society both structurally (in terms of what people do) and morally (in terms of what they believe).

But this approach assumes a singular vision of society that is simply not shared by everyone. For example, many women have traditionally worked outside the home out of economic necessity. Also, critics charge, Parsons's analysis ignores personal strains and social costs produced by rigid gender roles (Giele, 1988). Finally, this analysis legitimizes the status quo. Increasingly, as traditional norms and values have weakened, what Parsons saw as gender "complementarity" simply amounts to male "domination."

Social-Conflict Analysis

From a social-conflict point of view, gender involves not just differences in behavior but disparities in power. Conventional gender patterns have historically benefited men while subjecting women to prejudice and discrimination in a striking parallel to the treatment of racial and ethnic minorities (Hacker, 1951, 1974; Collins, 1971; Lengermann & Wallace, 1985). Thus gender promotes not cohesion but tension and conflict, as men seek to protect their privileges while women challenge the status quo.

A social-conflict analysis of gender also places sexism at center stage. A web of notions about female inferiority that justify depriving women of opportunities and subjecting them to manipulation and violence, sexism supports lower pay for women in the workplace, the exclusion of women from positions of power in national affairs, and the subordination of women in the home.

As was noted in earlier chapters, the social-conflict paradigm draws heavily on the ideas of Karl Marx. Yet Marx was a product of his time insofar as his writings focused almost exclusively on men. His friend and collaborator Friedrich Engels, however, did explore the link between gender and social classes (1902; orig. 1884).

Engels suggested that while the activities of women and men in hunting and gathering societies were different, the two sexes had comparable importance. As technological advances led to a productive surplus, however, social equality and communal sharing gave way to private property and, ultimately, a class hierarchy. At this point, men gained pronounced power over women. With surplus wealth to pass on to heirs, men took a keen interest in their offspring. This control of property, then, prompted the creation of monogamous marriage and the family. Ideally, men could be certain of their offspring—especially their sons—and the law ensured that wealth was passed on to them. For their part, women built their lives around bearing and raising children.

Engels contended that capitalism intensified male domination. First, capitalism created more wealth, which conferred greater power on men as the owners of property, the heirs of property, and the primary wage earners. Second, an expanding capitalist economy depended on defining people—especially women—as consumers and encouraging them to seek personal fulfillment through buying and owning products. Third, to support men working in factories, women were assigned the task of maintaining the home. The double exploitation of capitalism, then, lies in paying low wages for male labor and *no* wages for female work (Eisenstein, 1979; Barry, 1983; Jagger, 1983; Vogel, 1983).

Critical evaluation. The social-conflict analysis of gender highlights how society places the two sexes in unequal positions of privilege, prestige, and power.

Social-conflict analysis, too, has its critics. One problem, they suggest, is that this approach casts conventional families—historically defined by traditionalists as morally good—as a social evil. Second, from a more practical point of view, social-conflict analysis minimizes the extent to which women and men live together cooperatively, and often quite happily, in families. A third problem with this approach, at least for some critics, is the idea that capitalism stands at the root of gender stratification. Societies with socialist economic systems—including the People's Republic of China and the former Soviet Union—have also been strongly patriarchal.

FEMINISM

Feminism is *the advocacy of social equality for the sexes, in opposition to patriarchy and sexism.* The "first wave" of the feminist movement in the United States began in the 1840s as women opposed to slavery, including Elizabeth Cady Stanton and Lucretia Mott, drew parallels between the oppression of African Americans and the oppression of women (Randall, 1982). The primary objective of the early women's movement was securing the right to vote, which was achieved in 1920. But other disadvantages persisted and a "second wave" of feminism arose in the 1960s and continues today.

Basic Feminist Ideas

Feminism sees the personal experiences of women and men through the lens of gender. How we think of ourselves (gender identity), how we act (gender roles), and our sex's social standing (gender stratification) are all rooted in the operation of our society.

Although people who consider themselves feminists disagree about many things, most support the following five ideas:

1. **The importance of change.** Feminism, which is critical of the status quo, advocates equitable social standing for women and men. Feminist thinking about gender can be personally and socially transforming, and promises to enhance the dignity of both sexes in a society that values all people.

2. **Expanding human choice.** Feminists argue that cultural conceptions of gender divide the full range of human qualities into two opposing and limited spheres: the female world of emotions and cooperation and the male world of rationality and competition. As an alternative, feminists pursue a "reintegration of humanity" by which each human being can develop *all* human traits (French, 1985).

3. **Eliminating gender stratification.** Feminism opposes laws and cultural norms that limit the education, income, and job opportunities of women. For this reason, feminists have long advocated an Equal Rights Amendment (ERA) to the U.S. Constitution, which states simply:

Equality of rights under the law shall not be denied or abridged by the United States or any State on account of sex.

The ERA, first proposed in Congress in 1923, has the support of two-thirds of U.S. adults (N.O.R.C., 1991:279). Even so, it has yet to become law, which probably reflects the opposition of the men who dominate state legislatures around the country.

4. **Ending sexual violence.** A major objective of today's women's movement is eliminating sexual violence. Feminists argue that patriarchy distorts the relationships between women and men, encouraging violence against women, including rape, domestic abuse, sexual harassment, and pornography (Millet, 1970; J. Bernard, 1973; Dworkin, 1987). Thus feminism actively seeks to transform the power structure of society as a way to end violence against women.

5. **Sexual autonomy.** Finally, feminism promotes women's control over their sexuality and reproduction. Feminists advocate the free availability of birth control information, which, in some states, was illegal as recently as the 1960s. In addition, most feminists support a woman's right to choose whether to bear children or to terminate a pregnancy rather than allowing men—as husbands, physicians, and legislators—to control sexuality. Many feminists also support gay people's efforts to overcome prejudice and discrimination in a predominantly heterosexual culture. Lesbians, especially, suffer such social disadvantages because they violate both the cultural norm of heterosexuality and the norm that men should control the sexuality of women (Deckard, 1979; Barry, 1983; Jagger, 1983).

Variations Within Feminism

People pursue the goal of sexual equality in various ways, yielding three general types of feminism (Barry, 1983; Jagger, 1983; Stacey, 1983; Vogel, 1983).

Liberal feminism is rooted in classic liberal thinking that individuals should be free to develop their talents and pursue their interests. Liberal feminism accepts the basic organization of our society, while pointing out that women have yet to enjoy all the rights and opportunities that men have. Liberal feminism endorses the Equal Rights Amendment and stresses the need to eliminate the prejudice and discrimination that block the aspirations of women.

Liberal feminists also support reproductive freedom for all women. They respect the family as a social institution, but call for widely available maternity leave and child care for women who wish to work. Liberal feminists note that more than one hundred nations guarantee maternity leaves for all working women, but the United States has no such policy (Hewlett, 1986).

Socialist feminism evolved from the ideas of Karl Marx and Friedrich Engels, but partly developed in response to Marx's inattention to gender. From this point of view, capitalism intensifies patriarchy by concentrating wealth and power in the hands of a small number of men. Socialist feminists view the reforms sought by liberal feminism as insufficient. The bourgeois family fostered by capitalism must change, they argue, in favor of some collective means of carrying out housework and child care. The key to this goal, in turn, is a socialist revolution. (Further discussion of socialism is found in Chapter 11, "Economics and Politics.")

Radical feminism, too, finds the reforms of liberal feminism inadequate. Moreover, radical feminists claim that even a socialist revolution would not end patriarchy. Instead, this variant of feminism holds that gender equality can be realized only through the elimination of the cultural notion of gender itself. One possible way to achieve this goal is to utilize new reproductive technology (see Chapter 12, "Family and Religion") to separate women's bodies from the process of child bearing; in this way, people could reproduce without relying on the conventional family system. Furthermore, while the sexes will continue to differ biologically, radical feminists envision a culture that does not divide human capacities into feminine and masculine worlds—in short, a gender-free society.

Opposition to Feminism

Feminism—or, more correctly, a wide range of feminisms—has already brought dramatic change to the United States, providing opportunities for women to participate in our economic and political systems that simply did not exist a century ago. Not surprisingly, then, this social movement has also provoked spirited opposition.

Some people criticize feminism for the same reasons that many whites have historically opposed social equality for nonwhites: they do not want to lose privileges linked to their social position. Others criticize feminism for challenging the conventional family and rejecting what traditionalists see as time-honored male-female relationships that have guided social life for centuries.

Further, some men consider feminism a threat to an important basis of their status and self-respect: their masculinity. Men who have been socialized to value strength and dominance understandably feel uneasy about feminist contentions that they can also be gentle and warm (Doyle, 1983). Similarly, women who have centered their lives around their husbands and children may fear that feminism would deprive them of cherished social roles that have conferred meaning and identity (Marshall, 1985).

Finally, there is the question of *how* women's social standing should be improved. A large majority of people in the United States agree that women should have equal rights, but one survey found that 70 percent thought that women should advance individually, according to their abilities, while only 10 percent thought women should rely on the efforts of women's rights groups (N.O.R.C., 1991:387). Thus while support for feminism (its liberal version) is widespread, many people apparently object to the feminist label.

Gender: Looking Ahead

Predictions about the future are, at best, informed speculation. Just as economists disagree about the likely inflation rate a year from now, sociologists differ in their views of the future state of our society. Yet we can venture some general observations about gender, today and in the future.

To begin, change has been remarkable. The position of women a century ago was one of clear and striking subordination. Husbands controlled property in marriage, women were barred from most areas of the labor force, and no woman could vote. Although women remain socially disadvantaged, the movement toward greater equality has been dramatic.

Many factors have contributed to this change. Perhaps most important, industrialization has both broadened the range of human activity and shifted the nature of work—from physically demanding tasks that favored male strength to jobs that require human thought and imagination, placing the talents of women and men on an even footing. Additionally, medical technology has given us control over reproduction, so women's lives are less circumscribed by unwanted pregnancies.

Has there been a feminist backlash in the United States? Many feminists think so, and point to various kinds of evidence to support their contention. Television programming like *Civil Wars* may portray a successful woman lawyer, but actress Mariel Hemingway also resorts to traditional gender roles when she acts sexually and seductively (which, no doubt, keeps ratings high).

Many women and men have also made deliberate efforts to lessen the power of patriarchy. Feminism objects to assigning activities and channeling self-expression simply on the basis of sex. As these efforts continue, and as more women enter positions of power on the national level, the social changes in the twenty-first century may be even greater than those we have already witnessed.

In the midst of change, strong opposition to feminism persists. Many feminists are fearful of legal changes that will undercut women's reproductive options, setting back a generation of hard-won gains. On a broader front, gender still forms an important foundation of personal identity and family life, and it is deeply woven into the moral fabric of our society. Therefore, attempts to change cultural ideas about the two sexes will continue to provoke opposition.

On balance, while dramatic and radical change in the way we understand gender is unlikely in the short run, the movement toward a society in which women and men enjoy equal rights and opportunities seems certain to gain strength.

SUMMARY

1. Sex is a biological concept; a fetus is female or male from the moment of conception. People with the rare condition of hermaphroditism combine the biological traits of both sexes. Transsexuals are people who deliberately choose to surgically alter their sex.

2. Heterosexuality is the dominant sexual orientation in virtually every society in the world. Homosexuals make up a small but significant proportion of the U.S. population. Sexual orientation is not always clear cut, however; many people are bisexual.

3. Gender involves how cultures assign human traits and power to each sex. Gender varies historically and across cultures.

4. Some degree of patriarchy exists in every society. The ideology of sexism justifies male dominance, just as racism supports racial dominance.

5. The socialization process links gender to personal identity (gender identity) and distinctive activities (gender roles). The major agents of socialization— the family, peer groups, schools, and the mass media—reinforce cultural definitions of what is feminine and masculine.

6. Gender stratification entails numerous social disadvantages for women. Although most women are now in the paid labor force, a majority of working women hold clerical or service jobs. Unpaid housework remains predominantly a task performed by women.

7. On average, women earn about 70 percent as much as men do. This disparity stems from differences in jobs, family responsibilities, and discrimination.

8. Historically excluded from higher education, women now form a slight majority of all college students and receive half of all master's degrees. Men still earn a majority of doctorates and professional degrees.

9. The number of women in politics has increased sharply in recent decades. Still, the vast majority of national elected officials are men.

10. Minority women experience greater social disadvantages than white women. Overall, women of color earn only half as much as white men, and almost half the households headed by women of color are poor.

11. Because of their distinct identity and social disadvantages, women represent a social minority.

12. Violence against women is a widely recognized problem in the United States. Our society is also grappling with the issues of sexual harassment and pornography.

13. Structural-functional analysis suggests that distinct roles for females and males constitute a survival strategy in preindustrial societies. In industrial societies, pronounced gender inequality becomes dysfunctional, yet long-established gender norms change slowly. According to Talcott Parsons, complementary gender roles promote the social integration of the family.

14. Social-conflict analysis views gender as a dimension of social inequality and conflict. Friedrich Engels linked gender stratification to the development of private property. Engels claimed that capitalism increased male dominance by devaluing women and housework.

15. Feminism supports the social equality of the sexes and actively opposes patriarchy and sexism. Feminism advocates greater choice for women and men, eliminating gender stratification, ending sexual violence against women, and promoting women's control over their sexuality.

16. There are three variants of feminist thinking. Liberal feminism seeks equal opportunity for the two sexes within current social institutions; socialist feminism advocates abolishing private property as a means of achieving social equality; radical feminism seeks to create a gender-free society.

17. Because gender distinctions stand at the core of our way of life, feminism has encountered strong resistance. Although two-thirds of U.S. adults support the Equal Rights Amendment, this legislation—first proposed in Congress in 1923—has yet to become part of the U.S. Constitution.

KEY CONCEPTS

feminism the advocacy of social equality for the sexes, in opposition to patriarchy and sexism

gender human traits that are linked by culture to each sex

gender roles (sex roles) attitudes and activities that a culture links to each sex

gender stratification the unequal distribution of wealth, power, and privilege between the two sexes

hermaphrodite a human being with some combination of female and male internal and external genitalia

matriarchy a form of social organization in which females dominate males

patriarchy a form of social organization in which males dominate females

primary sex characteristics the genitals, used to reproduce the human species

secondary sex characteristics physical traits, other than the genitals, that distinguish physiologically mature females and males

sex the division of humanity into biological categories of female and male

sexism the belief that one sex is innately superior to the other

sexual harassment comments, gestures, or physical contact of a sexual nature that are deliberate, repeated, and unwelcome

sexual orientation the manner in which people experience sexual arousal and achieve sexual pleasure

transsexuals people who feel they are one sex though biologically they are the other

11

Economics and Politics

CHAPTER OUTLINE

"America First!" proclaimed the mayor of Greece, New York, an upstate community near Rochester. Amid bad economic news—a continuing recession, rising unemployment, and a deepening federal deficit—the town leaders had assembled for a symbolic act: voting to cancel the purchase of a $40,000 piece of excavating equipment from Japan's Komatsu corporation in order to give the business to U.S. manufacturer John Deere, even at a higher price.

The action prompted much applause, but the council's act only ended up revealing how complicated today's global economy really is. The Komatsu model, it turns out, is actually built in the United States, while the John Deere is powered by an engine—you guessed it—made in Japan. It appears that the emerging global economy is blurring conventional political boundaries.

This chapter examines the economy and politics, two vital dimensions of social life. First, we shall explore the economy, with special attention to the Industrial Revolution that ushered in the modern world, and the emerging global economy that is setting the stage for the future. Second, our attention will turn to politics, highlighting the growth and changing character of government in the United States, and surveying various types of political systems found elsewhere in the world.

The economic and political systems are each a major **social institution,** *an organized sphere of social life.* The two chapters that follow consider the other social institutions: Chapter 12 focuses on the family and religion, and Chapter 13 highlights education and medicine. These discussions show how social institutions function as strategies by which society meets its basic needs; at the same time, they also help maintain social inequality. We shall discover, too, that these institutions have been quite variable over human history.

THE ECONOMY: HISTORICAL OVERVIEW

The **economy** is *the institutionalized system for production, distribution, and consumption of goods and services.* To say that the economy is *institutionalized* means that it operates in a predictable and well-established manner. *Goods* are commodities ranging from necessities (such as food, clothing, and shelter) to luxury items (such as automobiles and swimming pools), while *services* refer to valued activities that benefit others (including the

work of religious leaders, physicians, and telephone operators).

The Agricultural Revolution

As Chapter 2 ("Culture") explained, the earliest societies relied on hunting and gathering to live off the land. There were no clearly distinct social institutions: production, distribution, and consumption of goods all took place as part of family life.

The development of agriculture brought revolutionary change to these societies beginning about five thousand years ago. Agriculture emerged as people harnessed animal power to plows, magnifying the productivity of hunting and gathering ten- to twentyfold. The resulting surplus meant that everyone no longer had to produce food, and many individuals began to assume specialized economic roles, forging crafts, designing tools, and constructing dwellings. This, in turn, allowed towns to spring up, which were soon linked by networks of traders dealing in food, animals, and other goods (Jacobs, 1970). These four factors—agricultural technology, productive specialization, permanent settlements, and trade—were the keys to a revolutionary expansion of the economy.

In agrarian societies, the world of work becomes distinct from family life, although production still occurs close to home. In medieval Europe, for instance, most people farmed nearby fields. People living in cities often worked in their homes—a pattern called *cottage industry*—producing goods sold in outdoor "flea markets" (a term suggesting that not everything was of the highest quality).

The Industrial Revolution

Beginning in mid–eighteenth-century England, industrialization introduced five revolutionary changes to the economies of Western societies.

1. **New forms of energy.** Throughout history, people had generated energy with their own muscles or those of animals. At the dawn of industrialization in 1765, however, the English inventor James Watt pioneered the application of steam power to machinery. Surpassing muscle power a hundred times over, steam engines soon made production far more efficient than ever before.

2. **The spread of factories.** Steam-powered machinery soon rendered cottage industries obsolete. Factories—centralized workplaces apart from the home—proliferated. A more productive system, factory work nonetheless lacked the personal ties that had characterized family-based cottage industries.

3. **Manufacturing and mass production.** Before the Industrial Revolution, most work involved cultivating and gathering raw materials, such as crops, wool, and wood. The industrial economy shifted that focus to manufacturing raw materials into a wide range of salable products. Factories mass produced clothing from wool and furniture from lumber.

4. **Specialization.** A skilled worker in a cottage industry fashioned a product from beginning to end. Factory work, by contrast, was highly specialized so that laborers repeated a single task, making only a small contribution to the finished product. Thus as factories raised productivity, they also lowered the skill level required of workers (Warner & Low, 1947).

5. **Wage labor.** Instead of people working for themselves or working together as households, factory workers became wage laborers. This means that they sold their labor to strangers who often cared less for them than for the machines they operated. Supervision became routine and intense.

The impact of the Industrial Revolution gradually rippled outward from the factories to transform all of society. Greater productivity steadily raised the standard of living as countless new products filled an expanding economy. Especially at the outset, however, these benefits were shared very unequally. Some factory owners made vast fortunes, while the majority of workers hovered perilously close to poverty. Children, too, worked in factories or deep in coal mines for pennies a day.

In time, however, the worst burdens were eased as workers organized into labor unions to represent their interests collectively. Pressure from the growing labor movement eventually prodded governments to outlaw child labor, bolster workplace safety, and extend political rights to more and more people.

The Postindustrial Society

By the mid-twentieth century, the United States was becoming a **postindustrial economy**, *a productive system based on service work and high technology.* Computerized machinery has reduced the role of human labor in production. Simultaneously, bureaucracy has expanded the ranks of clerical workers and managers. Service industries—such as public relations, advertising, banking, and sales—now employ most of our country's labor force. The postindustrial era, then, is marked by a shift from industrial production to service jobs.

The crucial technology of a postindustrial age concerns information. Computer technology forms the core of an *Information Revolution* generating a host of new, specialized occupations. Just as gaining technical skills held the key to success in the past, now workers must enhance their literacy skills.

The postindustrial society is also decentralizing work from factories as computers, facsimile (fax) machines, and other new information technologies allow people to perform many jobs at home or even while driving their cars. More educated and skilled workers also no longer require—and often do not tolerate—the close supervision characteristic of yesterday's factories.

Sectors of the Economy

The broad historical changes just described reflect a shifting balance among three sectors of a society's economy. The **primary sector** is *part of the economy that provides raw materials directly from the natural environment.* The primary sector, which includes agriculture, animal husbandry, fishing, forestry, and mining, predominates in preindustrial societies. Global Map 11–1 on page 260 shows that the primary sector is largest in the poorest nations of the world.

The **secondary sector** is *part of the economy that transforms raw materials into manufactured goods.* This sector stands out as societies industrialize. Such economic activity includes the refining of petroleum, and the use of metals to manufacture tools, building materials, and automobiles. Global Map 11–2 illustrates the scope of industrial production in global perspective.

The **tertiary sector** is *part of the economy involving services rather than goods.* Accounting for only a tiny share of work in preindustrial economies, the tertiary sector grows with industrialization and becomes dominant in postindustrial societies. Almost 70 percent of the U.S. labor force is now employed in service occupations, including secretarial and clerical work and positions in food service, sales, law, advertising, and teaching.

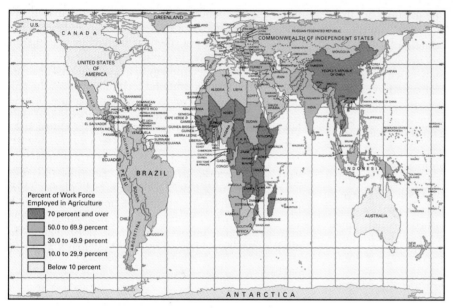

Global Map 11–1
Agricultural Employment in Global Perspective

The primary sector of the economy predominates in societies with the least economic development. Thus, in the poor countries of Africa and Asia, half, or even three-fourths, of all workers are farmers. The picture is altogether different among First-World nations—including the United States, Canada, Great Britain, and Australia—which have less than 10 percent of their work force in agriculture.

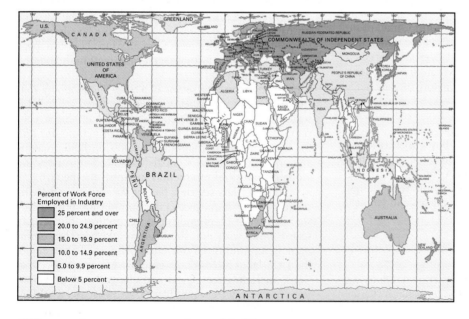

Global Map 11–2
Industrial Employment in Global Perspective

The Third World, by and large, has yet to industrialize. For this reason, in the countries of Latin America, Africa, and Asia, a small proportion of the labor force engages in industrial work. The industrial nations of the Second World—including the Commonwealth of Independent States—have the largest share of their workers in industry. In the First World, we see a reverse of this trend, with more and more workers moving from industrial jobs to service work. Thus, the postindustrial economy of the United States now has about the same share of workers in industrial jobs as the much poorer nation of Argentina.

GLOBAL ECONOMIC SYSTEMS

The economies of world societies can also be described in terms of two models: capitalism and socialism. These models represent two ends of a continuum on which an actual economy can be located.

Capitalism

Capitalism refers to *an economic system in which natural resources and the means of producing goods and services are privately owned*. Ideally, a capitalist economy has three distinctive features.

1. **Private ownership of property.** A capitalist economy supports the right of individuals to own almost anything. The more capitalist an economy is, the more private ownership there is of wealth-producing property like factories, real estate, and natural resources.

2. **Pursuit of personal profit.** A capitalist society promotes the accumulation of private property and defines a profit-minded orientation as a natural matter of "doing business." Further, claimed the Scottish economist Adam Smith (1723–1790), the drive of individuals pursuing their own self-interest helps an entire society prosper (1937; orig. 1776).

3. **Free competition and consumer sovereignty.** A purely capitalist economy would operate with no government interference, sometimes called a *laissez-faire* (a French expression meaning "to leave alone") approach. Adam Smith contended that a freely competitive economy regulates itself through the "invisible hand" of the laws of supply and demand.

   The market system is dominated by consumers, Smith maintained, who select goods and services offering the greatest value. Producers compete with one another by providing the highest-quality products at the lowest possible price. Thus, while entrepreneurs are motivated by personal gain, everyone benefits from more efficient production and ever-increasing value. In Smith's time-honored phrase, from narrow self-interest comes "greatest good for the greatest number of people." Government control of an economy would distort market forces, reducing producer motivation, di-

minishing the quality of goods, and shortchanging consumers.

The United States is the leading capitalist society, yet even here the guiding hand of government plays an extensive role in economic affairs. Government policies affect what companies produce, the quality and cost of merchandise, what businesses import and export, and how we consume or conserve natural resources. The federal government also owns and operates a host of productive organizations, including the U.S. Postal Service and the Amtrak railroad system. The entire U.S. military is also government-operated. Federal officials may step in to prevent the collapse of private businesses, as in the "bailout" of the savings and loan industry. Further, government policies set minimum wage levels and enforce workplace safety standards, regulate corporate mergers, provide farm price supports, and funnel income in the form of Social Security, public assistance, student loans, and veterans' benefits to a majority of people in the United States. Not surprisingly, local, state, and federal governments together make up this nation's biggest employer, with 15 percent of the labor force on their payrolls (U.S. Department of Labor, 1992).

Socialism

Socialism is *an economic system in which natural resources and the means of producing goods and services are collectively owned*. In its ideal form, a socialist economy opposes each of the three characteristics of capitalism just described.

1. **Collective ownership of property.** An economy is socialist to the extent that it limits the rights to private property, especially property used in producing goods and services. Laws prohibiting private ownership of property are designed to make housing and other goods available to all rather than just those with the most money.

   Karl Marx asserted that private ownership of productive property spawns social classes as it generates an economic elite. Socialism, then, holds out the promise of less social inequality and perhaps even a classless society.

2. **Pursuit of collective goals.** The individualistic pursuit of profit also stands at odds with the collective orientation of socialism. Socialist values and norms

The productivity of capitalist Hong Kong is evident in that city's omnipresent advertising and streets choked with shoppers. Socialist Beijing, by contrast, is dominated by government buildings rather than a central business district. Here bicyclists glide past the Great Hall of the People.

define as illegal what capitalists might call the entrepreneurial spirit.

3. **Government control of the economy.** Socialism rejects the notion that a free-market economy regulates itself. Instead of a laissez-faire approach, socialist governments oversee a *centrally controlled* or *command* economy.

   Socialism also opposes the idea that consumers guide capitalist production. From this point of view, consumers lack the information necessary to evaluate products and are manipulated by advertising to buy what is profitable rather than what they genuinely need. Commercial advertising thus plays little role in socialist economies.

The People's Republic of China and a number of societies in Asia, Africa, and Latin America—at least two dozen in all—model their economies on socialism, placing almost all wealth-generating property under state control (McColm et al., 1991). The extent of world socialism has declined in recent years, however, as societies in Eastern Europe and the former Soviet Union have been dramatically transformed. As change continues, these countries will eventually forge new economic systems from some combination of market forces and government regulation.

Socialism and Communism

Most people equate the terms *socialism* and *communism*. More precisely, as the ideal spirit of socialism, **communism** is *a hypothetical economic and political system in which all people have social equality*. The dominant political party in most socialist societies calls itself "communist," but nowhere in the world has the communist goal been realized.

Why? For one thing, social stratification involves differences of power as well as wealth. Socialist societies have generally succeeded in reducing disparities in wealth only by expanding government power, giving officials extensive control over the people. In the process, government has not "withered away" as Karl Marx imagined. On the contrary, during this century, members of political elites gained enormous power and privilege in socialist societies.

Marx would have been among the first to agree that communism is a *utopia* (derived from Greek words meaning "not a place"). Yet Marx considered communism to be a worthy goal, and would probably have disparaged existing "Marxist" societies such as North Korea, the former Soviet Union, the People's Republic of China, and Cuba for falling short of his communist ideal.

Democratic Socialism in Europe

Limited socialism, at least, does not necessarily stifle democracy. In fact, some of the nations of Western Europe—including Sweden and Italy—have merged socialist economic policies with a democratic political system. This hybrid is called **democratic socialism,** *a political and economic system that combines significant government control of the economy with free elections.*

Under democratic socialism, the government owns some of the largest industries and services, such as transportation, education, and health care. In Sweden and Italy, about 12 percent of total production is state-controlled. That leaves most industry in private hands but subject to extensive government regulation. High taxation (aimed especially at the rich) transfers wealth in the form of welfare programs to less advantaged members of society.

Relative Advantages of Capitalism and Socialism

In practice, how do economic systems differ? Assessing economic models is difficult because nowhere do they exist in their pure states. Societies mix capitalism and socialism to varying degrees, and each has distinctive cultural attitudes toward work, different natural resources, unequal levels of technological development, and disparate patterns of trade (Gregory & Stuart, 1985). Despite such complicating factors, some crude comparisons are revealing.

Productivity. Table 11–1 looks back at the economic performance in several societies that were predominantly socialist compared to several that are predominantly capitalist. "Gross Domestic Product" (GDP) is the total value of all goods and services produced annually within a nation's borders; "per capita" (per person) GDP allows us to compare societies of different size. Because each country uses its own currency, the table presents per capita GDP in U.S. dollars.

Among the predominantly capitalist societies (collectively dubbed the First World), the United States had the highest per capita GDP ($17,615), closely followed by Canada ($16,375) and the former West Germany ($14,730). Greece had the lowest per capita GDP ($5,500). An unweighted average (that is, ignoring population differences) puts capitalist per capita productivity at $13,345 annually.

Table 11–1 ECONOMIC PERFORMANCE OF CAPITALIST AND SOCIALIST ECONOMIES, 1988

Country	Per Capita GDP (U.S. dollars)
Predominantly Capitalist Economies	
Austria	12,386
Belgium	13,140
Canada	16,375
Federal Republic of Germany (the former West Germany)	14,730
France	13,961
Great Britain	12,270
Greece	5,500
Hong Kong	13,900
Japan	13,135
Sweden	13,780
United States	17,615
Unweighted average	13,345
Predominantly Socialist Economies	
Albania	2,000
Bulgaria	4,750
Czechoslovakia	7,750
German Democratic Republic (the former East Germany)	8,000
Hungary	4,500
Poland	4,000
Romania	3,000
Soviet Union	6,000
Yugoslavia	5,000
Unweighted average	5,000

SOURCE: United Nations Development Programme. *Human Development Report 1990.* New York: Oxford University Press, 1990, p. 129.

Looking at the former Soviet Union and other nations that were known as the Second World just before the upheavals at the end of the last decade, East Germany had the highest economic output per person ($8,000), while Albania had the lowest ($2,000). Overall, these socialist economies produced considerably less than their capitalist counterparts. The unweighted average for the Second World is $5,000, or 37 percent of the productivity of capitalist societies.

Income disparity. How resources are distributed is also important in comparing capitalist and socialist economies. Table 11–2 looks back at income inequality in selected societies with the two economic systems. The income ratios indicate how many times more income

Table 11–2 DISTRIBUTION OF INCOME IN CAPITALIST AND SOCIALIST ECONOMIES

Country	Income Ratio
Predominantly Capitalist Economies	
United States (1968)	12.7
Canada (1971)	12.0
Italy (1969)	11.2
Sweden (1971)	5.5
Great Britain (1969)	5.0
Unweighted average	9.3
Predominantly Socialist Economies	
Soviet Union (1966)	5.7
Czechoslovakia (1965)	4.3
Hungary (1964)	4.0
Bulgaria (1963–1965)	3.8
Unweighted average	4.5

SOURCE: Data are from P. J. D. Wiles, *Economic Institutions Compared* (New York: Halsted Press, 1977).

is received by highly paid people than is earned by poorly paid people.[1]

Of the five primarily capitalist societies listed in Table 11–2, the United States had the greatest income inequality, with a rich person earning almost thirteen times more than a poor person. Both Sweden (5.5) and Great Britain (5.0) had less income inequality, because these nations incorporate socialist principles into traditionally capitalist economies. The unweighted average shows a rich person earned more than nine times as much as a poor person in these predominantly capitalist societies.

With an unweighted average of 4.5, primarily socialist societies have about half as much income inequality. This comparison of economic performance supports two conclusions: first, *capitalist economies support a higher overall standard of living but with greater income disparity*; and, second, *socialist economies produce less income disparity, but offer a lower overall standard of living*.

Civil liberties. Economics and politics are closely linked. Capitalism depends on the freedom of producers

and consumers to interact without extensive interference from the state. Thus economic capitalism fosters broad political freedoms. Socialist governments try to maximize economic and social equality. This requires considerable state intervention in the economy, limiting the personal liberty of citizens. Humanity has yet to resolve the tension between the goals of political liberty and economic equality. The implications of this tension are nowhere more evident than in many socialist societies now striving to forge a new balance between these two goals.

Changes in Socialist Countries

During the last decade, a profound transformation has taken place in many socialist countries of the world. Beginning in the shipyards of Poland's port city of Gdansk in 1980, workers began organizing in opposition to their socialist government. Despite struggle and setback, the Solidarity movement eventually succeeded in dislodging the Soviet-backed party officials, electing its leader Lech Walesa as national president. This country is now in the process of introducing market principles to the nation's economy.

Other countries of Eastern Europe, all of which fell under the political control of the former Soviet Union at the end of World War II, also shook off socialist regimes during 1989 and 1990. These nations—including the former East Germany and the former Czechoslovakia, as well as Hungary, Romania, and Bulgaria—have likewise introduced capitalist elements into what had for decades been state-controlled economies. In 1992, the Soviet Union itself formally dissolved, a process that, along the way, liberated the Baltic states of Estonia, Latvia, and Lithuania and cast the remaining republics, except Georgia and Azerbaijan, into a new Commonwealth of Independent States.

The reasons for these sweeping changes are many and complex. In light of earlier discussion, however, two factors stand out. First, these predominantly socialist economies underproduced their capitalist counterparts. They were, as we have noted, successful in achieving economic equality; living standards for everyone, however, were low compared to those of Western European countries. Second, the brand of socialism that was imprinted on Eastern Europe by the former Soviet Union encouraged heavy-handed and unresponsive government that rigidly controlled the media as well as the ability of individuals to move about, even in their own nations. In short, the socialist systems in these societies did do

---

[1] Specifically, income ratio is derived from dividing the 95th percentile income by the 5th percentile income. The author is unaware of more recent data of this kind.

away with *economic* elites (as Karl Marx predicted), but, as Max Weber might have imagined, they expanded the clout of *political* elites as party bureaucracies grew to gargantuan proportions.

At this stage, the market reforms have been proceeding unevenly, with some nations faring better than others. For the short term at least, Eastern Europe has been buffeted by price increases, which have further eroded living standards. In the long term, however, officials in these countries hope that an expanding market will raise living standards through greater productivity. If this happens, based on the experience of Western societies, a rising standard of living may well be accompanied by increasing economic disparity.

WORK IN THE POSTINDUSTRIAL UNITED STATES

Change is not restricted to the socialist world; the last century has also dramatically transformed the economy of the United States. In 1991, 125 million people were in the labor force, representing two-thirds of those over the age of fifteen. As explained in Chapter 10 ("Sex and Gender"), a larger proportion of men (76.2 percent) than women (57.4 percent) had income-producing jobs, but this gap has diminished in recent decades. Among men, the proportion of people of African descent in the labor force (69.5 percent) is somewhat less than the proportion of whites (76.4 percent); among women, about the same share of African Americans (57.0 percent) and whites (57.4 percent) are gainfully employed.

The Changing Workplace

In 1900, 40 percent of the U.S. labor force engaged in farming. By 1993, this proportion had dropped to less than 3 percent. Figure 11–1 illustrates this rapid decline, which reflects the diminished role of the primary sector in the U.S. economy.

Industrialization swelled the ranks of blue-collar workers a century ago. By 1950, however, a white-collar revolution had carried a majority of workers into service occupations. By 1993, more than two-thirds of employed men and women held white-collar jobs. As Chapter 7 ("Social Stratification") explained, much so-called "white-collar" work is actually "service work," including sales positions, secretarial jobs, and positions in fast-food

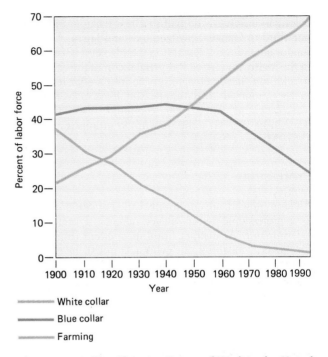

Figure 11–1 The Changing Pattern of Work in the United States, 1900–1990
(*U.S. Department of Labor*)

restaurants. Such work yields little of the income and prestige of professional white-collar occupations, and often provides fewer rewards than factory work. Therefore, more and more jobs in this postindustrial era provide a modest standard of living.

Labor Unions

The changing economy has been accompanied by a decline in **labor unions,** *organizations of workers seeking to improve wages and working conditions through various strategies, including negotiations and strikes.* Membership in labor unions increased rapidly after 1935 to more than one-third of non-farm workers by 1950. Union membership peaked during the 1970s at almost 25 million people. Since then, it has steadily declined to about 16 percent of the non-farm labor force, or about 20 million men and women.

In global perspective, unions are weaker in the United States than in other industrial societies. More than 90 percent of workers in Denmark and Sweden belong to unions, as do half in Great Britain, and about one-third in Canada, Switzerland, and Japan. One reason for our country's low union membership is a decrease in the highly unionized industrial sector of the economy. In addition, newly created service jobs are far less likely to be unionized. But unions still exert power in the workplace and, since 1990, economic uncertainty appears to have given some new life to unions (Goldfield, 1987; Marry, 1992).

Professions

All kinds of work are commonly called *professional*, such as a professional tennis player or even a professional exterminator. As distinct from an *amateur* (from Latin for "lover," meaning one who acts out of love for the activity itself), a professional pursues some task for a living.

More precisely, a **profession** is *a prestigious, white-collar occupation that requires extensive formal education.* The term signifies that certain work originally involved a profession—or public declaration—of faith or willingness to abide by certain principles. Traditional professions include the ministry, medicine, law, and academia (W. Goode, 1960). Today, more workers describe their occupations as professional to the extent that they have several characteristics (Ritzer, 1972). One is theoretical knowl-

edge of their field rather than mere technical training. Anyone can learn first aid, for example, but physicians draw on a theoretical knowledge of human health. Second, the typical professional is self-employed, "in practice" rather than working for a company. Third, based on extensive training, professionals claim authority over clients, and expect "lay people" to follow their direction. Fourth, professionals assert that they serve the community rather than merely seeking income. Codes of ethics bar some professionals, including physicians (but not lawyers), from advertising.

Self-Employment

Self-employment—in effect, earning a living without working for a large organization—was once commonplace in the United States. From about 80 percent of the labor force in 1800, self-employment now accounts for only 8 percent of workers: 9 percent of men and 6 percent of women (U.S. Bureau of Labor Statistics, 1992).

Lawyers and physicians and some other professionals have always been strongly represented among the self-employed because they possess valued education and skills. But most self-employed workers are small-business owners, plumbers, carpenters, freelance writers, editors, artists, and long-distance truck drivers. Overall, the self-

During the Great Depression, a time of catastrophic unemployment in the United States, Isaac Soyer (1907–1981) painted *Employment Agency*, a powerful statement of the personal collapse and private despair that can afflict men and women who are out of work.

Isaac Soyer, Employment Agency. *Collection of the Whitney Museum of American Art. Purchase 37.44. Photo by Geoffrey Clements, N.Y.*

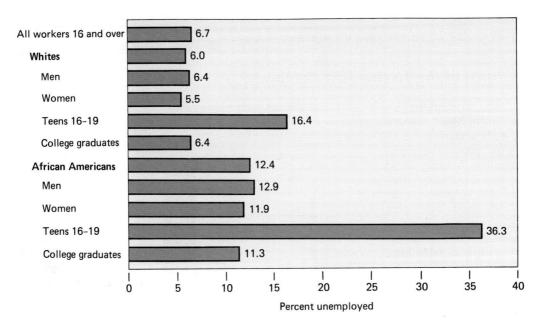

All workers 16 and over	6.7
Whites	6.0
Men	6.4
Women	5.5
Teens 16–19	16.4
College graduates	6.4
African Americans	12.4
Men	12.9
Women	11.9
Teens 16–19	36.3
College graduates	11.3

Percent unemployed

Figure 11–2 Official U.S. Unemployment Rate among Various Categories of Adults, 1991
(U.S. Department of Labor, 1992)

employed are more likely to have blue-collar jobs than white-collar work.

Unemployment

Every society has some unemployment. Few young people entering the labor force find a job right away; some older workers temporarily leave their jobs to seek new work, to have children, or because of a labor strike; others suffer from long-term illnesses; and still others are illiterate or without skills and cannot perform useful work.

But unemployment is also caused by the economy itself. Jobs disappear due to recession, as a result of occupations becoming obsolete, or because businesses close in the face of foreign competition. During the 1980s, for example, the decline of some U.S. industries increased unemployment among blue-collar workers; the recession in recent years has been especially hard on people with white-collar jobs.

In 1992, 8.5 million people over the age of sixteen were unemployed—about 7 percent of the civilian labor force. Unemployment declined through the 1980s, rising again with the recession of the early 1990s.

Figure 11–2 shows the official unemployment rate for various categories of U.S. workers in 1991 (U.S. Department of Labor, 1992). Unemployment among African Americans stood more than twice as high (12.4 percent) as among whites (6.0 percent). For both races, men now have higher unemployment than women—a reversal of a historical pattern. The economic recession in male-dominated blue-collar industries accounts for this change.

Social Diversity in the Workplace

Another revolution in the workplace concerns the composition of the U.S. labor force. In brief, this is designated as the *workplace diversity revolution.*

Traditionally, white men have been the mainstay of the U.S. labor force. As explained in Chapter 9 ("Race and Ethnicity"), however, our country's proportion of minorities is rising rapidly. During the 1980s, the increase in African Americans (13 percent) was twice as great as for whites (6 percent); even higher was the jump in the Hispanic population (more than 50 percent), and in the numbers of Asian Americans (topping 100 percent). Should these trends continue, there will be a

The Work Force of the Twenty-First Century

During the 1980s, the demographic profile of the United States changed significantly, with a marked rise in the share of the population represented by minorities. Looking ahead to the 1990s, continued transformation in the social composition of the population—and thus the labor force—is all but certain.

The figure shows that the number of white men in the U.S. labor force is projected to rise by a modest 8 percent during the 1990s. The rate of increase for African-American working men will be far greater, at 24 percent. Among Hispanic men, the rise will be a whopping 50 percent. Among women, projected increases across the board are larger than for men, meaning that a greater proportion of workers in the United States will be women as we approach the new century. But, here again, the gains among minorities will be greatest of all: a 19 percent rise among

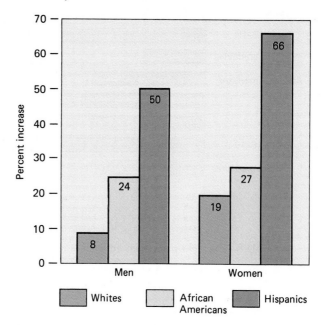

Projected Increase in Work Force Participation, by Gender and Race, 1990–2000

Hispanics can be of any race (U.S. Department of Labor)

"minority-majority" in the United States toward the end of the next century. The box takes a closer look at how increasing social diversity will affect the workplace through the 1990s.

Technology and Work

The central feature of the emerging postindustrial economy is the computer and related information technology. The Information Revolution is changing the conditions of work and the workplace.

Shoshana Zuboff (1982) points out four ways in which computers have already altered the character of work. First, she suggests, *computers are deskilling labor*. Just as industrial machines reduced worker skills in the past, so computers now threaten the skills of managers,

as computer programs are designed to make more decisions such as approving or rejecting a loan application. Second, *work is becoming more abstract*. Industrial workers generally have a "hands-on" relationship with their product; postindustrial workers manipulate symbols in pursuit of some abstract business goal. Third, Zuboff explains, *computers limit workplace interaction*. The Information Revolution is producing social isolation as employees perform most of their work at computer terminals. Fourth, *computers enhance the supervision and control of workers*. Using computers, supervisors can monitor worker output continuously. Workers now contend with ever-present management, more than their counterparts do in the industrial factory.

Making a broader point, Zuboff contends that technology is not socially neutral; rather, it shapes the way

whites will be surpassed by a 27 percent jump among African Americans, and a 66 percent increase in Hispanics.

When you add up all these factors, non-Hispanic white men—the traditional backbone of the U.S. labor force—will represent only 10 percent of new workers during the 1990s. By the end of the decade, they will amount to 40 percent of all workers, a figure that will continue to drop. In the twenty-first century, then, few businesses will be able to survive by relying solely on the efforts of white men. On the other hand, companies that begin now to plan for growing social diversity will enjoy a competitive advantage.

Responding effectively to workplace diversity means more than maintaining affirmative action programs, which are primarily aimed at recruiting. As important as fair hiring policies are, companies face a broader challenge—and a greater opportunity—that involves transforming the workplace environment to draw on the maximum potential of all workers. Employees, after all, are any company's most valuable resource, and developing this resource will require change in a number of key areas. First, companies must realize that the needs and concerns of women and people of color may not be the same as those of white men. For example, corporations will be pressed to offer workplace child care in the future; the ability to manage cultural diversity will also be vital. Second, businesses will have to devise in-house education programs aimed at defusing tensions that may arise from social differences. By establishing a corporate culture that does not tolerate harassment related to gender and race, companies will ensure the full efforts of all workers. Third, corporations will have to rethink current promotion practices. At present, only 2 percent of Fortune 500 executives are women, and just 1 percent are other minorities. In a broader survey of U.S. companies, the U.S. Equal Opportunity Commission confirmed that white men (40 percent of adults aged 20 to 64) hold 68 percent of management jobs; the comparable figures for white women are 41 and 23 percent; for African Americans, 12 and 5 percent; and, for Hispanics, 8 and 2 percent.

An informal "glass ceiling" that prevents advancement by skilled workers clearly discourages achievement. In the evolving labor market of the 1990s and beyond, any such barriers will deprive companies of their largest source of talent—women and other minorities.

SOURCES: Bureau of National Affairs (1990) and Crispell (1990).

---

we work. Understandably, then, while workers may hail some dimensions of the Information Revolution, they are likely to oppose others.

CORPORATIONS

At the core of today's capitalist economy lies the **corporation,** *an organization with a legal existence, including rights and liabilities, apart from those of its members.* By incorporating, an organization becomes a legal entity unto itself, able to enter into contracts and own property. Of roughly 20 million businesses in the United States, about 4 million are incorporated (*Statistics of Income Bulletin*, 1991).

The largest corporations are owned by millions of stockholders (including other corporations) rather than by single families. This dispersion of corporate ownership has spread wealth to some extent, making more people small-scale capitalists. Ralf Dahrendorf (1959) adds that the day-to-day operation of corporations falls to white-collar executives who may or may not be major stockholders. In practice, however, a great deal of corporate stock is owned by a small number of the corporation's top executives and directors (Useem, 1980).

Economic Concentration

About half of U.S. corporations are quite small, with assets worth less than $100,000. The largest corporations, however, dominate the nation's economy. Corporations of record in 1990 included 367 with assets exceeding $1 billion, representing 71 percent of all corporate assets and 73 percent of total corporate profits (U.S. Bureau of the Census, 1992).

The largest U.S. corporation in terms of sales is General Motors, which has $184 billion in total assets. GM's sales ($123 billion) equal the combined tax revenues of half the states and, even with recent layoffs, the corporation employs more people than the governments of all states on the West Coast.

Conglomerates and Corporate Linkages

Economic concentration has spawned *conglomerates*, giant corporations composed of many smaller corporations. Conglomerates emerge as corporations enter new markets, spinning off new companies or carrying out "takeovers" of existing companies. Beatrice Foods is a conglomerate encompassing more than fifty smaller companies that manufacture well-known products such as Reddi-Wip, Wesson cooking oils, Peter Pan peanut butter, Hunt's foods, Tropicana fruit juices, La Choy foods, Orville Redenbacher popcorn, Max Factor cosmetics, Playtex clothing, and Samsonite luggage (Beatrice, 1985).

Another type of corporate linkage is the *interlocking directorate*, a social network of people who serve simultaneously on the boards of directors of many corporations (Marlios, 1975; Herman, 1981; Scott & Griff, 1985). These connections give corporations access to valuable market information. Beth Mintz and Michael Schwartz (1981) found that General Motors is directly linked through board members to twenty-nine other major corporations, and indirectly to another seven hundred companies. Although corporate linkages do not necessarily run counter to the public interest, they certainly concentrate power and may encourage illegal activity such as price fixing.

Corporations and Competition

The capitalist model assumes that businesses operate independently in a competitive market. However, the *competitive sector* of the U.S. economy is mostly limited to smaller businesses and self-employed people. The corporate core of the economy, meanwhile, is largely a *noncompetitive sector*. Large corporations do not truly compete because, first, extensive linkages mean that they are not independent. Second, a small number of corporations dominate many large markets.

No large corporation can legally engage in **monopoly**, *domination of a market by a single producer*, because such a company could simply dictate prices. But a common practice is **oligopoly**, *domination of a market by a few producers*. Oligopoly results from the vast investment needed to enter a new market like the auto industry. Moreover, true competition means risk, which big business tries to avoid.

Although capitalism favors minimal government intervention in the economy, corporate power is now so great—and competition among corporations so limited—that government regulation is often the only way to protect the public interest. Yet, the government is also the corporate world's single biggest customer (Madsen, 1980). Washington also frequently intervenes to support struggling corporations, as in the savings and loan bailout of the late 1980s. Corporations and government typically work together to make the entire economy more stable and profitable.

The Global Economy: Looking Ahead

Corporations have grown in size so fast that they will soon account for most of the world's economic activity. The largest corporations—centered in the United States, Japan, and Western Europe—have spilled across national borders and view the world as one vast marketplace. Beatrice Foods, for example, operates factories in thirty countries and sells products in more than one hundred.

Corporations become multinational in order to make more money. Because three-fourths of the world's people and most of the planet's resources are found in Third-World societies, global corporations enter the Third World to gain access to raw materials, inexpensive labor, and vast markets. Developing an international profile also permits corporations to lower their tax liabilities and to move money from country to country, profiting from fluctuating currency rates.

The impact of multinationals on poor societies of the Third World is controversial, as Chapter 8 ("Global Inequality") explained in detail. On one side of the argument, modernization theorists claim that multinationals unleash the great productivity of the capitalist economic system to the benefit of poor nations (Rostow, 1978; Madsen, 1980; Berger, 1986). Advocates of modernization theory argue that corporations offer poor societies tax revenues, capital investment, new jobs, and advanced technology that combine to accelerate economic growth. On the other side, dependency theorists respond that multinationals have intensified global inequality (Vaughan, 1978; Wallerstein, 1979; Delacroix & Ragin, 1981; Bergesen, 1983). Multinational investment, they contend, actually creates few jobs and inhibits the development of local industries, a better source of employment. Further, critics charge, multinationals generally push developing countries to produce expensive consumer goods for export rather than food and other necessities that would bolster the standard of living in local communities. From this standpoint, multinationals make poor societies poorer and increasingly dependent on rich societies of the capitalist First World.

Finally, the emerging global economy cuts both ways. Foreign corporations now own more of the United States than U.S. corporations own abroad ("Buy America," 1989). Foreign investors currently have title to half of the commercial property in downtown Los Angeles, 40 percent in Houston, 35 percent in Minneapolis, and 25 percent in Manhattan (Selimuddin, 1989). Clearly, the national economies of the past are now being overshadowed by an interconnected global economic system.

POLITICS: HISTORICAL OVERVIEW

Closely related to economics is **politics,** *the institutionalized system by which a society distributes power and makes decisions.* Early in this century, Max Weber (1978; orig. 1921) defined **power** as *the ability to achieve desired ends despite opposition.*

History shows that force—physical or psychological coercion—is the most basic form of power. No society can long exist, however, if power *only* derives from force, because people will break the rules at the first opportunity. Social organization, therefore, depends on generating some consensus about proper goals (cultural values) and the suitable means of attaining them (cultural norms). The key to social stability and justice, Weber concluded, lies in **authority,** *power widely accepted as legitimate rather than coercive.*

The form authority takes depends partly on a society's economy. According to Weber, preindustrial societies rely on **traditional authority,** *power legitimized by respect for long-established cultural patterns.* Once woven into a traditional society's collective memory, power may seem almost sacred. The might of Chinese emperors

The expansion of Western multinational corporations has altered patterns of consumption throughout the world, creating a homogeneous "corporate culture" that is—for better or worse—undermining countless traditional ways of life.

In one of the most dramatic political transformations of this century, the former Soviet Union ended seventy-five years of centralized communist government in 1991. Hardly anyone was able to foresee this momentous change, and no one can be certain of its long-term consequences.

in antiquity was legitimized by tradition, as was the rule of nobles in medieval Europe. In both cases, hereditary family rule supported by tradition imbued leaders with almost godlike power.

Traditional authority declines as societies industrialize. Royal families still exist in several European societies, but a more democratic culture has shifted power to commoners elected to office. Yet, Weber continued, the expansion of rational bureaucracy enhances another, distinctly modern path to legitimizing power. **Rational-legal authority** (sometimes called *bureaucratic authority*), said Weber, is *power legitimized by legally enacted rules and regulations.*

Rationally enacted rules underlie most authority in the United States today. The authority of political leaders now flows from offices in vast governmental organizations. An office holder presumably exercises rational-

legal authority on the basis of talent and special training, not birth or family ties. A king's brother, for example, is a prince; but sisters and brothers of U.S. presidents often attract little public notice, and exercise no authority unless they, too, hold office.

Weber described one additional type of authority that has surfaced throughout history. Chapter 12 ("Family and Religion") explores *charisma*, exceptional personal qualities that play a key role in many religious movements. **Charismatic authority**, then, is *power legitimized by extraordinary personal abilities that inspire devotion and obedience.* Unlike its traditional and rational-legal counterparts, charismatic authority depends little on a person's ancestry or office; it is an expression of individual personality. Charisma may enhance the power of traditional or rational-legal rulers. More commonly, however, charismatics lead people away from traditional customs and established organizations. Followers line up behind someone with special magnetism, believing that the charismatic taps into a higher power. Charisma characterized leaders as different as Jesus of Nazareth, Adolph Hitler, and the Ayatollah Khomeini. But each of the three preached an alternative to the status quo and inspired followers to transform the existing social order.

Charismatic authority is inherently unstable, Weber warned, because it emanates from a single individual. Surviving the eventual loss of their leader depends on the **routinization of charisma**, *the transformation of charismatic authority into some combination of traditional and bureaucratic authority.* Christianity, for example, was spread by the personal charisma of Jesus of Nazareth. After the death of Jesus, the Roman Catholic Church gradually became established on a foundation of tradition and bureaucracy. But this routinization of charisma does not necessarily take place. Most charismatic movements disintegrate upon the departure of the inspirational leader. The nineteenth-century Christian sect in the Oneida region of upstate New York, founded by the charismatic clergyman John Humphrey Noyes, floundered soon after its aging leader left the community.

GLOBAL POLITICAL SYSTEMS

Government refers to *a formal organization that directs the political life of a society.* The governments of the world's 187 nations differ in countless ways. Yet virtually all bear a close resemblance to one of four political systems.

Monarchy

Monarchy (with Latin and Greek roots mean "ruling alone") is *a type of political system in which the power to rule is passed from generation to generation in a single family*. Monarchy dates back to earliest human history: the Bible, for example, tells of great kings such as David and Solomon; British monarchs trace their ancestry through centuries of nobility. In terms of Weber's analysis, monarchy is legitimized by tradition.

During the medieval era, *absolute monarchy*, in which hereditary rulers claimed a virtual monopoly of power based on divine right, flourished from England to China and in parts of the Americas. Monarchs in some nations—including Saudi Arabia—still exercise virtually absolute control over their people. During this century, however, elected officials have gradually replaced hereditary nobility. In those European societies where royal families remain—including Great Britain, Spain, Norway, Sweden, Belgium, Denmark, and the Netherlands—they now preside over *constitutional monarchies*, in which monarchs are little more than symbolic heads of state. Actual governing is the responsibility of elected officials, led by a prime minister, and guided by a constitution. In these countries, then, the nobility may reign, but elected officials rule (Roskin, 1982).

Democracy

The historical trend in the modern world has favored **democracy**, *a political system in which power is exercised by the people as a whole*. Members of democratic societies rarely participate directly in decision making; numbers alone make this an impossibility. Instead, a system of *representative democracy* places authority in the hands of elected leaders who are accountable to the people.

Affluent, industrial societies tend to embrace democratic political systems (Hannan & Carroll, 1981). Economic development and democratic government go together because both depend on a literate populace who turn away from traditions. Additionally, in every industrial society, a wide range of formal organizations tries to advance their interests within the political arena. Thus,

in contrast to the high concentration of power in the absolute monarchies common to preindustrial societies, industrial societies have a more complex and diffuse political system.

The traditional legitimation of power in a monarchy gives way in democratic political systems to rational-legal authority. A rational election process places leaders in offices regulated by law. Thus democracy and rational-legal authority are linked just as monarchy and traditional authority are. In addition, democratic societies are extensively bureaucratic. Most of the 17 million people who operate federal, state, and local governments in the United States are not elected. Thus much decision making in nominally democratic societies is actually performed in an undemocratic way (Scaff, 1981; Edwards, 1985; Etzioni-Halevy, 1985).

Democracy and Freedom: Contrasting Approaches

Virtually all industrialized nations in the world claim to be democratic and politically free, despite a history of widely differing political systems. This curious fact suggests the need for a closer look at what societies mean by their people being "free."

Capitalist societies, including the United States, Canada, and the nations of Western Europe, allow individuals a high level of personal freedom to pursue their self-interest. The capitalist approach to political freedom means personal *liberty*. Liberty refers to the *freedom to* vote for one's preferred leader or otherwise act with minimal interference from government. On the down side, capitalist liberty translates into some people being far more free than others because of a striking inequality of wealth.

In socialist societies, by contrast, political officials monitor social life more closely in order to provide every citizen with a job, housing, schooling, and medical care. The socialist approach to freedom thus emphasizes *freedom from* basic want. The problem here, as recent uprisings in Eastern Europe and the former Soviet Union suggest, is that such governments prohibit political opposition and can be unresponsive to the needs of people.

Change in much of the socialist world has led some Western analysts to trumpet the expansion of democracy. The box on page 274 reviews global political trends during the last decade, pointing out that an unprec-

The 1980s: A Decade of Democracy

Beginning with the rise of the Polish trade union Solidarity about 1980, popular opposition to socialist governments swelled throughout Eastern Europe. The "opening" of these tightly controlled societies intensified after 1985 when Mikhail Gorbachev came to power in the Soviet Union and initiated his program of *perestroika* or "restructuring." In the final months of 1989, the people of Eastern Europe toppled unpopular socialist governments like so many dominoes first in Poland, then in Hungary, East Germany, Bulgaria, Czechoslovakia, Romania, and, finally, in the Soviet Union itself. Although the political future of these countries is far from clear, political *pluralism*—in which many political parties compete for popular support—has replaced the monopoly of power held by communist parties since World War II.

Democratic forces have been making gains elsewhere as well. A trend toward political pluralism is swelling across Africa, Latin America, and South Asia. At the same time, there are also new threats to democracy—especially resurging nationalism and ethnic hatred that have fueled violence from Ireland to the former Soviet Union to the former Yugoslavia and India. But, on balance, the 1990s opened with greater prospects for political democracy in the world than have existed in recent memory.

According to Freedom House, a New York-based organization that tracks global political trends, 40 percent of the world's people—more than 2 billion out of a total of 5.3 billion—now live in free societies with extensive political rights. Another 28 percent of people (1.5 billion) are partially free with limited rights. The remaining one-third of the world's people live in countries in which government power strictly curbs individual choice.

During the 1980s, the trend toward global democracy was striking. In 1981, only 36 percent of the world's people were free, with 22 percent partially free, and 43 percent living in societies that were not free. This 1991 survey recorded for the first time in history, however, that more of the world's people are living in free than in rigidly controlled societies.

SOURCES: Based on Mathews (1991) and McColm et al. (1991).

edented share of the world's people now have sufficient political rights and civil liberties to be called "free," at least in the capitalist sense. A graphic representation of this transformation is provided in Global Map 11–3.

Authoritarianism and Totalitarianism

Authoritarianism refers to *a political system that denies popular participation in government.* No society involves all its citizens in the daily activities of government, so each is, to some degree, authoritarian. Truly authoritarian systems are indifferent to people's lives, and lack legal means to remove leaders from office. The absolute monarchies that remain in the world are highly authoritarian, as are the more common military juntas (as in Congo and Ethiopia) or the dictatorships that have ruled the Philippines, Haiti, and Panama.

The most intensely controlled political form is **totalitarianism,** *a highly centralized political system that extensively regulates people's lives.* Totalitarian government emerged only during this century along with the technological means to rigidly regulate people's lives. The Nazi regime in Germany, finally crushed at the end of World War II, was able to maintain extensive surveillance and terror. More recently, advanced electronic technology—especially computers for storing vast amounts of information—has increased the potential for government manipulation of a large population.

Although some totalitarian governments claim to represent the will of the people, most seek to bend people to the will of the government. Such governments are *total* concentrations of power, allowing no organized political opposition. Denying the populace the right to assemble for political purposes, these governments also limit the access of citizens to information: the former Soviet government, for example, restricted public access

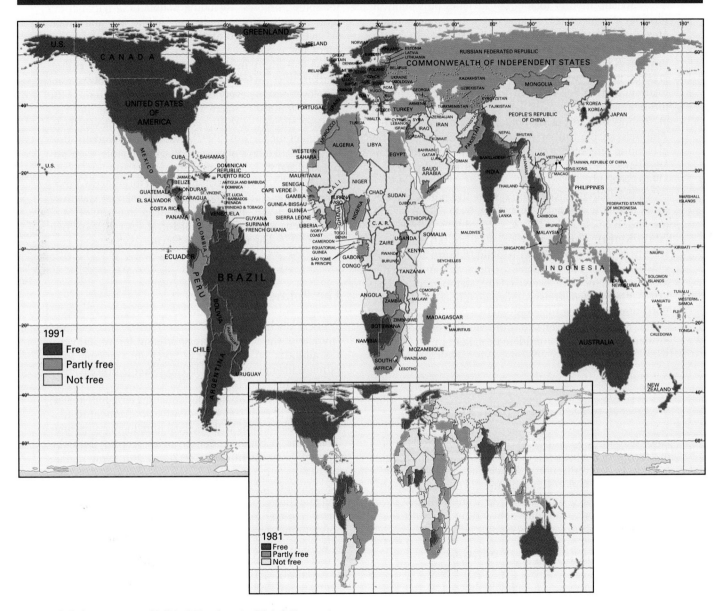

Global Map 11–3   Political Freedom in Global Perspective

In 1991, sixty-seven of the world's nations that contained almost 40 percent of all people were politically "free." Another fifty nations that included almost 30 percent of the world's people were "partly free." An additional thirty nations with about one-third of humanity remained "not free." Comparing the two maps shows that, during the 1980s, democratic gains were made in Eastern Europe, the former Soviet Union, and South America. Political rights are most extensive in the rich nations of the world and least extensive in poorer countries of Africa and Asia.

to telephone directories, copying machines, fax machines, and even city maps.

Socialization in totalitarian societies puts political ideology at center stage, seeking not just outward compliance but inward commitment to the system. In North Korea, one of the most totalitarian states in the world, pictures of leaders and political messages over loudspeakers crop up everywhere to remind citizens that they owe total support to the state. In the aftermath of China's pro-democracy movement, officials subjected students at Beijing universities to political "refresher" courses. The mass media further support totalitarian regimes by presenting only official versions of events (Arendt, 1958; Kornhauser, 1959; Friedrich & Brzezinski, 1965; Nisbet, 1966; Goldfarb, 1989).

Totalitarian governments span the political spectrum from the far right (including Nazi Germany) to the far left (such as the People's Republic of China and North Korea). This means that socialism (an economic system) is not synonymous with totalitarianism (a political system). While formal socialism does demand government involvement in everyday life, democratic socialism—as in Sweden—retains broad civil liberties. By contrast, some capitalist societies, such as South Africa and Chile, exercise sufficient control over the lives of most of their citizens to be considered totalitarian.

POLITICS IN THE UNITED STATES

After fighting a revolutionary war against Great Britain to gain political independence, early U.S. leaders sought to replace the British monarchy with a democratic political system. Our nation's commitment to democratic principles has persisted through two centuries, shaped by a distinctive history, economy, and cultural heritage.

Culture, Economics, and Politics

Our cultural emphasis on individualism is written into the Bill of Rights (the first ten amendments to the U.S. Constitution), which guarantees freedom from undue government interference. Many people in the United States, no doubt, share the sentiment of nineteenth-century philosopher and poet Ralph Waldo Emerson: "The government that governs best is the government that governs least."

Yet few of us would do away with government entirely because almost everyone thinks it is necessary for some purposes, including maintaining national defense, a system of schools, and public law and order. In fact, as the United States has become larger, government has expanded even faster, from a federal budget of $4.5 million in 1789 to well over the $1 trillion mark in 1991. In terms of numbers, from one government employee serving every eighteen hundred citizens at the nation's founding, today we have one official for every thirteen citizens, counting government at all levels (U.S. Bureau of the Census, 1992). Government workers serve the public in a host of ways, managing schools, monitoring civil rights, setting safety standards that protect consumers and workers, providing support for students, veterans, and the elderly, and overseeing our vast system of national defense. Just as important, a majority of U.S. adults depend on government for at least part of their income (Caplow et al., 1982; Devine, 1985).

The Political Spectrum

Political labels—including "conservative," "liberal," and "middle-of-the-roader"—are shorthand for an individual's attitudes on the *political spectrum*, ranging from extreme liberalism on the left to extreme conservatism on the right.

One cluster of attitudes concerns *economic issues*. Economic liberals support extensive government regulation of the economy with the goal of reducing disparities in income. Economic conservatives seek to limit the hand of government in the economy and allow market forces freer reign.

Social issues are moral questions ranging from abortion and the death penalty to gay rights and opportunities for minorities. Social liberals endorse equal rights and opportunities for all categories of people, view abortion as a matter of individual choice, and oppose the death penalty because it has been unfairly applied to minorities. The "family values" agenda of social conservatives includes maintaining traditional gender roles and opposing gay families, affirmative action, and other "special programs" for minorities. Social conservatives condemn abortion as a moral wrong and support the death penalty as a response to heinous crimes.

Of the two major political parties in the United States, the Republican Party is the more conservative on both economic and social issues while the Democratic

Party is the more liberal. Yet each party has conservative and liberal wings so that the difference between a liberal Republican and a conservative Democrat may be insignificant. Further, Republicans as well as Democrats favor big government—as long as it advances their aims. Liberal Democrats, for instance, support a national program extending health care to all; conservative Republicans, however, have long favored government action to ban abortion.

With wealth to protect, well-to-do people generally hold conservative views on economic issues. Yet their extensive schooling and secure social standing encourage them to be social liberals. Individuals of modest social position exhibit the opposite pattern, tending toward liberal views on economic policy and embracing a socially conservative agenda. They seek greater economic opportunity, but take pride in conforming to conventional cultural patterns (Nunn, Crocket, & Williams, 1978; Erikson, Luttbeg, & Tedin, 1980; Syzmanski, 1983; Humphries, 1984). People of color, regardless of social standing, tend to take a liberal stance both economically and socially and, for half a century, have voted Democratic. Historically, Hispanics and Jews have also supported the Democratic Party. Asian Americans, however, stand out as the only minority to vote Republican in the 1992 presidential election.

Because many people hold mixed political attitudes—espousing liberal views on some issues and conservative stands on others—party identification is weak in the United States. In this way, our nation differs from European democracies where people usually adhere strongly to one political party (Wolfinger, Shapiro, & Greenstein, 1980). Table 11–3 shows the results of a national survey of party identification among U.S. adults (N.O.R.C., 1991). About 45 percent identified themselves—to some degree—as Democrats and about 42 percent favored the Republicans. Twelve percent claimed to be independents, voicing no preference for either major party. Although more than eight in ten have a preference, however, most are not strongly committed to their party. In 1992, for example, Democrat Bill Clinton won the support of millions of people who had voted for Republican George Bush four years earlier.

Special-Interest Groups

In 1992, President George Bush proposed repealing the luxury tax on expensive boats. The boating industry,

Table 11–3 POLITICAL PARTY IDENTIFICATION IN THE UNITED STATES, 1991

Party Identification	Proportion of Respondents
Democrat	44.4%
Strong Democrat	14.8
Not very strong Democrat	21.0
Independent, close to Democrat	8.6
Republican	41.8%
Strong Republican	11.9
Not very strong Republican	18.8
Independent, close to Republican	11.1
Independent	12.4%
Other party, no response	1.3%

SOURCE: N.O.R.C., *General Social Surveys, 1972–1991* (Chicago: National Opinion Research Center, 1991), p. 96.

which had charged that this regulation was choking their business, applauded loudly.

The boating industry, as well as associations of elderly people, women's organizations, and environmentalists, each exemplify a **special-interest group,** *a political alliance of people interested in a particular economic or social issue.* Special-interest groups flourish in societies where political parties are weak, and the United States contains a vast array of them. Many special-interest groups employ *lobbyists* as their professional advocates in political circles.

Political action committees (PACs) are *organizations formed by special-interest groups, independent of political parties, to pursue political aims by raising and spending money.* Political action committees channel most of their funds directly to candidates likely to support their interests. Since the 1970s, the number of PACs has grown rapidly to more than six thousand (U.S. Bureau of the Census, 1991).

Because of the rising costs of campaigns, most candidates eagerly accept financial support from political action committees. More than half of all senators have received at least $1 million apiece from PACs, and these organizations now provide one-third of all Congressional campaign funding (U.S. Federal Election Commission, 1989). Supporters maintain that PACs represent the interests of a vast array of businesses, unions, and church groups, thereby increasing political participation. Critics claim that organizations supplying cash to politicians

African-American artist Thomas Waterman Wood (1823–1903) painted *American Citizens* (*To the Polls*) in 1867 to commemorate the 1866 elections—the first in which black men could vote. The painting features an affluent Yankee, a working-class Irishman, a Dutch public transportation worker, and an African American—new to the political scene—whose clothing provides little clue as to his occupation or his social standing. Despite differences of class, ethnicity, and race, in other words, Wood was optimistic that our political system would forge a representative, democratic government.

T. W. Wood, American Citizens (To the Polls). *1867. Watercolor on paper, 17½ x 35½ (44.5 x 90.2). Signed and dated in the lower left corner: T. W. Wood/1867. T. W. Wood Art Gallery.*

expect to be treated favorably in return so that, in effect, PACs try to buy political influence (Sabato, 1984).

Voter Apathy

In light of the courageous drive of people around the world to gain a greater voice in government—sometimes at the cost of their lives—a disturbing fact is that many people here in the United States seem indifferent to their own political rights. In fact, U.S. citizens are less likely to vote today than they were a century ago. The problem of *voter apathy* may well be worse in the United States than in most other industrialized democracies (Harvard/ABC News Symposium, cited in Piven & Cloward, 1988). In 1992—a year of heightened political interest—only 54 percent of eligible voters went to the polls in the presidential election.

Who is and is not likely to vote? After winning the right to vote in 1920, women cast ballots in lower proportions than men until 1988, when women outpolled men for the first time. Age makes an even bigger differ-

ence in voting behavior: people between eighteen and twenty-four years are half as likely to vote as those over sixty-five. Voting is also higher among whites than African Americans, with Hispanics the least likely of all to vote.

What accounts for nonvoting? First, at any given time, millions of people are sick or otherwise disabled; millions more are away from home having made no arrangement to submit an absentee ballot. Second, many people forget to re-register after moving from one election district to another. Third, registration and voting require the ability to read and write, which may discourage tens of millions of functionally illiterate men and women.

But the main reason for voter apathy, as conservatives see it, is *indifference* to politics, suggesting that people are by and large content with life in the United States. Liberals, and especially political radicals, counter that many people are so deeply dissatisfied with society that they doubt elections will make any real difference; thus, from this perspective, voter apathy signifies political *alienation*. Because we know that powerless people are least likely to vote, the second explanation is probably closer to the truth. A final possibility is that apathy flows from our two major parties having much in common. If the parties represented a wider spectrum of political opinion, some suggest, our population would have more reason to vote (Zipp & Smith, 1982; Zipp, 1985).

THEORETICAL ANALYSIS OF POLITICS

Sociologists have long debated the issue of how power is distributed in the United States. Power is one of the most difficult topics of scientific research because decision making is complex and often occurs behind closed doors. Moreover, as Plato recognized more than two thousand years ago, theories about power are inextricably bound up with the beliefs and interests of social thinkers themselves. From this mix of facts and values, two competing models of power in the United States have emerged.

The Pluralist Model: Structural-Functional Analysis

Formally, the **pluralist model** is *an analysis of politics that views power as dispersed among many competing interest groups.* Pluralists claim, first, that politics is an arena of negotiation. With limited resources, no organization can expect to achieve all its goals. Organizations, therefore, operate as *veto groups* realizing some objectives but mostly keeping opponents from achieving all of their ends. The political process, then, relies heavily on forging alliances and compromises that bridge differences among various interest groups so that policies gain wide support (Dahl, 1961, 1982).

Supporting the pluralists' vision of society, Nelson Polsby (1959) found in a study of New Haven, Connecticut, that key decisions involving urban renewal, selecting political candidates, and running the city's schools were made by different groups. Polsby also noted that few members of the New Haven upper class—high-prestige families listed in that city's *Social Register*—were also economic leaders. Thus, Polsby concluded, no one segment of society rules all the others.

The pluralist model implies that the United States is reasonably democratic, granting at least some power to everyone. Pluralists assert that the most influential individuals do not always get their way, and under this system even the disadvantaged are able to band together

to ensure that some of their political interests are addressed.

The Power-Elite Model: Social-Conflict Analysis

The **power-elite model** is *an analysis of politics that views power as concentrated among the rich.* The term *power elite* is the lasting contribution of C. Wright Mills (1956), who argued that the upper class (described in Chapter 7, "Social Stratification") holds the bulk of society's wealth, prestige, and power. The power elite constitutes this country's "super-rich," families linked through business and marriage who are able to turn the national agenda toward their own interests.

The power elite, claimed Mills, has historically dominated the three major sectors of U.S. society—the economy, the government, and the military. Elites circulate from one sector to another, Mills continued, consolidating power as they go. Alexander Haig, for example, has held top positions in private business, was secretary of state under Ronald Reagan as well as a 1988 presidential candidate, and is a retired army general. Haig is far from the exception: a majority of political leaders enter public life from powerful and highly paid positions in private business—and most return to the corporate world later on (Brownstein & Easton, 1983).

Power-elite theorists blast claims that the United States is a democracy; the concentration of wealth and power, they maintain, is just too great for the average person's voice to be heard. Rejecting pluralist assertions that various centers of power serve as checks and balances on one another, the power-elite model suggests that those at the top encounter no real opposition.

Supporting the power-elite position, Robert and Helen Lynd (1937) studied Muncie, Indiana (which they called "Middletown" to suggest that it was a typical city). They documented the fortune amassed by a single family—the Balls—from their business producing glass canning jars, and showed how the Ball family dominated many dimensions of the city's life. If anyone doubted the Balls' prominence, the Lynds explained, there was no need to look further than a local bank, a university, a hospital, and a department store, which all bear the family's name. In Muncie, according to the Lynds, the power elite more or less boiled down to a single family.

Critical evaluation. While these two models of power, summarized in Table 11–4, paint quite different pictures

Table 11–4 THE PLURALIST AND POWER-ELITE MODELS: A COMPARISON

	Pluralist Model	Power-Elite Model
How is power distributed in the United States?	Highly dispersed.	Highly concentrated.
How many centers of power are there?	Many, each with a limited scope.	Few, with power that extends to many areas.
How do centers of power relate to one another?	They represent different political interests and thus provide checks on one another.	They represent the same political interests and face little opposition.
What is the relation between power and the system of social stratification?	Some people have more power than others, but even minority groups can organize to gain power. Wealth, social prestige, and political office rarely overlap.	Most people have little power, and the upper class dominates society. Wealth, social prestige, and political office commonly overlap.
How important is voting?	Voting provides the public as a whole with a political voice.	Voting cannot promote significant political change.
What, then, is the most accurate description of the U.S. political system?	A pluralist democracy.	An oligarchy—rule by the wealthy few.

of U.S. politics, some evidence supports each interpretation. Reviewing all the research on this issue, we find greater support for the power-elite model. Even Robert Dahl (1982)—one of the stalwart supporters of the concept of pluralism—concedes that the marked concentration of wealth, as well as the barriers to equal opportunity faced by minorities, constitute basic flaws in our nation's quest for a truly pluralist democracy.

Does this mean that the pluralist model is entirely wrong? No, but it does suggest that our political system is not as democratic as most people think it is. The universal right to vote is a pluralist achievement; yet major candidates usually support only those positions acceptable to the most powerful segments of society (Bachrach & Baratz, 1970).

POWER BEYOND THE RULES

Politics is always a matter of disagreement about a society's goals and the means to achieve them. Yet a political system tries to resolve controversy within a system of rules. The foundation of the U.S. political system is the Constitution and its twenty-six amendments. Countless other regulations guide each political official from the president to the county tax assessor. But political activity sometimes exceeds—or tries to do away with—established practices.

Political Revolution

Political revolution is *the overthrow of one political system in order to establish another.* In contrast to reform, which involves change *within* a system, revolution implies change *of the system itself.* The extreme case of reform is the overthrow of one leader by another—a *coup d'état* (in French, literally "stroke concerning the state")—which involves only change at the top. Reform may also spark conflict, but it rarely escalates into violence. Revolution, by contrast, often generates widespread violence. The 1989 pro-democracy reform movement in China was brutally put down by the government; although the revolution throughout Eastern Europe was successful, it was violent in some countries (notably Romania), resulting in thousands of deaths.

No political system is immune to revolution; nor does revolution invariably produce any one kind of government. The U.S. Revolution transformed colonial rule by the British monarchy into democratic government. French revolutionaries in 1789 also overthrew a monarch, only to set the stage for the return of monarchy in the person of Napoleon. In 1917, the Russian Revolution replaced monarchy with a socialist government built on the ideas of Karl Marx. In 1992, the Soviet Union formally came to an end, as revolutionary change propelled the new Commonwealth toward political democracy and a market system.

Despite their striking variety, claim analysts, revolutions share a number of traits (Tocqueville, 1955, orig. 1856; Davies, 1962; Brinton, 1965; Skocpol, 1979; Lewis, 1984).

1. **Rising expectations.** Although common sense suggests that revolution is more likely when people are grossly deprived, history shows that revolutions generally occur when people's lives are improving. Rising expectations, rather than bitter resignation, fuel revolutionary fervor.

2. **Unresponsive government.** Revolutionary zeal gains strength to the extent that a government is unable or unwilling to reform, especially when such demands are made by powerful segments of society (Tilly, 1986).

3. **Radical leadership by intellectuals.** The English philosopher Thomas Hobbes (1588–1679) observed that rebellion is often centered at the universities. Students played a key role in China's recent pro-democracy movement, as they did in Eastern Europe. Intellectuals also articulate principles in support of revolution.

4. **Establishing a new legitimacy.** The overthrow of a political system rarely comes easily, but more difficult still is ensuring a revolution's long-term success. Some revolutionary movements are unified merely by hatred of the past regime, and may fall victim to internal division once new leaders are installed. Revolutionaries must also guard against counter-revolutionary drives led by past leaders. This explains the speed and ruthlessness with which victorious revolutionaries typically dispose of their predecessors.

Scientific research cannot pronounce the effects of revolution as good or bad; the full consequences of such upheaval depend on one's values and, in any case, become evident only after many years. In hindsight, we can see that revolutions have propelled many nations—including the United States—to world prominence. In the wake of recent revolution, the future of the Commonwealth of Independent States and the nations of Eastern Europe remains unsettled.

Terrorism

The 1980s was a decade of heightened concern over **terrorism,** *violence or the threat of violence employed by an individual or group as a political strategy.* Like revolution, terrorism is a political act beyond the rules of established political systems. Paul Johnson (1981) offers three insights about terrorism.

First, terrorism tries to paint violence as a legitimate political tactic, ignoring the fact that such acts are condemned by virtually every society. Terrorists also bypass (or are excluded from) established channels of political negotiation. Terrorism may therefore be used by weaker parties as a way of paralyzing a stronger foe. The people who held U.S. hostages in the Middle East until 1991 may have been morally wrong to do so, but they succeeded in directing the world's attention to that region of the globe.

Second, terrorism is not only a tactic employed by groups, it is also a strategy used by governments against their own people. *State terrorism* occurs when a government uses violence, usually without support of law, against individuals or groups. While contrary to democratic political principles, state terrorism may be enshrined in law in authoritarian and totalitarian governments, which survive by inciting fear and intimidation. The left-wing Stalinist regime in the former Soviet Union and the right-wing Nazi regime in Germany each incorporated widespread terror. More recently, Saddam Hussein has built his government on the use of terror to suppress those who oppose him.

Third, although democratic systems reject state terrorism, such societies are vulnerable to terrorism by individuals because these governments afford extensive civil liberties to their people and have minimal police networks. In striking contrast, totalitarian regimes make widespread use of state terrorism, yet their extensive police networks minimize opportunities for individual acts of terror.

For all but nine months of the 1980s, terrorists held U.S. citizens hostage somewhere in the world. Hostage-taking and outright killing provoke widespread anger, but devising an effective response to such acts poses several thorny problems. The immediate concern is identifying those responsible. Because terrorist groups are often shadowy organizations with no formal connection to any established state, targeting reprisals may be impossible. Yet, terrorism expert Brian Jenkins warns, the failure to respond "encourages other terrorist groups, who begin to realize that this can be a pretty cheap way to wage war on the United States" (cited in Whitaker, 1985:29). Then, too, a forcible military reaction to terrorism may broaden the scope of violence, increasing the risk of confrontation with other governments.

Finally, terrorism is always a matter of definitions. Governments claim the right to maintain order, even by force, and may brand opponents who use violence as "terrorists." Similarly, political differences may explain why one person's "terrorist" may be another's "freedom fighter."

WAR AND PEACE

Perhaps the most critical political issue is **war,** *armed conflict among the people of various societies, directed by their governments.* While war is as old as humanity, understanding it now takes on greater urgency. Because we now possess the technological capacity to destroy ourselves, war poses unprecedented danger to the entire planet. Most scholarly investigation of war has the aim of promoting **peace,** which is *the absence of war,* but not necessarily the end of all conflict.

Many people think of war as extraordinary, yet global peace is actually quite rare, existing for only brief periods during this century. In our nation's short history, we have participated in ten significant wars, which, as shown in Figure 11–3, resulted in the deaths of more than 1.3 million men and women and caused injury to many times that number (Vinovskis, 1989). Thousands more died in "undeclared wars" and limited military actions, in countries from the Dominican Republic to Lebanon, Grenada, and Panama.

Causes of War

The frequency of war in human affairs might suggest that there is something "natural" about armed confrontations. But while many animals are naturally aggressive (Lorenz, 1966), research provides no evidence that human beings inevitably go to war under any particular circumstances. As Ashley Montagu (1976) observes, governments around the world must resort to considerable coercion in order to mobilize their people for wars.

Like other forms of social behavior, warfare is a product of society that varies in purpose and intensity from culture to culture. The Semai of Malaysia, among the most peace-loving of the world's peoples, rarely resort to violence. In contrast, the Yąnomamö, described at

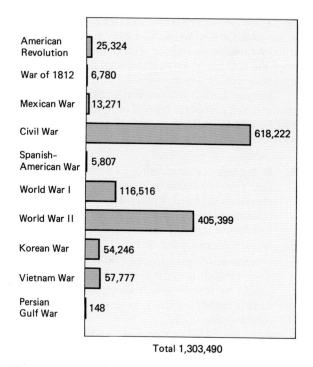

Figure 11–3 Deaths of U.S. Military Personnel in Ten U.S. Wars
(Compiled from various sources by Maris A. Vinovskis, 1989:37)

the beginning of Chapter 2 ("Culture"), are quick to wage war with others.

If society holds the key to war or peace, under what circumstances *do* humans engage in warfare? Quincy Wright (1987) cites five factors that promote war.

1. **Perceived threats.** Societies mobilize in response to a perceived threat to their people, territory, or culture. The likelihood of armed conflict with the former Soviet Union, for example, has subsided to the extent that our nation now defines that country as more friendly to us.

2. **Social problems.** Internal problems that cause widespread frustration prompt a society's leaders to become aggressive toward others. In this way, enemies are created as a form of scapegoating. The lack of economic development in the People's Republic of China, for example, sparked that nation's hostility toward Vietnam, Tibet, and the former Soviet Union.

3. **Political objectives.** Leaders sometimes settle on war as a desirable political strategy. Poor societies, such as Vietnam, have fought wars to end foreign domination. Powerful societies like the United States may employ a periodic "show of force" (toward, say, Iraq) to win concessions from opponents (Patchen, 1987).

4. **Moral objectives.** Nations rarely claim to fight simply to increase their wealth and power. They infuse military campaigns with moral urgency, rallying around visions of "freedom" or the "fatherland." Although few doubted that the Persian Gulf War was largely about *oil*, the United States portrayed the mission as a drive to halt a Hitler-like Saddam Hussein.

5. **The absence of alternatives.** A fifth factor promoting war is the lack of alternatives. Article 1 of the United Nations charter defines that global organization's goal as "maintaining international peace." Despite some notable successes, however, its ability to resolve tensions among self-interested societies has been limited.

Militarism and the Arms Race

The costs of warfare extend far beyond battlefield casualties and military hardware. Together, the world's nations spend more than $5 billion annually on militarism. While such expenditures, at least in part, may be justified, they divert resources from the desperate struggle for survival by millions of poor people throughout the world (see Chapter 8, "Global Inequality"). Assuming the will and the political wisdom of doing so, there is little doubt that the resources currently spent on militarism could be used to eradicate global poverty. A large share of the world's top scientists also direct their talents toward military research; this resource, too, is siphoned away from other work that might benefit humanity.

Defense has long been the largest single expenditure by the U.S. government. In 1990, military spending, about 25 percent of all expenditures, totaled $328 billion, or $1,300 for every man, woman, and child in the country. The historical reason for such high expenditures has been the *arms race*, a mutually reinforcing escalation of military power, between the United States and the former Soviet Union. By 1949, both the U.S. and the U.S.S.R. had nuclear arsenals, and both nations were convinced that they had to meet or exceed the other's nuclear threat. Ironically, for the next forty years, both sides pursued a policy of escalating military expenditures that neither nation wanted nor could afford.

To some analysts, this country is dominated by a **military-industrial complex,** *the close association between government, the military, and defense industries.* From this point of view, the U.S. economy has become so dependent on military spending as a source of jobs and corporate profits that large cuts in the current budget are unlikely (Marullo, 1987). Primarily in response to the dissolution of the Soviet Union, leaders are now calling for significant reductions in military spending during the 1990s. How deep these cuts will be—given the continuing need to maintain national security and the economic pressure by some special-interest groups to keep military spending high—will remain a pressing issue for some time to come.

Nuclear Weapons and War

The world now contains an estimated fifty thousand nuclear weapons, representing a destructive power equivalent to five tons of TNT for every person on the planet. Should even a small fraction of this arsenal be consumed in war, life as we know it might cease on much of the earth. Albert Einstein, whose genius contributed to the development of nuclear weapons, reflected: "The unleashed power of the atom has changed everything *save our modes of thinking,* and we thus drift toward unparalleled catastrophe." In short, nuclear weapons have rendered unrestrained war unthinkable in a world not yet capable of peace.

At present, the vast majority of nuclear weapons are held by the United States and the Commonwealth of Independent States. Great Britain, France, and the People's Republic of China also have a substantial nuclear capability. Even as the superpower rivalry has diminished, the danger of catastrophic war has increased along with *nuclear proliferation,* the acquisition of nuclear weapons by more and more societies. Most experts agree that Israel, India, Pakistan, and South Africa already possess some nuclear weapons, and other nations (including Argentina, Brazil, Iraq, Libya, and North Korea) are in the process of developing them. By the end of this decade, as many as fifty nations could have the ability to fight a nuclear war. Because many of these countries have longstanding conflicts with their neighbors, nuclear proliferation places the entire world at risk (Spector, 1988).

Social Diversity and the Military

Debate about our country's military does not focus solely on halting nuclear proliferation or curbing the arms race. A current national debate surrounds barriers that limit opportunity in the military for women and formally exclude gay people.

Military women. Women have been part of this country's armed forces since the Revolutionary War, even before the United States became an independent nation. Today, about 12 percent of all military personnel are women. In the 1991 war in the Persian Gulf, 35,000 women represented 6.5 percent of a total deployment of 540,000 U.S. troops. Five of the 148 Gulf War casualties were women.

Gender lies at the core of the historical underrepresentation of women in the military. Figure 11–4 shows that the extent of gender-based exclusion varies by branch of the service: while all jobs in the Coast Guard are open to women, only 20 percent of positions in the Marine Corps are made available to women.

The most widespread gender-based prohibition involves women in combat roles. Defenders of this policy argue that, on average, women lack the physical strength of men. Critics respond that military women are better educated and score higher on intelligence tests than their

male counterparts. The heart of the issue, however, turns on our society's deeply held view of women as *nurturers*—people who give life and help others. This way of thinking clashes intolerably with the image of women as professional killers.

Still, women are moving into more and more military assignments. One reason is legal change. In 1991, for example, Congress acted to allow (but not require) women to operate combat aircraft in all branches of the armed forces. More broadly, the technology of war has undermined traditional distinctions between combat and noncombat personnel. A combat pilot often fires missiles at a radar-screen target miles away; nonfighting medical evacuation teams often enter the immediate heat of battle (Moskos, 1985; Stiehm, 1989; May, 1991; McNeil, Jr., 1991).

Charges that military women have been sexually harassed and even assaulted by their male colleagues have deepened the debate over the role of women in the military. Commanding officers have acknowledged the need to rethink attitudes—and also revise policy—that affect military women and men.

Gays and the military. At present (1993), all military services formally bar homosexual men and women, although President Clinton is acting to end this exclusion. Tens of thousands of gay people have served their country in the military and continue to do so today, but even suspicion of a homosexual orientation can result in summary discharge. Roughly one thousand men and women are being expelled annually from the armed forces because of their sexual orientation.

Supporters of the status quo cite several reasons for this policy. First, soldiers live in close quarters with minimal privacy; the presence of homosexuals, the argument goes, puts discipline at risk and may undercut the military's morale and effectiveness. Second, officials worry that soldiers exposed as gay might be blackmailed into compromising military security. More recently, the danger of spreading the virus that causes AIDS has been added to the list.

As in the case of military women, policies relating to gays have more to do with traditional stereotypes than facts. Studies conducted by the military document that gay people have commendable performance records. Furthermore, gay people have rights to civilian jobs that are far more sensitive than those of rank-and-file soldiers.

Although change in this area has been slow, the exclusion of gay men and women from the military will probably end. Already a majority of the U.S. popula-

Figure 11–4 Gender Exclusion in the Armed Forces
(*U.S. Department of Defense, 1991*)

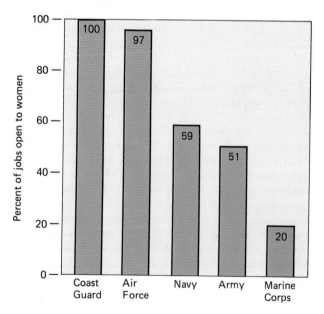

tion expresses disapproval of the current policy. And the policy is under attack more and more in the courts (Berube, 1990; Miller, 1991).

Prospects for Peace: Looking Ahead

Finally, how can the world reduce the dangers of war? We can briefly sketch several approaches to promoting peace.

1. **Maintaining the status quo.** The logic of the arms race holds that security derives from a balance of terror between the superpowers. Thus a principle of *mutually assured destruction* (MAD) demands that either side launching a first strike against the other sustain massive retaliation. This deterrence policy has kept the peace for forty years; yet it has encouraged the arms race and it cannot control nuclear proliferation, which poses a growing threat to peace.

2. **High-technology defense.** If technology created the weapons, perhaps it can also deliver us from the threat of war. This is the idea behind the *strategic defense initiative* (SDI), proposed by the Reagan administration a decade ago. SDI is a complex plan for satellites and ground installations to provide a protective shield or umbrella against enemy attack. Missiles would be detected soon after launch and destroyed by lasers and particle beams before re-entering the atmosphere. If perfected, advocates argue, the "star wars" defense would render nuclear weapons obsolete.

   Many analysts claim that, even after years and trillions of dollars, this program would produce at best a leaky umbrella. The collapse of the Soviet Union also calls into question the need for such an extensive—and expensive—defense scheme.

3. **Diplomacy and disarmament.** Perhaps the best approach to peace involves diplomacy rather than technology (Dedrick & Yinger, 1990). Diplomacy has the appeal of achieving security through reducing rather than increasing weapons stockpiles. But disarmament has its own dangers. No nation wishes to become vulnerable by reducing its defenses. Successful diplomacy, then, depends not on "soft" concession-making, or "hard" demands, but on everyone involved sharing responsibility for a common problem and working together to forge a solution (Fisher & Ury, 1988). The rising costs of the arms race, the pressing domestic social prob-

The tragic civil war in the former Yugoslavia is pointed evidence of the power of ethnic passion and religious fervor to fuel hatred and violence. This conflict also reveals that the world has yet to devise a system to resolve disputes of this kind without bloodshed.

lems of the United States and Russia, and their warming relations in recent years, offer hope for some disarmament during the 1990s.

4. **Resolving underlying conflict.** In the end, reducing the dangers of war may depend on resolving the issues that have fueled the arms race. Even in the "post–cold war" world, basic political differences between the United States and Commonwealth of Independent States will remain. Militarism also springs from regional conflicts in Latin America, Africa, Asia, and the Middle East. Why, then, does the world spend three thousand times as much money on militarism as it does on peace-keeping (Sivard, 1988)?

The danger of war remains great. We see vast stockpiles of weapons scattered around the world, a proliferation of nuclear technology, and a powerful military establishment at home. Forces working for peace also marshall great resources and the power of imagination: organizations such as the United Nations are promoting world stability, we see international cooperation in expanding trade worldwide, and the end of the cold war has lessened the threat of nuclear annihilation. Most crucial is the growing realization that the aspirations of billions of people for a better life depend on a nonviolent solution to the age-old problem of war.

SUMMARY

Economics

1. The economy is the institutional means by which a society produces, distributes, and consumes goods and services.
2. Industrialization expanded the economy with new sources of energy, specialization, and mass production. The postindustrial economy shifts production from goods to services.
3. The primary sector of the economy, generating raw materials, dominates in preindustrial societies. The secondary manufacturing sector prevails in industrial societies. The tertiary service sector has the greatest importance in postindustrial societies.
4. Capitalism is based on private ownership of productive property and the pursuit of profit in a competitive marketplace. Socialism is grounded in collective ownership of productive property with the goal of communal well-being through government control of the economy.
5. Capitalism is highly productive, providing a high overall standard of living; socialist economies are less productive but yield more economic equality.
6. Only a small percentage of U.S. workers are in agricultural jobs; just one-fourth remain in blue-collar work; two-thirds have white-collar service jobs.
7. A profession is a special category of white-collar work based on theoretical knowledge, occupational autonomy, and authority over clients, with an emphasis on community service.
8. About 7 percent of U.S. workers are unemployed, with young people and minorities most likely to be without jobs.
9. The workplace is becoming more socially diverse as women and people of color make up a rising share of all workers.
10. Corporations are the core of the U.S. economy. The largest corporations, which are conglomerates, account for most corporate assets and profits. Most large corporations are multinational in scope, with controversial effects for poorer nations in which they operate.

Politics

1. Politics is the institutional organization of societal power. Legitimate, rather than coercive, power is based in tradition, rationally enacted rules and regulations, and a leader's charisma.
2. Monarchy, based on traditional authority, is common to preindustrial societies. Although constitutional monarchies persist in some industrial nations, industrialization favors democracy.
3. Authoritarian political systems deny popular participation in government. Totalitarian political systems go even further, controlling people's everyday lives.
4. The political spectrum—from extreme liberalism on the left to extreme conservatism on the right—involves both economic and social issues. The former concerns the degree of government regulation of the economy; the latter involves moral questions about the rights and opportunities of all segments of the population.
5. Special-interest groups advance the political aims of specific segments of the population. These groups make use of lobbyists and political action committees to raise money to fund campaigns.
6. Most adults in the United States express a weak affiliation with the Republican or Democratic Party. Only about half of those eligible actually vote.
7. The pluralist model views political power as widely dispersed; the power-elite model claims that political power is concentrated in a small, wealthy segment of our society.
8. Political revolution radically transforms a political system. Terrorism, another unconventional political tactic, employs violence in pursuit of some goal. States as well as individuals engage in terrorism.
9. War is armed conflict between governments. The development of nuclear weapons, and their proliferation, has increased the threat of global catastrophe. Enhancing world peace ultimately depends on resolving the tensions that underlie militarism.

KEY CONCEPTS

Economics

capitalism an economic system in which natural resources and the means of producing goods and services are privately owned

communism a hypothetical economic and political system in which all people have social equality

corporation an organization with a legal existence, including rights and liabilities, apart from those of its members

democratic socialism a political and economic system that combines significant government control of the economy with free elections

economy the institutionalized system for production, distribution, and consumption of goods and services

labor unions organizations of workers seeking to improve wages and working conditions through various strategies, including negotiations and strikes

monopoly domination of a market by a single producer

oligopoly domination of a market by a few producers

postindustrial economy economic activity based on service work and high technology

primary sector part of the economy that generates raw materials directly from the natural environment

profession a prestigious, white-collar occupation that requires extensive formal education

secondary sector part of the economy that transforms raw materials into manufactured goods

social institution an organized sphere of social life such as the economy or the family

socialism an economic system in which natural resources and the means of producing goods and services are collectively owned

tertiary sector part of the economy involving services rather than goods

Politics

authoritarianism a political system that denies popular participation in government

authority power that is widely perceived as legitimate rather than coercive

charismatic authority power legitimized through extraordinary personal abilities that inspire devotion and obedience

democracy a political system in which power is exercised by the people as a whole

government a formal organization that directs the political life of a society

military-industrial complex the close association between the government, the military, and defense industries

monarchy a political system in which the power to rule is passed from generation to generation within a single family

peace the absence of war

pluralist model an analysis of politics that views power as dispersed among many competing interest groups

political action committee (PAC) an organization formed by a special-interest group, independent of political parties, to pursue political aims by raising and spending money

political revolution the overthrow of one political system in order to establish another

politics the institutionalized system by which a society distributes power and makes decisions

power the ability to achieve desired ends despite opposition

power-elite model an analysis of politics that views power as concentrated among the rich

rational-legal authority (bureaucratic authority) power legitimized by legally enacted rules and regulations

routinization of charisma the transformation of charismatic authority into some combination of traditional and bureaucratic authority

special-interest group a political alliance of people with an interest in a particular economic or social issue

terrorism violence or the threat of violence by an individual or a group as a political strategy

totalitarianism a highly centralized political system that extensively regulates people's lives

traditional authority power that is legitimized through respect for long-established cultural patterns

war armed conflict among the people of various societies, directed by their governments

12

Family and Religion

Verna Terry thought she had found the perfect apartment. But what started out as a simple matter of finding a place to live turned into a complicated legal tangle when John and Agnes Donahue, who own and reside on the Los Angeles property, discovered that Ms. Terry intended to live there with a man to whom she was not married. The Donahues, a very religious couple, are opposed to sex before marriage. To them, renting the property to Verna Terry meant helping someone commit the sin of fornication, an immoral situation for all concerned. Terry, on the other hand, felt she had been the victim of housing discrimination and filed suit.[1]

This case, which is currently winding its way through the court system, illustrates the controversy that surrounds the changing definition of families in the United States. We can see, too, how the current "family values" debate pits the issue of individual rights against the demands of religious doctrine.

This chapter examines the family and religion, which are closely linked as society's prominent *symbolic institutions*. Through both family and religious life, we establish morality, maintain traditions, and bond into durable social units. Not surprisingly, change in these institutions is sparking spirited disagreement. Not long ago, the cultural ideal in the United States was a family made up of a working father, a homemaker mother, and their young children; today, fewer people embrace such a singular vision of the family, and at any given time only about one in ten U.S. households fits that description. Similar changes have shaken the foundations of religion in the United States. Membership in most long-established churches is dwindling, while many new sects are flourishing.

The focus here is primarily on the United States and includes comparisons with other world societies. We will examine why, to some people, the family and religion are bedrock foundations of social life, while others predict—sometimes with faintly disguised approval—the demise of both institutions.

THE FAMILY: BASIC CONCEPTS

Kinship refers to *social relationships based on blood, marriage, or adoption*. We call our kin "relatives," suggesting that many of our social roles are performed *relative*

---

[1] This account is based on Niebuhr (1992).

to them. Especially in small preindustrial societies, people look to their kin to meet most everyday needs including food, shelter, and protection. The functional significance of kinship declines in industrial societies, as secondary ties play a greater role in everyday life.

Who falls within the family varies from place to place and over time. Generally, we can define the **family** as *a relatively permanent group of two or more people, who are related by blood, marriage, or adoption, and who usually live together*. In most societies, families are formed by **marriage,** *a legally sanctioned relationship involving economic cooperation, as well as normative sexual activity and childbearing, that people expect to be enduring*. Language offers a clue to understanding our cultural belief that marriage alone is the appropriate setting for procreation: traditionally, people have attached the label of "illegitimacy" to children born out of wedlock, and "matrimony," in Latin, means "the condition of motherhood." The link between childbearing and marriage has weakened, however, as the share of children born to single women (currently about one in four) has increased.

Yet few generalizations apply to every family, even in the United States. As suggested at the beginning of this chapter, some people object to applying the term "family" to an unmarried couple living together, or to gay couples or single parents and their children. But more people now think of kinship as *families of affinity*, that is, people with or without legal or blood ties who feel they belong together and want to define themselves as a family. What does or does not constitute a family, then, is the central issue in the current "family values" debate. The trend, in public opinion as well as in court decisions, is toward a wider and more inclusive definition of "family."

THE FAMILY: GLOBAL VARIATIONS

All societies contain families, although the precise nature of those family arrangements is a matter of cultural variation (Murdock, 1945). In one general pattern, preindustrial societies attach great importance to the **extended family,** *a social unit including parents, children, and other kin*. This is also called the *consanguine family*, meaning that it includes everyone with "shared blood." The onset of industrialization, a process detailed in Chapter 11 ("Economics and Politics"), gives rise to the **nuclear**

In modern industrial societies, the members of extended families usually live apart from one another. However, they may assemble for rituals such as weddings, funerals, and family reunions.

family, *a social unit containing one or, more commonly, two adults and any children*. Typically based on marriage, the nuclear family is also called the *conjugal family*. Although many members of our society live in extended families, the nuclear family has become the predominant form in the United States (Laslett, 1978; Degler, 1980).

Industrialization weakens extended families by moving productive work away from the home so that children grow up and leave home to pursue their careers (or as social scientists sometimes say, they leave their "family of orientation" to form a new "family of procreation"). Increasing geographical and social mobility both tug at kinship ties, distancing members of extended families from one another.

If this tells us something about the past, what about the future? Sweden is a progressive society that may point up some likely trends. Sociologist David Popenoe, who examined the state of the Swedish family, explains in the box on pages 292–93 that this nation may have the weakest families in the world.

Marriage Patterns

Cultural norms, and often laws, distinguish people suitable as marriage partners from those that are not. Some of these norms promote **endogamy**, *marriage between people of the same category*. Endogamy norms constrain marriage prospects to others of the same age, village, race, religion, or social class. Other norms encourage **exogamy**, *marriage between people of different categories*. In rural India, for example, people expect a person to marry someone from the same caste category but from a different village. In most of the world, societies pressure people to marry someone of the same social background but of the other sex.

In every industrial society, laws prescribe a form of marriage called **monogamy** (from the Greek meaning "one union"), *marriage involving two partners*. Global Map 12–1 on page 294 shows that while monogamy is the rule throughout the Americas and in Europe, many preindustrial societies—especially in Africa and southern Asia—permit **polygamy** (from Greek meaning "many unions"), *marriage that unites three or more people*. Polygamy takes two forms. By far the more common is *polygyny* (Greek meaning "many women" or "many wives"), a form of marriage that joins one male with more than one female. Islamic societies in the Middle East and Africa, for example, permit men up to four wives. In these societies, however, most families are monogamous all the same because few men have the wealth required to support several wives and even more children. *Polyandry* (from the Greek, meaning "many men" or "many husbands") unites one female with more than one male. This pattern appears only rarely; one example is among Tibetan Buddhists. In places where agriculture is difficult, polyandry discourages the division of land into parcels too small to support a family. It also functions to share the costs of supporting a wife among many men. Polyandry has also been linked to female infanticide—the abortion of female fetuses or the killing of female infants—so that the female population falls, forcing men to share women.

Looking at the issue historically and comparatively, we see that the majority of world societies have permitted more than one marital pattern. Even so, most marriages have been monogamous (Murdock, 1965). This predominance of monogamy reflects two key facts of life: first, the financial burden of supporting multiple spouses weighs heavily, and second, the rough numerical parity of the sexes limits the possibility for polygamy.

Sweden: The Weakest Families on Earth?

Sweden, one of the Scandinavian countries of northern Europe, has a proud record of avoiding many social problems that plague the United States. Violent crime is rare in Swedish cities, and the nightmare of drug abuse hardly touches the lives of Swedes. There is also little evidence of the grinding poverty that has blighted regions of our own cities. On the face of it, Sweden seems to fulfill the promise of the modern welfare state, with an extensive and professional government bureaucracy that sees to virtually all human needs.

According to David Popenoe, however, Sweden has another distinction: it has what are arguably the weakest families on earth. For one thing, the Swedes are less likely to marry than members of any other industrialized society; the country also has the highest share of adults living alone (20 percent versus about 12 percent in the United States). For another, a larger proportion of couples live together outside of marriage than anywhere else (25 percent versus about 3 percent in the United States), and half of all Swedish children (compared to one in four in the United States) are born to unmarried parents. Average household size is also the smallest in the world (2.2 persons versus 2.6 in the United States). Finally, Swedish families (based on marriage or consensual union) are more likely to dissolve than those elsewhere. Reviewing the evidence, Popenoe concludes that the family

has probably become weaker in Sweden than anywhere else—certainly among advanced Western nations. Individual family members are the most autonomous and least bound by the group, and the group as a whole is least cohesive. (1991:69)

The erosion of the Swedish family began in the 1960s, the product of several trends also at work in the United States. Popenoe claims that a growing culture of individualism and self-fulfillment, coupled with the declining influence of religion, set the stage for the weakening of Swedish families. In addition, Sweden has the lowest proportion of women who are full-time housewives (10 percent versus about 25 percent in the United States) and the highest percentage of women in the labor force (77 percent versus 57 percent in the United States). But underlying all these changes, Popenoe contends, is the expansion of the welfare state.

Government programs meet various human needs in every industrial society. Sweden, however, has enshrined in law the most far-reaching scheme of its kind. All Swedes are issued a national registration number at birth, and their citizenship entitles them to a lifetime of services—and high taxes. For example, they can

Residential Patterns

Just as societies regulate mate selection, so they designate where a couple resides. In preindustrial societies, most newlyweds live with one set of parents, gaining economic security and protection in the process. Most world societies have adopted *patrilocality* (Greek for "place of the father"), which guides a married couple to live with or near the husband's family (Murdock, 1965). But some societies endorse *matrilocality*, so that couples live with or near the wife's family. Which pattern exists often corresponds to warfare (warlike societies favor keeping married sons at home) and whether a society views sons or daughters as the greater economic asset (Ember & Ember, 1971, 1991).

Industrial societies show yet another pattern. When finances permit, at least, they favor *neolocality* (Greek meaning "new place"), by which a married couple lives apart from the parents of both spouses.

Patterns of Descent

Descent refers to *the system by which members of a society trace kinship over generations.* Most preindustrial societies trace kinship through only one side of the family —the father or the mother. The more prevalent pattern is *patrilineal descent*, meaning people trace their relations through males and pass property from fathers to sons. Patrilineal descent generally characterizes pastoral and

count on the government to give them jobs, to sustain their income, to deliver and educate their children, to provide health care, and, when the time comes, to pay for their funeral.

Many Swedes supported the creation of this vast welfare apparatus in the 1960s, Popenoe explains, as a means of *strengthening* families. But with the benefit of hindsight, he concludes, proliferating government programs have more accurately been *replacing* families. In other words, Swedish families are less an economic unit and more a cluster of individuals who look to the government for financial security.

Put differently, Swedish government policies effectively discourage families from looking out for their own. If a person does not want to tend to an aging parent in the home, the government will do it at a community facility—at no direct cost to that individual. Government child-care centers stand open to all working parents, but no subsidy is provided for those who wish to care for their children at home.

During the last several generations, then, Swedes have relaxed their family ties as they have become more dependent on their government. But if this system has apparently solved so many social problems, why should anyone be concerned about the erosion of family life? For two reasons, says Popenoe. First, government programs that replace the family are becoming astronomically expensive. Already a majority of Swedes have decided that their country must cut back on government programs because of skyrocketing costs. The second reason involves children. Government programs have lifted from adults much of the personal and financial responsibility for raising the young. But can competent professionals in large child-care centers provide children with the security and love possible in a family setting? It may turn out that small, intimate groups can accomplish some human tasks much better than formal organizations can.

Popenoe clearly thinks the Swedes have gone too far in delegating family responsibilities to government. But he also cautions that we in the United States—where the welfare state is least developed of all industrial societies—may not have gone far enough. Programs allowing time off from the workplace for new parents are a case in point. A Swedish parent can apply for up to eighteen months' work leave at 90 percent of salary; by early 1993, the United States still had no national program of this kind. In the end, the most effective way to meet human needs may turn out to be a thoughtful *partnership* between government and families themselves.

SOURCES: Popenoe (1991); also Herrstrom (1990).

---

agrarian societies, in which men produce the most valued resources. Less common is *matrilineal descent*, by which people define only the mother's side as kin, and daughters inherit property from mothers. Matrilineal descent is found more frequently in horticultural societies where women are the primary breadwinners (Haviland, 1985).

Industrial societies such as our own recognize *bilateral descent* ("two-sided descent"), and trace kinship through both men and women. In this pattern, children count among their relatives the families of both parents.

Patterns of Authority

The predominance of polygyny, patrilocality, and patrilineal descent in the world reflects the universal presence of patriarchy. Without denying that wives and mothers exercise considerable power in every society, as Chapter 10 ("Sex and Gender") explained, no truly matriarchal society is known to have existed. The universal pattern of patriarchy means that, to a greater or lesser extent, societies accord more wealth, power, and prestige to men than to women. In industrial societies like the United States, men usually head households, just as they dominate most areas of social life. More egalitarian family patterns are gradually evolving, especially as increasing numbers of women enter the labor force. However, the social power of wives remains lower than that of husbands. Parents in the United States also still prefer boys to girls, and typically give children their father's last name.

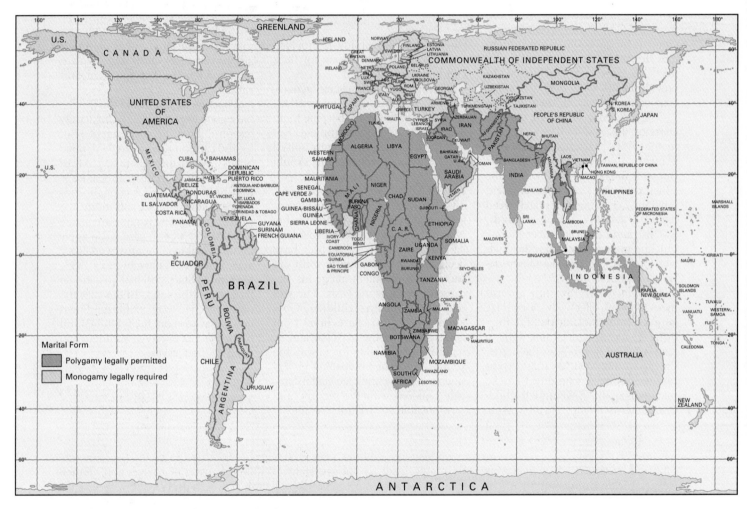

Global Map 12–1 Marital Form in Global Perspective

Monogamy is the legally required form of marriage in all industrial societies, and throughout the Western Hemisphere. In most African nations, as well as in southern Asia, however, polygamy is permitted by law. In the majority of cases, this reflects the historic influence of Islam, a religion that allows a man to have no more than four wives. Even so, most marriages in these societies are also monogamous.

THEORETICAL ANALYSIS OF THE FAMILY

As in earlier chapters, we draw on various theoretical approaches to provide useful insights into the family.

Functions of the Family: Structural-Functional Analysis

The structural-functional paradigm holds that the family performs several of society's basic tasks. This explains why we sometimes think of the family as "the backbone of society."

1. **Socialization.** As explained in Chapter 3 ("Socialization: From Infancy to Old Age"), the family is the first and most influential setting for socialization. In ideal terms, parents help their children learn to be well-integrated and contributing members of society (Parsons & Bales, 1955). Of course, family socialization continues throughout the life cycle. Adults change within marriage and, as any parent knows, mothers and fathers learn as much from their children as their children learn from them.

2. **Regulation of sexual activity.** Every culture regulates sexual activity because human reproduction is central to kinship organization and property rights. One universal regulation is the **incest taboo,** *a norm forbidding sexual relations or marriage between certain kin.* Precisely which kin fall within the incest taboo varies from one culture to another. The matrilineal Navajo, for example, forbid marrying any relative of one's mother. Our bilateral society applies the incest taboo to both sides of the family but limits it to close relatives, including parents, grandparents, siblings, aunts, and uncles. But even brother-sister marriages found approval among the ancient Egyptian, Incan, and Hawaiian nobility (Murdock, 1965).

    Reproduction between close relatives can adversely affect the mental and physical health of offspring. But this fact does not explain why, among all species of life, the incest taboo is observed only by human beings. The key reason to control incest, then, is social. Why? First, the incest taboo minimizes sexual competition within families by restricting legitimate sexuality to spouses. Second, it forces people to marry outside of their immediate families, forging links throughout the society. Third, since kinship defines people's rights and obligations toward each other, forbidding reproduction among close relatives protects kinship from collapsing into chaos.

3. **Social placement.** Of course, families are not biologically necessary for people to have children, but they do provide for the social placement of children. Social identity based on race, ethnicity, religion, and social class is ascribed at birth through the family. This fact explains the longstanding preference for so-called "legitimate" birth. Especially when parents are of similar social position, families clarify inheritance rights and allow for the stable transmission of social standing from parents to children.

The "family resemblance" of Martin and Charlie Sheen means more than sharing physical features. The range of any child's opportunities and interests depends on the social position of his or her parents. As sociologists have discovered, the family actually serves to reproduce the class structure, a fact suggested by the way in which children typically "follow in the footsteps" of the older generation.

4. **Material and emotional security.** The family has long been viewed as a "haven in a heartless world" because kin offer physical protection, emotional support, and financial assistance to "their own." To a greater or lesser extent, most families do all these things, although not without periodic conflict. In this connection, research confirms that people living in families tend to be healthier than those living alone.

Critical evaluation. Structural-functional analysis identifies a number of the family's major functions. From this point of view, it is easy to see that society as we know it could not exist without families.

But this approach rests on a rather narrow conception of family and overlooks the great diversity of U.S. family life. Moreover, the approach pays little attention to how other social institutions (say, government) could meet at least some of the same human needs. Finally, it overlooks the problems of family life. Established family forms support patriarchy, and also incorporate a surprising amount of violence with the dysfunctional effect of undermining individual self-confidence, health, and well-being.

Inequality and the Family: Social-Conflict Analysis

Like the structural-functional approach, the social-conflict paradigm also sees the family as central to the operation of society. But rather than concentrating on ways that this social unit benefits society, conflict theorists investigate how the family perpetuates social inequality. The role of families in the social reproduction of inequality takes several forms.

1. **Property and inheritance.** As noted in Chapter 10 ("Sex and Gender"), Friedrich Engels (1902; orig. 1884) traced the origin of the family to the need to identify heirs so that men (especially in the higher classes) could transmit property to their sons. Families thus support the concentration of wealth and reproduce the class structure in each succeeding generation (Mare, 1991).
2. **Gender.** Engels also emphasized how the family promotes patriarchy. The only way men can know who their heirs are is to control the sexuality of women. Thus, Engels continued, families transform women into the sexual and economic property

of men. A century ago in the United States, wives' earnings typically belonged to their husbands. Although this practice is no longer lawful, other examples of men's power over women remain. Despite moving rapidly into the paid work force, women still bear major responsibility for child rearing and housework (Haas, 1981; Schooler et al., 1984; Fuchs, 1986). Patriarchal families offer considerable benefits to men, but they also deprive men of the chance to share in the personal satisfaction and growth derived from interacting with children.

3. **Race and ethnicity.** Only because of endogamy—people marrying others like themselves—do racial and ethnic categories persist over generations. Thus traditional family life has also served to shore up the racial and ethnic hierarchy in our own society and elsewhere.

Later in this chapter, we will explore how the link between the traditional family and social inequality relates to a number of conflicts and changes, such as violence against women, divorce, and the trend of women choosing to raise their children outside of marriage.

Critical evaluation. Social-conflict analysis reveals another side of family life: its role in maintaining social inequality. During his era, Engels condemned the family as part and parcel of capitalism. Yet societies that have rejected the capitalist economy have families (and family problems) all the same. The family and social inequality are deeply intertwined, as Engels argued, but the family appears to carry out various societal functions that are not easily accomplished by other means.

Micro-Level Analysis

Both structural-functional and social-conflict analyses broadly view the family as a structural system with wide-ranging consequences for our lives. Micro-level approaches differ by exploring how individuals shape and experience family life.

Socially constructing family life. Seen from the inside, families are the setting for ongoing symbolic interaction. Individuals construct family life, and do so variably. Women and men, parents and children—all tend to see family life differently, and no two individuals experience precisely the same reality.

Family life also changes over time. A newlywed couple's initial expectations about their relationship will almost certainly change as they face the daily realities of life together. A new role for a spouse, such as a wife entering law school, alters the lives of all family members. Thus, from a symbolic-interaction point of view, marriage and the family are less rigid patterns than they are ongoing processes.

Family life as exchange. Social-exchange analysis is another micro-level approach that views courtship and marriage as ongoing negotiations (Blau, 1964). While dating, each person assesses the likely advantages and disadvantages of taking another person as a spouse, always with an eye toward what one has to offer in return. In essence, exchange analysts suggest, individuals seek to make the best "deal" they can in selecting a partner.

Physical attractiveness is one critical dimension of exchange. In patriarchal societies around the world, beauty has long been a commodity offered by women on the marriage market. The high value assigned to beauty explains women's traditional concern with physical appearance and their sensitivity about revealing their age. For his part, the man has traditionally been assessed according to the financial resources he commands (Melville, 1983). Now, however, the terms of exchange are converging for men and women because both are in the labor force and women are less dependent on men to support them and their children.

Critical evaluation. Micro-level analysis offers a useful balance to structural-functional and social-conflict visions of the family as an institutional system. Adopting an interactional or exchange viewpoint, we gain a better sense of the individual's experience of family life, and appreciate how people creatively shape this reality for themselves.

Using this approach, however, we run the risk of missing the bigger picture that family life is similar for people affected by any set of economic and cultural forces. That is, U.S. families vary in some predictable ways according to social class and ethnicity, and, as the next section explains, they typically evolve through stages linked to the life course.

STAGES OF FAMILY LIFE

The family shows marked changes over the life course. Members of our society recognize several stages of family life.

Courtship and Romantic Love

Adults in preindustrial societies generally consider courtship too important to be left to the young (Stone, 1977; Haviland, 1985). *Arranged marriages* represent an alliance made by two extended families, a negotiation involving wealth, power, and prestige. Romantic love has little to do with it, and parents may make such arrangements when their children are quite young. A century ago in India, for example, half of all girls married before reaching the age of fifteen (Mayo, 1927; Mace & Mace, 1960).

The Wedding Portrait (1434), by Flemish artist Jan Van Eyck (1390–1441), is a masterpiece of its time. Here we see a young couple solemnly reciting their wedding vows—a statement of the reverence with which people of that age approached marriage. The single candle in the chandelier above their heads symbolizes Christ, and the couple's removal of their shoes indicates that they are engaged in a holy ritual.

Jan Van Eyck, Giovanni Arnolfini and His Bride, 1434. Oil on wood. 33 x 22½". The National Gallery, London.

Industrialization erodes the importance of extended families, weakens traditions, and enhances personal choice in courtship. Young people now expect to choose mates for themselves, and they delay doing so until gaining the experience they need to select a suitable marriage partner. Dating sharpens their skills, and may serve as a period of sexual experimentation as well.

Our culture elevates *romantic love*—the experience of affection and sexual passion toward another person—as the basis for marriage. For us, marriage without love is difficult to imagine, and the mass media—from traditional fairy tales like "Cinderella" to today's paperback romance novels—portray love as the key to a successful marriage. Romantic love also motivates individuals to leave their original families to form new ones. Moreover, because romance is usually intense early in a relationship, it may carry a new couple through difficult adjustments to the realities of living together (Goode, 1959). Yet, because feelings wax and wane, romantic love makes for a less stable foundation for marriage than social and economic considerations—an assertion supported by our society's high divorce rate compared to others that afford people less choice about their partners.

But even in this age of choice, sociologists have long recognized that Cupid's arrow is aimed by society more than we like to think. Most people fall in love with others of the same race, of comparable age, and similar social class. All societies "arrange" marriages to the extent that they encourage **homogamy** (literally, "like marrying like"), *marriage between people with the same social characteristics.*

Settling In: Ideal and Real Marriage

Societies present marriage to the young in idealized, "happily-ever-after" terms. One consequence of such thinking is the danger of disappointment, especially for women—who, more than men, are taught to see in marriage the key to future happiness. Then, too, romantic love involves a good deal of fantasy: we fall in love with others, not necessarily as they are, but as we want them to be (Berscheid & Hatfield, 1983). Only after marriage do many spouses regularly confront each other as they carry out the day-to-day routines of maintaining a household.

Sexuality is one source of disappointment. In the romantic haze of falling in love, people may envision marriage as an endless sexual honeymoon, only to face the sobering realization that sex becomes less than an all-consuming passion. While about two in three married people claim to be satisfied with the sexual dimension of their relationship, marital sex does decline over time, as Table 12–1 shows (Blumstein & Schwartz, 1983).

Many experts agree that couples with the most fulfilling sexual relationships experience the greatest satisfaction in their marriages. This does not mean sex is the key to marital bliss, but rather that good sex and good relationships go together (Hunt, 1974; Tavris & Sadd, 1977; Blumstein & Schwartz, 1983).

Child Rearing

Almost all adults in the United States think that, ideally, a family should contain at least one child, as shown in Table 12–2. Few people desire more than four children, however—a marked change from two centuries ago, when *eight* children was the U.S. average (Newman & Matzke, 1984). Preindustrial families depend on children to provide labor, and having children is widely regarded as a wife's duty. This, coupled with unreliable or nonexistent birth control technology, makes childbearing a regular event. Finally, high infant mortality in such societies prevents many children from reaching adulthood; as late as 1900, about one-third of children in the United States died by age ten (Wall, 1980).

Industrialization transforms children, economically speaking, from a vital asset into a burdensome liability. The expense of raising even one child is well over $100,000, a figure that almost doubles if the child goes to college (*Family Economics Review*, 1989). This helps to explain the steady drop in U.S. family size during this century to about two children per woman today. Other industrial societies exhibit the same pattern: the median number of children is down from 4.5 in

Table 12–1 FREQUENCY OF SEXUAL ACTIVITY AMONG MARRIED COUPLES

Years Together	Sexual Intercourse (times per month)			
	1 or less	1–4	4–12	12 or more
0–2	6%	11%	38%	45%
2–10	6	21	46	27
10 or more	16	22	45	18

SOURCE: Adapted from Philip Blumstein and Pepper Schwartz, *American Couples* (New York: William Morrow, 1983), p. 196.

Table 12–2 THE IDEAL NUMBER OF CHILDREN FOR U.S. ADULTS, 1990

Number of Children	Proportion of Respondents
0	1.1%
1	2.7
2	52.4
3	21.6
4	10.1
5	1.4
6 or more	0.7
As many as you want	6.0
No response	3.9

SOURCE: N.O.R.C., *General Social Surveys, 1972–1991* (Chicago: National Opinion Research Center, 1991), p. 252.

1940 to 1.5 today. Such low rates of childbirth contrast sharply with poor societies in Latin America, Africa, and Asia where women have few alternatives to bearing and raising children. In such societies four to six children is still the norm.

Parenting is not only expensive but a lifetime commitment. As our society has afforded its members more choice about family life, more U.S. adults have opted to delay childbirth or to remain childless. In 1960, almost 90 percent of women between 25 and 29 who had ever married had at least one child; by 1990 this proportion had tumbled to 71 percent (U.S. Bureau of the Census, 1992). One recent survey indicated that about two-thirds of parents in the United States would like to devote far more of their time to child rearing (Snell, 1990). But, unless we are willing to suffer a decline in our material standard of living, economic realities demand that most parents pursue careers outside the home. Thus the child-rearing patterns we have described reflect ways of coming to terms with economic change.

As explained in Chapter 10 ("Sex and Gender"), most women with young children are now working for income. In 1991, 57 percent of all women over fifteen were in the work force; the proportion of women who have children under eighteen and who work for income is now up to 67 percent (U.S. Bureau of the Census, 1992). But while women and men share the burden of earning income, women continue to bear traditional responsibility for raising children and doing housework. Some men in our society are eager parents, yet most resist sharing responsibility for household tasks our cul-

ture historically has defined as "women's work" (Radin, 1982).

Old Age and Family Life

Increasing life expectancy in the United States means that, barring divorce, couples are likely to remain married for a long time. By age fifty to sixty, most parents have completed the task of raising children. The remaining years of marriage—the "empty nest"—bring a return to living with only one's spouse.

The departure of children requires adjustments, although the conjugal relationship often becomes closer and more satisfying (Kalish, 1982). A healthy marriage at this stage of life is generally characterized by companionship. Years of living together may have diminished a couple's sexual passion for each other, but mutual understanding and commitment are likely to have grown.

Contact with children usually continues, and most older adults live within a short distance of at least one of their adult children (Shanas, 1979). People's incomes peak in late middle age, when the expenses of child rearing are behind them. Parenting then may involve helping children make large purchases (a car or a house) and, of course, periodic babysitting of grandchildren.

Retirement brings further change to family life. If the wife has been a homemaker, the husband's retirement means spouses will be spending much more time together. Although the husband's presence may be a source of pleasure to both, it can dramatically change wives' established routines to the point of intrusion. As one woman bluntly put it: "I may have married him for better or worse, but not for lunch" (Kalish, 1982:96). Because retirement from the labor force is becoming common among women as well as men, this final stage of family life now provides ever-greater challenges as well as opportunities.

The final and surely the most difficult transition in married life comes with the death of a spouse. Wives typically outlive husbands because of women's greater life expectancy, and also because women usually marry men several years older to begin with. Wives can thus expect to spend a significant period of their lives as widows. The bereavement and loneliness accompanying the death of a spouse are always challenging. This experience may be even more difficult for widowers, who usually have fewer friends than widows do, and may well be unaccustomed to the responsibilities of housework (Berardo, 1970).

U.S. FAMILIES: CLASS, RACE, AND GENDER

Dimensions of inequality—social class, race and ethnicity, and gender—are powerful forces that shape marriage and family life. Keep in mind that while we will address each factor separately, they overlap in our lives.

Social Class

Social class molds a family's financial security and range of opportunities. Interviewing working-class women, Lillian Rubin (1976) found that wives deemed a good husband to be one who refrained from violence and excessive drinking and held a steady job. Rubin's middle-class informants, by contrast, never mentioned such things; these women simply *assumed* a husband would provide a safe and secure home. Their ideal husband was a man with whom they could communicate easily and share feelings and experiences. Clearly, what women (and men) feel they can hope for in marriage—and what they end up with—is substantially linked to the social level that circumscribes their entire lives (Komarovsky, 1967; Bott, 1971; Rubin, 1976).

Ethnicity and Race

Ethnicity, too, shapes the family. Hispanics are likely to enjoy the loyalty and support of extended families. Traditionally, too, Hispanic parents exercise somewhat greater control over their children's courtship, defining marriage as an alliance of families rather than a union based simply on romantic love. A third trait of the Hispanic heritage is stronger adherence to conventional gender roles. *Machismo*—masculine strength, daring, and sexual prowess—is pronounced in this culture, while women are both honored and closely supervised. Assimilation into the larger society is gradually tempering these traditional patterns, however. Many Puerto Ricans who migrate to New York, for example, do not maintain the strong extended families they knew in Puerto Rico. Especially among affluent Hispanic families—whose number has tripled in the last twenty years—the traditional authority of men over women has diminished (Fitzpatrick, 1971; Moore & Pachon, 1985; O'Hare, 1990).

Analysis of African-American families must begin with the stark reality of economic disadvantage: as explained in earlier chapters, the typical African-American family earned $21,548 in 1991, 60 percent of the national income standard. People of African ancestry are also

Hispanic cultures traditionally have maintained extended kinship ties. Carmen Lomas Garza's painting, *Family Pictures*, portrays the togetherness and shared responsibility that historically have been common to Hispanics.

Carmen Lomas Garza, Tamalda, 1988. Oil/linen mounted on wood. 24 x 32". Laguna Gloria Art Museum, Austin, TX.

three times as likely as whites to be poor so that family patterns reflect unemployment, underemployment, and, in some cases, a physical environment replete with crime and drug abuse.

One consequence of economic adversity is that more African-American individuals remain single. For example, 25 percent of black women now in their forties have never married, compared with about 10 percent of white women of the same age (Bennett, Bloom, & Craig, 1989). This means that women of color—often with children—are more likely to be heads of households. Figure 12–1 shows that women headed 46 percent of African-American families in 1991, compared with 24 percent of Hispanic families, 13 percent of Asian and Pacific Islander families, and 13 percent of white families (U.S. Bureau of the Census, 1992).

Regardless of race, however, one-parent families are at high risk of poverty: about one-third of families headed by white women are poor, and the proportion is closer to half among people of Hispanic or African descent—good evidence of how class, race, and gender overlap to create special disadvantages for many women. Note that African-American families with both wife and husband in the home—which represents half of the total—are not as economically vulnerable, earning about 84 percent as much as comparable white families. But two-thirds of African-American children are born to single women, and half of all African-American boys and girls are growing up poor, meaning that such families carry much of the burden of child poverty in the United States (Hogan & Kitagawa, 1985; U.S. Bureau of the Census, 1991).

Gender

Among all races, Jessie Bernard (1982) asserts, every marriage is actually *two* different marriages: a woman's marriage and a man's marriage. Although the extent of patriarchy has diminished with time, even today few marriages are composed of two equal partners. College students of both sexes reported to Mirra Komarovsky (1973, 1976) that their ideal marriage had a dominant husband, evidence that this pattern is deeply embedded in our culture. Thus even today most of us expect husbands to be older and taller than their wives, and to have more important careers (McRae, 1986).

What is curious, in light of these patterns, is the persistent notion that marriage is more beneficial to women than it is to men (Bernard, 1982). The positive

Figure 12–1   Family Form in the United States, 1991
(*U.S. Bureau of the Census*)

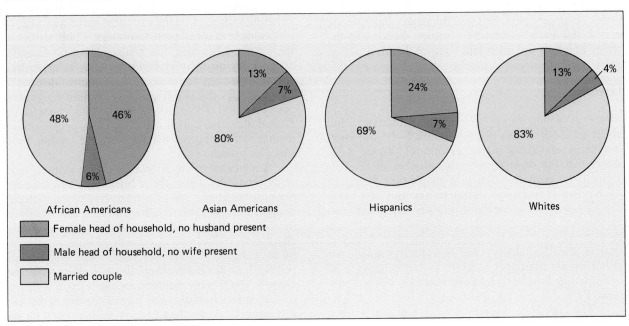

African Americans   48%   46%   6%

Asian Americans   13%   7%   80%

Hispanics   24%   7%   69%

Whites   13%   4%   83%

- Female head of household, no husband present
- Male head of household, no wife present
- Married couple

stereotype of the carefree bachelor contrasts sharply with the negative image of the lonely spinster. These ideas are rooted in women's historic exclusion from the labor force, which made a woman's financial security dependent on having a husband. But, Jessie Bernard explains, married women have poorer mental health and more passive attitudes than single women, and they report less personal happiness. Married men, by contrast, live longer than single men, are mentally better off, and report being happier. This suggests why, after divorce, many more women than men report happier lives and have less urge to remarry.

Bernard concludes that there is no better guarantor of long life, health, and happiness for a man than a woman well socialized to devote her life to taking care of him and providing the regularity and security of a well-ordered home. She is quick to add that marriage *could* be healthful for women if society would only end the "anachronistic way in which marriage is structured," meaning husbands dominating wives and leaving them to perform virtually all the housework.

TRANSITIONS AND PROBLEMS IN FAMILY LIFE

Ann Landers, a well-known observer of the U.S. scene, once remarked that "One marriage out of twenty is wonderful, four are good, ten are tolerable, and five are pure hell." Families can be a source of joy, but the reality of family life often falls short of the ideal.

Divorce

Members of our society strongly favor marriage, and about nine out of ten people eventually tie the knot. But many of today's marriages unravel. Figure 12–2 shows that the divorce rate—the number of divorces annually for every one thousand people over the age of fifteen—has risen tenfold during this century. By 1980, half of marriages in the United States were ending in divorce (for African Americans, about two-thirds); since then, the divorce rate has dropped somewhat. In global context, the U.S. divorce rate is second to none, and only here are marriages as likely to end by divorce as by death (Cherlin, 1981; Kitson & Raschke, 1981; Weitzman, 1985).

The high U.S. divorce rate is linked to a number

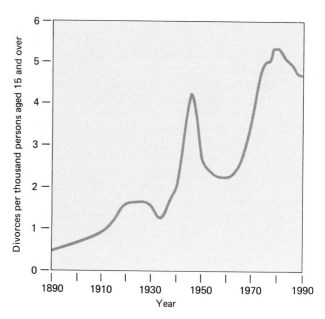

Figure 12–2 Divorce Rate in the United States, 1890–1990
(*U.S. Bureau of the Census*)

of factors (Huber & Spitze, 1980; Kitson & Raschke, 1981). First, members of our society now spend less time in family activities than in the past. We have become more individualistic, seemingly more concerned with personal happiness and success than with the well-being of families. Second, many marriages based on romantic love collapse as sexual passion subsides. Third, participation in the labor force has reduced women's financial dependency on their husbands so that, as a practical matter, marriages are easier to end. Fourth, divorce no longer carries the negative stigma common a century ago (Thornton, 1985; Gerstel, 1987). Fifth, because the United States has a high remarriage rate, people initiate divorce with confidence that they can find another, more suitable, partner.

At greatest risk of divorce are young spouses, especially those who marry after a brief courtship, have few financial resources, and have yet to mature emotionally. People in lower social classes are also more likely to divorce due to financial strains. At all social levels, the chance of divorce rises if a couple marries in response to an unexpected pregnancy, and when one or both partners have alcohol or other substance-abuse problems. Divorce also is more common among women with successful careers, probably less because of the strains of a two-career marriage than because such women do not

Because children learn so much from their families, divorce can be a lesson in conflict and hostility. This four-year-old, the object of a guardianship battle between his parents, bluntly expresses his opinion as the judge awards custody to his mother.

feel compelled to stay in an unhappy marriage. Moving, which weakens ties with family and friends, also raises the odds of divorce. Finally, people who divorce once tend to divorce again, presumably because problems follow them from one marriage to another (Booth & White, 1980; Yoder & Nichols, 1980; Glenn & Shelton, 1985).

Remarriage

Despite the rising divorce rate, marriage—and remarriage—remain as popular as ever. Four out of five people who divorce remarry, most within five years. Men, who derive greater benefits from marriage, are more likely to remarry than women are. Because we expect women to "marry up," the older a woman is, the more education she has, and the better her job, the more difficulty she will have in finding a suitable husband (Leslie & Korman, 1989).

Remarriage often creates *blended families*, composed of children and some combination of biological parents and stepparents. Members of blended families thus have to define precisely who is part of the child's nuclear family (Furstenberg, 1984). Blended families also present children with new challenges: an only child, for example, may suddenly find she has two older

brothers. And, as already noted, the risk of divorce is high for partners in such families. But blended families also have special joys since they sometimes free both young and old from rigid family roles.

Family Violence

The ideal family is a source of pleasure and support. The disturbing reality of many homes, however, is *family violence*, emotional, physical, or sexual abuse of one family member by another. Richard J. Gelles calls the family "the most violent group in society with the exception of the police and the military" (cited in Roesch 1984:75).

Violence against women. Family brutality often goes unreported to police, but researchers estimate that about 9 million couples—or one in six—experience violence each year. Investigators have also found that men tend to initiate most violence and women suffer most of the serious injuries (Straus & Gelles, 1986; Schwartz, 1987).

Government statistics show that almost 30 percent of women who are murdered—in contrast to 6 percent of men—are killed by partners or ex-partners. Nationwide, the death toll from family violence is four thousand women each year. This makes women more likely to be injured by a family member than to be mugged or raped by a stranger or injured in an automobile accident.

Historically, the law defined wives as the property of husbands, so that no man could be charged with raping his wife. By 1990, however, all but ten states had passed *marital rape* laws, although, in some cases, a marital rape charge is permissible only under specific circumstances such as after legal separation (Russell, 1982; O'Reilly, 1983; Margolick, 1984; Goetting, 1989).

Physically abused women traditionally have had few options. In the past, the law regarded domestic violence as a private family matter. Now, even without separation or divorce, a woman can obtain court protection to ensure that an abusive spouse will be punished. Since 1990, half the states have added "stalking laws" that prohibit an ex-partner from following or otherwise threatening a woman. Finally, communities across North America have established domestic abuse shelters that provide counseling as well as temporary housing for women and children driven from their homes by domestic violence.

Violence against children. Family violence also victimizes children. Child abuse entails more than physical

Nations, as well as parents, can abuse children. Prior to the fall of the Ceausescu regime in 1989, the Romanian government denied women any form of birth control and banned abortion. Tens of thousands of unwanted children were the result, many of whom remain warehoused in orphanages like this one.

injury: adults undermine a child's emotional well-being by misusing power and trust. Upwards of 2 million children each year suffer abuse, including several thousand who die as a result. Child abuse is most common among the youngest, most vulnerable children (Straus & Gelles, 1986; U.S. House of Representatives, 1987).

About 90 percent of child abusers are men, but

they conform to no simple stereotype. As one man who entered a therapy group reported, "I kept waiting for all the guys with raincoats and greasy hair to show up. But everyone looked like regular middle-class people" (Lubenow, 1984). Most abusers, however, share one common trait: having been abused themselves as children. Researchers have found that violent behavior in close personal relationships is learned; in families, then, violence begets violence (Gwartney-Gibbs, Stockard, & Bohmer, 1987).

ALTERNATIVE FAMILY FORMS

Most families in the United States are still composed of a married couple who raise children. But, in recent decades, our society has displayed increasing diversity in family life.

One-Parent Families

About three in ten families with children under eighteen years of age have only one parent in the household. *One-parent families*—four times more likely to include a mother than a father—may result from divorce or death, the inability to find a husband, or from the choice of an unmarried woman to have a child (Kantrowitz, 1985). Entering the labor force has bolstered women's financial capacity to be single mothers, but single parenthood still increases a woman's risk of poverty because it limits her ability to gain education or to work. At least one-third of the women in the United States now become pregnant as teenagers, and many decide to raise their children (Wallis, 1985). As shown earlier in Figure 12–1, 52 percent of African-American families are headed by a single parent. Single parenthood is less common among Hispanics (31 percent), Asian Americans (20 percent), and non-Hispanic whites (17 percent) (U.S. Bureau of the Census, 1992).

Most research supports the conclusion that growing up in a one-parent family can, but does not necessarily, disadvantage children. When divorce is involved, children sometimes grow up suffering from emotional scars that last for decades (Wallerstein & Blakeslee, 1989). But a more common problem among families with one parent—especially if that parent is a woman—is poverty. This, rather than the absence of a parent, probably results in such children being more likely to become low-income adults, to divorce, and to have children outside of marriage themselves (McLanahan, 1985; Weisner & Eiduson, 1986).

Cohabitation

Cohabitation is *the sharing of a household by an unmarried couple.* The number of cohabiting couples in the United States increased from about 500,000 in 1970 to almost 3 million by 1990, although this number represents only 3 percent of all couples (U.S. Bureau of the Census, 1991). Cohabiting is common on college and university campuses, where perhaps one-fourth of students cohabit for some period of time. Although most cohabitation does not lead to marriage, this living arrangement is unquestionably gaining popularity as a way to test a serious relationship while saving the expense of a second residence.

Gay and Lesbian Couples

In 1989, Denmark became the first country to lift the legal ban on homosexual marriages. This change extended to gay and lesbian couples advantages in inheritance, taxation, and joint property ownership as well as social legitimacy. Danish law, however, stopped short of permitting homosexual couples to adopt children. While our society legally prohibits homosexual marriage, laws enacted in San Francisco, New York, and elsewhere confer limited marital benefits on gay and lesbian couples.

Although a majority of people in the United States disapprove of homosexuality, many gay men and lesbians form long-term, committed partnerships and families (Bell, Weinberg, & Kiefer-Hammersmith, 1981). Like heterosexual couples, gays and lesbians enter relationships with romantic ideals and then adjust to day-to-day realities, and they share the burdens of financial and household responsibilities. Some homosexual couples also raise children from previous heterosexual relationships, adoption, or, among women, conceived through artificial insemination.

Gay men and lesbians who keep their relationships secret face special strains as they must turn to each other for much of the emotional, spiritual, and material support that heterosexual couples derive from family and friends. Yet, despite various disadvantages, many partnerships

between lesbians and between gay men are strong, resilient, and long-lasting.

Singlehood

Because nine out of ten people in the United States marry, singlehood is often seen as simply a transitory stage of life that ends with marriage. In recent decades, however, more people have deliberately chosen the freedom and independence of living alone, remaining both single and childless. In 1950 only one household in ten contained a single person. By 1990 this proportion had risen to about one in four: a total of 23 million single adults.

Most striking is the growing number of single young women. In 1960 28 percent of women aged twenty to twenty-four were single; by 1990, the proportion had soared to almost two-thirds. Underlying this trend is women's greater participation in the labor force: women who are economically secure view a husband as a matter of choice rather than a financial necessity.

By midlife, however, unmarried women sense a lack of available men. Because our culture discourages women from marrying partners much younger than they are (while endorsing a man's decision to do so), middle-aged women who wish to marry find the odds rising against them. In 1990, for example, there were eighty-three unmarried men aged forty to forty-four for every 100 unmarried women of the same age (U.S. Bureau of the Census, 1991).

New Reproductive Technology

Recent medical advances, generally called *new reproductive technology*, are changing families, too. In the twenty years since England's Louise Brown became the world's first "test-tube" baby, thousands of people have been conceived in this way. Early in the next century, 2 or 3 percent of the population of industrial societies may be the result of new birth technologies (Vines, 1986; Ostling, 1987).

Technically speaking, test-tube babies result from *in vitro fertilization*: uniting the male sperm and the female ovum "in glass" rather than in a woman's body. In this complex medical procedure, doctors use drugs to stimulate the woman's ovaries to produce more than one egg during a reproductive cycle. Then they surgically "harvest" the eggs and combine them with sperm in a laboratory dish. The successful fusion of eggs and sperm produces embryos, which are implanted in the womb of the woman who is to bear the child or, perhaps, frozen for use at a later time.

The immediate benefit of *in vitro* fertilization is to help some couples who cannot conceive children normally to become parents. Looking further ahead, new birth technologies may help reduce the incidence of birth defects. By genetically screening sperm and eggs, medical specialists expect to increase the odds for the birth of a healthy baby (Vines, 1986).

But gaining the ability to manipulate life in this way has sparked heated debate. The high cost (perhaps $10,000 per attempt) places this procedure in reach of only a small number of people. In addition, such technology allows medical experts to define what constitutes a proper "family." In most cases, doctors have restricted *in vitro* fertilization to women who are under forty years of age and are part of a heterosexual marriage. Single women, older women, and lesbian couples have been widely excluded from this opportunity.

But all new reproductive technologies—from laboratory fertilization to surrogate motherhood by which one woman bears a child for another—force us to consider whether what is scientifically possible is always morally desirable. The Catholic Church, for example, condemns any childbirth that is "the product of an intervention of medical or biological techniques." Such efforts, the Church claims, reduce human life to simply an object of research, and raise the specter of Nazi efforts to create a race of "superhumans." In support of this position, half the states in the U.S. and many European nations currently restrict genetic experimentation. Medical researchers, along with a large share of the public, take the opposing view that scientific work in this area can help people, which is a moral good.

The Family: Looking Ahead

Family life in the United States has changed in recent decades and will continue to do so. Transformation generates controversy, of course, with advocates of "traditional family values" locked in debate with supporters of new family forms and greater personal choice (Berger & Berger, 1983). Sociologists cannot predict the outcome of this debate but, more modestly, our discussions do suggest five directions of future change.

First, divorce has become an accepted—if regrettable—element of family life. This does not mean relationships are less durable today than they were a century ago, since back then death took a heavy toll (Kain, 1990). But more couples now *choose* to end their marriages. Although the divorce rate has recently stabilized, it is unlikely that marriage will regain the durability characteristic of the 1950s. One major reason is that increasing numbers of women are able to support themselves, and traditional marriages appeal to fewer of them. Men, as well, are seeking more satisfying relationships. The higher divorce rate of the last several decades should probably be viewed less as a threat to families than as a sign of change in family form. After all, most divorces still lead to remarriage, casting doubt on the notion that marriage is becoming obsolete.

Second, family life in the twenty-first century will be highly variable. We have noted an increasing number of cohabiting couples, one-parent families, gay and lesbian families, and blended families. Some alternatives, such as singlehood and childless marriage, are unlikely to be chosen by a majority of the population. Taken together, however, these options represent growing social diversity and a conception of family life as a matter of choice.

Third, in most families, men now play a limited role in child rearing. In the 1950s, a decade many people see as the "golden age" of families, men took a "hands-off" attitude toward parenting (Snell, 1990; Stacey, 1990). A counter-trend is emerging now as some fathers—older, on average, and more established in their careers—seek to become more involved in child care. But the rising divorce rate and a surge in single motherhood point to more children growing up with weak ties to fathers. Most research suggests that the absence of fathers is not directly and significantly detrimental to children, but there is little doubt that the absence of husbands and fathers from families contributes to the feminization of poverty in the United States.

Fourth, economic changes are reforming marriage and the family. In many families, both household partners must work to ensure their financial security. As Arlie Hochschild (1989) points out, economic changes reshape society in ways that people *feel* in family life. Marriage today is often the interaction of weary men and women; adults try their best to attend to children, yet worry that popular ideas like "quality time" may merely amount to justifications for minimal parenting (Dizard & Gadlin, 1990). Two-career couples may advance the goal of gender equality, but the long-term effects on families are likely to be mixed.

Fifth and finally, the importance of new reproductive technology will increase. While ethical concerns will surely slow these developments, new forms of reproduction will continue to alter the traditional meanings of parenthood.

Despite social changes that have buffeted the family in the United States, most people still report being happy as partners and parents (Cherlin & Furstenberg, 1983). Marriage and family life may now be more controversial, but both will likely remain the foundation of our society for some time to come.

RELIGION: BASIC CONCEPTS

Like the family, religion has played a central part in the drama of human history. Members of the earliest societies saw in their birth, death, and success or failure the workings of supernatural forces.

French sociologist Emile Durkheim explained that the focus of religion is "things that surpass the limits of our knowledge" (1965:62; orig. 1915). Humans, Durkheim explained, define ideas, objects, events, and experiences in one of two ways. Most we consider **profane** (from the Latin for "outside the temple"), meaning that they are *ordinary elements of everyday life*. A few, however, are set apart as **sacred**, defined as *extraordinary, inspiring a sense of awe, reverence, and even fear*. Distinguishing the sacred and the profane is the essence of all religious belief. **Religion**, in short, is *a system of belief and practice based on recognizing the sacred*.

In global perspective, matters of faith vary greatly, with nothing sacred to everyone on earth. Although most books are profane, the Torah (the first five books of the Hebrew Bible or the Old Testament) is sacred to Jews, as is the entire Bible to Christians, and the Quran (Koran) to Muslims.

However religious lines are drawn, Durkheim (1965:62) claimed, we understand profane things in terms of their usefulness: we sit down at a computer or turn the key of a car to accomplish everyday tasks. What is sacred, however, we reverently separate from daily life and denote as "set apart and forbidden." To make clear the boundary between the sacred and the profane, Muslims remove their shoes before entering a mosque to avoid defiling a sacred place with soles that have touched the profane ground outside.

The sacred is the focus of *ritual*, or formal, ceremonial behavior. Holy communion is the central ritual of

Every religion distinguishes the sacred from the secular. Followers of Islam reverently remove their shoes—which touch the profane ground—before entering this sacred mosque in the Persian Gulf nation of Brunei.

Christianity; to the Christian faithful, the wafer and wine consumed during communion symbolize the body and blood of Jesus Christ, and never food.

Further, since religion deals with ideas that transcend everyday experience, neither common sense nor science can point to religious truth. Religion is a matter of **faith**, *belief anchored in conviction rather than scientific evidence*. In the New Testament of the Bible, Christians are said to "walk by faith, not by sight" (II Corinthians 5:7), and faith is described as "the conviction of things not seen" (Hebrews 11:1).

For the same reason, some people with strong religious beliefs may be disturbed by the thought of sociologists studying what they hold to be sacred. Yet such study carries no threat to anyone's faith. Just as sociologists study the family, they seek to understand the common and distinctive features of religious experiences around the world and how religion is tied to other social institutions. In doing so, sociologists can make no claims about whether a particular religion is, in the absolute sense, right or wrong. Sociological analysis, then, investigates the social *consequences* of religious activity, but can never assess the *validity* of any religious doctrine because this involves faith rather than empirical evidence.

THEORETICAL ANALYSIS OF RELIGION

Sociologists have applied various theoretical paradigms to the study of religion. Each provides distinctive insights about religious life.

Functions of Religion: Structural-Functional Analysis

Emile Durkheim claimed that we confront the power of society every day. Society, he claimed, has an existence and power of its own beyond the life of any individual. Thus, society itself is "godlike," surviving the ultimate deaths of its members, whose lives it shapes. Durkheim concluded that religion is the celebration of the awesome potency of society (1965; orig. 1915).

This explains why, around the world, people transform everyday objects into sacred symbols of their collective life. Technologically simple societies do this with the **totem,** *a natural object collectively defined as sacred.* The totem—perhaps an animal or elaborate work of art—becomes the centerpiece of ritual. In our society, the flag is a quasi-religious totem that should never be used in a profane manner or allowed to touch the ground.

Durkheim pointed out three major functions of religion for the operation of society.

1. **Social cohesion.** Religion unites people through shared symbolism, values, and norms. Religious thought and ritual establish morality and rules of "fair play" that make organized social life possible.

2. **Social control.** Each society uses religious imagery and rhetoric to promote conformity. In medieval Europe, in fact, monarchs claimed to rule by divine right. Few of today's political leaders invoke religion so explicitly, but many publicly ask for God's blessing, implying to audiences that their efforts are both right and just.

3. **Providing meaning and purpose.** Religious beliefs offer the comforting sense that the vulnerable human condition serves a greater purpose. Strengthened by such beliefs, people are less likely to collapse in despair when confronted by life's calamities. For this reason, major life transitions—including birth, marriage, and death—are usually marked by religious observances.

Critical evaluation. Durkheim's structural-functional analysis of religion asserts that religious symbolism, in essence, makes society possible. This approach falls short, however, by downplaying the dysfunctional consequences of religion—especially the capacity of strong belief to generate destructive conflict. Nations have long marched to war under the banner of their god; few people would dispute that more killing has been done in the name of religious beliefs than for material gain.

Constructing the Sacred: Symbolic-Interaction Analysis

"Society," asserts Peter Berger (1967:3), "is a human product and nothing but a human product, that yet continuously acts back upon its producer." From a symbolic-interactionist point of view, religion, too, is socially constructed (although perhaps with divine inspiration). We construct the sacred, Berger explains, because placing life in a "cosmic frame of reference" confers on the fallible, transitory creations of human beings "the semblance of ultimate security and permanence" (1967:35–36).

For instance, to the extent that we define marriage as just a contract, it has no special hold on those involved. Defined as holy matrimony, however, marriage makes moral claims on us as it confers meaning on our lives. Especially when humans face uncertainty and life-threatening situations—such as illness, war, and natural disaster—sacred symbols come to the fore. By socially creating the sacred, humanity is also lifted above the ultimate reality of death, so that society—if not its individual members—becomes immortal.

Critical evaluation. The symbolic-interaction approach views religion as a social construction, placing everyday life under a "sacred canopy" of meaning (Berger, 1967). Of course, Berger adds, the sacred's ability to legitimize and stabilize society depends on its constructed character going unrecognized. After all, we could derive little strength from sacred beliefs we saw as mere devices for coping with tragedy. Then, too, this micro-level view pays little attention to religion's link to social inequality, to which we shall now turn.

Religion has always held a special promise for the poor, reaffirming the dignity of people flogged by famine and offering hope of a better life to come. Christian churches are currently thriving in the poorest regions of southern Africa, where Christian ideals are passionately expressed with some of the world's most inspiring religious art.

Religion and Inequality: Social-Conflict Analysis

The social-conflict paradigm highlights religion's support for social hierarchy. Religion, according to Karl Marx, serves elites by legitimizing the status quo and diverting people's attention from social inequities.

The British monarch, for example, is even today crowned by the head of the Church of England, illustrating the close alliance between religious and political hierarchy. In practical terms, working for political change may mean opposing the church—and, by implication, God. Religion also encourages people to look hopefully to a "better world to come," minimizing the social problems of *this* world. In one of his best-known statements, Marx offered a stinging criticism of religion as "the sigh of the oppressed creature, the sentiment of a heartless world, and the soul of soulless conditions. It is the opium of the people" (1964:27; orig 1848).

Religion reinforces social inequality in one other way: virtually all the world's major religions are patriarchal. For example, the Quran (Koran)—the sacred text of Islam—asserts that men are to have social dominance over women:

> Men are in charge of women. . . . Hence good women are obedient. . . . As for those whose rebelliousness you fear, admonish them, banish them from your bed, and scourge them. (cited in Kaufman, 1976:163)

Christianity—the dominant religion in the Western Hemisphere—has also supported patriarchy. Although Christians revere Mary, the mother of Jesus, the New Testament instructs us:

> A man . . . is the image and glory of God; but woman is the glory of man. For man was not made from woman, but woman from man. Neither was man created for woman, but woman for man. (I Corinthians 11:7–9)

> As in all the churches of the saints, the women should keep silence in the churches. For they are not permitted to speak, but should be subordinate, as even the law says. If there is anything they desire to know, let them ask their husbands at home. For it is shameful for a woman to speak in church. (I Corinthians 14:33–35)

> Wives, be subject to your husbands, as to the Lord. For the husband is the head of the wife as Christ is the head of the church. . . . As the church is subject to Christ, so let wives also be subject in everything to their husbands. (Ephesians 5:22–24)

Judaism, too, has traditionally supported patriarchy. Male Orthodox Jews include the following words in daily prayer:

> Blessed art thou, O Lord our God, King of the Universe, that I was not born a gentile.
> Blessed art thou, O Lord our God, King of the Universe, that I was not born a slave.
> Blessed art thou, O Lord our God, King of the Universe, that I was not born a woman.

Despite patriarchal traditions, many religious organizations are gradually placing women in leadership roles. Such developments, coupled with linguistic revisions in hymnals and prayers, have delighted progressives while outraging traditionalists. The consequences of such changes involve not just organizational patterns but conceptions of God. Theologian Mary Daly puts the matter bluntly: "If God is male, then male is God" (cited in Woodward, 1989:58).

Critical evaluation. Social-conflict analysis reveals how religion perpetuates social inequality. Yet religion has also promoted change and, sometimes, equality. Nineteenth-century religious groups in the United States, for example, played a key role in the abolition of slavery. During the 1950s and 1960s, religious organizations and their leaders stood at the core of the civil rights movement. During the 1960s and 1970s, clergy were active opponents of the Vietnam War and, as we shall explain presently, some have supported revolutionary change in Latin America and elsewhere.

RELIGION AND SOCIAL CHANGE

Religion is not just the conservative force portrayed by Karl Marx. Historically, as Max Weber (1958; orig. 1904–1905) explained, religion can promote dramatic social change.

Max Weber: Protestantism and Capitalism

Weber contended that particular religious ideas set into motion a wave of change that brought about the industrialization of Western Europe. Industrial capitalism, Weber noted, developed in the wake of Calvinism, a Christian movement within the Protestant Reformation.

Central to the religious thought of John Calvin (1509–1564) is the doctrine of *predestination.* This means that God, with complete control over the universe, has selected some people for salvation and others for damnation. Each individual's fate—known only to God—is thus predestined before birth. The only certainty for humans is what hangs in the balance: heavenly glory or hellfire for all of eternity.

Driven by anxious visions of salvation or damnation, Calvinists understandably sought signs of God's favor in *this* world. One sensible indication was worldly prosperity, leading many Calvinists to become absorbed in the pursuit of wealth. But riches could never lead to self-indulgent spending; nor were Calvinists moved to share their wealth with the poor, whose plight they saw as a mark of God's rejection. The Calvinist's lifelong "calling" was to be an agent of God's will.

Calvinists laid the groundwork for capitalism as they reinvested their profits, reaping ever-greater success. All the while they practiced personal thrift, and eagerly embraced technological advances that accompanied the Industrial Revolution.

Weber saw in the story of Calvinism striking evidence of the power of religious ideas to fuel social change. In time, the religious fervor that motivated early Calvinists weakened, but Weber noted that their success-seeking and personal discipline remained strong. So the pursuit of profit for its own sake rather than for the glory of God converted a religious ethic into a "work ethic." Thus Weber described industrial capitalism as a "disenchanted" religion. It is revealing that early Calvinists used the term *accounting* to refer to their written journal of daily moral deeds; today, of course, accounts are simply monetary records. In sum, what started out as the "Protestant ethic" ended up generating the "spirit of capitalism."

Liberation Theology

Christianity has a longstanding concern for the suffering of poor and oppressed people. Historically, the Christian response has been to strengthen the believer's faith in a better life to come. In recent decades, however, some church leaders and theologians have embraced **liberation theology,** *a fusion of Christian principles with political activism, often Marxist in character.*

This social movement started in the late 1960s in Latin America's Roman Catholic Church. In addition to the Church's efforts to free humanity from sin, Christian activists are helping Third-World people liberate themselves from abysmal poverty. Their message is simple: human suffering runs counter to Christian morality and is also preventable. Therefore, as a matter of faith and social justice, Christians must promote greater social equality.

This mix of religion and politics has attracted support among many church people (Neuhouser, 1989). Yet Pope John Paul II has condemned liberation theology because it leads church officials into the thick of worldly, political conflict. Despite the pontiff's objections, the liberation theology movement is growing stronger in

Latin America, fueled by the belief that Christian faith should propel the drive to improve the condition of the world's poor (Boff, 1984).

CHURCH, SECT, AND CULT

Sociologists analyze religious organization using three general types: church, sect, and cult. Drawing on the ideas of his teacher Max Weber, Ernst Troeltsch (1931) defined a **church** as *a formal religious organization well integrated into the larger society*. Church-like organizations typically persist for centuries and usually include generations of the same families. Churches favor formality with many rules and regulations, and expect their leaders to have approved training and formal ordination.

While concerned with the sacred, a church accepts the ways of the profane world, which gives it broad appeal. A church conceives of God in highly intellectualized terms (say, as a force for good) and favors general moral doctrine ("Do unto others as you would have them do unto you"). By teaching morality in safely abstract terms, a church need not engage in social controversies. For example, many churches with all-white memberships have historically celebrated the unity of all peoples. Such duality minimizes conflict between the church and political life (Troeltsch, 1931; O'Dea & Aviad, 1983).

A church generally takes one of two forms. An **ecclesia** is *a church that is formally allied with the state*. Ecclesias have been common in human history: for centuries the Catholic Church was allied with the Roman Empire; the Anglican Church is now the official Church of England; Confucianism was the state religion in China until early in this century; and Islam is today the official religion of Pakistan and Iran. State churches typically define everyone in a society as a member; tolerance of religious difference, therefore, is sharply limited.

A second type is a **denomination**, *a church, not linked to the state, that recognizes religious pluralism*. Denominations usually thrive in societies that formally separate church and state. Ours is a nation of religious diversity with dozens of Christian denominations—including Catholics, Baptists, Methodists, and Lutherans—as well as denominations of Judaism and other traditions. While members of any denomination hold certain religious beliefs, they recognize the right of others to disagree.

A second general religious form is the **sect**, *a type*

In global perspective, the range of human religious activity is truly astonishing. Members of one Christian cult in the Latin American nation of Guatemala observe Good Friday by vaulting over fire, an expression of faith that God will protect them.

of religious organization that stands apart from the larger society. Simply put, sect members place their own convictions ahead of what others around them may believe and, in extreme cases, may withdraw entirely from the society to practice their faith without interference from outsiders. The Amish are one example of a North American sect that has long isolated itself (Hostetler, 1980). Since our culture holds up religious tolerance as a virtue, members of sects are sometimes accused of being dogmatic in their insistence that they alone follow the true religion.

In organizational terms, sects are less formal than churches. Thus sect members often engage in highly spontaneous and emotional practices as they worship, while members of churches are more passive and attentive to their leader. Sects also reject the intellectualized religion of churches, stressing instead the personal experience of divine power. Rodney Stark (1985:314) points out that a church envisions a distant God found in prayer—"Our Father, who art in Heaven"—while a sect perceives a more immediate God—"Lord, bless this poor sinner kneeling before you now."

A further distinction between church and sect turns on patterns of leadership. The more church-like an organization, the more likely that its leaders are formally trained and ordained. Because more sect-like organizations celebrate the personal presence of God, members expect their leaders to exude divine inspiration in the form of **charisma** (from Greek meaning "divine favor"), *extraordinary personal qualities that can turn an audience into followers.*

Sects generally form as breakaway groups from established churches or other religious organizations (Stark & Bainbridge, 1979). Their psychic intensity and informal structure render them less stable than churches, and many sects blossom only to disappear soon after. The sects that do endure typically become more like churches, losing fervor as they become more bureaucratic and established.

To sustain their membership, sects rely on active recruitment, or *proselytizing*, of new members. Successful proselytizing leads to *conversion*, or religious rebirth. Members of Jehovah's Witnesses, for example, share their faith with others in the hope of attracting new members.

Finally, churches and sects differ in their social composition. Because they are more closely tied to the world, well-established churches tend to include people of high social standing. Sects, by contrast, attract more disadvantaged people. A sect's openness to new members and promise of salvation and personal fulfillment may be especially appealing to people who perceive themselves as social outsiders. However, as we shall explain presently, many established churches in the United States have lost membership in recent decades. As a result, a number of sects now find themselves with more affluent members.

A **cult** is *a religious organization with roots outside the cultural traditions of a society.* Whereas a sect emerges from within a conventional religious organization, a cult represents something else entirely. Because some cult principles or practices may seem unconventional, the popular view of cults pictures them as deviant or even evil. In recent decades, negative media publicity given to a few cults has raised suspicion about any unfamiliar religious group. Thus, some scholars note, to call a religious community a "cult" amounts to declaring it unworthy (Richardson, 1990).

This is unfortunate because there is nothing intrinsically wrong with this kind of religious organization. Many longstanding religions—Christianity, Islam, and Judaism included—began as cults. Of course, not all or even most cults exist for very long. One reason is that cults are even more at odds with the larger society than sects. Many cults demand that members not only accept their doctrine but embrace a radically new lifestyle. This is why cults are sometimes accused of brainwashing new members, although research suggests that most people who join cults experience no psychological harm (Barker, 1981; Kilbourne, 1983).

Cults typically form around a highly charismatic leader who offers a compelling message. Such was the case when Jesus of Nazareth attracted followers in a remote part of the Roman Empire two millennia ago. More recently, Joseph Smith founded the Church of Jesus Christ of Latter-Day Saints (the Mormons) in New York State in 1830. Smith accepted many established Christian principles, but he distinguished early Mormonism with several novel ideas, including the practice of polygynous marriage. During this century, however, Mormons steadily became more church-like, abandoning unorthodox practices. Spurred by a doctrine of proselytizing, Mormonism is now one of the fastest-growing religious organizations in the United States (Stark, 1984).

RELIGION IN HISTORY

Like the family, religion is a part of every known society. But, also like the family, religion shows marked historical and cross-cultural variation.

Religion in Preindustrial Societies

Religion predates written history. Archaeological evidence suggests that our human ancestors routinely engaged in religious rituals some forty thousand years ago.

Early hunters and gatherers embraced **animism** (from Latin meaning "the breath of life"), *the belief that natural objects are conscious life forms that affect humanity.* Animistic people view forests, oceans, mountains, and the wind as spiritual forces. Many Native-American societies were animistic, which accounts for their historical reverence for the natural environment.

Belief in a single divine power responsible for creating the world marked the rise of pastoral and horticultural societies. Pastoralists typically recognize a deity directly involved in the well-being of the universe. This view of God is widespread among members of our society because Christianity, Judaism, and Islam all emerged among pastoral peoples. In agrarian societies, the institution of religion gains in prominence, as evidenced by the centrality of the church in medieval Europe. The physical design of the medieval city even casts this dominance in stone, with the cathedral rising above all other structures.

Religion in Industrial Societies

The Industrial Revolution ushered in a growing emphasis on science. Even so, religious thought persists simply because science cannot address issues of ultimate meaning in human life. In other words, *how* this world works is a matter for scientists; but *why* we and the rest of the universe exist at all is a question about which science has nothing to say. Whatever the benefits of science, then, religion has a unique capacity to address essential dimensions of human existence.

Still, because they both offer powerful but distinctive visions of the universe, science and religion have often fallen into an uneasy relationship. Throughout this century, the question of human origins provoked spirited debate, with scientific facts about human evolution appearing to stand at odds with religious beliefs commonly called *creationism*. The box on page 314 provides details.

RELIGION IN THE UNITED STATES

Is religion becoming weaker in the United States? Research reveals that beliefs are changing, but confirms the ongoing role of religion in social life (Collins, 1982; Greeley, 1989).

Religious Commitment

National surveys show that 90 percent of adults identify with a particular religion (N.O.R.C., 1991). As we see in Table 12–3, Protestants account for almost two-thirds of the population, with one-fourth of the nation claiming to be Catholics, and 2 percent saying they are Jews. In addition, significant numbers of people adhere to dozens of other religions—from animism to Zen Buddhism—making our society more religiously diverse than virtually any on earth. This religious variety stems from our lack of any government-sponsored religion and a high rate of immigration.

Religiosity is *the importance of religion in a person's*

Table 12–3 RELIGIOUS IDENTIFICATION IN THE UNITED STATES, 1991

Religion	Proportion Indicating Preference
Protestant denominations	63.7%
Baptist	20.1
Methodist	9.0
Lutheran	6.7
Presbyterian	4.9
Episcopalian	2.1
All others or no denomination	20.9
Catholic	25.4%
Jewish	2.1%
Other or no answer	2.1%
No religious preference	6.7%

life. By global standards, North Americans are a relatively religious people, more so, for example, than Europeans or the Japanese. Quantitative measures of religiosity, however, depend on precisely how this concept is operationalized (see Chapter 1, "Sociology: Perspective, Theory, and Method"). Almost everyone in the United States (95 percent) claims to believe in a divine power of some kind, although only about 65 percent assert that they "know that God exists and have no doubts about it" (N.O.R.C., 1991:401). We have already noted that 90 percent of adults identify with a specific religion. Asked "How close do you feel to God most of the time?" one-third of respondents said "extremely close," while half replied "somewhat close." At the same time, half say they pray at least once a day, but only one-third claim they attend religious services on a weekly or almost-weekly basis (N.O.R.C., 1991).

Assessing the degree of our society's religiosity, then, is no simple matter. Because belief in God is normative in our culture, many people may make such a claim simply to conform. A safe conclusion, then, is that most U.S. adults are marginally religious, and a sizable minority are deeply religious. This estimation squares with the survey results presented in Figure 12–3.

Finally, religiosity varies among denominations. Research suggests that, overall, Catholics are more religious than Protestants, and members of sects are the most religious of all (Stark & Glock, 1968).

Does Science Threaten Religion? The Creation Debate

"In the beginning God created the heavens and the earth." A literal reading of this passage from the biblical book of Genesis puts the origin of life on earth at the third day when God created vegetation; on the fifth and sixth days, God created animal life, including human beings fashioned in God's own image.

For centuries, this account of creation held sway in many Western societies. But, in 1859, the English scientist Charles Darwin published *On the Origin of Species*, a biological theory of human origins. Darwin's account of evolution states that, far from being present at the earth's creation, humans evolved from lower forms of life over a billion years.

Darwin's theory brought him fame and immediate notoriety. What some celebrated as a scientific breakthrough, others condemned as an attack on sacred beliefs. On the surface, Darwin's science seems to contradict the Bible, setting the stage for the creation debate.

A major event in the course of this conflict occurred in 1925 in the town of Dayton, Tennessee. At that time, state law forbid teaching "any theory that denies the story of the Divine Creation of man as taught in the Bible," and especially claiming that "man descended from a lower order of animals." One afternoon in Doc Robinson's drugstore, John Thomas Scopes, a high-school science teacher, conceded that he had, on occasion, taught evolution. To challenge the law, Scopes agreed to stand trial for his crime.

Public interest in the "Scopes Monkey Trial" was heightened by the presence of three-time presidential candidate William Jennings Bryan, a fundamentalist Christian who detested evolutionary science. Bryan enthusiastically prosecuted the case. Clarence Darrow, a renowned criminal lawyer, sat across the aisle to defend Scopes.

The trial proved to be one of Darrow's finest performances, while Bryan, aging, ill, and only days from death, did little to advance the creationist cause. Yet most people applauded when the court found Scopes guilty and fined him $100. His conviction was reversed on appeal (perhaps to prevent the case from reaching the U.S. Supreme Court), and Tennessee law banned teaching evolution until 1967. Soon after, the U.S. Supreme Court struck down all such laws as violating the Constitution's ban on government-supported religion.

But creationists were quick to regroup: if evolution was to be taught in schools, creationism must be included to provide balance. Creationism, stripped of obvious religious qualities, emerged as *creation science*. Creationists won over some state legislatures that mandated the inclusion of creation science in school curricula. But again the Court stepped in, rejecting such teaching as violating the constitutional separation of church and state.

But this time, the Court went further, declaring creation science itself to be invalid *as science*. A science, the justices claimed, has a provisional character so that theory changes as new evidence appears. The theory of evolution had been altered by research, but creation science has not, making creationism religion, not science.

Members of our society remain divided over creationism. But many, including church leaders, insist that the conflict rests on faulty thinking. John S. Spong, the Episcopal bishop of Newark, New Jersey, argues that scientists and biblical scholars alike must accept the "enormous amount of evidence" that humanity did evolve over a billion years. But, he adds, science merely investigates *how* the natural world operates; only religion can address *why* we exist and God's role in this process. Human creation, then, can be approached from the perspective of both scientific fact and religious faith.

SOURCES: Based on Gould (1981), Numbers (1982), and Nelson & Jermain (1985). Professor J. Kenneth Smail of Kenyon College also contributed ideas to this section.

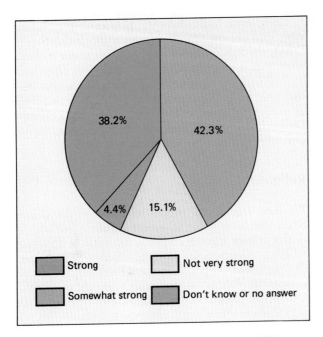

Figure 12–3 Degree of Religious Commitment, 1991
(National Opinion Research Center)

Pie chart segments:
- 42.3% Strong
- 15.1% Not very strong
- 4.4% Somewhat strong
- 38.2% Don't know or no answer

Legend:
- Strong
- Somewhat strong
- Not very strong
- Don't know or no answer

Religion and Social Stratification

Religious affiliation is related to a number of other factors. Of special interest is how religions are linked to dimensions of social stratification.

Class. Wade Roof (1979) found that Jews, Episcopalians, and Presbyterians had the highest overall social standing in the United States. In a middle position were Congregationalists and Methodists; lower social standing was typical of Catholics, Lutherans, Baptists, and members of sects. All categories, of course, show internal variation.

Ethnicity. Throughout the world, religion is tied to ethnicity, largely because one religion may predominate in a single region or society. The Arab cultures of the Middle East, for example, are mostly Islamic; Hinduism is closely fused with the culture of India. Christianity and Judaism diverge from this pattern: while primarily grounded in Western societies, followers are found in numerous cultures.

The link between religion and ethnicity also comes through at home. Our society encompasses *Anglo-Saxon*

Protestants, *Irish* Catholics, *Russian* Jews, and *Greek* Orthodox. This fusion of nationality and religion derives from an influx of immigrants from societies with a single major religion. Still, nearly every U.S. ethnic group incorporates at least some religious diversity. People of English ancestry, for instance, may be members of a Protestant denomination, Roman Catholics, Jews, or affiliated with some other religion.

Race. The church has historically been central to the lives of African Americans. Transported to the Western Hemisphere, most people of African descent became Christians—the dominant religion in the Americas—but they blended Christian belief and practice with elements of African religions. Guided by this multicultural religious heritage, many people of color even today participate in rituals that, by European standards, seem emotional and spontaneous (Frazier, 1965; Roberts, 1980).

As African Americans migrated from the rural South to the industrial cities of the North, the church played a key role in addressing problems of dislocation, prejudice, and poverty. Further, black churches have provided an important avenue of achievement for talented men and women. Ralph Abernathy, Martin Luther King, Jr., and Jesse Jackson each gained world recognition as a religious leader.

RELIGION IN A CHANGING SOCIETY

As we have seen with family life, religion continues to change in the United States. Analysis of religious change revolves around the concept of *secularization*.

Secularization

Secularization refers to *the historical decline in the influence of religion.* Secularization (derived from the Latin, meaning "the present age") is commonly associated with modern, technologically advanced societies (Cox, 1971; O'Dea & Aviad, 1983). Conventional wisdom holds that secularization results from the increasing importance of science in understanding human affairs.

More adults today, for example, experience the transitions of birth, illness, and death in the presence of physicians (with scientific knowledge) than church leaders (whose knowledge is based on faith). This seems to suggest that religion's sphere of influence has diminished. Harvey Cox elaborates:

> The world looks less and less to religious rules and rituals for its morality or its meanings. For some, religion provides a hobby, for others a mark of national or ethnic identification, for still others an aesthetic delight. For fewer and fewer does it provide an inclusive and commanding system of personal and cosmic values and explanations. (1971:3)

If Cox is right, should we expect that religion will someday completely disappear? The consensus among sociologists is "no" (Hammond, 1985; McGuire, 1987). Recall that the vast majority of people in the United States continue to profess a belief in God and two-thirds avow an affiliation with a religious organization—actually four times the share that did so in 1850.

Secularization does not, then, signal the impending death of religion. More accurately, a decline in some dimensions of religion (like belief in life after death) is being accompanied by an increase in others (like church attendance). Similarly, our society is of two minds about whether secularization is good or bad. Many conservative people see any erosion of religion as a mark of moral decline. But progressives view secularization as liberation from the all-encompassing beliefs of the past, so that people can take greater responsibility for what they choose to believe. Secularization has also nudged the practices of many religious organizations more in line with widespread social attitudes. The Catholic Church, for example, abandoned Latin in religious services in favor of commonly spoken languages, and many religions allow the ordination of women.

Civil Religion

Secularization takes many forms, including what Robert Bellah (1975) calls **civil religion**, *quasi-religious loyalty based on citizenship.* Bellah argues that our citizenship has many religious qualities.

Certainly, most people in the United States consider our way of life to be morally good and see our nation's involvement in the world as beneficial to other societies. Of course, the social diversity of the United States allows for no single vision of our moral purpose or destiny; various political movements—liberal and conservative alike—draw strength from civil religion (Williams & Demerath, 1991).

Civil religion also involves a range of rituals, from rising to sing the National Anthem at sporting events to sitting down to watch public parades several times a year. And like the Christian cross or the Jewish Star of David, the flag serves as a sacred symbol of our national identity that we expect people to treat with reverence.

Finally, participants in patriotic events often feel the same sense of reverence and awe shared by people at a religious service. The explanation lies in Emile Durkheim's insight that all rituals allow us to experience our collective identity—the power of society.

Religious Revival

We have argued that overall religiosity in the United States has been stable in recent decades. But a great deal of change is going on inside the world of organized religion. Membership in established, "mainstream" churches like the Episcopalian and Presbyterian denominations has plummeted by almost 50 percent since 1960. During the same period, affiliation with other religious organizations (including the Mormons, Seventh-Day Adventists, and especially Christian sects) has risen just as dramatically. Perhaps secularization is self-limiting: as church-like organizations become more worldly, many people abandon them in favor of sect-like communities that better address their spiritual concerns (Stark & Bainbridge, 1981; Roof & McKinney, 1987; Jacquet & Jones, 1991).

A key dimension of this change is the growth of **religious fundamentalism,** *a conservative doctrine that opposes intellectualism and worldly accommodation in favor of restoring traditional, otherworldly religion.* In the United States, fundamentalism has made the greatest gains among Protestants. Southern Baptists, one such organization, form the largest religious community in the United States. But fundamentalist groups have also proliferated among Roman Catholics and Jews.

In response to what they see as the growing influence of science and the erosion of the conventional family, religious fundamentalists defend their version of traditional values. From this point of view, the liberal churches are simply too tolerant of religious diversity and too open to change. One way fundamentalism opposes secularization is by insisting on a literal interpretation of the Bible as the one true voice of God. Thus, fundamentalism offers the promise of truth in an uncertain world. What some—including many faithful Christians—consider dogmatic, then, others find distinctly reassuring.

Fundamentalism also places a sect-like emphasis

The painting *Arts of the South* by Thomas Hart Benton (1889–1975) suggests that religious fundamentalism is strongly integrated into the community life of rural people in the southern United States.

Thomas Hart Benton, Arts of the South. Tempera with oil glaze, 8 x 13 feet, 1953.20. From the collection of the New Britain Museum of American Art, Connecticut. Harriet Russell Stanley Fund.

on the personal experience of religion. In contrast to the reserve and self-control found in "mainstream" churches, fundamentalism seeks to propagate "good old-time religion" and expects members to display their personal relationship with Jesus Christ in daily life. To do so often encourages a sect-like detachment from the world; however, some fundamentalist leaders have weighed into the political arena to oppose what they see as the "liberal agenda" of passing the Equal Rights Amendment, ensuring abortion as a matter of choice, and expanding the definition of legitimate families. They have also sought to return prayer to public schools, which they view as awash in moral permissiveness, while scolding the mass media for coloring stories with liberal sentiments (Viguerie, 1981; Hunter, 1983; Speer, 1984; Ostling, 1985).

Which religious organizations are "fundamentalist"? This term is most correctly applied to conservative organizations in the larger evangelical tradition, including Southern Baptists, Pentecostals, Seventh-Day Adventists, and the Assembly of God. Asking people who identified themselves as Protestants to describe their religious orientation, the *General Social Survey* (1991:161) found the term "fundamentalist" was preferred by 33 percent of respondents, "moderate" was chosen by 42 percent, and "liberal" was favored by the remaining 25 percent.

In contrast to small village congregations of years past, some fundamentalist organizations have become *electronic churches* dominated by "prime-time preachers"

(Hadden & Swain, 1981). Electronic religion, a pattern that developed only in the United States, has propelled Oral Roberts, Jim and Tammy Bakker, and others to greater prominence than all but a few clergy in the past. Perhaps 5 percent of the national television audience (about 10 million people) are regular viewers of religious television, while 20 percent (about 40 million) watch at least some religious programming every week (Martin, 1981; Gallup, 1982; N.O.R.C., 1991).

During the 1980s, regular solicitation of contributions brought a financial windfall to some religious organizations. Broadcasting with thirty-two hundred stations in half the countries in the world, for example, Jimmy Swaggart raised as much as $180 million in annual contributions. But some media-based ministries were corrupted by the power of money. In 1989, Jim Bakker (who began his television career in 1965, with his wife Tammy, hosting a children's puppet show) was jailed following a conviction for defrauding contributors. Such cases, although few in number, attracted enormous national attention as people began to wonder whether television preachers were more interested in raising cash or moral standards.

Religion: Looking Ahead

The power of media ministries, the rapid growth of sects, and the adherence of millions more people to "mainstream" churches show that religion will remain a central element of modern society (Stark & Bainbridge, 1981; Bateson & Ventis, 1982; Hunter, 1985). The world is becoming more complex, with rapid change almost outstripping our ability to keep pace. But rather than undermining belief, these processes end up firing the religious imagination of people who seek a sense of religious community and ultimate purpose.

Science is simply unable to provide answers to the most central human needs and questions. Moreover, science also creates problems of its own. Four in ten adults in the United States are troubled that science makes the world change too quickly, breaking down our sense of right and wrong (N.O.R.C., 1991). Against this backdrop of uncertainty, it is little wonder that many people turn to their faith for assurance and hope (Cox, 1977; Barker, 1981).

SUMMARY

Family

1. All societies are built on kinship, although the form families take varies across cultures and over time.

2. In industrial societies such as the United States, marriage is monogamous. Many preindustrial societies, however, permit polygamy, of which there are two types: polygyny and polyandry.

3. In global perspective, patrilocality is most common, while industrial societies favor neolocality, and a few cultures have matrilocal residence. Industrial societies utilize bilateral descent, while preindustrial societies tend to be either patrilineal or matrilineal.

4. Structural-functional analysis identifies major family functions: socializing the young, regulating sexual activity, and providing social placement and emotional support. Social-conflict theories explore how the family perpetuates inequality by strengthening divisions based on class, ethnicity, race, and gender. Symbolic-interaction analysis highlights the dynamic and changeable nature of family life.

5. In the United States and elsewhere, family life evolves over the life course beginning with courtship, extending through child rearing, and ending with the loss of a spouse, usually in old age.

6. Families also differ according to class position, race, ethnicity, and gender. Few family patterns apply to all household groups.

7. The divorce rate today is ten times higher than it was a century ago; half of current marriages will end in divorce. Most people who divorce—especially men—remarry.

8. Family violence, victimizing both women and children, is an important public issue.

9. Our society's family life is becoming more varied. Singlehood, cohabitation, and one-parent families are on the rise. While homosexual men and women cannot legally marry, many form long-lasting relationships.

10. Although ethically controversial, new reproductive technology is altering traditional notions of parenthood.

Religion

1. Religion is based on distinguishing the sacred and the profane.

2. Religion is a matter of faith, not scientific evidence. Therefore, sociologists study religion's role in society while making no claim as to the ultimate truth of any religious belief.

3. Emile Durkheim argued that, in religion, individuals express the power of their society. His structural-functional analysis suggests that religion promotes social cohesion and conformity, and confers meaning and purpose on life.

4. Using the symbolic-interaction paradigm, Peter Berger explains that religious beliefs are socially constructed as a response to life's disruptions.

5. Social-conflict analyst Karl Marx claimed that religion supports inequality. Yet religious ideals, as Max Weber explained, can trigger change and even promote social equality.

6. Churches, formal religious organizations well integrated into their societies, fall into two categories—ecclesias and denominations. Sects, the result of religious division, are marked by suspicion of the

larger society as well as charismatic leadership. Cults are religious organizations that embrace new and unconventional beliefs and practices.

7. Almost all U.S. adults identify with a religion and claim to believe in God; about 60 percent claim a religious affiliation, and half say they engage in daily prayer. About one-third regularly attend religious services.

8. The concept of secularization refers to the diminishing importance of religion in U.S. life. But while some measures of religiosity (including membership in "mainstream" churches) have weakened, others (such as membership in sects) are on the rise.

9. Fundamentalist Christianity stresses literal interpretation of the Bible and pursues the personal experience of God's presence. Many fundamentalists support traditional "family values" and a conservative social agenda.

KEY CONCEPTS

Family

cohabitation the sharing of a household by an unmarried couple

descent the system by which members of a society trace kinship over generations

endogamy marriage between people of the same category

exogamy marriage between people of different categories

extended family (consanguine family) a social unit including parents, children, and other kin

family a relatively permanent group of two or more people, who are related by blood, marriage, or adoption, and who usually live together

homogamy marriage between people with the same social characteristics

incest taboo a norm forbidding sexual relations or marriage between certain kin

kinship social relationships based on blood, marriage, or adoption

marriage a legally sanctioned relationship involving economic cooperation as well as normative sexual activity and child-bearing, that people expect to be enduring

monogamy marriage involving two partners

nuclear family (conjugal family) a social unit containing one or, more commonly, two adults and any children

polygamy marriage that unites three or more people

Religion

animism the belief that natural objects are conscious forms of life that affect humanity

charisma extraordinary personal qualities that can turn an audience into followers

church a formal religious organization well integrated into the larger society

civil religion a quasi-religious loyalty based on citizenship

cult a religious organization with roots outside the cultural traditions of a society

denomination a church, not linked to the state, that recognizes religious pluralism

ecclesia a church that is formally allied with the state

faith belief anchored in conviction rather than scientific evidence

liberation theology a fusion of Christian principles with political (often Marxist) activism

profane that which people define as an ordinary element of everyday life

religion a system of beliefs and practices based on recognizing the sacred

religiosity the importance of religion in a person's life

religious fundamentalism a conservative religious doctrine that opposes intellectualism and worldly accommodation in favor of restoring traditional, otherworldly religion

sacred that which is defined as extraordinary, inspiring a sense of awe, reverence, and even fear

sect a type of religious organization that stands apart from the larger society

secularization the historical decline in the influence of religion

totem a natural object collectively defined as sacred

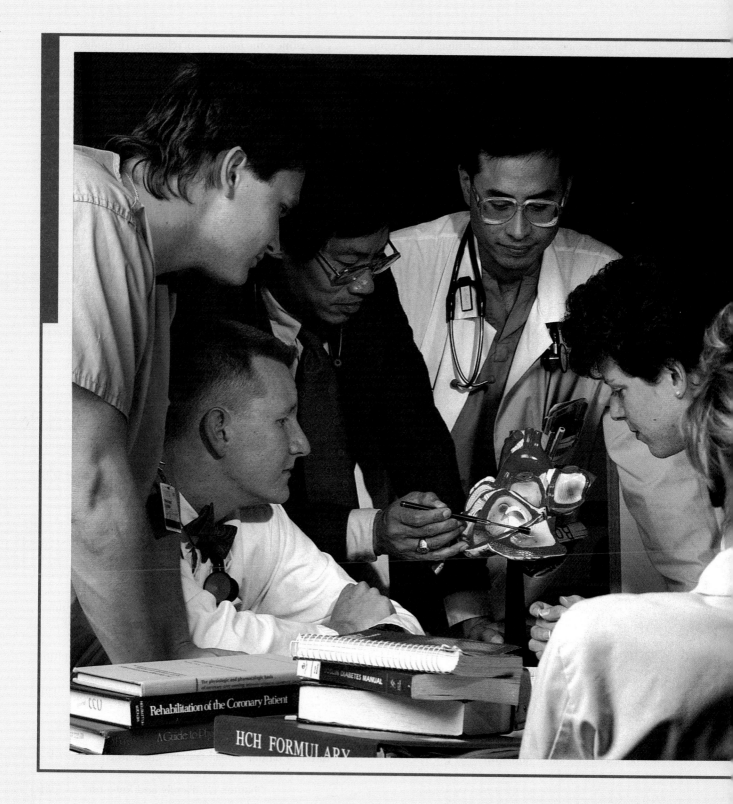

13

Education and Medicine

Thirteen-year-old Naoko Masuo has just returned from school to her home in suburban Yokohama, Japan. Instead of dropping off her books and beginning an afternoon of fun, she settles in to do her homework. Several hours later, her mother reminds her that it is time to leave for the *juku* or "cram school" that she attends three evenings a week. After a short subway trip downtown, Naoko joins dozens of other girls and boys for intensive training in Japanese, English, math, and science.

Attending *juku* costs the Masuo family several hundred dollars a month. They know, however, that the realities of Japanese schooling will make the investment pay off when Naoko takes a national examination to determine her school placement. In three years, she will face another hurdle with the high-school placement exam. Then will come the final test: earning admission to an exclusive national university, a prize awarded only to the one-third of Japanese students who perform best on this examination (Simons, 1989).

Why do the Japanese pay such attention to schooling? Because in this modern, industrial society, admission to an elite university virtually ensures a high-paying, prestigious career. This chapter begins by exploring *education*, a vital institution in societies such as Japan and the United States. We shall explain *why* schooling is important in modern societies, as well as *who* reaps most educational benefits. The second half of the chapter examines *medicine*, another social institution that has great importance in the modern world. Good health, like quality schooling, is distributed unequally through-

out our society's population. And like education, medicine reveals striking variation from society to society.

EDUCATION: A GLOBAL SURVEY

Education refers to *various ways in which society ensures that its members gain relevant knowledge—including facts, skills, and values.* Education takes place in a host of ways, many of them as informal as a family discussion. A vital type of education in industrial societies, however, is **schooling,** *formal instruction under the direction of specially trained teachers.*

Preindustrial and Third-World Societies

In preindustrial societies, families and local communities teach their members specialized productive skills, but schooling—especially learning not directly linked to work—is generally available only to the wealthy. The English word *school*, in fact, is derived from a Greek word for "leisure." In ancient Greece, renowned teachers such as Plato, Socrates, and Aristotle taught aristocratic men to the exclusion of everyone else. Similarly, in ancient China, the wisdom of the famous philosopher Confucius was shared only with a privileged few (Rohlen, 1983).

We find marked diversity in schooling throughout the Third World today. In part, this reflects the influence

The popularity of "cram schools" to supplement regular classes in Japan is one reason for the educational achievement of young people there. In addition, these children are socialized to work hard and are given strong parental guidance. Although Japan can boast of the greater share of children completing high school, however, a larger proportion of young people in the United States earns a college degree.

of hundreds of local cultural traditions. In Iran, for example, education and religion are closely linked, so that Islam figures prominently in schooling there. Bangladesh in Asia, Zimbabwe in Africa, and Nicaragua in Latin America have each molded schooling to reflect their cultural heritage. Schooling in poor societies also reflects historic colonialism by which various European nations—or the United States—imposed their culture on others. But all poor societies have one trait in common: limited access to schooling. In the poorest nations (including several in Central Africa), half of all elementary-aged children are not in school; throughout the Third World, no more than half of children attend secondary school (Najafizadeh & Mennerick, 1992). Overall, then, illiteracy disadvantages about one-third of Latin Americans, almost half of Asians, and about two-thirds of Africans. Global Map 13–1 on page 324 displays the extent of illiteracy around the world.

Industrial Societies

Industrial societies, by contrast, embrace the principle of mass education. Industrial production demands that workers gain at least basic skills in reading, writing, and arithmetic. Our society has also looked to schooling as a way to forge a literate citizenry able to actively participate in political life. More recently, the Information Revolution and the postindustrial economy have made schooling even more important.

In 1850 half the U.S. population between the ages of five and nineteen were enrolled in school. By 1918, however, every state had a *mandatory education law*, most requiring schooling to age sixteen or completion of the eighth grade. These laws drew children from farms and factories to classrooms. Table 13–1 shows that a milestone was reached in the mid-1960s when a majority of adults had completed high school. In 1991, almost four in five adults had a high-school education and more than one in five had completed four years of college.

Schooling in Japan

Until industrialization brought mandatory education to Japan in 1872, only a privileged few received schooling. Today's educational system in Japan is widely praised for generating some of the world's highest achievers.

The early grades concentrate on transmitting Japanese traditions including obligation to family (Benedict,

Table 13–1 EDUCATIONAL ACHIEVEMENT IN THE UNITED STATES, 1910–1991*

Year	High-School Graduates	College Graduates	Median Years of Schooling
1910	13.5%	2.7%	8.1
1920	16.4	3.3	8.2
1930	19.1	3.9	8.4
1940	24.1	4.6	8.6
1950	33.4	6.0	9.3
1960	41.1	7.7	10.5
1970	55.2	11.0	12.2
1980	68.7	17.0	12.5
1991	78.4	21.4	12.7

* For persons twenty-five years of age and over.
SOURCE: U.S. Bureau of the Census, 1992.

1974). By their early teens, students encounter Japan's system of rigorous and competitive examinations. These written tests, which resemble the Scholastic Aptitude Tests (SATs) used for college admissions in the United States, all but determine a young Japanese student's future.

More men and women graduate from high school in Japan (90 percent) than in the United States (78 percent). But competitive examinations sharply curb the number of college-bound youths, so that only 30 percent of high-school graduates—half the proportion for our society—end up entering college (Simons, 1989). Understandably, then, Japanese students take these examinations with the utmost seriousness and about half attend *juku* "cram schools" to better prepare for them. Japanese women, who are only now entering the labor force in large numbers, often devote themselves to their children's success in school (Brinton, 1988; Simons, 1989).

Despite—or perhaps because of—the pressure it places on students, Japanese schooling produces impressive results. In a number of fields, notably mathematics and science, young Japanese outperform students in every other industrial society, including the United States (Hayneman & Loxley, 1983; Rohlen, 1983).

Schooling in Great Britain

During the Middle Ages, schooling was a privilege of the British nobility, who studied classical subjects unrelated to earning a living. As the Industrial Revolution

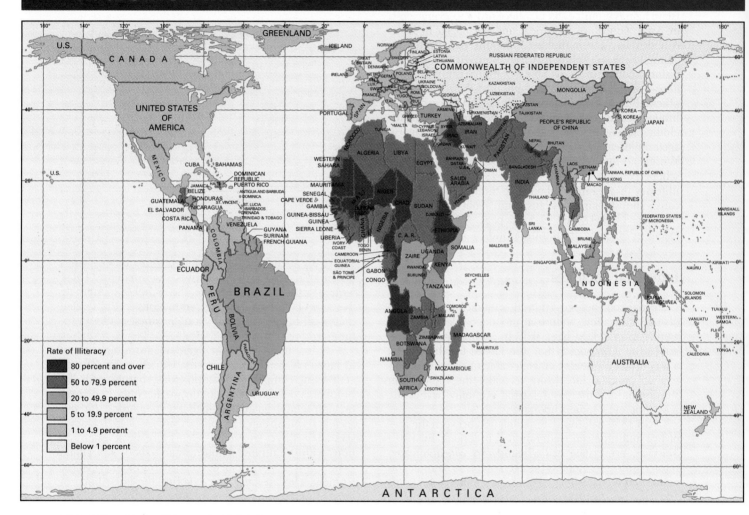

Global Map 13–1 Illiteracy in Global Perspective

Reading and writing skills are widespread in every industrial society, with illiteracy rates generally below 5 percent. Throughout Latin America, however, illiteracy is more commonplace—one consequence of limited economic development. In about a dozen nations of the world—many of them in Africa—illiteracy is the rule rather than the exception. In such societies, people rely on what sociologists call "the oral tradition" of face-to-face communication rather than communicating through the written word.

created a need for educated workers, and as working-class people demanded access to schools, a rising share of the British population entered the classroom. Law now requires every British child to attend school until age sixteen.

Traditional social distinctions, however, persist in British education. Many wealthy families send their children to what the British call *public schools*, the equivalent of private boarding schools here. Such elite schools teach not only academic subjects, they also convey to children from wealthy (especially *new rich*) families the distinctive patterns of speech, mannerisms, and social graces of the British upper class. These schools are far too expensive for most students, however, who attend state-supported schools.

To lessen the influence of social background on schooling, the British expanded their university system during the 1960s and 1970s and inaugurated a system of competitive examinations for admission (Sampson, 1982). For those who score highest, the government pays most of the cost of tuition and living expenses. Still, class differences figure more prominently in British education than they do in Japan, where more meritocratic policies have taken hold. A disproportionate number of well-to-do British children continue to attend Oxford and Cambridge, the British universities with the highest social prestige (roughly comparable to Yale, Harvard, and Princeton in the United States). These "Oxbridge" graduates assume their place at the heart of the British power elite.

Schooling in the United States

The educational system in the United States, too, has been shaped by our cultural tradition, which stresses political participation. Thomas Jefferson thought the new nation could become democratic only if schooling enabled people to "read and understand what is going on in the world" (cited in Honeywell, 1931:13). The United States now has a larger proportion of its people attending colleges and universities than any other industrial society (Rubinson, 1986).

Schooling in the United States also reflects the value of *equal opportunity*. National surveys show that most people think schooling is crucial to personal success (Gallup, 1982; N.O.R.C., 1991). We also like to think that our society offers educational opportunity: 70 percent endorse the notion that people have the chance to get an education consistent with their abilities and talents

Wealth and power in Great Britain have long been linked to "public" schools—actually privately funded boarding schools for young men and, to a lesser extent, women. The most elite of these schools transmit the way of life of the upper class not so much in the classroom as on the playing fields, in the dining halls, and in the dormitories, where informal socialization goes on continuously. Elite boarding schools are especially important to new-rich families; parents with modest backgrounds and large bank accounts send their children to these schools to mix with and learn from the offspring of "old-money" families.

(N.O.R.C., 1991). But this view better expresses our aspirations than our achievement. Until this century, women were all but excluded from higher education, and only among the wealthy do a majority of young people attend college even today.

Besides trying to make schooling more accessible, our educational system has also stressed the value of *practical* learning, that is, knowledge that has a direct bearing on people's work and interests. The educational philosopher John Dewey (1859–1952) maintained that children would readily learn those things that they found useful, rather than a fixed body of knowledge passed on from generation to generation. Thus Dewey (1968;

Following the Jobs: Trends in Bachelor's Degrees

College attendance in the United States has never been higher, and the 1980s saw a particular increase in the number of bachelor's degrees earned by women. For both sexes, however, college education retains an emphasis on practicality, with people pursuing degrees in fields where they think jobs are plentiful.

Looking across the 1980s, the figure shows that the greatest surge in bachelor's degrees—reflecting the Information Revolution—was in computer science, which soared almost fivefold over the previous ten years. The number of degrees in law and communications, both central to the postindustrial economy, also doubled during this decade. Business, management, and accounting—the most popular fields of study for students—also made gains.

By and large, students shied away from majors in areas where the demand for workers has slipped. Library science heads the list of fields posting reductions, followed by agriculture and education. Note, too, a modest decline in the number of bachelor's degrees in the social sciences; however, the data show that these disciplines (including sociology) enjoyed an upswing late in the 1980s.

SOURCE: National Center for Education Statistics (1991).

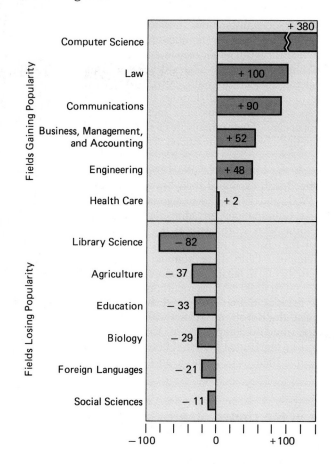

Percentage Changes in Bachelor's Degrees Earned, 1987–1988 Compared with 1977–1978

(*National Center for Education Statistics, 1980, 1991*)

orig. 1938) championed *progressive education* that addressed people's changing concerns and needs.

Reflecting this practical emphasis, today's college students select areas of major study with an eye toward future jobs. The box takes a look at how student interests changed during the 1980s.

THE FUNCTIONS OF SCHOOLING

Structural-functionalism focuses attention on ways in which schooling enhances the operation of society.

1. **Socialization.** In technologically simple societies, the family transmits a way of life from one generation to another. As societies acquire complex technology, formal systems of education emerge with specially trained teachers conveying specialized knowledge.

2. **Social integration.** Schools help to forge a mass of people into a unified whole with common norms and values. This is especially important in societies like ours that encompass great cultural diversity. In this connection, mandatory education laws paralleled the arrival of millions of immigrants a century ago. In many of today's cities, a majority of students are racial and ethnic minorities; schools help them blend their traditions with the larger culture.

3. **Social placement.** We expect schools to identify the talents of students and see that they receive appropriate instruction. Schooling thus acts as a social "leveler" that develops individual abilities, ideally with little regard for people's social background. Historically, schooling has been the key to upward social mobility in the United States (Hurn, 1978).

4. **Cultural innovation.** Educational systems create as well as transmit culture. Schools—especially centers of higher education—promote critical inquiry and research that lead to discovery and innovation.

5. **Latent functions of schooling.** Formal education has additional functions that are less widely recognized. Schools serve the rising number of one-parent families and two-career marriages by providing child care. Among teens, schooling consumes much time and considerable energy, inhibiting deviant behavior. Schooling also usefully occupies thousands of young people in their twenties for whom few jobs may be available. High schools, colleges, and universities bring together people of marriageable age, many of whom meet their future spouse in these settings. School networks provide not only friendship, but valuable career opportunities and resources for later life.

Schooling is a way of teaching the values and attitudes that a society deems important. It is also a means favored by governments to instill in children conformity and compliance. Holding portraits of a revered leader, these children in Taiwan participate in a lesson in "political correctness."

Critical evaluation. The structural-functional analysis of formal education stresses the various ways in which this social institution supports the operation of an industrial society. However, functionalism overlooks the extent of inequality inherent in our educational system, which provides quality schooling to some people and makes it barely available to others. In the next section, social-conflict analysis examines precisely this issue.

SCHOOLING AND SOCIAL INEQUALITY

Social-conflict analysis links formal education to social inequality. From this point of view, schooling perpetuates social inequality and acceptance of the status quo.

1. **Social control.** Samuel Bowles and Herbert Gintis (1976) claim that the expansion of public education in the late nineteenth century provided U.S. capitalists with a docile and disciplined work force. Mandatory education laws ensured that immigrants learned the English language as well as cultural values supportive of capitalism. Compliance, punctuality, and discipline were—and still are—

From a functionalist point of view, schooling provides children with the information and skills they will need as adults. A conflict analysis adds that schooling also instills discipline and respect for authority, thereby molding the children of today into the docile labor force of tomorrow.

part of what is sometimes called a school's *hidden curriculum*.

2. **Testing and social inequality.** In effect, standardized testing transforms privilege into personal merit. Intelligence and aptitude tests were developed early in this century to evaluate innate ability, not social background. But such tests have questionable validity insofar as scores also reflect a subject's cultural environment. In the United States, tests designed by white, affluent educators are likely to contain some bias in favor of white, affluent students (Owen, 1985; Crouse & Trusheim, 1988; Putka, 1990).

3. **Tracking and social inequality.** Despite their deficiencies, tests are the basis for educational **tracking,** *assigning students to different educational programs.* Defenders claim that tracking allows teachers to tailor schooling to a student's individual aptitude and interests. Thus some enroll in college preparatory classes, others receive a general education, and still others gain vocational and technical training. Critics charge that tracking undermines meritocracy because, in practice, students from privileged backgrounds typically enter higher tracks and receive the best the school can offer. Those from disadvantaged backgrounds, by contrast, end up in lower tracks in which rote memorization and classroom drill are commonplace. Because

the classroom also shapes friendships, tracking promotes segregation of privileged and disadvantaged students (Bowles & Gintis, 1976; Persell, 1977; Davis & Haller, 1981; Oakes, 1982, 1985; Hallinan & Williams, 1989; Kilgore, 1991).

Public and Private Education

Just as students are treated differently within schools, so do schools vary among themselves. In 1990 almost 90 percent of the 65 million primary and secondary school children in the United States attended state-funded public schools. The remainder were enrolled in private schools.

Most private-school students attend Christian church schools. A majority of these are *parochial* schools (from the Latin meaning "of the parish"), operated by the Catholic Church as a way to impress Catholic doctrine upon young people living in the predominantly Protestant United States. The network of Catholic schools originated a century ago with widespread immigration. Today, after millions of whites have fled the inner cities, many African-American students attend parochial schools seeking a better education than the public schools provide. More recently, fundamentalist Protestants have also started religious schools that offer religious instruction, a more rigorous academic environment, and—sometimes—a racially exclusive classroom (James, 1989).

A small number of private schools enroll young people mostly from the upper classes. These prestigious and expensive preparatory schools not only provide a strong academic program, but inculcate the mannerisms, attitudes, and social graces of the well-to-do. "Preppies" also derive numerous advantages from lifelong social networks with other graduates of their school.

Private schools, research suggests, teach more effectively than public schools. Two influential reports (Coleman, Hoffer, & Kilgore, 1981; Coleman & Hoffer, 1987) indicate that, holding social background constant, students in private schools perform better than public-school students. Smaller classes, more rigorous curricula, and greater discipline appear to account for this disparity.

But even the public schools are not all the same. For example, Winnetka, Illinois, one of the richest areas in the United States, spends more than $8,000 annually per student, compared to $3,000 spent in Socorro, Texas, one of the poorest. Some of this variation reflects cost-of-living differences, but it also indicates real differences of opportunity among our nation's 15,000 school districts (Carroll, 1990).

Generally, suburban districts offer better schooling than those in central cities. This pattern—which benefits whites—has prompted a policy of *busing*—transporting students to achieve racial balance and equal opportunity in schools. Although this policy currently affects only

5 percent of U.S. school children, it has generated enormous controversy. Advocates claim that, given the reality of racial segregation, governments will provide adequate funding to schools in poor neighborhoods only if children from across the city attend them. Critics respond that busing is expensive and undermines the concept of neighborhood schools. But both sides acknowledge that inner cities today contain too few white students to generate racial parity, whatever schools they attend. To be effective, then, busing would have to join cities (where people of color are concentrated) and suburbs (which are overwhelmingly white). Rarely has this been politically feasible.

A report by a research team headed by James Coleman (1966) confirmed that the handicap of predominantly black schools ranges from larger class size to insufficient libraries and fewer science labs. But the Coleman report concluded that increased funding alone would not bolster academic quality. More important are the attitudes and enthusiasm of teachers, parents, and children themselves. Supporting this conclusion, Christopher Jencks (1972) claimed that even if schools were exactly the same for all, some students would perform better than others because of broader social advantages. These two studies were conducted several decades ago, but conditions in the public schools have not changed substantially since that time.

Figure 13–1 College Attendance and Family Income, 1991 (*U.S. Bureau of the Census, 1992*)

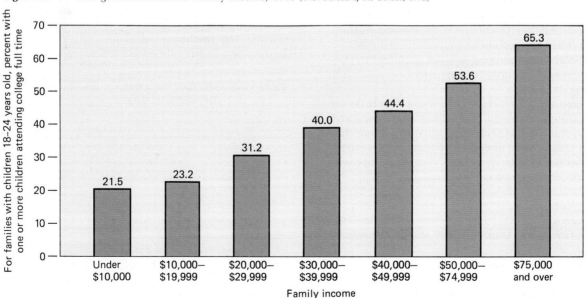

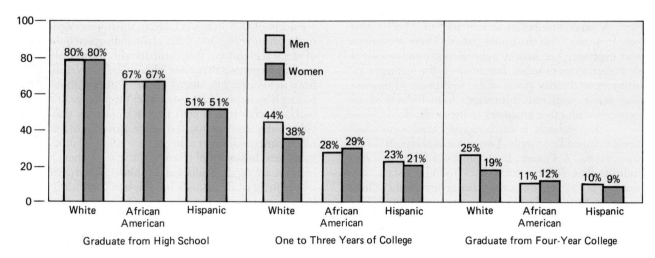

Figure 13–2 Educational Achievement for Various Categories of People, 1991 *(U.S. Bureau of the Census, 1992)*

One conclusion is clear: schools alone cannot overcome marked social inequality in the United States. Yet our society can hardly afford to ignore the educational needs of poor minority children, who represent a steadily increasing proportion of the future work force (Cohen, 1989).

Access to Higher Education

Higher education is a path to occupational achievement; not surprisingly, then, the vast majority of parents would send their children to college if they could (Gallup, 1982). Yet only 60 percent of high-school graduates enroll in college the following fall and, among the U.S. population aged twenty-five and older, only one-fifth are college graduates.

There are many reasons that more people do not enter or complete college. Not all high-school students want to continue their schooling, and the intellectual rigors of college may discourage others. But, a crucial factor affecting access is money. College is expensive and the price is going up rapidly. Even at state-supported colleges and universities, tuition averages about $2,500 annually, and the most expensive private colleges and universities top $20,000 a year. Thus, as Figure 13–1 on page 329 shows, family income is a good predictor of college attendance.

The financial burden of higher education dissuades many minorities, typically with below-average incomes, from attending college. Figure 13–2 shows that whites are overly represented both as high-school and college graduates. During the 1980s, however, the number of Hispanics in college rose by about 40 percent and African-American enrollments rose by 18 percent; the white increase was a modest 6 percent (U.S. Bureau of the Census, 1992).

For those who do complete college, rewards include not just intellectual and personal growth. College graduates also end up with more income. Table 13–2 presents 1990 median income for full-time workers aged 25 and over according to their education. Women with an eighth-grade education typically earned about $12,000; income rose above $18,000 for high-school graduates and reached $28,000 for college graduates. The numbers in parentheses are ratios, showing that a

Table 13–2 MEDIAN INCOME BY SEX AND YEARS OF SCHOOLING*

Schooling	Men	Women
Graduate school	$49,304 (2.8)	$33,750 (2.8)
College graduate	39,238 (2.3)	28,017 (2.3)
1–3 years college	31,734 (1.8)	22,227 (1.8)
High-school graduate	26,653 (1.5)	18,319 (1.5)
9–12 years	20,902 (1.2)	14,429 (1.2)
8 years or less	17,394 (1.0)	12,251 (1.0)

* Persons age twenty-five years and over, working full time, 1990. The earnings ratio, in parentheses, indicates how many times the lowest income level is earned by an individual with additional schooling.

SOURCE: U.S. Bureau of the Census, 1991.

woman with at least some graduate school earns 2.8 times as much as her counterpart with only an eighth-grade education. More schooling boosts men's income at the same rate, although men earn about 40 percent more across the board. Finally, bear in mind that the high earnings of college graduates have to do with more than education, since these people are likely to come from relatively well-to-do families to begin with.

Credentialism

Sociologist Randall Collins (1979) has dubbed the United States a *credential society*, because people view degrees as evidence of ability to perform specialized occupational roles. In modern, technologically advanced societies, credentials now say "who you are" as much as family background.

Credentialism, then, means *evaluating people on the basis of educational degrees.* Functionally speaking, credentialism helps fill jobs with well-trained people. But social-conflict analysis contends that credentials often bear little relation to the responsibilities of a specific job. Collins (1979) argues that advanced degrees serve as a shorthand way to sort out people with the manners, attitudes, and even color desired by many employers. Credentialism is thus a gatekeeping strategy that restricts important occupations to a small segment of the population.

Critical evaluation. Social-conflict analysis links formal education to social inequality. A key insight drawn from this point of view is that schooling transforms privilege into personal worthiness, and disadvantage into personal deficiency.

Critics claim that the social-conflict approach minimizes the extent to which schooling has provided upward mobility for talented women and men of all backgrounds. Further, especially in recent years, educational curricula are challenging the status quo on many fronts, including the multicultural initiative described in Chapter 2 ("Culture").

PROBLEMS IN THE SCHOOLS

An intense debate revolves around schooling in the United States. Few people think schools are doing an excellent job; about half give our schools a grade of C or below (Elam, Rose, & Gallup, 1991).

In some cities of the United States, the level of violence has escalated to the point that parents fear for their children's safety not only while traveling to and from school but also while *in* the classroom. These two five-year-old brothers set off for school in New York City wearing bulletproof jackets.

Discipline and Violence

While most people think schools should instill personal discipline (N.O.R.C., 1991:490), many suspect that the job is not being done well. The government estimates that several hundred thousand students and at least one thousand teachers are physically assaulted on school grounds every year.

Disorder spills into schools from the surrounding society. Nevertheless, schools do have the power to effect change for the better. The key to success appears to be firm disciplinary policies, supported by parents and, if necessary, law enforcement officials (Burns, 1985). Schools are unlikely to solve problems of violence that have roots deep in society itself (Reed, 1983), but they can control violence by forging alliances with parents and community leaders.

Student Passivity

Schools themselves are grappling with a pervasive problem of *student passivity*. Low interest in learning characterizes students in both public and private schools and at all grade levels (Coleman, Hoffer, & Kilgore, 1981).

Too many students perceive the opportunity to learn not as a privilege, but as a series of hurdles to be cleared in pursuit of credentials. In short, students are bored. Some of the blame must be placed on students themselves, and on other factors such as television, which now consumes more of young people's time than school does. Even so, much student passivity is caused by the schools themselves.

Small, personal schools found in countless local communities a century ago have been replaced by huge educational factories. A study of high schools across the United States led Theodore Sizer (1984) to identify five ways in which large, bureaucratic schools undermine education (1984:207–9).

1. **Rigid uniformity.** Bureaucratic schools are typically insensitive to cultural diversity in local communities. Outsider "specialists" operate schools with too little understanding of the everyday lives of students.

2. **Numerical ratings.** School officials focus on attendance rates, dropout rates, and achievement test scores. In doing so, they overlook dimensions of schooling difficult to quantify, such as the creativity of students and the energy and enthusiasm of teachers.

3. **Rigid expectations.** Fifteen-year-olds are expected to be in the tenth grade, and eleventh-grade students are expected to score at a certain level on a standardized verbal achievement test. Rarely are exceptionally bright and motivated students permitted to graduate early. Likewise, the system demands that students who have learned little graduate with their class.

4. **Specialization.** High-school students learn English from one teacher, receive guidance from another, and are coached in sports by still others. No school official comes to know the "complete" student. Students experience this division of labor as a continual shuffling among fifty-minute periods throughout the school day.

5. **Little individual responsibility.** Highly bureaucratic schools do not empower students to learn on their own. Similarly, teachers have little latitude in what and how they teach their classes; they dare not accelerate learning for fear of disrupting "the system."

Of course, some formal organization in schools is inevitable given the immense size of the task. The number of students in the New York City public schools alone now exceeds the population of the entire country a century ago. But, Sizer maintains, schools can be made more responsive and humane. He recommends eliminating fixed class schedules, reducing class size, and training teachers more broadly to help them become fully involved in the lives of their students. Perhaps his most radical suggestion is that graduation from high school should depend on what a student has learned rather than simply on the length of time spent in school.

College: The Silent Classroom[1]

Passivity is also common among college and university students. Sociologists have done little research on the college classroom—a curious fact considering how much time they spend there.

In one study, David Karp and William Yoels (1976) systematically observed classes at a coeducational university. Even in small classes, they found, only a few students actively participate. Sometimes, they noticed, students themselves become irritated with one of their peers who is especially talkative.

Survey responses revealed that most students consider classroom passivity to be their own failing. But, Karp and Yoels reasoned, the educational system itself teaches students to passively view instructors as "experts" who impart "truth." Students come to see their proper role as simply listening and taking notes. As a result, the researchers estimate, only a scant 10 percent of college class time is devoted to discussion. Students soon realize that most instructors enter a classroom ready to deliver a lecture, and dislike being sidetracked by student questions or comments (Boyer, 1987). Early in a course, then, a handful of students is recognized by everyone as the ones ready to offer whatever limited responses instructors may seek.

Dropping Out

If many students are passive in class, others are not there at all. The problem of *dropping out*—quitting school before earning a high-school diploma—leaves young people (many of whom are disadvantaged to begin with) ill-equipped for the world of work and at high risk for poverty.

---

[1] The phrase "silent classroom" is taken from Martha E. Gimenez (1989).

The dropout rate has eased slightly in recent decades; currently, 11.0 percent of people between the ages of 15 and 24 leave school, a total of some 4 million young women and men. Dropping out is least pronounced among whites (11.0 percent), slightly greater among African Americans (12.0 percent), and the most serious among Hispanics (29.4 percent) (U.S. Bureau of the Census, 1992).

For many Spanish-speaking students, a limited ability to speak, read, or write English prompts the decision to leave school (Suro, 1990). Women of all racial and ethnic categories who become pregnant may view attending school as an insurmountable barrier. For both women and men who are poor, the need to work sometimes crowds out the time and energy needed to do homework and go to class. In addition, many young people who drop out have parents with little schooling themselves, so their elders may provide little encouragement to continue.

For young people who drop out of school in a credential-based society, the risks of unemployment or becoming stuck in a low-paying job are easy to imagine. Faced with this reality, approximately one-third of those who leave school return to the classroom at a later time.

Academic Standards

Perhaps the biggest educational issue confronting our society involves the quality of schooling. A *Nation at Risk*, a 1983 study of the quality of U.S. schools prepared by the National Commission on Excellence in Education, began with an alarming statement:

> If an unfriendly foreign power had attempted to impose on America the mediocre educational performance that exists today, we might well have viewed it as an act of war. As it stands, we have allowed this to happen to ourselves. (1983:5)

Supporting this conclusion, the report notes that "nearly 40 percent of 17-year-olds cannot draw inferences from written material; only one-fifth can write a persuasive essay; and only one-third can solve mathematical problems requiring several steps" (1983:9). Furthermore, scores on the Scholastic Aptitude Test (SAT) have declined since the early 1960s. Then, median scores for students were 500 on the mathematical test and 480 on the verbal test; by 1991, the averages had slipped to 474 and 422. Some of this decline may stem from the

Paco learned to read last year. So did Dad.

Literacy Volunteers of America, Inc.

The problem of illiteracy in the United States is most serious among Hispanics. In part this is due to a dropout rate among fourteen to twenty-four-year-olds of almost 30 percent, which is three times the rate among whites or African Americans. The broader issue is that schools fail to teach many Spanish-speaking people to read and write any language very well.

growing number of students taking the standardized test, not all of whom are well prepared (Owen, 1985). But few doubt that schooling has suffered a setback.

A *Nation at Risk* also notes with alarm the extent of **functional illiteracy**, *reading and writing skills inadequate for everyday needs*. Roughly one in eight children—one in three people of color—completes secondary school without learning to read or write very well. The result of this poor schooling is 25 million adults (15 percent) who read and write at no better than a fourth-grade level. Functional illiteracy costs our society an estimated $100 billion a year in decreased productivity, accidents, and unnecessary welfare or prison costs (Kozol, 1980, 1985).

A *Nation at Risk* recommends drastic reform. First, it calls for rigorous requirements: all students should complete several years of English, mathematics, social studies, general science, and computer science courses. Second, schools should keep students as long as necessary to teach basic skills. Third, teacher training must improve and teachers' salaries should rise to attract talent into the profession. *A Nation at Risk* concludes that educators must ensure that schools meet public expectations, and we citizens must be prepared to bear the costs of good schools.

Finally, consider that young people in the United States spend 180 days annually in school, compared to 190 in Germany and 240 in Japan. Some educational experts think that we could remedy our schools' poor performance, at least in part, simply by making education a higher priority for our young people.

CONTEMPORARY ISSUES IN U.S. EDUCATION

America's schools must respond to new challenges and technological innovation. The following section explores several significant contemporary educational issues.

School Choice

Some analysts claim that our schools do not teach very well because they have no competition. Thus, giving parents a range of options about where to school their children may force all schools to do a better job. This is the essence of the *school choice* proposal.

Proponents of school choice advocate creating a market for schooling, so that parents and students can shop for the best value. According to one proposal, the government would provide vouchers to all families with school-aged children, allowing them to spend the money at public, private, or parochial schools. Milwaukee began such a plan in 1990 in the hope that public schools would be forced to perform better in order to win the confidence of families. But critics fear that school choice amounts to abandoning our nation's commitment to public schools and will do little to improve schooling where the need is greatest—in central cities.

Within the school choice movement, however, still other proposals for change have emerged. One calls for creating more *magnet schools*; some 1,000 such schools have been operating in U.S. cities and towns since the 1970s. These schools offer special facilities

and programs to promote educational excellence in areas as diverse as computer science, foreign languages, or science and mathematics. In municipalities where several magnet schools exist, parents are able to choose the one best suited to a particular student's talents and interests.

Another recent development in the school choice movement is *schooling for profit*. According to advocates of this proposal, school systems can be operated by private profit-making companies more effectively than by local governments. Of course, private schooling is nothing new; more than ten thousand schools are currently operated by private organizations and religious groups. What is new, however, is the assertion that private companies can carry out *mass* education in the United States. Chris Whittle, head of a large media corporation that includes a commercial television channel for the classroom, has taken the lead in this area with plans to open some two hundred schools-for-profit in the next five years.

Research confirms that many public school systems suffer from bureaucratic bloat, spending far too much and teaching far too little. Further, in a society that has long looked to competition as a strategy to improve quality, it is not surprising that various "choice" proposals are gaining favor. But whether education is consistent with commercialism and whether such plans will improve schools for everyone or only for some of our population are questions that remain, for now, unanswered (Putka, 1991; Toch, 1991).

Schooling People With Disabilities

Mandatory education embodies our society's commitment to provide a basic education to everyone. Nevertheless, millions of people with mental or physical disabilities receive little or no schooling. A highly bureaucratized system of mass education simply does not readily meet the special needs of some children.

Educating children with disabilities clearly poses a challenge. Many children with physical impairments have difficulty getting to and from school and those with crutches or wheelchairs cannot negotiate stairs and other obstacles inside school buildings. Children with developmental disabilities like mental retardation require extensive personal attention from specially trained teachers. As a result, many children with mental and physical disabilities have received a public education only because of persistent efforts by parents and other concerned citizens. In 1990, about 5 million children, with a wide range of disabilities, were attending school in the United States.

About one-fourth of these children are schooled in special facilities; the rest attend public schools, many participating in regular classes. This reflects the policy of *mainstreaming* or integrating students with disabilities into the overall educational program. An alternative to segregated "special education" classes, mainstreaming works best for physically impaired students who have no difficulty keeping up with the rest of the class. As an added advantage, children with disabilities learn how to interact with others just as other children interact with them. Mainstreaming is typically less effective for students who have serious mental or emotional impairments. These children may have difficulty matching the performance of other students, and they may simultaneously be deprived of appropriate special education. In any case, mainstreaming is expensive, requiring changes in physical facilities and hiring teachers capable of meeting the special needs of children with disabilities.

Adult Education

Most schooling involves young people. However, an increasing share of students are adults, many of whom return to the classroom after a considerable period of time.

By 1992, more than 25 million U.S. adults were enrolled in school. They range in age from the mid-twenties to well past the age of sixty-five. Adult students are generally a fairly privileged slice of the population: most are white and have above-average incomes.

What propels adults to go back to school? The reasons are as varied as the students, but usually the motivation is work-related. Most pursue study to enhance their careers, enrolling in courses in business, health, and engineering. Others return to school simply for the pleasure of learning.

Education: Looking Ahead

We in the United States are justifiably proud of our educational system: nowhere on earth, for example, does a larger share of the population attend college. At the same time, few people doubt that our system of public schooling—the first of its kind in the world—is laboring (and sometimes collapsing) under great strains. Public leaders all agree that more needs to be done; however,

while prospects for real improvement are widely discussed, far-reaching solutions still elude us.

Despite many people's best efforts, there will be no quick fix for the problems that beset schools in the United States. Firm discipline may lessen the level of school violence; proposals for choice may shake up complacent school officials. But our schools are part of the larger society and reflect its problems. As long as neighborhoods are burdened by poverty, children will carry a host of disadvantages into the schools. Similarly, as long as we fail to provide jobs for hundreds of thousands of young people, they will see little point in pursuing an education. In sum, our modern society can take pride in having created an expansive educational system, but our challenge for the future lies in making it work to the benefit of all.

HEALTH

Another social institution that expands greatly in modern societies is **medicine**, *the institutionalized means of combating disease and improving health*. In ideal terms, according to the World Health Organization, **health** is *a state of complete physical, mental, and social well-being* (1946:3).

Health and Society

The remainder of this chapter demonstrates that health is as much a social as a biological issue. To begin, society affects health in three basic ways.

1. **Cultural patterns define health.** Standards of health vary from culture to culture. René Dubos (1980; orig. 1965) points out that, early in this century, the contagious skin disease yaws was so common in tropical Africa that people there considered it normal.

   What members of a society view as healthful also reflects what they think is morally good; by the same token, illness has much to do with what they think is morally wrong. People who believe homosexuality is wrong, for example, may view this sexual orientation as "sick," although it is medically quite natural. Many people in the United States, especially men, tend to define a competitive, stressful way of life as normal, despite strong evidence that such behavior accounts for most physician visits and heart disease—this nation's leading cause of death (Wallis, 1983). Ideas about health, therefore, act as a form of social control encouraging conformity to cultural standards.

2. **Technology and resources affect health.** Even a century ago, the United States was ravaged by malnutrition, poor sanitation, and infectious disease—at least by current standards. Similarly, what we think of as poor health, many Third-World people today take as the norm.

3. **Social inequality affects health.** Resources that promote well-being are distributed unequally everywhere. The physical, mental, and emotional health of well-to-do people is far better than that of the poor. Affluent people also live years longer than those racked by poverty.

HEALTH: A GLOBAL SURVEY

The marked variations in health from place to place confirm the link between health and society. Historical patterns, likewise, reinforce this connection.

Preindustrial Societies

Simple technology limits the ability of hunting and gathering societies to generate a healthful environment. As Gerhard and Jean Lenski (1991) suggest, a food shortage sometimes forced a nursing mother to abandon a child. Children fortunate enough to survive infancy were still vulnerable, and perhaps half died before age twenty. Few lived to forty.

The agricultural revolution expanded the supply of food and other resources. Yet, due to increasing social inequality, elites enjoyed better health while peasants and slaves faced hunger and crowded, unsanitary shelters. Especially in the growing cities of medieval Europe, human waste and other refuse fueled infectious diseases, including plagues that periodically wiped out entire towns (Mumford, 1961).

Third-World Health Today

Striking poverty throughout the Third World (see Chapter 8, "Global Inequality") limits life expectancy to between forty and sixty years, much as was true in Europe

Medieval medical practice was heavily influenced by astrology, so that physicians and lay people alike attributed disease to astral influence; this is the root of our word "influenza." In this woodcut (1580) by Swiss artist Jost Amman (1539–1591), midwives attend a childbirth as astrologers cast a horoscope for the newborn.

centuries ago. Paul Harrison (1984) estimates that, around the world, 10 percent of children die during their first year of life and, in the poorest societies, half do not survive to adulthood.

According to the World Health Organization, 1 billion people around the world suffer from serious illness. Poverty coupled with poor sanitation creates the cruel reality of hunger and breeds infectious disease. The leading causes of death in the United States in 1900 are still major killers in poor societies. Thus, while most people in our society die in old age from heart disease and cancer, most people in the Third World die at any time in the life cycle from infectious and parasitic diseases.

Improving dismal Third-World health presents a monumental challenge. First, in a classic vicious cycle, poverty breeds disease, which, in turn, undermines people's ability to earn income (Harrison, 1984). Second, when medical technology does combat infectious disease, the populations of poor societies soar. Without resources to ensure the well-being of the people they have now, poor countries can ill afford population growth. Thus, efforts to reduce death rates will have little beneficial effect without programs to reduce birth rates as well.

Industrial Societies

Industrialization dramatically changes patterns of human health. Looking to Europe, where the Industrial Revolution first took hold in the mid-eighteenth century, factories swelled the cities as people from the countryside streamed in seeking greater economic opportunities. This massive concentration of people in a small area produced serious problems of sanitation and overcrowding. Factories continuously fouled the air with smoke, a health threat unrecognized until well into the twentieth century. Accidents in the workplace were common.

But as the nineteenth century progressed, health in Western Europe and North America began to improve, mainly because of a rising standard of living that translated into better nutrition and safer housing for the majority of people. After 1850, scientific advances in medicine promoted even better health, primarily by controlling infectious diseases in cities. To illustrate, in 1854 John Snow noted the street addresses of cholera victims in London and traced the source of this disease to contaminated drinking water (Mechanic, 1978). Soon after, scientists linked cholera to specific bacteria and developed a protective vaccine against the deadly disease. Armed with this knowledge, early environmentalists campaigned against age-old practices such as discharging raw sewage into rivers used for drinking water. By the early twentieth century, death rates from infectious diseases had declined sharply.

Over the long term, industrialization has had a dramatic, beneficial effect on people's health. Leading killers in 1900—influenza and pneumonia—accounted for one-fourth of all deaths. Today these diseases cause fewer than 3 percent of deaths in the United States. As Table 13–3 indicates, other infectious diseases that were once major causes of death no longer pose a threat to health.

Chronic illnesses including heart disease, stroke, and cancer now claim almost two-thirds of the population of the United States, generally in old age. Changing social patterns play a part here, too: the increasing use of work-saving devices reduces healthful exercise, our

Table 13–3   THE CHANGING CAUSES OF DEATH IN THE UNITED STATES

The Ten Leading Causes of Death in 1900
1. Influenza and pneumonia
2. Tuberculosis
3. Stomach and intestinal diseases
4. Heart disease
5. Cerebral hemorrhage
6. Kidney disease
7. Accidents
8. Cancer
9. Diseases of early infancy
10. Diphtheria

The Ten Leading Causes of Death in 1990
1. Heart disease
2. Cancer
3. Cerebrovascular diseases
4. Accidents
5. Lung disease (noncancerous)
6. Pneumonia and influenza
7. Diabetes
8. Suicide
9. Cirrhosis and related liver disease
10. Homicide

SOURCES: Information for 1900 is from William C. Cockerham, *Medical Sociology*, 2nd ed. (Englewood Cliffs, NJ: Prentice-Hall, 1986), p. 24; information for 1990 is from U.S. National Center for Health Statistics, *Monthly Vital Statistics Report*, Vol. 39, No. 11 (March 8, 1991): 14–15.

diet draws heavily on meat and eggs producing excessive levels of blood cholesterol, and many people smoke cigarettes, a practice rare a century ago. In short, while nothing alters the reality of death, industrial societies manage to delay our demise until old age.

HEALTH IN THE UNITED STATES

Living in an affluent, industrial society, people in the United States have good health by world standards. Still, some categories of people are far healthier than others.

Social Epidemiology: Who Is Healthy?

Social epidemiology is *the study of how health and disease are distributed throughout a population.* Just as early social epidemiologists examined the origin and spread

Table 13–4 ASSESSMENT OF PERSONAL HEALTH BY INCOME, 1990

Family Income	Excellent	Very Good	Good	Fair	Poor
$35,000 and over	49.7%	29.3%	17.2%	3.1%	0.8%
$20,000–$34,999	39.2	30.5	22.3	6.2	1.8
$10,000–$19,999	30.4	27.6	27.9	10.3	3.8
Under $10,000	25.8	23.4	29.2	14.2	7.4

SOURCE: U.S. National Center for Health Statistics, *Current Estimates from the National Health Interview Survey United States*, 1990, Series 10, No. 181 (Washington, DC: U.S. Government Printing Office, 1991), Table 70, p. 113.

of epidemic diseases, researchers today link health to the physical and social environments (Cockerham, 1986). Such analysis compares the health of different categories of people.

Age and gender.   In general, death is now rare among young people, with two notable exceptions: a rise in mortality resulting from accidents and, more recently, from acquired immune deficiency syndrome (AIDS). Across the life course, women fare better than men. Females have a slight biological advantage that renders them less likely to die at or soon after birth. Then, as socialization takes over, males learn to be more aggressive and individualistic, resulting in higher rates of accidents, violence, and suicide. Our cultural conception of masculinity also encourages adult men to be more competitive, to repress their emotions, and to engage in hazardous behavior like smoking cigarettes and drinking alcohol to excess.

Social class and race.   Infant mortality—the death rate among newborns—is twice as high for disadvantaged children as for children born to privilege. While the health of the richest children in our society rivals that of anyone in the world, our poorest children are as vulnerable as those in many Third-World nations including Sudan and Lebanon.

Table 13–4 shows that almost 80 percent of people in the United States with family incomes over $35,000 evaluate their health as excellent or very good, while fewer than half of those in families earning less than $10,000 make this claim. Conversely, while only about 4 percent of higher-income people described their own health as fair or poor, almost one-fourth of the poor respond this way. Bear in mind that just as income shapes health, so does health affect income. Members of low-income families miss twenty-seven days of school or work each year due to illness, while higher-income

people lose only ten days annually for this reason (U.S. National Center for Health Statistics, 1991).

Because people of color are three times as likely as whites to be poor, they are more likely to die in infancy and to suffer illness as adults. Table 13–5 shows the life expectancy for U.S. children born in 1990. Whites can expect to live more than seventy-six years; African Americans, about seventy-one years. Sex is a stronger predictor of health than race, since African-American females can expect to outlive males of either race. The table also indicates that 75 percent of white men—but only about 63 percent of African-American men—will live to sixty-five. The comparable chances for women are about 86 percent for whites and 78 percent for African Americans.

Regardless of race, many poor people live in crowded, unsanitary dwellings that breed infectious diseases. Many also suffer from nutritional deficiencies. Twenty percent of our population—some 50 million people—can afford neither a healthful diet nor adequate medical care. As a result, while wealthy people can

Table 13–5   LIFE EXPECTANCY FOR U.S. CHILDREN BORN IN 1990

	Females	Males	Both Sexes
Whites	79.6	72.7	76.2
	(86%)	(75%)	(81%)
African Americans	75.0	67.7	71.4
	(78%)	(63%)	(70%)
All races	79.0	72.1	75.6
	(85%)	(73%)	(79%)

Figures in parentheses indicate the chances of living to age 65.

SOURCE: U.S. Bureau of the Census, 1991.

expect to die of long-range chronic illnesses such as heart disease and cancer, the poor are likely to die younger from infectious diseases and illnesses linked to poor nutrition.

Poverty also breeds stress and violence. The leading cause of death among African-American men aged fifteen to twenty-four—who figure prominently in the urban underclass—is homicide. In 1990 about five thousand people of African descent were killed by others of their race—more than half the number of black soldiers killed in the entire Vietnam War.

Environment and Health

Health also rises or falls according to the quality of the physical environment. Without denying its benefits, industrial technology has also generated some serious environmental hazards to health. Few of us can imagine living without automobiles and factories, but they both pollute the air. In Los Angeles, officials warn that the air itself poses a health risk half the days of the year. Across the country, industries have polluted the soil and ground water with a host of chemicals.

Some thirty thousand waste sites in the United States threaten water supplies. The Environmental Protection Agency has targeted 1,200 of these for immediate action, but fewer than fifty have been cleaned up because of bureaucratic delays, disagreement over who should pay the costs, and a lack of national resolve to tackle this problem.

An additional source of environmental concern is nuclear power. This form of energy has the advantage of not depleting finite resources like coal and oil. In 1990, 111 nuclear reactors produced about 20 percent of this country's electricity. Concerns over nuclear power abound, however: a major malfunction could spew radiation into the atmosphere for hundreds of miles, as deadly as fallout from an atomic bomb. Nuclear power plants also produce waste materials that remain highly radioactive for hundreds of thousands of years. Currently, no means of disposing of such wastes eliminates the danger of future radioactive contamination.

Economic development is desperately needed in much of the world. Yet, if even half of the Third World reached a standard of living comparable to that of the United States, the consumption of energy, utilization of finite resources, and output of pollution and solid waste would place our planet in imminent danger. Thus we face the vexing dilemma of how to raise living standards in much of the world without irreparably ruining the global environment.

Cigarette Smoking

Many threats to health are matters of individual behavior, and cigarette smoking tops the list of preventable hazards. Smoking became popular in the United States after World War I. Despite evidence of its dangers, smoking was still fashionable even a generation ago. Today smoking has been redefined as a mild form of social deviance.

Consumption of cigarettes has fallen since 1960, when almost 45 percent of U.S. adults smoked. By 1990, only 27 percent were smokers (National Institute of Drug Abuse, 1991). Quitting is difficult because cigarette smoke contains nicotine, which is physically addictive. People also smoke to cope with stress. This psychological dependence suggests why divorced and separated people are more likely to smoke, as are the unemployed, and people in the armed forces. Generally speaking, the less education people have, the greater their chances of smoking. In terms of gender, a larger proportion of men (30 percent) smoke than women (24 percent). But cigarettes—the only form of tobacco use to gain popularity among women—have taken a growing toll on women's health. By 1987, lung cancer surpassed breast cancer as a cause of death among women in the United States.

Some 430,000 men and women die each year as a result of cigarette smoking—about the same number of U.S. soldiers who died in all of World War II. Smoking leads to heart disease, cancer of the mouth, throat, and lungs, and emphysema. Smokers also suffer from frequent minor illnesses such as flu, and pregnant women who smoke increase the likelihood of spontaneous abortion and prenatal death. Even nonsmokers exposed to tobacco smoke have a higher risk of smoking-related diseases (Shephard, 1982).

Tobacco was a $25 billion industry in the United States in 1990. The tobacco industry maintains that, since the precise link between cigarettes and disease cannot be specified, the health effects of smoking must remain "an open question" (Rudolph, 1985). But the tobacco industry is not breathing as easily today as it once did. Laws mandating a smoke-free environment are spreading rapidly. Furthermore, courts have increased the liability of cigarette manufacturers in lawsuits brought by victims of smoking-related illnesses, or their survivors.

Experts—as well as the general public—disagree as to the best strategy for combating the spread of HIV. Liberals support the distribution of condoms to young people because condom use significantly reduces the chances for sexual transmission of the virus. Conservatives object to this policy, claiming it encourages casual sex, which, to them, is the heart of the problem. From this point of view, rethinking the notion that young people should be sexually active is a better approach.

In response to these antismoking drives in the United States, the tobacco industry has been selling more products in the Third World, where tobacco sales and advertising are less strictly regulated. In the United States, however, more and more smokers are trying to break the habit, taking advantage of the fact that someone who has not smoked for ten years has about the same pattern of health as a lifelong nonsmoker.

Sexually Transmitted Diseases

Sexual activity, while both pleasurable and vital to our species, can transmit some fifty illnesses. Sometimes called *venereal diseases* (from Venus, the Roman goddess of love), these ailments date back to humanity's beginnings. Our culture has long linked sex to sin; therefore, some people regard venereal diseases not only as illness, but also as a mark of immorality.

Sexually transmitted diseases (STDs) became a national issue during the "sexual revolution" of the 1960s. STDs stand out as a notable exception to the general decline in infectious ailments during this century. In global perspective, STDs constitute a serious health prob-

lem; the World Health Organization estimates that 250 million new cases are contracted annually.

Gonorrhea and syphilis. Gonorrhea and syphilis, among the oldest diseases, are caused by a microscopic organism almost always transmitted by sexual contact. Untreated, gonorrhea can cause sterility, while syphilis can damage major organs and result in blindness, mental disorders, and death.

Roughly 600,000 cases of gonorrhea and 40,000 instances of syphilis are reported each year, and the actual numbers may be several times higher (Masters, Johnson, & Kolodny, 1988). Both diseases are more common among people of color than whites. Reporting suggests that almost 80 percent of infections involve African Americans, 15 percent affect whites, and 5 percent afflict Hispanics (Moran et al., 1989; Centers for Disease Control, 1991).

Most cases of gonorrhea and syphilis are easily cured with penicillin, an antibiotic drug developed in the 1940s. Thus neither disease currently represents a major health problem in the United States.

Genital herpes. An estimated 20 to 30 million adults in the United States (one in seven) are infected with the genital herpes virus. The infection rate among people of color is about twice as high as among whites (Moran et al., 1989).

Although far less serious than gonorrhea and syphilis, herpes is incurable. People may exhibit no symptoms or they may experience periodic, painful blisters on the genitals accompanied by fever and headache. Although not fatal to adults, women with active genital herpes can transmit the disease during a vaginal delivery to infants, to whom it may be deadly. Such women, therefore, often give birth by caesarean section.

AIDS. The most serious sexually transmitted disease is acquired immune deficiency syndrome, or AIDS. Identified in 1981, this disease is incurable and fatal. AIDS is caused by a human immunodeficiency virus (HIV). This virus attacks white blood cells, the core of the immune system, rendering a person vulnerable to a wide range of infectious diseases that eventually cause death. About 47,000 new cases were reported in the United States during 1992, raising the total to almost 250,000. More than 160,000 of these people have already died (Centers for Disease Control, 1992).

In global perspective, as many as 10 million people are infected with HIV, a figure that could increase three- or fourfold by the end of this decade. Global Map 13–2 shows that the African continent (more specifically,

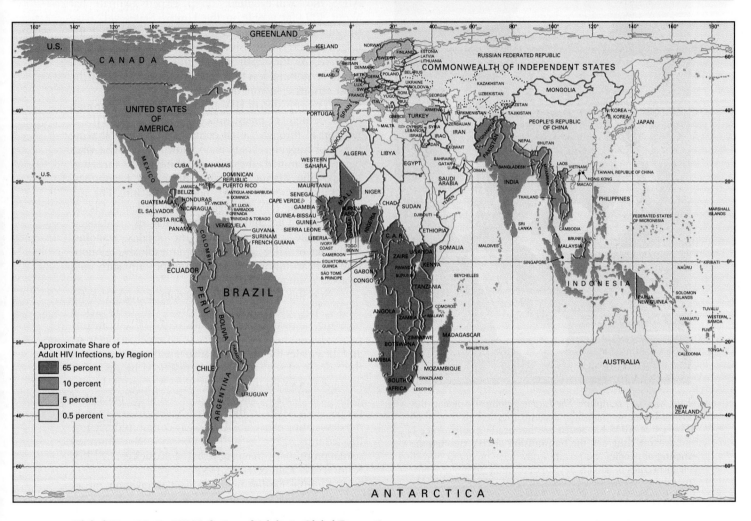

Global Map 13–2   HIV Infection of Adults in Global Perspective

Infection of adults with HIV is not spread evenly around the world. Approximately two-thirds of all cases in the world are recorded in sub-Saharan Africa where, in many countries, HIV has become a runaway epidemic. Such a high infection rate reflects the prevalence of other venereal diseases and infrequent use of condoms, both of which promote heterosexual transmission of HIV. Regions of the world with moderate rates of infection include South and Southeast Asia, which together account for 10 percent of global infections, and South and North America, which each represent another 10 percent of all cases of HIV. The incidence of infection is lower still in Europe. Least affected by HIV are the societies of North Africa and the Middle East and also the nations of Australia and New Zealand.

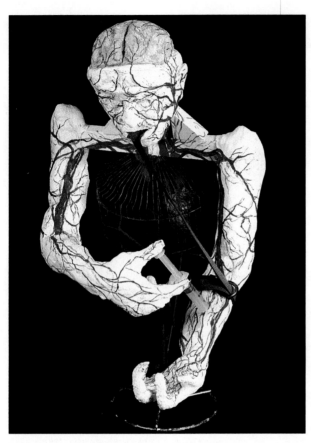

Paul Marcus's sculpture *The Junkie* graphically depicts the loss of humanity that often accompanies serious drug abuse. The age of AIDS has added another deadly consequence of intravenous drug use: the transmission of HIV through the sharing of needles. Some cities now have programs providing clean needles to addicts despite opposition on the grounds that doing so encourages illegal drug use.

countries south of the Sahara Desert) has the highest HIV infection rate and currently accounts for almost two-thirds of all world cases. In the cities of central African nations such as Burundi, Rwanda, Uganda, and Kenya, roughly one-fifth of all young adults are infected with HIV (Tofani, 1991). North America represents about 10 percent of global HIV. In the United States, estimates placed the number of infected people in 1992 at around 1 million.

People with HIV do not immediately contract AIDS. On the contrary, most initially display no symptoms and are unaware of their infection. Symptoms of

AIDS usually do not appear for at least a year; in five years, some 25 percent of infected persons will develop AIDS; most will eventually do so. Experts estimate that about 400,000 people in the United States will have the disease by the end of 1993. This means that the infection rate is still rising, although at a slower rate of increase. As the death toll mounts, AIDS has turned out to be nothing less than catastrophic—potentially the most serious epidemic of modern times.

Transmission of HIV almost always occurs through blood, semen, or breast milk. This means that HIV is not spread through casual contact—that is, by shaking hands or hugging. There is no known case of the virus being transmitted through coughing and sneezing, through the sharing of towels, dishes, or telephones, or through water in a bath, pool, or hot tub. The risk of transmitting HIV through saliva (as in kissing) is extremely low. Oral and especially genital sex are dangerous, but the risk is reduced by use of latex condoms. In the age of AIDS, abstinence or an exclusive relationship with an uninfected person are the only sure ways to avoid contracting HIV.

Specific behaviors place people at high risk for AIDS. The first is *anal sex*, which can cause rectal bleeding, allowing easy transmission of HIV from one person to another. This practice is extremely dangerous, and the greater the number of sexual partners, the greater the risk. Anal sex is commonly practiced by gay men, in some cases with multiple partners. As a result, homosexual and bisexual men comprise about 57 percent of people with AIDS in the United States. In response to the devastating effect of AIDS on gay communities across this country, gays (as well as nongays) have shunned sexual promiscuity in recent years (McKusick et al., 1985; Kain, 1987; Kain & Hart, 1987).

Sharing needles used to inject intravenous drugs is a second high-risk behavior. At present, intravenous drug users account for 25 percent of people with AIDS. Sex with a drug user is also very risky. Because intravenous drug use is more common among poor people in the United States, AIDS is becoming a disease of the socially disadvantaged. Overall, 53 percent of AIDS patients are white, with African Americans (12 percent of the population) accounting for 30 percent. Hispanics (7 percent of the population) represent 17 percent of AIDS cases. Asian Americans and Native Americans each account for less than 1 percent of people with AIDS. The rise of AIDS among young women of color stands out as a recent trend: for them, this disease is now the leading cause of death. Finally, almost 80 percent of young children with AIDS are African Americans (Bowles & Robinson, 1989; U.S. Department of Health and Human Services, 1989; Centers for Disease Control, 1992).

Using any drug, including alcohol, also increases the risk of being infected with HIV to the extent that it impairs judgment. In other words, even people who understand what places them at risk may act irresponsibly (say, by having unprotected sex) once they are under the influence of alcohol, marijuana, or some other drug.

In 1991, only 6 percent of people with AIDS in the United States were infected with HIV through heterosexual contact (although heterosexuals, infected in various ways, account for almost 30 percent of AIDS cases). So the likelihood of a runaway "breakout" of AIDS into the heterosexual population seems less likely than it did several years ago (Fumento, 1989). But heterosexual activity can and does transmit AIDS, and the risk rises with the number of sexual partners, especially if they fall into high-risk categories.

AIDS is throwing our health-care system into crisis. The cost of treatment for one person has already soared to hundreds of thousands of dollars. Government health programs, private insurance, and personal savings will be able to cover only a small fraction of this total. There is little doubt, then, that AIDS represents both a medical and a social problem of staggering proportions.

Initially, the government response to the AIDS crisis was slow, largely because gays and intravenous drug users are widely viewed as deviant. More recently, funding for AIDS research has increased rapidly, and progress toward effective treatment and a cure is being made. For example, researchers have found that some drugs, such as AZT, suppress the symptoms of the disease. But educational programs remain our most effective weapon against AIDS, since prevention is the only way to stop a disease that currently has no cure.

Ethical Issues: Confronting Death

Health issues always involve ethical considerations. Moral questions are more pressing than ever now that technological advances have given human beings the power to define life and death. We now grapple with deciding how to use these new powers, or whether to use them at all.

When is a person dead? Common sense suggests that life ceases when breathing and heartbeat stop. But now that a heart can be revived or replaced, and respiration can be artificially sustained, such notions of death have become obsolete. Medical and legal experts in the United States now define death as an *irreversible* state involving no response to stimulation, no movement or breathing, no reflexes, and no indication of brain activity (Ladd, 1979; Wall, 1980).

Do people have a right to die? Today, medical personnel, family members, and patients themselves face the agonizing burden of deciding when a terminally ill person should die. Who should assume this responsibility? In 1990, twenty-six-year-old Nancy Cruzan fell into an irreversible coma after an automobile accident. Physicians exhausted their efforts and solemnly assured Cruzan's parents that their daughter would never recover. Certain that their daughter would not wish to live in a permanent vegetative state, the Cruzans sought a legal decision to let Nancy die, which required taking their case all the way to the U.S. Supreme Court. In 1990, the court issued a judgment supporting a patient's right to die by declaring that any person deemed competent could choose to refuse medical treatment or nutrition. Because the Cruzans were able to present "clear and convincing evidence" that this would be Nancy's wish, the court permitted removal of the feeding tube keeping her alive. Nancy Cruzan died twelve days later (Mauro, 1990).

Ten thousand people in the United States are in the same kind of permanent vegetative state as Nancy Cruzan (Howlett, 1990). Thousands more, faced with a terminal illness that may cause terrible suffering, consider ending their own lives. Courts and government commissions continue to weigh patients' rights against the obligation to provide all appropriate care to those in need. A 1983 presidential commission noted that the first responsibility of physicians and hospitals is to protect the patient's life. Doctors must explain every medical option available to patients or, when a patient is incapacitated, to family members. Even so, terminally ill patients can refuse heroic treatment that may extend their lives but offer no hope of recovery. According to the commission, however, a family decision such as that faced by the Cruzans must be made in the interest of the patient—no one else. The commission also endorsed honoring a *living will*, a statement of a person's intention regarding heroic treatment in the event of catastrophic illness.

What about mercy killing? *Mercy killing* is the common term for **euthanasia**, *assisting in the death of a*

The vexing problem of whether or when a society should allow suffering people to die is nowhere better illustrated than in the life of Dax Cowart. After being critically burned in a propane-gas explosion, Cowart begged for a gun to shoot himself, and protested every effort by medical specialists to save him. Now, almost twenty years later, Cowart has forged a life worth living—he graduated from law school and is married. But he still maintains that doctors should have complied with his wishes and let him die.

person suffering from an incurable disease. Euthanasia (from the Greek, meaning "a good death") poses the ethical dilemma of being both an act of kindness and a form of killing.

Although a patient's right to die has widespread support in the United States, assisting in the death of another person still provokes controversy. In 1992, for example, Jack Kevorkian, a Michigan physician who helped two women end their lives with his "suicide machine," was arrested on charges of murder. No one thinks that the women involved—both suffering from terminal illnesses—looked on Kevorkian as their murderer. But our society remains uneasy about empowering physicians to actively end a life in response to a patient's request.

The debate breaks down roughly as follows. Those who view life—even with suffering—as preferable to death categorically reject euthanasia. People who recognize circumstances under which death is preferable to life support euthanasia, but they face the practical problem of determining just when life is no longer worth living. Such a decision can be an enormous burden on family members who are already emotionally strained. Then, too, they must confront the reality of medical costs, which skyrocket when heroic care is involved. Opponents of euthanasia voice fears that such costs will enter into a family's decision regarding life-sustaining treatment, perhaps compromising the interests of the patient.

THE MEDICAL ESTABLISHMENT

Through most of human history, health care was the responsibility of individuals and their families. Members of preindustrial societies consult various health practitioners—from herbalists to acupuncturists—who are still helping to improve health in much of the Third World (Ayensu, 1981).

As a society industrializes, health care becomes the responsibility of specially trained and legally licensed healers. The medical establishment of modern, industrial societies took form 150 years ago as healers and researchers applied the logic of science to their work.

The Rise of Scientific Medicine

In colonial times, the herbalists, druggists, midwives, and ministers who each engaged in some form of healing arts in this country agreed on few principles or procedures (Stevens, 1971). Unsanitary instruments, lack of anesthesia, and simple ignorance made surgery a terrible ordeal in which doctors killed as many patients as they saved.

Medical specialists gradually learned about human anatomy, physiology, and biochemistry. By about 1850, doctors had established themselves as self-regulating professionals with medical school degrees. The American Medical Association (AMA), founded in 1847, symbolized the growing acceptance of a scientific model of medicine. The AMA widely publicized the medical successes of its members in identifying the cause of life-threatening diseases—bacteria and viruses—and developing vaccines to combat illness.

Still, other approaches to health care, such as regulating nutrition, also had defenders. The AMA responded boldly—some thought arrogantly—to these alternative ideas in health care, trumpeting the superiority of its practitioners. By the early 1900s, state licensing boards agreed to certify only physicians trained in the scientific programs approved by the AMA (Starr, 1982). With control of the certification process, the AMA effectively closed down schools teaching other healing skills, limiting the practice of medicine mainly to those with an M.D. degree. In the process, both the prestige and income of physicians rose dramatically. Men and women with M.D. degrees are now among the highest-paid workers in the United States, with 1990 average earnings of about $150,000.

Practitioners of other approaches, such as osteopathic physicians, concluded that they had no choice but to fall in line and follow AMA standards. Thus osteopaths (with D.O. degrees), originally concerned with manipulating the skeleton and muscles, today treat illness much as medical doctors (with M.D. degrees) do. Other practitioners—such as chiropractors, herbal healers, and midwives—have held more to their traditional practices at the cost of being relegated to the fringe of the medical profession (Gordon, 1980).

Scientific medicine, taught in expensive, urban medical schools, also changed the social profile of doctors. Most physicians soon came from privileged backgrounds and practiced in cities. Furthermore, women had played a key role in many forms of healing denigrated by the AMA. Some early medical schools did train women and African Americans but, with few financial resources, most of these schools soon closed their doors. Only in recent decades have women and people of color increased their representation in medicine (Stevens, 1971; Starr, 1982; Huet-Cox, 1984).

Holistic Medicine

The scientific model of medicine has recently been tempered by the more traditional notion of **holistic medicine,** *an approach to health care that emphasizes prevention of illness and takes account of the person's entire physical and social environment.*

Holistic practitioners also embrace the use of drugs, surgery, artificial organs, and high technology, but they caution that these developments risk transforming medicine into narrow specialties concerned with symptoms rather than people, and with disease instead of health.

The rise of scientific medicine sparked stunning achievements in our ability to control disease. But it also effectively reduced the number of African Americans in the medical professions and opposed many kinds of healers who traditionally have served rural areas. Michael Cheers, M.D. has tried to turn the tide by transforming an abandoned restaurant into a medical clinic in Tchula, Mississippi. Cheers, who is also an ordained minister and jazz pianist, accepts donations and works overtime in hospital emergency rooms to enable him to treat people who cannot afford to pay for care.

The following are foundations of holistic health care (Gordon, 1980).

1. **Patients are people.** Holistic practitioners are concerned not only with symptoms, but with how each person's environment and lifestyle affect health. For example, the likelihood of illness increases under stress caused by poverty or intense competition at work (Duhl, 1980). Holistic practitioners extend the bounds of conventional medicine, taking an active role in combating environmental pollution and other dangers to public health.

2. **Responsibility, not dependency.** The complexity of contemporary medicine fosters patients' dependence on physicians. Holistic medicine tries to shift some responsibility for health from physicians to people themselves by enhancing their abilities to engage in health-promoting behavior (Ferguson, 1980). Holistic medicine favors a more *active* approach to *health*, not a *reactive* approach to *illness*.

3. **Personal treatment.** Conventional medicine locates medical care not in homes but in impersonal offices and hospitals, which are disease-centered settings. Holistic practitioners favor, as much as possible, a personal and relaxed setting. Holistic medicine seeks to re-establish the personal social ties that united healers and patients before the era of specialists. The AMA currently recognizes more than fifty specialized areas of medical practice, and a growing proportion of M.D.s are entering these high-paying specialties rather than family practice. Thus, there is a need for practitioners who are concerned with the patient in the holistic sense.

Clearly, holistic care does not oppose scientific medicine but simply changes the emphasis in health care. To supporters, this approach moves away from narrowly treating disease toward the goal of achieving the highest possible level of well-being for everyone.

Paying the Costs: A Global Survey

Especially as medicine has come to rely on high technology, the costs of health care in industrial societies have skyrocketed. Countries use various strategies to meet these costs.

The People's Republic of China. The People's Republic of China, a poor, agrarian society only beginning to industrialize, faces the daunting task of attending to the health of more than a billion people. Traditional healing arts, including acupuncture and the prescription of medicinal herbs, are still widely practiced in China. In addition, a holistic concern for the interplay of mind and body marks the Chinese approach to health (Sidel & Sidel, 1982b; Kaptchuk, 1985).

China recently experimented with private medical care, but by 1990 the government had re-established tight control over every area of life. China's famed barefoot doctors, roughly comparable to U.S. paramedics, have brought some modern methods of medical care to millions of peasants in remote rural villages.

The Commonwealth of Independent States. The former Soviet Union is currently struggling to transform a state-dominated economy into more of a market system. For this reason, the scheme for providing medical care is in transition. Currently, the government provides medical care funded from taxes. As is the case in the People's

Republic of China, people do not choose a physician, but report to a local government health facility.

Physicians in the former Soviet Union have had lower prestige and income than their counterparts in the United States. They have received about the same salary as skilled industrial workers, a reflection of socialist attempts at economic equality. Worth noting, too, is that about 70 percent of Commonwealth physicians are women, compared with about 20 percent in the United States, and, as in our society, occupations dominated by women yield fewer financial rewards (Fuchs, 1974; Knaus, 1981).

The Soviet system has trained enough physicians to meet the basic needs of a large population. However, rigid bureaucracy still results in highly standardized and impersonal care. As market reforms are adopted, uniformity will likely diminish, and disparities in the quality of care among various segments of the population may well increase.

Sweden. In 1891 Sweden instituted a compulsory, comprehensive system of government medical care. Citizens of this Scandinavian country pay for this program with their taxes, which are among the highest in the world. Typically, physicians receive salaries from the government rather than fees from patients, and most hospitals are government-managed. Because this medical system resembles that of socialist societies, it is often described as **socialized medicine,** *a medical-care system in which the government owns most facilities and employs most physicians.*

Great Britain. In 1948 Great Britain, too, instituted socialized medicine. The British did not do away with private care, however, creating a "dual system" of medical services. All British citizens are entitled to medical care provided by the National Health Service, but those who can afford to may purchase more extensive care from doctors and hospitals that operate privately.

Canada. Like a vast insurance company, the Canadian government pays doctors and hospitals, which operate privately, according to scheduled fees. Some physicians work entirely outside of the government-funded system, charging whatever fees they wish (Grant, 1984; Vayda & Deber, 1984).

Japan. Physicians and hospitals in Japan operate privately. In general, employers provide comprehensive health coverage as an employee benefit. For those without such programs, government medical insurance covers most costs, and the elderly receive free care (Vogel, 1979).

Medicine in the United States

As of 1993, the United States was unique among the industrialized societies in having no government-subsidized medical program for everyone. On average, European governments pay about 75 percent of medical costs; the U.S. government pays 40 percent (Lohr, 1988). For the most part, then, medicine in this country is handled as a private, profit-making industry. Called a **direct-fee system**, ours is *a medical-care system in which patients pay directly for the services of physicians and hospitals.*

Affluent people in the United States can purchase outstanding medical care, yet the poor fare worse than their counterparts in Europe. This translates into relatively high death rates among both infants and adults in the United States compared to many European countries (Fuchs, 1974; United Nations, 1991).

Why does the United States have no national health-care program? First, our society has historically favored limited government. Second, support for a national medical program has not been strong even among labor unions, which have concentrated on winning health-care benefits from employers. Third, the AMA and the insurance industry have strongly and consistently opposed any such program (Starr, 1982).

Figure 13–3 shows that medical expenditures in the United States increased dramatically from $12 billion (5 percent of the gross national product) in 1950 to $666 billion (12 percent of GNP) by 1990. Who pays the medical bills?

Private insurance programs. In 1990, 150 million people in the United States (61 percent) received medical-care benefits from a family member's employer or labor union. Another 35 million people (14 percent) purchased some private coverage on their own. Private insurance (including Blue Cross and Blue Shield) rarely pays all medical costs, but three-fourths of our population has some private medical insurance (Health Insurance Association of America, 1991).

Public insurance programs. In 1965 Congress created Medicare and Medicaid. Medicare pays some of the medical costs for people over sixty-five; in 1990 it covered almost 33 million men and women, about 13 percent of the population. Medicaid, a medical insurance program for the poor, provided benefits for some 24 million

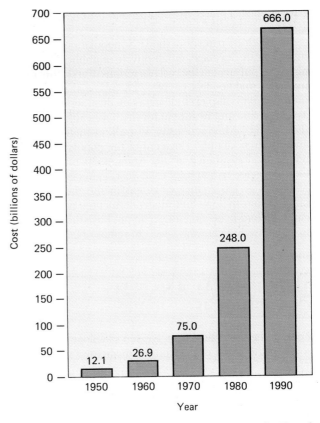

Figure 13–3 The Rising Cost of Medical Care in the United States

(*U.S. Bureau of the Census, 1970; Health Insurance Association of America, 1991*)

people, about 10 percent of the population. An additional 10 million veterans (4 percent) can obtain free care in government-operated hospitals. In all, about 30 percent of this country's people enjoy some medical benefits from the government, although most are also covered to some extent by private insurance programs.

Health maintenance organizations. An increasing number of people in the United States belong to a **health maintenance organization** (HMO), *an association that provides comprehensive medical care for a fixed fee.* In 1990, 556 HMOs enrolled some 33 million individuals, about 13 percent of the population. HMOs vary in costs and benefits, and none provides full coverage. But fixed costs give these organizations a financial interest in keeping their subscribers healthy; therefore, many have adopted a preventive approach to health (Ginsburg, 1983).

In all, 85 percent of the U.S. population has some medical-care coverage, either private or public. Yet most plans pay only part of the cost of a serious illness, threatening even middle-class people with financial ruin. And most programs also exclude many medical services, such as dental care and treatment for mental-health problems (Eve, 1984). Most seriously, 35 million men, women, and children (about 14 percent of the population) have no medical insurance at all. Another 30 million lose their coverage temporarily each year, generally because of layoffs or job changes. Caught in the medical-care bind are mostly low- and moderate-income people who cannot afford to become ill yet do not have the resources to purchase the care they need to remain healthy.

THEORETICAL ANALYSIS OF MEDICINE

Each of the theoretical paradigms in sociology highlights some of the social dimensions of medicine.

Structural-Functional Analysis

Talcott Parsons (1951) viewed medicine as a social system's means of keeping its members healthy. In this view, illness is a form of system dysfunction, undermining the performance of social roles.

The sick role.   One response to illness, Parsons argued, is to assume the **sick role**, *patterns of behavior defined as appropriate for those who are ill.* Insofar as people suffer from poor health, the sick role exempts them from everyday responsibilities. However, Parsons added, people cannot simply declare themselves ill; this assessment falls to a recognized medical expert. Parsons noted further that on assuming the sick role the patient is obligated to do whatever is needed to regain good health, including cooperating with health professionals.

The physician's role.   Physicians function to assess claims of sickness, and to restore sick people to normal routines. The physician's power and responsibility in relation to the patient derive from specialized knowledge, Parsons explained. Physicians expect patients to follow "doctor's orders," and to provide whatever personal information may reasonably assist their efforts. Although it

is invariably hierarchical, the doctor-patient relationship varies from society to society, as the box explains with a look to Japan.

Critical evaluation.   Parsons's work links illness and medicine to the broader organization of society. Others have extended the useful concept of the sick role to some non-illness situations such as pregnancy (Myers & Grasmick, 1989). Bear in mind, however, that a sick person's ability to regain health depends on available resources. Many impoverished people can ill afford either effective health care or time off from work.

Critics charge that Parsons's view of the physician's role supports the idea that doctors rather than patients bear primary responsibility for health. Treatment-oriented physicians respond to acute illness, of course, but a more prevention-minded approach would cast physicians and patients as partners in the pursuit of health.

Symbolic-Interaction Analysis

Viewed according to the symbolic-interaction paradigm, society is less a grand system than a complex and changing reality. Both health and medical care are thus human constructions, which we, in turn, perceive subjectively.

Socially constructing illness.   Since we socially construct both health and illness, members of a society where most people go hungry may view malnutrition as quite normal. Similarly, members of our own society defined smoking cigarettes as fashionable for decades, and we remain complacent about the unhealthful effects of a rich diet.

How we respond to illness, too, is based on social definitions that may or may not square with medical facts. For instance, people with AIDS contend with fear and sometimes outright bigotry that has no basis in medical fact.

How people define a medical situation can sometimes affect how someone actually feels. Medical experts have long noted the existence of *psychosomatic* disorders (a fusion of Greek words for "mind" and "body"), in which state of mind guides physical sensations (Hamrick, Anspaugh, & Ezell, 1986). As sociologist W. I. Thomas (1931) pointed out, a situation defined as real becomes real in its consequences.

Socially constructing treatment.   In Chapter 4 ("Social Interaction in Everyday Life"), we used the dramaturgical approach of Erving Goffman to explain how physicians

Breaking Bad News: Comparing Japanese and U.S. Physicians

Japanese emperor Hirohito died in 1988 without even knowing why. The world learned that the traditional Japanese ruler succumbed to intestinal cancer, but doctors never told him the bad news. This is the rule in Japan, where physicians routinely conceal the fact of terminal illness from patients. A Japanese specialist in bioethics explains:

> In Japan, the art of medicine is regarded as an expression of loving kindness—part of the art of *Jin*, the fundamental teaching of Confucian ideas. There is the belief that giving the patient hope until the last minute will give him a fighting spirit.

Out of kindness, then, Japanese physicians take charge of every decision that affects a patient's well-being. Their professional standards demand that doctors withhold information about the seriousness of an illness. The Japanese are not alone in this practice; physicians in most of the less-developed nations of the world follow the same precepts.

Physicians in the United States acted the same way three decades ago. In 1961 an article in the *Journal of the American Medical Association* reported that just one in eight U.S. physicians believed in discussing a terminal illness with a dying patient. What changed this practice? The *patients' rights movement*, which has gathered the greatest support in the

John Collier's (1913–) painting *Sentence of Death* portrays perhaps the most difficult ordeal a physician can face: informing a patient of impending death. Until recently, U.S. physicians routinely withheld such a diagnosis in the belief that the patient was better off not knowing of a terminal condition. Although now this practice is far less common in the United States, it continues in Japan and in many other countries of the world.

United States, has rewritten the rules for the physician-patient relationship. The public has steadily demanded—often with support from the courts—that physicians readily disclose more and more medical information and assist patients in making decisions for themselves. Researchers have backed up this policy by demonstrating that such disclosure reduces patients' anxieties, strengthens their bond with physicians, and allows terminally ill people to better plan how to use whatever time is left.

This example illustrates how ethics—like technology—varies from place to place and is subject to change. European societies are now following the U.S. lead in advancing patients' rights. Japan, too, is reconsidering its stance, debating the physician's duty to tell people the truth, even when the news is bad.

SOURCE: Based on Darnton & Hoshia (1989).

---

craft their physical surroundings ("the office") and present themselves to others to foster specific impressions of competence and power.

Sociologist Joan Emerson (1970) further illustrates this process of reality construction by analyzing a situation familiar to women, a gynecological examination carried out by a male doctor. After observing seventy-five such examinations, she explains that this situation is precarious

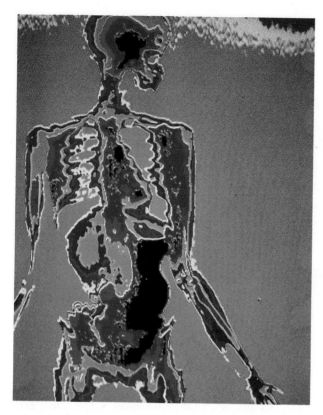

Advances in medicine utilizing computers and other new technology offer significant health benefits to many people. But they have also contributed to the soaring cost of medical care. This country is now developing a national health care package in response to charges that we have two standards of health: one for those who can afford the best care and another for everyone else.

because it is vulnerable to serious misinterpretation. Why? Simply because the man's touching of a woman's genitals—conventionally viewed as a sexual act and possibly even an assault—must, in this case, be defined as impersonal and professional. To ensure that reality is constructed in this way, the medical staff carefully removes any sexual connotations from their performances.

To accomplish this task, they furnish the examination room with nothing but medical equipment, and all personnel wear uniforms. The staff also acts as if such examinations are simply routine although, from the patient's point of view, they may be quite unusual. Further, although rapport between physician and patient is important, this is established before the examination

begins. Once under way, the doctor's performance is strictly professional, suggesting to the patient that inspecting the genitals is no different from surveying any other part of the body. A nurse is often present during the examination not only to assist the physician, but to dispel any impression that a man and woman are "alone in a room" (Emerson, 1970:81).

The need to manage situational definitions has long been overlooked by medical schools. This omission is unfortunate because, as Emerson's analysis shows, understanding how reality is socially constructed in the examination room is just as crucial as mastering the medical skills required for effective treatment.

Critical evaluation. One strength of the symbolic-interaction paradigm lies in revealing the relativity of sickness and health. What people view as normal or deviant, healthful or harmful, depends on a host of factors, many of which are not, strictly speaking, medical. This approach also shows that all medical procedures involve subtle interaction between patient and physician.

Yet this approach seems to deny that there are any objective standards of well-being. Certain physical conditions do indeed cause specific changes in human capacities, whether we think so or not. And people who lack sufficient nutrition and safe water, for example, suffer from their unhealthy environment however they define their surroundings.

Social-Conflict Analysis

Social-conflict analysis draws a connection between health and social inequality and, following Karl Marx, ties health to the operation of capitalism. Researchers have focused on three main issues: access to medical care, the effects of the profit motive, and the politics of medicine.

Unequal access. Personal health is the foundation of social life. Yet by making health a commodity, capitalist societies allow health to follow wealth. As already noted, the access problem is more serious in the United States than in most other industrial societies since we have no comprehensive medical-care system.

Marxist critics contend that capitalist health problems are rooted in class conflict. These critics claim that the concentration of wealth makes equal medical care impossible, even if some comprehensive government health-care program were enacted. Only a redistribution of economic resources would make medical care uniformly available (Bodenheimer, 1977; Navarro, 1977).

The profit motive. Some social-conflict analysts go further, arguing that the real problem is not access to medical care but the character of capitalist medicine itself. The profit motive turns physicians, hospitals, and the pharmaceutical industry into multibillion-dollar corporate conglomerates (Ehrenreich, 1978). The quest for ever-increasing profits encourages unnecessary tests and surgery and an overreliance on drugs (Kaplan et al., 1985).

Of the 30 million surgical operations performed in the United States each year, three-fourths are "elective," meaning that they are intended to promote long-term health rather than being prompted by a medical emergency. Critics charge that the decision to perform surgery reflects the financial interests of surgeons and hospitals as well as the medical needs of patients (Illich, 1976). Perhaps 10 percent of this elective surgery could safely be refused or deferred, saving patients more than $1 billion each year. More important, since about one in two hundred patients dies from elective surgery (because surgery is itself dangerous), thirteen thousand lives a year are needlessly lost (Sidel & Sidel, 1982a). Finally, from this point of view, our society is too tolerant of physicians having a direct, financial interest in the tests and procedures they order for their patients (Pear & Eckholm, 1991). In short, critics conclude, health care should be motivated by a concern for people, not profits.

Medicine as politics. Although science declares itself to be politically neutral, scientific medicine frequently takes sides on significant social issues. For example, the medical establishment strongly opposes government health-care programs. The history of medicine, critics

contend, is replete with racial and sexual discrimination based on "scientific" facts about women and other minorities. For example, a century ago, medical men declared women unfit for higher education, lest learning harm their reproductive systems (Zola, 1978; Brown, 1979; Leavitt, 1984).

Even today critics see political mischief in scientific medicine. Scientific medicine explains illness in terms of bacteria and viruses rather than showing the effects on health of social inequality. In this way, scientific medicine depoliticizes health in the United States by reducing social issues to simple biology.

Critical evaluation. Social-conflict analysis provides still another view of the relationships among health, medicine, and society. There is little doubt that many people benefit from CAT scans, chemotherapy, and even artificial hearts. But, just as important, millions of people still lack basic medical care.

The most common objection to the conflict approach is that it minimizes the advances in U.S. health supported by scientific medicine and higher living standards. Though there is plenty of room for improvement, health indicators for our population have risen steadily over the course of this century.

To sum up, sociology's three major theoretical paradigms convincingly argue that health and medicine are social issues. The famous French scientist Louis Pasteur (1822–1895) spent much of his life studying how bacteria cause disease. Yet just before his death, he concluded that health depends less on bacteria than on the social environment in which bacteria operate (Gordon, 1980:7). Explaining Pasteur's insight is sociology's contribution to human health.

SUMMARY

Education

1. Education is a major social institution for transmitting knowledge and skills as well as norms and values. In preindustrial societies, education occurs informally within the family; industrial societies develop formal systems of schooling.

2. The United States was among the first societies to institute compulsory mass education, reflecting

both democratic political ideals and the needs of the industrial-capitalist economy.

3. The functions of schooling include socialization, social placement, and fostering both social integration and innovation. Additional latent functions involve child care and forging social networks.

4. Social-conflict analysis points out how class, race,

and gender promote unequal opportunities for schooling. Formal education also serves to instill conformity to produce compliant adult workers.

5. Based on standardized testing, tracking places students in classes corresponding to their ability. Critics charge that tracking is keyed to students' social background and allocates more resources to privileged students.

6. The great majority of young people in the United States attend state-funded public schools. Most privately funded schools are affiliated with religious organizations. A small proportion of young people—generally well-to-do—attend elite private preparatory schools.

7. One-fifth of U.S. adults over the age of twenty-five are now college graduates, marking the emergence of a credential society.

8. Most adults in the United States are critical of public schools. Violence permeates many schools, especially those in poor neighborhoods. The bureaucratic character of schools has also fostered high dropout rates and widespread student passivity.

9. Declining academic standards are reflected in lower average scores today on academic achievement tests and the functional illiteracy of a significant proportion of high-school graduates.

10. The school choice movement seeks to make educational systems more responsive to the public. Innovative options include magnet schools and schools for profit, which have improved education in some cities and towns.

11. Children with mental or physical disabilities historically have been schooled in special classes or not at all. Mainstreaming affords broader opportunities to students with disabilities.

Medicine

1. Health is a social and biological issue and depends on a society's technology and distribution of resources. Culture shapes definitions of health as well as patterns of health care.

2. Health improved dramatically in Western Europe and North America in the nineteenth century, first due to industrialization and later because of medical advances.

3. Infectious diseases were leading killers at the beginning of this century. Today most people in the United States die in old age of chronic illnesses like heart disease, cancer, or stroke.

4. Third-World health suffers from inadequate sanitation, hunger, and other problems linked to poverty. Life expectancy is about twenty years less than in the United States; in the poorest nations, half of all children do not survive to adulthood.

5. Three-fourths of U.S. children born today can expect to reach age sixty-five. Throughout the life course, women have relatively better health than men, and people of high social position enjoy better health than others.

6. While industrialization has raised our living standards, environmental pollution threatens the future health of our population.

7. Cigarette smoking has increased during this century to become the greatest preventable cause of death in the United States.

8. Unlike other kinds of infections, sexually transmitted diseases are on the rise. As a result, there has been a reduction in casual sexual relations.

9. Because of advancing medical technology, an increasing number of ethical decisions surround how and when death should occur.

10. Historically a family concern, health care is now the responsibility of trained specialists. The model of scientific medicine underlies the U.S. medical establishment. The holistic approach seeks to give people greater responsibility for their own health.

11. Socialist societies define medical care as a right that governments offer equally to everyone. Capitalist societies view medical care as a commodity to be purchased, although most capitalist governments support medical care through socialized medicine or national health insurance. The United States is the only industrial society with no comprehensive medical-care program.

12. Central to the structural-functional analysis of health is the concept of the sick role, in which illness allows release from routine responsibilities. The symbolic-interaction paradigm investigates the social construction of both health and medical treatment. Social-conflict analysis focuses on the unequal access to health care and criticizes our medical system for emphasizing biological rather than social causes of illness.

KEY CONCEPTS

Education

credentialism evaluating people on the basis of educational degrees

education various ways in which a society ensures that its members gain relevant knowledge—including facts, skills, and values

functional illiteracy reading and writing skills inadequate for everyday needs

schooling formal instruction under the direction of specially trained teachers

tracking assigning students to different educational programs

Medicine

direct-fee system a medical-care system in which patients pay directly for the services of physicians and hospitals

euthanasia (mercy killing) assisting in the death of a person suffering from an incurable illness

health a state of complete physical, mental, and social well-being

health maintenance organization (HMO) an organization that provides comprehensive medical care for a fixed fee

holistic medicine an approach to health care that emphasizes prevention of illness and takes account of a person's entire physical and social environment

medicine the institutionalized means of combating disease and improving health

sick role patterns of behavior defined as appropriate for those who are ill

social epidemiology the study of how health and disease are distributed throughout a society's population

socialized medicine a health-care system in which the government owns most facilities and employs most physicians

14

Population and Urbanization

In 1519 a band of Spanish conquistadors led by Hernando Cortés reached Tenochtitlán, the capital of the Aztec empire. What they saw stunned them. Here was a lake-encircled city, teeming with over 300,000 people—more people than could be found in any European city at that time. Gazing down broad streets, exploring magnificent stone temples, and examining the golden treasures of the royal palace, Cortés and his soldiers wondered if they were dreaming.

Cortés soon woke up and set his mind to looting the city. Unable at first to overcome the superior forces of the Aztecs and their leader Montezuma, Cortés spent two years raising a vast army and finally destroyed Tenochtitlán. In its place, Cortés constructed a new city in the European fashion—*Ciudad Imperial de México*—Mexico City.

Today Mexico City is once more fighting for its life. Its soaring population will reach 30 million by the end of the 1990s—one hundred times the number that astonished Cortés. This huge population is grappling with a host of problems common to Third-World societies, including poverty, foreign debt, and a deteriorating environment.

A triple burden of rising population, urban sprawl, and desperate poverty weighs on much of today's world. This chapter examines both population growth and urbanization—two powerful forces that have shaped and reshaped our planet for thousands of years. Increasing population will be one of the most serious challenges facing the world in the coming century, and this compelling drama will be played out in cities of unprecedented size.

DEMOGRAPHY: THE STUDY OF POPULATION

From the point at which the human species emerged some 200,000 years ago until several centuries ago, the earth's population remained at some 20 million—about the same number as the population of southern California today. Life was uncertain at best; people were vulnerable to countless diseases and frequent natural disasters. For ten thousand generations, however, our species has managed to flourish. Ironically, perhaps, global population is now so large (5.5 billion in 1993), and growing so rapidly (by almost 100 million annually), that the future of humanity is again uncertain.

The causes and consequences of this growth form the core of **demography,** *the study of human population.* Demography (from Greek meaning "descripton of people"), a close cousin of sociology, analyzes the size and composition of a population, as well as how people move from place to place. Although much demographic research is a numbers game, the discipline also poses crucial questions about the effects of population growth and how it can be controlled.

The following sections explain basic demographic concepts.

Fertility

The study of human population begins with how many people are born. **Fertility** is *the incidence of childbearing in a society's population.* During their childbearing years, from the onset of menstruation (typically in the early teens) to menopause (usually in the late forties), women are capable of bearing over twenty children. But *fecundity*, or potential childbearing, is sharply reduced by illness, finances, and personal choice.

Demographers measure fertility using the **crude birth rate,** *the number of live births in a given year for every thousand people in a population.* They calculate a crude birth rate by dividing the number of live births in a year by a society's total population, and multiplying the result by 1,000. In the United States in 1990, there were 4.2 million live births in a population of 253 million (U.S. Bureau of the Census, 1991). According to this formula, then, the crude birth rate was 16.6.

This birth rate is "crude" because it is based on the entire population, not just women and men in their childbearing years. Comparing the crude birth rates of various countries can be misleading, then, if one society has a larger share of women of childbearing age than another. A crude birth rate also tells us nothing about how birth rates differ among people of various races, ethnicities, and religions. But this measure is easy to calculate and serves as a good indicator of a society's overall fertility. Table 14–1 shows that the crude birth rate of the United States is low in world context.

Mortality

Population size is also affected by **mortality,** *the incidence of death in a society's population.* Corresponding to the crude birth rate, demographers use a **crude death**

Table 14–1 FERTILITY AND MORTALITY RATES IN GLOBAL PERSPECTIVE, 1991

	Crude Birth Rate	Crude Death Rate	Infant Mortality Rate
North America			
United States	17	9	10
Canada	14	8	7
Europe			
Belgium	12	11	6
Commonwealth of Independent States	17	10	23
Denmark	12	11	6
France	14	9	6
Spain	11	8	6
United Kingdom	14	11	7
Latin America			
Chile	21	6	18
Cuba	18	7	12
Haiti	44	15	106
Mexico	29	5	30
Nicaragua	37	7	60
Puerto Rico	19	8	17
Africa			
Algeria	32	7	57
Cameroon	41	15	118
Egypt	33	10	82
Ethiopia	45	15	114
Nigeria	46	16	118
South Africa	34	8	51
Asia			
Afghanistan	44	20	164
Bangladesh	36	13	118
India	30	11	84
Israel	22	6	9
Japan	10	7	4
Vietnam	30	8	48

SOURCE: U.S. Bureau of the Census, *Statistical Abstract of the United States 1992* (Washington, DC: U.S. Government Printing Office, 1992).

rate, *the number of deaths in a given year for every thousand people in a population.* This time, we take the number of deaths in a year, and again divide by the total population, multiplying the result by 1,000. In 1990 there were 2.2 million deaths in the U.S. population of 253 million, yielding a crude death rate of 8.7. As Table 14–1 shows, this rate is low by world standards.

Another common demographic measure is the **infant mortality rate,** *the number of deaths among infants under one year of age for each thousand live births in a given year.* This rate is derived by dividing the number of deaths of children under one year of age by the number of live births during the same year and multiplying the result by 1,000. In 1990 there were 42,600 infant deaths and about 4.2 million live births in the United States. Dividing the first number by the second and multiplying the result by 1,000 produces an infant mortality rate of 10.4. Here again, bear in mind variation among different categories of people. For example, African-Americans, with three times the burden of poverty as whites, have an infant mortality rate of about 18—twice the white rate (U.S. Bureau of the Census, 1992). But infant mortality offers a good general measure of overall quality of life. Table 14–1 shows that infant mortality in the United States, while low by global standards, is somewhat higher than in Canada, Denmark, and other nations that make medical care more widely available to their people.

Low infant mortality greatly increases **life expectancy,** *the average life span of a society's population.* Males born in 1990 can expect to live 72.1 years, while females can look toward 79.0 years. In Third-World societies with high infant mortality, however, life expectancy is about twenty years less.

Migration

Population size is also affected by **migration,** *the movement of people into and out of a specific territory.* Migration is sometimes involuntary, such as the forcible transport of 10 million Africans to the Western Hemisphere as slaves (Sowell, 1981). Voluntary migration is usually motivated by complex "push-pull" factors. Dissatisfaction with life may "push" people to move, while a common "pull" factor is the opportunity for a better life in a big city. As explained later in this chapter, this situation is causing rapid urban growth in the Third World.

People's movement into a territory—commonly termed *immigration*—is measured as an *in-migration rate,* calculated as the number of people entering an area for every thousand people in the population. Movement out of a territory—or *emigration*—is measured in terms of the *out-migration rate,* the number leaving for every thousand people. Both types of migration usually occur simultaneously, their difference being the *net-migration rate.*

African-American artist Jacob Lawrence completed a series of paintings that he titled *The Migration of the Negro* (1941) to document a major population movement among people of color from the rural South to the urban centers of the Northeast and Midwest.

Jacob Lawrence, The Migration of the Negro. *Panel 1: During the World War There Was a Great Migration North by Southern Negroes, 1940–41. Tempera on masonite. 11½ x 17½". The Phillips Collection.*

Population Growth

Fertility, mortality, and migration all affect the size of a society's population. Demographers calculate a population's natural growth rate by subtracting the crude death rate from the crude birth rate. The natural growth rate of the U.S. population in 1990 was 7.9 (the crude birth rate of 16.6 minus the crude death rate of 8.7), which is about 0.8 percent annual growth.

Global Map 14–1 shows that population growth in the United States and other industrialized nations is well below the world average. In Europe, the current rate of growth is just 0.2 percent, and in Japan it is falling rapidly. By contrast, annual growth rates equal or exceed the global average throughout the Third World—including Asia (currently about 1.7 percent) and Latin America (overall, about 1.8 percent). The greatest population surge is occurring in Africa, where population growth averages 3.1 percent. Keep in mind that an annual growth of 2 percent (as in Latin America) doubles a population in thirty-five years, and a 3 percent growth rate (as in Africa) pares the *doubling time* to only twenty-four years. The rapid population growth of the poorest countries is deeply troubling because they can barely support the populations they have now.

Later in this chapter, we detail reasons for this striking pattern. For the moment, we can note that industrialized nations offer more widespread birth control, greater options out of the home for women, and higher costs for raising children. Less-developed nations, by contrast, provide less birth control, limit women's choices more, and look on children as economic assets.

Population Composition

Demographers also study the composition of a society's population at a given point in time. One simple variable is the **sex ratio**, *the number of males for every hundred females in a given population.* In 1990 the sex ratio in the United States was 95.0, or 95 males for every 100 females. Sex ratios are usually below 100 because women typically outlive men.

A more complex measure is the **age-sex pyramid**, *a graphic representation of the age and sex of a population.* Figure 14–1 on page 360 presents the age-sex pyramid for the United States. The left side shows the number of males of various ages, while the right side shows the corresponding number of females. The rough pyramid shape results from higher mortality as people age. The bulge corresponding to ages twenty through forty-four reflects high birth rates from the mid-1940s to the late

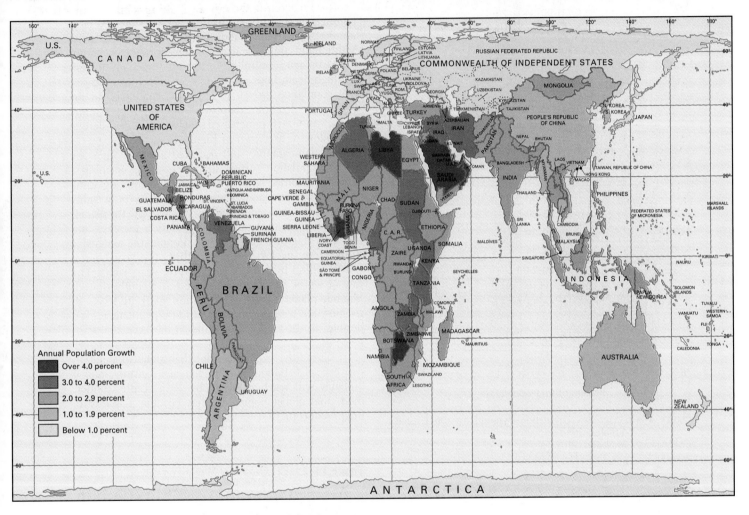

Global Map 14–1 Population Growth in Global Perspective

The richest societies of the world—including the United States, Canada, and the nations of Europe—have growth rates below 1 percent. The nations of Latin America and Asia typically have growth rates of about 2 percent, which double a population in thirty-five years. The continent of Africa has an overall growth rate of 3.1 percent, which cuts the doubling time to less than twenty-four years. In global perspective, we see that a society's standard of living is closely related to its rate of population growth, meaning that population is rising fastest in the world regions that can least afford to support more people.

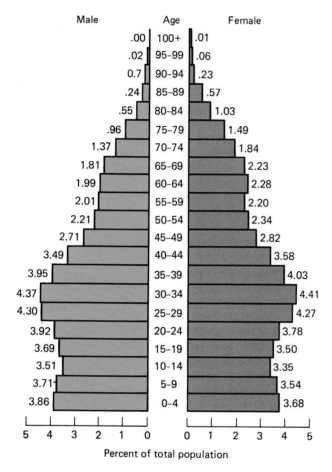

Male   **Age**   **Female**

.00	100+	.01
.02	95–99	.06
0.7	90–94	.23
.24	85–89	.57
.55	80–84	1.03
.96	75–79	1.49
1.37	70–74	1.84
1.81	65–69	2.23
1.99	60–64	2.28
2.01	55–59	2.20
2.21	50–54	2.34
2.71	45–49	2.82
3.49	40–44	3.58
3.95	35–39	4.03
4.37	30–34	4.41
4.30	25–29	4.27
3.92	20–24	3.78
3.69	15–19	3.50
3.51	10–14	3.35
3.71	5–9	3.54
3.86	0–4	3.68

5   4   3   2   1   0   0   1   2   3   4   5

Percent of total population

Figure 14–1 Age-Sex Population Pyramid for the United States, 1990
(U.S. Bureau of the Census, 1991)

1960s, commonly called the *baby boom*. The contraction just below shows the *baby bust* that followed. From a peak of 25.3 in 1957, the crude birth rate dipped to 15.3 in 1986 (and rose again to 16.6 by 1990).

Bulges and contractions in age-sex pyramids reveal a society's demographic history and likely future. Compared to the age-sex pyramids of industrial societies, those of Third-World nations are wider at the bottom (reflecting higher birth rates) and narrow quickly by what we would term middle age (due to higher mortality). In poor societies, the majority of females have yet to enter their childbearing years, setting the stage for exploding population unless measures are taken to control births.

HISTORY AND THEORY OF POPULATION GROWTH

Through most of human history, societies favored large families since human labor was the key to productivity. Additionally, until the development of rubber condoms 150 years ago, controlling birth was uncertain at best. But high death rates, resulting from infectious diseases, kept population growth low. World population at the dawn of civilization, about 6000 B.C.E., was no more than 25 million; this increased slowly across the millennia that followed, as shown in Figure 14–2.

A demographic shift occurred about 1750 as the earth's population turned sharply upward, reaching 1 billion a century later. This increase (requiring some forty thousand years) was repeated by 1930 (only eighty years later) when a second billion was added to the planet. In other words, not only did population increase, but the *rate* of growth accelerated. Population reached a third billion by 1962 (after just thirty-two years) and a fourth billion by 1974 (a scant twelve years later). The rate of world population increase has recently slowed, but our planet passed the 5 billion mark in 1987. In no previous century did the world's population even double. In the twentieth century, it has increased *four-fold*.

Currently, experts predict that global population will exceed 6 billion early in the next century, and it probably will reach 8 billion by 2025. Little wonder, then, that global population has become a matter of urgent concern.

Figure 14–2 The Growth of World Population

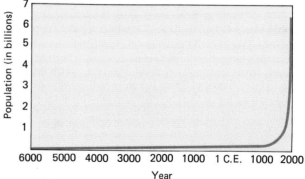

Malthusian Theory

It was the sudden population growth two centuries ago that sparked the development of demography. Thomas Robert Malthus (1766–1834), an English clergyman and economist, devised a demographic theory that warned of impending social chaos. Malthus (1926; orig. 1798) began by claiming that population growth was the simple result of timeless passion between the sexes. Population increase, he predicted, would approximate what mathematicians call a geometric progression, illustrated by the series of numbers 2, 4, 8, 16, 32, and so on. Malthus reached the sobering conclusion that world population would soon soar out of control.

Food production would also increase, Malthus reasoned, but only in arithmetic progression (as in the series 2, 3, 4, 5, 6) because, even with agricultural innovation, farmland is limited. Malthus's analysis yielded a troubling vision of the future: people reproducing beyond what the planet could feed, leading ultimately to catastrophic starvation.

What of limits to population growth? Malthus foresaw what he called *positive checks* such as famine, disease, and war; and *preventive checks* like artificial birth control, sexual abstinence, and delayed marriages. He rejected birth control on religious grounds, and his common sense told him people would not abstain from sex or marry later. Famine stalked the future of humanity, in Malthus's scheme, a vision that earned him the title of the "dismal parson."

Critical evaluation. Fortunately, Malthus's prediction was flawed. First, by 1850 the birth rate in Europe began to drop, partly because children were becoming less of an economic asset and more of a liability, and partly because people did adopt artificial birth control. Second, Malthus underestimated human ingenuity: irrigation, fertilizers, and pesticides have greatly increased farm production just as factories have generated a bounty of other products.

Critics also chided Malthus for ignoring the role of social inequality in world abundance and famine. Karl Marx (1967; orig. 1867) objected to viewing suffering as a "law of nature," rather than the mischief of capitalism.

Still, we should not entirely dismiss Malthus's dire prediction. First, habitable land, clean water, and fresh air are certainly limited. And greater productivity has also worsened problems like environmental pollution.

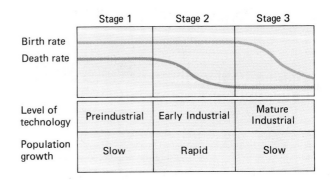

Figure 14–3   Demographic Transition Theory

Finally, medical advances have lowered death rates but, in so doing, have boosted world population. This is especially true in poor societies, which are experiencing some of the catastrophe Malthus envisioned.

In principle, conclude some analysts, while recent global population growth may be below that feared by Malthus, no growth is acceptable in the long run (Ehrlich, 1978). Thus, the entire planet must remain alert to the long-range dangers of population increase.

Demographic Transition Theory

Malthus's rather crude analysis has been superseded by **demographic transition theory,** *a thesis linking population patterns to a society's level of technological development.*

Figure 14–3 shows the demographic consequences of three stages of technological development. Preindustrial agrarian societies—those at Stage 1—have high birth rates because of the economic value of children and the absence of effective birth control. Death rates are also high, the result of low living standards and the lack of medical technology. But deaths neutralize births, so population increase is modest, as it was for thousands of years before the Industrial Revolution in Europe.

Stage 2—the onset of industrialization—brings a demographic transition as population surges upward. Technology expands food supplies and combats disease. Birth rates remain high, but death rates fall sharply, resulting in rapid population growth. It was in an era like this that Malthus formulated his ideas, which explains his pessimism. Most Third-World societies today are still in this high-growth stage.

Il paraît que je suis
un phénomène socio-culturel.

LA FRANCE
A BESOIN
D'ENFANTS.

The birth rate in Europe has dropped so low that some analysts foresee an absolute drop in population in this world region. In France, a nation that sees children not as the concern of families but as a national resource, the government has turned to advertising to encourage people to reproduce. The ad implies children are becoming so rare that this baby can remark: "It appears that I am a sociocultural phenomenon." At the bottom right is added, "France needs children."

In Stage 3—a fully industrialized economy—the birth rate drops, curbing population growth once again. First, a high standard of living makes raising children expensive, so large families become an economic liability rather than an asset. Smaller families are also favored by women working outside the home. Furthermore, birth control becomes increasingly effective. As birth rates follow death rates downward, population growth again slows. Western industrial societies have been in this stage for much of this century. Most Third-World societies, however, appear to be locked in a dangerously high population-growth spiral.

Critical evaluation. Demographic transition theory suggests that technology holds the key to population control. Instead of the runaway population increase Malthus feared, this analysis foresees technology both controlling population growth and ensuring material plenty.

Demographic transition theory dovetails with modernization theory, one approach to global development discussed in Chapter 8 ("Global Inequality"). Modernization theorists take the optimistic view that poor societies will solve their population problems as they industrialize.

But critics—notably dependency theorists—argue that current economic arrangements will only ensure continued poverty in much of the world. Unless there is a significant redistribution of global resources, they claim, our planet will become increasingly divided into industrialized "haves," enjoying low population growth, and nonindustrialized "have-nots," struggling in vain to feed soaring populations.

WORLD POPULATION TODAY

What demographic patterns exist in today's world? Drawing on the discussion so far, we can highlight a number of key patterns and reach several conclusions.

The Low-Growth North

When the Industrial Revolution began, population growth in Western Europe and North America peaked at 3 percent annually. But, in the centuries since, it steadily declined in countries of the Northern Hemisphere and, in 1970, fell below 1 percent in the United States. Having now reached Stage 3, the U.S. birth rate is close to the replacement level of 2.1 children per woman, a point termed **zero population growth,** *the level of reproduction that maintains population at a steady state.* Several countries in Europe have already shown even greater dips in the birth rate, prompting some analysts to anticipate a fourth demographic stage, characterized by population *decline* (van de Kaa, 1987). Because our population is still relatively young—with a median age of thirty-three in 1990—modest population growth is expected to continue during the next several decades. Yet the "graying of the United States," discussed in Chapter 3 ("Socialization: From Infancy to Old Age"), may eventually bring us to zero population growth.

Factors holding down population include the high costs of raising children, the rising proportion of women in the labor force, trends toward later marriages and more singlehood, and use of contraceptives by about two-thirds of women of childbearing age. Voluntary sterilization has increased dramatically to become the most common form of birth control in the United States. Even U.S. Catholics, whose religious doctrine prohibits the use of artificial birth control, no longer differ from others in their contraceptive practices (Westoff & Jones, 1977; Moore & Pachon, 1985).

Finally, abortion has been legal in the United States since 1973, and each year women decide to terminate some 1.4 million pregnancies in this fashion (Centers for Disease Control, 1991). Poor families are still somewhat larger than average, which contributes to the problem of child poverty in this country. Overall, however, population growth here and in other industrial nations does not present the pressing problem that it does in poor societies.

The High-Growth South

Population growth remains a serious problem in the poor societies of the Southern Hemisphere. Only a few societies, lacking any industrial technology, are at demographic transition theory's Stage 1. Most countries in Latin America, Africa, and Asia have agrarian economies with some industry, placing them in Stage 2. Advanced medical technology supplied by First-World societies has sharply reduced death rates, but birth rates remain high. Figure 14–4 shows the result. These societies now account for two-thirds of the earth's people and the proportion continues to rise.

Third-World birth rates remain high because children are still economic assets, frequently working eight- or ten-hour days to generate income; later, as adults, they care for aging parents. Throughout the Third World, families average four or five children; in rural areas, the number may reach six or eight (The World Bank, 1991).

Worldwide, we see that societies that define women's primary responsibilities as bearing children have high population growth. In Latin America, a combination of economic need, traditional patriarchy, and Roman Catholic doctrine discourages women from using birth control devices, with predictable demographic results. In much of Africa, many women in poor villages have no access to effective birth control (Salas, 1985). Asia is a study in contrasts: many rural women are unable to acquire contraceptive devices, but some—notably in China—are the target of aggressive campaigns by government to control birth rates. The box on page 364 reviews the current situation in the People's Republic of China, the world's most populous society.

In the long run, a key to population control may turn out to be giving people more economic and educational opportunities. Simply put, women restricted to traditional child-rearing roles have many children; similarly, men lacking jobs and schooling are likely to define

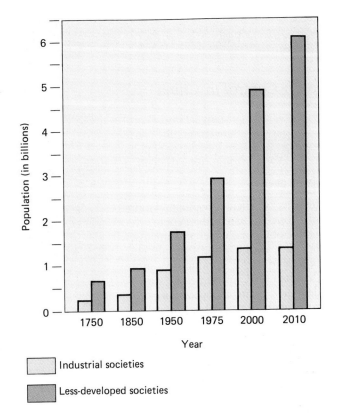

Figure 14–4 Population Distribution, Industrial and Less-Developed Societies, 1750–2010
(Piotrow, 1980; U.S. Bureau of the Census, 1991)

their masculinity in terms of virility. Research in Sudan (Africa) and Colombia (South America) suggests that women with seven years of schooling had half as many children as those without any education (Ross, 1985; Salas, 1985).

Efforts to control fertility have met with some success in many poor countries, with family size falling by 20 percent between 1975 and 1985 (Salas, 1985). But birth rates are still high, and now death rates are falling too, neutralizing some of the gain.

In point of fact, population growth in the Third World is due *primarily* to declining death rates. After about 1920, when Europe and North America began to export advances in scientific medicine, nutrition, and sanitation to poor societies, mortality tumbled. Since then, inoculations against infectious diseases and the use of antibiotics and insecticides have continued to curb death rates with stunning effectiveness. For example, in Sri Lanka, malaria caused half of all deaths in

Birth Control in China

P. R. China

Many Third-World governments have responded to population growth with a variety of programs aimed at reducing fertility. Nowhere is population more of a concern than in the People's Republic of China, which encompasses one-fifth of the world's people (1.2 billion in 1990). Ominously, more than half the Chinese people are under thirty, raising the specter of a baby boom without parallel in human history. As a result, since 1979, the Chinese government has pursued a tough policy limiting couples to a single child.

Local officials strongly encourage people to delay childbirth and, once a child is born, to submit to sterilization or abort subsequent pregnancies. One-baby couples enjoy income bonuses, and single children are promised priority in school enrollment, health care, and, later, in employment and housing. The results of this program have included a drop in annual population growth from 2.0 percent in the 1960s to about 1.8 percent

Government policies often have unanticipated consequences. Now that regulations limit couples to a single child on which parents and grandparents can lavish attention, some Chinese wonder if they may be raising a generation of "little empresses" and "little emperors."

in the 1980s.

But this policy spawned a number of unexpected problems. First, a decade ago, some nations charged China with forcing sterilization on its people. Second, the one-child policy has encouraged parents to abort female fetuses or even kill female infants. Chinese traditions give sons the duty of caring for elderly parents; daughters serve their husband's parents. Thus most Chinese couples shudder at the thought of growing old without a son. Third, privileges accorded to only-children are now disproportionately enjoyed by sons, increasing sexual inequality in China.

By 1990, the government reacted to these strains with some leniency. Yet the price of unregulated growth could be high since, at the present rate of increase, China's population will double by 2025, undermining the struggle of a vast society to raise its standard of living.

SOURCES: The World Bank (1984), Brophy (1989a, 1989b), and Tien (1989).

---

the mid-1930s; a decade later, use of insecticide to kill malaria-carrying mosquitoes cut the malaria death toll in half (Ehrlich, 1978). Although we hail such an achievement, over the long run, this technological advance sent Sri Lanka's population soaring. Similarly, India's infant mortality rate fell from 130 in 1975 to 90 in 1990, a decline that helped boost that nation's population to more than 850 million.

In short, both infant mortality and life expectancy have improved in much of the Third World. But birth control policies are now vital in countries where "death

control" programs worked well several generations ago (Piotrow, 1980).

Demography: Looking Ahead

Demographic analysis sheds light on how and why the earth is gaining unprecedented population. Only through such study can humankind address this pressing problem.

But even if we grasp the causes of the problem, controlling global population in the next century will be a monumental task. As we have seen, population growth is currently greatest in the poorest societies of the world, those that lack productive capacity to support their present populations, much less their future ones. Most of the privileged inhabitants of rich societies are spared the trauma of poverty. But adding almost 100 million people to our planet each year—80 million of these to poor societies—will require a global commitment to provide not only food, but housing, schools, and employment—all of which are in tragically short supply. The well-being of the entire world may ultimately depend on resolving many of the economic and social problems of poor, overly populated countries and bridging the widening gulf between the "have" and "have-not" societies. Describing recent population growth as "a great wave," one official of the United States government concluded:

I see the world population movement as the effort to construct a breakwater—a structure that will stop the wave and prevent it from engulfing and sweeping away centuries of human development and civilization. (cited in Gupte, 1984:323)

URBANIZATION: THE GROWTH OF CITIES

For most of human history, the small populations found around the world lived in nomadic groups, moving as they depleted vegetation or searched for migratory game. Small settlements marked the emergence of civilization in the Middle East some ten thousand years ago, but they held only a small fraction of the earth's people. Today the largest single cities contain as many people as the entire planet did then.

Urbanization is *the concentration of humanity into cities.* Urbanization both redistributes population within a society and also transforms many patterns of social life. We will trace these changes in terms of three urban revolutions—the emergence of cities, the development of industrial cities, and the explosive growth of Third-World cities.

The Evolution of Cities

Cities have existed for only a fraction of human history. Only about ten thousand years ago did our ancestors

Early urban settlement in Latin America often took the form of ceremonial centers. Here is the massive Pyramid of the Sun at Teotihuacán, a short drive from Mexico City.

found a permanent settlement, setting the stage for the *first urban revolution.*

Preconditions of cities. The first precondition of urban development was *a favorable ecology*: as glaciers began to melt at the end of the last ice age, people were drawn to warm regions with fertile soil. The second was *changing technology*: at about the same time, humans discovered how to cultivate animals and crops. Whereas hunting and gathering demanded continual movement, raising food required people to remain in one place (Lenski, Lenski, & Nolan, 1991). Domesticating animals and plants also produced a material surplus, which freed some people from concentrating on food production, allowing them to build shelters, make tools, weave clothing, and lead religious rituals. In this context, the founding of cities was truly revolutionary, raising living standards and enhancing specialization as never before.

The first cities. Historians think the first city was Jericho, a settlement to the north of the Dead Sea in disputed land currently occupied by Israel. About 8000 B.C.E., Jericho contained about 600 people (Kenyon, 1957; Hamblin, 1973). By 4000 B.C.E., numerous cities were flourishing in the Fertile Crescent between the Tigris and Euphrates rivers in present-day Iraq and, soon afterward, along the Nile River in Egypt. Some, with populations as high as 50,000, became centers of urban empires. Priest-kings wielded absolute power over lesser nobles,

Table 14–2 POPULATION GROWTH IN SELECTED INDUSTRIAL CITIES OF EUROPE (IN THOUSANDS)

City	Year			
	1700	1800	1900	1991*
Amsterdam	172	201	510	725
Berlin	100	172	2,424	3,021
Lisbon	188	237	363	2,426
London	550	861	6,480	9,115
Madrid	110	169	539	4,513
Paris	530	547	3,330	8,720
Rome	149	153	487	3,033
Vienna	105	231	1,662	2,344

* For urban area

SOURCES: Based on data from Tertius Chandler and Gerald Fox, *3000 Years of Urban History* (New York: Academic Press, 1974), pp. 17–19; and U.S. Bureau of the Census, *World Population Profile*, Washington, DC: U.S. Government Printing Office, 1992.

administrators, artisans, soldiers, and farmers. Slaves, captured in frequent military campaigns, labored to build monumental structures like the pyramids of Egypt (Wenke, 1980; Stavrianos, 1983; Lenski, Lenski, & Nolan, 1991).

Cities originated independently in at least three other areas of the world. Several large, complex cities dotted the Indus River region of present-day Pakistan starting about 2500 B.C.E. Scholars date Chinese cities from 2000 B.C.E. And, in Central and South America, urban centers began about 1500 B.C.E. In North America, however, Native American societies rarely formed settlements; significant urbanization did not begin until the arrival of European settlers in the sixteenth century (Lamberg-Karlovsky, 1973; Change, 1977; Coe & Diehl, 1980).

Preindustrial European cities. Urbanization in Europe began about 1800 B.C.E. on the Mediterranean island of Crete. Cities soon spread throughout Greece, resulting in more than one hundred city-states, of which Athens is the most famous. During its Golden Age, lasting barely a century after 500 B.C.E., some 300,000 people living within roughly one square mile made major contributions to the Western way of life in philosophy, the arts, and politics. Despite such achievements, Athenian society rested on the labor of slaves, perhaps one-third of the population. Their democratic principles notwith-

standing, Athenian men also denied the rights of citizenship to women and foreigners (Mumford, 1961; Gouldner, 1965; Stavrianos, 1983).

As Greek civilization faded, the city of Rome grew to almost 1 million inhabitants and became the center of a vast empire. By the first century C.E., the militaristic Romans subdued much of northern Africa, Europe, and the Middle East. In the process, Rome spread its language, arts, and technological innovations. Four centuries later, the Roman Empire fell into disarray, a victim of its own gargantuan size, internal corruption, and militaristic appetite. Yet, between them, the Greeks and Romans had founded cities across Europe, including London, Paris, and Vienna.

The fall of the Roman Empire initiated an era of urban decline and stagnation lasting 600 years. Cities drew back within defensive walls; few encompassed more than 25,000 people. Competing warlords battled for territory, inhibiting urban trade. About the eleventh century, the "Dark Ages" came to an end as a semblance of peace allowed trade to bring life to cities once again.

Medieval cities slowly removed their walls as trade expanded. The narrow and winding streets of London, Brussels, and Florence soon teemed with merchants, artisans, priests, peddlers, jugglers, nobles, and servants. Typically, occupational groups such as bakers, keymakers, and carpenters clustered together in distinct sections or "quarters." In the medieval cities of Europe, cathedrals towered above all other buildings, signifying the preeminence of the Christian church.

By today's standards, medieval cities were surprisingly personal (Sjoberg, 1965). Family ties were strong, and people inside each "quarter" shared a trade and sometimes a religious and ethnic tradition. In some cases, this clustering was involuntary, as laws restricted minorities to certain districts. Jews were targets of extensive prejudice and discrimination in an era dominated by the Roman Catholic Church. First in Venice and later in most of Europe, laws confined Jews to areas known as *ghettos.*

Industrial European cities. Throughout the Middle Ages, steadily increasing commerce created an affluent urban middle class or *bourgeoisie* (French meaning "of the town"). By the fifteenth century, the wealth-based power of the bourgeoisie rivaled the dominance of the hereditary nobility.

By about 1750 the Industrial Revolution was under way, triggering a *second urban revolution,* first in Europe and then in North America. Factories unleashed productive power as never before, causing cities to grow to unprecedented size, as Table 14–2 shows. During the nineteenth century the population of Paris soared from 500,000 to over 3 million, and that of London exploded from 800,000 to 6.5 million (A. Weber, 1963, orig. 1899; Chandler & Fox, 1974). Most of this increase was due to migration from rural areas by people seeking a better standard of living.

Cities changed in other ways as well during this time. So dominant was commerce, that the industrial-capitalist city evolved a new urban form. Broad, straight boulevards replaced the old irregular streets to accommodate the flow of commercial traffic and, eventually, motor vehicles. Steam and electric trolleys crisscrossed the expanding European cities. Lewis Mumford (1961) explains that developers divided the city into regular-sized lots, making land a commodity to be bought and sold. Finally, the cathedrals that had guided the life of medieval cities were soon dwarfed by towering, brightly lit, and frantic central business districts made up of banks, retail stores, and office buildings.

Urban social life also changed. Focused on business, cities became impersonal and increasingly crowded. Crime rates rose. Especially at the outset, a small number of industrialists lived in grand style, while for most men, women, and children, factory work proved exhausting and provided bare subsistence.

Table 14–2 shows that European cities continued to grow during this century, although at a slower rate. Organized efforts by workers to improve their plight led to legal regulation of the workplace, better housing, and the right to vote. Public services such as water, sewage, and electricity further enhanced urban living. Today some urbanites still live in poverty, but a rising standard of living has partly fulfilled the city's historical promise of a better life.

The Growth of U.S. Cities

Inhabiting this continent for tens of thousands of years, Native Americans were migratory people, establishing few permanent settlements. Cities first sprang up, then, as a product of European colonization. The Spanish made an initial settlement at St. Augustine, Florida, in 1565, and the English founded Jamestown, Virginia, in 1607. New Amsterdam (later called New York) was settled in 1624 by the Dutch, and soon overshadowed these smaller settlements. In 1990, the United States had 195 cities with more than 100,000 inhabitants. How

we became an urban society is explained in the brief history that follows.

Colonial settlement: 1624–1800. The metropolises of New York and Boston were, at their founding, tiny villages in a vast wilderness. Dutch New Amsterdam at the tip of Manhattan Island (1624) and English Boston (1630) each resembled medieval towns of Europe, with narrow, winding streets that still exist in lower Manhattan and downtown Boston. New Amsterdam was walled on the north, the site of today's Wall Street. In 1700, Boston was the largest U.S. city, with just 7,000 people.

The rational and expansive culture of capitalism soon transformed these quiet villages into thriving towns with grid-like streets. Figure 14–5 on page 368 contrasts the medieval shape of New Amsterdam with the modern grid system of Philadelphia, founded in 1680 after another half-century of economic development.

On the heels of independence from Great Britain, the United States was still an overwhelmingly rural society. In 1790 the government's first census tallied roughly 4 million people. As Table 14–3 shows, just 5 percent of them resided in cities.

Urban expansion: 1800–1860. Early in the nineteenth century, towns began springing up as transportation routes opened the American West. In 1818 the National Road (now Route 40) funneled Easterners from Baltimore to the Ohio Valley. A decade later the Baltimore and Ohio Railroad and the Erie Canal (1825) from New

Table 14–3	THE URBAN POPULATION OF THE UNITED STATES, 1790–1990	
Year	Population (millions)	Percent Urban
1790	3.9	5.1
1800	5.3	6.1
1820	9.6	7.3
1840	17.1	10.5
1860	31.4	19.7
1880	50.2	28.1
1900	76.0	39.7
1920	105.7	51.3
1940	131.7	56.5
1960	179.3	69.9
1980	226.5	73.7
1990	253.0	75.2

SOURCE: U.S. Bureau of the Census.

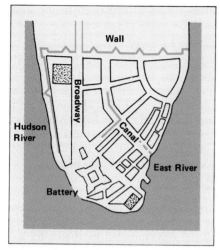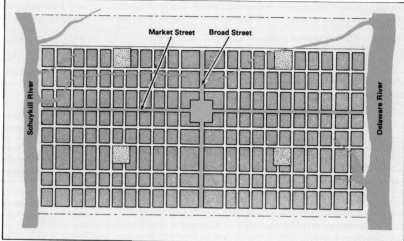

Figure 14–5 The Street Plans of Colonial New Amsterdam and Philadelphia

The plan of colonial New Amsterdam, shown at left, exemplifies the preindustrial urban pattern of walls enclosing a city of narrow, irregular streets. Colonial Philadelphia, founded fifty years later, reflects the industrial urban pattern of accessible cities with wide, regularly spaced, parallel and perpendicular streets to facilitate economic activity.

York touched off the development of cities along the Great Lakes, including Buffalo, Cleveland, and Detroit. The historical importance of water transportation for commerce accounts for the proliferation of U.S. cities by lakes and rivers.

By 1860 about one-third of the U.S. population lived in cities. Underlying this urban expansion was the Industrial Revolution, which was transforming primarily the northern states. In 1850, for example, New York City had a population ten times greater than that of Charleston, South Carolina. This division of the United States into the industrial-urban North and the agrarian-rural South was one key cause of the Civil War (Schlesinger, 1969).

The metropolitan era: 1860–1950.   The Civil War gave an enormous boost to urbanization, as factories strained to produce the tools of combat. Now waves of people fled the countryside for cities in hopes of obtaining better jobs. To their numbers were added tens of millions of immigrants—most from Europe—whose various backgrounds combined to form a culturally diverse urban mix. Table 14–4 shows the rapid growth of U.S. cities in the late nineteenth century.

In 1900 New York boasted 4 million residents, and Chicago—a city of scarcely 100,000 people in 1860—was closing in on 2 million. This growth marked the era of the **metropolis,** *a large city that socially and economically dominates an urban area.* Dozens of metropolises (with Greek roots meaning "mother city") became the manufacturing, commercial, and residential centers of the United States.

Industrial technology further changed the physical shape of cities, pushing buildings well above the three or four stories common up to this point. By the 1880s, steel girders and mechanical elevators raised structures over ten stories high. In 1930, New York's Empire State Building became an urban wonder, a true "skyscraper" stretching 102 stories into the clouds. Railroads and highways drew cities outward so that, by 1920, the United States was a predominantly urban society.

Urban decentralization: 1950–present.   The industrial metropolis reached its peak about 1950. Since then, something of a turnaround has occurred as people have deserted the downtowns in a process known as *urban decentralization* (Edmonston & Guterbock, 1984). As Table 14–4 shows, large cities of the Northeast and Midwest stopped growing—and some even lost population—in the decades after 1950. The 1990 census count found New York, for example, to have half a million fewer people than at mid-century.

But decentralization has not brought an end to urbanization; cities simply continue to change their form.

Instead of densely populated central cities, the urban landscape now looks more and more like vast urban regions, a trend closely tied to the expansion of suburbs.

Suburbs and Central Cities

Just as central cities flourished a century ago, we have recently witnessed the expansion of **suburbs,** *urban areas beyond the political boundaries of a city.* Suburbs began to grow late in the nineteenth century as railroad and trolley lines enabled people to live beyond the commotion of the city while still being able to commute "downtown" to work (Warner, 1962). The first suburbanites were well-to-do people, imitating the pattern of the European nobility who shuttled between their country estates and town houses (Baltzell, 1979). But the growth of suburbs was also fueled by racial and ethnic intolerance. Rising immigration was adding to the social diversity of central cities, prompting many to flee to homogeneous, high-prestige enclaves beyond the reach of the masses. In time, of course, less wealthy people also came to view a single-family house on its own piece of leafy suburban ground as part of the American Dream.

The postwar economic boom of the late 1940s, coupled with the mobility offered by increasingly affordable automobiles, placed suburbia within the grasp of the average household. After World War II, men and women eagerly returned to family life, igniting the baby boom described earlier in this chapter. Since central cities afforded little space for new housing construction, suburbs blossomed almost overnight. The government weighed in with guaranteed bank loans, and developers offered new, prefabricated homes at unheard-of low prices.

Levittown is the most famous of the low-cost suburbs. Built on potato fields on New York's Long Island in the late 1940s, Abraham Levitt's homes were dismissed by some as lookalike boxes, but buyers snatched up these homes as fast as Levitt could build them. By 1970, more of our population lived in the suburbs than in the central cities.

Not surprisingly, business, too, began eyeing the suburbs, and soon the suburban mall had largely replaced downtown stores of the metropolitan era (Rosenthal, 1974; Tobin, 1976; Geist, 1985). Manufacturing companies also decentralized into industrial parks far from the high taxes, congested streets, and soaring crime rates of inner cities. The interstate highway system with its beltways encircling central cities made moving out to the suburbs almost irresistible for residents and business people alike.

Decentralization was not good news for everyone, however. Rapid suburban growth soon threw older cities of the Northeast and Midwest into financial chaos. Population decline meant reduced tax revenues. Further, cities that were losing more affluent people to the suburbs were still left with the burden of providing expensive

Table 14–4 POPULATION GROWTH IN SELECTED U.S. CITIES, 1870–1990

City	Population (in thousands)						
	1870	1890	1910	1930	1950	1970	1990
Baltimore	267	434	558	805	950	905	736
Boston	251	448	671	781	801	641	574
Chicago	299	1,100	2,185	3,376	3,621	3,369	2,784
Dallas	7	38	92	260	434	844	1,007
Detroit	80	206	466	1,569	1,850	1,514	1,028
Los Angeles	6	50	319	1,238	1,970	2,812	3,485
Milwaukee	71	204	374	578	637	717	628
New Orleans	191	242	339	459	570	593	497
New York*	942	2,507	4,767	6,930	7,892	7,896	7,323
Philadelphia	674	1,047	1,549	1,951	2,072	1,949	1,586
St. Louis	311	452	687	822	857	622	397
San Francisco	149	299	417	634	775	716	724

* Population figures for New York in 1870 and 1890 reflect that city as presently constituted.

SOURCE: U.S. Bureau of the Census.

social programs to the poor who stayed behind (Gluck & Meister, 1979). These factors led to inner-city decay beginning about 1950 (Sternlieb & Hughes, 1983). Some major cities, such as Cleveland and New York, actually plummeted to the brink of bankruptcy. Especially to whites, the deteriorating inner cities became synonymous with slum housing, crime, drugs, unemployment, the poor, and minorities. This perception fed on itself, fueling wave after wave of "white flight" and urban decline. Suburbs may have their share of poor housing, congestion, and crime, but they still appeal to many people because they remain largely white, unlike the inner cities, whose populations encompass a greater share of people of color (Clark, 1979; Logan & Schneider, 1984; Stahura, 1986; Galster, 1991).

The official response to the plight of the central cities was **urban renewal,** *government programs intended to revitalize cities.* Federal and local funds have paid for the rebuilding of many inner cities. Yet critics of urban renewal charge that these programs have benefited business communities while doing little to meet the housing needs of low-income residents (Jacobs, 1961; Greer, 1965; Gans, 1982).

Postindustrial Sunbelt Cities

In the new postindustrial economy (see Chapter 11, "Economics and Politics"), people are not only moving beyond the boundaries of central cities, they are also migrating from the Snowbelt to the Sunbelt. The Snowbelt—the traditional industrial heartland of the United States—runs from the Northeast to the Midwest. Here almost 60 percent of the U.S. population lived in 1940. By 1975, however, the Sunbelt—the South and the West—passed the Snowbelt in overall population and, by 1990, it was home to 55.6 percent of U.S. residents.

This demographic shift is shown in Table 14–5, which compares the ten largest cities in the United States in 1950 and in 1990. In 1950, eight of the top ten were industrial cities of the Snowbelt whereas, in 1990, six out of ten were postindustrial cities of the Sunbelt. The box provides a snapshot of how our nation's urban profile changed during the 1980s.

Why are Sunbelt cities faring so well? Unlike their counterparts in the Snowbelt, the postindustrial cities of the Sunbelt grew *after* urban decentralization began. Since Snowbelt cities have long been closed in by a ring of politically independent suburbs, outward migration took place at the expense of the central city. Suburbs

Table 14–5 THE TEN LARGEST CITIES IN THE UNITED STATES, 1950 AND 1990

Rank	City	Population
1950		
1	New York	7,892,000
2	Chicago	3,621,000
3	Philadelphia	2,072,000
4	Los Angeles	1,970,000
5	Detroit	1,850,000
6	Baltimore	950,000
7	Cleveland	915,000
8	St. Louis	857,000
9	Boston	801,000
10	San Francisco	775,000
1990		
1	New York	7,323,000
2	Los Angeles	3,485,000
3	Chicago	2,784,000
4	Houston	1,631,000
5	Philadelphia	1,586,000
6	San Diego	1,111,000
7	Detroit	1,028,000
8	Dallas	1,007,000
9	Phoenix	983,000
10	San Antonio	936,000

SOURCE: U.S. Bureau of the Census.

have played a much smaller role in the history of Sunbelt cities, which have simply expanded outward, gaining population in the process. Chicago, for example, covers 228 square miles, whereas Houston sprawls over 565. Through physical expansion, Sunbelt cities have retained population even as people have moved outward from the urban center.

The great sprawl of the typical Sunbelt city does have drawbacks, however. Traveling across town is time-consuming, and automobile ownership is almost a necessity. Lacking a dense center, Sunbelt cities also generate far less of the excitement and intensity that draw people to New York or Chicago. Critics have long tagged Los Angeles, for example, as a vast cluster of suburbs in search of a center.

The Burgeoning Sunbelt Cities

Just as the twentieth century opened with tremendous urban growth in the North and Midwest, the twenty-first century will almost surely begin with rapid urbanization in the South and West. The official count from the 1990 census indicates that, taken as a whole, Snowbelt cities suffered a moderate drop in population while Sunbelt population is soaring.

The figure shows how the largest Snowbelt and Sunbelt cities fared during the 1980s. Two of the six most populous Snowbelt cities posted slight increases in population, while the remaining four recorded substantial losses. Each of these six cities is now well below its 1950 size, when Snowbelt cities reached their peak population.

The picture is very different if we turn to the cities of the Sunbelt, where population has grown rapidly since mid-century. All six of the largest Sunbelt cities registered population gains during the 1980s—even Houston and Dallas, which were hard hit by the economic downturn. The population growth in the other four is dramatic—similar to the explosive increases found in the Snowbelt a century ago.

Which cities—of any size—grew fastest of all during the 1980s? Across

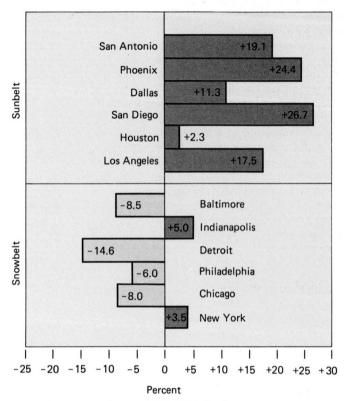

Percent Population Change, 1980–1990, for the Six Largest Snowbelt and Sunbelt Cities

(U.S. Bureau of the Census, 1993)

the United States, Mesa, Arizona, led the way with an 89 percent gain (to 288,000). Nine other cities had population increases of over 60 percent during the 1980s—every one in the Sunbelt.

Megalopolis: Regional Cities

The decentralization of U.S. cities has produced vast urban areas that contain numerous municipalities. In 1990 the Bureau of the Census (1991) recognized 284 regional cities, which they call *metropolitan statistical areas* (MSAs). Each MSA includes at least one city with 50,000 or more people plus densely populated surrounding counties. Almost all of the fifty fastest-growing MSAs are in the Sunbelt.

The biggest MSAs, containing more than 1 million people, are called *consolidated metropolitan statistical areas* (CMSAs). In 1990, there were twenty CMSAs. Heading the list was New York and adjacent urban areas in Long Island, western Connecticut, and northern New Jersey, with a total population of some 18 million. Next in size was the CMSA in southern California that includes Los Angeles, Riverside, and Anaheim, with a population of almost 15 million (U.S. Bureau of the Census, 1991).

Some regional cities have grown so large that they have collided with one another. The East Coast now contains a 400-mile supercity extending from New England to Virginia. In the early 1960s, French geographer Jean Gottmann (1961) coined the term **megalopolis** to designate *a vast urban region containing a number of cities and their surrounding suburbs.* A megalopolis is composed of hundreds of politically independent cities and suburbs; from an airplane at night, however, it appears to be a single continuous city. Other supercities of this kind are on the eastern coast of Florida, and the land extending from Cleveland to Chicago. Future urban regions will undoubtedly emerge, especially in the fast-growing Sunbelt.

URBANISM AS A WAY OF LIFE

Various sociologists in Europe and the United States were among the first to contrast urban and rural life. We will briefly present their accounts of urbanism as a way of life.

Ferdinand Toennies: *Gemeinschaft* and *Gesellschaft*

In the late nineteenth century, the German sociologist Ferdinand Toennies (1855–1937) set out to chronicle the social traits emerging in the industrial metropolis. He contrasted rural and urban life using two concepts that have become a lasting part of sociology's terminology.

Toennies (1963; orig. 1887) used the German word *Gemeinschaft* (meaning roughly "community") to refer to *a type of social organization by which people are bound closely together by kinship and tradition.* Rural villagers, Toennies explained, are joined by kinship, neighborhood, and friendship. *Gemeinschaft*, then, describes any social setting in which people form what amounts to a single primary group.

By and large, argued Toennies, *Gemeinschaft* is not found in the modern city. On the contrary, urbaniza-tion enhances *Gesellschaft* (a German word meaning roughly "association"), *a type of social organization by which people have weak social ties and considerable self-interest.* In the *Gesellschaft* scheme, women and men are motivated by their own needs and desires rather than a drive to enhance the well-being of everyone. City dwellers, Toennies suggested, have little sense of community or common identity and look to others mostly as a means of advancing their individual goals. Thus Toennies saw in urbanization the erosion of primary social relations in favor of the temporary, impersonal ties typical of business.

Emile Durkheim: Mechanical and Organic Solidarity

The French sociologist Emile Durkheim agreed with much of Toennies's thinking about cities. Yet Durkheim's analysis highlighted patterns of social solidarity: that is, what binds people together. Traditional, rural life Durkheim conceptualized as **mechanical solidarity,** *social bonds based on collective conformity to tradition.* Durkheim's concept of mechanical solidarity bears a striking similarity to Toennies's *Gemeinschaft*.

But if urbanization erodes some mechanical solidarity, Durkheim explained, it also generates a new type of bonding, which he termed **organic solidarity,** *social bonds based on specialization and interdependence.* This concept, which parallels Toennies's *Gesellschaft*, reveals a key difference between the two thinkers. While each thought the expansion of industry and cities would undermine traditional social patterns, Durkheim was more optimistic about this historical transformation. Where societies had been built on *likeness*, in short, Durkheim now saw social life based on *difference*. And Durkheim did not miss the fact that urban society typically offers more individual choice, moral tolerance, and greater personal privacy than people find in rural villages. In short, Durkheim concluded, something may be lost in urbanization, but much is gained.

Georg Simmel: The Blasé Urbanite

German sociologist Georg Simmel (1858–1918) offered a micro-analysis of cities by asking how urban life shaped people's behavior and attitudes (1964; orig. 1905). From the point of view of the individual, Simmel explained, the city is a crush of people, objects, and events. Under-

Marc Chagall's (1887–1985) painting *I and the Village* (1911) conveys the essential unity of rural life forged by tradition and common work on the land. By contrast, in his painting *The City* (1919), Fernand Léger (1881–1955) communicates the disparate images and discontinuity of experience that are commonplace in urban areas. Taken together, these two paintings capture Toennies's distinction between *Gemeinschaft* and *Gesellschaft*.

Marc Chagall, I and the Village, *1911. Oil on canvas, 63⅝ x 59⅝". Collection, The Museum of Modern Art, New York. Mrs. Simon Guggenheim Fund; Fernand Léger,* The City, *1919. 91 x 117½. The Philadelphia Museum of Art (The A. E. Gallatin Collection).*

standably, he continued, the urbanite is easily overwhelmed with stimulation and develops a *blasé attitude*. In the city, in other words, people learn to respond selectively by tuning out much of what goes on around them. City dwellers are not without sensitivity and compassion for others, although they sometimes seem "cold and heartless." But urban detachment, as Simmel saw it, is better understood as a strategy for social survival by which people stand aloof from most others so they can devote their time and energy to those who really matter.

Robert Park: Studying the City

Sociologists in the United States soon joined the exploration of rapidly growing cities. Robert Park (1864–1944), a leader of the first major U.S. sociology program at the University of Chicago, studied the European thinkers. But he sought to give urban studies in this country a more empirical emphasis and urged urbanists to get

out and study real cities. In one of his most memorable comments Park said of himself:

> I suspect that I have actually covered more ground, tramping about in cities in different parts of the world, than any other living man. (1950:viii)

What did Park conclude from his lifetime of travel? He found the city to be a carefully organized mosaic of distinctive ethnic communities, vice districts, and industrial sectors. Over time, he observed, these "natural areas" develop and change in relation to each other. To Park, then, the city was a living organism, truly the human kaleidoscope.

Louis Wirth: Urbanism as a Way of Life

A second major figure in the Chicago School of urban sociology was Louis Wirth (1897–1952). Wirth's (1938) best-known contribution is a brief essay in which he systematically blended the ideas of Toennies, Simmel, Durkheim, and Park into a comprehensive theory of urban life.

Wirth began by defining the city as a setting with a large population, dense settlement, and social diversity. These traits, he argued, yield a distinctive way of life that is impersonal, superficial, and transitory. Living among millions of others, urbanites come into contact with many more people than rural residents do. Thus, if city people notice others at all, they usually know them only in terms of *what they do*: as bus driver, florist, or grocery store clerk, for instance. But urban relationships are not only specialized, they are also founded on self-interest. For example, shoppers see grocers as the source of goods, while grocers view shoppers as a source of income. These men and women may pleasantly exchange greetings, but friendship is not the reason for their interaction. Finally, limited social involvement coupled with great social diversity also make city dwellers more tolerant than rural villagers. Rural communities often jealously enforce their narrow traditions, but the heterogeneous population of a city rarely shares any single code of moral conduct (Wilson, 1985).

Critical evaluation.   Wirth offers a mixed view of urban living. On the one hand, the rapid urbanization of Europe and North America troubled him, as it did Toennies. Wirth recognized that the close personal ties and traditional morality of rural life are lost in the anonymous rush of the city. On the other hand, Wirth echoed Durkheim and Park as he noted urbanism's positive face, including greater personal autonomy and a wider range of life choices.

And what of Wirth's specific claims about urbanism? Decades of research have provided support for only some of his conclusions. Wirth correctly maintained that urban settings do sustain a weaker sense of community than do rural areas. But one can easily forget that conflict is found in the countryside as well as the city. Furthermore, while urbanites treat most people impersonally, they typically welcome such privacy and, of course, they do maintain close personal relationships with a select few (Keller, 1968; Cox, 1971; Macionis, 1978; Wellman, 1979; Lee et al., 1984).

Wirth's analysis falls short, however, in overlooking how urbanism varies according to class, race, and gender. Herbert Gans (1968) explains that there are many brands of urbanites: rich and poor, white and black, Anglo and Hispanic, women and men—all leading distinctive lives in cities. In fact, cities can intensify these social differences. That is, we see the extent of social diversity most clearly in cities where social forces of class, race, ethnicity, and gender are most clearly at work (Spates & Macionis, 1987).

Urban Ecology

Sociologists also embrace **urban ecology,** *the study of the link between the physical and social dimensions of cities.* Chapter 2 ("Culture") spotlighted cultural ecology, the study of how cultural patterns are related to the physical environment. Urban ecology is one application of this approach, revealing how the physical and social forms of cities are closely linked.

Consider, for example, why cities are located where they are. The first cities emerged in fertile regions where the ecology favored raising crops and, thus, settlement. Preindustrial societies, concerned with defense, built their cities on mountains (Athens was situated on an outcropping of rock) or surrounded by water (Paris and Mexico City were founded on islands). After the Industrial Revolution, the unparalleled importance of economics situated cities near rivers and natural harbors that facilitated trade.

Urban ecologists also study the physical design of cities. In 1925 Ernest W. Burgess, a student and colleague of Robert Park, described land use in Chicago in terms of *concentric zones.* City centers, Burgess observed, are business districts bordered by a ring of factories, followed by residential rings that become more expensive with greater distance from the noise and pollution of the city's center.

Homer Hoyt (1939) refined Burgess's observations by noting that distinctive districts often form *wedge-shaped sectors.* For example, one fashionable area may develop next to another, or neighborhoods may extend outward from a city's center along a train or trolley line.

Chauncy Harris and Edward Ullman (1945) added yet another insight: decentralization results in *multicentered cities.* As cities grow, residential areas, industrial parks, and shopping districts typically push away from one another. Few people wish to live close to industrial areas, for example, so the city becomes a mosaic of distinct districts.

Social area analysis adds another twist to urban ecology by investigating what people in specific neighborhoods have in common. Three factors seem to explain most of the variation—family patterns, social class, and race and ethnicity (Shevky & Bell, 1955; Johnston, 1976).

Families with children gravitate to areas offering large apartments or single-family homes and good schools. The rich generally seek high-prestige neighborhoods, often in the central city near many of the city's cultural attractions. People with a common social heritage tend to cluster together or, just as often, they are relegated involuntarily to certain areas.

Finally, Brian Berry and Philip Rees (1969) tie all these insights together. They explain that distinct family types tend to settle in the concentric zones described by Ernest Burgess. Specifically, households with few children tend to cluster toward the city's center, while those with more children live farther away. Social class differences generate the sector-shaped districts described by Homer Hoyt as, for instance, the rich occupy one "side of the tracks"; the poor, the other. And racial and ethnic neighborhoods are found at various points throughout the city, consistent with Harris and Ullman's multiple-center model.

Critical evaluation. After almost a century of research, urban ecologists have succeeded in linking the physical and social dimensions of urban life. But, as ecologists themselves concede, their conclusions paint an overly simplified picture of urban life. Critics chime in that urban ecology errs to the extent it implies that cities take shape simply from the choices people make. More correctly, they continue, urban development responds more to power elites than to ordinary citizens (Molotch, 1976; Feagin, 1983). A final criticism holds that urban

Many Third-World cities provide striking social contrasts: Rio de Janeiro is both a playground for the world's rich and home to millions who are desperately poor. Perhaps not surprisingly, a recent crime wave in this city has been directed largely at affluent tourists.

ecologists have studied only U.S. cities and only during a single historical period. What we have learned about industrial cities may not apply to preindustrial towns; similarly, even among industrial cities, socialist settlements differ from their capitalist counterparts. In sum, there is good reason to doubt that any single ecological model will account for the full range of urban diversity.

THIRD-WORLD URBANIZATION

Twice in human history the world has experienced a revolutionary expansion of cities. The first urban revolution began about 8000 B.C.E. with the first urban settlements, and continued as permanent settlements later appeared on different continents. The second urban revolution began about 1750 and lasted for two centuries as the Industrial Revolution touched off rapid growth of cities in Europe and North America.

A third urban revolution was under way by 1950, but this time the change is taking place not in industrial societies where, as Global Map 14–2 shows, 75 percent of people are already city dwellers. Extraordinary urban growth is now occurring in the Third World. In 1950, about 25 percent of Third-World people inhabited cities; by 1990, the proportion had risen to 40 percent; by 2000, it will exceed 50 percent. Put in other words, in 1950, only seven cities in the world had populations over 5 million, and just two of these were in the Third World. By 1990, thirty-three cities had passed this mark, and twenty-four of them were in the Third World (U.S. Bureau of the Census, 1992). By the end of this century, some of these Third-World cities will dwarf all but a few cities in industrial societies.

Table 14–6 looks back to 1980 and ahead to 2000, comparing the size of the world's ten largest urban areas (cities and surrounding suburbs). In 1980, six of the top ten were in industrialized societies; three were in the United States. By the beginning of the next century, however, only four of the ten will be situated in industrialized nations: two in Japan, one in South Korea, and one in the United States. The majority will be in less economically developed societies of the Third World. These urban areas not only will be the world's largest, they will encompass unprecedented populations. Relatively rich societies such as Japan may have the resources to provide for cities with upwards of 30 million people, but for poor societies, such as Mexico and Brazil, such supercities will tax resources that are already severely strained.

Table 14–6 THE WORLD'S TEN LARGEST URBAN AREAS, 1980 AND 2000

1980	
Urban Area	Population (in millions)
New York, U.S.A.	16.5
Tokyo–Yokohama, Japan	14.4
Mexico City, Mexico	14.0
Los Angeles–Long Beach, U.S.A.	10.6
Shanghai, China	10.0
Buenos Aires, Argentina	9.7
Paris, France	8.5
Moscow, U.S.S.R.	8.0
Beijing, China	8.0
Chicago, U.S.A.	7.7

2000 (projected)	
Urban Area	Population (in millions)
Tokyo–Yokohama, Japan	30.0
Mexico City, Mexico	27.9
São Paulo, Brazil	25.4
Seoul, South Korea	22.0
Bombay, India	15.4
New York, U.S.A.	14.7
Osaka–Kobe–Kyoto, Japan	14.3
Tehran, Iran	14.3
Rio de Janeiro, Brazil	14.2
Calcutta, India	14.1

SOURCES: United Nations and U.S. Bureau of the Census.

Causes of Third-World Urbanization

To understand the third urban revolution, recall that many nonindustrial societies are now entering the high-growth stage of demographic transition. Falling death rates have fueled a population explosion in Latin America, Africa, and Asia. For urban areas, the rate of growth is *twice* as high because, in addition to natural increase, millions of migrants leave the countryside each year in search of jobs, health care, education, and conveniences like running water and electricity. Political events can also "push" migration as, for example, when elites seize land from peasants (London, 1987).

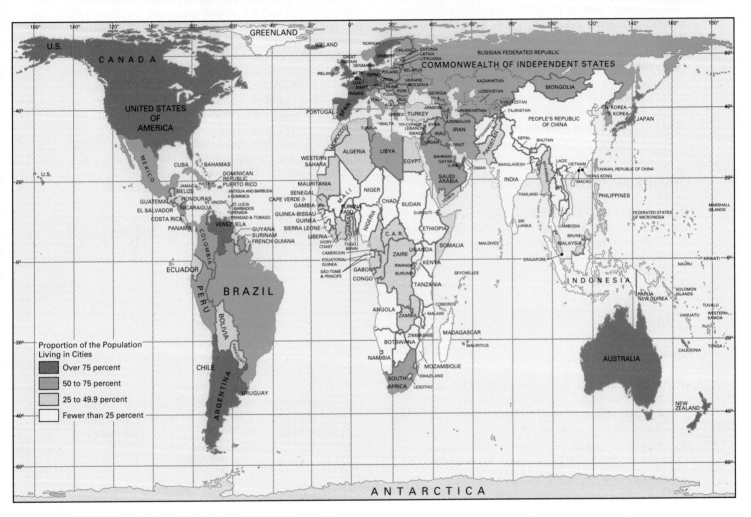

Global Map 14–2 Urbanization in Global Perspective

Urbanization is closely linked to economic development. Thus First-World nations—including the United States and Canada—have more than three-fourths of their populations in cities, while in the poorest countries of the Third World—found in Africa and Asia—fewer than one-fourth of the people live in urban centers. Urbanization is now extremely rapid in the Third World, however, with emerging "supercities" of unprecedented size.

Cities do offer more opportunities than rural areas, but they provide no quick fix for the massive problems of escalating population and grinding poverty. Many Third-World centers—including Mexico City, described at the beginning of this chapter—are simply unable to meet the basic needs of much of their population. Thousands of rural people stream into Mexico City every day, although more than 10 percent of *current* residents have no running water in their homes, 15 percent lack sewerage facilities, and half the trash and garbage produced each day cannot be processed. To make matters worse, exhaust from factories and cars chokes everyone, rich and poor alike (Friedrich, 1984). Like other major cities throughout Latin America, Africa, and Asia, Mexico City is surrounded by wretched shantytowns—settlements of makeshift homes built from discarded materials. As explained in Chapter 8 ("Global Inequality"), even city dumps are home to thousands of poor people, who pick through the waste hoping to find enough to ensure their survival for another day.

Urbanization: Looking Ahead

The problems now facing Third-World cities seem to defy solution, and the end of this remarkable urban growth is nowhere in sight. What hope is there of relieving the plight of people in emerging megacities like Mexico City, São Paulo, and Bombay?

Earlier chapters point up two different answers to this question. One view, linked with modernization theory, holds that as the Third World undergoes industrialization (as Western Europe and North America did a century ago), greater productivity will simultaneously raise living standards and this, in turn, will reduce population growth. A second view, associated with dependency theory, argues that such progress is unlikely as long as Third-World societies remain economically dependent on rich societies.

We know that, throughout history, the city has improved people's living standards more than any other settlement pattern. The question facing humanity now is whether cities in poor societies will be able to meet the needs of vastly larger populations in the coming century. The answer—which rests on issues of international relations, global economic ties, and simple justice—will affect us all.

SUMMARY

Population

1. Fertility and mortality are major factors affecting population size. In global terms, fertility, mortality, and population growth in North America are relatively low.

2. Migration, another key demographic concept, has special importance to the historical growth of cities.

3. Demographers employ age-sex pyramids to graphically represent the composition of a population and to project population trends.

4. Historically, world population grew slowly because high birth rates were largely offset by high death rates. About 1750, a demographic transition began as world population rose sharply, mostly due to declining death rates.

5. Malthus warned that population growth would outpace food production, resulting in social calamity. Contradicting Malthus's ominous predictions, demographic transition theory holds that technological advances gradually prompt a drop in birth rates. Although this leveling off has occurred in industrial societies, in the Third World declining death rates coupled with continued high birth rates are swelling population to unprecedented levels.

6. World population is expected to reach 8 billion by the year 2025. Such an increase will likely overwhelm many poor societies, where most of the increase will take place.

Urbanization

1. Closely related to population growth is urbanization. The first urban revolution began with the appearance of cities after 8000 B.C.E.; by the start of the common era, cities had emerged in most regions of the world except for North America.

2. Preindustrial cities are characterized by small buildings, narrow, winding streets, and strong interpersonal social ties.

3. A second urban revolution began about 1750 as the Industrial Revolution propelled rapid urban growth in Europe. The structure of cities changed,

as planners created wide, regular streets to facilitate trade. Their business emphasis and increasing size rendered cities less personal.

4. Urbanism came to North America with European settlers. A string of colonial towns dotting the Atlantic coastline gave way by 1850 to hundreds of new settlements from coast to coast. By 1920, a majority of the U.S. population lived in urban settings, and several metropolises contained millions of inhabitants. About 1950, cities began to decentralize so that, by 1970, most urbanites lived in suburbs.

5. Rapid urbanization in Europe during the nineteenth century led early sociologists to contrast rural and urban life. Ferdinand Toennies built his analysis on the concepts of *Gemeinshaft* and *Gesell-*

schaft. Emile Durkheim's concepts of mechanical solidarity and organic solidarity closely parallel those of Toennies. Georg Simmel claimed that overstimulation produced a blasé attitude in urbanites.

6. At the University of Chicago, Robert Park hailed cities for permitting greater social freedom. Louis Wirth gave a more mixed review, suggesting that their size, density, and heterogeneity render urban life impersonal, self-interested, and tolerant. Other researchers have explored urban ecology, the interplay of social and physical dimensions of cities.

7. A third urban revolution is now occurring in the Third World, where most of the world's largest cities will soon be found.

KEY CONCEPTS

Population

age-sex pyramid a graphic representation of the age and sex of a population

crude birth rate the number of live births in a given year for every thousand people in a population

crude death rate the number of deaths in a given year for every thousand people in a population

demographic transition theory a thesis linking population patterns to a society's level of technological development

demography the study of human population

fertility the incidence of childbearing in a society's population

infant mortality rate the number of deaths among infants under one year of age for each thousand live births in a given year

life expectancy the average life span of a society's population

migration the movement of people into and out of a specific territory

mortality the incidence of death in a society's population

sex ratio the number of males for every hundred females in a given population

zero population growth the level of reproduction that maintains population at a steady state

Urbanization

Gemeinschaft a type of social organization by which people are bound together by kinship and tradition

Gesellschaft a type of social organization by which people have weak social ties and considerable self-interest

mechanical solidarity social bonds based on collective conformity to tradition

megalopolis a vast urban region containing a number of cities and their surrounding suburbs

metropolis a large city that socially and economically dominates an urban area

organic solidarity social bonds based on specialization and interdependence

suburbs urban areas beyond the political boundaries of a city

urban ecology study of the link between the physical and social dimensions of cities

urbanization the concentration of humanity into cities

urban renewal government programs intended to revitalize cities

15

Social Change and Modernity

CHAPTER OUTLINE

The firelight flickers in the gathering darkness. Chief Kanhonk sits, as he has every evening for many years, to begin an evening of animated talk and storytelling.[1] This is the hour when the Kaiapo, a small society in Brazil's Amazon region, celebrate their heritage. Because the Kaiapo are a traditional people with no written language, the elders rely on evenings by the fire to teach their culture to the grandchildren. In the past, nights like this have been filled with tales of brave Kaiapo warriors fighting off Portuguese traders in pursuit of slaves and gold.

But as the minutes pass, only a few older villagers assemble for the evening ritual. None of the children is drawn by the chief's storytelling. "It is the Big Ghost," one man grumbles, explaining the poor turnout. The "Big Ghost" has indeed descended upon them: its presence is marked by the soft glow spilling from windows of homes throughout the village. The Kaiapo children—and many adults as well—are watching television. The consequences of installing a satellite dish three years ago have turned out to be greater than anyone imagined. In the end, what their enemies failed to do to the Kaiapo with guns, they may do to themselves with prime-time programming.

The Kaiapo are some of the 230,000 native peoples who inhabit the country we call Brazil. They stand out because of their striking body paint and ornate ceremonial dress. Recently, they have become rich, as profits from gold mining and harvesting mahogany trees have flowed into the settlement. Now the Kaiapo must decide whether their new-found fortune is a blessing or a curse. To some, affluence means the opportunity to learn about the outside world through travel and television. Others, like Chief Kanhonk, are not so sure. Sitting by the fire, he thinks aloud, "I have been saying that people must buy useful things like knives and fishing hooks. Television does not fill the stomach. It only shows our children and grandchildren white people's things." Bebtopup, the oldest priest, agrees: "The night is the time the old people teach the young people. Television has stolen the night" (Simons, 1989:37).

The transformation of the Kaiapo raises profound questions about the causes of change and whether change—even toward a higher standard of living—is al-

ways for the better. Moreover, the dilemma of the Kaiapo is being played out around the globe as more and more traditional societies are lured away from their past by the materialism and affluence of the First World.

This chapter examines social change as a process with both positive and negative consequences. Of particular interest to people in the United States is what sociologists call *modernity*, changes brought on by the Industrial Revolution. But we shall also consider how rich and powerful nations, like the United States, are affecting the rest of the world.

WHAT IS SOCIAL CHANGE?

Earlier chapters have explored human societies in terms of both stability and change. Relatively *static* social patterns include status and role, social stratification, and the various social institutions. The *dynamic* patterns that have recast humanity's consciousness, behavior, and needs range from technological innovation to the growth of bureaucracy and the expansion of cities. These are all dimensions of **social change**, *the transformation of culture and social institutions over time.* This complex process has four general characteristics.

1. **Social change happens everywhere; however, the rate of change varies from place to place.** "Nothing is certain except death and taxes," as the saying goes. But social patterns related to death have changed dramatically as life expectancy in the United States has doubled since 1850. Moreover, the principal causes of death now differ from what they were then, and even the definition of death has shifted in response to new life-prolonging technology. Taxes, meanwhile, were unknown through most of human history, emerging only with complex social organization several thousand years ago. In short, one is hard pressed to identify anything not subject to the twists and turns of change.

   Still, some societies change faster than others. As Chapter 2 ("Culture") explained, hunting and gathering societies changed quite slowly; members of technologically complex societies, on the other hand, can sense significant change even within a single lifetime. In all societies, moreover, some cultural elements change faster than others. William Ogburn's (1964) theory of *cultural lag*

---

[1] This opening is a selective adaptation of the account provided by Simons (1989).

Increasing technological sophistication and the expansion of multinational corporations have made the world seem smaller, as products familiar to us are now eagerly consumed all around the globe. Does this mean that thousands of historically distinctive ways of life will become a single global McCulture? What are the advantages and drawbacks of this expansion of First-World influence?

Early automobile manufacturers understood that cars would allow people to travel in a single day distances that had required weeks or months a century before. But no one foresaw how profoundly the mobility provided by automobiles would affect the environment and reshape cities and suburbs. In addition, automotive pioneers could hardly have predicted the 50,000 deaths each year in car accidents in the United States alone.

3. **Social change often generates controversy.** As the history of the automobile demonstrates, most social change yields both good and bad consequences. Capitalists welcomed the Industrial Revolution because advancing technology increased productivity and profits. Many workers, however, fearing that machines would make their skills obsolete, strongly resisted "progress." In the United States, changing social patterns between people of color and whites, between women and men, and between gays and heterosexuals give rise to misunderstandings, tensions, and, sometimes, hostility.

4. **Some changes matter more than others.** Some changes have only passing significance, whereas other transformations resonate for generations. At one extreme, fads, such as the "Teenage Mutant Ninja Turtles," arise and dissipate quickly. At the other, we are still adjusting to powerful technological advances such as television half a century after its introduction. Looking ahead as the computer-based Information Revolution unfolds, who can predict with any certainty how this technology will transform the entire world during the next century?

(see Chapter 2) asserts that material culture (that is, things) usually changes faster than nonmaterial culture (ideas and attitudes). For example, medical devices that prolong life have developed more rapidly than have ethical standards for deciding when and how to employ them.

2. **Social change is sometimes intentional but often unplanned.** Industrial societies actively promote many kinds of change. For example, political candidates promise new policies and programs, scientists seek more efficient forms of energy, and advertisers try to convince consumers that a new gadget is a "necessity." Yet even the experts rarely envision all the consequences of the changes they propose.

CAUSES OF SOCIAL CHANGE

There are many causes of social change. And in a world linked by sophisticated communication and transportation technology, change in one place often begets change elsewhere.

Culture and Change

Culture is a dynamic system of symbols that continually gains and loses elements. Chapter 2 ("Culture") identified three important sources of cultural change. First, *inven-*

tion produces objects, ideas, and social patterns that reshape society to varying degrees. Rocket-propulsion research, which began in the 1940s, has now produced sophisticated vehicles for space flight. Today we take such technology for granted; during the next century, a significant number of people may well travel in space.

A second process, *discovery*, occurs when people first take notice of existing elements of the world or learn to see them in a new way. For example, medical advances offer a growing understanding of how the human body operates. Beyond the direct effects for human health, medical discoveries have also stretched life expectancy, setting in motion the "graying of the United States" (see Chapter 3, "Socialization: From Infancy to Old Age").

Third, *diffusion* creates change as trade, migration, and mass communication spread cultural elements from one society to another. Ralph Linton (1937) recognized that many familiar aspects of our culture came from other lands—for example, cloth (developed in Asia), clocks (invented in Europe), and coins (devised in Turkey). In general, material things diffuse more easily than nonmaterial traits. The Kaiapo, described at the beginning of this chapter, have been quick to adopt television, but they have been reluctant to embrace the materialism and individualism that sometimes seizes those who spend hours watching Western, commercial programming.

During its entire history, the United States has been transformed by cultural diffusion accompanying immigration. In recent decades, people from Latin America and Asia have introduced new cultural patterns, evident in the sights, smells, and sounds of cities across the country (Fallows, 1983; Muller & Espenshade, 1985). Conversely, the global power of the United States ensures that many elements of our culture—from the taste of hamburgers to the sounds of Harlem rap music to the skills of Harvard M.B.A.s—are being diffused to other societies.

Conflict and Change

Tension and conflict within a society also produce change. Karl Marx heralded class conflict as the engine that drives societies from one historical era to another. In industrial-capitalist societies, he maintained, the struggle between capitalists and workers propels society toward a system of socialist production. In the century since Marx's death, this model has proven simplistic; yet, he correctly foresaw that conflict arising from inequality

(involving race and gender as well as class) would reshape every society, including the United States.

The Natural Environment and Change

Because human societies interact with their natural environment, change in one tends to produce change in the other. Many Native American cultures viewed the natural world with reverence, living according to natural rhythms. European settlers who came to North America generally saw nature in a strikingly different way: as an adversary to be tamed and then molded to human purposes. Confronting a wilderness, these newcomers systematically cut down forests to provide space and materials for building, established towns, extended roads in every direction, and dammed rivers as a source of water and energy.

Despite its benefits, technological development increasingly threatens the natural environment. With our high standard of living, the people of the United States generate more than 300 billion pounds of refuse annually. Where is it to go? In operating more than a hundred million motor vehicles and tens of thousands of factories, and in routinely using dozens of household products, we regularly release hazardous chemicals into the air. Only in the last few decades have we begun to recognize the potentially poisonous effects on the environment of our way of life; devising workable solutions to this problem will likely require decades more.

Our patterns of culture also consume very high levels of energy. As Global Map 15–1 shows, residents of rich countries including the United States use one hundred times as much oil as people who live in the world's poorest societies. This fact raises concerns not only about conserving our finite resources, but also about the pressing issue of material disparity that divides the world's peoples.

The natural environment can also lash out at human societies, sometimes with devastating effects. Throughout history, entire civilizations have succumbed to natural disasters in the form of floods, volcanic eruptions, and earthquakes. Today, life is still periodically disrupted by such events. In recent years major earthquakes have killed tens of thousands in Armenia and Iran, and droughts have taken an even greater human toll in central Africa. In rich societies, loss of life from natural disasters is low, but property damage, as the 1992 hurricane devastation in southern Florida suggests, is far higher than in the Third World.

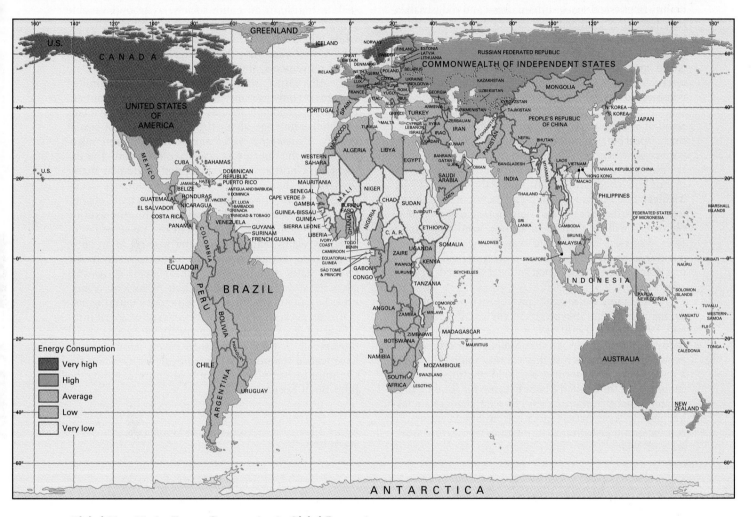

Global Map 15–1 Energy Consumption in Global Perspective
The members of industrial societies consume far more energy than others on the planet.
The typical U.S. resident uses the same amount of energy in a year as one hundred
people in the Central African Republic. This means that the most economically productive
societies are also those that place the greatest burden on the natural environment.

Demographic Change

Demographic factors (described in Chapter 14, "Population and Urbanization") also steer social change. Population growth places escalating demands on the environ- ment and, as research in the Netherlands and Japan reveals, high density living affects virtually every facet of life. For example, homes in Amsterdam are small and narrow compared to those in the United States, and staircases are extremely steep to make efficient use of space. In Tokyo, commuters routinely endure subway crowding far greater than that found in the United States. Although North American societies have enjoyed a bounty of physical space, urbanization and industrialization have also changed our way of life. About three-fourths of North Americans live in cities, which cover only a small percentage of the land surface. The fast-paced and anonymous way of life that results barely resembles that found in the rural villages and small towns common to our past.

Profound change also results from the shifting composition of a population. Our nation's population, collectively speaking, is growing older. In 1991 almost 13 percent were over sixty-five, triple the proportion in 1900. By the year 2030, seniors will account for about one in four U.S. residents (U.S. Bureau of the Census, 1992). Medical research and health-care services are already focusing on the elderly, and common stereotypes about old people will be challenged as more men and women enter this stage of life. Life may change in countless additional ways, with homes and household products increasingly being redesigned to meet the needs of older consumers.

Migration within and among societies is another demographic factor that promotes change. Between 1870 and 1930, tens of millions of immigrants swelled the industrial cities in the United States. Millions of rural people from towns across this country joined them. As a result, farm communities declined, metropolises burgeoned, and the United States became for the first time a predominantly urban society. Similar changes are taking place today as people moving from Snowbelt to Sunbelt states mingle with new immigrants from Latin America and Asia.

Social Movements and Change

A final cause of social change lies in people's own initiatives. People commonly band together to form **social movements,** *organized efforts encouraging or opposing some dimension of change.* Our national history is replete with social movements of all kinds, from the colonial drive for independence to contemporary movements that advocate various positions on feminism, gay rights, and the environment.

Types of social movements.   Researchers have classified social movements according to the kind of change they seek (Aberle, 1966; Cameron, 1966; Blumer, 1969). One variable is *breadth*: some movements limit their efforts to changing only a specific category of people; others seek to transform an entire society. A second variable is *depth*: some crusades attempt only superficial change, while others aspire to remake society in a fundamental way. Combining these variables produces four types of social movements, shown in Figure 15–1.

Alternative social movements pursue limited change in only certain individuals. As an example, Planned Parenthood focuses on educating individuals of childbearing age about the consequences of sexual activity. *Redemptive social movements* also aim selectively, but they pursue radical transformation. Fundamentalist Christian organizations that invite new members to be "born again" exemplify redemptive social movements. *Reformative social movements* try to change the entire society, generally working within the existing political system. The "Buy American" movement, for instance, teams manufacturers and workers in an effort to persuade consumers to favor products made in the United States. Finally, *revolutionary social movements* advocate a sweeping transformation of society. Sometimes advancing specific plans, sometimes spinning utopian dreams, such movements reject existing social institutions in favor of radical change. Revolutionary social movements that have flourished in the United States have leaned toward both the political left (consider the Communist Party) and the political right (including the John Birch Society).

Figure 15–1   Four Types of Social Movements
(Aberle, 1966)

Understanding social movements. Sociologists have devised several ways of looking at social movements. One approach, *deprivation theory*, suggests that advocates of social change are people who see themselves as deprived of something they deserve. Research points to no absolute level of deprivation that triggers activism. Rather, people react to **relative deprivation**, *a perceived disadvantage relative to some standard of comparison.* Drawing on deprivation theory, we can see why revolutionary movements have surfaced in both good and bad times: it is not people's absolute standing that counts but how they subjectively perceive their situation (Tocqueville, 1955, orig. 1856; Davies, 1962; Merton, 1968).

Mass-society theory, a second approach, locates organized efforts toward change among rootless individuals who seek, through collective activity, a sense of membership and purpose. From this point of view, social movements have a personal as well as a political agenda (Kornhauser, 1959; Melucci, 1989).

Resource-mobilization theory, a third theoretical scheme, links the success of any social movement to available resources—including money, human labor, access to the mass media, and even moral confidence. Most social movements are small, at least at the outset, and must look beyond themselves to mobilize the resources needed to increase their chances for success (McCarthy & Zald, 1977; Killian, 1984; Snow, Rochford, Jr., Worden, & Benford, 1986).

Fourth, and finally, *new social movements theory* points out the distinctive character of recent social movements. Not only are they typically national or international in scope, but they are likely to focus on quality-of-life issues—including global ecology, world peace, or animal rights—rather than economic issues. This broader scope of contemporary social movements mirrors the closer ties among governments and the growing global influence of the mass media (Melucci, 1980; McAdam, McCarthy, & Zald, 1988; Kriesi, 1989).

Stages in social movements. We can discern patterns even in the process of change. The *emergence* of social movements typically parallels the perception that society is in some way flawed. In certain cases (the women's movement), activism may be rooted in the everyday experiences of countless people; in others (the AIDS crisis), a small vanguard may mobilize the public.

The *coalescence* of a social movement is often a matter of available resources. A newly formed movement must clearly define itself, recruit new members, and

Environmentalists are a prominent example of what are called "new social movements." Such efforts for change typically involve people in many countries and are concerned with "quality-of-life" issues that participants believe are vital to the future of humanity. Here, throngs of people in New York take part in a recent Earth Day demonstration.

devise policies and tactics. Leaders must also gain access to the mass media and forge alliances with other organizations.

As it marshalls resources, a social movement may undergo *bureaucratization*. This means that it grows more established, depending less on the charisma and talents of a few leaders and more on a professional staff. As movements become more bureaucratic, members may lose some of their initial fervor, but the movement as a whole will have a better chance of long-term survival.

Finally, social movements *decline* for a variety of reasons. Resources may dry up, the group may face overwhelming opposition, or members may become victims of their own success. Some well-established organizations outlive their original causes, moving on to new crusades; others lose touch with the idea of changing society and choose, instead, to become part of the "system" (Piven & Cloward, 1977; Miller, 1983).

MODERNITY

A central concept in the study of social change is **modernity,** *social patterns caused by industrialization.* In everyday usage, modernity (its Latin root means "lately") refers to the present in relation to the past. Sociologists include within this catch-all concept social patterns set in motion by the Industrial Revolution beginning in Western Europe in the mid-eighteenth century. **Modernization,** then, is *the process of social change initiated by industrialization.* Peter Berger (1977) notes four general characteristics of modernization.

1. **The decline of small, traditional communities.** Modernity involves "the progressive weakening, if not destruction, of the . . . relatively cohesive communities in which human beings have found solidarity and meaning throughout most of history" (Berger, 1977:72). For thousands of years, in the camps of hunters and gatherers and in the rural villages of early North American settlers, people lived in small-scale communities based on family and neighborhood. Such traditional worlds afford each individual a well-defined place; while such small primary groups limited the range of personal experience, they provided a strong sense of personal identity, belonging, and purpose.

Small, isolated communities still exist in the United States, of course, but they are now home to only a small percentage of our nation's people. Even for rural families, efficient communication and rapid transportation have brought individuals in touch with the pulse of the larger society and even the entire world. For everyone, too, the family is no longer the unrivaled center of daily life. As Talcott Parsons (1966) noted, modern living is carried out in distinct institutional settings including schools, businesses, and places of worship.

2. **The expansion of personal choice.** People in traditional, preindustrial societies view their lives as being shaped by forces beyond human control—gods, spirits, or, put simply, fate. Jealously protecting their traditions, these societies grant members a narrow range of personal choices.

   As the power of tradition erodes, people come to see their lives as an unending series of options. Berger calls this process *individualization.* Many people in the United States, for instance, adopt one "lifestyle" or another because the way of life one person finds suitable may hold little appeal for another. Recognizing alternatives in everyday life, of course, parallels a willingness to embrace change. Modern people, then, easily imagine the world being different from the way it is now.

In response to the accelerated pace of social change in the late nineteenth century, Paul Gauguin (1848–1903) deserted his native France for the South Seas, where he was captivated by a simpler and seemingly timeless way of life. He romanticized this environment in his 1894 painting *Mahana no Atua (Day of the Gods).*

Paul Gauguin, Day of the Gods (Mahana no Atua), *1894. Oil on canvas, 68.3 x 91.5 cm. The Art Institute of Chicago. Helen Birch Bartlett Memorial Collection.*

3. **Increasing social diversity.** In preindustrial societies, strong family ties and powerful religious beliefs enforce conformity, discouraging diversity and change. Modernization promotes a more rational, scientific world view, in which traditional beliefs lose their force and morality becomes a matter of individual attitude. The growth of cities, the expansion of impersonal organizations, and the social mix of people from various backgrounds combine to foster a diversity of beliefs and behavior as well as a tolerant openness to those who differ from ourselves.

   Chapter 12 ("Family and Religion") spotlighted *secularization*, the historical decline in the importance of religion. The weakening of religious doctrine, and especially the official separation of religion and politics, helps expand the range of personal beliefs in modern societies.

4. **Future orientation and growing awareness of time.** People in modern societies share a distinctive appreciation of time. First, we tend to think more about the future, while premodern people focus more on the past. Modern people are not only forward-looking but optimistic that life will be enhanced by new inventions and discoveries. Second, modern societies organize daily routines according to precise units of time. With the introduction of clocks in the late Middle Ages, Europeans began to think not in terms of sunlight and seasons but in terms of hours and minutes. Why? Because of the growing importance of economic activity. Industrial technology demands increasingly precise measurement of time; in addition, the Industrial Revolution prompted capitalists, preoccupied with profits, to exclaim, "Time is money!" Berger suggests that one gauge of a society's degree of industrialization is the proportion of people wearing wristwatches.

Finally, recall that modernization touched off the development of sociology itself. As Chapter 1 ("Sociology: Perspective, Theory, and Method") explained, the discipline originated in the wake of the Industrial Revolution in Western Europe, at a time and place where social change was proceeding most intensely. Early European and U.S. sociologists tried to analyze the rise of modern society and its consequences—both good and bad—for human beings.

Ferdinand Toennies: The Loss of Community

The German sociologist Ferdinand Toennies produced a highly influential account of modernization, detailed in Chapter 14 ("Population and Urbanization"). Like Peter Berger, whose work he influenced, Toennies viewed modernization as the progressive loss of human community, or *Gemeinschaft*. As Toennies saw it, the Industrial Revolution undermined the strong social fabric of family and tradition by introducing a business-like emphasis on facts and efficiency. European and North American societies gradually became rootless and impersonal as people came to associate mostly on the basis of self-interest—a state Toennies termed *Gesellschaft* (1963; orig. 1887).

At least some of the United States early in this century approximated Toennies's concept of *Gemeinschaft*. Families that had lived in small villages and towns for many generations were integrated into a hard-working, slow-moving way of life. Telephones (invented in 1876) were rare, and the first coast-to-coast call was placed only in 1915. Living without television (introduced in 1939, and widespread after 1950), families entertained themselves, often gathering with friends in the evening—much like Brazil's Kaiapo—to share stories, sorrows, or song. Without rapid transportation (Henry Ford's assembly line began in 1908, and cars became common only after World War II), many people perceived their own town as their entire world.

Inevitable tensions and conflicts—sometimes based on race, ethnicity, and religion—characterized small communities of the past. According to Toennies, however, the traditional ties of *Gemeinschaft* bound people together as a community "essentially united in spite of all separating factors" (1963:65).

Modernity turns society inside out so that, as Toennies put it, people are "essentially separated in spite of uniting factors" (1963:65). This is the world of *Gesellschaft* where, especially in large cities, most people live among strangers and ignore those they pass on the street. Trust is hard to come by in a mobile and anonymous society; one recent survey found that a majority of U.S. adults agreed that "you can't be too careful" in dealing with people (N.O.R.C., 1991:195). No wonder, as one recent news report indicated, 15 million men and women attend weekly support groups (also made up of strangers) in which they establish temporary emotional ties and find someone who is willing simply to *listen* (Leerhsen, 1990).

Geographic mobility underlies much of our soci-

Table 15–1 MOVING ON IN THE MODERN UNITED STATES

Region	Residence in 1990				
	Same House as 1989	Different House than in 1989	Different House Same County	Different County Same State	Different State
Northeast	87.4%	11.9%	7.6%	2.4%	2.0%
Midwest	83.9	15.8	9.6	3.1	3.1
South	80.6	18.8	11.1	3.7	3.9
West	77.2	21.7	14.0	3.8	3.9
Total U.S.	82.1	17.3	10.6	3.3	3.3

SOURCE: U.S. Census Bureau, *Geographical Mobility. March 1989 to March 1990* (Washington, DC: U.S. Government Printing Office, 1991), pp. 19–20.

ety's rootlessness. Table 15–1 shows that one in six households in the United States moves in a given year because of a new job, divorce, or perhaps simply in search of warmer weather.

Modern life is not completely devoid of *Gemeinschaft*. Even in a world of strangers, friendships are often strong and lasting. Traditions are also especially pronounced in many ethnic neighborhoods where residents maintain close community ties. But in cosmopolitan districts of large cities, an indifference to those outside of a person's immediate circle—the attitude that disturbed Toennies in the 1880s—continues to present an ethical dilemma today, as the box explains.

Critical evaluation. Toennies's theory of *Gemeinschaft* and *Gesellschaft* is the most widely cited model for describing modernization. The theory's strength lies in its synthesis of various dimensions of change—growing population, the rise of cities, greater impersonality. However, Toennies's theory says little about which factors are cause and which are effect. Critics also assert that Toennies favored—perhaps even romanticized—traditional societies.

Emile Durkheim: The Division of Labor

The French sociologist Emile Durkheim shared Toennies's interest in the profound social changes wrought by the Industrial Revolution. For Durkheim, the rise of modernity is marked by increasing **division of labor,** meaning *specialized economic activity* (1964b; orig. 1893). Whereas everyone in traditional societies performs more or less the same activities, modern societies function by having people carry out highly distinctive roles.

As the last chapter explained, Durkheim claimed preindustrial societies were held together by *mechanical solidarity*, social bonds resting on shared moral sentiments. Thus members of such societies have a sense that everyone is basically alike and belongs together. Mechanical solidarity—or what Toennies called *Gemeinschaft*—depends on a minimal division of labor, so that every person's life follows much the same path.

Modernization takes place as the division of labor becomes more and more pronounced. Modern societies, then, are held together by *organic solidarity*, bonds of mutual dependency among people who engage in specialized work. Put simply, modern societies are held together

A sure sign of modernization is that people shun traditional activities such as farming in favor of specialized productive roles. Hoping to secure a day's work in Mexico City, these men offer their services as electricians, contractors, painters, and plumbers.

CRITICAL THINKING

Modern Society: What Do We Owe One Another?

In today's society, how involved should we become in the lives of others? Few would want to go back to the "tyranny of the tribe," by which people in traditional communities suspiciously monitor each other's every activity. But does the modern notion of "individual freedom" mean that we should be indifferent to everyone around us, including those in need?

Modern society poses a dilemma which pits our desire for privacy against our need for human community. The 1964 murder of Kitty Genovese in New York City helps us sort out our obligations to others. Returning from work late at night, Ms. Genovese was stalked and stabbed to death by a stranger in the parking lot of her apartment building.

Investigators were later stunned to learn that at least thirty-eight people in the building had witnessed the attack, which had lasted more than thirty minutes. Not one of these witnesses came to her assistance or even called the police. The behavior of these "neighbors," even more than the killing itself, provoked people across the country to consider just what members of modern societies owe one another.

For some, the murder of Kitty Genovese brought to mind the New Testament book of Luke (10:30–37), in which Jesus responds to the question "Who is my neighbor?" by offering the tale of the Good Samaritan. The story begins with a man on the road to Jericho being robbed and left for dead; several travelers pass by without offering him any help. Then a Samaritan stops, attends to the man's wounds, takes him to an inn, and leaves money to pay for further care. The Samaritan makes no effort to establish a personal relationship with the victim; he does not even try to learn his name. The victim, it seems, is just another stranger. But while the Samaritan behaves impersonally, he also acts compassionately, doing what is necessary for a fellow human being in need.

This ancient Biblical parable holds an important lesson for today's world. We certainly do not want to become personally involved with everyone we meet. But if we become indifferent to the humanity of those around us, we risk losing our own.

---

not by likeness but by difference. Organic solidarity corresponds to Toennies's concept of *Gesellschaft*.

Despite clear similarities, Durkheim and Toennies interpreted modernity somewhat differently. To Toennies, modern *Gesellschaft* incorporates almost no social solidarity—the result of the gradual change from the "natural" and "organic" bonds of the past to the "artificial" and "mechanical" ties of today. Durkheim disagreed, reversing Toennies's language: he labeled modern social life as "organic," suggesting that today's world is no less "natural" than before, and traditional societies are "mechanical" because they are so regimented. Thus Durkheim viewed modernization not so much as a loss of community as a change in the basis of community—from bonds of likeness (kinship and neighborhood) to ties of economic interdependence (the division of labor). Durkheim's view of modernity is thus both more complex and more positive than that of Toennies.

Critical evaluation. Durkheim's work stands alongside that of Toennies, which it closely resembles, as a highly influential analysis of modernity. Of the two, Durkheim is clearly the more optimistic; still, he feared that modern societies might become so internally diverse that they would collapse into **anomie,** *a condition in which society provides little moral guidance to individuals.* In the midst of weak moral claims from society, modern people tend to be egocentric, placing our own needs above those of the community.

Evidence supports Durkheim's contention that anomie plagues modern societies. Suicide rates, which Durkheim considered to be an index of anomie, have risen during this century. Moreover, the vast majority of U.S. adults report that they see moral questions not in clear terms of right and wrong but as "shades of gray" (N.O.R.C., 1991:403). On the other hand, shared norms and values are still strong enough to give most people a sense of meaning and purpose. Additionally, whatever the hazards of anomie and atomization, most people value the privacy and personal autonomy modern society affords.

Max Weber: Rationalization

For Max Weber, modernity amounts to the progressive replacement of a traditional world view with a rational way of thinking. In preindustrial societies, tradition acts as a constant brake to change. To traditional people, "truth" is roughly synonymous with *what has always been* (1978:36; orig. 1921). In modern societies, however, people see truth as the product of deliberate calculation. Because they value efficiency more than reverence toward the past, individuals embrace whatever social patterns will allow them to achieve their goals. A rational view of the world, then, leads people to seek out and assess various options according to their specific consequences rather than based on any absolute standard of rightness.

Echoing the claim by Toennies and Durkheim that industrialization weakens tradition, Weber declared that modern society had become "disenchanted." What were once unquestioned truths have become subject to matter-of-fact calculations. Embracing rational, scientific thought, in short, modern society turns away from the gods. Throughout his life, then, Weber explored various modern "types"—the capitalist, the scientist, the bureaucrat—all of whom share the detached world view that he believed was coming to dominate humanity.

Critical evaluation. Compared with Toennies, and especially Durkheim, Weber was a profound critic of modern society. He recognized that science could produce technological and organizational wonders, yet he worried that it was carrying us away from more basic questions about the meaning and purpose of human existence. Weber feared that rationalization, especially in bureaucracies, would erode the human spirit with endless rules and regulations.

Some of Weber's critics think that the alienation he attributed to bureaucracy actually stemmed from social inequality. This leads us to the work of Karl Marx.

Karl Marx: Capitalism

While other analysts of modernity examined shifting patterns of social order, Karl Marx focused on social conflict. For Marx, modern society was synonymous with capitalism; he saw the Industrial Revolution primar-

ily as a *capitalist revolution.* Marx claimed that the bourgeoisie emerged in medieval Europe as a social class intent on wresting control of society from the feudal nobility. The bourgeoisie were finally successful when the Industrial Revolution placed a powerful new productive system under their control.

Marx agreed that modernity weakened small-scale communities (as described by Toennies), increased the division of labor (as noted by Durkheim), and fostered a rational world view (as asserted by Weber). But he saw these factors simply as conditions necessary for capitalism to flourish. Capitalism, according to Marx, draws population from farms and small towns into an ever-expanding market system centered in the cities; specialization underlies efficient factories; and rationality is exemplified by the capitalists' relentless quest for profits.

Earlier chapters have painted Marx as a spirited critic of capitalist society, but his vision of modernity also incorporates a considerable measure of optimism. Unlike Weber, who viewed modern society as an "iron cage" of bureaucracy, Marx believed that social conflict in capitalist societies would sow the seeds of revolutionary change, leading to an egalitarian socialism. Such a society, he claimed, would harness the wonders of industrial technology to enrich the lives of the many rather than the few—and thereby rid the world of the prime source of conflict and dehumanization. While Marx's evaluation of modern capitalist society was highly negative, then, he envisioned a future with greater human freedom, blossoming human creativity, and renewed human community.

Critical evaluation. Marx's theory of modernization draws together many threads in a fabric dominated by capitalism. Yet Marx underestimated the significance of bureaucracy in shaping modern societies. The stifling effects of bureaucracy on humanity turned out to be as bad—or worse—in socialist societies, as their government apparatus expanded, than the dehumanizing impact of capitalism. The recent upheavals in Eastern Europe and the former Soviet Union reveal the depth of popular opposition to rigid state bureaucracies.

UNDERSTANDING MODERNITY: THE THEORY OF MASS SOCIETY

The rise of modernity is a complex process involving many dimensions of change, described in previous chapters and summarized in Table 15–2. How is one to

Table 15-2 TRADITIONAL AND MODERN SOCIETIES: DIMENSIONS OF DIFFERENCE

Elements of Society	Traditional Societies	Modern Societies
Cultural Patterns		
Values	Homogeneous; sacred character; few subcultures and countercultures	Heterogeneous; secular character; many subcultures and countercultures
Norms	High moral significance; little tolerance of diversity	Variable moral significance; high tolerance of diversity
Time orientation	Present linked to past	Present linked to future
Technology	Preindustrial; human and animal energy	Industrial; advanced energy sources
Social Structure		
Status and role	Few statuses, most ascribed; few specialized roles	Many statuses, some ascribed and some achieved; many specialized roles
Relationships	Typically primary; little anonymity and privacy	Typically secondary; considerable anonymity and privacy
Communication	Face to face	Face-to-face communication supplemented by mass media
Social control	Informal gossip	Formal police and legal system
Social stratification	Rigid patterns of social inequality; little mobility	Fluid patterns of social inequality; considerable mobility
Gender patterns	Pronounced patriarchy; women's lives centered on the home	Declining patriarchy; increasing number of women in the paid labor force
Economy	Based on agriculture; some manufacturing in the home; little white-collar work	Based on industrial mass production; factories become centers of production; increasing white-collar work
State	Small-scale government; little state intervention in society	Large-scale government; considerable state intervention in society
Family	Extended family as the primary means of socialization and economic production	Nuclear family retains some socialization functions but is more a unit of consumption than of production
Religion	Religion guides world view; little religious pluralism	Religion weakens with the rise of science; extensive religious pluralism
Education	Formal schooling limited to elites	Basic schooling becomes universal, with growing proportion receiving advanced education
Health	High birth and death rates; brief life expectancy because of low standard of living and simple medical technology	Low birth and death rates; longer life expectancy because of higher standard of living and sophisticated medical technology
Settlement patterns	Small scale; population typically small and widely dispersed in rural villages and small towns	Large scale; population typically large and concentrated in cities
Social Change	Slow; change evident over many generations	Rapid; change evident within a single generation

make sense of so many changes going on at once? One broad approach—drawing on the ideas of Toennies, Durkheim, and Weber—understands modernity as the emergence of *mass society* (Dahrendorf, 1959; Kornhauser, 1959; Nisbet, 1966, 1969; Baltzell, 1968; Stein, 1972; Berger, Berger, & Kellner, 1974).

A **mass society** is *a society in which industry and bureaucracy have eroded traditional social ties.* A mass society is marked by weak kinship and neighborhood ties so that individuals are socially atomized. In their isolation, members of mass societies typically experience feelings of moral uncertainty and personal powerlessness.

The Mass Scale of Life

Mass-society theory argues, first, that the scale of modern life has increased greatly. Before the Industrial Revolution, Europe and North America formed an intricate mosaic of countless rural villages and small towns. In these small communities, which inspired Toennies's concept of *Gemeinschaft*, people lived out their lives surrounded by kin and guided by a shared heritage. Gossip was an informal, yet highly effective, means of maintaining rigid conformity to community standards. Limited community size, coupled with strong moral values, combined to stifle social diversity—the mechanical solidarity described by Durkheim. For example, in England before 1690, law and local custom demanded that everyone regularly participate in the Christian ritual of Holy Communion (Laslett, 1984). Similarly, only Rhode Island among the New England colonies offered any support for the notion of religious dissent. Because social differences were repressed, subcultures and countercultures rarely flourished and change proceeded slowly. Social stratification was more or less set at birth, with little social mobility.

A surge in population, the growth of cities, and specialized economic activity during the Industrial Revolution gradually changed all this. People came to be known by their function (for example, as the "doctor" or the "bank clerk") rather than by their kin group or home town. The majority of people looked on others as simply a mass of strangers. The face-to-face communication of the village was eventually replaced by the mass media—newspapers, radio, and television—that furthered social atomization. Large organizations steadily assumed more and more responsibility for daily needs that had once been fulfilled by family, friends, and neighbors; universal public education enlarged the scope of learning; police, lawyers, and courts supervised a formal criminal justice system. Even charity became the work of faceless bureaucrats working for various social welfare agencies.

Geographical mobility, mass communications, and exposure to diverse ways of life undermined traditional values. Less certain about what was worth believing, people became more tolerant of social diversity, trumpeting the merits of individual rights and freedom of choice. Subcultures and countercultures multiplied. Making categorical distinctions among people fell out of favor; to treat someone a particular way based on race, sex, or religion came to be defined as backwards and unjust. In the process, minorities who had long lived at the margins of society gained greater power and broader participation. Yet, mass society theorists fear, transforming people of various backgrounds into a generic mass may end up dehumanizing everyone.

The Ever-Expanding State

In the small-scale, preindustrial societies of Europe, government amounted to little more than a local noble. A royal family formally reigned over an entire nation, but without efficient transportation and communication, the power of even absolute monarchs fell far short of that wielded by today's political leaders.

As technological innovation allowed government to expand, the centralized state grew in size and importance. At the time the United States gained independence from Great Britain, the federal government was a tiny organization whose prime function was national defense. Since then, government has entered more and more areas of social life—regulating wages and working conditions, establishing standards for products of all sorts, schooling the population, and providing financial assistance to the ill and the unemployed. Taxes have correspondingly soared, so that today's average worker labors four months a year to pay for various government services.

In a mass society, power resides in large bureaucracies, leaving people in local communities little control over their lives. For example, a local school must have a standardized education program, local products must carry government-mandated labels, and every citizen must maintain extensive records for purposes of taxation. While such regulations may protect people and enhance uniformity of treatment, they depersonalize human decision making and limit the autonomy of neighborhoods, families, and individuals.

Critical evaluation. The theory of mass society concedes that the transformation of small-scale societies has positive aspects, but tends to see in historical change the loss of an irreplaceable heritage. Modern societies increase individual rights, magnify tolerance of social differences, and raise living standards. But they seem prone to what Max Weber feared most—excessive bureaucracy—as well as Toennies's self-centeredness and Emile Durkheim's anomie. The size, complexity, and tolerance of diversity in modern society all but doomed traditional values and family patterns, leaving individuals isolated, powerless, and materialistic. As noted in Chapter 11 ("Economics and Politics"), voter apathy has be-

Edvard Munch (1863–1944), a Norwegian artist who lived for most of his career in Paris, captured in his painting *The Scream* (1893) the terror of feeling utterly alone. While this sensation probably was fueled by the artist's own psychological problems, it has a sociological side as well—the isolation of the individual that was becoming more pronounced in the modern world.

come a serious problem in the United States. But should we be surprised that individuals in vast, impersonal societies end up thinking that their one voice makes no difference?

Critics of mass-society theory contend that it romanticizes the past. They remind us that many people in the small towns of our past were actually quite eager to set out for a better standard of living in cities. Critics also point out that this approach pays little attention to problems of social inequality. Mass-society analysis, these critics conclude, attracts social and economic conservatives who defend conventional morality and often seem indifferent to the historical plight of women and other minorities.

ANOTHER APPROACH: THE THEORY OF CLASS SOCIETY

A second interpretation of modernity derives largely from the ideas of Karl Marx. From this point of view, modernity takes the form of a **class society**, *a stratified, capitalist society*. This theory holds that feelings of powerlessness in modern society stem from social inequality. While acknowledging that modern societies have grown to a mass scale, this approach views the heart of modernization as an expanding capitalist economy, which prevents modern technology from fulfilling its promise of a good life for everyone by concentrating wealth in the hands of a few. Thus further social revolution is needed to eradicate the social inequality wrought by capitalism (Miliband, 1969; Habermas, 1970; Polenberg, 1980; Blumberg, 1981; Harrington, 1984).

Capitalism

Class-society theory follows Marx in claiming that the increasing scale of social life in modern times has resulted from the insatiable appetite of capitalism. Because a capitalist economy pursues ever-increasing profits, both production and consumption expand.

According to Marx, capitalism rests on "naked self-interest" and greed (1972:337; orig. 1848). This self-centeredness erodes the social ties that once cemented small-scale communities. Capitalism also fosters impersonality and anonymity by transforming people into commodities, as both a source of labor and a market for capitalist production. The net result is that capitalism reduces human beings to cogs in the machinery of material production.

Capitalism also transforms science, the key to greater productivity, into an ideology that justifies the status quo. In preindustrial Europe, the nobility defended their rule with traditional notions of moral obligation and responsibility. In modern societies, capitalists legitimize their way of life by encouraging people to view well-being as a *technical* puzzle to be solved by engineers and other experts rather than through the pursuit of *social* justice (Habermas, 1970). A capitalist culture, for example, seeks to improve health through scientific medicine rather than by eliminating poverty, which undermines many people's health in the first place.

Businesses also raise the banner of scientific logic, claiming that efficiency is achieved only through continual growth. As Chapter 11 ("Economics and Politics") explained, capitalist corporations have reached enormous size and control almost unimaginable wealth. They have done so by "going global," that is, by becoming multinationals that operate throughout the world. From the class-society point of view, then, the expanding scale of life is less a function of *Gesellschaft* than the inevitable and destructive consequence of capitalism.

Persistent Inequality

Modernity has gradually eroded some of the rigid categorical distinctions that divided preindustrial societies. Class-society theorists maintain, however, that elites persist albeit in a different form: capitalist millionaires rather than family-based nobility. In the United States, we may have no hereditary monarchy, but the richest 5 percent of the population nevertheless controls more than half of all property. And, during the 1980s, the concentration of wealth actually increased.

What of the state, which mass-society theorists suggest has an expanding role in combating social problems? The capitalist state, Marx argued, has little incentive to address social ills because it is designed to defend the wealth and privileges of capitalists. Other theorists add that, while working people and minorities enjoy greater political rights and a higher standard of living today, these changes are the fruits of political struggle, not expressions of government benevolence. And, they continue, despite our pretensions of democracy, power still rests primarily in the hands of those with wealth. Throughout the 1980s conservative political leaders, in the name of economic growth and free-market efficiency, curtailed government funding for programs that benefited less privileged families (Harrington, 1984; Jacob, 1986).

Critical evaluation. Table 15–3 spells out key differences between the interpretations of modernity offered by mass-society theory and class-society theory. While the former focuses on the increasing scale of social life and growth of government, the latter stresses the expansion of capitalism and the persistence of inequality. Class-society theory also dismisses Durkheim's argument that people in modern societies suffer from anomie claiming, instead, that they contend with alienation and powerlessness. Not surprisingly, then, the class-society interpreta-

Table 15–3 TWO INTERPRETATIONS OF MODERNITY: A SUMMARY

	Key Process of Modernization	Key Effects of Modernization
Mass-society theory	Industrialization; growth of bureaucracy	Increasing scale of life; rise of the state and other formal organizations
Class-society theory	Rise of capitalism	Expansion of capitalist economy; persistence of social inequality

tion of modernity enjoys widespread support among social and economic liberals and radicals who favor greater equality and seek extensive regulation (or abolition) of the capitalist marketplace.

A core criticism of class-society theory holds that this analysis overlooks the many ways in which modern societies have grown more egalitarian. After all, although discrimination based on race, ethnicity, religion, and sex may still exist, they are now illegal and widely viewed as social problems. Further, most people in the United States favor unequal rewards, at least insofar as they reflect personal differences in talent and effort. Second, few observers think that a centralized economy would cure the ills of modernity in light of socialism's failure to generate a high overall standard of living. Many other problems in the United States—from unemployment, homelessness, and industrial pollution to unresponsive government—have also been commonplace in socialist nations like the former Soviet Union (Young, 1990).

MODERNITY AND THE INDIVIDUAL

Both mass- and class-society theories focus on broad patterns of change since the Industrial Revolution. From each "macro-level" approach we can also draw "micro-level" insights into how modernity shapes individual lives.

Mass Society: Problems of Identity

Modernity liberated individuals from small, tightly knit communities of the past. Most members of modern societies possess unprecedented privacy and freedom to ex-

Affluent people in the United States have such a wide range of choices about how to live that they often speak of their "lifestyles" as something they shape for themselves. For most of humanity, however, tradition and lack of opportunity combine to generate a more steady existence and a more well-defined personal identity.

press their individuality. Mass-society theory suggests, however, that extensive social diversity, atomization, and rapid social change make it difficult for many people to establish any coherent identity at all (Wheelis, 1958; Riesman, 1970; Berger, Berger, & Kellner, 1974).

Chapter 3 ("Socialization: From Infancy to Old Age") explained that people forge distinctive personalities based on their social experience. The small, homogeneous, and slowly changing societies of the past provided a firm (if narrow) foundation for building meaningful identity. Even today, the Amish communities that flourish in the United States and Canada confer on members a strong sense of roots. There, young Amish men and women know the meaning of being Amish—that is, how they should think and behave—and they learn to embrace this life as "natural" and right. Not everyone born into an Amish community can tolerate these demands for conformity, but most members establish a

coherent and satisfying personal identity (Hostetler, 1980).

Mass societies, with their characteristic diversity and rapid change, provide only shifting sands on which to build a personal identity. Left to make most of our own life decisions, many of us—especially those with greater affluence—confront a bewildering range of options. Autonomy has little value without standards for making choices, however, and in a tolerant mass society, no one path seems more compelling than the next. Not surprisingly, many people shuttle from one identity to another, changing their lifestyle in search of an elusive "true self." They may fall in and out of relationships, experiment with various religions, or join one or another social movement in search of purpose and belonging. This difficulty in developing an identity is not psychological, although it is often treated as an individual problem. More accurately, such people are suffering from the widespread "relativism" of modern societies; without a working moral compass, they have lost the security and certainty once provided by tradition.

For David Riesman (1970; orig. 1950), modernization brings on changes in **social character,** *personality patterns common to members of a society.* Preindustrial societies promote what Riesman calls **tradition-direction,** *rigid conformity to time-honored ways of living.* Members of such societies model their lives on what has gone before so that what is viewed as "good" is equivalent to "what has always been." Tradition-directedness, then, carries to the level of individual experience Toennies's *Gemeinschaft* and Durkheim's mechanical solidarity. Culturally conservative, tradition-directed people think and act alike. Unlike the conformity found in modern societies, this uniformity is not an effort to mimic one another. Instead, traditional conformity exists because everyone draws on the same cultural foundation. Amish women and men exemplify tradition-direction; in the Amish culture, conformity ties everyone to ancestors and descendants in an unbroken chain of righteous living (Hostetler, 1980).

A tradition-directed personality is likely to be defined as deviant by members of a culturally diverse and rapidly changing society. Modern people, by and large, prize personal flexibility, the capacity to adapt, and sensitivity to others. Riesman calls this type of social character **other-direction,** *an openness to change and tendency to imitate others.* Because their socialization occurs within societies that are continuously in flux, other-directed people develop fluid identities marked by superficiality, inconsistency, and change. They try on different "selves," almost like so many pieces of new clothing, seek out "role models," and engage in varied "performances" from setting to setting (Goffman, 1959). In a rigid, traditional society, such "shiftiness" marks a person as untrustworthy; but in a changing, modern society, the chameleon-like ability to fit in virtually anywhere stands as a valued personal trait (Wheelis, 1958).

In societies that value the up-to-date rather than the traditional, people look to members of their own generation, rather than elders, as significant role models. Following the same reasoning, "peer pressure" can sometimes seem irresistible to people with no enduring standards to guide them. Our society urges people to be true to themselves. But when social surroundings change so rapidly, how can people determine to which self they should be true? This problem lies at the root of the identity crisis so widespread in industrial societies today. "Who am I?" is a nagging question that many of us struggle to answer. In sociological terms, this personal problem reflects the inherent instability of modern mass society.

Class Society: Problems of Powerlessness

Class-society theory paints a different picture of modernity's effects on individuals. This approach maintains that persistent inequality undermines modern society's promise of individual freedom. For some, modernity delivers great privilege, but, for the majority, everyday life means coping with a gnawing sense of powerlessness. For people of color, the problem of relative disadvantage looms even larger. Similarly, women enjoy increasing participation in modern societies, but they continue to run up against traditional barriers of sexism. In short, this approach rejects mass-society theory's claim that people suffer from too much freedom. Instead, class-society theory holds, a majority of people in our society are still denied full participation in social life.

Class-society theorists hail the struggle to empower individuals, which has been gaining strength in recent years. For example, employees seek greater control of the workplace, consumers press for more say in the marketplace, and citizens try to make government more responsive to their needs (Toffler, 1981).

On a global scale, as Chapter 8 ("Global Inequality") explained, the expanding scope of world capitalism has placed more of the earth's population under the influence of multinational corporations. As a result, about two-thirds of the world's income is concentrated

Mass-society theory explains the collapse of the social fabric in U.S. cities as the result of rapid social change and the erosion of tradition. Class-society theory, by contrast, suggests that social inequality diminishes the likelihood of meaningful human community.

in the richest societies, where only about 15 percent of its people live. Is it any wonder, class-society theorists ask, that throughout the Third World people are also seeking greater power to shape their own lives?

Such problems led Herbert Marcuse (1964) to challenge Max Weber's contention that modern society is rational. Marcuse condemns modern society as irrational because it fails to meet the needs of so many people. While modern capitalist societies produce unparalleled wealth, poverty remains the daily plight of more than a billion people. Moreover, Marcuse argues, technological advances rarely empower people; instead, technology tends to reduce their control over their own lives. High technology generally means that a core of specialists—not the vast majority of people—controls events and dominates discussion, whether the issue is energy production for communities or health care for individuals. Specialists define ordinary people as ill-equipped for decision making, urging the public to defer to elites. And elites, from this point of view, have little concern for the common interest. Despite the popular view that technology *solves* the world's problems, Marcuse concludes, it may be more accurate to say it *causes* them. In sum, class-society theory asserts that people suffer because modern societies have concentrated both wealth and power in the hands of a privileged few.

THE IDEA OF PROGRESS

In modern societies, most people expect—and applaud—social change. People link modernity to the idea of *progress* (from Latin, meaning "a moving forward"), a state of continual improvement. By contrast, we denigrate stability as stagnation.

This chapter began by describing the Kaiapo of Brazil, for whom affluence has broadened opportunities but weakened traditional heritage. In examining the Kaiapo, we see that social change, with all its beneficial and detrimental consequences, is too complex to be simply equated with progress. More precisely, whether or not we see a given change as progress depends on our underlying values. A rising standard of living among the Kaiapo—or, historically, among the people in the United States—has helped make our lives longer and more comfortable. But affluence has also fueled materialism at the expense of spiritual life, creating ambivalence toward change in the minds of many people. In a recent survey, most adults in the United States expressed mixed feelings on the subject of scientific change; aware of its benefits, many nonetheless think that science "makes our way of life change too fast" (N.O.R.C., 1991:388).

Many people also celebrate modern society's recognition of basic human rights. The assertion that people have rights simply by virtue of their humanity is a distinctly modern idea found in the U.S. Declaration of Independence and the United Nations' *Declaration of Human Rights*. But, as Chapter 2 ("Culture") explained, we now have something of a "culture of rights" that tends to overlook our obligations to one another. The box on page 400 offers another angle on this issue by contrasting the modern idea of individual dignity and the traditional notion of personal honor.

In principle, the idea that individuals should have considerable autonomy in shaping their own lives has widespread support in the United States. Thus, many people will applaud the demise of traditional conceptions of honor, viewing this trend as a sign of progress. Yet, as people exercise their freedom of choice they inevitably challenge social patterns cherished by others who maintain a more traditional way of life. For example, people may choose not to marry, to live with someone without

marrying, perhaps even to form a partnership with someone of their own sex. To those who support individual choice, such changes symbolize progress; to those who value traditional family patterns, however, these developments signal societal decay (Wallis, 1985).

Even new technology remains controversial. More rapid transportation or more efficient communication may improve our lives in some respects. However, complex technology has also eroded traditional attachments to home towns and maybe even to family. Industrial technology has also unleashed an unprecedented threat to the natural environment. In short, social change gives rise to uncertainty, complexity, and controversy, making sweeping assumptions about the effect of change risky at best.

MODERNIZATION: OUR GLOBAL FUTURE

Sometimes social change proceeds haphazardly, sometimes deliberately. Some change that is desperately needed has not occurred at all, as in much of the Third World, where almost 1 billion people struggle daily against life-threatening poverty.

Two competing views of the causes of global poverty are detailed in Chapter 8 ("Global Inequality"). *Modernization theory* claims that in the past the entire world was poor and that technological change, especially the Industrial Revolution, has enhanced human productivity and raised living standards. From this point of view, the solution to global poverty lies in encouraging technological development in poor regions.

For reasons suggested earlier, however, global modernization may be difficult. Recall that David Riesman portrayed preindustrial people as tradition-directed and likely to resist change. So some modernization theorists advocate that the world's rich societies deliberately intervene in poor societies to encourage productive innovation. First-World nations can speed development by exporting technology to the Third World, welcoming students from abroad, and providing foreign aid to stimulate economic growth.

The review of modernization theory in Chapter 8 suggests that the success of these policies has been limited. Even where the greatest efforts have been made, resistance to change has compromised the results. Traditional people such as Brazil's Kaiapo have gained wealth by selling their natural resources on world markets, but

What Happened to Honor?

Honor occupies about the same place in contemporary usage as chastity. An individual asserting it hardly invites admiration, and one who claims to have lost it is an object of amusement rather than sympathy. (1974:83)

Honor is a human virtue that seems distinctly out of place in modern society. Honor means acting according to traditional cultural norms. Since norms used to be quite different for various categories of people, men claim honor by being masculine as women do by being feminine. Honor, then, is acting like the kind of person you are in a world of rigid social distinctions—between females and males, nobles and serfs, one's own family and outsiders.

Through observing the rules that apply to them, however, honor is available to people of any social station. During the Middle Ages, European nobles claimed honor when they performed their feudal obligations toward their social inferiors and displayed proper respect for their peers.

Similarly, commoners acted honorably to the extent that they fulfilled their duties to their superiors and everyone else. Honorable men assumed the cultural ideal of a fatherly, protective role toward women, while never "taking advantage" of them. For their part, women honorably observed proper morals and manners in the presence of men.

With modernization, cultural norms have become weaker and more variable, and categorical distinctions among people have been challenged by drives for social equality. Modern culture holds that all people should treat others as equals. Therefore, although the concept of honor survives in some ethnic communities and traditional occupations like the military, it has less appeal to most members of modern societies.

Modernization enhances concern for people as *individuals*, which leads us to the concept of *dignity*. Whereas various categories of people have distinctive codes of honor, dignity is a universal human trait, resting on the inherent value of everyone. We recognize the dignity of others when we acknowledge our common humanity by overlooking social differences.

In the spirit of modern dignity, women may object to men treating them as women rather than as individuals. The male practices of holding open a door for a woman and paying for a shared meal may be honorable by traditional standards, but now they are more likely to be viewed as affronts to the dignity of women by underscoring gender differences.

As a result, honor is fading from modern societies. The cultural diversity and rapid change sweeping across the modern world renders all traditional scripts for living suspect. In contrast to codes of honor that guided people in the past, human beings now value individual self-worth and self-determination—the essence of dignity.

SOURCE: Based on Berger, Berger, & Kellner (1974).

---

only at the cost of being drawn into the "global village" where concern for money supersedes traditional values. In some societies, including Iran and Ethiopia, rapid modernization has set off a powerful backlash from groups that want to restore traditional culture.

Modernization theory thus leaves unresolved a contemporary dilemma: modernity may bring higher living standards but, in the process, it sweeps a society into the global mass culture of Western pop music, trendy clothes, and fast food. One Brazilian anthropologist expressed uncertainty about the future of the Kaiapo: "At least they quickly understood the consequences of watching television. . . . Now [they] can make a choice" (Simons, 1989:37).

But not everyone agrees that modernization is even a choice. According to a second approach to global inequality, *dependency theory*, today's poor societies have little ability to modernize, even if they want to. From this point of view, the major barrier to economic development is not traditionalism but the global domination by rich, capitalist societies. Initially, as Chapter 8 explained, this system took the form of colonialism, whereby European societies seized control of much of Latin America, Africa, and Asia. Trading relationships

The future of our world lies not in isolation, by which societies jealously protect their culture, nor in confederation, by which everyone enthusiastically embraces a single way of life. The challenge of the next century will be *managing diversity*, a skill made more necessary as communications technology, economic expansion, and the need to confront global problems draw the disparate peoples of the world closer together. In the emerging conversation of nations, we should not assume that the richest and most powerful countries should do all the talking. On the contrary, the keys to long-term peace and ecological survival may well lie in rediscovering many of the human truths that form the common sense of our more traditional neighbors.

soon enriched England, Spain, and other colonial powers, as their colonies grew poorer. Almost all societies subjected to this form of domination are now politically independent, but colonial-style ties continue in the form of First-World corporations operating around the globe.

In effect, dependency theory asserts, rich societies achieved their modernization at least partly at the expense of poor nations, which provided valuable natural resources and human labor. Even today, the Third World remains locked in a disadvantageous economic relationship with the First World, dependent on rich societies to buy their raw materials and in return to provide them with whatever manufactured goods they can afford. Continuing ties with rich societies appear likely to perpetuate current patterns of global inequality.

Dependency theory implies that social change occurs outside the control of individual societies. On the contrary, the fate and fortune of individual nations worldwide is tied to their position in the global economy. Thus, change to improve the plight of people in the Third World will involve corresponding changes in First-World societies.

Whichever approach one finds more convincing, we can no longer study the United States in isolation from the rest of the world. At the beginning of the twentieth century, a majority of people in even the richest societies lived in relatively small settlements with limited awareness of others. Now, at the threshold of the twenty-first century, people everywhere are playing out a far larger human drama. The world seems smaller because the lives of all its people are increasingly linked. We now discuss the relationships among societies in the same way that people a century ago talked about the expanding ties among towns and cities.

The century now coming to an end has witnessed unparalleled human achievement. Yet solutions to many problems of human existence—including finding meaning in life, eradicating poverty, and resolving conflict among societies—remain elusive. To this list of pressing matters, new concerns have been added, such as controlling population growth and managing the global environment. Yet as we approach the twenty-first century, we can look ahead with optimism, because of our unprecedented understanding of human society.

SUMMARY

1. Every society changes continuously, although with varying speed and consequences. Whether social change is intentional or unplanned, it often generates controversy.

2. Social change is the result of invention, discovery, and cultural diffusion as well as social conflict.

3. Social movements amount to deliberate efforts to promote or resist change. Analysts link social movements to relative deprivation, the rootlessness of mass society, and an organization's ability to muster resources. So-called "new social movements" are international in scope.

4. Modernity refers to the social consequences of industrialization. According to Peter Berger, distinctive traits of modernity include the erosion of traditional communities, expanding personal choice, increasingly diverse beliefs, and a keen awareness of time, especially the future.

5. Ferdinand Toennies described modernization as the transition from *Gemeinschaft* to *Gesellschaft*: the loss of community amid growing individualism.

6. Emile Durkheim saw modernization as a function of society's expanding division of labor. Mechanical solidarity, based on shared activities and beliefs, gradually gives way to organic solidarity, in which specialization makes people interdependent.

7. Max Weber explained modernity as the replacement of traditional thought by rationality. He feared the dehumanizing effect of rational organization.

8. In Karl Marx's view, modernity emerged in the triumph of capitalism over feudalism. Because cap-

italist societies are fraught with conflict, Marx advocated revolutionary change leading to a more egalitarian, socialist system.

9. According to mass-society theory, modernity increases the scale of life, enlarging the role of government and other formal organizations in carrying out tasks previously performed by family members and neighbors. Mass-society theory holds that cultural diversity and rapid social change prevent people in modern societies from developing a stable identity and finding certainty and meaning in their lives.

10. Class-society theory states that capitalism is central to Western modernization. This approach charges that by concentrating wealth, capitalism generates widespread feelings of powerlessness.

11. Although we sometimes equate modernity with social progress, social change is a complex process whose outcomes are rarely entirely good.

12. In a global context, modernization theory claims that global poverty is caused primarily by traditionalism. Therefore, some modernization theorists advocate intentional intervention by rich societies to stimulate the development of poor nations.

13. Dependency theory argues that a society's potential for development depends on its present position in the world economic system. Poor societies are unlikely to duplicate the modernization of rich societies because, through neocolonialism, they have become economically dependent on these rich societies.

KEY CONCEPTS

anomie a condition in which society provides little moral guidance to individuals

class society a stratified, capitalist society

division of labor specialized economic activity

mass society a society in which industry and bureaucracy erode traditional social ties

modernity social patterns caused by industrialization

modernization the process of social change initiated by industrialization

other-direction a personality pattern marked by openness to change and a tendency to imitate others

relative deprivation a perceived disadvantage relative to some standard of comparison

social change the transformation of culture and social institutions over time

social character personality patterns common to members of a society

social movement an organized effort to encourage or oppose some dimension of change

tradition-direction a personality pattern marked by rigid conformity to time-honored ways of living

Glossary

absolute poverty a deprivation of resources that is life-threatening

achieved status a social position that a person assumes voluntarily and that reflects a significant measure of personal ability and choice

Afrocentrism the dominance of African cultural patterns

ageism prejudice and discrimination against the elderly

age-sex pyramid a graphic representation of the age and sex of a population

agriculture a way of life based on large-scale cultivation using animal-drawn plows

alienation the experience of powerlessness in social life

animism the belief that natural objects are conscious forms of life that affect humanity

anomie a condition in which society provides little moral guidance to individuals

anticipatory socialization social learning directed toward gaining a desired position

ascribed status a social position that a person receives at birth or assumes involuntarily later in the life course

assimilation the process by which minorities gradually adopt patterns of the dominant culture

authoritarianism a political system that denies popular participation in government

authority power that is widely perceived as legitimate rather than coercive

blue-collar occupation lower-prestige work that involves mostly manual labor

bureaucracy an organizational model designed to perform tasks efficiently

bureaucratic inertia the tendency of bureaucratic organizations to persist over time

bureaucratic ritualism a preoccupation with organizational rules and regulations to the point of obstructing organizational goals

capitalism an economic system in which natural resources and the means of producing goods and services are privately owned

capitalist one who owns a factory or other productive enterprise

caste system social stratification based on ascription

cause and effect a relationship between two variables in which change in one (the independent variable) causes change in another (the dependent variable)

charisma extraordinary personal qualities that can turn an audience into followers

charismatic authority power legitimized through extraordinary personal abilities that inspire devotion and obedience

church a formal religious organization well integrated into the larger society

civil religion a quasi-religious loyalty based on citizenship

class society a stratified, capitalist society

class system social stratification based on individual achievement

cohabitation the sharing of a household by an unmarried couple

colonialism the process by which some nations enrich themselves through political and economic control of other nations

communism a hypothetical economic and political system in which all people have social equality

concept an abstract idea that represents some aspect of the world, inevitably in a somewhat simplified form

concrete operational stage Piaget's term for the level of human development at which individuals begin logical reasoning

corporation an organization with a legal existence, including rights and liabilities, apart from those of its members

correlation a relationship between two (or more) variables

counterculture cultural patterns that strongly oppose conventional culture

credentialism evaluating people on the basis of educational degrees

crime the violation of norms formally enacted into criminal law

crimes against the person (violent crimes) crimes against people that involve violence or the threat of violence

crimes against property (property crimes) crimes that involve theft of property belonging to others

criminal justice system a reaction to alleged violations of the law through the use of police, courts, and state-sanctioned punishment

criminal recidivism subsequent offenses committed by people previously convicted of crimes

crude birth rate the number of live births in a given year for every thousand people in a population

crude death rate the number of deaths in a given year for every thousand people in a population

cult a religious organization with roots outside the cultural traditions of a society

cultural ecology a theoretical paradigm that explores the relationship between human culture and the physical environment

cultural integration the close relationship among various parts of a cultural system

cultural lag inconsistencies in a cultural system resulting from the unequal rates at which various cultural elements change

cultural relativism the practice of evaluating any culture by its own standards

cultural transmission the process by which culture is passed from one generation to the next

cultural universals traits found in every culture

culture the beliefs, values, behavior, and material objects shared by a particular people

culture shock the personal disorientation accompanying exposure to an unfamiliar way of life

democracy a type of political system in which power is exercised by the people as a whole

democratic socialism a political and economic system that combines significant government control of the economy with free elections

demographic transition theory a thesis linking population patterns to a society's level of technological development

demography the study of human population

denomination a church, not linked to the state, that recognizes religious pluralism

dependency theory a model of economic and social development that explains global inequality in terms of the exploitation of poor societies by rich societies

dependent variable a variable that is changed by another (independent) variable

descent the system by which members of a society trace kinship over generations

deterrence the attempt to discourage criminality through punishment

deviance the recognized violation of cultural norms

direct-fee system a medical-care system in which patients pay directly for the services of physicians and hospitals

discrimination treating various categories of people unequally

division of labor specialized economic activity

dramaturgical analysis the investigation of social interaction in terms of theatrical performance

dyad a social group with two members

ecclesia a church that is formally allied with the state

economy the institutionalized system for production, distribution, and consumption of goods and services

education various ways in which a society ensures that its members gain relevant knowledge—including facts, skills, and values

ego Freud's designation of a person's conscious attempts to balance the pleasure-seeking drives of the human organism and the demands of society

empirical evidence facts we are able to verify with our senses

endogamy marriage between people of the same category

ethnicity a shared cultural heritage

ethnocentrism the practice of judging another culture by the standards of our own culture

ethnomethodology the study of the everyday, common-sense understandings that people have of the world

Eurocentrism the dominance of European (especially English) cultural patterns

euthanasia (mercy killing) assisting in the death of a person suffering from an incurable illness

exogamy marriage between people of different categories

experiment a research method that investigates cause-and-effect relationships under highly controlled conditions

expressive leadership group leadership that emphasizes collective well-being

extended family (consanguine family) a social unit including parents, children, and other kin

faith belief anchored in conviction rather than scientific evidence

family a relatively permanent group of two or more people, who are related by blood, marriage, or adoption, and who usually live together

feminism the advocacy of social equality for the sexes, in opposition to patriarchy and sexism

feminization of poverty the trend by which women represent an increasing proportion of the poor

fertility the incidence of childbearing in a society's population

First World industrial societies with predominantly capitalist economies

folkways norms that have little moral significance

formal operational stage Piaget's term for the level of human development at which individuals think abstractly and with imagination

formal organization a large secondary group that is organized to achieve specific goals

functional illiteracy reading and writing skills inadequate for everyday needs

Gemeinschaft a type of social organization by which people are bound together by kinship and tradition

gender human traits that are linked by culture to each sex

gender roles (sex roles) attitudes and activities that a culture links to each sex

gender stratification the unequal distribution of wealth, power, and privilege between the two sexes

generalized other George Herbert Mead's term for widespread cultural norms and values used as a reference in evaluating ourselves

genocide the systematic killing of one category of people by another

gerontocracy a form of social organization in which the elderly have the most wealth, power, and privileges

gerontology the study of aging and the elderly

Gesellschaft a type of social organization by which people have weak social ties and considerable self-interest

government a formal organization that directs the political life of a society

"groupthink" limited understanding of some issue due to group conformity

health a state of complete physical, mental, and social well-being

health maintenance organization (HMO) an organization that provides comprehensive medical care for a fixed fee

hermaphrodite a human being with some combination of female and male internal and external genitalia

holistic medicine an approach to health care that emphasizes prevention of illness and takes account of a person's entire physical and social environment

homogamy marriage between people with the same social characteristics

horticulture a way of life based on the use of hand tools to raise crops

humanizing bureaucracy organizational efforts to develop human resources

hunting and gathering a way of life based on the use of simple tools to hunt animals and gather vegetation

hypothesis an unverified statement of a relationship between two (or more) variables

id Freud's designation of the human being's basic drives

ideology cultural beliefs that reflect and support the interests of certain categories of people

incest taboo a norm forbidding sexual relations or marriage between certain kin

income wages or salary from work and earnings from investments

independent variable a variable that causes change in another (dependent) variable

industrial society a society that produces goods using sophisticated machinery powered by advanced fuels

infant mortality rate the number of deaths among infants under one year of age for each thousand live births in a given year

ingroup an esteemed social group commanding a member's loyalty

institutional discrimination patterns of discrimination that are a normative and routine part of the operation of a society

instrumental leadership group leadership that emphasizes the completion of tasks

intergenerational social mobility the social standing of children in relation to their parents

interview a series of questions or items administered personally by a researcher to respondents

intragenerational social mobility a change in social position occurring during a person's lifetime

kinship social relationships based on blood, marriage, or adoption

labeling theory the assertion that deviance and conformity arise in the response of others to some act

labor unions organizations of workers seeking to improve wages and working conditions through various strategies, including negotiations and strikes

language a system of symbols with standard meanings that allows members of a society to communicate with one another

latent functions the unrecognized and unintended consequences of any social pattern

liberation theology a fusion of Christian principles with political (often Marxist) activism

life expectancy the average life span of a society's population

looking-glass self Cooley's term referring to a conception of self derived from the responses of others

macro-level orientation a concern with large-scale patterns that characterize society as a whole

manifest functions the recognized and intended consequences of any social pattern

marriage a legally sanctioned relationship, involving economic cooperation as well as normative sexual activity and childbearing, that people expect to be enduring

mass media impersonal communications directed to a vast audience

mass society a society in which industry and bureaucracy erode traditional social ties

master status a social position with exceptional importance for identity, often shaping a person's entire life

matriarchy a form of social organization in which females dominate males

mean the arithmetic average of a series of numbers

measurement the process of determining the value of a variable in a specific case

mechanical solidarity social bonds based on collective conformity to tradition

median the value that occurs midway in a series of numbers or, simply, the middle case

medicalization of deviance the transformation of moral and legal issues into medical matters

medicine the institutionalized means of combating disease and improving health

megalopolis a vast urban region containing a number of cities and their surrounding suburbs

meritocracy stratification linking rewards to personal merit

metropolis a large city that socially and economically dominates an urban area

micro-level orientation a concern with small-scale patterns of social interaction in specific settings

migration the movement of people into and out of a specific territory

military-industrial complex the close association between the government, the military, and defense industries

minority a category of people, distinguished by physical or cultural traits, who are socially disadvantaged

miscegenation the biological process of interbreeding among racial categories

mode the value that occurs most often in a series of numbers

modernity social patterns caused by industrialization

modernization the process of social change initiated by industrialization

modernization theory a model of economic and social development that explains global inequality in terms of differing levels of technological development among world societies

monarchy a type of political system in which the power to rule is passed from generation to generation in a single family

monogamy marriage involving two partners

monopoly domination of a market by a single producer

mores norms that have great moral significance

mortality the incidence of death in a society's population

multiculturalism the recognition of our society's cultural diversity coupled with efforts to promote the equality of all cultural traditions

multinational corporation a large business that operates in many countries

neocolonialism a new form of economic exploitation involving not formal political control but the operation of multinational corporations

network a web of weak social ties

nonverbal communication communication using body movements, gestures, and facial expressions rather than spoken words

norms rules by which a society guides the behavior of its members

nuclear family (conjugal family) a social unit containing one or, more commonly, two adults and any children

oligarchy the rule of the many by the few

oligopoly domination of a market by a few producers

organic solidarity social bonds based on specialization and interdependence

organizational environment any external factors that affect the operation of an organization

other-direction a personality pattern marked by openness to change and a tendency to imitate others

outgroup a scorned social group toward which one feels competition or opposition

participant observation a research method in which investigators systematically observe people while joining in their routine activities

pastoralism a way of life based on the domestication of animals

patriarchy a form of social organization in which males dominate females

peace the absence of war

peer group a group whose members have interests, social position, and age in common

personality a person's fairly consistent patterns of thinking, feeling, and acting

personal space the surrounding area over which a person makes some claim to privacy

plea bargaining a legal negotiation in which the prosecution reduces a charge in exchange for a defendant's guilty plea

pluralism a state in which people of all races and ethnicities are distinct but have social parity

pluralist model an analysis of politics that views power as dispersed among many competing interest groups

political action committee (PAC) an organization formed by a special-interest group, independent of political parties, to pursue political aims by raising and spending money

political revolution the overthrow of one political system in order to establish another

politics the institutionalized system by which a society distributes power and makes decisions

polygamy marriage that unites three or more people

population the people about whom a researcher seeks knowledge

positivism a path to understanding based on science

postindustrial economy economic activity based on service work and high technology

power the ability to achieve desired ends despite opposition

power-elite model an analysis of politics that views power as concentrated among the rich

prejudice a rigid and irrational generalization about a category of people

preoperational stage Piaget's term for the level of human development at which individuals first use language and other symbols

presentation of self Goffman's term for the ways in which individuals, in various settings, try to create specific impressions in the minds of others

primary group a small social group in which relationships are personal and enduring

primary sector part of the economy that generates raw materials directly from the natural environment

primary sex characteristics the genitals, used to reproduce the human species

profane that which people define as an ordinary element of everyday life

profession a prestigious, white-collar occupation that requires extensive formal education

proletariat people who sell their productive labor

public opinion the attitudes of people throughout a society about one or more controversial issues

questionnaire a series of written questions or items to which subjects respond

race a category composed of men and women who share biologically transmitted traits that are defined as socially significant

racism the belief that one racial category is innately superior or inferior to another

rationality deliberate, matter-of-fact calculation of the most efficient means to accomplish any particular task

rationalization Max Weber's term for the change from tradition to rationality as the dominant mode of human thought

rational-legal authority (bureaucratic authority) power legitimized by legally enacted rules and regulations

reference group a social group that serves as a point of reference for making evaluations and decisions

rehabilitation reforming the offender to preclude further offenses

relative deprivation a perceived disadvantage relative to some standard of comparison

relative poverty deprivation in relation to the greater resources of others

reliability the quality of consistency in measurement

religion a system of beliefs and practices based on recognizing the sacred

religiosity the importance of religion in a person's life

religious fundamentalism a conservative religious doctrine that opposes intellectualism and worldly accommodation in favor of restoring traditional, otherworldly religion

research method a strategy for systematically carrying out research

resocialization deliberate socialization intended to radically alter the individual's personality

retribution inflicting on an offender suffering comparable to that caused by the offense

retrospective labeling the interpretation of someone's past consistent with present deviance

role normative patterns of behavior for those holding a particular status

role conflict incompatibility among the roles corresponding to two or more statuses

role set a number of roles attached to a single status

role strain incompatibility among roles corresponding to a single status

routinization of charisma the transformation of charismatic authority into some combination of traditional and bureaucratic authority

sacred that which is defined as extraordinary, inspiring a sense of awe, reverence, and even fear

sample a relatively small number of cases selected to be representative of an entire population

Sapir-Whorf hypothesis the assertion that people perceive the world only in terms of the symbols provided by their language

scapegoat a person or category of people, typically with little power, unfairly blamed for the troubles of others

schooling formal instruction under the direction of specially trained teachers

science a logical system that derives knowledge from direct, systematic observation

secondary group a large and impersonal social group based on some special interest or activity

secondary sector part of the economy that transforms raw materials into manufactured goods

secondary sex characteristics physical traits, other than the genitals, that distinguish physiologically mature females and males

Second World industrial societies that are transforming socialist economies into market systems

sect a type of religious organization that stands apart from the larger society

secularization the historical decline in the influence of religion

segregation the physical and social separation of categories of people

self George Herbert Mead's term for the dimension of

personality composed of an individual's active self-awareness

sensorimotor stage Piaget's term for the level of human development at which individuals have only sensory-based experience

sex the division of humanity into biological categories of female and male

sexism the belief that one sex is innately superior to the other

sex ratio the number of males for every hundred females in a given population

sexual harassment comments, gestures, or physical contact of a sexual nature that are deliberate, repeated, and unwelcome

sexual orientation the manner in which people experience sexual arousal and achieve sexual pleasure

sick role patterns of behavior defined as appropriate for those who are ill

social change the transformation of culture and social institutions over time

social character personality patterns common to members of a society

social-conflict paradigm a theoretical framework based on the assumption that society is a complex system characterized by inequality and conflict that generate social change

social construction of reality the process by which individuals creatively build reality through social interaction

social control attempts by society to regulate the thought and behavior of individuals

social dysfunction the undesirable consequences of any social pattern for the operation of society

social epidemiology the study of how health and disease are distributed throughout a society's population

social function the consequences of any social pattern for the operation of society as a whole

social group two or more people who identify and interact with one another

social institution an organized sphere of social life such as the economy or the family

social interaction the process by which people act and react in relation to others

socialism an economic system in which natural resources and the means of producing goods and services are collectively owned

socialization the lifelong process of social experience by which individuals develop their human potential and learn patterns of their culture

socialized medicine a health-care system in which the government owns most facilities and employs most physicians

social mobility a change of position in a stratification system

social movement an organized effort to encourage or oppose some dimension of change

social protection rendering an offender incapable of further offenses either temporarily through incarceration or permanently by execution

social stratification a system by which a society ranks categories of people in a hierarchy

social structure any relatively stable pattern of social behavior

society people interacting within a limited territory guided by their culture

sociobiology a theoretical paradigm that explains cultural patterns in terms of biological forces

sociocultural evolution the historical process of cultural change caused by technological innovation

socioeconomic status a composite social ranking based on various dimensions of social inequality

sociology the scientific study of human social activity

special-interest group a political alliance of people with an interest in a particular economic or social issue

status a recognized social position that an individual occupies

status consistency consistent standing across various dimensions of social inequality

status set all the statuses a person holds at a particular time

stereotype a prejudiced description of some category of people

stigma a powerfully negative label that radically changes a person's social identity and self-concept

structural-functional paradigm a theoretical framework based on the assumption that society is a complex system whose parts work together to promote stability

structural social mobility social mobility of large numbers of people due more to changes in society itself than to individual efforts

subculture cultural patterns that distinguish some segment of a society's population

suburbs urban areas beyond the political boundaries of a city

superego Freud's designation of the presence of culture within the individual in the form of internalized values and norms

survey a research method in which subjects respond to a series of statements or questions in a questionnaire or interview

symbol anything that carries a particular meaning recognized by members of a society

symbolic-interaction paradigm a theoretical framework based on the view that society is the product of the everyday interaction of individuals

technology the application of knowledge to the practical tasks of living

terrorism violence or the threat of violence by an individual or a group as a political strategy

tertiary sector part of the economy involving services rather than goods

theoretical paradigm a set of fundamental assumptions that guides thinking and research

theory an explanation of how and why specific facts are related

Third World primarily agrarian societies in which most people are poor

Thomas theorem the assertion that situations that are defined as real are real in their consequences

total institution a setting in which individuals are isolated from the rest of society and manipulated by an administrative staff

totalitarianism a highly centralized political system that extensively regulates people's lives

totem a natural object collectively defined as sacred

tracking assigning students to different educational programs

tradition sentiments and beliefs about the world that are passed from generation to generation

traditional authority power that is legitimized through respect for long-established cultural patterns

tradition-direction a personality pattern marked by rigid conformity to time-honored ways of living

transsexuals people who feel they are one sex though biologically they are the other

triad a social group with three members

urban ecology study of the link between the physical and social dimensions of cities

urbanization the concentration of humanity into cities

urban renewal government programs intended to revitalize cities

validity the quality of measurement gained by measuring exactly what one intends to measure

values culturally defined standards of desirability, goodness, and beauty that serve as broad guidelines for social life

variable a concept whose value changes from case to case

victimless crime violation of law in which there is no readily apparent victim

war armed conflict among the people of various societies, directed by their governments

wealth the total amount of money and valuable goods that any person or family controls

white-collar crime crimes committed by people of high social position in the course of their occupations

white-collar occupation higher-prestige work that involves mostly mental activity

zero population growth the level of reproduction that maintains population at a steady state

References

ABERLE, DAVID F. *The Peyote Religion Among the Navaho.* Chicago: Aldine, 1966.

ADORNO, T. W., ET AL. *The Authoritarian Personality.* New York: Harper & Brothers, 1950.

ALAM, SULTANA. "Women and Poverty in Bangladesh." *Women's Studies International Forum.* Vol. 8, No. 4 (1985):361–71.

ALBON, JOAN. "Retention of Cultural Values and Differential Urban Adaptation: Samoans and American Indians in a West Coast City." *Social Forces.* Vol. 49, No. 3 (March 1971):385–93.

ALLAN, EMILIE ANDERSEN, and DARRELL J. STEFFENS-MEIER. "Youth, Underemployment, and Property Crime: Differential Effects of Job Availability and Job Quality on Juvenile and Young Adult Arrest Rates." *American Sociological Review.* Vol. 54, No. 1 (February 1989):107–23.

AMERICAN COUNCIL ON EDUCATION. "Senior Women Administrators in Higher Education: A Decade of Change, 1975–1983." Washington, DC: 1984.

AMERICAN SOCIOLOGICAL ASSOCIATION. "Code of Ethics." Washington, DC: 1984.

ANDERSON, DANIEL R., and ELIZABETH PUGZLES LORCH. "Look at Television: Action or Reaction?" In Jennings Bryant and Daniel R. Anderson, eds., *Children's Understanding of Television: Research on Attention and Comprehension.* New York: Academic Press, 1983:1–33.

ANDO, FAITH H. "Women in Business." In Sara E. Rix, ed., *The American Woman: A Status Report 1990–91.* New York: Norton, 1990:222–30.

ANG, IEN. *Watching Dallas: Soap Opera and the Melodramatic Imagination.* London: Methuen, 1985.

ARCHER, DANE, and ROSEMARY GARTNER. *Violence and Crime in Cross-National Perspective.* New Haven, CT: Yale University Press, 1987.

ARENDT, HANNAH. *The Origins of Totalitarianism.* Cleveland, OH: Meridian Books, 1958.

ARIÈS, PHILIPPE. *Centuries of Childhood: A Social History of Family Life.* New York: Vintage Books, 1965.

———. *Western Attitudes Toward Death: From the Middle Ages to the Present.* Baltimore, MD: The Johns Hopkins University Press, 1974.

ASANTE, MOLEFI KETE. *The Afrocentric Idea.* Philadelphia: Temple University Press, 1987.

———. *Afrocentricity.* Trenton, NJ: Africa World Press, 1988.

ASCH, SOLOMON. *Social Psychology.* Englewood Cliffs, NJ: Prentice Hall, 1952.

AYENSU, EDWARD S. "A Worldwide Role for the Healing Powers of Plants." *Smithsonian.* Vol. 12, No. 8 (November 1981):87–97.

BACHRACH, PETER, and MORTON S. BARATZ. *Power and Poverty.* New York: Oxford University Press, 1970.

BAILEY, WILLIAM C., and RUTH D. PETERSON. "Murder and Capital Punishment: A Monthly Time-Series Analysis of Execution Publicity." *American Sociological Review.* Vol. 54, No. 5 (October 1989):722–43.

BAKER, MARY ANNE, CATHERINE WHITE BERHEIDE, FAY ROSS GRECKEL, LINDA CARSTARPHEN GUGIN, MARCIA J. LIPETZ, and MARCIA TEXLER SEGAL. *Women Today: A Multidisciplinary Approach to Women's Studies*. Monterey, CA: Brooks/Cole, 1980.

BALES, ROBERT F. "The Equilibrium Problem in Small Groups." In Talcott Parsons et al., eds., *Working Papers in the Theory of Action*. New York: Free Press, 1953:111–15.

BALES, ROBERT F., and PHILIP E. SLATER. "Role Differentiation in Small Decision-Making Groups." In Talcott Parsons and Robert F. Bales, eds., *Family, Socialization and Interaction Process*. New York: Free Press, 1955:259–306.

BALTZELL, E. DIGBY. *The Protestant Establishment: Aristocracy and Caste in America*. New York: Vintage Books, 1964.

_____, ed. *The Search for Community in Modern America*. New York: Harper & Row, 1968.

_____. "The Protestant Establishment Revisited." *The American Scholar*. Vol. 45, No. 4 (Autumn 1976):499–518.

_____. *Philadelphia Gentlemen: The Making of A National Upper Class*. Philadelphia: University of Pennsylvania Press, 1979; orig. 1958.

_____. *Puritan Boston and Quaker Philadelphia*. New York: Free Press, 1979.

_____. "The WASP's Last Gasp." *Philadelphia Magazine*. Vol. 79 (September 1988):104–7, 184, 186, 188.

BANFIELD, EDWARD C. *The Unheavenly City Revisited*. Boston: Little, Brown, 1974.

BARASH, DAVID. *The Whispering Within*. New York: Penguin Books, 1981.

BARKER, EILEEN. "Who'd Be a Moonie? A Comparative Study of Those Who Join the Unification Church in Britain." In Bryan Wilson, ed., *The Social Impact of New Religious Movements*. New York: Rose of Sharon Press, 1981:59–96.

BARRY, KATHLEEN. "Feminist Theory: The Meaning of Women's Liberation." In Barbara Haber, ed., *The Women's Annual 1982–1983*. Boston: G. K. Hall, 1983:35–78.

BASSUK, ELLEN J. "The Homelessness Problem." *Scientific American*. Vol. 251, No. 1 (July 1984):40–45.

BATESON, C. DANIEL, and W. LARRY VENTIS. *The Religious Experience: A Social-Psychological Perspective*. New York: Oxford University Press, 1982.

BAUER, P. T. *Equality, the Third World, and Economic Delusion*. Cambridge, MA: Harvard University Press, 1981.

BEATRICE COMPANY, INC. *Annual Report 1985*. Chicago: Beatrice, 1985.

BECKER, HOWARD S. *Outside: Studies in the Sociology of Deviance*. New York: Free Press, 1966.

BEEGHLEY, LEONARD. *The Structure of Social Stratification in the United States*. Needham Heights, MA: Allyn and Bacon, 1989.

BELL, ALAN P., MARTIN S. WEINBERG, and SUE KIEFER-HAMMERSMITH. *Sexual Preference: Its Development in Men and Women*. Bloomington: Indiana University Press, 1981.

BELLAH, ROBERT N. *The Broken Covenant*. New York: Seabury Press, 1975.

BELLAH, ROBERT N., RICHARD MADSEN, WILLIAM M. SULLIVAN, ANN SWIDLER, and STEVEN M. TIPTON. *Habits of the Heart: Individualism and Commitment in American Life*. New York: Harper & Row, 1985.

BELSKY, JAY, RICHARD M. LERNER, and GRAHAM B. SPANIER. *The Child in the Family*. Reading, MA: Addison-Wesley, 1984.

BEM, SANDRA LIPSITZ. "Gender Schema Theory: A Cognitive Account of Sex-Typing." *Psychological Review*. Vol. 88, No. 4 (July 1981):354–64.

BENEDICT, RUTH. "Continuities and Discontinuities in Cultural Conditioning." *Psychiatry*. Vol. 1 (May 1938):161–67.

_____. *The Chrysanthemum and the Sword: Patterns of Japanese Culture*. New York: New American Library, 1974; orig. 1946.

BENNETT, NEIL G., DAVID E. BLOOM, and PATRICIA H. CRAIG. "The Divergence of Black and White Marriage Patterns." *American Journal of Sociology*. Vol. 95, No. 3 (November 1989):692–722.

BENOKRAITIS, NIJOLE, and JOE FEAGIN. *Modern Sexism: Blatant, Subtle, and Overt Discrimination*. Englewood Cliffs, NJ: Prentice Hall, 1986.

BERARDO, F. M. "Survivorship and Social Isolation: The Case of the Aged Widower." *The Family Coordinator*. Vol. 19 (January 1970):11–25.

BERGER, BRIGITTE, and PETER L. BERGER. *The War Over the Family: Capturing the Middle Ground*. Garden City, NY: Anchor/Doubleday, 1983.

BERGER, PETER L. *Invitation to Sociology*. New York: Anchor Books, 1963.

_____. *The Sacred Canopy: Elements of a Sociological Theory of Religion*. Garden City, NY: Doubleday, 1967.

_____. *Facing Up to Modernity: Excursions in Society, Politics, and Religion*. New York: Basic Books, 1977.

_____. *The Capitalist Revolution: Fifty Propositions About Prosperity, Equality, and Liberty*. New York: Basic Books, 1986.

BERGER, PETER, BRIGITTE BERGER, and HANSFRIED KELLNER. *The Homeless Mind: Modernization and Consciousness*. New York: Vintage Books, 1974.

BERGER, PETER L., and THOMAS LUCKMANN. *The Social Con-*

struction of Reality: A Treatise in the Sociology of Knowledge. Garden City, NY: Anchor Books, 1967.

BERGESEN, ALBERT, ED. Crises in the World-System. Beverly Hills, CA: Sage, 1983.

BERNARD, JESSIE. The Female World. New York: Free Press, 1981.

————. The Future of Marriage. New Haven, CT: Yale University Press, 1982; orig. 1973.

BERNARD, LARRY CRAIG. "Multivariate Analysis of New Sex Role Formulations and Personality." Journal of Personality and Social Psychology. Vol. 38, No. 2 (February 1980):323–36.

BERRY, BRIAN L., and PHILIP H. REES. "The Factorial Ecology of Calcutta." American Journal of Sociology. Vol. 74, No. 5 (March 1969):445–91.

BERSCHEID, ELLEN, and ELAINE HATFIELD. Interpersonal Attraction. 2nd ed. Reading, MA: Addison-Wesley, 1983.

BERUBE, ALLAN. Coming Out Under Fire: The History of Gay Men and Women in World War Two. New York: Free Press, 1990.

BEST, RAPHAELA. We've All Got Scars: What Boys and Girls Learn in Elementary School. Bloomington: Indiana University Press, 1983.

BLAU, JUDITH R., and PETER M. BLAU. "The Cost of Inequality: Metropolitan Structure and Violent Crime." American Sociological Review. Vol. 47, No. 1 (February 1982):114–29.

BLAU, PETER M. Exchange and Power in Social Life. New York: Wiley, 1964.

————. Inequality and Heterogeneity: A Primitive Theory of Social Structure. New York: Free Press, 1977.

BLAU, PETER M., TERRY C. BLUM, and JOSEPH E. SCHWARTZ. "Heterogeneity and Intermarriage." American Sociological Review. Vol. 47, No. 1 (February 1982):45–62.

BLAU, PETER M., and OTIS DUDLEY DUNCAN. The American Occupational Structure. New York: Wiley, 1967.

BLAUSTEIN, ALBERT P., and ROBERT L. ZANGRANDO. Civil Rights and the Black American. New York: Washington Square Press, 1968.

BLOOM, LEONARD. "Familial Adjustments of Japanese-Americans to Relocation: First Phase." In Thomas F. Pettigrew, ed., The Sociology of Race Relations. New York: Free Press, 1980:163–67.

BLUM, ALAN, and GARY FISHER. "Women Who Kill." In Delos H. Kelly, ed., Criminal Behavior: Readings in Criminology. New York: St. Martin's Press, 1980:291–301.

BLUMBERG, ABRAHAM S. Criminal Justice. Chicago: Quadrangle Books, 1970.

BLUMBERG, PAUL. Inequality in an Age of Decline. New York: Oxford University Press, 1981.

BLUMER, HERBERT G. "Collective Behavior." In Alfred McClung Lee, ed., Principles of Sociology. 3rd ed. New York: Barnes & Noble Books, 1969:65–121.

BLUMSTEIN, PHILIP, and PEPPER SCHWARTZ. American Couples. New York: Morrow, 1983.

BODENHEIMER, THOMAS S. "Health Care in the United States: Who Pays?" In Vicente Navarro, ed., Health and Medical Care in the U.S.: A Critical Analysis. Farmingdale, NY: Baywood, 1977:61–68.

BOFF, LEONARD and CLODOVIS. Salvation and Liberation: In Search of a Balance Between Faith and Politics. Maryknoll, NY: Orbis Books, 1984.

BOGARDUS, EMORY S. "Comparing Racial Distance in Ethiopia, South Africa, and the United States." Sociology and Social Research. Vol. 52, No. 2 (January 1968):149–56.

BOHLEN, CELESTINE. "Where the Fires of Hatred are Easily Stoked." New York Times (August 4, 1991):E3.

BONILLA-SANTIAGO, GLORIA. "A Portrait of Hispanic Women in the United States." In Sara E. Rix, ed., The American Woman 1990–91: A Status Report. New York: Norton, 1990:249–57.

BONNER, JANE. Research presented in "The Two Brains." Public Broadcasting System telecast, 1984.

BOOTH, ALAN, and LYNN WHITE. "Thinking About Divorce." Journal of Marriage and the Family. Vol. 42, No. 3 (August 1980):605–16.

BOSWELL, TERRY E. "A Split Labor Market Analysis of Discrimination Against Chinese Immigrants, 1850–1882." American Sociological Review. Vol. 51, No. 3 (June 1986):352–71.

BOTT, ELIZABETH. Family and Social Network. New York: Free Press, 1971; orig. 1957.

BOWLES, JACQUELINE, and WILLIAM A. ROBINSON. "PHS Grants for Minority Group HIV Infection Education and Prevention Efforts." Public Health Reports. Vol. 104, No. 6 (November–December 1989):552–59.

BOWLES, SAMUEL, and HERBERT GINTIS. Schooling in Capitalist America: Educational Reform and the Contradictions of Economic Life. New York: Basic Books, 1976.

BOYER, ERNEST L. College: The Undergraduate Experience in America. Prepared by The Carnegie Foundation for the Advancement of Teaching. New York: Harper & Row, 1987.

BRAITHWAITE, JOHN. "The Myth of Social Class and Criminality Reconsidered." American Sociological Review. Vol. 46, No. 1 (February 1981):36–57.

BRINTON, CRANE. The Anatomy of Revolution. New York: Vintage Books, 1965.

BRINTON, MARY C. "The Social-Institutional Bases of Gender Stratification: Japan as an Illustrative Case." American Journal of Sociology. Vol. 94, No. 2 (September 1988):300–34.

BROPHY, GWENDA. "China, Part I." *Population Today.* Vol. 17, No. 3 (March 1989a):12.

———. "China: Part II." *Population Today.* Vol. 17. No. 4 (April 1989b):12.

BROWN, E. RICHARD. *Rockefeller Medicine Men: Medicine and Capitalism in America.* Berkeley: University of California Press, 1979.

BROWNMILLER, SUSAN. *Against Our Will: Men, Women and Rape.* New York: Simon and Schuster, 1975.

BROWNMILLER, SUSAN. *Femininity.* New York: Linden Press, Simon and Schuster, 1984.

BROWNSTEIN, RONALD, and NINA EASTON. *Reagan's Ruling Class: Portraits of the President's Top One Hundred Officials.* New York: Pantheon Books, 1983.

BURCH, ROBERT. Testimony to House of Representatives Hearing in "Review: The World Hunger Problem." October 25, 1983, Serial 98–38.

BUREAU OF NATIONAL AFFAIRS. "The Challenge of Diversity: Equal Employment and Managing Difference in the 1990s." Summary report. Washington, DC: The Bureau of National Affairs, 1990.

BURNS, JAMES A. "Discipline: Why Does It Continue To Be a Problem? Solution Is in Changing School Culture." *National Association of Secondary School Principals Bulletin.* Vol. 69, No. 479 (March 1985):1–47.

BUSBY, LINDA J. "Sex Role Research on the Mass Media." *Journal of Communications.* Vol. 25 (Autumn 1975):107–13.

BUTTERWORTH, DOUGLAS, and JOHN K. CHANCE. *Latin American Urbanization.* Cambridge: Cambridge University Press, 1981.

"Buy America while Stocks Last." *The Economist.* Vol. 313, No. 7633 (December 16, 1989):63–66.

CAMERON, WILLIAM BRUCE. *Modern Social Movements: A Sociological Outline.* New York: Random House, 1966.

CANTOR, MURIAL G., and SUZANNE PINGREE. *The Soap Opera.* Beverly Hills, CA: Sage, 1983.

CAPLOW, THEODORE, ET AL. *Middletown Families.* Minneapolis: University of Minnesota Press, 1982.

CARLSON, NORMAN A. "Corrections in the United States Today: A Balance Has Been Struck." *The American Criminal Law Review.* Vol. 13, No. 4 (Spring 1976):615–47.

CARMICHAEL, STOKELY, and CHARLES V. HAMILTON. *Black Power: The Politics of Liberation in America.* New York: Vintage Books, 1967.

CARROLL, GINNY. "Who Foots the Bill?" *Newsweek.* Special Issue (Fall–Winter, 1990):81–85.

CENTER FOR THE STUDY OF SPORT IN SOCIETY. *1991 Racial Report Card: A Study in the NBA, NFL, and Major League Baseball.* Boston: Northeastern University, 1991.

CENTERS FOR DISEASE CONTROL. Report included in "Blacks'

Syphilis Rate Up Sharply." *New York Times* (May 17, 1991):A19.

———. *HIV/AIDS Surveillance.* Vol. 40, Nos. 51 & 52 (January 3, 1992). Atlanta: The Centers, 1992.

CHAGNON, NAPOLEON A. *Yqnomamö.* 3rd ed. New York: Holt, Rinehart & Winston, 1983.

CHANDLER, TERTIUS, and GERALD FOX. *3000 Years of Urban History.* New York: Academic Press, 1974.

CHANGE, KWANG-CHIH. *The Archaeology of Ancient China.* New Haven, CT: Yale University Press, 1977.

CHERLIN, ANDREW. *Marriage, Divorce, Remarriage.* Cambridge, MA: Harvard University Press, 1981.

CHERLIN, ANDREW, and FRANK F. FURSTENBERG, JR. "The American Family in the Year 2000." *The Futurist.* Vol. 17, No. 3 (June 1983):7–14.

CHILDREN'S DEFENSE FUND. *Child Poverty in America.* Washington, DC: 1991.

CLARK, JUAN M., JOSE I. LASAGA, and ROSE S. REGUE. *The 1980 Mariel Exodus: An Assessment and Prospect: Special Report.* Washington, DC: Council for Inter-American Security, 1981.

CLARK, THOMAS A. *Blacks in Suburbs.* New Brunswick, NJ: Rutgers University Center for Urban Policy Research, 1979.

CLINARD, MARSHALL B. *Cities with Little Crime: The Case of Switzerland.* Cambridge: Cambridge University Press, 1978.

CLINARD, MARSHALL, and DANIEL ABBOTT. *Crime in Developing Countries.* New York: Wiley, 1973.

CLOWARD, RICHARD A., and LLOYD E. OHLIN. *Delinquency and Opportunity: A Theory of Delinquent Gangs.* New York: Free Press, 1966.

COAKLEY, JAY J. *Sport in Society: Issues and Controversies.* 3rd ed. St. Louis, MO: Mosby, 1986; 4th ed., 1990.

COCKERHAM, WILLIAM C. *Medical Sociology.* 3rd ed. Englewood Cliffs, NJ: Prentice Hall, 1986.

COE, MICHAEL D., and RICHARD A. DIEHL. *In the Land of the Olmec.* Austin: University of Texas Press, 1980.

COHEN, ALBERT K. *Delinquent Boys: The Culture of the Gang.* New York: Free Press, 1971; orig. 1955.

COHEN, LLOYD R. "Sexual Harassment and the Law." *Society.* Vol. 28, No. 4 (May–June 1991):8–13.

COHEN, MICHAEL. "Restructuring the System." *Transaction.* Vol. 26, No. 4 (May–June 1989):40–48.

COHN, BOB. "The Lawsuit Cha-Cha." *Newsweek* (August 26, 1991):58–59.

COLEMAN, JAMES S., and THOMAS HOFFER. *Public and Private High Schools: The Impact of Communities.* New York: Basic Books, 1987.

COLEMAN, JAMES, THOMAS HOFFER, and SALLY KILGORE.

Public and Private Schools: An Analysis of Public Schools and Beyond. Washington, DC: National Center for Education Statistics, 1981.

COLEMAN, RICHARD P., and BERNICE L. NEUGARTEN. *Social Status in the City.* San Francisco: Jossey-Bass, 1971.

COLEMAN, RICHARD P., and LEE RAINWATER. *Social Standing in America.* New York: Basic Books, 1978.

COLLINS, RANDALL. "A Conflict Theory of Sexual Stratification." *Social Problems.* Vol. 19, No. 1 (Summer 1971):3–21.

_____. *The Credential Society: An Historical Sociology of Education and Stratification.* New York: Academic Press, 1979.

_____. *Sociological Insight: An Introduction to Non-obvious Sociology.* New York: Oxford University Press, 1982.

COLLOWAY, N. O., and PAULA L. DOLLEVOET. "Selected Tabular Material on Aging." In Caleb Finch and Leonard Hayflick, eds., *Handbook of the Biology of Aging.* New York: Van Nostrand Reinhold, 1977:666–708.

COMTE, AUGUSTE. *Auguste Comte and Positivism: The Essential Writings.* Gertrud Lenzer, ed. New York: Harper Torchbooks, 1975.

CONTRERAS, JOSEPH. "A New Day Dawns." *Newsweek* (March 30, 1992):40–41.

COOLEY, CHARLES HORTON. *Human Nature and the Social Order.* New York: Schocken Books, 1964; orig. 1902.

COPPOCK, MARJORIE L. "Women's Leadership Involvement in Community Volunteer Organizations." Paper presented to Southwestern Sociological Association, Dallas, TX, 1987.

CORSARO, WILLIAM A., and THOMAS A. RIZZO. "Discussione and Friendship: Socialization Processes in the Peer Culture of Italian Nursery School Children." *American Sociological Review.* Vol. 53, No. 6 (December 1988):879–94.

COUNCIL ON INTERNATIONAL EDUCATIONAL EXCHANGE. *Educating for Global Competence: The Report of the Advisory Committee for International Educational Exchange.* New York: The Council, 1988.

COUNTS, G. S. "The Social Status of Occupations: A Problem in Vocational Guidance." *School Review.* Vol. 33 (January 1925):16–27.

COURTNEY, ALICE E., and THOMAS W. WHIPPLE. *Sex Stereotyping in Advertising.* Lexington, MA: Heath, 1983.

COX, HARVEY. *The Secular City.* Rev. ed. New York: Macmillan, 1971; orig. 1965.

_____. *Turning East: The Promise and Peril of the New Orientalism.* New York: Simon and Schuster, 1977.

CRISPELL, DIANE. "Working in 2000." *American Demographics.* Vol. 12, No. 3 (March 1990):36–40.

CROUSE, JAMES, and DALE TRUSHEIM. *The Case Against the SAT.* Chicago: University of Chicago Press, 1988.

CURRIE, ELLIOTT. *Confronting Crime: An American Challenge.* New York: Pantheon Books, 1985.

DAHL, ROBERT A. *Who Governs?* New Haven, CT: Yale University Press, 1961.

_____. *Dilemmas of Pluralist Democracy: Autonomy vs. Control.* New Haven, CT: Yale University Press, 1982.

DAHRENDORF, RALF. *Class and Class Conflict in Industrial Society.* Stanford, CA: Stanford University Press, 1959.

DALY, MARTIN, and MARGO WILSON. *Homicide.* New York: Aldine De Gruyter, 1988.

DANIELS, ROGER. "The Issei Generation." In Amy Tachiki et al., eds., *Roots: An Asian American Reader.* Los Angeles: UCLA Asian American Studies Center, 1971:138–49.

DANNEFER, DALE. "Adult Development and Social Theory: A Reappraisal." *American Sociological Review.* Vol. 49, No. 1 (February 1984):100–116.

DARNTON, NINA, and YURIKO HOSHIA. "Whose Life Is It, Anyway?" *Newsweek.* Vol. 113, No. 4 (January 13, 1989):61.

DAVIES, CHRISTIE. *Ethnic Humor Around the World: A Comparative Analysis.* Bloomington: Indiana University Press, 1990.

DAVIES, JAMES C. "Toward a Theory of Revolution." *American Sociological Review.* Vol. 27, No. 1 (February 1962):5–19.

DAVIES, MARK, and DENISE B. KANDEL. "Parental and Peer Influences on Adolescents' Educational Plans: Some Further Evidence." *American Journal of Sociology.* Vol. 87, No. 2 (September 1981):363–87.

DAVIS, KINGSLEY. "Extreme Social Isolation of a Child." *American Journal of Sociology.* Vol. 45, No. 4 (January 1940):554–65.

_____. "Final Note on a Case of Extreme Isolation." *American Journal of Sociology.* Vol. 52, No. 5 (March 1947):432–37.

DAVIS, KINGSLEY, and WILBERT MOORE. "Some Principles of Stratification." *American Sociological Review.* Vol. 10, No. 2 (April 1945):242–49.

DAVIS, SHARON A., and EMIL J. HALLER. "Tracking, Ability, and SES: Further Evidence on the 'Revisionist-Meritocratic Debate.'" *American Journal of Education.* Vol. 89 (May 1981):283–304.

DECKARD, BARBARA SINCLAIR. *The Women's Movement: Political, Socioeconomic, and Psychological Issues.* 2nd ed. New York: Harper & Row, 1979.

DEDRICK, DENNIS K., and RICHARD E. YINGER. "MAD, SDI, and the Nuclear Arms Race." Manuscript in development. Georgetown, KY: Georgetown College, 1990.

DEGLER, CARL. *At Odds: Women and the Family in America From the Revolution to the Present.* New York: Oxford University Press, 1980.

DELACROIX, JACQUES, and CHARLES C. RAGIN. "Structural Blockage: A Crossnational Study of Economic Dependency, State Efficacy, and Underdevelopment." *American Journal of Sociology.* Vol. 86, No. 6 (May 1981):1311–47.

DEPARLE, JASON. "Painted by Numbers, 1980s are Rosy to G.O.P., While Democrats See Red." *New York Times* (September 26, 1991a):B10.

————. "Poverty Rate Rose Sharply Last Year as Incomes Slipped." *New York Times* (September 27, 1991b):A1, A11.

Der Spiegel. "Third World Metropolises Are Becoming Monsters; Rural Poverty Drives Millions to the Slums." In *World Press Review* (October 1989).

DEVINE, JOEL A. "State and State Expenditure: Determinants of Social Investment and Social Consumption Spending in the Postwar United States." *American Sociological Review.* Vol. 50, No. 2 (April 1985):150–65.

DEWEY, JOHN. *Experience and Education.* New York: Collier Books, 1968; orig. 1938.

DIZARD, JAN E., and HOWARD GADLIN. *The Minimal Family.* Amherst: University of Massachusetts Press, 1990.

DOBYNS, HENRY F. "An Appraisal of Techniques with a New Hemispheric Estimate." *Current Anthropology.* Vol. 7, No. 4 (October 1966):395–446.

DOLLARD, JOHN, ET AL. *Frustration and Aggression.* New Haven, CT: Yale University Press, 1939.

DOMHOFF, G. WILLIAM. *Who Rules America Now? A View of the '80s.* Englewood Cliffs, NJ: Prentice Hall, 1983.

DONOVAN, VIRGINIA K., and RONNIE LITTENBERG. "Psychology of Women: Feminist Therapy." In Barbara Haber, ed., *The Women's Annual 1981: The Year in Review.* Boston: G. K. Hall, 1982:211–35.

DOW, UNITY. Personal communication, 1990.

DOYLE, JAMES A. *The Male Experience.* Dubuque, IA: Wm. C. Brown, 1983.

DUBOS, RENE. *Man Adapting.* New Haven, CT: Yale University Press, 1980; orig. 1965.

DUHL, LEONARD J. "The Social Context of Health." In Arthur C. Hastings et al., eds., *Health for the Whole Person: The Complete Guide to Holistic Medicine.* Boulder, CO: Westview Press, 1980:39–48.

DURKHEIM, EMILE. *The Division of Labor in Society.* New York: Free Press, 1964a; orig. 1895.

————. *The Rules of Sociological Method.* New York: Free Press, 1964b; orig. 1893.

————. *The Elementary Forms of Religious Life.* New York: Free Press, 1965; orig. 1915.

————. *Suicide.* New York: Free Press, 1966; orig. 1897.

DWORKIN, ANDREA. *Intercourse.* New York: Free Press, 1987.

EASTERLIN, RICHARD A. "Immigration: Economic and Social Characteristics." In *Harvard Encyclopedia of American Ethnic Groups.* Cambridge, MA: Harvard University Press, 1980:476–86.

EBAUGH, HELEN ROSE FUCHS. *Becoming an EX: The Process of Role Exit.* Chicago: University of Chicago Press, 1988.

ECKHOLM, ERIK. "Malnutrition in Elderly: Widespread Health Threat." *New York Times* (August 13, 1985):19–20.

EDMONSTON, BARRY, and THOMAS M. GUTERBOCK. "Is Suburbanization Slowing Down? Recent Trends in Population Deconcentration in U.S. Metropolitan Areas." *Social Forces.* Vol. 62, No. 4 (June 1984):905–25.

EDWARDS, DAVID V. *The American Political Experience.* 3rd ed. Englewood Cliffs, NJ: Prentice Hall, 1985.

EDWARDS, RICHARD. *Contested Terrain: The Transformation of the Workplace in the Twentieth Century.* New York: Basic Books, 1979.

EHRENREICH, BARBARA. *The Hearts of Men: American Dreams and the Flight from Commitment.* Garden City, NY: Anchor Books, 1983.

EHRENREICH, JOHN. "Introduction." In John Ehrenreich, ed., *The Cultural Crisis of Modern Medicine.* New York: Monthly Review Press, 1978:1–35.

EHRLICH, PAUL R. *The Population Bomb.* New York: Ballantine Books, 1978.

EICHLER, MARGRIT. *Nonsexist Research Methods: A Practical Guide.* Winchester, MA: Unwin Hyman, 1988.

EISENSTEIN, ZILLAH R., ED. *Capitalist Patriarchy and the Case for Socialist Feminism.* New York: Monthly Review Press, 1979.

EKMAN, PAUL. "Biological and Cultural Contributions to Body and Facial Movements in the Expression of Emotions." In A. Rorty, ed., *Explaining Emotions.* Berkeley: University of California Press, 1980a:73–101.

————. *Face of Man: Universal Expression in a New Guinea Village.* New York: Garland Press, 1980b.

————. *Telling Lies: Clues to Deceit in the Marketplace, Politics, and Marriage.* New York: Norton, 1985.

EKMAN, PAUL, WALLACE V. FRIESEN, and JOHN BEAR. "The International Language of Gestures." *Psychology Today* (May 1984):64–69.

ELAM, STANLEY M., LOWELL C. ROSE, and ALEC M. GALLUP. "The 23rd Annual Gallup Poll of the Public's Attitudes Toward Public Schools." *Phi Delta Kappan,* Vol. 73 (September 1991):41–56.

ELIAS, ROBERT. *The Politics of Victimization: Victims, Victimology and Human Rights.* New York: Oxford University Press, 1986.

ELKIND, DAVID. *The Hurried Child: Growing Up Too Fast Too Soon*. Reading, MA: Addison-Wesley, 1981.

ELLIOT, DELBERT S., and SUZANNE S. AGETON. "Reconciling Race and Class Differences in Self-Reported and Official Estimates of Delinquency." *American Sociological Review*. Vol. 45, No. 1 (February 1980):95–110.

EMBER, MELVIN, and CAROL R. EMBER. "The Conditions Favoring Matrilocal versus Patrilocal Residence." *American Anthropologist*. Vol. 73, No. 3 (June 1971):571–94.

EMBER, MELVIN M., and CAROL R. EMBER. *Anthropology*. 6th ed. Englewood Cliffs, NJ: Prentice Hall, 1991.

EMERSON, JOAN P. "Behavior in Private Places: Sustaining Definitions of Reality in Gynecological Examinations." In H. P. Dreitzel, ed., *Recent Sociology*. Vol. 2. New York: Collier, 1970:74–97.

ENGELS, FRIEDRICH. *The Origin of the Family*. Chicago: Charles H. Kerr, 1902; orig. 1884.

ERIKSON, ROBERT S., NORMAN R. LUTTBEG, and KENT L. TEDIN. *American Public Opinion: Its Origins, Content, and Impact*. 2nd ed. New York: Wiley, 1980.

ETZIONI, AMITAI. *A Comparative Analysis of Complex Organization: On Power, Involvement, and Their Correlates*. Revised and enlarged ed. New York: Free Press, 1975.

————. "Too Many Rights, Too Few Responsibilities." *Society*. Vol. 28, No. 2 (January–February 1991):41–48.

ETZIONI-HALEVY, EVA. *Bureaucracy and Democracy: A Political Dilemma*. Rev. ed. Boston: Routledge & Kegan Paul, 1985.

EVE, SUSAN BROWN. "Age Strata Differences in Utilization of Health Care Services among Adults in the United States." *Sociological Focus*. Vol. 17, No. 2 (April 1984):105–20.

FALK, GERHARD. Personal communication, 1987.

FALLOWS, JAMES. "Immigration: How It's Affecting Us." *The Atlantic Monthly*. Vol. 252 (November 1983):45–52, 55–62, 66–68, 85–90, 94, 96, 99–106.

Family Economics Review. "Updated Estimates of the Cost of Raising a Child." Vol. 2, No. 4 (1989):30–31.

FARRELL, MICHAEL P., and STANLEY D. ROSENBERG. *Men at Midlife*. Boston: Auburn House, 1981.

FEAGIN, JOE. *The Urban Real Estate Game*. Englewood Cliffs, NJ: Prentice Hall, 1983.

FEAGIN, JOE R. "The Continuing Significance of Race: Antiblack Discrimination in Public Places." *American Sociological Review*. Vol. 56, No. 1 (February 1991):101–16.

FEATHERMAN, DAVID L., and ROBERT M. HAUSER. *Opportunity and Change*. New York: Academic Press, 1978.

FENNELL, MARY C. "The Effects of Environmental Characteristics on the Structure of Hospital Clusters." *Administrative Science Quarterly*. Vol. 29, No. 3 (September 1980):489–510.

FERGUSON, TOM. "Medical Self-Care: Self Responsibility for Health." In Arthur C. Hastings et al., eds., *Health for the Whole Person: The Complete Guide to Holistic Medicine*. Boulder, CO: Westview Press, 1980:87–109.

FERGUSSON, D. M., L. J. HORWOOD, and F. T. SHANNON. "A Proportional Hazards Model of Family Breakdown." *Journal of Marriage and the Family*. Vol. 46, No. 3 (August 1984): 539–49.

FINKELSTEIN, NEAL W., and RON HASKINS. "Kindergarten Children Prefer Same-Color Peers." *Child Development*. Vol. 54, No. 2 (April 1983):502–8.

FIORENTINE, ROBERT. "Men, Women, and the Premed Persistence Gap: A Normative Alternatives Approach." *American Journal of Sociology*. Vol. 92, No. 5 (March 1987):1118–39.

FISHER, ELIZABETH. *Woman's Creation: Sexual Evolution and the Shaping of Society*. Garden City, NY: Anchor/Doubleday, 1979.

FISHER, ROGER, and WILLIAM URY. "Getting to YES." In William M. Evan and Stephen Hilgartner, eds., *The Arms Race and Nuclear War*. Englewood Cliffs, NJ: Prentice Hall, 1988:261–68.

FITZPATRICK, JOSEPH P. *Puerto Rican Americans: The Meaning of Migration to the Mainland*. Englewood Cliffs, NJ: Prentice Hall, 1971.

————. "Puerto Ricans." In *Harvard Encyclopedia of American Ethnic Groups*. Cambridge, MA: Harvard University Press, 1980:858–67.

FLAHERTY, MICHAEL G. "A Formal Approach to the Study of Amusement in Social Interaction." *Studies in Symbolic Interaction*. Vol. 5. New York: JAI Press, 1984:71–82.

————. "Two Conceptions of the Social Situation: Some Implications of Humor." *The Sociological Quarterly*. Vol. 31, No. 1 (Spring 1990).

FLORIDA, RICHARD, and MARTIN KENNEY. "Transplanted Organizations: The Transfer of Japanese Industrial Organization to the U.S." *American Sociological Review*. Vol. 56, No. 3 (June 1991):381–98.

Forbes. "The 400 Richest People in America." Special Issue. (October 19, 1992).

FORD, CLELLAN S., and FRANK A. BEACH. *Patterns of Sexual Behavior*. New York: Harper & Row, 1951.

FRANK, ANDRE GUNDER. *On Capitalist Underdevelopment*. Bombay: Oxford University Press, 1975.

————. *Crisis: In the World Economy*. New York: Holmes & Meier, 1980.

————. *Reflections on the World Economic Crisis*. New York: Monthly Review Press, 1981.

FRANKLIN, JOHN HOPE. *From Slavery to Freedom: A History of Negro Americans*. 3rd ed. New York: Vintage Books, 1967.

Frazier, E. Franklin. *Black Bourgeoisie: The Rise of a New Middle Class.* New York: Free Press, 1965.

Fredrickson, George M. *White Supremacy: A Comparative Study in American and South African History.* New York: Oxford University Press, 1981.

French, Marilyn. *Beyond Power: On Women, Men, and Morals.* New York: Summit Books, 1985.

Friedrich, Carl J., and Zbigniew Brzezinski. *Totalitarian Dictatorship and Autocracy.* 2nd ed. Cambridge, MA: Harvard University Press, 1965.

Friedrich, Otto. "A Proud Capital's Distress." *Time.* Vol. 124, No. 6 (August 6, 1984):26–30, 33–35.

———. "United No More." *Time.* Vol. 129, No. 18 (May 4, 1987):28–37.

Fuchs, Victor R. *Who Shall Live.* New York: Basic Books, 1974.

———. "Sex Differences in Economic Well-Being." *Science.* Vol. 232 (April 25, 1986):459–64.

Fugita, Stephen S., and David J. O'Brien. "Structural Assimilation, Ethnic Group Membership, and Political Participation among Japanese Americans: A Research Note." *Social Forces.* Vol. 63, No. 4 (June 1985):986–95.

Fujimoto, Isao. "The Failure of Democracy in a Time of Crisis." In Amy Tachiki et al., eds., *Roots: An Asian American Reader.* Los Angeles: UCLA Asian American Studies Center, 1971:207–14.

Fumento, Michael. *The Myth of Heterosexual AIDS.* New York: Basic Books, 1989.

Furstenberg, Frank F., Jr. "The New Extended Family: The Experience of Parents and Children after Remarriage." Paper presented to the Changing Family Conference XIII: The Blended Family. University of Iowa, 1984.

Gagliani, Giorgio. "How Many Working Classes?" *American Journal of Sociology.* Vol. 87, No. 2 (September 1981):259–85.

Gallup, George, Jr. *Religion in America.* Princeton, NJ: Princeton Religion Research Center, 1982.

Galster, George. "Black Suburbanization: Has It Changed the Relative Location of Races?" *Urban Affairs Quarterly.* Vol. 26, No. 4 (June 1991):621–28.

Gans, Herbert J. *People and Plans: Essays on Urban Problems and Solutions.* New York: Basic Books, 1968.

———. *Deciding What's News: A Study of CBS Evening News, NBC Nightly News, Newsweek and Time.* New York: Vintage Books, 1980.

———. *The Urban Villagers: Group and Class in the Life of Italian-Americans.* New York: Free Press, 1982; orig. 1962.

Garfinkel, Harold. "Conditions of Successful Degradation Ceremonies." *American Journal of Sociology.* Vol. 61, No. 2 (March 1956):420–24.

———. *Studies in Ethnomethodology.* Cambridge: Polity Press, 1967.

Geertz, Clifford. "Common Sense as a Cultural System." *The Antioch Review.* Vol. 33, No. 1 (Spring 1975):5–26.

Geist, William. *Toward a Safe and Sane Halloween and Other Tales of Suburbia.* New York: Times Books, 1985.

Gelles, Richard J., and Claire Pedrick Cornell. *Intimate Violence in Families.* 2nd ed. Newbury Park, CA: Sage, 1990.

Gerstel, Naomi. "Divorce and Stigma." *Social Problems.* Vol. 43, No. 2 (April 1987):172–86.

Geschwender, James A. *Racial Stratification in America.* Dubuque, IA: Wm. C. Brown, 1978.

Gibbons, Don C. *Delinquent Behavior.* 3rd ed. Englewood Cliffs, NJ: Prentice Hall, 1981.

Gibbons, Don C., and Marvin D. Krohn. *Delinquent Behavior.* 4th ed. Englewood Cliffs, NJ: Prentice Hall, 1986.

Gibbs, Nancy. "When Is It Rape?" *Time.* Vol. 137, No. 22 (June 3, 1991a):48–54.

———. "The Clamor on Campus." *Time.* Vol. 137, No. 22 (June 3, 1991b):54–55.

Giddens, Anthony. *Sociology: A Brief but Critical Introduction.* New York: Harcourt Brace Jovanovich, 1982.

Giele, Janet Z. "Gender and Sex Roles." In Neil J. Smelser, ed., *Handbook of Sociology.* Newbury Park, CA: Sage, 1988:291–323.

Gilbert, Dennis, and Joseph A. Kahl. *The American Class Structure: A New Synthesis.* 3rd ed. Homewood, IL: Dorsey Press, 1987.

Gilligan, Carol. *In a Different Voice: Psychological Theory and Women's Development.* Cambridge, MA: Harvard University Press, 1982.

Gimenez, Martha E. "Silence in the Classroom: Some Thoughts about Teaching in the 1980s." *Teaching Sociology.* Vol. 17, No. 2 (April 1989):184–91.

Ginsburg, Paul B. "Market-Oriented Options in Medicare and Medicaid." In Jack B. Meyer, ed., *Market Reforms in Health Care: Current Issues, New Directions, Strategic Decisions.* Washington, DC: American Enterprise Institute for Public Policy Research, 1983:103–18.

Giovannini, Maureen. "Female Anthropologist and Male Informant: Gender Conflict in a Sicilian Town." In John J. Macionis and Nijole V. Benokraitis, eds., *Seeing Ourselves: Classic, Contemporary, and Cross-Cultural Readings in Sociology.* 2nd ed. Englewood Cliffs, NJ: Prentice Hall, 1992:27–32.

Gladue, Brian A., Richard Green, and Ronald E. Hellman. "Neuroendocrine Response to Estrogen and Sexual Orientation." *Science.* Vol. 225, No. 4669 (September 28, 1984):1496–99.

GLENN, CHARLES L., and FRANMARIE KENNEDY-KEEL. "Commentary." *Education Week*. Vol. V, No. 21 (February 5, 1986):21.

GLENN, NORVAL D., and BETH ANN SHELTON. "Regional Differences in Divorce in the United States." *Journal of Marriage and the Family*. Vol. 47, No. 3 (August 1985):641–52.

GLUCK, PETER R., and RICHARD J. MEISTER. *Cities in Transition*. New York: New Viewpoints, 1979.

GLUECK, SHELDON, and ELEANOR GLUECK. *Unraveling Juvenile Delinquency*. New York: Commonwealth Fund, 1950.

GOETTING, ANN. Personal communication, 1989.

GOFFMAN, ERVING. *The Presentation of Self in Everyday Life*. Garden City, NY: Anchor Books, 1959.

_____. *Asylums: Essays on the Social Situation of Mental Patients and Other Inmates*. Garden City, NY: Anchor Books, 1961.

_____. *Stigma: Notes on the Management of Spoiled Identity*. Englewood Cliffs, NJ: Prentice Hall, 1963.

_____. *Interactional Ritual: Essays on Face to Face Behavior*. Garden City, NY: Anchor Books, 1967.

GOLD, ALLAN R. "Increasingly, Prison Term is the Price for Polluters." *New York Times* (February 15, 1991):B6.

GOLDBERG, STEVEN. *The Inevitability of Patriarchy*. New York: Morrow, 1974.

_____. Personal communication, 1987.

GOLDFARB, JEFFREY C. *Beyond Glasnost: The Post-Totalitarian Mind*. Chicago: University of Chicago Press, 1989.

GOLDFIELD, MICHAEL. *The Decline of Organized Labor in the United States*. Chicago and London: University of Chicago Press, 1987.

GOLDSMITH, H. H. "Genetic Influences on Personality from Infancy." *Child Development*. Vol. 54, No. 2 (April 1983):331–35.

GOODE, WILLIAM J. "The Theoretical Importance of Love." *American Sociological Review*. Vol. 24, No. 1 (February 1959):38–47.

_____. "Encroachment, Charlatanism, and the Emerging Profession: Psychology, Sociology and Medicine." *American Sociological Review*. Vol. 25, No. 6 (December 1960):902–14.

GORDON, JAMES S. "The Paradigm of Holistic Medicine." In Arthur C. Hastings et al., eds., *Health for the Whole Person: The Complete Guide to Holistic Medicine*. Boulder, CO: Westview Press, 1980:3–27.

GORDON, JOHN STEELE. "Numbers Game." *Forbes* (October 19, 1992):48, 52, 56.

GORDON, MILTON M. *Assimilation in American Life*. New York: Oxford University Press, 1964.

GORING, CHARLES BUCKMAN. *The English Convict: A Statistical Study*. Montclair, NJ: Patterson Smith, 1972; orig. 1913.

GORTMAKER, STEVEN L. "Poverty and Infant Mortality in the United States." *American Journal of Sociology*. Vol. 44, No. 2 (April 1979):280–97.

GOTTMANN, JEAN. *Megalopolis*. New York: Twentieth Century Fund, 1961.

GOUGH, KATHLEEN. "The Origin of the Family." *Journal of Marriage and the Family*. Vol. 33, No. 4 (November 1971):760–71.

GOULD, STEPHEN J. "Evolution as Fact and Theory." *Discover*. (May 1981):35–37.

GOULDNER, ALVIN. *Enter Plato*. New York: Free Press, 1965.

_____. "The Sociologist as Partisan: Sociology and the Welfare State." In Larry T. Reynolds and Janice M. Reynolds, eds., *The Sociology of Sociology*. New York: McKay, 1970a:218–55.

_____. *The Coming Crisis of Western Sociology*. New York: Avon Books, 1970b.

GRANOVETTER, MARK. "The Strength of Weak Ties." *American Journal of Sociology*. Vol. 78, No. 6 (May 1973):1360–80.

GRANT, KAREN R. "The Inverse Care Law in the Context of Universal Free Health Insurance in Canada: Toward Meeting Health Needs Through Public Policy." *Sociological Focus*. Vol. 17, No. 2 (April 1984):137–55.

GRAY, PAUL. "Whose America?" *Time*. Vol. 137, No. 27 (July 8, 1991):12–17.

GREELEY, ANDREW M. *Why Can't They Be Like Us? America's White Ethnic Groups*. New York: Dutton, 1971.

_____. *Ethnicity in the United States: A Preliminary Reconnaissance*. New York: Wiley, 1974.

_____. *Religious Change in America*. Cambridge, MA: Harvard University Press, 1989.

GREENBERG, DAVID F. *The Construction of Homosexuality*. Chicago: University of Chicago Press, 1988.

GREER, SCOTT. *Urban Renewal and American Cities*. Indianapolis, IN: Bobbs-Merrill, 1965.

GREGORY, PAUL R., and ROBERT C. STUART. *Comparative Economic Systems*. 2nd ed. Boston: Houghton Mifflin, 1985.

GRISWOLD, WENDY. "The Fabrication of Meaning: Literary Interpretation in the United States, Great Britain, and the West Indies." *American Journal of Sociology*. Vol. 92, No. 5 (March 1987):1077–117.

GUPTE, PRANAY. *The Crowded Earth: People and the Politics of Population*. New York: Norton, 1984.

GURAK, DOUGLAS T., and JOSEPH P. FITZPATRICK. "Intermarriage among Hispanic Ethnic Groups in New York City." *American Journal of Sociology*. Vol. 87, No. 4 (January 1982):921–34.

GWARTNEY-GIBBS, PATRICIA A., JEAN STOCKARD, and SUSANNE BOHMER. "Learning Courtship Aggression: The Influence of Parents, Peers, and Personal Experiences." *Family Relations.* Vol. 36, No. 3 (July 1987):276–82.

HAAS, LINDA. "Domestic Role Sharing in Sweden." *Journal of Marriage and the Family.* Vol. 43, No. 4 (November 1981):957–67.

HABERMAS, JURGEN. *Toward a Rational Society: Student Protest, Science, and Politics.* Jeremy J. Shapiro, trans. Boston: Beacon Press, 1970.

HACKER, HELEN MAYER. "Women as a Minority Group." *Social Forces.* Vol. 30 (October 1951):60–69.

———. "Women as a Minority Group: 20 Years Later." In Florence Denmark, ed., *Who Discriminates Against Women.* Beverly Hills, CA: Sage, 1974:124–34.

HADDEN, JEFFREY K., and CHARLES E. SWAIN. *Prime Time Preachers: The Rising Power of Televangelism.* Reading, MA: Addison-Wesley, 1981.

HAGAN, JOHN, A. R. GILLIS, and JOHN SIMPSON. "The Class Structure of Gender and Delinquency: Toward a Power-control Theory of Common Delinquent Behavior." *American Journal of Sociology.* Vol. 90, No. 6 (May 1985):1151–78.

HAGAN, JOHN, and PATRICIA PARKER. "White-Collar Crime and Punishment: The Class Structure and Legal Sanctioning of Securities Violations." *American Sociological Review.* Vol. 50, No. 3 (June 1985):302–16.

HAGAN, JOHN, JOHN SIMPSON, and A. R. GILLIS. "Class in the Household: A Power-Control Theory of Gender and Delinquency." *American Journal of Sociology.* Vol. 92, No. 4 (January 1987):788–816.

HAIG, ROBIN ANDREW. *The Anatomy of Humor: Biopsychosocial and Therapeutic Perspectives.* Springfield, IL: Charles C Thomas, 1988.

HALBERSTAM, DAVID. *The Reckoning.* New York: Avon Books, 1986.

HALLINAN, MAUREEN T., and RICHARD A. WILLIAMS. "Interracial Friendship Choices in Secondary Schools." *American Sociological Review.* Vol. 54, No. 1 (February 1989):67–78.

HAMBLIN, DORA JANE. *The First Cities.* New York: Time-Life, 1973.

HAMMOND, PHILIP E. "Introduction." In Philip E. Hammond, ed., *The Sacred in a Secular Age: Toward Revision in the Scientific Study of Religion.* Berkeley: University of California Press, 1985:1–6.

HAMRICK, MICHAEL H., DAVID J. ANSPAUGH, and GENE EZELL. *Health.* Columbus, OH: Merrill, 1986.

HANDLER, JOEL F., and YEHESKEL HASENFELD. *The Moral Construction of Poverty: Welfare Reform in America.* Newbury Park, CA: Sage, 1991.

HANDLIN, OSCAR. *Boston's Immigrants 1790–1865: A Study in Acculturation.* Cambridge, MA: Harvard University Press, 1941.

HANNAN, MICHAEL T., and GLENN R. CARROLL. "Dynamics of Formal Political Structure: An Event-History Analysis." *American Sociological Review.* Vol. 46, No. 1 (February 1981):19–35.

HARDEN, MIKE. "Rest Assured that Eventually You'll Get Your Money's Worth." *The Columbus Dispatch* (November 19, 1989):C1.

HAREVEN, TAMARA K. "The Life Course and Aging in Historical Perspective." In Tamara K. Hareven and Kathleen J. Adams, eds., *Aging and Life Course Transitions: An Interdisciplinary Perspective.* New York: Guilford Press, 1982:1–26.

HARLOW, CAROLINE WOLF. *Female Victims of Violent Crime.* Bureau of Justice Statistics report. Washington, DC: U.S. Government Printing Office, 1991.

HARLOW, HARRY F., and MARGARET KUENNE HARLOW. "Social Deprivation in Monkeys." *Scientific American.* Vol. 207 (November 1962):137–46.

HARRINGTON, MICHAEL. *The New American Poverty.* New York: Penguin Books, 1984.

HARRIS, CHAUNCEY D., and EDWARD L. ULLMAN. "The Nature of Cities." *The Annals.* Vol. 242 (November 1945):7–17.

HARRIS, MARVIN. *Cows, Pigs, Wars and Witches: The Riddles of Culture.* New York: Vintage Books, 1975.

———. "Why Men Dominate Women." *New York Times Magazine* (November 13, 1977):46, 115–23.

———. *Good to Eat: Riddle of Food and Culture.* New York: Simon and Schuster, 1985.

———. *Cultural Anthropology.* 2nd ed. New York: Harper & Row, 1987.

HARRISON, PAUL. *Inside the Third World: The Anatomy of Poverty.* 2nd ed. New York: Penguin Books, 1984.

HARTMANN, BETSY, and JAMES BOYCE. *Needless Hunger: Voices from a Bangladesh Village.* San Francisco: Institute for Food and Development Policy, 1982.

HAVILAND, WILLIAM A. *Anthropology.* 4th ed. New York: Holt, Rinehart & Winston, 1985.

HAYNEMAN, STEPHEN P., and WILLIAM A. LOXLEY. "The Effect of Primary-School Quality on Academic Achievement Across Twenty-nine High- and Low-Income Countries." *American Journal of Sociology.* Vol. 88, No. 6 (May 1983):1162–94.

HEALTH INSURANCE ASSOCIATION OF AMERICA. *Source Book of Health Insurance Data.* Washington DC: The Association, 1991.

HELMUTH, JOHN W. "World Hunger Amidst Plenty." *USA Today.* Vol. 117, No. 2526 (March 1989):48–50.

HENLEY, NANCY, MYKOL HAMILTON, and BARRIE THORNE.

"Womanspeak and Manspeak: Sex Differences in Communication, Verbal and Nonverbal." In John J. Macionis and Nijole V. Benokraitis, eds., *Seeing Ourselves: Classic, Contemporary, and Cross-Cultural Readings in Sociology*, 2nd ed. Englewood Cliffs, NJ: Prentice Hall, 1992:10–15.

HERITAGE, JOHN. *Garfinkel and Ethnomethodology.* Cambridge: Polity Press, 1984.

HERMAN, DIANNE F. "The Rape Culture." In John J. Macionis and Nijole V. Benokraitis, eds., *Seeing Ourselves: Classic, Contemporary, and Cross-Cultural Readings in Sociology.* 2nd ed. Englewood Cliffs, NJ: Prentice Hall, 1992.

HERMAN, EDWARD S. *Corporate Control, Corporate Power: A Twentieth Century Fund Study.* New York: Cambridge University Press, 1981.

HERRSTROM, STAFFAN. "Sweden: Pro-Choice on Child Care." *New Perspectives Quarterly.* Vol. 7, No. 1 (Winter 1990):27–28.

HEWLETT, SYLVIA ANN. *A Lesser Life: The Myth of Women's Liberation in America.* New York: Morrow, 1986.

HIRSCHI, TRAVIS. *Causes of Delinquency.* Berkeley: University of California Press, 1969.

HIRSCHI, TRAVIS, and MICHAEL GOTTFREDSON. "Age and the Explanation of Crime." *American Journal of Sociology.* Vol. 89, No. 3 (November 1983):552–84.

HOCHSCHILD, ARLIE, with ANNE MACHUNG. *The Second Shift: Working Parents and the Revolution at Home.* New York: Viking Books, 1989.

HODGE, ROBERT W., DONALD J. TREIMAN, and PETER H. ROSSI. "A Comparative Study of Occupational Prestige." In Reinhard Bendix and Seymour Martin Lipset, eds., *Class, Status, and Power: Social Stratification in Comparative Perspective.* 2nd ed. New York: Free Press, 1966:309–21.

HOERR, JOHN. "The Payoff from Teamwork." *Business Week*, No. 3114 (July 10, 1989):56–62.

HOGAN, DENNIS P., and EVELYN M. KITAGAWA. "The Impact of Social Status and Neighborhood on the Fertility of Black Adolescents." *American Journal of Sociology.* Vol. 90, No. 4 (January 1985):825–55.

HOLLAND, DOROTHY C., and MARGARET A. EISENHART. *Educated in Romance: Women, Achievement, and College Culture.* Chicago: University of Chicago Press, 1990.

HOLT, THOMAS C. "Afro-Americans." In *Harvard Encyclopedia of American Ethnic Groups.* Cambridge, MA: Harvard University Press, 1980:5–23.

HONEYWELL, ROY J. *The Educational Work of Thomas Jefferson.* Cambridge, MA: Harvard University Press, 1931.

HOOK, ERNEST B. "Behavioral Implications of the XYY Genotype." *Science.* Vol. 179 (January 12, 1973):139–50.

HOSTETLER, JOHN A. *Amish Society.* 3rd ed. Baltimore, MD: The Johns Hopkins University Press, 1980.

HOUSE OF REPRESENTATIVES. *A.I.D. and Third World Women, the Unmet Potential.* Hearing held May 11, 1988. Washington, DC: U.S. Government Printing Office, 1988.

HOWE, NEIL, and WILLIAM STRAUSS. "America's 13th Generation." *New York Times* (April 16, 1991).

HOWLETT, DEBBIE. "Cruzan's Struggle Left Imprint: 10,000 Others in Similar State." *USA Today* (December 27, 1990):3A.

HOYT, HOMER. *The Structure and Growth of Residential Neighborhoods in American Cities.* Washington, DC: Federal Housing Administration, 1939.

HSU, FRANCIS L. K. *The Challenge of the American Dream: The Chinese in the United States.* Belmont, CA: Wadsworth, 1971.

HUBER, JOAN, and GLENNA SPITZE. "Considering Divorce: An Expansion of Becker's Theory of Marital Instability." *American Journal of Sociology.* Vol. 86, No. 1 (July 1980):75–89.

HUET-COX, ROCIO. "Medical Education: New Wine in Old Wine Skins." In Victor W. Sidel and Ruth Sidel, eds., *Reforming Medicine: Lessons of the Last Quarter Century.* New York: Pantheon Books, 1984:129–49.

HULS, GLENNA. Personal communication, 1987.

HUMPHRIES, HARRY LEROY. *The Structure and Politics of Intermediary Class Positions: An Empirical Examination of Recent Theories of Class.* Unpublished Ph.D. dissertation. Eugene: University of Oregon, 1984.

HUNT, MORTON. *Sexual Behavior in the 1970s.* Chicago: Playboy Press, 1974.

HUNTER, JAMES DAVISON. *American Evangelicalism: Conservative Religion and the Quandary of Modernity.* New Brunswick, NJ: Rutgers University Press, 1983.

———. "Conservative Protestantism." In Philip E. Hammond, ed., *The Sacred in a Secular Age.* Berkeley: University of California Press, 1985:50–66.

HURN, CHRISTOPHER. *The Limits and Possibilities of Schooling.* Needham Heights, MA: Allyn and Bacon, 1978.

ILLICH, IVAN. *Medical Nemesis: The Expropriation of Health.* New York: Pantheon Books, 1976.

IRWIN, JOHN. *Prison in Turmoil.* Boston: Little, Brown, 1980.

ISAY, RICHARD A. *Being Homosexual: Gay Men and Their Development.* New York: Farrar, Straus & Giroux, 1989.

JACOB, JOHN E. "An Overview of Black America in 1985." In James D. Williams, ed., *The State of Black America 1986.* New York: National Urban League, 1986:i–xi.

JACOBS, DAVID. "Inequality and Police Strength." *American Sociological Review.* Vol. 44, No. 6 (December 1979):913–25.

422   References

JACOBS, JANE. *The Death and Life of Great American Cities.* New York: Random House, 1961.

_____. *The Economy of Cities.* New York: Vintage Books, 1970.

JACOBS, JERRY, ED. *Deviance: Field Studies and Self-Disclosures.* Palo Alto, CA: National Press Books, 1974:69–72.

JACQUET, CONSTANT H., and ALICE M. JONES. *Yearbook of American and Canadian Churches 1991.* Nashville, TN: Abingdon Press, 1991.

JAEGER, ART, and ROBERT GREENSTEIN. "Poverty Rate and Household Income Stagnate as Rich-Poor Gap Hits Post-War High." Washington, DC: Center on Budget and Policy Priorities, 1989.

JAGGER, ALISON. "Political Philosophies of Women's Liberation." In Laurel Richardson and Verta Taylor, eds., *Feminist Frontiers: Rethinking Sex, Gender, and Society.* Reading, MA: Addison-Wesley, 1983.

JAMES, DAVID R. "City Limits on Racial Equality: The Effects of City-Suburb Boundaries on Public-School Desegregation, 1968–1976." *American Sociological Review.* Vol. 54, No. 6 (December 1989):963–85.

JANIS, IRVING. *Victims of Groupthink.* Boston: Houghton Mifflin, 1972.

_____. *Crucial Decisions: Leadership in Policymaking and Crisis Management.* New York: Free Press, 1989.

JAYNES, GERALD DAVID, and ROBIN M. WILLIAMS, EDS. *A Common Destiny: Blacks and American Society.* Washington, DC: National Academy Press, 1989.

JENCKS, CHRISTOPHER. "Genes and Crime." *New York Review* (February 12, 1987):33–41.

JENCKS, CHRISTOPHER, ET AL. *Inequality: A Reassessment of the Effect of Family and Schooling in America.* New York: Basic Books, 1972.

JOHNSON, DIRK. "Census Finds Many Claiming New Identity: Indian." *New York Times* (March 5, 1991):A1, A16.

JOHNSON, JULIE. "Do We Have Too Many Lawyers?" *Time.* Vol. 138, No. 8 (August 26, 1991):54–55.

JOHNSON, PAUL. "The Seven Deadly Sins of Terrorism." In Benjamin Netanyahu, ed., *International Terrorism.* New Brunswick, NJ: Transaction Books, 1981:12–22.

JOHNSTON, R. J. "Residential Area Characteristics." In D. T. Herbert and R. J. Johnston, eds., *Social Areas in Cities. Vol. 1: Spatial Processes and Form.* New York: Wiley, 1976:193–235.

JOINT ECONOMIC COMMITTEE. *The Concentration of Wealth in the United States: Trends in the Distribution of Wealth Among American Families.* Washington, DC: United States Congress, 1986.

JONES, DAVID A. *History of Criminology: A Philosophical Perspective.* Westport, CT: Greenwood Press, 1986.

JONES, TERRY. "Foul Ball in the Front Office: Racial Practices in Baseball Management." *The Black Scholar.* Vol. 18, No. 3 (May–June 1987):16–24.

JOSEPHY, ALVIN M., JR. *Now That the Buffalo's Gone: A Study of Today's American Indians.* New York: Knopf, 1982.

KAELBLE, HARTMUT. *Social Mobility in the 19th and 20th Centuries: Europe and America in Comparative Perspective.* New York: St. Martin's Press, 1986.

KAIN, EDWARD L. "A Note on the Integration of AIDS Into the Sociology of Human Sexuality." *Teaching Sociology.* Vol. 15, No. 4 (July 1987):320–23.

_____. *The Myth of Family Decline: Understanding Families in a World of Rapid Social Change.* Lexington, MA: Lexington Books, 1990.

KAIN, EDWARD L., and SHANNON HART. "AIDS and the Family: A Content Analysis of Media Coverage." Presented to National Council on Family Relations, Atlanta, GA, 1987.

KALISH, CAROL B. "International Crime Rates." In Bureau of Justice Statistics, *Special Report,* May 1988. Washington, DC: U.S. Government Printing Office, 1988.

KALISH, RICHARD A. *Late Adulthood: Perspectives on Human Development.* 2nd ed. Monterey, CA: Brooks/Cole, 1982.

KAMINER, WENDY. "Volunteers: Who Knows What's in It for Them." *Ms.* (December 1984):93–94, 96, 126–28.

KANTER, ROSABETH MOSS. *Men and Women of the Corporation.* New York: Basic Books, 1977.

_____. *The Change Masters: Innovation and Entrepreneurship in the American Corporation.* New York: Simon and Schuster, 1983.

_____. *When Giants Learn to Dance: Mastering the Challenges of Strategy, Management, and Careers in the 1990s.* New York: Simon and Schuster, 1989.

KANTER, ROSABETH MOSS, and BARRY A. STEIN. "The Gender Pioneers: Women in an Industrial Sales Force." In R. M. Kanter and B. A. Stein, eds., *Life in Organizations.* New York: Basic Books, 1979:134–60.

KANTER, ROSABETH MOSS, and BARRY STEIN. *A Tale of "O": On Being Different in an Organization.* New York: Harper & Row, 1980.

KANTROWITZ, BARBARA. "Mothers on Their Own." *Newsweek* (December 23, 1985):66–67.

KAPLAN, ERIC B., ET AL. "The Usefulness of Preoperative Laboratory Screening." *Journal of the American Medical Association.* Vol. 253, No. 24 (June 28, 1985):3576–81.

KAPTCHUK, TED. "The Holistic Logic of Chinese Medicine." In Shepard Bliss et al., eds., *The New Holistic Health Handbook.* Lexington, MA: Steven Greene Press/Penguin Books, 1985:41.

KARP, DAVID A., and WILLIAM C. YOELS. "The College Classroom: Some Observations on the Meaning of Student

Participation." *Sociology and Social Research*. Vol. 60, No. 4 (July 1976):421–39.

KAUFMAN, POLLY WELTS. "Women and Education." In Barbara Haber, ed., *The Women's Annual, 1981: The Year in Review*. Boston: G. K. Hall, 1982:24–55.

KAUFMAN, WALTER. *Religions in Four Dimensions: Existential, Aesthetic, Historical and Comparative*. New York: Reader's Digest Press, 1976.

KELLER, SUZANNE. *The Urban Neighborhood*. New York: Random House, 1968.

KEMP, ALICE ABEL, and SHELLEY COVERMAN. "Marginal Jobs or Marginal Workers: Identifying Sex Differences in Low-Skill Occupations." *Sociological Focus*. Vol. 22, No. 1 (February 1989):19–37.

KENNICKELL, ARTHUR, and JANICE SHACK-MARQUEZ. "Changes in Family Finances from 1983 to 1989: Evidence from the Survey of Consumer Finances." *Federal Reserve Bulletin* (January 1992):1–18.

KENYON, KATHLEEN. *Digging Up Jericho*. London: Ernest Benn, 1957.

KERCKHOFF, ALAN C., RICHARD T. CAMPBELL, and IDEE WINFIELD-LAIRD. "Social Mobility in Great Britain and the United States." *American Journal of Sociology*. Vol. 91, No. 2 (September 1985):281–308.

KILBOURNE, BROCK K. "The Conway and Siegelman Claims Against Religious Cults: An Assessment of Their Data." *Journal for the Scientific Study of Religion*. Vol. 22, No. 4 (December 1983):380–85.

KILGORE, SALLY B. "The Organizational Context of Tracking in Schools." *American Sociological Review*. Vol. 56, No. 2 (April 1991):189–203.

KILLIAN, LEWIS M. "Organization, Rationality and Spontaneity in the Civil Rights Movement." *American Sociological Review*. Vol. 49, No. 6 (December 1984):770–83.

KING, KATHLEEN PIKER, and DENNIS E. CLAYSON. "The Differential Perceptions of Male and Female Deviants." *Sociological Focus*. Vol. 21, No. 2 (April 1988):153–64.

KING, MARTIN LUTHER, JR. "The Montgomery Bus Boycott." In Walt Anderson, ed., *The Age of Protest*. Pacific Palisades, CA: Goodyear, 1969:81–91.

KINSEY, ALFRED, ET AL. *Sexual Behavior in the Human Male*. Philadelphia: Saunders, 1948.

———. *Sexual Behavior in the Human Female*. Philadelphia: Saunders, 1953.

KIPP, RITA SMITH. "Have Women Always Been Unequal?" In Beth Reed, ed., *Towards a Feminist Transformation of the Academy: Proceedings of the Fifth Annual Women's Studies Conference*. Ann Arbor, MI: Great Lakes Colleges Association, 1980:12–18.

KIRK, MARSHALL, and PETER MADSEN. *After the Ball: How America Will Conquer its Fear and Hatred of Gays in the '90s*. New York: Doubleday, 1989.

KITANO, HARRY H. L. *Race Relations*. 3rd ed. Englewood Cliffs, NJ: Prentice Hall, 1985.

KITSON, GAY C., and HELEN J. RASCHKE. "Divorce Research: What We Know, What We Need to Know." *Journal of Divorce*. Vol. 4, No. 3 (Spring 1981):1–37.

KITTRIE, NICHOLAS N. *The Right To Be Different: Deviance and Enforced Therapy*. Baltimore, MD: The Johns Hopkins University Press, 1971.

KLEIN, SUSAN SHURBERG. "Education." In Sarah M. Pritchard, ed., *The Women's Annual, Number 4, 1983–1984*. Boston: G. K. Hall, 1984:9–30.

KLEUGEL, JAMES R., and ELIOT R. SMITH. *Beliefs About Inequality: Americans' Views of What Is and What Ought to Be*. New York: Aldine de Gruyter, 1986.

KLUCKHOHN, CLYDE. "As An Anthropologist Views It." In Albert Deuth, ed., *Sex Habits of American Men*. New York: Prentice Hall, 1948.

KNAUS, WILLIAM A. *Inside Russian Medicine: An American Doctor's First-Hand Report*. New York: Everest House, 1981.

KOHLBERG, LAWRENCE, and CAROL GILLIGAN. "The Adolescent as Philosopher: The Discovery of Self in a Postconventional World." *Daedalus*. Vol. 100 (Fall 1971):1051–86.

KOHN, MELVIN L. *Class and Conformity: A Study in Values*. 2nd ed. Homewood, IL: Dorsey Press, 1977.

KOMAROVSKY, MIRRA. *Blue Collar Marriage*. New York: Vintage Books, 1967.

———. "Cultural Contradictions and Sex Roles: The Masculine Case." *American Journal of Sociology*. Vol. 78, No. 4 (January 1973):873–84.

———. *Dilemmas of Masculinity: A Study of College Youth*. New York: Norton, 1976.

KORNHAUSER, WILLIAM. *The Politics of Mass Society*. New York: Free Press, 1959.

KOZOL, JONATHAN. *Prisoners of Silence: Breaking the Bonds of Adult Illiteracy in the United States*. New York: Continuum, 1980.

———. "A Nation's Wealth." *Publisher's Weekly* (May 24, 1985):28–30.

———. *Illiterate America*. Garden City, NY: Doubleday, 1985.

———. *Rachel and Her Children: Homeless Families in America*. New York: Crown, 1988.

KRAMARAE, CHERIS, BARRIE THORNE, and NANCY HENLEY. "Sex Similarities and Differences in Language, Speech, and Nonverbal Communication: An Annotated Bibliography." In Barrie Thorne, Cheris Kramarae, and Nancy Henley, eds., *Language, Gender and Society*. Rowley, MA: Newbury House, 1983:150–331.

KRIESI, HANSPETER. "New Social Movements and the New Class in the Netherlands." *American Journal of Sociology*. Vol. 94, No. 5 (March 1989):1078–116.

KRISBERG, BARRY, and IRA SCHWARTZ. "Rethinking Juvenile Justice." *Crime and Delinquency.* Vol. 29, No. 3 (July 1983):333–64.

KÜBLER-ROSS, ELISABETH. *On Death and Dying.* New York: Macmillan, 1969.

KUHN, THOMAS. *The Structure of Scientific Revolutions.* 2nd ed. Chicago: University of Chicago Press, 1970.

KUZNETS, SIMON. "Economic Growth and Income Inequality." *The American Economic Review.* Vol. XLV, No. 1 (March 1955):1–28.

_____. *Modern Economic Growth: Rate, Structure, and Spread.* New Haven, CT: Yale University Press, 1966.

LADD, JOHN. "The Definition of Death and the Right to Die." In John Ladd, ed., *Ethical Issues Relating to Life and Death.* New York: Oxford University Press, 1979:118–45.

LAI, H. M. "Chinese." In *Harvard Encyclopedia of American Ethnic Groups.* Cambridge, MA: Harvard University Press, 1980:217–33.

LAMBERG-KARLOVSKY, C. C., and MARTHA LAMBERG-KARLOVSKY. "An Early City in Iran." In *Cities: Their Origin, Growth, and Human Impact.* San Francisco: Freeman, 1973:28–37.

LAPPÉ, FRANCES MOORE, and JOSEPH COLLINS. *World Hunger: Twelve Myths.* New York: Grove Press/Food First Books, 1986.

LAPPÉ, FRANCES MOORE, JOSEPH COLLINS, and DAVID KINLEY. *Aid as Obstacle: Twenty Questions about Our Foreign Policy and the Hungry.* San Francisco: Institute for Food and Development Policy, 1981.

LASLETT, BARBARA. "Family Membership, Past and Present." *Social Problems.* Vol. 25, No. 5 (June 1978):476–90.

LASLETT, PETER. *The World We Have Lost: England Before the Industrial Age.* 3rd ed. New York: Scribner's, 1984.

LEACOCK, ELEANOR. "Women's Status in Egalitarian Societies: Implications for Social Evolution." *Current Anthropology.* Vol. 19, No. 2 (June 1978):247–75.

LEAVITT, JUDITH WALZER. "Women and Health in America: An Overview." In Judith Walzer Leavitt, ed., *Women and Health in America.* Madison: University of Wisconsin Press, 1984:3–7.

LEE, BARRETT A., R. S. OROPESA, BARBARA J. METCH, and AVERY M. GUEST. "Testing the Decline of Community Thesis: Neighborhood Organization in Seattle, 1929 and 1979." *American Journal of Sociology.* Vol. 89, No. 5 (March 1984):1161–88.

LEERHSEN, CHARLES. "Unite and Conquer." *Newsweek* (February 5, 1990):50–55.

LEMERT, EDWIN M. *Social Pathology.* New York: McGraw-Hill, 1951.

_____. *Human Deviance, Social Problems, and Social Control.* 2nd ed. Englewood Cliffs, NJ: Prentice Hall, 1972.

LENGERMANN, PATRICIA MADOO, and RUTH A. WALLACE. *Gender in America: Social Control and Social Change.* Englewood Cliffs, NJ: Prentice Hall, 1985.

LENSKI, GERHARD. *Power and Privilege: A Theory of Social Stratification.* New York: McGraw-Hill, 1966.

LENSKI, GERHARD, JEAN LENSKI, and PATRICK NOLAN. *Human Societies: An Introduction to Macrosociology.* 6th ed. New York: McGraw-Hill, 1991.

LEONARD, EILEEN B. *Women, Crime, and Society: A Critique of Theoretical Criminology.* New York: Longman, 1982.

LESLIE, GERALD R., and SHEILA K. KORMAN. *The Family in Social Context.* 7th ed. New York: Oxford University Press, 1989.

LESTER, DAVID. *The Death Penalty: Issues and Answers.* Springfield, IL: Charles C Thomas, 1987.

LEVER, JANET. "Sex Differences in the Complexity of Children's Play and Games." *American Sociological Review.* Vol. 43, No. 4 (August 1978):471–83.

LEVINSON, DANIEL J., with CHARLOTTE N. DARROW, EDWARD B. KLEIN, MARIA H. LEVINSON, and BRAXTON McKEE. *The Seasons of a Man's Life.* New York: Knopf, 1978.

LEVITAN, SARAH, and ISAAC SHAPIRO. *Working but Poor: America's Contradiction.* Baltimore, MD: The Johns Hopkins University Press, 1987.

LEVY, FRANK. *Dollars and Dreams: The Changing American Income Distribution.* New York: Russell Sage Foundation, 1987.

LEWIS, FLORA. "The Roots of Revolution." *New York Times Magazine* (November 11, 1984):70–71, 74, 77–78, 82, 84, 86.

LEWIS, OSCAR. *The Children of Sanchez.* New York: Random House, 1961.

LIAZOS, ALEXANDER. "The Poverty of the Sociology of Deviance: Nuts, Sluts and Preverts." *Social Problems.* Vol. 20, No. 1 (Summer 1972):103–20.

LICHTER, DANIEL R. "Race, Employment Hardship, and Inequality in the American Nonmetropolitan South." *American Sociological Review.* Vol. 54, No. 3 (June 1989):436–46.

LIEBERSON, STANLEY. *A Piece of the Pie: Black and White Immigrants Since 1880.* Berkeley: University of California Press, 1980.

LIN, NAN, WALTER M. ENSEL, and JOHN C. VAUGHN. "Social Resources and Strength of Ties: Structural Factors in Occupational Status Attainment." *American Sociological Review.* Vol. 46, No. 4 (August 1981):393–405.

LING, PYAU. "Causes of Chinese Emigration." In Amy Tachiki et al., eds., *Roots: An Asian American Reader.* Los Angeles: UCLA Asian American Studies Center, 1971:134–38.

LINK, BRUCE G., FRANCIS T. CULLIN, JAMES FRANK, and JOHN F. WOZNIAK. "The Social Rejection of Former Mental

Patients: Understanding Why Labels Matter." *American Journal of Sociology*. Vol. 92, No. 6 (May 1987):1461–1500.

LINTON, RALPH. "One Hundred Percent American." *The American Mercury*. Vol. 40, No. 160 (April 1937):427–29.

———. *The Study of Man*. New York: Appleton-Century, 1937.

LIPSET, SEYMOUR MARTIN, and REINHARD BENDIX. *Social Mobility in Industrial Society*. Berkeley: University of California Press, 1967.

LISKA, ALLEN E. *Perspectives on Deviance*. 3rd ed. Englewood Cliffs, NJ: Prentice Hall, 1991.

LISKA, ALLEN E., and MARK TAUSIG. "Theoretical Interpretations of Social Class and Racial Differentials in Legal Decision Making for Juveniles." *Sociological Quarterly*. Vol. 20, No. 2 (Spring 1979):197–207.

LISKA, ALLEN E., and BARBARA D. WARNER. "Functions of Crime: A Paradoxical Process." *American Journal of Sociology*. Vol. 96, No. 6 (May 1991):1441–63.

LITTMAN, MARK S. "Poverty in the 1980s: Are the Poor Getting Poorer?" *Monthly Labor Review*. Vol. 112, No. 6 (June 1989):13–18.

LOGAN, JOHN R., and MARK SCHNEIDER. "Racial Segregation and Racial Change in American Suburbs, 1970–1980." *American Journal of Sociology*. Vol. 89, No. 4 (January 1984):874–88.

LOHR, STEVE. "British Health Service Faces A Crisis in Funds and Delays." *New York Times* (August 7, 1988):1, 12.

LONDON, BRUCE. "Structural Determinants of Third World Urban Change: An Ecological and Political Economic Analysis." *American Sociological Review*. Vol. 52, No. 1 (February 1987):28–43.

LONG, EDWARD V. *The Intruders: The Invasion of Privacy by Government and Industry*. New York: Praeger, 1967.

LORD, WALTER. *A Night to Remember*. Rev. ed. New York: Holt, Rinehart & Winston, 1976.

LORENZ, KONRAD. *On Aggression*. New York: Harcourt, Brace & World, 1966.

LOY, PAMELA HEWITT, and LEA P. STEWART. "The Extent and Effects of Sexual Harassment of Working Women." *Sociological Focus*. Vol. 17, No. 1 (January 1984):31–43.

LUBENOW, GERALD C. "A Troubling Family Affair." *Newsweek* (May 14, 1984):34.

LUTZ, CATHERINE, and GEOFFREY M. WHITE. "The Anthropology of Emotions." In Bernard J. Siegel, Alan R. Beals, and Stephen A. Tyler, eds., *Annual Review of Anthropology*. Palo Alto, CA: Annual Reviews, 1986: Vol. 15, 405–36.

LUTZ, CATHERINE A. *Unnatural Emotions: Everyday Sentiments on a Micronesia Atoll and Their Challenge to Western Theory*. Chicago: University of Chicago Press, 1988.

LYND, ROBERT S. *Knowledge For What? The Place of Social Science in American Culture*. Princeton, NJ: Princeton University Press, 1967.

LYND, ROBERT S., and HELEN MERRELL LYND. *Middletown in Transition*. New York: Harcourt, Brace & World, 1937.

McADAM, DOUG, JOHN D. McCARTHY, and MAYER N. ZALD. "Social Movements." In Neil J. Smelser, ed., *Handbook of Sociology*. Newbury Park, CA: Sage, 1988:695–737.

McCARTHY, JOHN D., and MAYER N. ZALD. "Resource Mobilization and Social Movements: A Partial Theory." *American Journal of Sociology*. Vol. 82, No. 6 (May 1977):1212–41.

MACCOBY, ELEANOR EMMONS, and CAROL NAGY JACKLIN. *The Psychology of Sex Differences*. Palo Alto, CA: Stanford University Press, 1974.

McCOLM, R. BRUCE, JAMES FINN, DOUGLAS W. PAYNE, JOSEPH E. RYAN, LEONARD R. SUSSMAN, and GEORGE ZARYCKY. *Freedom in the World: Political Rights & Civil Liberties, 1990–1991*. New York: Freedom House, 1991.

MACE, DAVID, and VERA MACE. *Marriage East and West*. Garden City, NY: Doubleday (Dolphin), 1960.

McGUIRE, MEREDITH B. *Religion: The Social Context*. 2nd ed. Belmont, CA: Wadsworth, 1987.

MACIONIS, JOHN J. "Intimacy: Structure and Process in Interpersonal Relationships." *Alternative Lifestyles*. Vol. 1, No. 1 (February 1978):113–30.

———. "The Search for Community in Modern Society: An Interpretation." *Qualitative Sociology*. Vol. 1, No. 2 (September 1978):130–43.

———. "A Sociological Analysis of Humor." Presentation to the Texas Junior College Teachers Association, Houston, 1987.

MacKAY, DONALD G. "Prescriptive Grammar and the Pronoun Problem." In Barrie Thorne, Cheris Kramarae, and Nancy Henley, eds., *Language, Gender and Society*. Rowley, MA: Newbury House, 1983:38–53.

MacKINNON, CATHARINE A. *Feminism Unmodified: Discourses on Life and Law*. Cambridge, MA: Harvard University Press, 1987.

McLANAHAN, SARA. "Family Structure and the Reproduction of Poverty." *American Journal of Sociology*. Vol. 90, No. 4 (January 1985):873–901.

McNEIL, DONALD G., JR. "Should Women Be Sent Into Combat?" *New York Times* (July 21, 1991):E3.

McRAE, SUSAN. *Cross-Class Families: A Study of Wives' Occupational Superiority*. New York: Oxford University Press, 1986.

McROBERTS, HUGH A., and KEVIN SELBEE. "Trends in Occupational Mobility in Canada and the United States: A Comparison." *American Sociological Review*. Vol. 46, No. 4 (August 1981):406–21.

MADSEN, AXEL. *Private Power: Multinational Corporations*

for the Survival of Our Planet. New York: Morrow, 1980.

MAJKA, LINDA C. "Sexual Harassment in the Church." *Society.* Vol. 28. No. 4 (May–June, 1991):14–21.

MAJOR, BRENDA. "Gender Patterns in Touching Behavior." In Clara Mayo and Nancy M. Henley, eds., *Gender and Nonverbal Behavior.* New York: Springer Verlag, 1981: 15–37.

MALTHUS, THOMAS ROBERT. *First Essay on Population 1798.* London: Macmillan, 1926; orig. 1798.

MANGAN, J. A., and ROBERTA J. PARK. *From Fair Sex to Feminism: Sport and the Socialization of Women.* London: Frank Cass, 1987.

MARCUSE, HERBERT. *One-Dimensional Man.* Boston: Beacon Press, 1964.

MARE, ROBERT D. "Five Decades of Educational Assortative Mating." *American Sociological Review.* Vol. 56, No. 1 (February 1991):15–32.

MARGOLICK, DAVID. "Rape in Marriage Is No Longer Within the Law." *New York Times* (December 13, 1984):6E.

MARKOFF, JOHN. "Remember Big Brother? Now He's a Company Man." *New York Times* (March 31, 1991):7.

MARLIOS, PETER. "Interlocking Directorates and the Control of Corporations: The Theory of Bank Control." *Social Science Quarterly.* Vol. 56, No. 3 (December 1975):425–39.

MARRY, MARCUS. "New Hope for Old Unions?" *Newsweek* (February 24, 1992):39.

MARSDEN, PETER. "Core Discussion Networks of Americans." *American Sociological Review.* Vol. 52, No. 1 (February 1987):122–31.

MARSHALL, SUSAN E. "Ladies Against Women: Mobilization Dilemmas of Antifeminist Movements." *Social Problems.* Vol. 32, No. 4 (April 1985):348–62.

MARTIN, WILLIAM. "The Birth of a Media Myth." *The Atlantic.* Vol. 247, No. 6 (June 1981):7, 10, 11, 16.

MARULLO, SAM. "The Functions and Dysfunctions of Preparations for Fighting Nuclear War." *Sociological Focus.* Vol. 20, No. 2 (April 1987):135–53.

MARX, KARL. *Karl Marx: Selected Writings in Sociology and Social Philosophy.* T. B. Bottomore, trans. New York: McGraw-Hill, 1964.

——. *Capital.* Friedrich Engels, ed. New York: International Publishers, 1967; orig. 1867.

——. "Theses on Feuer." In Robert C. Tucker, ed., *The Marx-Engels Reader.* New York: Norton, 1972:107–9; orig. 1845.

MARX, KARL, and FRIEDRICH ENGELS. "Manifesto of the Communist Party." In Robert C. Tucker, ed., *The Marx-Engels Reader.* New York: Norton, 1972:331–62; orig. 1848.

——. *The Marx-Engels Reader.* Robert C. Tucker, ed. New York: Norton, 1977.

MASHEK, JOHN W., and PATRICIA AVERY. "Women Politicians Take Off the White Gloves." *U.S. News and World Report* (August 15, 1983):41–42.

MASSEY, DOUGLAS S., and NANCY A. DENTON. "Hypersegregation in U.S. Metropolitan Areas: Black and Hispanic Segregation Along Five Dimensions." *Demography.* Vol. 26, No. 3 (August 1989):373–91.

MASTERS, WILLIAM H., VIRGINIA E. JOHNSON, and ROBERT C. KOLODNY. *Human Sexuality.* 3rd ed. Glenview, IL: Scott, Foresman/Little, Brown, 1988.

MATTHIESSEN, PETER. *In the Spirit of Crazy Horse.* New York: Viking Press, 1983.

——. *Indian Country.* New York: Viking Press, 1984.

MAURO, TONY. "Cruzan's Struggle Left Imprint: Private Case Triggered Public Debate." *USA Today* (December 27, 1990):3A.

MAY, ELAINE TYLER. "Women in the Wild Blue Yonder." *New York Times* (August 7, 1991):21.

MAYO, KATHERINE. *Mother India.* New York: Harcourt, Brace, 1927.

MCKUSICK, LEON, ET AL. "Reported Changes in the Sexual Behavior of Men at Risk for AIDS, San Francisco, 1982–84—The AIDS Behavioral Research Project." *Public Health Reports.* Vol. 100, No. 6 (November–December 1985):622–29.

MEAD, GEORGE HERBERT. *Mind, Self, and Society.* Charles W. Morris, ed. Chicago: University of Chicago Press, 1962; orig. 1934.

MEAD, MARGARET. *Sex and Temperament in Three Primitive Societies.* New York: Morrow, 1963; orig. 1935.

MECHANIC, DAVID. *Medical Sociology.* 2nd ed. New York: Free Press, 1978.

MELTZER, BERNARD N. "Mead's Social Psychology." In Jerome G. Manis and Bernard N. Meltzer, eds., *Symbolic Interaction: A Reader in Social Psychology.* 3rd ed. Needham Heights, MA: Allyn and Bacon, 1978.

MELUCCI, ALBERTO. "The New Social Movements: A Theoretical Approach." *Social Science Information.* Vol. 19, No. 2 (May 1980):199–226.

——. *Nomads of the Present: Social Movements and Individual Needs in Contemporary Society.* Philadelphia: Temple University Press, 1989.

MELVILLE, KEITH. *Marriage and Family Today.* 3rd ed. New York: Random House, 1983.

MERTON, ROBERT K. "Social Structure and Anomie." *American Sociological Review.* Vol. 3, No. 6 (October 1938):672–82.

——. *Social Theory and Social Structure.* New York: Free Press, 1968.

——. "Discrimination and the American Creed." In *Sociological Ambivalence and Other Essays.* New York: Free Press, 1976:189–216.

MICHELS, ROBERT. *Political Parties*. Glencoe, IL: Free Press, 1949; orig. 1911.

MILGRAM, STANLEY. "Behavioral Study of Obedience." *Journal of Abnormal and Social Psychology*. Vol. 67, No. 4 (1963):371–78.

_____. "Group Pressure and Action Against a Person." *Journal of Abnormal and Social Psychology*. Vol. 69, No. 2 (August 1964):137–43.

_____. "Some Conditions of Obedience and Disobedience to Authority." *Human Relations*. Vol. 18 (February 1965):57–76.

MILIBAND, RALPH. *The State in Capitalist Society*. London: Weidenfield and Nicolson, 1969.

MILLER, ARTHUR G. *The Obedience Experiments: A Case of Controversy in Social Science*. New York: Praeger, 1986.

MILLER, FREDERICK D. "The End of SDS and the Emergence of Weatherman: Demise Through Success." In Jo Freeman, ed., *Social Movements of the Sixties and Seventies*. New York: Longman, 1983:279–97.

MILLER, MARK. "Under Cover, In the Closet." *Newsweek* (January 14, 1991):25.

MILLER, MICHAEL. "Lawmakers Begin to Heed Calls to Protect Privacy." *Wall Street Journal* (April 11, 1991):A16.

MILLER, WALTER B. "Lower Class Culture as a Generating Milieu of Gang Delinquency." In Marvin E. Wolfgang, Leonard Savitz, and Norman Johnston, eds., *The Sociology of Crime and Delinquency*. 2nd ed. New York: Wiley, 1970:351–63; orig. 1958.

MILLET, KATE. *Sexual Politics*. Garden City, NY: Doubleday, 1970.

MILLS, C. WRIGHT. *The Power Elite*. New York: Oxford University Press, 1956.

_____. *The Sociological Imagination*. New York: Oxford University Press, 1959.

MINK, BARBARA. "How Modernization Affects Women." *Cornell Alumni News*. Vol. III, No. 3 (April 1989):10–11.

MINTZ, BETH, and MICHAEL SCHWARTZ. "Interlocking Directorates and Interest Group Formation." *American Sociological Review*. Vol. 46, No. 6 (December 1981):851–69.

MIROWSKY, JOHN. "The Psycho-Economics of Feeling Underpaid: Distributive Justice and the Earnings of Husbands and Wives." *American Journal of Sociology*. Vol. 92, No. 6 (May 1987):1404–34.

MOLNAR, STEPHEN. *Human Variation: Races, Types, and Ethnic Groups*. 2nd ed. Englewood Cliffs, NJ: Prentice Hall, 1983.

MOLOTCH, HARVEY. "The City as a Growth Machine." *American Journal of Sociology*. Vol. 82, No. 2 (September 1976):309–33.

MOLOTCH, HARVEY L., and DEIRDRE BODEN. "Talking Social Structure: Discourse, Domination, and the Watergate Hearings." *American Sociological Review*. Vol. 50, No. 3 (June 1985):273–88.

MONTAGU, ASHLEY. *The Nature of Human Aggression*. New York: Oxford University Press, 1976.

MOORE, JOAN, and HARRY PACHON. *Hispanics in the United States*. Englewood Cliffs, NJ: Prentice Hall, 1985.

MOORE, WILBERT E. "Modernization as Rationalization: Processes and Restraints." In Manning Nash, ed., *Essays on Economic Development and Cultural Change in Honor of Bert F. Hoselitz*. Chicago: University of Chicago Press, 1977:29–42.

_____. *World Modernization: The Limits of Convergence*. New York: Elsevier, 1979.

MORAN, JOHN S., S. O. ARAL, W. C. JENKINS, T. A. PETERMAN, and E. R. ALEXANDER. "The Impact of Sexually Transmitted Diseases on Minority Populations." *Public Health Reports*. Vol. 104, No. 6 (November–December 1989):560–65.

MOSKOS, CHARLES C. "Female GIs in the Field." *Society*. Vol. 22, No. 6 (September–October 1985):28–33.

MULLER, THOMAS, and THOMAS J. ESPENSHADE. *The Fourth Wave: California's Newest Immigrants*. Washington, DC: Urban Institute Press, 1985.

MUMFORD, LEWIS. *The City in History: Its Origins, Its Transformations, and Its Prospects*. New York: Harcourt, Brace & World, 1961.

MURDOCK, GEORGE P. "Comparative Data on the Division of Labor by Sex." *Social Forces*. Vol. 15, No. 4 (May 1937):551–53.

_____. "The Common Denominator of Cultures." In Ralph Linton, ed., *The Science of Man in World Crisis*. New York: Columbia University Press, 1945:123–42.

MURDOCK, GEORGE PETER. *Social Structure*. New York: Free Press, 1965; orig. 1949.

MURRAY, PAULI. *Proud Shoes: The History of an American Family*. New York: Harper & Row, 1978.

MYERS, SHEILA, and HAROLD G. GRASMICK. "The Social Rights and Responsibilities of Pregnant Women: An Application of Parsons' Sick Role Model." Paper presented to Southwestern Sociological Association, Little Rock, Arkansas, March 1989.

MYRDAL, GUNNAR. *An American Dilemma: The Negro Problem and Modern Democracy*. New York: Harper & Brothers, 1944.

NAJAFIZADEH, MEHRANGIZ, and LEWIS A. MENNERICK. "Sociology of Education or Sociology of Ethnocentrism: The Portrayal of Education in Introductory Sociology Textbooks." *Teaching Sociology*. Vol. 20, No. 3 (July 1992): 215–21.

Education Statistics: 1990. Washington, DC: U.S. Government Printing Office, 1991:244.

NATIONAL COMMISSION ON EXCELLENCE IN EDUCATION. *A Nation at Risk.* Washington, DC: U.S. Government Printing Office, 1983.

NATIONAL INSTITUTE OF DRUG ABUSE. U.S. Department of Health and Human Services. *National Household Survey on Drug Abuse: Main Findings 1990.* Rockville, MD: U.S. Government Printing Office, 1991.

NAVARRO, VICENTE. "The Industrialization of Fetishism or the Fetishism of Industrialization: A Critique of Ivan Illich." In Vicente Navarro, ed., *Health and Medical Care in the U.S.: A Critical Analysis.* Farmingdale, NY: Baywood, 1977:38–58.

NEIDERT, LISA J., and REYNOLDS FARLEY. "Assimilation in the United States: An Analysis of Ethnic and Generation Differences in Status and Achievement." *American Sociological Review.* Vol. 50, No. 6 (December 1985):840–50.

NELSON, HARRY, and ROBERT JERMAIN. *Introduction to Physical Anthropology.* 3rd ed. St. Paul, MN: West, 1985:22–24.

NEUHOUSER, KEVIN. "The Radicalization of the Brazilian Catholic Church in Comparative Perspective." *American Sociological Review.* Vol. 54, No. 2 (April 1989):233–44.

NEWMAN, JAMES L., and GORDON E. MATZKE. *Population: Patterns, Dynamics, and Prospects.* Englewood Cliffs, NJ: Prentice Hall, 1984.

NEWMAN, WILLIAM M. *American Pluralism: A Study of Minority Groups and Social Theory.* New York: Harper & Row, 1973.

NIEBUHR, R. GUSTAV. "California Top Court to Wrestle With 'Sin' vs. Tenants' Rights." *Wall Street Journal* (August 25, 1992):B1, B8.

NISBET, ROBERT. "Sociology as an Art Form." In *Tradition and Revolt: Historical and Sociological Essays.* New York: Vintage Books, 1970.

NISBET, ROBERT A. *The Sociological Tradition.* New York: Basic Books, 1966.

_____. *The Quest for Community.* New York: Oxford University Press, 1969.

N.O.R.C. *General Social Surveys, 1972–1991: Cumulative Codebook.* Chicago: National Opinion Research Center, 1991.

NUMBERS, RONALD L. "Creationism in 20th-Century America." *Science.* Vol. 218, No. 5 (November 1982):538–44.

NUNN, CLYDE Z., HARRY J. CROCKETT, JR., and J. ALLEN WILLIAMS, JR. *Tolerance for Nonconformity.* San Francisco: Jossey-Bass, 1978.

OAKES, JEANNIE. "Classroom Social Relationships: Exploring the Bowles and Gintis Hypothesis." *Sociology of Education.* Vol. 55, No. 4 (October 1982):197–212.

_____. *Keeping Track: How High Schools Structure Inequality.* New Haven, CT: Yale University Press, 1985.

O'DEA, THOMAS F., and JANET O'DEA AVIAD. *The Sociology of Religion.* 2nd ed. Englewood Cliffs, NJ: Prentice Hall, 1983.

OFFIR, CAROLE WADE. *Human Sexuality.* New York: Harcourt Brace Jovanovich, 1982.

OGBURN, WILLIAM F. *On Culture and Social Change.* Chicago: University of Chicago Press, 1964.

O'HARE, WILLIAM. "In the Black." *American Demographics.* Vol. 11, No. 11 (November 1989):25–29.

_____. "The Rise of Hispanic Affluence." *American Demographics.* Vol. 12, No. 8 (August 1990):40–43.

O'HARE, WILLIAM, and JAN LARSON. "Women in Business: Where, What, and Why." *American Demographics.* Vol. 13, No. 7 (July 1991):34–38.

OKIMOTO, DANIEL. "The Intolerance of Success." In Amy Tachiki et al., eds., *Roots: An Asian American Reader.* Los Angeles: UCLA Asian American Studies Center, 1971:14–19.

OLZAK, SUSAN. "Labor Unrest, Immigration, and Ethnic Conflict in Urban America, 1880–1914." *American Journal of Sociology.* Vol. 94, No. 6 (May 1989):1303–33.

O'REILLY, JANE. "Wife Beating: The Silent Crime." *Time.* Vol. 122, No. 10 (September 5, 1983):23–24, 26.

ORLANSKY, MICHAEL D., and WILLIAM L. HEWARD. *Voices: Interviews with Handicapped People.* Columbus, OH: Merrill, 1981:85, 92, 133–34, 172.

OSTLING, RICHARD N. "Jerry Falwell's Crusade." *Time.* Vol. 126, No. 9 (September 2, 1985):48–52, 55, 57.

_____. "Technology and the Womb." *Time.* Vol. 129, No. 12 (March 23, 1987):58–59.

OSTRANDER, SUSAN A. "Upper Class Women: The Feminine Side of Privilege." *Qualitative Sociology.* Vol. 3, No. 1 (Spring 1980):23–44.

_____. *Women of the Upper Class.* Philadelphia: Temple University Press, 1984.

OUCHI, WILLIAM. *Theory Z: How American Business Can Meet the Japanese Challenge.* Reading, MA: Addison-Wesley, 1981.

OWEN, DAVID. *None of the Above: Behind the Myth of Scholastic Aptitude.* Boston: Houghton Mifflin, 1985.

PARCEL, TOBY L., CHARLES W. MUELLER, and STEVEN CUVELIER. "Comparable Worth and Occupational Labor Market: Explanations of Occupational Earnings Differentials." Paper presented to the American Sociological Association, New York, 1986.

PARK, ROBERT E. *Race and Culture.* Glencoe, IL: Free Press, 1950.

PARKINSON, C. NORTHCOTE. *Parkinson's Law and Other Studies in Administration*. New York: Ballantine Books, 1957.

PARSONS, TALCOTT. *Essays in Sociological Theory*. New York: Free Press, 1954.

_____. *The Social System*. New York: Free Press, 1964; orig. 1951.

_____. *Societies: Evolutionary and Comparative Perspectives*. Englewood Cliffs, NJ: Prentice Hall, 1966.

PARSONS, TALCOTT, and ROBERT F. BALES, EDS. *Family, Socialization and Interaction Process*. New York: Free Press, 1955.

PATCHEN, MARTIN. "The Escalation of Inter-Nation Conflicts." *Sociological Focus*. Vol. 20, No. 2 (April 1987):95–110.

PATTERSON, GREGORY A. "Black Middle Class Debates Merits of Cities and Suburbs." *Wall Street Journal* (August 6, 1991):B1.

PAUL, ELLEN FRANKEL. "Bared Buttocks and Federal Cases." *Society*. Vol. 28. No. 4 (May–June, 1991):4–7.

PEAR, ROBERT. "Women Reduce Lag in Earnings, But Disparities With Men Remain." *New York Times* (September 4, 1987):1, 7.

PEAR, ROBERT, with ERIK ECKHOLM. "When Healers are Entrepreneurs: A Debate Over Costs and Ethics." *New York Times* (June 2, 1991):1, 17.

PENNINGS, JOHANNES M. "Organizational Birth Frequencies: An Empirical Investigation." *Administrative Science Quarterly*. Vol. 27, No. 1 (March 1982):120–44.

PEREZ, LISANDRO. "Cubans." In *Harvard Encyclopedia of American Ethnic Groups*. Cambridge, MA: Harvard University Press, 1980:256–60.

PERSELL, CAROLINE HODGES. *Education and Inequality: A Theoretical and Empirical Synthesis*. New York: Free Press, 1977.

PETER, LAURENCE J., and RAYMOND HULL. *The Peter Principle: Why Things Always Go Wrong*. New York: Morrow, 1969.

PETERS, THOMAS J., and ROBERT H. WATERMAN, JR. *In Search of Excellence: Lessons From America's Best-Run Companies*. New York: Warner Books, 1982.

PHYSICIANS' TASK FORCE ON HUNGER IN AMERICA. "Hunger Reaches Blue-Collar America." Report issued 1987.

PIOTROW, PHYLLIS T. *World Population: The Present and Future Crisis*. Headline Series 251 (October 1980). New York: Foreign Policy Association.

PIRANDELLO, LUIGI. "The Pleasure of Honesty." In *To Clothe the Naked and Two Other Plays*. New York: Dutton, 1962:143–98.

PIVEN, FRANCES FOX, and RICHARD A. CLOWARD. *Poor People's Movements: Why They Succeed, How They Fail*. New York: Pantheon Books, 1977.

_____. *Why Americans Don't Vote*. New York: Pantheon Books, 1988.

PLOMIN, ROBERT, and TERRYL T. FOCH. "A Twin Study of Objectively Assessed Personality in Childhood." *Journal of Personality and Social Psychology*. Vol. 39, No. 4 (October 1980):680–88.

POLENBERG, RICHARD. *One Nation Divisible: Class, Race, and Ethnicity in the United States Since 1938*. New York: Pelican Books, 1980.

POLSBY, NELSON W. "Three Problems in the Analysis of Community Power." *American Sociological Review*. Vol. 24, No. 6 (December 1959):796–803.

POMER, MARSHALL I. "Labor Market Structure, Intragenerational Mobility, and Discrimination: Black Male Advancement Out of Low-Paying Occupations, 1962–1973." *American Sociological Review*. Vol. 51, No. 5 (October 1986):650–59.

POPENOE, DAVID. "Family Decline in the Swedish Welfare State." *The Public Interest*. No. 102 (Winter 1991):65–77.

POPKIN, SUSAN J. "Welfare: Views from the Bottom." *Social Problems*. Vol. 17, No. 1 (February 1990):64–79.

PORTES, ALEJANDRO. "The Rise of Ethnicity: Determinants of Ethnic Perceptions Among Cuban Exiles in Miami." *American Sociological Review*. Vol. 49, No. 3 (June 1984):383–97.

PORTES, ALEJANDRO, and LEIF JENSEN. "The Enclave and the Entrants: Patterns of Ethnic Enterprise in Miami Before and After Mariel." *American Sociological Review*. Vol. 54, No. 6 (December 1989):929–49.

POWELL, CHRIS, and GEORGE E. C. PATON, EDS. *Humour in Society: Resistance and Control*. New York: St. Martin's Press, 1988.

PUTKA, GARY. "SAT To Become A Better Gauge." *Wall Street Journal* (November 1, 1990):B1.

QUEENAN, JOE. "The Many Paths to Riches." *Forbes*. Vol. 144, No. 9 (October 23, 1989):149.

QUINNEY, RICHARD. *Class, State and Crime: On the Theory and Practice of Criminal Justice*. New York: David McKay, 1977.

RADIN, NORMA. "Primary Caregiving and Role-Sharing Fathers." In Michael E. Lamb, ed., *Nontraditional Families: Parenting and Child Development*. Hillsdale, NJ: Lawrence Erlbaum, 1982:173–204.

RANDALL, VICKI. *Women and Politics*. London: Macmillan, 1982.

RAPHAEL, RAY. *The Men from the Boys: Rites of Passage in Male America*. Lincoln and London: University of Nebraska Press, 1988.

RECKLESS, WALTER C. "Containment Theory." In Marvin E. Wolfgang, Leonard Savitz, and Norman Johnstone, eds., *The Sociology of Crime and Delinquency.* 2nd ed. New York: Wiley, 1970:401–5.

RECKLESS, WALTER C., and SIMON DINITZ. "Pioneering with Self-Concept as a Vulnerability Factor in Delinquency." *Journal of Criminal Law, Criminology, and Police Science.* Vol. 58, No. 4 (December 1967):515–23.

REED, RODNEY J. "Administrator's Advice: Causes and Remedies of School Conflict and Violence." *National Association of Secondary School Principals Bulletin.* Vol. 67, No. 462 (April 1983):75–79.

REICH, ROBERT B. "As the World Turns." *The New Republic* (May 1, 1989):23, 26–28.

REID, SUE TITUS. *Crime and Criminology.* 3rd ed. New York: Holt, Rinehart & Winston, 1982; 6th ed. Fort Worth, TX: Holt, Rinehart & Winston, 1991.

REIMAN, JEFFREY H. *The Rich Get Richer and the Poor Get Prison: Ideology, Class, and Criminal Justice.* 2nd ed. New York: Wiley, 1984; 3rd ed., 1990.

REIMERS, CORDELIA W. "Sources of the Family Income Differentials Among Hispanics, Blacks, and White Non-Hispanics." *American Journal of Sociology.* Vol. 89, No. 4 (January 1984):889–903.

REMOFF, HEATHER TREXLER. *Sexual Choice: A Woman's Decision.* New York: Dutton/Lewis, 1984.

RICHARDSON, JAMES T. "Definitions of Cult: From Sociological-Technical to Popular Negative." Paper presented to the American Psychological Association, Boston, August, 1990.

RIDGEWAY, CECILIA, and DAVID DIEKEMA. "Dominance and Collective Hierarchy Formation in Male and Female Task Groups." *American Sociological Review.* Vol. 54, No. 1 (February 1989):79–93.

RIDGEWAY, CECILIA L. *The Dynamics of Small Groups.* New York: St. Martin's Press, 1983.

RIESMAN, DAVID. *The Lonely Crowd: A Study of the Changing American Character.* New Haven, CT: Yale University Press, 1970; orig. 1950.

RILEY, MATILDA WHITE, ANNE FONER, and JOAN WARING. "Sociology of Age." In Neil J. Smelser, ed., *Handbook of Sociology.* Newbury Park, CA: Sage, 1988:243–90.

RITZER, GEORGE. *Man and His Work: Conflict and Change.* New York: Appleton-Century-Crofts, 1972.

ROBERTS, J. DEOTIS. *Roots of a Black Future: Family and Church.* Philadelphia: Westminster Press, 1980.

ROBINSON, VERA M. "Humor and Health." In Paul E. McGhee and Jeffrey H. Goldstein, eds., *Handbook of Humor Research, Vol II, Applied Studies.* New York: Springer-Verlag, 1983:109–28.

ROESCH, ROBERTA. "Violent Families." *Parents.* Vol. 59, No. 9 (September 1984):74–76, 150–52.

ROETHLISBERGER, F. J., and WILLIAM J. DICKSON. *Management and the Worker.* Cambridge, MA: Harvard University Press, 1939.

ROHLEN, THOMAS P. *Japan's High Schools.* Berkeley: University of California Press, 1983.

ROOF, WADE CLARK. "Socioeconomic Differentials Among White Socioreligious Groups in the United States." *Social Forces.* Vol. 58, No. 1 (September 1979):280–89.

_____. "Unresolved Issues in the Study of Religion and the National Elite: Response to Greeley." *Social Forces.* Vol. 59, No. 3 (March 1981):831–36.

ROOF, WADE CLARK, and WILLIAM McKINNEY. *American Mainline Religion: Its Changing Shape and Future.* New Brunswick, NJ: Rutgers University Press, 1987.

ROOS, PATRICIA. "Marriage and Women's Occupational Attainment in Cross-Cultural Perspective." *American Sociological Review.* Vol. 48, No. 6 (December 1983):852–64.

ROSEN, ELLEN ISRAEL. *Bitter Choices: Blue-Collar Women In and Out of Work.* Chicago: University of Chicago Press, 1987.

ROSENTHAL, JACK. "The Rapid Growth of Suburban Employment." In Lois H. Masotti and Jeffrey K. Hadden, eds., *Suburbia in Transition.* New York: New York Times Books, 1974:95–100.

ROSKIN, MICHAEL G. *Countries and Concepts: An Introduction to Comparative Politics.* Englewood Cliffs, NJ: Prentice Hall, 1982.

ROSS, SUSAN. "Education: A Step Ladder to Mobility." *Popline.* Vol. 7, No. 7 (July 1985):1–2.

ROSSI, ALICE S. "Gender and Parenthood." In Alice S. Rossi, ed., *Gender and the Life Course.* New York: Aldine, 1985:161–91.

ROSSIDES, DANIEL W. *Social Stratification: The American Class System in Comparative Perspective.* Englewood Cliffs, NJ: Prentice Hall, 1990.

ROSTOW, WALT W. *The World Economy: History and Prospect.* Austin: University of Texas Press, 1978.

ROWE, DAVID C. "Biometrical Genetic Models of Self-Reported Delinquent Behavior: A Twin Study." *Behavior Genetics.* Vol. 13, No. 5 (1983):473–89.

ROWE, DAVID C., and D. WAYNE OSGOOD. "Heredity and Sociological Theories of Delinquency: A Reconsideration." *American Sociological Review.* Vol. 49, No. 4 (August 1984):526–40.

RUBIN, LILLIAN BRESLOW. *Worlds of Pain: Life in the Working-Class Family.* New York: Basic Books, 1976.

RUBINSON, RICHARD. "Class Formation, Politics, and Institutions: Schooling in the United States." *American Journal of Sociology.* Vol. 92, No. 3 (November 1986):519–48.

RUDOLPH, BARBARA. "Tobacco Takes a New Road." *Time.* Vol. 126, No. 20 (November 18, 1985):70–71.

RUSSELL, DIANA E. H. *Rape in Marriage.* New York: Macmillan, 1982.

RYAN, WILLIAM. *Blaming the Victim.* Rev. ed. New York: Vintage Books, 1976.

RYTINA, JOAN HUBER, WILLIAM H. FORM, and JOHN PEASE. "Income and Stratification Ideology: Beliefs About the American Opportunity Structure." *American Journal of Sociology.* Vol. 75, No. 4 (January 1970):703–16.

SABATO, LARRY J. *PAC Power: Inside the World of Political Action Committees.* New York: Norton, 1984.

SALAS, RAFAEL M. "The State of World Population 1985: Population and Women." *Popline.* Vol. 7, No. 7 (July 1985):4–5.

SALE, KIRKPATRICK. *The Conquest of Paradise: Christopher Columbus and the Columbian Legacy.* New York: Knopf, 1990.

SALHOLZ, ELOISE. "The Future of Gay America." *Newsweek* (March 12, 1990):20–25.

SALTMAN, JULIET. "Maintaining Racially Diverse Neighborhoods." *Urban Affairs Quarterly.* Vol. 26, No. 3 (March 1991):416–41.

SAMPSON, ANTHONY. *The Changing Anatomy of Britain.* New York: Random House, 1982.

SAMPSON, ROBERT J. "Urban Black Violence: The Effects of Male Joblessness and Family Disruption." *American Journal of Sociology.* Vol. 93, No. 2 (September 1987):348–82.

SAMPSON, ROBERT J., and JOHN H. LAUB. "Crime and Deviance Over the Life Course: The Salience of Adult Social Bonds." *American Sociological Review.* Vol. 55, No. 5 (October 1990):609–27.

SAPIR, EDWARD. "The Status of Linguistics as a Science." *Language.* Vol. 5 (1929):207–14.

————. *Selected Writings of Edward Sapir in Language, Culture, and Personality.* David G. Mandelbaum, ed. Berkeley: University of California Press, 1949.

SCAFF, LAWRENCE A. "Max Weber and Robert Michels." *American Journal of Sociology.* Vol. 86, No. 6 (May 1981):1269–86.

SCHEFF, THOMAS J. *Being Mentally Ill: A Sociological Theory.* 2nd ed. New York: Aldine, 1984.

SCHLESINGER, ARTHUR. "The City in American Civilization." In A. B. Callow, Jr., ed., *American Urban History.* New York: Oxford University Press, 1969:25–41.

SCHLESINGER, ARTHUR, JR. "The Cult of Ethnicity: Good and Bad." *Time.* Vol. 137, No. 27 (July 8, 1991):21.

SCHOOLER, CARMI, JOANNE MILLER, KAREN A. MILLER, and CAROL N. RICHTAND. "Work for the Household: Its Nature and Consequences for Husbands and Wives." *American Journal of Sociology.* Vol. 90, No. 1 (July 1984):97–124.

SCHREINER, TIM. "Your Cost to Bring Up Baby: $142,700." *USA Today* (October 19, 1984):1D.

SCHUR, EDWIN M. *Labeling Women Deviant: Gender, Stigma, and Social Control.* New York: Random House, 1984.

SCHUTT, RUSSELL K. "Objectivity versus Outrage." *Society.* Vol. 26, No. 4 (May–June 1989):14–16.

SCHWARTZ, FELICE N. "Management, Women, and the New Facts of Life." *Harvard Business Review.* Vol. 89, No. 1 (January–February 1989):65–76.

SCHWARTZ, JOE. "Rising Status." *American Demographics.* Vol. 11, No. 1 (January 1989):10.

SCHWARTZ, MARTIN D. "Gender and Injury in Spousal Assault." *Sociological Focus.* Vol. 20, No. 1 (January 1987):61–75.

SCHWARTZ-NOBEL, LORETTA. *Starving in the Shadow of Plenty.* New York: McGraw-Hill, 1981.

SCOTT, JOHN, and CATHERINE GRIFF. *Directors of Industry: The British Corporate Network, 1904–1976.* New York: Blackwell, 1985.

SCOTT, W. RICHARD. *Organizations: Rational, Natural, and Open Systems.* Englewood Cliffs, NJ: Prentice Hall, 1981.

SELIMUDDIN, ABU K. "The Selling of America." *USA Today.* Vol. 117, No. 2525 (March 1989):12–14.

SELLIN, THORSTEN. *The Penalty of Death.* Beverly Hills, CA: Sage, 1980.

SENGOKU, TAMOTSU. *Willing Workers: The Work Ethics in Japan, England, and the United States.* Westport, CT: Quorum Books, 1985.

SENNETT, RICHARD, and JONATHAN COBB. *The Hidden Injuries of Class.* New York: Vintage Books, 1973.

SHANAS, ETHEL. "Social Myth as Hypothesis: The Case of the Family Relations of Old People." *The Gerontologist.* Vol. 19, No. 1 (February 1979):3–9.

SHAPIRO, NINA. "Botswana Test Case." *Chicago Tribune* (September 15, 1991):1.

SHAWCROSS, WILLIAM. *Sideshow: Kissinger, Nixon and the Destruction of Cambodia.* New York: Pocket Books, 1979.

SHEEHAN, TOM. "Senior Esteem as a Factor in Socioeconomic Complexity." *The Gerontologist.* Vol. 16, No. 5 (October 1976):433–40.

SHELDON, WILLIAM H., EMIL M. HARTL, and EUGENE McDERMOTT. *Varieties of Delinquent Youth.* New York: Harper & Brothers, 1949.

SHEPHARD, ROY J. *The Risks of Passive Smoking.* London: Croom Helm, 1982.

SHERRID, PAMELA. "Hot Times in the City of London." *U.S. News & World Report* (October 27, 1986):45–46.

SHEVKY, ESHREF, and WENDELL BELL. *Social Area Analysis.* Stanford, CA: Stanford University Press, 1955.

SHIPLEY, JOSEPH T. *Dictionary of Word Origins.* Totowa, NJ: Roman & Allanheld, 1985.

SIDEL, RUTH, and VICTOR W. SIDEL. *The Health Care of China*. Boston: Beacon Press, 1982b.

_____. *A Healthy State: An International Perspective on the Crisis in United States Medical Care*. Rev. ed. New York: Pantheon Books, 1982a.

SILVERSTEIN, MICHAEL. In Jon Snodgrass, ed., *A Book of Readings for Men Against Sexism*. Albion, CA: Times Change Press, 1977:178–79.

SIMMEL, GEORG. *The Sociology of Georg Simmel*. Kurt Wolff, ed. New York: Free Press, 1950:118–69.

_____. "The Mental Life of the Metropolis." In Kurt Wolff, ed., *The Sociology of Georg Simmel*. New York: Free Press, 1964:409–24; orig. 1905.

SIMON, DAVID R., and D. STANLEY EITZEN. *Elite Deviance*. 3rd ed. Needham Heights, MA: Allyn and Bacon, 1990.

SIMONS, CAROL. "Japan's *Kyoiku* Mamas." In John J. Macionis and Nijole V. Benokraitis, eds., *Seeing Ourselves: Classic, Contemporary, and Cross-Cultural Readings in Sociology*. Englewood Cliffs, NJ: Prentice Hall, 1989:281–86.

SIMONS, MARLISE. "The Amazon's Savvy Indians." *The New York Times Magazine* (February 26, 1990):36–37, 48–52. Copyright © 1989 by the New York Times Company.

SINGER, DOROTHY. "A Time to Reexamine the Role of Television in Our Lives." *American Psychologist*. Vol. 38, No. 7 (July 1983):815–16.

SINGER, JEROME L., and DOROTHY G. SINGER. "Psychologists Look at Television: Cognitive, Developmental, Personality, and Social Policy Implications." *American Psychologist*. Vol. 38, No. 7 (July 1983):826–34.

SIVARD, RUTH LEGER. *World Military and Social Expenditures, 1987–88*. 12th ed. Washington, DC: World Priorities, 1988.

SIZER, THEODORE R. *Horace's Compromise: The Dilemma of the American High School*. Boston: Houghton Mifflin, 1984.

SJOBERG, GIDEON. *The Preindustrial City*. New York: Free Press, 1965.

SKOCPOL, THEDA. *States and Social Revolutions: A Comparative Analysis of France, Russia, and China*. Cambridge: Cambridge University Press, 1979.

SKOLNICK, ARLENE. *The Psychology of Human Development*. New York: Harcourt Brace Jovanovich, 1986.

SKOLNICK, ARLENE S. *The Intimate Environment: Exploring Marriage and the Family*. 5th ed. New York: HarperCollins, 1992.

SLATER, PHILIP. *The Pursuit of Loneliness*. Boston: Beacon Press, 1976.

SLATER, PHILIP E. "Contrasting Correlates of Group Size." *Sociometry*. Vol. 21, No. 2 (June 1958):129–39.

SMITH, ADAM. *An Inquiry into the Nature and Causes of the Wealth of Nations*. New York: Modern Library, 1937; orig. 1776.

SMITH, DOUGLAS A. "Police Response to Interpersonal Violence: Defining the Parameters of Legal Control." *Social Forces*. Vol. 65, No. 3 (March 1987):767–82.

SMITH, DOUGLAS A., and PATRICK R. GARTIN. "Specifying Specific Deterrence: The Influence of Arrest on Future Criminal Activity." *American Sociological Review*. Vol. 54, No. 1 (February 1989):94–105.

SMITH, DOUGLAS A., and CHRISTY A. VISHER. "Street-Level Justice: Situational Determinants of Police Arrest Decisions." *Social Problems*. Vol. 29, No. 2 (December 1981):167–77.

SMITH, ROBERT ELLIS. *Privacy: How to Protect What's Left of It*. Garden City, NY: Anchor/Doubleday, 1979.

SMITH-LOVIN, LYNN, and CHARLES BRODY. "Interruptions in Group Discussions: The Effects of Gender and Group Composition." *American Journal of Sociology*. Vol. 54, No. 3 (June 1989):424–35.

SNELL, MARILYN BERLIN. "The Purge of Nurture." *New Perspectives Quarterly*. Vol. 7, No. 1 (Winter 1990):1–2.

SNOW, DAVID A., E. BURKE ROCHFORD, JR., STEVEN K. WORDEN, and ROBERT D. BENFORD. "Frame Alignment Processes, Micromobilization, and Movement Participation." *American Sociological Review*. Vol. 51, No. 4 (August 1986):464–81.

SOUTH, SCOTT J., and STEVEN F. MESSNER. "Structural Determinants of Intergroup Association: Interracial Marriage and Crime." *American Journal of Sociology*. Vol. 91, No. 6 (May 1986):1409–30.

SOWELL, THOMAS. *Ethnic America*. New York: Basic Books, 1981.

SPATES, JAMES L. "Sociological Overview." In Alan Milberg, ed., *Street Games*. New York: McGraw-Hill, 1976a:286–90.

_____. "Counterculture and Dominant Culture Values: A Cross-National Analysis of the Underground Press and Dominant Culture Magazines." *American Sociological Review*. Vol. 41, No. 5 (October 1976b):868–83.

_____. "The Sociology of Values." In Ralph Turner, ed., *Annual Review of Sociology*. Vol. 9. Palo Alto, CA: Annual Reviews, 1983:27–49.

SPATES, JAMES L., and JOHN J. MACIONIS. *The Sociology of Cities*. 2nd ed. Belmont, CA: Wadsworth, 1987.

SPATES, JAMES L., and H. WESLEY PERKINS. "American and English Student Values." *Comparative Social Research*. Vol. 5. Greenwich, CT: JAI Press, 1982:245–68.

SPECTOR, LEONARD S. "Nuclear Proliferation Today." In William M. Evan and Stephen Hilgartner, eds., *The Arms Race and Nuclear War*. Englewood Cliffs, NJ: Prentice Hall, 1988:25–29.

SPEER, JAMES A. "The New Christian Right and Its Parent Company: A Study in Political Contrasts." In David G.

Bromley and Anson Shupe, eds., *New Christian Politics.* Macon, GA: Mercer University Press, 1984:19–40.

SPEIZER, JEANNE J. "Education." In Barbara Haber, ed., *The Women's Annual 1982–1983.* Boston: G. K. Hall, 1983:29–54.

SPENCER, GARY. *Projections of the Population of the United States, by Age, Sex, and Race: 1988 to 2080.* Washington, DC: U.S. Government Printing Office, 1989.

SPITZER, STEVEN. "Toward a Marxian Theory of Deviance." In Delos H. Kelly, ed., *Criminal Behavior: Readings in Criminology.* New York: St. Martin's Press, 1980:175–91.

SRINIVAS, M. N. *Social Change in Modern India.* Berkeley: University of California Press, 1971.

STACEY, JUDITH. *Patriarchy and Socialist Revolution in China.* Berkeley: University of California Press, 1983.

STACEY, JUDITH. *Brave New Families: Stories of Domestic Upheaval in Late Twentieth-Century America.* New York: Basic Books, 1990.

STACK, CAROL B. *All Our Kin: Strategies for Survival in a Black Community.* New York: Harper & Row, 1975.

STAHURA, JOHN M. "Suburban Development, Black Suburbanization and the Black Civil Rights Movement Since World War II." *American Sociological Review.* Vol. 51, No. 1 (February 1986):131–44.

STAPLES, BRENT. "Where Are the Black Fans?" *New York Times Magazine* (May 17, 1987):26–34, 36.

STARK, RODNEY. "The Rise of a New World Faith." *Review of Religious Research.* Vol. 26, No. 1 (September 1984):18–27.

———. *Sociology.* Belmont, CA: Wadsworth, 1985.

STARK, RODNEY, and WILLIAM SIMS BAINBRIDGE. "Of Churches, Sects, and Cults: Preliminary Concepts for a Theory of Religious Movements." *Journal for the Scientific Study of Religion.* Vol. 18, No. 2 (June 1979):117–31.

———. "Secularization and Cult Formation in the Jazz Age." *Journal for the Scientific Study of Religion.* Vol. 20, No. 4 (December 1981):360–73.

STARK, RODNEY, and CHARLES Y. GLOCK. *American Piety: The Nature of Religious Commitment.* Berkeley: University of California Press, 1968.

STARR, PAUL. *The Social Transformation of American Medicine.* New York: Basic Books, 1982.

Statistics of Income Bulletin. Vol. 11, No. 3 (Winter 1991–92).

STAVRIANOS, L. S. *A Global History: The Human Heritage.* 3rd ed. Englewood Cliffs, NJ: Prentice Hall, 1983.

STEELE, SHELBY. *The Content of Our Character: A New Vision of Race in America.* New York: St. Martin's Press, 1990.

STEIN, MARUICE R. *The Eclipse of Community: An Interpreta-*

tion of American Studies. Princeton, NJ: Princeton University Press, 1972.

STEPHENS, JOHN D. *The Transition from Capitalism to Socialism.* Urbana: University of Illinois Press, 1986.

STERNLIEB, GEORGE, and JAMES W. HUGHES. "The Uncertain Future of the Central City." *Urban Affairs Quarterly.* Vol. 18, No. 4 (June 1983):455–72.

STEVENS, GILLIAN, and GRAY SWICEGOOD. "The Linguistic Context of Ethnic Endogamy." *American Sociological Review.* Vol. 52, No. 1 (February 1987):73–82.

STEVENS, ROSEMARY. *American Medicine and the Public Interest.* New Haven, CT: Yale University Press, 1971.

STIEHM, JUDITH HICKS. *Arms and the Enlisted Woman.* Philadelphia: Temple University Press, 1989.

STONE, LAWRENCE. *The Family, Sex and Marriage in England 1500–1800.* New York: Harper & Row, 1977.

STONE, ROBYN. *The Feminization of Poverty and Older Women.* Washington, DC: U.S. Department of Health and Human Services, 1986.

STOUFFER, SAMUEL A., ET AL. *The American Soldier: Adjustment During Army Life.* Princeton, NJ: Princeton University Press, 1949.

STRAUS, MURRAY A., and RICHARD J. GELLES. "Societal Change and Change in Family Violence from 1975 to 1985 as Revealed by Two National Surveys." *Journal of Marriage and the Family.* Vol. 48, No. 4 (August 1986):465–79.

SUDNOW, DAVID N. *Passing On: The Social Organization of Dying.* Englewood Cliffs, NJ: Prentice Hall, 1967.

SUMNER, WILLIAM GRAHAM. *Folkways.* New York: Dover, 1959; orig. 1906.

SUNG, BETTY LEE. *Mountains of Gold: The Story of the Chinese in America.* New York: Macmillan, 1967.

SURO, ROBERTO. "Hispanics in Despair." *New York Times: Education Life* (November 4, 1990):section 4a, page 25.

SUTHERLAND, EDWIN H. "White Collar Criminality." *American Sociological Review.* Vol. 5, No. 1 (February 1940):1–12.

SUTHERLAND, EDWIN H., and DONALD R. CRESSEY. *Criminology.* 10th ed. Philadelphia: Lippincott, 1978.

SUZUKI, DAVID, and PETER KNUDTSON. *Genethics: The Clash Between the New Genetics and Human Values.* Cambridge, MA: Harvard University Press, 1989.

SWARTZ, STEVE. "Why Michael Milken Stands to Qualify for Guinness Book." *Wall Street Journal.* Vol. LXX, No. 117 (March 31, 1989):1, 4.

SYZMANSKI, ALBERT. *Class Structure: A Critical Perspective.* New York: Praeger, 1983.

SZASZ, THOMAS S. *The Manufacturer of Madness: A Comparative Study of the Inquisition and the Mental Health Movement.* New York: Dell, 1961.

———. *The Myth of Mental Illness: Foundations of a Theory*

of Personal Conduct. New York: Harper & Row, 1970; orig. 1961.

TAJFEL, HENRI. "Social Psychology of Intergroup Relations." Annual Review of Psychology. Palo Alto, CA: Annual Reviews, 1982:1–39.

TANNENBAUM, FRANK. Slave and Citizen: The Negro in the Americas. New York: Vintage Books, 1946.

TAVRIS, CAROL, and SUSAN SADD. The Redbook Report on Female Sexuality. New York: Delacorte Press, 1977.

TAYLOR, JOHN. "Don't Blame Me: The New Culture of Victimization." New York Magazine (June 3, 1991):26–34.

THEEN, ROLF H. W. "Party and Bureaucracy." In Erik P. Hoffmann and Robbin F. Laird, eds., The Soviet Polity in the Modern Era. New York: Aldine, 1984:131–65.

THOITS, PEGGY A. "Self-labeling Processes in Mental Illness: The Role of Emotional Deviance." American Journal of Sociology. Vol. 91, No. 2 (September 1985):221–49.

THOMAS, PIRI. Down These Mean Streets. New York: Signet, 1967.

THOMAS, W. I. "The Relation of Research to the Social Process." In Morris Janowitz, ed., W. I. Thomas on Social Organization and Social Personality. Chicago: University of Chicago Press, 1966:289–305; orig. 1931.

THORNBERRY, TERRANCE, and MARGARET FARNSWORTH. "Social Correlates of Criminal Involvement: Further Evidence on the Relationship Between Social Status and Criminal Behavior." American Sociological Review. Vol 47, No. 4 (August 1982):505–18.

THORNE, BARRIE, CHERIS KRAMARAE, and NANCY HENLEY, EDS. Language, Gender and Society. Rowley, MA: Newbury House, 1983.

THORNTON, ARLAND. "Changing Attitudes Toward Separation and Divorce: Causes and Consequences." American Journal of Sociology. Vol. 90, No. 4 (January 1985):856–72.

THUROW, LESTER C. "A Surge in Inequality." Scientific American. Vol. 256, No. 5 (May 1987):30–37.

TIEN, H. YUAN. "Second Thoughts on the Second Child." Population Today. Vol. 17, No. 4 (April 1989):6–9.

TIENDA, MARTA, and DING-TZANN LII. "Minority Concentration and Earnings Inequality: Blacks, Hispanics, and Asians Compared." American Journal of Sociology. Vol. 93, No. 1 (July 1987):141–65.

TIGER, LIONEL, and JOSEPH SHEPHER. Women in the Kibbutz. New York: Harcourt Brace Jovanovich, 1975.

TILLY, CHARLES. "Does Modernization Breed Revolution?" In Jack A. Goldstone, ed., Revolutions: Theoretical, Comparative, and Historical Studies. New York: Harcourt Brace Jovanovich, 1986:47–57.

TITTLE, CHARLES R., and WAYNE J. VILLEMEZ. "Social Class and Criminality." Social Forces. Vol. 56, No. 22 (December 1977):474–502.

TITTLE, CHARLES R., WAYNE J. VILLEMEZ, and DOUGLAS A. SMITH. "The Myth of Social Class and Criminality: An Empirical Assessment of the Empirical Evidence." American Sociological Review. Vol. 43, No. 5 (October 1978):643–56.

TOBIN, GARY. "Suburbanization and the Development of Motor Transportation: Transportation Technology and the Suburbanization Process." In Barry Schwartz, ed., The Changing Face of the Suburbs. Chicago: University of Chicago Press, 1976.

TOCH, THOMAS. "The Exodus." U.S. News and World Report. Vol. 111, No. 24 (December 9, 1991):68–77.

TOCQUEVILLE, ALEXIS DE. The Old Regime and the French Revolution. Stuart Gilbert, trans. Garden City, NY: Doubleday Anchor Books, 1955; orig. 1856.

TOENNIES, FERDINAND. Community and Society (Gemeinschaft und Gesellschaft). New York: Harper & Row, 1963; orig. 1887.

TOFANI, LORETTA. "AIDS Ravages a Continent, and Sweeps a Family." Philadelphia Inquirer (March 24, 1991):1, 15-A.

TOFFLER, ALVIN. The Third Wave. New York: Bantam Books, 1981.

TROELTSCH, ERNST. The Social Teaching of the Christian Churches. New York: Macmillan, 1931.

TROIDEN, RICHARD R. Gay and Lesbian Identity: A Sociological Analysis. Dix Hills, NY: General Hall, 1988.

TUMIN, MELVIN M. "Some Principles of Stratification: A Critical Analysis." American Sociological Review. Vol. 18, No. 4 (August 1953):387–94.

————. Social Stratification: The Forms and Functions of Inequality. 2nd ed. Englewood Cliffs, NJ: Prentice Hall, 1985.

TYGIEL, JULES. Baseball's Great Experiment: Jackie Robinson and His Legacy. New York: Oxford University Press, 1983.

TYLER, S. LYMAN. A History of Indian Policy. Washington, DC: U.S. Department of the Interior, Bureau of Indian Affairs, 1973.

UNITED NATIONS. World Economic Survey 1988: Current Trends and Policies in the World Economy. New York: United Nations, 1988.

UNITED NATIONS DEVELOPMENT PROGRAMME. Human Development Report 1991. New York: Oxford University Press, 1991.

UNNEVER, JAMES D., CHARLES E. FRAZIER, and JOHN C. HENRETTA. "Race Differences in Criminal Sentencing." The Sociological Quarterly. Vol. 21, No. 2 (Spring 1980):197–205.

UNRUH, JOHN D., JR. The Plains Across. Urbana: University of Illinois Press, 1979.

U.S. BUREAU OF THE CENSUS. Statistical Abstract of the United States: 1970. 91st ed. Washington, DC: U.S. Government Printing Office, 1970.

U.S. BUREAU OF THE CENSUS. Household and Family Characteristics: *March 1990 and 1989*. Current Population Reports, Series P-20, No. 447. Washington, DC: U.S. Government Printing Office, 1990.

U.S. Bureau of the Census. "Get the Scoop on 1990 Metro Area Population." *Census and You*. Vol. 29, No. 9 (September 1991). Washington, DC: U.S. Government Printing Office, 1991.

U.S. Bureau of the Census. *Money Income of Households, Families, and Persons in the United States: 1990*. Current Population Reports, Series P-60, No. 174. Washington, DC: U.S. Government Printing Office, 1991.

U.S. Bureau of the Census. *Statistical Abstract of the United States: 1991*. 111th ed. Washington, DC: U.S. Government Printing Office, 1991.

U.S. Bureau of the Census. Current Population Survey. Unpublished data for March 1991. Supplied by the bureau, 1992.

U.S. Bureau of the Census. *Money Income of Households, Families, and Persons in the United States: 1991*. Current Population Reports, Series P-60, No. 174. Washington, DC: U.S. Government Printing Office, 1992.

U.S. Bureau of the Census. *Statistical Abstract of the United States: 1992*. 112th ed. Washington, DC: U.S. Government Printing Office, 1992.

U.S. Bureau of Justice Statistics. *Recidivism of Prisoners Released in 1983*. Washington, DC: U.S. Government Printing Office, 1989.

U.S. Bureau of Justice Statistics. *Sourcebook of Criminal Justice Statistics 1989*. Timothy J. Flanagan and Kathleen Maguire, eds. Washington, DC: U.S. Government Printing Office, 1990.

U.S. Bureau of Labor Statistics. *Employment and Earnings*. Vol. 38, No. 9 (September). Washington, DC: U.S. Government Printing Office, 1991.

U.S. Bureau of Labor Statistics. *Employment and Earnings*. Vol. 39, No. 1 (January). Washington, DC: U.S. Government Printing Office, 1992.

U.S. Department of Health and Human Services. *Alcohol, Drug Abuse, and Mental Health News*. Vol. 15, No. 8 (October 1989).

U.S. Department of Justice. *Criminal Victimization in the United States, 1987*. Washington, DC: U.S. Government Printing Office, 1987.

U.S. Department of Labor. Bureau of Labor Statistics. *Employment and Earnings*. Vol. 38, No. 9 (September). Washington, DC: U.S. Government Printing Office, 1991.

U.S. Department of Labor. Bureau of Labor Statistics. *Employment and Earnings*. Vol. 39, No. 1 (January). Washington, DC: U.S. Government Printing Office, 1992.

Useem, Michael. "Corporations and the Corporate Elite." In Alex Inkeles et al., eds., *Annual Review of Sociology*. Vol. 6. Palo Alto, CA: Annual Reviews, 1980:41–77.

U.S. Federal Bureau of Investigation. *Crime in the United States 1991*. Washington, DC: U.S. Government Printing Office, 1992.

U.S. Federal Election Commission. *Federal Election Commission Record*. Vol. 15, No. 8 (August 1989).

U.S. House of Representatives, Select Committee on Children, Youth, and Families. *Abused Children in America: Victims of Neglect*. Washington, DC: U.S. Government Printing Office, 1987.

U.S. House of Representatives. *1991 Green Book*. Washington, DC: U.S. Government Printing Office, 1991.

U.S. National Center for Health Statistics. *Current Estimates from the National Health Survey, 1989*. Washington, DC: U.S. Government Printing Office, 1990.

U.S. National Center for Health Statistics. *Vital Statistics of the United States, 1988, Vol. 1: Natality*. Washington DC: U.S. Government Printing Office, 1990.

Van De Kaa, Dirk J. "Europe's Second Demographic Transition." *Population Bulletin*. Vol. 42, No. 1 (March 1987). Washington, DC: Population Reference Bureau.

Van Den Haag, Ernest, and John P. Conrad. *The Death Penalty: A Debate*. New York: Plenum Press, 1983.

Vatz, Richard E., and Lee S. Weinberg. *Thomas Szasz: Primary Values and Major Contentions*. Buffalo, NY: Prometheus Books, 1983.

Vaughan, Mary Kay. "Multinational Corporations: The World as a Company Town." In Ahamed Idris-Soven et al., eds., *The World as a Company Town: Multinational Corporations and Social Change*. The Hague: Mouton, 1978:15–35.

Vayda, Eugene, and Raisa B. Deber. "The Canadian Health Care System: An Overview." *Social Science and Medicine*. Vol. 18, No. 3 (1984):191–97.

Viguerie, Richard A. *The New Right: We're Ready to Lead*. Falls Church, VA: Viguerie, 1981.

Vines, Gail. "Whose Baby Is It Anyway?" *New Scientist*. No. 1515 (July 3, 1986):26–27.

Vinovskis, Maris A. "Have Social Historians Lost the Civil War? Some Preliminary Demographic Speculations." *Journal of American History*. Vol. 76, No. 1 (June 1989):34–58.

Vogel, Ezra F. *Japan as Number One: Lessons for America*. Cambridge, MA: Harvard University Press, 1979.

Vogel, Lise. *Marxism and the Oppression of Women: Toward a Unitary Theory*. New Brunswick, NJ: Rutgers University Press, 1983.

Vold, George B., and Thomas J. Bernard. *Theoretical Criminology*. 3rd ed. New York: Oxford University Press, 1986.

Von Hirsh, Andrew. *Past or Future Crimes: Deservedness and Dangerousness in the Sentencing of Criminals*. New Brunswick, NJ: Rutgers University Press, 1986.

WALL, THOMAS F. *Medical Ethics: Basic Moral Issues.* Washington, DC: University Press of America, 1980.

WALLERSTEIN, IMMANUEL. *The Modern World-System: Capitalist Agriculture and the Origins of the European World-Economy in the Sixteenth Century.* New York: Academic Press, 1974.

_____. *The Capitalist World-Economy.* New York: Cambridge University Press, 1979.

_____. "Crises: The World Economy, the Movements, and the Ideologies." In Albert Bergesen, ed., *Crises in the World-System.* Beverly Hills, CA: Sage, 1983:21–36.

_____. *The Politics of the World Economy: The States, the Movements, and the Civilizations.* Cambridge: Cambridge University Press, 1984.

WALLERSTEIN, JUDITH S., and SANDRA BLAKESLEE. *Second Chances: Men, Women, and Children a Decade after Divorce.* New York: Ticknor & Fields, 1989.

WALLIS, CLAUDIA. "Stress: Can We Cope?" *Time.* Vol. 121, No. 23 (June 6, 1983):48–54.

_____. "Children Having Children." *Time.* Vol. 126, No. 23 (December 9, 1985):78–82, 84, 87, 89–90.

WARNER, SAM BASS, JR. *Streetcar Suburbs.* Cambridge, MA: Harvard University and M.I.T. Presses, 1962.

WARNER, W. LLOYD, and J. O. LOW. *The Social System of the Modern Factory.* Yankee City Series, Vol. 4. New Haven, CT: Yale University Press, 1947.

WARNER, W. LLOYD, and PAUL S. LUNT. *The Social Life of a Modern Community.* New Haven, CT: Yale University Press, 1941.

WAXMAN, CHAIM I. *The Stigma of Poverty: A Critique of Poverty Theories and Policies.* 2nd ed. New York: Pergamon Press, 1983.

WEBER, ADNA FERRIN. *The Growth of Cities.* New York: Columbia University Press, 1963; orig. 1899.

WEBER, MAX. *The Protestant Ethic and the Spirit of Capitalism.* New York: Scribner's, 1958; orig. 1904–1905.

_____. *Economy and Society.* G. Roth and C. Wittich, eds. Berkeley: University of California Press, 1978.

WEINBERG, GEORGE. *Society and the Healthy Homosexual.* Garden City, NY: Anchor Books, 1973.

WEISNER, THOMAS S., and BERNICE T. EIDUSON. "The Children of the 60s as Parents." *Psychology Today* (January 1986):60–66.

WEITZMAN, LENORE J. *The Divorce Revolution: The Unexpected Social and Economic Consequences for Women and Children in America.* New York: Free Press, 1985.

WEITZMAN, LENORE J., DEBORAH EIFLER, ELIZABETH HODAKA, and CATHERINE ROSS. "Sex-Role Socialization in Picture Books for Preschool Children." *American Journal of Sociology.* Vol. 77, No. 6 (May 1972):1125–50.

WELLFORD, CHARLES. "Labeling Theory and Criminology: An Assessment." In Delos H. Kelly, ed., *Criminal Behavior: Readings in Criminology.* New York: St. Martin's Press, 1980:234–47.

WELLMAN, BARRY. "The Community Question: Intimate Networks of East Yorkers." *American Journal of Sociology.* Vol. 84, No. 5 (March 1979):1201–31.

WENKE, ROBERT J. *Patterns of Prehistory.* New York: Oxford University Press, 1980.

WERMAN, JILL. "Who Makes What?" *Working Woman* (January 1989):72–76, 80.

WESTERMAN, MARTY. "Death of the Frito Bandito." *American Demographics.* Vol. 11, No. 3 (March 1989):28–32.

WESTOFF, CHARLES F., and ELISE F. JONES. "The Secularization of U.S. Catholic Birth Control Practices." *Family Planning Perspective.* Vol. X, No. 5 (September/October 1977):203–7.

WHEELIS, ALLEN. *The Quest for Identity.* New York: Norton, 1958.

WHITAKER, MARK. "Ten Ways to Fight Terrorism." *Newsweek* (July 1, 1985):26–29.

WHITE, RALPH, and RONALD LIPPITT. "Leader Behavior and Member Reaction in Three 'Social Climates.' " In Dorwin Cartwright and Alvin Zander, eds., *Group Dynamics.* Evanston, IL: Row, Peterson, 1953:586–611.

WHITMAN, DAVID. "Shattering Myths about the Homeless." *U.S. News & World Report* (March 20, 1989):26, 28.

WHORF, BENJAMIN LEE. "The Relation of Habitual Thought and Behavior to Language." In *Language, Thought, and Reality.* Cambridge, MA: The Technology Press of M.I.T.; New York: Wiley, 1956:134–59; orig. 1941.

WHYTE, WILLIAM H., JR. *The Organization Man.* Garden City, NY: Anchor Books, 1957.

WIARDA, HOWARD J. "Ethnocentrism and Third World Development." *Society.* Vol. 24, No. 6 (September–October 1987):55–64.

WIATROWSKI, MICHAEL A., DAVID B. GRISWOLD, and MARY K. ROBERTS. "Social Control Theory and Delinquency." *American Sociological Review.* Vol. 46, No. 5 (October 1981):525–41.

WILL, GEORGE F. "No Psycho-Socio Babble Lessens the Fact That Evil Was the Crux of Central Park Rape." *Philadelphia Inquirer* (May 1, 1989).

WILLIAMS, RHYS H., and N. J. DEMERATH III. "Religion and Political Process in an American City." *American Sociological Review.* Vol. 56, No. 4 (August 1991):417–31.

WILLIAMS, ROBIN M., JR. *American Society: A Sociological Interpretation.* 3rd ed. New York: Knopf, 1970.

WILLIAMSON, JEFFREY G., and PETER H. LINDERT. *American Inequality: A Macroeconomic History.* New York: Academic Press, 1980.

WILSON, CLINT C., II, and FELIX GUTIÉRREZ. *Minorities and*

Media: Diversity and the End of Mass Communication. Beverly Hills, CA: Sage, 1985.

WILSON, EDWARD O. *Sociobiology: The New Synthesis.* Cambridge, MA: Belknap Press of the Harvard University Press, 1975.

_____. *On Human Nature.* New York: Bantam Books, 1978.

WILSON, JAMES Q. *Bureaucracy: What Government Agencies Do and Why They Do It.* New York: Basic Books, 1991.

WILSON, JAMES Q., and RICHARD J. HERRNSTEIN. *Crime and Human Nature.* New York: Simon and Schuster, 1985.

WILSON, THOMAS C. "Urbanism and Tolerance: A Test of Some Hypotheses Drawn from Wirth and Stouffer." *American Sociological Review.* Vol. 50, No. 1 (February 1985):117–23.

WILSON, WILLIAM JULIUS. "The Black Underclass." *The Wilson Quarterly.* Vol. 8 (Spring 1984):88–99.

_____. "Studying Inner-City Social Dislocations: The Challenge of Public Agenda Research." *American Sociological Review.* Vol. 56, No. 1 (February 1991):1–14.

WINN, MARIE. *Children Without Childhood.* New York: Pantheon Books, 1983.

WIRTH, LOUIS. "Urbanism As a Way of Life." *American Journal of Sociology.* Vol. 44, No. 1 (July 1938):1–24.

WITKIN-LANOIL, GEORGIA. *The Female Stress Syndrome: How to Recognize and Live with It.* New York: Newmarket Press, 1984.

WOLF, NAOMI. *The Beauty Myth: How Images of Beauty Are Used Against Women.* New York: Morrow, 1990.

WOLFE, DAVID B. "Killing the Messenger." *American Demographics.* Vol. 13, No. 7 (July 1991):40–43.

WOLFGANG, MARVIN E., and FRANCO FERRACUTI. *The Subculture of Violence: Towards an Integrated Theory in Criminology.* Beverly Hills, CA: Sage, 1982.

WOLFGANG, MARVIN E., ROBERT M. FIGLIO, and THORSTEN SELLIN. *Delinquency in a Birth Cohort.* Chicago: University of Chicago Press, 1972.

WOLFGANG, MARVIN E., TERRENCE P. THORNBERRY, and ROBERT M. FIGLIO. *From Boy to Man, From Delinquency to Crime.* Chicago: University of Chicago Press, 1987.

WOLFINGER, RAYMOND E., MARTIN SHAPIRO, and FRED J. GREENSTEIN. *Dynamics of American Politics.* 2nd ed. Englewood Cliffs, NJ: Prentice Hall, 1980.

WONG, BUCK. "Need for Awareness: An Essay on Chinatown, San Francisco." In Amy Tachiki et al., eds., *Roots: An Asian American Reader.* Los Angeles: UCLA Asian American Studies Center, 1971:265–73.

WOODWARD, C. VANN. *The Strange Career of Jim Crow.* 3rd rev. ed. New York: Oxford University Press, 1974.

WOODWARD, KENNETH L. "Feminism and the Churches." *Newsweek.* Vol. 13, No. 7 (February 13, 1989):58–61.

THE WORLD BANK. *World Development Report 1984.* New York: Oxford University Press, 1984.

_____. *World Development Report 1991: The Challenge of Development.* New York: Oxford University Press, 1991.

WORLD HEALTH ORGANIZATION. *Constitution of the World Health Organization.* New York: World Health Organization Interim Commission, 1946.

WREN, CHRISTOPHER S. "In Soweto-by-the-Sea, Misery Lives On as Apartheid Fades." *New York Times* (June 9, 1991):1, 7.

WRIGHT, ERIK OLIN, and BILL MARTIN. "The Transformation of the American Class Structure, 1960–1980." *American Journal of Sociology.* Vol. 93, No. 1 (July 1987):1–29.

WRIGHT, JAMES D. "Address Unknown: Homelessness in Contemporary America." *Society.* Vol. 26, No. 6 (September–October 1989):45–53.

WRIGHT, QUINCY. "Causes of War in the Atomic Age." In William M. Evan and Stephen Hilgartner, eds., *The Arms Race and Nuclear War.* Englewood Cliffs, NJ: Prentice Hall, 1987:7–10.

WRONG, DENNIS H. "The Oversocialized Conception of Man in Modern Sociology." *American Sociological Review.* Vol. 26, No. 2 (April 1961):183–93.

YODER, JAN D., and ROBERT C. NICHOLS. "A Life Perspective: Comparison of Married and Divorced Persons." *Journal of Marriage and the Family.* Vol. 42, No. 2 (May 1980):413–19.

YOUNG, CATHY. "Notes From the Underclass: 'Bomzh' Away." *The New Republic.* Vol. 202, No. 5 (January 29, 1990):18–20.

ZASLAVSKY, VICTOR. *The Neo-Stalinist State: Class, Ethnicity, and Consensus in Soviet Society.* Armonk, NY: M.E. Sharpe, 1982.

ZHOU, MIN, and JOHN R. LOGAN. "Returns of Human Capital in Ethnic Enclaves: New York City's Chinatown." *American Sociological Review.* Vol. 54, No. 5 (October 1989):809–20.

ZIPP, JOHN F. "Perceived Representativeness and Voting: An Assessment of the Impact of 'Choices' vs. 'Echoes.'" *The American Political Science Review.* Vol. 79, No. 1 (March 1985):50–61.

ZIPP, JOHN F., and JOEL SMITH. "A Structural Analysis of Class Voting." *Social Forces.* Vol. 60, No. 3 (March 1982):738–59.

ZOLA, IRVING KENNETH. "Medicine as an Institution of Social Control." In John Ehrenreich, ed., *The Cultural Crisis of Modern Medicine.* New York: Monthly Review Press, 1978:80–100.

ZUBOFF, SHOSHANA. "New Worlds of Computer-Mediated Work." *Harvard Business Review.* Vol. 60, No. 5 (September–October 1982):142–52.

Photo Credits

Granger Collection, 158; Michael Grecco/Stock Boston, 168; Roger Prigent/Sygma, 170; FPG International, 173; John George Brown/Art Resource, 175 (left); *Street Arabs in the Area of Mulberry Street,* circa 1889, The Jacob A. Riis Collection, #123, Museum of the City of New York, 175 (right); Henry O. Tanner/Philadelphia Museum of Art, 176.

CHAPTER 8   David Alfaro Siquieros/Museum of Modern Art, 180; Pablo Bartholomew/Gamma-Liaison, 185; Paul Liebhardt, 189, 191, 194; ARCHIV/Photo Researchers, 193; Diego Rivera/Granger Collection, 196; AP/Wide World Photos, 199.

CHAPTER 9   Ruby Newman & Selma Brown/Norman Prince, 204; Paul Liebhardt, 207 (top, left; top, middle; bottom, left; bottom, middle); Robert Caputo/Stock Boston, 207 (top, right); Lisl Dennis/The Image Bank, 207 (bottom, right); Raveendran/Agence France Press, 211; Chester Higgins, Jr./Photo Researchers, 214; Bettman, 215; Eric Haase/CONTACT/Woodfin Camp & Associates, 217; UPI/Bettman, 219; National Archives/Courtesy of National Japanese American Historical Society, 223; Randy Taylor/Sygma, 226.

CHAPTER 10   Larry Fried/The Image Bank, 230; Michael Tcherevkoff/The Image Bank, 233; Co Rentmeester/The Image Bank, 235; Revlon, 239; Jacob Lawrence/Terry Distenfass Gallery, NYC, 243; Charles Gupton/Stock Boston, 245; AP/Wide World Photos, 247; Courtesy NOW, 250; Robert Fox/Impact Visuals, 248; Bob D'Amico/ABC, 253.

CHAPTER 11   Vince DeWitt/Impact Visuals, 256; Harald Sung/The Image Bank, 262 (left); Sygma, 262 (right); Isaac Soyer/Whitney Museum of American Art, 266; Mayer/Gamma-Liaison, 271; Andy Hernandez/SIPA, 272; T. W. Wood/T. W. Wood Art Gallery, 278; Jay Colton/SABA, 285.

CHAPTER 12   Louinès Mentor/Courtesy Howard and Judy Sacks, 288; Farrell Grehan/Photo Researchers, 291; Steve Sands/Outline Press, 295; Jan Van Eyck/National Gallery, London, 297; Carmen Lomas Garza/Laguna Gloria Art Museum, Austin, TX, 300; David Schrieber/Torrance *Daily Breeze,* 303; James Skovmand/San Diego *Union-Tribune,* 304; Hans Hoefer/Woodfin Camp & Associates, 307; William Campbell/*Time* Magazine, 309; Gilles Peress/Magnum Photos, 311; Thomas Hart Benton/New Britain Museum of American Art, 317.

CHAPTER 13   Robert Burke/Liaison International, 320; Richard Kalvar/Magnum Photos, 322; Hans Neleman/The Image Bank, 325; Paul Liebhardt, 327; AP/Wide World Photos, 331; Literacy Volunteers of America, 333; Granger Collection, 336; Marty Katz, 340; Ruven Afanadore, 344; D. Michael Cheers from *Songs of My People,* © New African Visions, Inc., 345; John Collier/Mansell Collection Limited, 349; Howard Sochurek/Woodfin Camp & Associates, 350.

CHAPTER 14   Paul Liebhardt, 354; Jacob Lawrence/The Phillips Collection, 358; N. Macesschal/The Image Bank, 362; Anderson/Gamma-Liaison, 364; Erich Hartmann/Magnum Photos, 365; Marc Chagall/Museum of Modern Art, 373 (left); Fernand Leger/Philadelphia Museum of Art, 373 (right); Allen Tannenbaum/Sygma, 375.

CHAPTER 15   James Willis/Toby Stone Worldwide/Chicago, 380; G. V. Faint/The Image Bank, 383; Donna Binder/Impact Visuals, 387; Paul Gauguin/Art Institute of Chicago, 388; Stephanie Maze/Woodfin Camp & Associates, 390; Munch, Eduard (1863–1944) *Grido, il,* Galleria Nazionale, Oslo, Scala/Art Resource, 395; Paul Liebhardt, 397; Andrew Holbrooke/Black Star, 398; Kevin Bubriski/The Film Study Center, Harvard University, 401.

Index

Index   445

Subject Index